A DOCUMENTARY HISTORY OF JEWISH–CHRISTIAN RELATIONS

Jews and Christians have interacted for two millennia, yet there is no comprehensive, global study of their shared history. This book offers a chronological and thematic approach to that 2,000-year history, based on some 200 primary documents chosen for their centrality to the encounter. A systematic and authoritative work on the relationship between the two religions, it reflects both the often troubled history of that relationship and the massive changes of attitude and approach in more recent centuries. Written by a team of leading international scholars in the field, each chapter introduces the context of its historical period, draws out the key themes arising from the relevant documents, and provides a detailed commentary on each document to shed light on its significance in the history of Jewish–Christian relations. The volume is aimed at scholars, teachers and students, clerics and lay people, and anyone interested in the history of religion.

EDWARD KESSLER MBE is Founder President of the Woolf Institute and a leading thinker in interfaith relations, primarily Jewish–Christian–Muslim relations. He founded the Woolf Institute in 1998 and was described by *The Times Higher Education Supplement* (London) as 'probably the most prolific interfaith figure in British academia'. He received the 2024 Seelisberg Prize for his contributions to Jewish–Christian relations.

NEIL WENBORN is a full-time writer and publishing consultant who has published widely in both the UK and the US. He is the author of several biographies and is co-editor of the highly respected *History Today Companion to British History* (1995) and *A Dictionary of Jewish–Christian Relations* (2005).

A DOCUMENTARY HISTORY OF JEWISH–CHRISTIAN RELATIONS

From Antiquity to the Present Day

EDITED BY

Edward Kessler

and

Neil Wenborn

CAMBRIDGE
UNIVERSITY PRESS

Shaftesbury Road, Cambridge CB2 8EA, United Kingdom

One Liberty Plaza, 20th Floor, New York, NY 10006, USA

477 Williamstown Road, Port Melbourne, VIC 3207, Australia

314–321, 3rd Floor, Plot 3, Splendor Forum, Jasola District Centre, New Delhi – 110025, India

103 Penang Road, #05–06/07, Visioncrest Commercial, Singapore 238467

Cambridge University Press is part of Cambridge University Press & Assessment, a department of the University of Cambridge.

We share the University's mission to contribute to society through the pursuit of education, learning and research at the highest international levels of excellence.

www.cambridge.org
Information on this title: www.cambridge.org/9781009292160

DOI: 10.1017/9781009292146

First published 2024

A catalogue record for this publication is available from the British Library

A Cataloging-in-Publication data record for this book is available from the Library of Congress

ISBN 978-1-009-29216-0 Hardback

Dedicated to
Trisha Oakley Kessler
and
Sue Black

Contents

Contributors

PHILIP ALEXANDER
Emeritus Professor, Religions and Theology, University of Manchester

VICTORIA BARNETT
Former Director of the Programs on Ethics, Religion and the Holocaust, United States Holocaust Memorial Museum

KARMA BEN-JOHANAN
Senior Lecturer in Comparative Religion, Hebrew University of Jerusalem

MARY C. BOYS
Skinner and McAlpin Professor of Practical Theology, Union Theological Seminary in the City of New York

JAMES CARLETON PAGET
Reader in Ancient Judaism and Early Church History, Faculty of Divinity, University of Cambridge

PAUL KERRY
Visiting Fellow, Programme for the Foundations of Law and Constitutional Government, Faculty of Law, University of Oxford, and Associate Director, International Center for Law and Religion Studies and Associate Professor of History, Brigham Young University

MATTHEW V. NOVENSON
Professor of Biblical Criticism and Biblical Antiquities, University of Edinburgh

MARC SAPERSTEIN
Emeritus Professor of Jewish History, George Washington University, and Professor of Jewish History and Homiletics, Leo Baeck College

Editors' Preface

The history of the relationship between Jews and Christians stretches over 2,000 years, but it is still a relatively young subject of academic study. Although the distinctiveness, even uniqueness, of the relationship has long been noted, historical studies have tended to focus on particular moments or brief periods, individual figures or geographical regions. There are, of course, many theological works which consider the relationship, often from the perspective of a shared scriptural culture, as well as a small but increasing number of introductory works which demonstrate growing interest in the field. Yet, remarkably, there has until now existed no single collection of primary documents which offers a chronological and thematic approach to the entire history of Jewish–Christian relations worldwide.

A Documentary History of Jewish–Christian Relations is a history of Jewish–Christian relations told through a collection of key documents from 2,000 years of encounter between the two faiths. These documents include a wide range of different types of writing: biblical texts, theological writings, political tracts, newspaper articles, diaries, sermons and speeches, letters, novels and plays, a trial record, as well as conference proceedings and scholarly works. Each document, which is accompanied by a detailed commentary, has been chosen because it fulfils one or more of the following criteria: it sheds light on the Jewish–Christian relationship at the time it was written; it is influential on the historical development of Jewish–Christian relations; it addresses a central theme in the Jewish–Christian relationship. The documents' value therefore lies in their significance to the *encounter between* Jews and Christians, rather than simply to the understanding of Jews and Judaism or Christians and Christianity.

As the title of the book suggests, the dominant principle of organisation is chronological. The contents are divided into three parts: Part I covers the period up to the end of the ninth century, Part II the period from the tenth to the end of the eighteenth century, and Part III the period from the beginning of the nineteenth century to the present. Within these parts the nine chapters, each of which is written by a leading scholar in the field and contains a minimum of fifteen documents and accompanying commentaries, form a chronological progression, from New Testament times to the present day. The only exceptions to this principle are Chapters 2 and 3, which offer contrasting perspectives on the period from the second/third to the end of the ninth century CE, Chapter 2 from the viewpoint of eastern and western writings in Greek and Latin, Chapter 3 from that of classic rabbinic literature. In addition to the chronological chapters, we include two appendices which present (at the end of Part I) case studies of exegetical encounters between Judaism and Christianity during the first millennium and (at the end of Part III) a series of institutional statements on Jewish–Christian relations since the end of World War II.

Each chapter begins with an extended introduction which provides the context for the specific historical period under review, outlining its particularities and significance for the Jewish–Christian encounter, introducing the documents that follow, weaving together the key themes arising from them and providing a bibliography for the chapter as a whole. The body of each chapter consists of the documents and commentaries themselves.

One of the challenges of preparing a documentary history is to contextualise the documents, in order, for example, to help the reader understand the role of institutions and practices of the pre-modern world which are not always easily intelligible today. To this end, each document is followed by a commentary which sets it in its historical/theological context; educes its significance to the Jewish–Christian encounter in terms of its contemporary importance, the historical/theological tradition within which it sits and its legacy for the later history of the relationship; explains any technical terms; and includes a short bibliography. In exceptional cases, where documents are interrelated or otherwise thematically connected, they have been grouped under a portmanteau heading and treated in a single, sometimes extended, commentary (e.g., Bauer's and Marx's writings on the so-called 'Jewish question' in Chapter 6 or the responses of Pope Pius XII, William Temple, the World Council of Churches and the World Jewish Congress to the confirmation of the genocide of European Jews in Chapter 7).

Otherwise, the documents and commentaries within each chapter are organised chronologically, insofar as that chronology can be established. (The only exception is Chapter 3 which, given the difficulty of dating the traditions on which the rabbinic literature is based, takes a thematic approach to its subject.) They thus cover the entire history of the Jewish–Christian encounter from Paul's First Letter to the Thessalonians in the 40s CE – probably the earliest text in the New Testament – to the statement on Jewish–Christian relations released jointly by the Office of the Chief Rabbi of the United Hebrew Congregations of the Commonwealth and the Church of Scotland in 2023.

Most of the documents in the book are excerpted from longer documents, with omissions indicated by square-bracketed ellipses (unbracketed ellipses are part of the original document). Authorial interpolations have likewise been indicated by square brackets, with any square-bracketed phrases that were part of the original document indicated after the source reference. Where authors have translated documents themselves, they also identify important original words in added parentheses. (The terms 'author' and 'authorial' in relation to the source references denote interpolations and translations by the contributor of the chapter concerned.) The documents preserve the style and conventions of the originals even where they are at variance with those of the book as a whole, although we have silently corrected one or two typographical errors. Source references are provided at the end of the documents (except in the Appendix to Part I, where they are given in footnotes for reasons explained on p. 165). Where a document has a title, it appears under that title. Where the original titles are in a language other than English, they are translated, with the title given first in English if the English title is the more familiar and vice versa, for example Albert of Aix's *History of the Journey to Jerusalem* (*Historia Ierosolimitana*) but *Constitutio pro Judeis* (An Edict in Favour of the Jews). Where it seemed artificial to give the original title in full, it is given in the source reference, and where the English version of the title is the universally established form (e.g., Martin Luther's *That Jesus Christ Was Born a Jew*), the original title is omitted altogether. Where the original document had no title, a description is given instead (e.g., Stephen Wise to John Haynes Holmes: Letter on Palestine).

As will be evident from the Introduction, the history of Jewish–Christian relations is in many ways an echo chamber, with resonances sounding from the earliest period to the latest and between voices and events at every stage between. We have aimed to create a network of cross-references between different parts of the book to reflect this profound interconnectedness. Cross-references to documents within chapters are by document number; cross-references between chapters are by page number. Every chapter contains both kinds of cross-reference, which we hope will provide helpful routes of access for the reader between documents, periods and themes.

A Documentary History of Jewish–Christian Relations reflects the massive changes of attitude and approach to the question of Jewish–Christian relations that have taken place over the centuries, most strikingly since the beginning of modern Zionism and the Christian rediscovery of a more constructive relationship with Jews and Judaism in the late nineteenth century. As such, it embodies the latest scholarly thinking in the field of Jewish–Christian relations and the many other disciplines on which it draws. We and the contributors have been at pains to ensure, however, that it remains accessible not only to scholars but also to anyone interested in the historical and continuing encounter between Judaism and Christianity. We hope the decisions we have made about the structure and presentation of the material will have gone some way towards achieving that aim, but we would always be interested to hear suggestions from readers as to how its accessibility might be enhanced in future editions.

Acknowledgements

A book like this is by its very nature a collaborative project, and we are delighted to be able to express our gratitude to the many people and institutions who have helped it come to fruition.

Our greatest debt is of course to the contributors, Philip Alexander, Vicki Barnett, Karma Ben-Johanan, Mary Boys, James Carleton Paget, Paul Kerry, Matt Novenson and Marc Saperstein, without whom it is far more than a truism to say that the *Documentary History* could never have been written. They have from the outset given their time and energy to a project which must often have seemed to demand more of both than they had anticipated and have put up with our editorial suggestions, queries and deadlines with a grace, a patience and a conscientiousness for which we cannot thank them enough.

Our warmest thanks are also due to Ahreum Kim for the eagle eye and meticulous attention to detail she brought to the proofreading of the documents and the compilation of the index, and to Sharon Cunningham for her unflappable tenacity in tracking down copyright owners through the labyrinth of changes in the configuration of publishers and imprints. We gratefully acknowledge the authors, editors and publishers of all the documents which appear in the book, further details of whom appear in the source references for individual documents.

We are grateful to all those who helped in the shaping and development of the book, including Anna Sapir Abulafia, Josh Ahrens, Harvey Hames, Susannah Heschel, Daniel Langton and John Pawlikowski. Particular thanks are due to Philip Cunningham and Miri Rubin, who reviewed sections of the manuscript and offered wise and helpful advice, and to Sami Everett and Iris Koch, who lent their translation skills to documents that appear here in English for the first time.

The project would have been a very different experience without the active interest and moral support during the research and writing process of the staff of the Woolf Institute, including Esther-Miriam Wagner, Emma Harris, Seherish Abrar, Sally Adelman, Mohammed Ahmed, Claire Curran, Dunya Habash, Julian Hargreaves, Emma Heyn, Flora Moffie, Kitty O'Lone, Danielle Padley, David Perry, Beth Phillips and Amy Rhys-Davies.

Our thanks are also due to the present and former Trustees who believed in the vision of a Centre for Jewish–Christian Relations (CJCR), now called the Woolf Institute, including Ian Blair, Trixie Brenninkmeijer, Alex Carlile, Simon Dangoor, Dominic Fenton, Bob Glatter, Peter Halban, Brenda Hale, Khalid Hameed, Richard Harries, David Leibowitz,

Julius Lipner, John Lyon, Clemens Nathan, Martin Paisner, John Pickering, Shabir Randeree, Tim Stevens, Ed Williams, Jeremy Woolf and Sarah Yamani.

Any book is of course the product of the experience, advice and support over the years of many more people than were directly involved in its creation. We therefore also extend our grateful thanks:

To friends and mentors who encouraged Ed Kessler in the study of Jewish–Christian relations from the inception of the Woolf Institute to the present day, including Martin Forward, Prince Hassan of Jordan, Susie and Tim Sainsbury, Robert and Edie Sansom and Harry and Marguerite Woolf.

To those who jointly taught courses on Jewish–Christian relations with Ed and supported the teaching of Jewish–Christian relations within the Cambridge Theological Federation, including Anna Abram, Gorazd Andrejč, Dan Ava, Anders Bergquist, Chris Chivers, Chris Cocksworth, Dragos Herescu, Hannah Holtschneider, Susanne Jennings, Ian McIntosh, Oonagh O'Brien, Beth Phillips, Sue Price, John Proctor, Martin Seeley, Gemma Simmonds, Mary Tanner, Mike Thompson, Austin Tiffany, Margie Tolstoy, Sam Victor, Michael Volland and George Wilkes.

To the CJCR teachers of Jewish–Christian relations who passed away too young: Jim Aitken and Melanie Wright.

To friends at the Council of Centers on Jewish–Christian Relations (CCJR), the Council of Christians and Jews (CCJ) and the International Council of Christians and Jews (ICCJ), for whom the study of Jewish–Christian relations is central to Jewish and Christian self-understanding, including Judy Banki, Alan Berger, James Bernauer, Alice and Roy Eckardt (of blessed memory), Eugene Fisher, Elena Procario-Foley, Adam Gregerman, Katharina von Kellenbach, Björn Krondorfer, Mike McGarry, Peter Pettit, Jim Rudin, Christian Rutishauser, David Sandmel, Frank Sherman (of blessed memory), Joe Sievers, Abraham Skorka, Kevin Spicer, Etienne Vetö, Burton Visotzky and Murray Watson.

To those engaged in Jewish–Christian dialogue in Israel, including Avital Erez, Jamal Khader, Ron Kronish, Diana Lipton, David Neuhaus, Amnon Ramon, David and Sharon Rosen, Richard Sewell and Debbie Weissman.

To Christian and Jewish religious leaders who combine pastoral and academic interest in Jewish–Christian relations and offered encouragement at different times, including George Carey, Toby Howarth, Basil Hume (of blessed memory), Walter Kasper, Kurt Koch, Ephraim Mirvis, Cormac Murphy-O'Connor (of blessed memory), Vincent Nichols, Jonathan Sacks (of blessed memory), Richard Sudworth, Justin Welby, Guy Wilkinson and Rowan Williams.

To the Sisters of Sion, who demonstrate the dramatic shift in Christian attitudes to Jews and Judaism in modern times, especially Teresa Brittain, Maureen Cusick, Celia Deutsch, Clare Jardine, Margaret Shepherd and Lucy Thorson.

To Westminster College for their hospitality, and in particular to Nigel Appleton, Susan Durber, Alison Gray, Neil Thorogood and Nigel Uden.

To Rick Sopher, in the hope he will produce a documentary history of Jewish–Muslim relations; to Mark Goodridge, for advice over many years and for being more like his father than he realises; and to Norman Solomon, academic and practitioner of Jewish–Christian dialogue who led the way with the Selly Oak Centre.

To friends and colleagues at the School of Religion, Theology and Peace Studies at Trinity College Dublin, where Ed spent a very happy Fellowship in 2022/3, especially Carlo Aldrovandi, Siobhán Garrigan, Zohar Hadromi-Allouche, Andrew Pierce, Aideen Woods; and to Jane Ohlmeyer, for her kind hospitality.

Thank you all.

The publishers, Cambridge University Press, and especially Beatrice Rehl and Bethany Johnson, provided encouragement and advice at every stage of the project and saw the book through to completion with their customary care, while Alwyn Harrison was the most meticulous of copy-editors. We would also like to express our grateful appreciation for the support of the British Academy, the Headley Trust, the Spalding Trust and the Woolf Institute, who made generous contributions towards the funding of the research and editorial process.

Finally, our deepest appreciation goes to our families: from Ed, to my mother Jo Kessler and father Willie (of blessed memory), my brothers George, Charles and James, my children Shoshana, Asher and Eliana, and especially to my wife, Trisha; and from Neil, as always, to Sue and Edward, and remembering Henry.

Vladimir Soloviev: 'The Jews and the Christian Question'. Reprinted by permission from *Freedom, Faith, and Dogma: Essays by V. S. Soloviev on Christianity and Judaism* by V. S. Soloviev, the State University of New York Press © 2008, State University of New York. All rights reserved.

Leo Baeck: *The Essence of Judaism*. From Leo Baeck, *The Essence of Judaism*, trans. Victor Grubwieser and Leonard Pearl (London: Macmillan, 1936). Reproduced courtesy of James N. Dreyfus and family, the descendants of Rabbi Leo Baeck.

Gerhard Kittel: 'The Jewish Question'; Siegfried Leffler: 'Christ in Germany's Third Reich'; Evangelical Church of the Old Prussian Union: The Godesberg Declaration. From Mary Solberg (ed. and trans.), *A Church Undone: Documents from the German Christian Faith Movement, 1932–1940*. Reproduced by permission of Augsburg Fortress. Copyright © 2015 Fortress Press. All rights reserved.

Marc Boegner: Address to a Protest Meeting in the Hall of Chopin, Paris; William Temple, Archbishop of Canterbury: Speeches; Aide-mémoire from the Secretariats of the World Council of Churches and the World Jewish Congress. Reprinted by permission of the Snoek family from *The Grey Book: A Collection of Protests against Anti-Semitism and the Persecution of the Jews issued by Non-Roman Catholic Churches and Church Leaders during Hitler's Rule* by Johan M. Snoek, published by Van Gorcum & Co. Copyright © 1969 Johan M. Snoek.

Richard Rubenstein: *After Auschwitz: Radical Theology and Contemporary Judaism*. From Richard Rubenstein, *After Auschwitz: History, Theology, and Contemporary Judaism*. Copyright © 1966, 1992 by Richard L. Rubenstein. All rights reserved. Reproduced with permission of the Licensor through PLSclear.

Rosemary Radford Ruether: *Faith and Fratricide: The Theological Roots of Anti-Semitism*. Copyright © 1974 by the Seabury Press Inc. Used by permission of Wipf and Stock Publishers, www.wipfandstock.com.

Irving Greenberg: *For the Sake of Heaven and Earth: The New Encounter between Judaism and Christianity*. Reproduced from *For the Sake of Heaven and Earth: The New Encounter between Judaism and Christianity* by Irving Greenberg by permission of the University of Nebraska Press. Copyright © 2004 by Irving Greenberg. Published by The Jewish Publication Society, Philadelphia.

The Lambeth Conference: *Jews, Christians and Muslims: The Way of Dialogue*. From *The Truth Shall Make You Free: The Lambeth Conference 1988: The Reports, Resolutions & Pastoral Letters from the Bishops*. Copyright © The Secretary of the Anglican Consultative Council 1998. Reproduced by permission of the Anglican Consultative Council.

Kairos Palestine: *A Moment of Truth: A Word of Faith, Hope and Love from the Heart of Palestinian Suffering*. © 2018 Kairos Palestine. Reproduced by permission of Kairos Palestine.

Abbreviations of Rabbinic Literature and Scripture

RABBINIC LITERATURE

b.	Babylonian Talmud
y.	Jerusalem/Palestinian Talmud
m.	Mishnah
t.	Tosefta
Gen. Rab.	Genesis Rabbah
Lam. Rab.	Lamentations Rabbah
Lev. Rab.	Leviticus Rabbah
Num. Rab.	Numbers Rabbah
Song Rab.	Song of Songs Rabbah

HEBREW BIBLE/OLD TESTAMENT

Gen.	Genesis	Song	Song of Songs
Exod.	Exodus	Isa.	Isaiah
Lev.	Leviticus	Jer.	Jeremiah
Num.	Numbers	Lam.	Lamentations
Deut.	Deuteronomy	Ezek.	Ezekiel
Josh.	Joshua	Dan.	Daniel
Judg.	Judges	Hos.	Hosea
Ruth	Ruth	Joel	Joel
1–2 Sam.	1–2 Samuel	Amos	Amos
1–2 Kgs	1–2 Kings	Obad.	Obadiah
1–2 Chr.	1–2 Chronicles	Jon.	Jonah
Ezra	Ezra	Mic.	Micah
Neh.	Nehemiah	Nah.	Nahum
Esth.	Esther	Hab.	Habakkuk
Job	Job	Zeph.	Zephaniah
Ps.	Psalms	Hag.	Haggai
Prov.	Proverbs	Zech.	Zechariah
Eccl.	Ecclesiastes	Mal.	Malachi

NEW TESTAMENT

Matt.	Matthew	1–2 Thess.	1–2 Thessalonians
Mark	Mark	1–2 Tim.	1–2 Timothy
Luke	Luke	Titus	Titus
John	John	Phlm.	Philemon
Acts	Acts	Heb.	Hebrews
Rom.	Romans	Jas	James
1–2 Cor.	1–2 Corinthians	1–2 Pet.	1–2 Peter
Gal.	Galatians	1–3 John	1–3 John
Eph.	Ephesians	Jude	Jude
Phil.	Philippians	Rev.	Revelation
Col.	Colossians		

Documents

Chapter 3: Classic Rabbinic Literature up to the Ninth Century

Chapter 5: From the Reformation to the Enlightenment

Chapter 8: The State of Israel to the Election of Pope John Paul II

Chapter 9: The Flourishing of Jewish–Christian Relations

Appendix to Part III: Institutional Statements

Introduction

It is sometimes said that Jews and Christians are divided by a common Bible. The remark is not as glib as it first appears, because scripture provides a common ground for the Jewish–Christian encounter and also, historically, has resulted in deep division.

Is the Hebrew Bible the same as the Old Testament? Since Jews and Christians regard scripture as a revelatory text, is it their common heritage? There are of course differences, not least because the text is read differently by each tradition. Even the name 'Hebrew Bible' indicates difference, since the vast majority of Christians (and significant numbers of Jews) read not the 'Hebrew' Bible but translations. Although the term 'Hebrew Bible' draws attention to its origins within Judaism, it is not the designation most commonly used by Jews, most of whom prefer 'Tanakh'. Christians prefer the designation 'Old Testament'; moreover, as the church traditionally relied on the Greek Septuagint (LXX) the Christian canon differs from the Hebrew in the order of the books, and in the inclusion of the Apocrypha. Perhaps it is best to conclude that the written heritage of biblical Israel is too complex to admit of a single adequate title.

A similar problem of terminology applies to the strip of land along the Mediterranean that became the birthplace of both Testaments. Located between Mesopotamia to the north and Egypt to the south, with the Mediterranean to the west and to the east a mountainous, virtually impassable stony desert, it offers the only available land route between Asia and Africa. As a result, whoever controlled that strip in biblical times controlled the major land route for trade or military activity between the great empires that rose and fell in the surrounding area. Today, some call the land Israel and others Palestine. Promised Land and Holy Land are also common; Occupied Land is sometimes used, too.

This variety of nomenclature, of both scripture and territory, is one conspicuous example of the complex reality which characterises the mutually entangled and often difficult history of Jewish–Christian relations. We hope that, in seeking to shed light on this complexity, the *Documentary History* may illuminate some of the recurring themes of that 2,000-year history – for example, scripture and its interpretation, polemic and argument, identity and self-understanding, mission and dialogue, the land (and, later, State) of Israel. The documents in the book present these themes among others, sometimes in combination, giving them prominence at different historical moments and providing a lens through which to understand relations between Jews and Christians right up to the present day.

PART I: TO 900 CE

Conflicting interpretations lie at the heart of the Jewish–Christian encounter. The overwhelmingly Christological interpretation that Christians have traditionally brought to the Bible renders it, according to Jews, an almost completely different book. For their part, Jewish interpreters appeared inward-looking, producing a combination of literal interpretations alongside a bewildering array of legal, ethical and mystical layers which seemed unconnected to the text, making it unintelligible to Christians. And both communities have claimed it for themselves exclusively.

During the first millennium, much of the Jewish–Christian debate revolved around scripture. The Septuagint had acquired the status of an inspired text in Christianity as reflecting the words of God more precisely than the Hebrew, leading to a neglect of Hebrew among Christians in favour of Latin and Greek. The canonisation of the exclusively Christian New Testament further widened the separation of Jews and Christians.

The *Documentary History* begins with the New Testament, since the early Jesus-followers were rooted in first-century Judaism and the twenty-seven books exhibit a close relationship with many aspects of traditional Jewish interpretation. Although some scholars argue that the New Testament should be defined as a collection of Jewish rather than Christian writings, these books symbolise both divergence and convergence. As Matthew Novenson explains in Chapter 1, 'although most of the authors of the texts comprising the New Testament were Jewish, almost all of their readers down the centuries have been gentile Christians'.

The destruction of the Jerusalem temple in 70 CE was one step in what has become known as the parting, or sometimes partings, of the ways, a concept explored further in Chapter 2. Left to ask where God would be found if there were no temple, Jews were divided; some found the answer in the Torah as taught by rabbis, others found it in Jesus as fulfilment of the Torah and still others in the scriptures alone, whether Torah (e.g., Samaritans) or Tanakh (e.g., Karaites). While the Old Testament is indispensable for understanding the earliest claims about Jesus, the New Testament, with its eschatological orientation, generally applies the biblical text to some aspect of Jesus' life. This is unlike rabbinic interpretation, which seeks to discover some 'hidden' element in the biblical text itself, because for the rabbis the biblical text is primary; for the New Testament writers and the church fathers, however, Jesus is primary.

As the demography of Christianity became increasingly gentile, some, such as the second-century theologian Marcion, questioned the value of the Old Testament altogether. For others it was vital testimony to the truth of Christian faith as God's fulfilment of the promises to biblical Israel. An example of this divergence can be seen in the two main strands of thought about the messianic understanding of Jesus. One strand emphasises a break with scripture involving a new covenant with God (e.g., Heb. 8:8–13); this approach depicts Judaism as an old and superseded covenant. A second strand describes Jesus as a fulfilment of what was prophesied in the Bible (e.g., Jer. 31:31) which remains in a typological relationship to it (e.g., Matt. 5:17). Before long, what was seen as having foreshadowed Jesus Christ in the Old Testament had become overshadowed in him, contributing to a tendency towards supersessionism, commonly found from the writings of the early church fathers onwards.

Naturally, the (Christian) question as to why Jews rejected the messiah became a preoccupation of Jewish–Christian relations. While both Jews and Christians accepted that some passages referred to the coming of the messiah, the latter believed them to be fulfilled by Jesus and the former did not, a divergence which, from the time of the earliest Jesus-followers, contributed to the parting of the ways.

As the first missionary for Christ to the gentiles, Paul has a unique place in the history of Jewish–Christian relations. Convinced that God had called gentiles to be members of his people, Paul insisted that what had happened as a consequence of the death and resurrection of Christ was the fulfilment of God's promises to Israel. Later generations would lose sight of his emphasis on continuity, however, misinterpreting his words as an attack on Judaism, a perspective that, as we shall see, would be challenged only in the twentieth century. It is an index of Paul's enduring significance to the encounter that his writings are (as being the earliest in the New Testament) the earliest texts in the *Documentary History* and reflections on them among the most recent, and their interpretation, misinterpretation and reinterpretation over the centuries is one of the central threads that runs throughout the book.

The parting of the ways between Jews and Christians became defined by the end of the fourth century, by which time Christianity had become the dominant religion in the Roman empire and Rabbinic Judaism the mainstream voice within the Jewish world. The most important historical event in this process after the first century was the decision of the Roman emperor Constantine (*r.* 306–37) to become a Christian. The Christianisation of the Roman empire would be a long and complex process, but with Constantine's assumption of control of the eastern empire and his construction of a new Christian capital, Constantinople, the setting in which Jews and Christians had dealings with one another changed profoundly. As James Carleton Paget writes in Chapter 2, this period, 'not least through the writings of the church fathers, moulds the character of Jewish–Christian relations as these developed in the Middle Ages and beyond, that is, relations marked predominantly by hostility and mutual recrimination but intermittently hinting also at something more positively interactive'.

Hostility towards Jews is demonstrated by Christian polemical writings in various literary forms, the most popular being the dialogue, of which Chapter 2 discusses several examples. This genre occasionally reflects actual conversations in encounters between Christians and Jews and demonstrates a good knowledge of contemporary Jewish practice. It also reflects recurring polemical motifs, such as Jews' inability to read the prophecies correctly, their rejection and killing of Christ, and controversy about religious observance and the election of Israel. As early as the late second century, Christian self-understanding was intrinsically linked to an opposition to Judaism. Yet even though anti-Jewish discourse sought to keep Jews and Christians apart, a separation reinforced by legal restrictions from the secular authorities, evidence shows that words were not always followed by action and in numerous cities and regions Jews and Christians lived side by side and face to face, seemingly contentedly.

In addition, the legacy of Augustinian toleration of Jews facilitated the survival of Judaism because, in contrast to its attitude to early Christian heresies and paganism, Augustine's argument that Jews should be preserved, if only to witness Christian truth, was accepted by the church. This teaching, sometimes called 'witness theology' since it taught that Jewish subservience witnessed the victory of Christianity as the true Israel, continued to guide teaching about Jews and Judaism into the medieval period, extending from the realm of theology into the domain of law.

Condemnatory discourse was not limited to Christian writings. Although there are few explicit references to Christians and Christianity in rabbinic literature, Philip Alexander argues in Chapter 3 that Christianity was viewed by the rabbis as 'an existential threat to the Jewish people, and so had to be vigorously countered'. From the rabbinic perspective, Christians were heretics and their theological claims required rebuttal. Those rabbinic texts that do explicitly mention Jesus and the early church, such as the *Toledot Yeshu*, are highly critical and dismissive (views taken up by post-rabbinic medieval commentators such as Maimonides and in the anonymous *Nizzahon Vetus*, both examined in Chapter 4). They mocked Christian interpretations that abandoned the literal meaning of Hebrew words in favour of giving them messianic significance. Thus, both Jewish and Christian writings in the first millennium consist, in the main, of a collection of polemical accounts of the 'other'.

The problem of polemic has provided one of the major challenges in Jewish–Christian relations. It is a problem compounded by the fact that Jesus was a Jew who taught fellow Jews, some of whom followed his teaching while others did not. The New Testament bears witness to debates and arguments which were vigorous and sometimes bitter, but what became forgotten was that these arguments were primarily between Jews, about a Jew or about Jewish issues. It was a family argument which led to fracture (and which perhaps helps explain the intensity of hostility in the Gospels towards the Pharisees, the contemporary Jewish group whom New Testament scholars view as being closer to Jesus than any other). As a result, the church fathers soon read polemical passages in the New Testament as 'Christian' arguments against 'Jews', resulting in what Jules Isaac would come to call a 'teaching of contempt' of Judaism.

The Appendix to Part I reveals a different side to the Jewish–Christian relationship in the first millennium – a side hinted at in Chapters 2 and 3 – by uncovering more positive interaction, as witnessed in the writings of Jewish and Christian biblical commentators. Their interpretations of scripture indicate that relations were closer than the polemical texts may imply. Edward Kessler shows that 'even though Jewish and Christian interpretations are put to different uses, some demonstrate mutual awareness, influence and encounter', and that Jewish and Christian interpretations were themselves mutually influential.

This exegetical interaction, over hundreds of years, not only sheds light on Jewish–Christian relations historically but retains significance in the present day, because Jews and Christians still inhabit a common biblical culture, a theme that runs through all the chapters of this *Documentary History*.

PART II: 900 TO 1800

By the beginning of the second millennium the theology of toleration of Jews had been incorporated into papal legislation that offered both protection (such as a ban on forced baptism) and also restrictions (such as the barring of Jews from holding public office). However, the gap between statements and actions was thrown into stark relief by the First Crusade of 1096, a year which serves as a demarcation for the beginning of a new era – one in which Christendom had become more homogeneous and Jews were one of the last 'different' groups remaining. Jews suffered mass violence during the Crusades and during the fourteenth-century Black Death (for which they were often blamed) and, beginning with England in 1290, by the end of the sixteenth century they had experienced expulsion from most of western Europe.

This was the time of the Inquisition, when Christians became aware of the existence of post-biblical Jewish writings such as the Talmud and denounced them; of the disputation and the burning of Jewish books; of blood libel accusations and conspiracy theories – all developments to which documents in Chapter 4 attest. Jews were described as carnal, lustful, gluttonous, greedy, a source of danger (notably to Christian children) and would-be torturers of the body of Christ. They were compelled to listen to Christian preachers, sometimes themselves converts, delivering conversionary sermons that sought to convince them of the truth of Christianity. In the Iberian Peninsula the sermon became a component of the *auto-da-fé* (the ritual of public penance imposed before execution), when those convicted by the Inquisition were forced to listen to a sermon intended to prompt confession and repentance.

For their part, Jews identified Christianity as *avodah zarah* ('foreign worship'), a designation for an idolatrous religion. Jewish religious leaders, like their Christian counterparts, sought to maintain boundaries and, not always successfully, to minimise Jewish–Christian interaction. A wide range of Jewish polemical writings were circulated, portraying Jesus as irrational and immoral.

Yet, as in the first millennium, there were also positive encounters between Jews and Christians. As Marc Saperstein and Edward Kessler write in Chapter 4, 'there was more social interaction between Jews and Christians than the restrictions enacted by religious authorities might imply', with regular contact between Jewish and Christian neighbours and through trade. This seems to have been true even at the darkest moments, as witnessed by Bernard of Clairvaux's intervention to protect German Jews from being killed during the Second Crusade.

In the Muslim Iberian Peninsula Jews, like Christians, had become an accepted part of the religious landscape during the centuries of *convivencia* (literally 'living together' but generally translated as 'coexistence'), subject to some restrictions but widely tolerated, as in Córdoba and Toledo. For a while a similar openness existed in Christian Iberia, where Jews (and Muslims) were accepted as part of the fabric of society, until Christian kingdoms, particularly after the anti-Jewish riots of 1391, began to assert their Christian identity more aggressively and to pursue anti-Jewish and anti-Muslim policies.

However, the most important historical event impacting Jewish–Christian relations during the centuries covered by Part II of the *Documentary History* was the Reformation, which broke the religious monopoly of the Roman Catholic Church, introducing alternative theologies and churches. Moreover, several of its outcomes – not least the growth of religious pluralism – can be seen, in the words of the Reformation historian Diarmaid MacCulloch, as 'a prehistory of the Enlightenment', which would in turn catalyse arguably the most significant reconfiguration in the position of Jews in society since the Christianisation of the Roman empire. Jews viewed the Reformation as a positive development, partly because of its challenge to the unity of the church, which at first diverted Christian attention away from Judaism. This was reinforced by the Protestant return to the Hebrew Bible (*sola scriptura*, 'by scripture alone') and some Reformers' awareness of Jewish biblical commentaries. As Chapter 5 shows, Luther's early writings suggested a dramatic change in Christian perceptions of Judaism, but Jewish hopes were short-lived and the bitter anti-Jewish treatises written towards the end of Luther's life served to reinforce Jewish loyalty to the Catholic emperor – as in the case of Josel of Rosheim, leader of German Jews during the Reformation, whose initial sympathy with Luther, from whom he hoped for an amelioration in the position of Jews, subsequently soured to the point where he described him, in a play on words, as *lo-tahar*, which means 'impure'. While for the most part the Christian teaching of contempt therefore continued unabated, however, some Reformers held more positive views, including Calvin, whose belief that God had not abrogated the covenant with Israel, for example, would influence Calvinist churches through the centuries and contribute to the tolerance extended to Jews in the Netherlands and, later, in the American colonies.

The Enlightenment challenged the assumptions of the church and the political role of its leaders. The religious life of Jews was affected in similar ways to that of the Christians among whom they lived. Although many of the dramatic changes in Jewish–Christian relations caused by the Enlightenment occurred in the nineteenth century, the seventeenth and eighteenth centuries witnessed the start of Jewish emancipation and increased contact between Jews and Christians. Jews gained civil rights on a more or less equal footing with other citizens of the countries in which they lived, such as in England and France. Yet attitudes were often ambivalent, as illustrated by the case of Voltaire who, while advocating certain universal human rights such as religious tolerance and freedom of speech, has been seen by some scholars as the father of secular, racial antisemitism. The Enlightenment concept of religious toleration made it easier for Jews and Christians to meet and converse, but, as Paul Kerry writes in Chapter 5, 'such discussions also saw Jews caught in a new dilemma: some Christians found comfort in religious retrenchment and challenged Jews for not converting, while others embraced enlightened rationalism and attacked Jews for remaining part of what they saw as a retrograde, even barbaric faith'.

PART III: 1800 TO THE PRESENT DAY

By 1800 both Jews and Christians were struggling to come to terms with the new socio-cultural norms, attitudes and practices associated with modernity, which continued to influence Jewish–Christian relations in the next century and beyond. Part III of the book opens with the emancipation of Jews, which took place alongside that of other religious minorities (Protestants in some countries, Catholics in others). The focus, however, was on the rights of Jews as individuals rather than as a group. Any emphasis on Jewish people-hood, or even the wider Jewish community, could (and sometimes did) undermine Jews' desire for equal rights. Underlying this position is a tension between the nation state and its minority communities, which led to a narrowing of identity. Edward Kessler explains in Chapter 6 how the development of the modern concept of nationhood impacted on the relationship between Jews and Christians, 'sometimes prompting new forms of Christian intolerance of Jews, as well as secular attacks on Judaism and Christianity (and on all religious belief)'.

An upsurge of antisemitism began in the second half of the nineteenth century, epitomised in France by the Dreyfus affair of 1894–9. Albert Dreyfus, the only Jewish member of the French General Staff, was blamed for (and found guilty of) passing military secrets to a German military attaché. The evidence was fabricated, as Emile Zola showed in his famous 1897 newspaper article '*J'accuse …!*', but when Dreyfus was tried again in 1899, a military court again found him guilty. (Ten days later, the President of France pardoned him.) The affair polarised the country, demonstrating a religious divide between Catholics and Protestants – the former generally in opposition to and the latter in support of Dreyfus – while French Jews, for the most part, stayed silent. Among the journalists who covered the trial was Theodor Herzl, the Budapest-born father of political Zionism, for whom it was profoundly influential.

In Orthodox Christianity, with its veneration of tradition, the legacy of *adversus Judaeos* (against Jews), a term which refers to a genre of Christian anti-Jewish writings from the second to the eighteenth centuries, remained central to its approach to Jews and Judaism. Throughout the nineteenth and early twentieth century there were serious outbreaks of antisemitism in Russia, where half the world's Jewish population lived. While violent attacks on Jews in Russia – pogroms, so called after the Russian word for 'devastation' – were prompted by social and economic factors, they were dressed in the garb of Orthodox religious zeal, although a few church leaders, such as Antonii Vadkovskii (1846–1912), Metropolitan of St Petersburg, condemned the violence.

This period also saw a surge in missionary activity and the founding of new societies such as the London Society for Promoting Christianity amongst the Jews. One legacy of the Reformation was a desire among some Christians (already prefigured in humanist circles during the Renaissance) for a knowledge of Hebrew, which the missionary orders regarded as essential: if Jews were to be won for Christ, Judaism and Jewish interpretation of scripture had to be better understood (and refuted). Some missionaries were also Christian restorationists, who offered public support for a new Jewish movement – Zionism (see below) – and missionary activity and Christian Zionism ran in parallel and sometimes overlapped. Indeed, Christian support was a key element in the formative years of Zionism, as illustrated by the help Theodor Herzl received from the Anglican priest and restorationist William Hechler, who attended the first World Zionist Conference in 1897. Notably, Lloyd George (British prime minister, 1916–22) and Arthur Balfour (prime minister 1902–5 and foreign secretary 1916–19), were brought up with an intimate familiarity with scripture which, they both acknowledged, contributed to a positive view of Zionism. Although it would be simplistic to regard the government's support in 1917 for the Jewish claim of sovereignty in Palestine, known as the Balfour Declaration, in terms of religious agendas, the intersection of religion and politics undoubtedly played a role.

During the nineteenth and early twentieth century, Christian understanding of Jews and Judaism became more informed, leading both to Jewish–Christian encounters at the scholarly level and to the foundations of modern dialogue. In Britain, the writings of Claude Montefiore and Travers Herford represented the first serious modern challenge to the traditional negative Christian stereotypes of Rabbinic Judaism as a form of barren legalism. In Germany, Abraham Geiger proposed that Jesus was a Pharisee, part of a liberalising Jewish movement, generating public controversy and, for the most part, a critical response from contemporary Christian theologians such as Franz Delitzsch and Julius Wellhausen.

This period witnessed more Jews actively engaging in wider society, but many were assimilating or converting to Christianity, some to avoid the strictures of antisemitism, others for the purpose of social advancement, others still for both reasons. Heinrich Heine famously called his conversion a 'ticket of admission to European culture'. On the whole, assimilation was the preferred choice where feasible, especially when it was possible to maintain a Jewish religious identity. Nevertheless, later generations often witnessed conversions to Christianity and an abandonment of Judaism, as illustrated by the fact that while Moses Mendelssohn rejected Lavater's call to convert to Christianity in 1769, his son Abraham brought up his own children, including the composer Felix, as Christian.

The nineteenth and early twentieth century also saw the rise of modern nationalism and the growth of pseudo-scientific race theory. However, while the logic of nationalism, with its romantic concept of the unique soul of a particular 'folk' rooted in a specific land and language, threatened integration, it also fostered, in Zionism, a Jewish nationalism which offered Jews an alternative path to a place in the modern world as a particular nation like all other nations – a trajectory that would have significant consequences for Jewish–Christian relations in the second half of the twentieth century. Accusations of disloyalty against Jews made by political activists were intensified by some nationalist churches which viewed Jewish rejection of Christianity (i.e., Jews who remained Jewish) with disdain. These churches' often close alliance with the state contributed to an increasingly virulent antisemitic environment, until the rights accorded to Jews over the course of the preceding century and more began to be suspended, most heinously with the rise of Adolf Hitler and his National Socialist Party. As Victoria Barnett writes in Chapter 7, 'the German Jewish community experienced a traumatic and unexpected transition from an era of emancipation and assimilation to persecution'. This transition led, ultimately, to the Holocaust, which represents the first of two major historical events in the centuries covered by Part III of the book which had, and continue to have, an enormous influence on Jewish–Christian relations.

Of course, race and not religion was the dominant motive for the Nazis' genocide. They aimed at identifying and murdering every single person they considered to be a Jew – without exception. They included Jews who had converted to Christianity, such as Edith Stein, who became a Carmelite nun and with her sister Rosa perished at Auschwitz. (Controversy about Stein erupted with her canonisation in 1998, which, while acknowledging her Jewishness, recognised her as a Christian martyr.) Yet if race provided the mythology and motivation, secularised religious language provided the justification. In *Mein Kampf* (1924) Hitler did not hesitate to use overtly Christian language to appeal to a pious audience. Many Christians came to agree with him and many more stood by when the Nazis enacted policies that built on existing racist and religious attitudes towards Jews in Europe, helping to pave the way to Auschwitz. The Third Reich neutralised the Protestant churches as effectively as it did the Roman Catholic Church, for example by proclaiming a new Reich Church which forcibly brought together all Protestant churches under Bishop Ludwig Müller.

By the time World War II ended in 1945, so had a whole way of life for European Jews. Their numbers were decimated – 6 million had perished. Fewer than 10 per cent of the pre-war Jewish populations of Poland, Latvia, Lithuania, Estonia, Germany and Austria survived, and fewer than 30 per cent of Jews in occupied Russia, Ukraine, Belgium, Yugoslavia, Norway and Romania.

In the Holocaust the morality of many Christians, including leaders of the churches, was tried and found wanting, though a few Christians (and some Muslims) helped their Jewish neighbours, with rescuers later reporting a mixture of motivations, from Christian beliefs to simple humanitarianism; in some instances it was even possible for individuals to hold antisemitic beliefs and still engage in rescue. Eugenio Pacelli, Pope Pius XII from 1939 to 1958, remains an especially controversial figure, with some scholars claiming that he knew much and yet did nothing of importance to help Jews during the Holocaust, while others retort that he did what he could and encouraged others to do more. Widely agreed to be an exception to the prevailing inaction was Angelo Giuseppe Roncalli (Pope John XXIII from 1958 to 1963) who, as Papal nuncio for Turkey and Greece, made available baptismal certificates to thousands of Hungarian Jews in a bid to persuade Germans to leave them unmolested.

The theological problems raised by the Holocaust for Christianity were immense since most Europeans were, at least nominally, Christian. While the perpetrators were relatively few in number, most Christians, from the highest to the lowest, were bystanders and looked aside. Since the end of World War II, there has been increasing reflection on the Holocaust, contributing to a fundamental shift in Christian attitudes towards Jews. As Karma Ben-Johanan writes in Chapter 8, 'From high-ranking Vatican officials to independent theologians, Christian thinkers and leaders listened to the claims of their Jewish critics and used them, from around the mid-1960s, to call for an overarching revision of Christian theology.' This revision led, most notably, to the document *Nostra aetate*, promulgated at the Second Vatican Council in 1965, which symbolised a transformation in Jewish–Christian relations and ushered in a new era, a new discourse concerning Jews never previously heard in the Catholic Church. The concept of a dialogue now entered the mainstream of the relationship and began to be institutionalised, and institutional statements, several of which are collected in the Appendix to Part III, became a common feature of formal Jewish–Christian encounters.

The second major historical event in this period to influence Jewish–Christian relations was the creation in 1948 of the State of Israel. As Karma Ben-Johanan comments, 'The question of how to relate to the State of Israel stood at the heart of the Jewish–Christian relationship and was second only to the issue of Christian responsibility (or lack thereof) for the Holocaust.' Indeed, the challenge to Christian thinking presented by the Holocaust was, while profoundly difficult and disturbing, in some ways a clearer one than that presented by the shift, among some Jews, from waiting for a divine solution to anti-Jewish violence to seeking to take their destiny into their own hands and create a Jewish homeland in Palestine.

The approach of the Roman Catholic Church to Zionism had changed since Herzl's meeting with Pius X in 1904, when the pope rejected his request for support, and the Vatican formally recognised the State of Israel in 1993. In 2000 Pope John Paul II made a pilgrimage to Israel, a practice followed by his successors Benedict XVI and Francis, in 2009 and 2014, respectively. Protestantism was, and remains, deeply divided on Zionism. There are some who conclude, like the Palestinian Anglican priest Naim Ateek, that it represents a profane corruption of Judaism's true prophetic mission; others, including evangelicals such as the International Christian Embassy in Jerusalem, fervently support Israel and turn to scripture, for example the promises to Abraham in Genesis 12, as justification.

In the first decades of the twenty-first century, the subject of Israel remains a major area of tension in Jewish–Christian relations. For Jews, the uniqueness of the land of the Bible, as well as 40 per cent of the world's Jewish population, is at stake. At the same time, however, trends show that Jews in the diaspora, and particularly young people, are increasingly divided and alienated from engaging with Israel. Divergence of views towards Israel can also be found among Christians, who of course feel particular concern for fellow Christians living in the nation state of Israel as well as for Palestinians as a whole. The long-lasting Israeli–Palestinian conflict, especially during war or even outbursts of violence, makes the topic even more difficult to discuss. The 2023–4 war in Gaza, for example, resulted in huge pressure on Jewish–Christian relationships and even fractured some dialogue groups.

One factor to reckon with is Christian status as a minority in the Middle East as a whole. Not only are Christians a minority within the State of Israel – approximately 200,000 in a population of 9 million – they also represent only 10 per cent of the Arab population of 2 million (as of 2023). Purely on the psychological level, church representatives feel under pressure. Yet Christian Arabs and Muslim Arabs, whatever their religious differences might be, live in one society, speak one language and share one culture. Dialogue with Muslims is sometimes a priority for Christians, especially in places where there are no Jews.

In addition, there has been a small but increasing number of violent attacks on Christians and Christian properties by extremist nationalist Jews. In the 1970s the attacks were linked to Meir Kahane and his party, Kach ('power'), which was banned for its overt racism, but the assimilation of the next generation of Kahanists into government from 2022 has coincided with an increase in anti-Christian violence.

With this exception, however, it seems that Jews and Christians have reached a stage where many of the main divisive issues have been either eliminated or taken to the furthest point at which agreement is possible. The efforts of Christians towards respect for Judaism project attitudes that would have been unthinkable a few decades earlier. Even in the Global South, where few Jews live, Christians are better informed by the churches about these new perspectives. Jewish attitudes to Christianity have, for the most part, also become more positive, as epitomised by the cross-denominational Jewish statement *Dabru Emet* (*Speak Truth*), published in 2000 and included in the Appendix to Part III. The Jewish people, this document asserts, need to learn about the efforts of Christians to honour Judaism and to reflect on what Judaism may now say about Christianity. Since then, statements have been issued by various Jewish denominations, including Orthodox Judaism, although ultra-Orthodox Jews continue to show little or no interest in Christianity.

And so we come to the final chapter of this volume, in which Mary Boys highlights the 'significant scholarly literature that demonstrates the flourishing of Jewish–Christian relations across a range of significant issues, perspectives, authors and methods' and points to 'a more nuanced understanding of the historical matrix in which Judaism and Christianity emerged through mutually formative processes'. The documents in Chapter 9 reflect on many of the themes that the *Documentary History* charts over 2,000 years. Some of these, such as the land and State of Israel discussed above, have come to the fore of the Jewish–Christian encounter as a result of recent historical developments. Others, such as the question of scripture and its interpretation, have persisted throughout. Others still are deeply intertwined, as witness the way polemic and argument have, since the earliest period, been closely related to identity and self-understanding.

One such close interrelationship, between mission and dialogue, can be traced to New Testament times and has once again become a subject of theological discussion between Jews and Christians in the form of the role of covenant. German scholar Friedrich-Wilhelm Marquardt viewed covenant as the most constructive biblical concept to explore Christian–Jewish relations and help develop a positive Christian identity. The church can only hope to become a partner in a covenantal relationship with the people of Israel, Marquardt argued, if it joins in the calling of Israel to restore the world and embarks on a joint journey to the 'new covenant' with God. In other words, rather than a mission *to* Jews, Marquardt called for a mission *with* Jews. Similarly, the rediscovery of the

Jewishness of Jesus, which began in the late nineteenth century, has been followed since the second half of the twentieth by a rereading of Paul's writings in their Jewish context, as exemplified by the Lutheran scholar Krister Stendahl, who argued that Paul could not accept the idea that Jews as a people and a religion are totally and forever outside the people of God. According to Stendahl, Paul suggests that both Israel and the church are elect and both participate in the covenant of God.

Perhaps the most notable shift in the contemporary Jewish–Christian encounter has been that from polemic to dialogue, requiring a genuine hearing of 'the other' and taking the other as seriously as one demands to be taken oneself. This means asking to what extent Christians can view Judaism as a valid religion in its own terms (and vice versa). Polemic of course still exists, but there is a growing recognition that it is best tackled together. The New Testament shares a problem with the Hebrew Bible (and all holy texts), that polemical writings, against a named other, once enshrined in sacred documents, carry a weight and authority throughout history. Moreover, they are constantly available to justify appalling actions in the name of God. Their very existence is and remains the problem. Clearly, they are not going to be expurgated. Tackling polemical texts, sometimes called 'difficult texts', is thus a challenge faced by Jews and Christians alike. One response has been reading texts within their proper historical context, since it demonstrably makes a difference if the reader understands something of the background and context from which these texts came. Although this cannot render a text innocent or change the history of its effect, the joint study of the reception history (*Wirkungsgeschichte*) of the text may begin the process of overcoming its negative impact, showing that questions can be jointly addressed, not in enmity but in partnership. If the collection of documents included in this book can help in furthering that process, it will have achieved one of its aims.

Bibliography

Flannery, Edward H., *The Anguish of the Jews: Twenty-Three Centuries of Antisemitism*, rev. ed. (New York: Paulist Press, 1985).

Fry, Helen (ed.), *Christian–Jewish Dialogue: A Reader* (Exeter: University of Exeter Press, 1996).

Homolka, Walter, Kampling, Rainer, Levine, Amy-Jill, Markschies, Christoph, Schäfer, Peter and Thurner, Martin (eds.), *Encyclopedia of Jewish–Christian Relations Online* (De Gruyter, 2019–24), www.ejcr-project.com/.

www.jcrelations.net. Published by the International Council of Christians and Jews.

Kessler, Edward, *An Introduction to Jewish–Christian Relations* (Cambridge: Cambridge University Press, 2010).

Kessler, Edward, and Wenborn, Neil (eds.), *A Dictionary of Jewish–Christian Relations* (Cambridge: Cambridge University Press, 2005).

Marcus, Jacob Rader, and Saperstein, Marc, *The Jews in Christian Europe: A Source Book, 315–1791* (Pittsburgh: Hebrew Union College Press; University of Pittsburgh Press, 2015).

Mendes-Flohr, Paul, and Reinharz, Jehuda (eds.), *The Jew in the Modern World: A Documentary History*, 3rd ed. (New York: Oxford University Press, 2011).

Osten-Sacken, Peter von der, *Christian–Jewish Dialogue: Theological Foundations*, trans. Margaret Cole (Philadelphia: Fortress Press, 1986).

Rubin, Alexis P. (ed.), *Scattered among the Nations: Documents Affecting Jewish History, 49 to 1975* (Toronto: Wall & Emerson, 1993).

Studies in Christian–Jewish Relations, www.ccjr.us/journal-christian-studies (2001–). (*Studies in Christian–Jewish Relations* is the journal of the Council of Centers on Jewish–Christian Relations and is published by the Center for Christian–Jewish Learning at Boston College.)

Talmage, Frank E. (ed.), *Disputation and Dialogue: Readings in the Jewish–Christian Encounter* (New York: Ktav Publishing House, 1975).

PART I

To 900 CE

I

The New Testament
The First to the Early Second Century
MATTHEW V. NOVENSON

INTRODUCTION

The history of Jewish–Christian relations is as old as Christianity. Jews and Judaism are much older, of course. But as soon as there were Christians, they had to reckon with Jews, and Jews with them. In the *very* earliest period, in fact, more or less all 'Christians' were Jews, and the name 'Christian' did not exist yet. What we call Christianity was, in the beginning, just one minor messianic sect within the Judaism of the early Roman empire. Jesus of Nazareth was a Jewish teacher and wonderworker from Galilee, latterly acclaimed as messiah by his (likewise Galilean, Jewish) band of disciples. After Jesus' execution by the Roman provincial administration under Tiberius (early 30s CE), this band of disciples continued to teach his message of the kingdom of God, and other, latecomer messengers (also Jewish: people like Paul, Barnabas, Andronicus, Junia and Apollos) joined them.

By the reign of Nero in the 60s CE – about a generation after the death of Jesus – many, perhaps most, participants in this new Christ religion were gentiles, a demographic shift whose importance is hard to overstate. But even in the 60s, the name 'Christianity' was not yet current. These people were just gentiles-in-Christ, gentile devotees of the Jewish God and his son, the risen messiah Jesus. The name 'Christian' first occurs in sources from around the turn of the second century CE (1 Pet. 4:16; Acts 11:26, 26:28; Josephus, *Jewish Antiquities* 18.63–64; Pliny, *Epistles* 10.96; Tacitus, *Annals* 15.44; Suetonius, *Nero* 16). In some of these sources it is used of people living in the mid-first century, but this may be anachronistic, since sources from the mid-first century do not yet use, or show any knowledge of, the term. The abstract noun 'Christianity' is a little later still, a coinage of the Bishop Ignatius of Antioch in the early second century (Ignatius, *Epistle to the Romans* 3:3; *Epistle to the Magnesians* 10:1–3; *Epistle to the Philadelphians* 6:1).

When Ignatius coins the Greek word *Christianismos* ('Christianity'), he coins it, tellingly, in contrast to *Ioudaismos* ('Judaism'). Already in Ignatius, Christian self-understanding is dependent on and derivative from a concept of Jews and Judaism. Ancient Christian thinkers from Ignatius onwards were deeply invested in at least one aspect of (what we call) Jewish–Christian relations because, given the actual historical origins of Christianity, Christians did not know who they were, religiously, apart from Jews and Judaism. By contrast, Jewish thinkers of this early period (the *tannaim*, in particular) went on their merry way without thinking of Christians most of the time, if their literary sources are any indication. Only in the fourth century and later, when Christian state power was ascendant, did Jewish literary sources begin to pay reciprocal attention to Christians, once it became politically urgent to do so.

This late antique encounter between rabbis and church fathers is documented in Chapters 2 and 3 below. In the present chapter, however, we are concerned only with the very earliest period, the first to early second centuries CE. The documents in this chapter differ from those in all the subsequent chapters inasmuch as they come from a time when the terms 'Jewish' and 'Christian' did not yet mark out separate identities. Of the twenty-three documents in this chapter, twenty-two are excerpted from texts in the canonical New Testament, and one comes from the Jewish-Roman historian Flavius Josephus. None of these documents calls itself 'Christian', and only two of the authors represented here even know of the word 'Christian'. Most, perhaps all, of the authors of these documents were Jews. All of them – except Josephus – also venerated Christ, but it does not follow that they considered themselves 'Christian'. That is our later label for them, not their own.

As we shall see, this change of labels has yielded some strange (and sometimes tragic) moments in the subsequent history of interpretation. For although most of the authors of the texts comprising the New Testament were Jewish, almost all of their readers down the centuries have been gentile Christians. And when gentile Christians in the second, fifth, sixteenth or twenty-first century make new, canonical, Christian meanings out of these ancient Jewish texts, these new meanings are often many miles away from the original meanings, often (though not always) in a conspicuously anti-Jewish direction. In the commentary accompanying each respective document below, we shall try to unpick these layers of interpretation: to show both what sense the document makes in its original, first-century context and also the senses it has made to later readers down the centuries.

As regards the history of Jewish–Christian relations, then, the documents in this chapter have a twofold function. In their first-century context, they are artefacts of what we could, with only slight anachronism, call Jewish–Christian relations in that period: the encounter between the earliest Christ-believers (many of them Jewish, some gentile) and the Jewish majority. Also in their first-century context, these documents attest the historically unusual combination of traditional Jewish piety and Christ-devotion in a single Jewish thinker, as in the case of the apostle Paul, John of Patmos or the author of the Gospel of Matthew. But the documents in this chapter also have an equally important second function: they are canonical resources for a great deal of later reflection on Jewish–Christian relations from antiquity to the present. In this latter capacity, these documents will pop up again and again throughout this book, as snippets of them are picked up and reused by church fathers, rabbis, councils, polemicists, theologians and other interested parties.

The ideas of these various interested parties are products of their own widely varying historical contexts, as the later chapters in this volume amply demonstrate. But the seeds of some of these ideas, at least, appear already in the texts collected in the New Testament. For example: although supersessionism proper – the theological idea that the church succeeds and replaces Israel in God's affections – is arguably a second-century innovation, several of our first-century texts invoke the prophet Jeremiah's notion (Jer. 31:31–4) of a 'new covenant' that rectifies some supposed deficiency in the 'old covenant' made with Israel at Mount Sinai; and this contrast of old and new covenants has a long afterlife in many Christian supersessionist theologies. Interestingly, however, the first-century texts do not yet imagine the related idea – which we find earliest attested in Justin Martyr (see Chapter 2, p. 75) – of an ostensible 'true, spiritual Israel' (comprising the church) in contrast to 'carnal Israel' (comprising Jews). Another example: although the idea of a perpetual pan-Jewish bloodguilt for the killing of Jesus is a later Christian innovation, at least one New Testament text (Matthew 27:15–26; see document 16 below) does attribute the Roman destruction of Jerusalem in 70 CE to God's judgement upon that generation of Jews who assented to the crucifixion of Jesus; and later bloodguilt theorists were all too happy to point to the Gospel in support of their claims. One last, more edifying, example: all of the many variations on a 'family tree' model of Jewish–Christian relations are indebted – most of them knowingly and expressly – to one extraordinarily influential first-century text: the apostle Paul's Letter to the Romans, which figures God's people as an olive tree, with Israel as the natural branches and the gentiles as branches artificially grafted in (see document 6 below). Here, too, as in the uglier examples noted above, a first-century text provides the fodder for centuries' worth of Jewish–Christian engagement.

In the commentaries and bibliographies that follow, readers will encounter quite a lot of modern New Testament scholarship, the results of which we have tried to make as clear and accessible as possible. For most of its roughly 250-year history, modern New Testament scholarship has been a rather niche project undertaken by gentile Christian academics working in historically Christian universities. Before the mid-twentieth century, there were only relatively rare exceptions to this rule, but in the decades since the academic study of the New Testament has significantly expanded to include a wide variety of non-sectarian institutions and non-Christian scholars. It has, in short, become a much more *public* discipline than it once was, undertaken by academics of all faiths and none. One upshot of this development is that today many of the world's leading scholars of the New Testament – Adele Reinhartz, Amy-Jill Levine, Paula Fredriksen, Mark Nanos, Yair Furstenberg and others, all of whom appear in the bibliographies in this chapter – are themselves Jewish, which has made the whole discourse around Jews and Judaism in the New Testament a great deal more intellectually honest and morally accountable than it has often been in years past.

Not unrelated to this demographic shift in the field has been the rediscovery – especially in post-Holocaust scholarship – of the Jewishness of the New Testament itself. There were occasional, praiseworthy exceptions in older scholarship, but the dominant tradition by far was to read the New Testament *over against* Judaism, as a foil or a rival. Historians of the New Testament today, however, recognise most or all of the texts comprising the New Testament as originally Jewish works, written by Jewish authors, about Jewish ideas, for Jewish audiences (as well as some gentile audiences). The transformation of these Jewish texts into Christian scripture – important as it was and is – was a later, secondary development. Groundbreaking studies like Krister Stendahl's 'The Apostle Paul and the Introspective Conscience of the West' (1963) (see Chapter 8, p. 418), Geza Vermes' *Jesus the Jew* (1973) and E. P. Sanders' *Paul and Palestinian Judaism* (1977) paved the way for this new consensus, a monument to which is Amy-Jill Levine and Marc Zvi Brettler's remarkable *Jewish Annotated New Testament* (2011) (see also Chapter 9, p. 499). The influence of this sea change in scholarship will be very evident in the commentaries below.

Here it will be helpful to say a word about the organisation of the documents and commentaries in this chapter. Many people are accustomed to seeing New Testament texts in their received *canonical* order: Matthew, Mark, Luke, John, Acts, Romans, 1 Corinthians and so on. In this chapter, however, we discuss our excerpted documents in (their most likely, reconstructed) *chronological* order: Paul (40s–50s CE), Mark (70s CE), Matthew (80s–90s CE) and so on. The reason for this is that some of our documents almost certainly know, build on, or even react against other, earlier ones. So we can only see the relations between them clearly if we take them in the order in which they were probably written. This is the approach taken in the other chapters of this *Documentary History* as well (with the exception of Chapter 3, for reasons explained in the Introduction to that chapter; see p. 118), so it makes good sense to follow it here. Readers who may at first find this disorientating will soon see how it makes a lot of things fall into place.

Documents 1–7 below are all excerpted from the undisputed letters of Paul. Whereas many of the texts comprising the New Testament are anonymous, the undisputed letters of Paul permit us at least a degree of prosopography: the possibility of connecting up certain texts to a particular, known historical person. Importantly for our topic, too, Paul is the only New Testament author who certainly wrote before 70 CE, the year the Roman army sacked Jerusalem and destroyed the Second Temple, and a fundamental watershed in Jewish history. That also puts him in the first generation of the Christ groups, a period when some – including Paul – still expected the arrival of the kingdom of God and the end of all things within their own lifetime. In a number of passages, Paul reflects directly on the question of the relation of Israel to the gentiles in the kingdom of God, and these reflections have been put to quite diverse uses in the history of Jewish–Christian relations. Document 8, an excerpt from the Letter to the Hebrews, was not written by Paul but is indebted to him, and was received by many ancient Christians as if it were by Paul, hence its inclusion here.

From there we move to the Gospels, taking them in chronological order. Documents 9–12 are excerpted from Mark, the earliest of the four canonical Gospels, written around 70 CE. Mark is the earliest extant narrative of the life of Jesus (about which Paul says very little), written some four decades or so after the events. It is thus a record of the time about which it purports to write, c. 30 CE, as well as the time when it was written, c. 70 CE. Mark is important both as a literary work in its own right and as the principal source for subsequent Gospel writers: certainly Matthew and Luke, and very probably John as well. Documents 13–16 are excerpted from the Gospel of Matthew, written sometime in the last quarter of the first century. Matthew's many additions to Mark include, among other things, some quite loaded passages pertaining to Jews and Judaism, all of which are discussed below.

With document 17, we take an intermission from the Gospels and consider an excerpt from the Apocalypse of John (also known as the Book of Revelation), a text written around the same time as the Gospel of Matthew – hence its chronological place here – by a Jewish author, John of Patmos, for an audience of probably Jewish Christ-followers. Documents 18–20 are excerpted from a structurally unusual book which modern critics call Luke–Acts: the Gospel of Luke and the Acts of the Apostles, which were originally two volumes of a single work by one anonymous author (whom tradition calls 'Luke'). This 'Luke' was either a Jew himself or an exceptionally well-informed gentile, and he draws upon Mark and possibly Matthew as well, to tell the life of Jesus and his first-generation disciples. Documents 21 and 22 come from the Gospel of John, the fourth and most literarily distinctive of the canonical Gospels. Its author, who probably uses at least Mark as a source, is – like Luke, but in his own quite different way – tremendously well-informed about Jews and Judaism (perhaps as an ethnic insider) but also writes some very harsh polemic about Jews, as we explain in the commentaries below.

The one excerpt from Josephus (document 23), the so-called *Testimonium Flavianum*, is the obvious outlier; it is the only document in this chapter that is not part of the canonical New Testament. But it is a very important text, and it makes better sense here than anywhere else. Like the other documents in this chapter, it is a late first- or early second-century Jewish text about Jesus of Nazareth, even if its author was not a follower of Jesus. What is more, arguably at least one New Testament author (the author of Luke–Acts) actually knew and used Josephus. For all these reasons, we include Josephus alongside Paul, Mark, Matthew, Luke and the rest as a witness to this earliest chapter in the history of Jewish–Christian relations.

Bibliography

Carleton Paget, James, *Jews, Christians, and Jewish Christians in Antiquity* (Tübingen: Mohr Siebeck, 2010).

Chilton, Bruce, and Neusner, Jacob, *Judaism in the New Testament: Practices and Beliefs* (London: Routledge, 1995).

Donaldson, Terence L., *Jews and Anti-Judaism in the New Testament: Decision Points and Divergent Interpretations* (London: SPCK, 2010).

Fredriksen, Paula, *When Christians Were Jews: The First Generation* (New Haven: Yale University Press, 2018).

Fredriksen, Paula, and Reinhartz, Adele (eds.), *Jesus, Judaism, and Christian Anti-Judaism: Reading the New Testament after the Holocaust* (Louisville: Westminster John Knox, 2002).

Gager, John G., *The Origins of Anti-Semitism: Attitudes toward Judaism in Pagan and Christian Antiquity* (Oxford: Oxford University Press, 1985).

Levine, Amy-Jill, *The Misunderstood Jew: The Church and the Scandal of the Jewish Jesus* (San Francisco: Harper, 2006).

Levine, Amy-Jill, and Brettler, Marc Zvi, *The Bible with and without Jesus: How Jews and Christians Read the Same Stories Differently* (San Francisco: Harper, 2020).

Levine, Amy-Jill, and Brettler, Marc Zvi (eds.), *The Jewish Annotated New Testament*, 2nd ed. (Oxford: Oxford University Press, 2017).

Murray, Michele, *Playing a Jewish Game: Gentile Christian Judaizing in the First and Second Centuries*
 CE (Waterloo, ON: Wilfrid Laurier University Press, 2004).
Stendahl, Krister, *Paul among Jews and Gentiles, and Other Essays* (Philadelphia: Fortress, 1976).
Tomson, Peter J., and Schwarz, Joshua (eds.), *Jews and Christians in the First and Second Centuries:
 How to Write Their History* (Leiden: Brill, 2014).
Vermes, Geza, *Jesus and the World of Judaism* (London: SCM, 1983).

DOCUMENTS

I

1 Thessalonians 2:13–16 (mid-first century CE)

Text

$^{2:13}$ We also constantly give thanks to God for this, that when you received the word of God that you heard from us you accepted it not as a human word but as what it really is, God's word, which is also at work in you believers. ^{14} For you, brothers and sisters, became imitators of the churches of God in Christ Jesus that are in Judea, for you suffered the same things from your own compatriots as they did from the Jews ^{15} who killed both the Lord Jesus and the prophets and drove us out; they displease God and oppose everyone ^{16} by hindering us from speaking to the gentiles so that they may be saved. Thus they have constantly been filling up the measure of their sins, but wrath has overtaken them at last.

Commentary

Paul, apostle of Christ to the gentiles, was born around the turn of the era, a near-contemporary to Philo of Alexandria and Jesus of Nazareth. The Acts of the Apostles says that his Hebrew name was Saul and that he was from Tarsus in Cilicia, Asia Minor, but his own letters say nothing about either of these biographical questions. He is simply Paul, Greek-speaking diaspora Jew and apostle of Christ. The First Letter to the Thessalonians is probably the earliest of his extant letters, making it also the earliest text in the New Testament – written in the 40s CE and sent to the assembly of gentiles-in-Christ at Thessalonike in Macedonia. (The Greek word *ekklēsia*, usually translated as 'church', is an old Greek civic term meaning 'assembly'. The 'assemblies' to which Paul writes are, on the evidence of the letters themselves, mostly or entirely composed of gentiles who have been baptised into Christ.) In this letter, Paul praises them for turning away from idols to the true God (1 Thess. 1:9–10) and encourages them not to despair for their comrades who die while they wait for the appearance of Christ (1 Thess. 4:13–18).

In the document here excerpted, Paul draws a parallel between the social opprobrium suffered by the Thessalonians-in-Christ from their (Thessalonian) neighbours and that suffered by the Judeans-in-Christ from their (Judean) neighbours. In Macedonia as in the Jewish homeland, he says, the Christ assemblies find themselves harassed by outsiders. In Judea, however, those outsiders are of course Judeans (or Jews, since there is only one Greek word, *Ioudaioi*, underlying both English words). Paul then itemises a number of bad things they have supposedly done: killing Jesus, killing the prophets, expelling Paul, displeasing God, hindering Paul preaching to gentiles, filling up the measure of their sins. (This lattermost phrase is an old biblical idiom for doing wrong to so great an extent that God's wrath is forced to intervene [e.g., Gen. 15:16; Dan. 8:23].)

There is a famous problem to do with the so-called antisemitic comma at the end of v. 14, which is printed in the widely used NRSV translation (though not in the NRSVue translation given above): 'you suffered the same things from your own compatriots as they did from the Jews, who killed both the Lord Jesus and the prophets' (NRSV). Punctuated thus, the text seems to suggest that *the Jews* – without qualification – killed Jesus and the prophets, a notion that would feed into the later Christian myth of Jews as Christ-killers. This, together with a common reading of v. 16 – 'wrath has overtaken them at last' – as an allusion to the destruction of Jerusalem in 70 CE (several years after the death of Paul!), has persuaded some that this passage is a later interpolation: not an original part of Paul's letter, but a gloss inserted by an anti-Jewish Christian scribe. That hypothesis could be true, but there are no manuscripts of 1 Thessalonians that lack the offending verses. It could be, then, that the passage is original to Paul, but that it refers not to all Jews, but only to those Judeans who opposed Jesus and the apostles in the earliest days of the Christ movement. The wrath overtaking them, in that case, would refer not to the destruction of 70 CE but to some lesser, local catastrophe.

Bibliography

Bockmuehl, Markus, '1 Thessalonians 2:14–16 and the Church in Jerusalem', *Tyndale Bulletin* 52 (2001), 1–31.

Gilliard, Frank D., 'The Problem of the Antisemitic Comma between 1 Thessalonians 2.14 and 15', *New Testament Studies* 35 (1989), 481–502.

Pearson, Birger A., '1 Thessalonians 2:13–16: A Deutero-Pauline Interpolation', *Harvard Theological Review* 64 (1971), 79–94.

2

Galatians 2:15–3:14, 4:21–5:10 (mid-first century CE)

Text

2:15 We ourselves are Jews by birth and not gentile sinners, 16 yet we know that a person is justified not by the works of the law but through the faith of Jesus Christ. And we have come to believe in Christ Jesus, so that we might be justified by the faith of Christ and not by doing the works of the law, because no one will be justified by the works of the law. [17] But if, in our effort to be justified in Christ, we ourselves have been found to be sinners, is Christ then a servant of sin? Certainly not! [18] But if I build up again the very things that I once tore down, then I demonstrate that I am a transgressor. [19] For through the law I died to the law, so that I might live to God. I have been crucified with Christ, [20] and it is no longer I who live, but it is Christ who lives in me. And the life I now live in the flesh I live by the faith of the Son of God, who loved me and gave himself for me. [21] I do not nullify the grace of God, for if righteousness comes through the law, then Christ died for nothing.

[3:1] You foolish Galatians! Who has bewitched you? It was before your eyes that Jesus Christ was publicly exhibited as crucified! [2] The only thing I want to learn from you is this: Did you receive the Spirit by doing the works of the law or by believing what you heard? [3] Are you so foolish? Having started with the Spirit, are you now ending with the flesh? [4] Did you experience so much for nothing? – if it really was for nothing. [5] Well then, does God supply you with the Spirit and work miracles among you by your doing the works of the law or by your believing what you heard?

[6] Just as Abraham 'believed God, and it was reckoned to him as righteousness,' [Gen. 15:6] [7] so, you see, those who believe are the descendants of Abraham. [8] And the scripture, foreseeing that God would reckon as righteous the gentiles by faith, declared the gospel beforehand to Abraham, saying, 'All the gentiles shall be blessed in you.' [Gen. 12:3; 22:18] [9] For this reason, those who believe are blessed with Abraham who believed.

[10] For all who rely on the works of the law are under a curse, for it is written, 'Cursed is everyone who does not observe and obey all the things written in the book of the law.' [Deut. 27:26] [11] Now it is evident that no one is reckoned as righteous before God by the law, for 'the one who is righteous will live by faith.' [Hab. 2:4] [12] But the law does not rest on faith; on the contrary, 'Whoever does the works of the law will live by them.' [Lev. 18:5] [13] Christ redeemed us from the curse of the law by becoming a curse for us – for it is written, 'Cursed is everyone who hangs on a tree' [Deut. 21:23] – [14] in order that in Christ Jesus the blessing of Abraham might come to the gentiles, so that we might receive the promise of the Spirit through faith […]

[4:21] Tell me, you who desire to be subject to the law, will you not listen to the law? [22] For it is written that Abraham had two sons, one by an enslaved woman and the other by a free woman. [23] One, the child of the enslaved woman, was born according to the flesh; the other, the child of the free woman, was born through the promise. [24] Now this is an allegory: these women are two covenants. One woman, in fact, is Hagar, from Mount Sinai, bearing children for slavery. [25] Now Hagar is Mount Sinai in Arabia and corresponds to the present Jerusalem, for she is in slavery with her children. [26] But the other woman corresponds to the Jerusalem above; she is free, and she is our mother. [27] For it is written,

'Rejoice, you childless one, you who bear no children,
    burst into song and shout, you who endure no birth pangs,
 for the children of the desolate woman are more numerous
    than the children of the one who is married.' [Isa. 54:1]

[28] Now you, my brothers and sisters, are children of the promise, like Isaac. [29] But just as at that time the child who was born according to the flesh persecuted the child who was born according to the Spirit, so it is now also. [30] But what does the scripture say? 'Drive out the enslaved woman and her child, for the child of the enslaved woman will not share the inheritance with the child of the free woman.' [Gen. 21:10] [31] So then, brothers and sisters, we are children, not of an enslaved woman but of the free woman. [5:1] For freedom Christ has set us free. Stand firm, therefore, and do not submit again to a yoke of slavery.

[2] Listen! I, Paul, am telling you that, if you let yourselves be circumcised, Christ will be of no benefit to you. [3] Once again I testify to every man who lets himself be circumcised that he is obliged to obey the entire law. [4] You who want to be reckoned as righteous by the law have cut yourselves off from Christ; you have fallen away from grace. [5] For through the Spirit, by faith, we eagerly wait for the hope of righteousness. [6] For in Christ Jesus neither circumcision nor uncircumcision counts for anything; the only thing that counts is faith working through love.

[7] You were running well; who prevented you from obeying the truth? [8] Such persuasion does not come from the one who calls you. [9] A little yeast leavens the whole batch of dough. [10] I am confident about you in the Lord that you will not think otherwise. But whoever it is that is confusing you will pay the penalty.

Commentary

Paul's Letter to the Galatians is arguably the single most important New Testament text for later forms of Christian *theological* anti-Judaism. The letter's stark binaries of law versus promise, works of the law versus Christ-faith and flesh versus spirit have been used by many Christian readers (especially Martin Luther and his Protestant heirs) to frame an equally stark binary between Judaism and Christianity. The irony here is that Paul himself, in the letter, rages not against Judaism but against another form of (what we moderns would call) Christianity. Galatians is another relatively early letter of Paul, sent in the 50s CE to a cluster of gentile Christ-assemblies (*ekklēsiai*) in Galatia in central Asia Minor. The whole burden of the letter is to dissuade the gentile, Christ-believing men in the assembly from undergoing Jewish proselyte circumcision (thus the warning in Gal. 5:2, near the end of the excerpt above: 'if you let yourselves be circumcised, Christ will be of no benefit to you'). In between Paul's earlier, in-person visit to Galatia and the writing of the letter, some other apostles of Christ had come telling the men in the assemblies that they should undergo circumcision in order to become proper sons of Abraham. Paul hears of this and writes a letter angrily insisting that they not do so.

In Galatians 2, the beginning of the excerpt above, Paul makes one major point of the letter: that justification (Paul's technical term for transferral into the perfect righteousness of the eschaton) comes only from Christ, the messiah, not from the law of Moses. The law of Moses is righteous, he says, but it cannot transfer anyone into the age to come (what Paul calls the 'inheritance' that God promised to father Abraham); only the messiah can do that. This is the point on which he thinks the rival apostles are misleading people. Galatians 3 comprises a dense cluster of arguments from proof-texts in the Torah and prophets. Paul claims that the Torah itself testifies that it was only meant to legislate for people who sin and die. But Habakkuk prophesies a kind of righteousness from faith by which people will live forever. The messiah 'redeem[s] us from the curse of the law' – namely, the curse of dying – by dying himself and then rising again, thereby triggering the new creation. In Galatians 4, Paul draws an elaborate allegory (similar in form, but not in content, to Philo of Alexandria's allegorical readings of Genesis) about Ishmael being born to Hagar and Isaac to Sarah. The proselyte-circumcised Galatians-in-Christ are like Ishmael the slave, Paul says, while the foreskinned gentiles-in-Christ are like Isaac the heir. Both are sons of Abraham, strictly speaking, but only the latter stand to inherit God's promise, which for Paul is the immortal life of the spirit (Gal. 3:14). Later interpreters, by using categories and contexts that were unavailable to Paul, have often read this as a supersessionist allegory for Judaism and Christianity (thus, e.g., Marius Victorinus, Chrysostom, Jerome, Thomas Aquinas, Luther). With hindsight, we can see how these Christian thinkers made such an interpretation of this text, but it is historically as well as morally dubious.

Bibliography

Bachmann, Michael, *Anti-Judaism in Galatians?*, trans. Robert L. Brawley (Grand Rapids: Eerdmans, 2008).

Elliott, Mark W., Hafemann, Scott J., Wright, N. T., and Frederick, John (eds.), *Galatians and Christian Theology: Justification, the Gospel, and Ethics in Paul's Letter* (Grand Rapids: Baker, 2014).

Johnson Hodge, Caroline, *If Sons, Then Heirs: A Study of Kinship and Ethnicity in the Letters of Paul* (Oxford: Oxford University Press, 2007).

Sanders, E. P., *Paul, the Law, and the Jewish People* (Philadelphia: Fortress, 1983).

3

2 Corinthians 3:5–16 (mid-first century CE*)*

Text

3:5 Not that we are qualified of ourselves to claim anything as coming from us; our qualification is from God, [6] who has made us qualified to be ministers of a new covenant, not of letter but of spirit, for the letter kills, but the Spirit gives life.

[7] Now if the ministry of death, chiseled in letters on stone tablets, came in glory so that the people of Israel could not gaze at Moses's face because of the glory of his face, a glory now set aside, [8] how much more will the ministry of the Spirit come in glory? [9] For if there was glory in the ministry of condemnation, much more does the ministry of justification abound in glory! [10] Indeed, what once had glory has in this respect lost its glory because of the greater glory, [11] for if what was set aside came through glory, much more has the permanent come in glory!

[12] Since, then, we have such a hope, we act with complete frankness, [13] not like Moses, who put a veil over his face to keep the people of Israel from gazing at the end of the glory

that was being set aside. [14] But their minds were hardened. Indeed, to this very day, when they hear the reading of the old covenant, the same veil is still there; it is not unveiled since in Christ it is set aside. [15] Indeed, to this very day whenever Moses is read, a veil lies over their minds, [16] but when one turns to the Lord, the veil is removed.

Commentary

In this excerpt from his Second Letter to the Corinthians, the apostle Paul commends himself to his audience of gentiles-in-Christ by identifying his own apostolic work as the fulfilment of the prophet Jeremiah's promise of a new covenant: [31] 'The days are surely coming, says the LORD, when I will make a new covenant with the house of Israel and the house of Judah. [32] It will not be like the covenant that I made with their ancestors [...] [33] [T]his is the covenant that I will make with the house of Israel after those days, says the LORD: I will put my law within them, and I will write it on their hearts' (Jer. 31:31–3, NRSVue). Paul believes that his own announcement of Christ *is* this new covenant, and he contrasts it – following the contrast drawn by Jeremiah – with the covenant at Mount Sinai.

The covenant at Mount Sinai Paul calls the 'the ministry of death', 'the ministry of condemnation' and 'the old covenant'. Indeed, it is from this passage – via the north African Latin Christian writer Tertullian – that Christians get their habit of referring to the Hebrew Bible or Tanakh as 'the Old Testament', *testamentum* being the Latin gloss for 'covenant' here. Like Jeremiah, Paul imagines that under the new covenant people will be perfectly righteous all the time. (Thus there will be no more death or condemnation, as there was under the 'ministry of death' and 'ministry of condemnation'.) But whereas for Jeremiah that miraculous change lay in a utopian future, Paul is convinced that it is a present reality, and that *he himself* is bringing it about. This would become a puzzle for later Christian interpreters, who realised – as Paul did not – that the present age of sin and death is still, sadly, very much with us. Thus many Christian readers took, and still take, this text to be about not the perfect age to come but rather a current 'Christian' covenant with God, one supposedly more glorious than the covenant at Mount Sinai.

Which is why this text has been a bugbear in Jewish–Christian relations, because, interpreted in the way just described, it strikes a plainly supersessionist and triumphalist note. That is not really what Paul meant, but that fact hardly matters, since it is the history of interpretation that determines a text's impact in the world. Christians (who are, almost all of them, gentiles) have long used this passage to tell Jews that they, Jews, do not know how to read their own scriptures (quoting Paul: 'to this very day, when they hear the reading of the old covenant, the same veil is still there'). Some recent Christian statements have done better, as, for instance, the 2001 Pontifical Biblical Commission document *The Jewish People and Their Sacred Scriptures in the Christian Bible* (see Appendix to Part III, p. 528), which comments on our passage: 'Paul clearly states that "the very words of God were entrusted" to the Israelites (Rm 3:2) and he takes it for granted that these words of God could be read and understood before the coming of Christ. Although he speaks of a blindness of the Jews with regard to "the reading of the Old Testament" (2 Co 3:14), he does not mean a total incapacity to read, only an inability to read it in the light of Christ.' This interpretation is far more humane, not to mention historically accurate, than many earlier Christian ones. But even so, arguably a degree of offence remains in this text no matter how one reads it.

Bibliography

Boyarin, Daniel, *A Radical Jew: Paul and the Politics of Identity* (Berkeley: University of California Press, 1994), 86–105.

Cover, Michael, *Lifting the Veil: 2 Corinthians 3:7–18 in Light of Jewish Homiletic and Commentary Traditions* (Berlin: De Gruyter, 2015).

Duff, Paul B., *Moses in Corinth: The Apologetic Context of 2 Corinthians 3* (Leiden: Brill, 2015).

Fisch, Yael, *Written for Us: Paul's Interpretation of Scripture and the History of Midrash* (Leiden: Brill, 2022).

4

Romans 2:25–9 (mid-first century CE)

Text

²:²⁵ Circumcision indeed is of value if you obey the law, but if you are a transgressor of the law your circumcision has become uncircumcision. ²⁶ So, if the uncircumcised keep the requirements of the law, will not their uncircumcision be regarded as circumcision? ²⁷ Then the physically uncircumcised person who keeps the law will judge you who, though having the written code and circumcision, are a transgressor of the law. ²⁸ For a person is not a Jew who is one outwardly, nor is circumcision something external and physical. ²⁹ Rather, a person is a Jew who is one inwardly, and circumcision is a matter of the heart, by the Spirit, not the written code. Such a person receives praise not from humans but from God.

Commentary

This document is one of several which have caused considerable trouble in Jewish–Christian relations due to poor translations, including, in this case, the NRSVue quoted here (though at least it improves on its predecessors the RSV and NRSV). In most standard English versions of the Bible, this text seems to actually *redefine* who is a Jew and who is circumcised. It seems to suggest that Jewishness and circumcision are inner, spiritual realities, not outward, empirical, bodily marks of identity. It seems to suggest, in fact, that the only *real* 'Jew' and the only *truly* 'circumcised' person is a Christian. To make such a claim would be a barefaced appropriation of Jewish identity for Christians, a move which many Christian thinkers down the centuries have been all too happy to make.

But that is not actually what Paul writes in his Letter to the Romans. In this letter to a group of gentiles-in-Christ at Rome, where Paul hopes to visit and be warmly received, he argues that the only viable way for gentiles to be put right by the Jewish God is through trust in the messiah, not – as some gentiles-in-Christ themselves argued – through proselyte circumcision and adoption of the law of Moses. In Romans 2, Paul reasons with a hypothetical gentile man who has gone and got himself circumcised in order to demonstrate his devotion to the Jewish God. Paul says that such a man would have been far better off remaining in his naturally foreskinned state and keeping only those commandments that pertain to gentiles (similar to the rabbinic 'Noahide commandments'). Jews, for their part, should indeed seek the moral circumcision of the heart, as Moses taught (Deut. 10:16, 30:6), but a proselyte's ostentatious circumcision of his flesh will not win him any praise from God.

The key verses 28–9, then, are better translated as follows: 'For it is not the Jew on display, nor the circumcision on display in the flesh, but the Jew in secret, and the circumcision of the heart in *pneuma* ["spirit"] not letter, whose praise comes from God rather than humans.' The big idea – which this document has in common with the classical Hebrew prophets, the teaching of Jesus in the Gospels and the ethics of *Pirkei Avot* (the collection of rabbinic moral aphorisms in the Mishnah) – is that God sees the heart and rewards sincere piety. Our text, which has been used as one plank in the platform of supersessionist Christian theologies of a 'true, spiritual Israel', actually says nothing of the sort, as recent research has begun to recognise. Those supersessionist theologies are still current in some Christian circles, but now they have to compete with other, more humane theologies of religious coexistence.

Bibliography

Barclay, John M. G., 'Paul and Philo on Circumcision: Romans 2.25–9 in Social and Cultural Context', *New Testament Studies* 44 (1998), 536–56.

Novenson, Matthew V., 'The Self-Styled Jew of Romans 2 and the Actual Jews of Romans 9–11', in *Paul, Then and Now* (Grand Rapids: Eerdmans, 2022), 91–117.

Stowers, Stanley K., *A Rereading of Romans: Justice, Jews, and Gentiles* (New Haven: Yale University Press, 1994), 159–75.

Thiessen, Matthew, 'Paul's Argument against Gentile Circumcision in Romans 2:17–29', *Novum Testamentum* 56 (2014), 373–91.

5

Romans 9:1–8 (mid-first century CE)

Text

9:1 I am speaking the truth in Christ – I am not lying; my conscience confirms it by the Holy Spirit – 2 I have great sorrow and unceasing anguish in my heart. 3 For I could wish that I myself were accursed and cut off from Christ for the sake of my own brothers and sisters, my own flesh and blood. 4 They are Israelites, and to them belong the adoption, the glory, the covenants, the giving of the law, the worship, and the promises; 5 to them belong the patriarchs, and from them, according to the flesh, comes the Christ, who is over all, God blessed forever. Amen.

6 It is not as though the word of God has failed. For not all those descended from Israel are Israelites, 7 and not all of Abraham's children are his descendants, but 'it is through

Isaac that descendants shall be named for you' [Gen. 21:12]. [8] This means that it is not the children of the flesh who are the children of God, but the children of the promise are counted as descendants.

Commentary

This document comprises the opening verses of Romans 9, while the following document (no. 6) comprises the concluding movement of Romans 11. These two are bookends of a lengthy section of Paul's Letter to the Romans, chapters 9–11, which is the single longest discourse on Jews and Judaism anywhere in the New Testament. It is not, however, an abstract treatise on Jews and Judaism, but rather a quite contingent reflection, by the (Jewish) apostle Paul, on the real-time successes and failures of the apostles' announcement of the risen Jesus. Contrary to his and others' expectations, their movement preaching the Jewish messiah and the resurrection of the dead seemed to be doing quite well among gentiles, but not among Jews. How could this be?

Paul's perplexity and distress at this state of affairs – 'I have great sorrow and unceasing anguish' – is all the greater precisely because of (what he recognises as) Israel's tremendous privileges. Unlike the gentiles, they already have the status of God's children, the presence ('glory') of God in the Jerusalem temple, the covenants of old, the Torah of Moses, the service of the Levitical priests, the ancestors, God's promises to the ancestors and, indeed, the Christ (literally: 'messiah') himself. (Recall, Paul writes all of this a decade or so before 70 CE, with the temple cult still flourishing in Jerusalem as it had done for centuries.) Paul might have expected his fellow Jews to welcome (the man he thinks is) the messiah with open arms, but by the mid-first century, several decades after the death of Jesus, they had not done so. One possible explanation is that Jesus was not in fact the messiah, but this is unthinkable for Paul. Perhaps, then, even more impiously, one might conclude that God's promises to Israel have failed: God sent the messiah, but Israel did not receive him, so all is lost. But that, too, Paul refuses to believe: 'It is not as though the word of God has failed' (Rom. 9:6).

Paul's explanation, which he will go on to develop in Romans 9–11, is that the current state of affairs is some kind of divine mystery. In vv. 6–8 above, his argument is that the small minority of first-century Jews who recognise Jesus as messiah are a remnant, a group chosen by God to carry the divine promises even while the majority are (as Paul sees it) hardened and darkened. But this is only temporary, because by the end of Romans 11 Paul declares that God will bring the majority around in due course. Here in Romans 9, however, his argument is that, just as God chose Isaac over Ishmael, so too, at the present moment, God has chosen a remnant over the majority of Israel. If the discourse stopped there, one might possibly reason – and some supersessionist Christian theologies have reasoned – that Israel has been dispossessed and replaced. But Paul, for his part, certainly does not stop there. If Israel were dispossessed, he reckons, that would make God either impotent or dishonest, neither of which can be true. Israel's majority indifference to Jesus is, for Paul, a test of the faithfulness of God, but a test that God must surely pass.

Bibliography

Fredriksen, Paula, *Paul: The Pagans' Apostle* (New Haven: Yale University Press, 2017).

Gaston, Lloyd, 'Israel's Misstep in the Eyes of Paul', in *Paul and the Torah* (Vancouver: University of British Columbia Press, 1987), 135–50.

Räisänen, Heikki, 'Paul, God, and Israel: Romans 9–11 in Recent Research', in Neusner, Jacob, Borgen, Peter, Frerichs, Ernest S., and Horsley, Richard (eds.), *The Social World of Formative Christianity and Judaism* (Philadelphia: Fortress, 1988), 178–206.

Wagner, J. Ross, *Heralds of the Good News: Isaiah and Paul in Concert in the Letter to the Romans* (Leiden: Brill, 2002), 43–118.

6

Romans 11:1–36 (mid-first century CE)

Text

[11:1] I ask, then, has God rejected his people? By no means! I myself am an Israelite, a descendant of Abraham, a member of the tribe of Benjamin. [2] God has not rejected his people whom he foreknew. Do you not know what the scripture says of Elijah, how he pleads with God against Israel? [3] 'Lord, they have killed your prophets, they have demolished your altars; I alone am left, and they are seeking my life.' [1 Kgs 19:10, 14] [4] But what is the divine reply to him? 'I have kept for myself seven thousand who have not bowed the knee to Baal.' [1 Kgs 19:18] [5] So, too, at the present time there is a remnant chosen by grace. [6] But if it is by grace, it is no longer on the basis of works, otherwise grace would no longer be grace.

[7] What then? Israel has not achieved what it was pursuing. The elect have achieved it, but the rest were hardened, [8] as it is written,

> 'God gave them a sluggish spirit,
> eyes that would not see
> and ears that would not hear,
> down to this very day.' [Deut. 29:3; Isa. 29:10]

[9] And David says,

> 'Let their table become a snare and a trap,
> a stumbling block and a retribution for them;
> [10] let their eyes be darkened so that they cannot see,
> and keep their backs forever bent.' [Ps. 68:23 LXX]

[11] So I ask, have they stumbled so as to fall? By no means! But through their stumbling salvation has come to the gentiles, so as to make Israel jealous. [12] Now if their stumbling means riches for the world and if their loss means riches for gentiles, how much more will their full inclusion mean!

[13] Now I am speaking to you gentiles. Inasmuch then as I am an apostle to the gentiles, I celebrate my ministry [14] in order to make my own people jealous and thus save some of them. [15] For if their rejection is the reconciliation of the world, what will their

acceptance be but life from the dead? [16] If the part of the dough offered as first fruits is holy, then the whole batch is holy; and if the root is holy, then the branches also are holy.

[17] But if some of the branches were broken off, and you, a wild olive shoot, were grafted among the others to share the rich root of the olive tree, [18] do not boast over the branches. If you do boast, remember: you do not support the root, but the root supports you. [19] You will say, 'Branches were broken off so that I might be grafted in.' [20] That is true. They were broken off on account of unbelief, but you stand on account of belief. So do not become arrogant, but be afraid. [21] For if God did not spare the natural branches, neither will he spare you. [22] Note then the kindness and the severity of God: severity toward those who have fallen but God's kindness toward you, if you continue in his kindness; otherwise you also will be cut off. [23] And even those of Israel, if they do not continue in unbelief, will be grafted in, for God has the power to graft them in again. [24] For if you have been cut from what is by nature a wild olive tree and grafted, contrary to nature, into a cultivated olive tree, how much more will these natural branches be grafted back into their own olive tree.

[25] I want you to understand this mystery, brothers and sisters, so that you may not claim to be wiser than you are: a hardening has come upon part of Israel until the full number of the gentiles has come in. [26] And in this way all Israel will be saved, as it is written,

> 'Out of Zion will come the Deliverer;
>   he will banish ungodliness from Jacob.' [Isa. 59:20]
> [27] 'And this is my covenant with them,
>   when I take away their sins.' [Isa. 27:9]

[28] As regards the gospel they are enemies for your sake, but as regards election they are beloved for the sake of their ancestors, [29] for the gifts and the calling of God are irrevocable. [30] Just as you were once disobedient to God but have now received mercy because of their disobedience, [31] so also they have now been disobedient in order that, by the mercy shown to you, they also may now receive mercy. [32] For God has imprisoned all in disobedience so that he may be merciful to all.

[33] O the depth of the riches and wisdom and knowledge of God! How unsearchable are his judgments and how inscrutable his ways!

> [34] 'For who has known the mind of the Lord?
>   Or who has been his counselor?' [Isa. 40:13 LXX]
> [35] 'Or who has given a gift to him,
>   to receive a gift in return?' [Job 41:3]

[36] For from him and through him and to him are all things. To him be the glory forever. Amen.

Commentary

This document is the end of Paul's long discourse on Israel comprising all of Romans 9–11 (cf. document 5 above, the beginning of that discourse). Whereas he begins Romans 9 by lamenting a present (mid-first-century CE) division within Israel – a minority who trust Jesus as the messiah, a majority who do not – he ends Romans 11 by expressing his confidence that all Israel is safe in God's hands. Paul reasons, in fact, that the current state of affairs must be the consequence of a mysterious divine purpose: God, in his inscrutable wisdom, has *deliberately* made Israel disbelieve the apostles, just to allow time and space for the fullness of the gentile nations to turn from their idols and trust in the living God and his messiah Jesus.

In vv. 13–24, Paul paints what would become a tremendously influential picture of Israel and the gentiles as branches of one great olive tree, of which God is the gardener (see, e.g., Vatican II, *Lumen gentium* 1.6). The tree is the whole people of God, and the Jewish people are its 'natural branches', who have always had a home there as God's covenant people (cf. 'to them belong[s] the adoption' in Rom. 9:4). The gentiles, by contrast, are 'wild branches', not naturally part of the tree. But the divine gardener, in his great mercy, is grafting the gentiles into his tree, giving them a place among his people; this is what Paul thinks is happening through his own announcement of Jesus the messiah. His contemporary fellow Jews who disbelieve the apostles Paul portrays here as natural branches which are temporarily broken off, but will be grafted in again. The allegory of the olive tree illustrates the fine line that Paul walks in Romans 9–11: all the gentiles being baptised into Christ are, he is certain, full members of the eschatological people of God, but this does not mean that Israel is displaced, disinherited or otherwise cast aside. Paul has his cake and eats it, too: God has hardened Israel to allow time for the gentiles; God can never abandon Israel.

In this context, the much-debated phrase 'All Israel will be saved' (v. 26) is best interpreted to mean that the whole of the Jewish people, not just the tiny remnant of Rom. 9:6–8 and 11:1–5, will surely survive the day of judgement and inherit the kingdom of God. It is, in other words, very similar to the sentiment expressed by the rabbis in m.Sanh. 10:1: 'All Israel have a share in the world to come.' By Paul's lights, the unshakeable faithfulness of God entails such an outcome. Some later gentile Christian thinkers took a different view. They claimed that God *had* in fact disinherited Israel and replaced them with the church. But if so, then these Christian thinkers had to find a different meaning for Rom. 11:26: 'All Israel will be saved', they reasoned, must mean that *the church* will be saved, perhaps as some kind of 'spiritual' Israel. But more recent interpretation, especially since the Holocaust, has recognised how strained such an interpretation is. Thus, to cite perhaps the most important example, the Second Vatican Council wrote about our passage in their declaration *Nostra aetate* (see Appendix to Part III, p. 512): 'God holds the Jews most dear for the sake of their Fathers; He does not repent of the gifts He makes or of the calls He issues – such is the witness of the Apostle.'

Bibliography

Stendahl, Krister, *Final Account: Paul's Letter to the Romans* (Minneapolis: Fortress, 1995).
Still, Todd D. (ed.), *God and Israel: Providence and Purpose in Romans 9–11* (Waco: Baylor University Press, 2017).

Wagner, J. Ross, *Heralds of the Good News: Isaiah and Paul in Concert in the Letter to the Romans* (Leiden: Brill, 2002), 219–305.

Wilk, Florian, and Wagner, J. Ross (eds.), *Between Gospel and Election: Explorations in the Interpretation of Romans 9–11* (Tübingen: Mohr Siebeck, 2010).

7

Philippians 3:2–9 (mid-first century CE)

Text

[3:2] Beware of the dogs, beware of the evil workers, beware of those who mutilate the flesh! [3] For it is we who are the circumcision, who worship in the Spirit of God and boast in Christ Jesus and have no confidence in the flesh – [4] even though I, too, have reason for confidence in the flesh.

If anyone else has reason to be confident in the flesh, I have more: [5] circumcised on the eighth day, a member of the people of Israel, of the tribe of Benjamin, a Hebrew born of Hebrews; as to the law, a Pharisee; [6] as to zeal, a persecutor of the church; as to righteousness under the law, blameless.

[7] Yet whatever gains I had, these I have come to regard as loss because of Christ. [8] More than that, I regard everything as loss because of the surpassing value of knowing Christ Jesus my Lord. For his sake I have suffered the loss of all things, and I regard them as rubbish, in order that I may gain Christ [9] and be found in him, not having a righteousness of my own that comes from the law but one that comes through faith in Christ, the righteousness from God based on faith.

Commentary

The NRSVue translation quoted here handles this passage reasonably well, though many familiar English versions cause problems similar to those noted in Romans 2:25–9 (document 4 above), suggesting that the apostle Paul appropriates the names 'Jew', 'Israel' or 'circumcision' for Christians. Paul writes here, 'we […] are the circumcision, who worship in the Spirit of God and boast in Christ Jesus' (Phil. 3:3), but this is often translated: 'We are the *true* circumcision, the ones who worship in the spirit of God', as if Paul were snatching the title 'circumcision' away from Jews and awarding it to Christians. As with Romans 2:25–9, that is not in fact what this passage says, but in its long Christian reception it has often been taken in that way.

The actual context of this passage in Paul's Letter to the Philippians is that, as in Galatians, Paul is aware of some rival apostles suggesting to his audience of gentiles-in-Christ that they ought to undergo Jewish proselyte circumcision in order to follow the Jewish God. As in Galatians, Paul insists that they should not do so. But his argument here is different from the one in Galatians. Here Paul boasts that he himself, as a native-born Jew, circumcised on the eighth day, from the school of the Pharisees, a virtuoso in the Torah, is to be trusted over against his rivals, who, he strongly implies, are not thus qualified. This passage is an important piece of evidence for the likely hypothesis that Paul's rivals are not Jews but gentile proselytes. In any case, what Paul opposes in this passage is certainly not traditional Jewish circumcision (which he praises here: 'circumcised on the eighth day'), but proselyte circumcision. When, therefore, he writes 'we are the circumcision', he means *not* 'we Christians, not those Jews' but rather 'we Jewish apostles, not those proselyte interlopers'.

The denouement of our passage (vv. 7–9) is a rhetorical devaluation of Paul's formidable credentials in comparison to metamorphosis into the image of the heavenly Christ: 'I regard everything as loss […] I regard them as rubbish'. This is a comparison between the life of the present age (righteousness in the law) and the life of the age to come (gaining the messiah, the righteousness of God). But here, once again, the long history of Christian reception has often read our passage as a comparison between Judaism and Christianity, as if Paul were simply rejecting one religion for the other. This, together with the misreading that takes 'we are the circumcision' as an appropriation of a title from Jews for Christians, has made this document another problem text in the history of Jewish–Christian relations.

Bibliography

Campbell, William S., 'I Rate All Things as Loss: Paul's Puzzling Accounting System', in *Unity and Diversity in Christ: Interpreting Paul in Context* (Eugene: Cascade, 2013), 203–24.

Collman, Ryan D., 'Beware the Dogs! The Phallic Epithet in Philippians 3.2', *New Testament Studies* 67 (2021), 105–20.

Munck, Johannes, *Paul and the Salvation of Mankind* (London: SCM, 1959).

Sanders, E. P., 'Paul on the Law, His Opponents, and the Jewish People in Philippians 3 and 2 Corinthians 11', in Richardson, Peter (ed.), *Anti-Judaism in Early Christianity*, vol. 1 (Waterloo, ON: Wilfrid Laurier University Press, 1986), 75–90.

8

Hebrews 8:1–13 (late first century CE*)*

Text

8:1 Now the main point in what we are saying is this: we have such a high priest, one who is seated at the right hand of the throne of the Majesty in the heavens, 2 a minister in the sanctuary and the true tent that the Lord, and not any mortal, has set up. 3 For every high priest is appointed to offer gifts and sacrifices; hence it is necessary for this priest also to have something to offer. 4 Now if he were on earth, he would not be a priest at all, since there are already those who offer gifts according to the law. 5 They offer worship in a sanctuary that is a sketch and shadow of the heavenly one, just as Moses was warned when he was about to erect the tent. For, God said, 'See that you make everything according to the pattern that was shown you on the mountain.' [Exod. 25:40] 6 But Jesus has now obtained a more excellent ministry, and to that degree he is the mediator of a better covenant, which has been enacted on the basis of better promises. 7 For if that first covenant had been faultless, there would have been no need to look for a second one.

⁸ God finds fault with them when he says:
'The days are surely coming, says the Lord,
    when I will establish a new covenant with the house of Israel
    and with the house of Judah,
⁹ not like the covenant that I made with their ancestors
    on the day when I took them by the hand to lead them out of the land of Egypt,
for they did not continue in my covenant,
    and so I had no concern for them, says the Lord.
¹⁰ This is the covenant that I will make with the house of Israel
    after those days, says the Lord:
I will put my laws in their minds
    and write them on their hearts,
and I will be their God,
    and they shall be my people.
¹¹ And they shall not teach one another
    or say to each other, "Know the Lord,"
for they shall all know me,
    from the least of them to the greatest.
¹² For I will be merciful toward their iniquities,
    and I will remember their sins no more.' [Jer. 31:31–4]

¹³ In speaking of a new covenant, he has made the first one obsolete, and what is obsolete and growing old will soon disappear.

Commentary

The Epistle to the Hebrews is one of the most mysterious texts in the New Testament. It was received in the ancient church as the Epistle *of Paul* to the Hebrews, but it almost certainly was not written by Paul (the text itself does not claim to be), nor is it actually addressed to 'the Hebrews', nor is it even an epistle. It is a high literary homily or sermon (with an ersatz epistolary ending, Heb. 13:22–5), whose author and audience are both formally anonymous, which constructs an elaborate contrast between God's new covenant mediated by his son the messiah and God's old covenant mediated by the Levitical priesthood.

Hebrews is often read, not altogether unreasonably, as a supersessionist contrast between Judaism and Christianity. The strange thing about it, however, is that Hebrews quarrels not with (what we normally think of as) Judaism – that is, the everyday piety of Jewish laypeople – nor even with the priestly cultus of the late Second Temple, which was still a relatively recent memory at the time Hebrews was written (late first century CE, within a generation of the destruction of the temple by the Roman army). Instead, Hebrews quarrels with *Leviticus*, that is, the ancient Israelite priestly Torah. The quarrel takes the form of a highly literary *synkrisis* ('comparison' in the technical sense of Graeco-Roman rhetoric), but it is hard to see how, or indeed whether, it mapped onto the actual religious practice of any of Hebrews' original readers. We do not know who these readers were, but we do know that they were not ancient Israelite priests!

The excerpt above quotes at length from Jeremiah's prophecy of a new covenant in contrast to the ostensibly old covenant at Mount Sinai (cf. document 3 above). But whereas, for Jeremiah, the difference between the covenants is simply Israel's obedience, for Hebrews the new covenant entails a new priesthood, new sacrifices and a new sanctuary. (Following the idiom of Leviticus, Hebrews speaks in archaic terms of 'sanctuary' and 'tent', not in the more contemporary terms of 'temple'.) Whereas Jeremiah's focus was ethical, Hebrews' focus is cultic. For Hebrews – unlike any other text in the New Testament – the essential thing about Christ is that he is a high priest. Hebrews argues that, when the Israelite priests offered sacrifices to God in the tabernacle in the wilderness, that was only a shadow of the original heavenly sanctuary (cf. Exod. 25:40), where Christ is now both high priest and sacrifice. For Hebrews, Christ's heavenly priesthood supersedes and renders obsolete the earthly priesthood prescribed in Leviticus.

We can perhaps imagine why, especially after the destruction of the Jerusalem temple in 70 CE, the author might have thought along these lines. But it is still far from clear what relation, if any, Hebrews had to the religious lives of actual Jewish people at the time he was writing. In any case, his loaded language of shadows, obsolescence, disappearance, passing away, etc., applied by later Christian readers to the religious lives of actual Jewish people, became fodder for some stridently supersessionist Christian theologies down the centuries. But recent church statements – e.g., *God's Unfailing Word* (2019), from the Church of England Faith and Order Commission – have rightly criticised such interpretations of Hebrews on both exegetical and theological grounds.

Bibliography

Bauckham, Richard, Driver, Daniel R., Hart, Trevor A., and MacDonald, Nathan (eds.), *The Epistle to the Hebrews and Christian Theology* (Grand Rapids: Eerdmans, 2009).

Docherty, Susan, *The Use of the Old Testament in Hebrews* (Tübingen: Mohr Siebeck, 2009).

Klassen, William, 'To the Hebrews or Against the Hebrews? Anti-Judaism in the Epistle to the Hebrews', in Wilson, Stephen G. (ed.), *Anti-Judaism in Early Christianity*, vol. 2 (Waterloo, ON: Wilfrid Laurier University Press, 1986), 1–16.

Moffitt, David M., *Reading Hebrews after Supersessionism* (Eugene: Cascade, forthcoming).

9

Mark 7:1–23 (late first century CE)

Text

7:1 Now when the Pharisees and some of the scribes who had come from Jerusalem gathered around him, ² they noticed that some of his disciples were eating with defiled hands, that is, without washing them. ³ (For the Pharisees, and all the Jews, do not eat unless they wash their hands, thus observing the tradition of the elders, ⁴ and they do not eat anything from the market unless they wash, and there are also many other traditions that they observe: the washing of cups and pots and bronze kettles and beds.) ⁵ So the Pharisees and the scribes asked him, 'Why do your disciples not walk according to the tradition of the elders but eat with defiled hands?' ⁶ He said to them, 'Isaiah prophesied rightly about you hypocrites, as it is written,

> "This people honors me with their lips,
>   but their hearts are far from me;
> ⁷ in vain do they worship me,
>   teaching human precepts as doctrines." [Isa. 29:13]

⁸ 'You abandon the commandment of God and hold to human tradition.'

⁹ Then he said to them, 'You have a fine way of rejecting the commandment of God in order to keep your tradition! ¹⁰ For Moses said, "Honor your father and your mother," [Exod. 20:12; Deut. 5:16] and, "Whoever speaks evil of father or mother must surely die." [Exod. 21:17; Lev. 20:9] ¹¹ But you say that if anyone tells father or mother, "Whatever support you might have had from me is Corban" (that is, an offering to God), ¹² then you no longer permit doing anything for a father or mother, ¹³ thus nullifying the word of God through your tradition that you have handed on. And you do many things like this.'

¹⁴ Then he called the crowd again and said to them, 'Listen to me, all of you, and understand: ¹⁵ there is nothing outside a person that by going in can defile, but the things that come out are what defile.'

¹⁷ When he had left the crowd and entered the house, his disciples asked him about the parable. ¹⁸ He said to them, 'So, are you also without understanding? Do you not see that whatever goes into a person from outside cannot defile, ¹⁹ since it enters not the heart but the stomach and goes out into the sewer?' (Thus he declared all foods clean.) ²⁰ And he said, 'It is what comes out of a person that defiles. ²¹ For it is from within, from the human heart, that evil intentions come: sexual immorality, theft, murder, ²² adultery, avarice, wickedness, deceit, debauchery, envy, slander, pride, folly. ²³ All these evil things come from within, and they defile a person.'

Commentary

The Gospel of Mark is the earliest of the numerous early Christian Gospels, four of which are canonised in the New Testament. Mark was probably written around 70 CE, roughly concurrent with the Roman destruction of Jerusalem. The author is anonymous, as is his audience, although the fact that he sometimes pauses to explain Jewish customs (e.g., Mark 7:3–4 above) suggests that he expects that gentiles will read his life of Jesus.

This document relates a halakhic dispute between Jesus and his disciples on the one hand and the Pharisees and their disciples on the other. At issue is the legal question of whether ritual impurity can flow from food, through hands, to a person's body. The Pharisees think so, hence they undertake a ritual hand-washing before eating. Jesus thinks not, hence he and his disciples do not. Jesus argues that this practice of the Pharisees is their own innovation, not part of the Torah of Moses. Strictly speaking, this is true. In the most relevant text, the food laws of Leviticus 11, certain *prohibited* foods (e.g., carrion animal flesh) can contaminate a person, but they would do so whether the person washed his hands or not. *Permitted* foods, however, cannot contaminate a person, even if they happen to have come into contact with ritual impurity (e.g., food prepared by a menstruating woman). (The general term for food laws like these is *kashrut*: a system for discerning proper from improper foods, and proper from improper ways of preparing food.) Hand-washing before eating, then, is irrelevant to the transferral of ritual impurity. Jesus' legal opinion on this issue agrees exactly with Rashi's (Rashi at b.Shabbat 13b); but the Pharisees here and some *tannaim* in the Mishnah take the opposing view.

The moral of the story is that here, as often in the Gospels, Jesus' notorious conflicts with the Pharisees are actually traditional intra-Jewish halakhic disputes and not (as Christians frequently read them) stories of Jesus overthrowing Judaism to make way for Christianity. (Christianity, of course, does not yet exist in the Gospels.) Sometimes this Christian reading tradition even leads to translation problems, as in Mark 7:19 above. The NRSVue puts the final clause of the verse outside the quotation marks, in parentheses, and translates it 'Thus he [Jesus] declared all foods clean', as if Jesus were nullifying the whole biblical system of kosher and non-kosher foods. But that contradicts what Jesus actually says in the passage (which is about hand-washing, not *kashrut*), and it is a dubious translation of the Greek. The final clause literally reads simply 'purifying all the foods', and it makes better sense as the end of Jesus' own sentence: '[Food] enters not the heart but the stomach and goes out into the sewer, purifying all the foods.' Jesus does not abolish *kashrut*; he simply takes a more biblicist position on mealtime hand-washing than some of his Jewish contemporaries. Christians generally do not observe *kashrut*, of course, but this has to do with a later policy of the apostles (see document 20 below).

Bibliography

Avemarie, Friedrich, 'Jesus and Purity', in *Neues Testament und frührabbinisches Judentum* (Tübingen: Mohr Siebeck, 2013), 407–32.

Furstenberg, Yair, 'Defilement Penetrating the Body: A New Understanding of Contamination in Mark 7:15', *New Testament Studies* 54 (2008), 176–200.

Thiessen, Matthew, *Jesus and the Forces of Death* (Grand Rapids: Baker, 2020).

Williams, Logan A., 'The Stomach Purifies All Foods: Jesus' Anatomical Argument in Mark 7:18–19', *New Testament Studies* (2024).

10

Mark 12:1–12 (late first century CE)

Text

12:1 Then he began to speak to them in parables. 'A man planted a vineyard, put a fence around it, dug a pit for the winepress, and built a watchtower; then he leased it to tenants and went away. 2 When the season came, he sent a slave to the tenants to collect from them his share of the produce of the vineyard. 3 But they seized him and beat him and sent him away empty-handed. 4 And again he sent another slave to them; this one they beat over the head and insulted. ⁵ Then he sent another, and that one they killed. And so it was with many others; some they beat, and others they killed. ⁶ He had still one other, a beloved son. Finally he sent him to them, saying, "They will respect my son." ⁷ But those tenants said to one another, "This is the heir; come, let us kill him, and the inheritance will be ours." ⁸ So they seized him, killed him, and threw him out of the vineyard. ⁹ What then will the owner of the vineyard do? He will come and destroy the tenants and give the vineyard to others. ¹⁰ Have you not read this scripture:

> "The stone that the builders rejected
> has become the cornerstone;
> ¹¹ this was the Lord's doing,
> and it is amazing in our eyes"?' [Ps. 118:22]

¹² When they realized that he had told this parable against them, they wanted to arrest him, but they feared the crowd. So they left him and went away.

Commentary

By this point in Mark's Gospel, Jesus and his disciples have reached Jerusalem, where he will die at the hands of the Romans. This scene takes place in the temple's outer court, and the 'them' to whom Jesus here speaks in parables are the chief priests, scribes and elders (Mark 11:27), that is, the Jewish ruling class. (The Pharisees, Jesus' usual interlocutors back in Galilee, are largely absent from the Jerusalem-set passion narratives.)

In the Synoptic Gospels, Jesus frequently teaches in parables. This polemical parable, directed 'against them' (Mark 12:12), is a retelling of the prophet Isaiah's parable of the vineyard (Isa. 5:1–7). Jesus' version, like Isaiah's, is about God hoping to find righteousness in Israel but being disappointed. (So, too, the rabbis' version, which interprets the watchtower as the Jerusalem temple and the winepress as the high altar (t.Sukkah 3:15). In short, both Jews and Christians have used this prophetic image to criticise injustice in their own communities, and sometimes also to criticise one another.) Jesus adds, however, the characters of the tenants and the messengers, thus ascribing guilt to the ruling class in particular. The tenants in the story are the elders of Israel and the messengers are the prophets of old, whose message of repentance fell on deaf ears. Jesus himself comes preaching repentance like the prophets before him. But in a twist, he is more than a prophet; he is God's own son. (In Mark's Gospel, 'son of God' does not yet have the maximal Nicene Christian sense of 'second person of the Godhead'. It is a biblical, messianic title, which also has resonances with the contemporary Roman emperors who, like Jesus, ascended to heaven after their deaths.)

With obvious dramatic foreshadowing, Mark's Jesus declares that the elders will kill him as they did the prophets, stirring up God's anger against them. God's vineyard, Israel, will of course survive, but it will be given to other tenants who do repent – perhaps alluding to the tax collectors, sinners and others who receive Jesus' message of the kingdom of God in Mark's Gospel. (Some later Christian supersessionist theologies would make the parable mean that God revoked his favour from Israel entirely and transferred it to the gentile church.) The quotation here of Psalm 118:22 ('The stone that the builders rejected has become the cornerstone') to represent Jesus' rejection by the elders but later vindication by God becomes very influential in subsequent New Testament passages, appearing again in Matt. 21:42, Luke 20:17, Acts 4:11, 1 Pet. 2:7 and frequently in Christian texts thereafter. Psalm 118 is also one of the Hallel psalms used, from antiquity down to the present, in the Jewish liturgy for festivals (including Passover, the very context where Jesus cites it in Mark 12). What is more, rabbinic texts also keep alive the messianic interpretation of the psalm that originally underlay its use here in Mark 12: the stone is King David (the messiah), while the builders are his father Jesse, the prophet Samuel and other leaders who overlooked the young David (b.Pesah. 119a).

Bibliography

Kloppenborg, John S. *The Tenants in the Vineyard* (Tübingen: Mohr Siebeck, 2006).

Levine, Amy-Jill, 'Matthew, Mark, and Luke: Good News or Bad?', in Fredriksen, Paula, and Reinhartz, Adele (eds.), *Jesus, Judaism, and Christian Anti-Judaism: Reading the New Testament after the Holocaust* (Louisville: Westminster John Knox, 2002), 77–98.

Levine, Amy-Jill, *Short Stories by Jesus: The Enigmatic Parables of a Controversial Rabbi* (San Francisco: HarperOne, 2014).

Thoma, Clemens, and Wyschogrod, Michael (eds.), *Parable and Story in Judaism and Christianity* (New York: Paulist, 1989).

11

Mark 14:53–65 (late first century CE)

Text

14:53 They took Jesus to the high priest, and all the chief priests, the elders, and the scribes were assembled. 54 Peter had followed him at a distance, right into the courtyard of the high priest, and he was sitting with the guards, warming himself at the fire. 55 Now the chief priests and the whole council were looking for testimony against Jesus to put him to death, but they found none. 56 For many gave false testimony against him, and their testimony did not agree. 57 Some stood up and gave false testimony against him, saying, 58 'We heard him say, "I will destroy this temple that is made with hands, and in three days I will build another, not made with hands."' 59 But even on this point their testimony did not agree. 60 Then the high priest stood up before them and asked Jesus, 'Have you no answer? What is it that they testify against you?' 61 But he was silent and did not answer. Again the high priest asked him, 'Are you the Messiah, the Son of the Blessed One?' 62 Jesus said, 'I am, and

> "you will see the Son of Man
> seated at the right hand of the Power"
> and "coming with the clouds of heaven."' [Dan. 7:13]

63 Then the high priest tore his clothes and said, 'Why do we still need witnesses? 64 You have heard his blasphemy! What is your decision?' All of them condemned him as

deserving death. [65] Some began to spit on him, to blindfold him, and to strike him, saying to him, 'Prophesy!' The guards also took him and beat him.

Commentary

In our previous document, Jesus told a parable against the Jerusalem chief priests, scribes and elders; here he appears before them in chains. This scene is often called a trial, which is not quite right, since – as the subsequent narrative bears out – any actual capital proceedings against Jesus have to happen before the Roman governor. What this scene does give us, though, is Mark's idea of what the Jerusalem ruling class has against Jesus: namely, that he is the messiah son of God.

When Jesus admits to being the messiah son of God, the high priest accuses him of blasphemy (Mark 14:64), which is a famous problem. Blasphemy in ancient Judaism – as in modern Judaism, and Islam, and even Christianity for that matter – means to slander God himself. But if so, to claim to be the messiah is not blasphemy. (For a human to claim to be *God* might be blasphemy, but that is not what Jesus does in our text, or anywhere in Mark's Gospel.) There were numerous Jews in antiquity who claimed to be, or were said by others to be, the messiah (e.g., Herod the Great, Bar Kokhba, Rabbi Judah the Patriarch), and none of them is ever charged with blasphemy. So it is not altogether clear why the high priest draws this conclusion in Mark 14. It could be that this is simply a misunderstanding of Judaism by the author of Mark's Gospel: Jews in the first century CE did not think that a messianic claim was blasphemy, but Mark mistakenly thought that they did.

Alternatively, Mark might mean to draw attention to one part of Jesus' confession in particular: messiah *son of the Blessed One*, that is, messiah son of God. There are several kinds of messiahs in Jewish tradition (see Chapter 3, pp. 141–5): the very well known messiah son of David (a king), but also messiah son of Aaron (a priest), messiah son of Joseph (a warrior) and – as here – messiah son of God. What exactly 'messiah son of God' means is ambiguous (in some Hebrew Bible texts, the messiah son of David *is* the messiah son of God). But Mark may take it to mean that Jesus, at least after his death and resurrection, has become a god, like the Roman emperors who underwent apotheosis. And this he might take, rightly or wrongly, to amount to blasphemy from a Jewish perspective. Quite apart from the blasphemy issue, however, the rabbis also take the verse here quoted by Jesus – Dan. 7:13: 'the Son of Man [...] "coming with the clouds of heaven"' – as a reference to a triumphant messiah: if Israel is meritorious, then the messiah will come with the clouds of heaven (b.Sanh. 98a). In later Jewish–Christian relations, writers on both sides would draw an oft-repeated contrast between a Jewish *political* messiah and a Christian *spiritual* messiah, but that contrast is nowhere to be found in this earliest period.

Bibliography

Anderson, Charles P., 'The Trial of Jesus as Jewish–Christian Polarization: Blasphemy and Polemic in Mark's Gospel', in Richardson, Peter (ed.), *Anti-Judaism in Early Christianity*, vol. 1 (Waterloo, ON: Wilfrid Laurier University Press, 1986), 107–26.

Boyarin, Daniel, *The Jewish Gospels: The Story of the Jewish Christ* (New York: New Press, 2012).

Juel, Donald, *Messiah and Temple: The Trial of Jesus in the Gospel of Mark* (Missoula: Scholars Press, 1977).

Marcus, Joel, 'Mark 14:61: Are You the Messiah-Son-of-God?', *Novum Testamentum* 31 (1989), 125–41.

Winter, Paul, *On the Trial of Jesus* (Berlin: De Gruyter, 1961).

12

Mark 15:1–15 (late first century CE)

Text

15:1 As soon as it was morning, the chief priests held a consultation with the elders and scribes and the whole council. They bound Jesus, led him away, and handed him over to Pilate. 2 Pilate asked him, 'Are you the King of the Jews?' He answered him, 'You say so.' 3 Then the chief priests accused him of many things. 4 Pilate asked him again, 'Have you no answer? See how many charges they bring against you.' 5 But Jesus made no further reply, so that Pilate was amazed.

6 Now at the festival he used to release a prisoner for them, anyone for whom they asked. 7 Now a man called Barabbas was in prison with the insurrectionists who had committed murder during the insurrection. 8 So the crowd came and began to ask Pilate to do for them according to his custom. 9 Then he answered them, 'Do you want me to release for you the King of the Jews?' 10 For he realized that it was out of jealousy that the chief priests had handed him over. 11 But the chief priests stirred up the crowd to have him release Barabbas for them instead. 12 Pilate spoke to them again, 'Then what do you wish me to do with the man you call the King of the Jews?' 13 They shouted back, 'Crucify him!' 14 Pilate asked them, 'Why, what evil has he done?' But they shouted all the more, 'Crucify him!' 15 So Pilate, wishing to satisfy the crowd, released Barabbas for them, and after flogging Jesus he handed him over to be crucified.

Commentary

In our previous document (Mark 14:53–65), Jesus faced questioning by the Jewish priests and elders in Jerusalem. Here, however, there is a transfer of custody to the Roman provincial governor, Pontius Pilate. The chief priests could opine that Jesus was *deserving of death* (Mark 14:64), but only the Roman administration could actually put him to death, as they go on to do by the end of Mark 15. Long gone by this point in Mark's Gospel are the Pharisees, who had been Jesus' closest interlocutors and competitors back home in Galilee (Mark 1–10). In Jerusalem, by contrast, Jesus has to reckon, first, with the priestly aristocracy and, second and finally, with the Romans. With the Pharisees, Jesus had had sectarian disputes over interpretations of the law (sabbath allowances, ritual purifications, etc.). The only concern of the chief priests and the Romans, however, is whether Jesus poses a political threat.

We leave aside for now the argument over the two Jesuses, Christ and Barabbas, which Matthew narrates in more elaborate detail (see Matt. 27:15–26; document 16 below). More important for our present purposes is the fact that Pilate's worry about Jesus of Nazareth is that he is supposed to be *king of the Jews* (Mark 15:2, 9, 12). But the Jerusalem chief priests had not said this. In the previous scene, the high priest had asked whether Jesus was the *messiah son of the Blessed One* (Mark 14:61). To that question, Jesus had answered, 'I am'. But when Pilate asks if he is king of the Jews, he only answers, 'You say so'. His answer to Pilate does not affect the outcome, however. What gets Jesus crucified is the fact that the Roman governor worries he *might* be a kind of would-be king, a rival to Roman imperial government, or that his followers have that dangerous idea. (There are striking parallels a century later in the Bar Kokhba revolt under Hadrian, but Bar Kokhba was a Jewish king who *did* take up arms against Rome.) Most of what Jesus does during his ministry in Mark (and the other Gospels) is not characteristically messianic or royal: he teaches, heals people, exorcises demons. Ironically, the fact that Jesus goes down in history as Christ, or messiah, is due to the Romans' perception of him as a would-be king of the Jews.

The Talmud, in its only express mention of the execution of Jesus (b.Sanh. 43a), seems to show an awareness of this Gospel account. Interestingly, however, the rabbis claim that Jesus was executed not for being 'king of the Jews' but rather for committing certain capital offences specified in the Torah: practising sorcery and enticing Israel to apostasy (Deut. 13:1–11). This story, however, was redacted out of many medieval Talmud manuscripts under the widespread policy of Christian censorship of Jewish books.

Bibliography

Cho, Bernardo K., *Royal Messianism and the Jerusalem Priesthood in the Gospel of Mark* (London: T&T Clark, 2019).

Dahl, Nils A., 'The Crucified Messiah', in *The Crucified Messiah, and Other Essays* (Minneapolis: Augsburg, 1974), 10–36.

Fredriksen, Paula, *Jesus of Nazareth, King of the Jews* (New York: Knopf, 1999).

Schäfer, Peter, *Jesus in the Talmud* (Princeton: Princeton University Press, 2007).

13

Matthew 5:17–22, 27–48 (late first century CE)

Text

5:17 Do not think that I have come to abolish the Law or the Prophets; I have come not to abolish but to fulfill. [18] For truly I tell you, until heaven and earth pass away, not one letter, not one stroke of a letter, will pass from the law until all is accomplished. [19] Therefore, whoever breaks one of the least of these commandments and teaches others to do the same will be called least in the kingdom of heaven, but whoever does them and teaches them will be called great in the kingdom of heaven. [20] For I tell you, unless your righteousness exceeds that of the scribes and Pharisees, you will never enter the kingdom of heaven.

[21] You have heard that it was said to those of ancient times, 'You shall not murder,' [Exod. 20:13; Deut. 5:17] and 'whoever murders shall be liable to judgment.' [Lev. 24:17] [22] But I say to you that if you are angry with a brother or sister, you will be liable to judgment, and if you insult a brother or sister, you will be liable to the council, and if you say, 'You fool,' you will be liable to the hell of fire [...]

[27] You have heard that it was said, 'You shall not commit adultery.' [Exod. 20:14; Deut. 5:18] [28] But I say to you that everyone who looks at a woman with lust has already committed adultery with her in his heart [...]

[31] It was also said, 'Whoever divorces his wife, let him give her a certificate of divorce.' [Deut. 24:1] [32] But I say to you that anyone who divorces his wife, except on the ground of sexual immorality, causes her to commit adultery, and whoever marries a divorced woman commits adultery.

[33] Again, you have heard that it was said to those of ancient times, 'You shall not swear falsely, but carry out the vows you have made to the Lord.' [Lev. 19:12] [34] But I say to you: Do not swear at all, either by heaven, for it is the throne of God, [35] or by the earth, for it is his footstool, or by Jerusalem, for it is the city of the great King. [36] And do not swear by your head, for you cannot make one hair white or black. [37] Let your word be 'Yes, Yes' or 'No, No'; anything more than this comes from the evil one.

[38] You have heard that it was said, 'An eye for an eye and a tooth for a tooth.' [Exod. 21:24; Lev. 24:20] [39] But I say to you: Do not resist an evildoer. But if anyone strikes you on the right cheek, turn the other also, [40] and if anyone wants to sue you and take your shirt, give your coat as well, [41] and if anyone forces you to go one mile, go also the second mile. [42] Give to the one who asks of you, and do not refuse anyone who wants to borrow from you.

[43] You have heard that it was said, 'You shall love your neighbor [Lev. 19:18] and hate your enemy.' [44] But I say to you: Love your enemies and pray for those who persecute you, [45] so that you may be children of your Father in heaven, for he makes his sun rise on the evil and on the good and sends rain on the righteous and on the unrighteous. [46] For if you love those who love you, what reward do you have? Do not even the tax collectors do the same? [47] And if you greet only your brothers and sisters, what more are you doing than others? Do not even the gentiles do the same? [48] Be perfect, therefore, as your heavenly Father is perfect.

Commentary

The Gospel of Matthew comes first in the canonical order of the books of the New Testament, but in chronological terms it was actually the *second* Gospel written. Matthew (the name attached to the Gospel in Christian tradition, though not in the text itself), written in the last quarter of the first century, knows and uses the Gospel of Mark, which was written around 70 CE. (Luke and John come later and use at least Mark, and possibly also Matthew, to write their Gospels.) Matthew reproduces most of what is in Mark, though with some changes, but he also adds a great deal of material, especially large blocks of Jesus' teachings, including the so-called Sermon on the Mount, from which the excerpt above is taken.

This document, which is conventionally styled 'the Antitheses' (for the repeated formula: 'You have heard that it was said ... but I say to you'), illustrates Matthew's close but complicated relation to Judaism. It is because of passages such as this that Matthew is often called the most Jewish of the four canonical Gospels. Only in this Gospel does Jesus emphatically insist that he does not abolish the law of Moses, that not a single letter of the law can pass away. Many interpreters have detected in this saying a veiled argument against Paul or Pauline Christ-believers, on the assumption that he or they *did* abolish the law of Moses (though, as we have discussed above, things with Paul are not nearly as simple as that).

Matthew's Jesus does not annul any of the commandments of Moses, but he does add further ones. That is the point of the antithesis formula, 'You have heard that it was said ... but I say to you'. Moses prohibited murder, but Jesus prohibits even angry words. Moses prohibited adultery, but Jesus prohibits even lust and divorce. Moses prohibited false oaths, but Jesus prohibits all oaths. Moses prohibited excessive retaliation, but Jesus prohibits all retaliation. Moses commanded love of neighbours, but Jesus commands love even of enemies. In short, Matthew's Jesus builds a fence around the law (as in the early rabbinic saying in m.Avot 1:1: 'The men of the Great Synagogue said three things: Be deliberate in judgment, raise up many disciples, and make a fence around the Law'). He confirms the law of Moses, but then adds even stricter interpretations of the commandments, what later Jewish tradition would call *chumrot* (religious stringency). In all three Synoptic Gospels (and, much less so, John), Jesus teaches halakhah, but the halakhah in Matthew is the most demanding. In Matthew, Jesus' disciples are commanded to be more righteous than the gentiles, more righteous even than the Pharisees and scribes.

In short, whereas Christians have often thought of Jesus as bringing a new message *in place of* the Jewish law, in Matthew's Gospel he actually teaches *a rigorist interpretation of* the Jewish law. Interestingly, on this particular point early modern Christian interpreters (e.g., Luther, Calvin, Bullinger) generally improved upon their ancient and medieval forebears (e.g., Irenaeus, Chrysostom, Thomas). Where those earlier interpreters tended to pit the law of Christ against the law of Moses, the Reformers took Jesus to be quarrelling with contemporary Pharisaic interpretation, not with Moses himself.

Bibliography

Allison, Dale C., 'The Configuration of the Sermon on the Mount and Its Meaning', in *Studies in Matthew* (Grand Rapids: Baker, 2005), 173–216.

Kampen, John, *Matthew within Sectarian Judaism* (New Haven: Yale University Press, 2019).

Runesson, Anders, and Gurtner, Daniel M. (eds.), *Matthew within Judaism: Israel and the Nations in the First Gospel* (Atlanta: SBL Press, 2020).

Sigal, Phillip, *The Halakhah of Jesus of Nazareth According to the Gospel of Matthew* (Atlanta: SBL Press, 2007).

14

Matthew 6:7–15 (late first century CE)

Text

⁶:⁷ When you are praying, do not heap up empty phrases as the gentiles do, for they think that they will be heard because of their many words. ⁸ Do not be like them, for your Father knows what you need before you ask him.

⁹ Pray then in this way:

> Our Father in heaven,
>   may your name be revered as holy.
> ¹⁰ May your kingdom come.
>   May your will be done
>   on earth as it is in heaven.
> ¹¹ Give us today our daily bread.
> ¹² And forgive us our debts,
>   as we also have forgiven our debtors.
> ¹³ And do not bring us to the time of trial,
>   but rescue us from the evil one.

¹⁴ For if you forgive others their trespasses, your heavenly Father will also forgive you, ¹⁵ but if you do not forgive others, neither will your Father forgive your trespasses.

Commentary

Sometimes called the Paternoster after its opening words in Latin, the Lord's Prayer (Matt. 6:9–13; shorter form Luke 11:2–4) is one of the most familiar passages in the New Testament and is widely regarded as the Christian prayer *par excellence*. It offers a window into the liturgical origins of Christianity within Judaism partly because of its possible Aramaic origins and partly because, in both form and content, it is a Jewish prayer. It is Jesus who prescribes it, and Christians still pray it, but there is nothing uniquely Christian (e.g., trinitarian) about it.

From this document we learn that the very early Christ-followers were, and prayed as, Jews, and that Jesus himself prayed as a Jew. What is more, inasmuch as Christian liturgy in all the mainstream churches (Orthodox, Catholic and Protestant) still gives pride of place to the Lord's Prayer, that liturgy retains its many ancient biblical and Jewish (even rabbinic) resonances. For instance, the petition for 'daily bread' is an allusion to Prov. 30:8–9, and the address to God as 'our father' (*pater noster*) appears already in the Hebrew Bible (Isa. 63:16) and continues in the Talmud (e.g., b.Ber. 32b; b.Sotah 10a; b.Ta'anit 25b) and Jewish liturgy. The Lord's Prayer is of course familiar to many Jews from long cultural exposure, but it is also the case that, in terms of content, there is nothing in it that would be religiously objectionable to even strictly observant Jews.

Close examination of the text also reveals parallels to contemporary Jewish liturgical practice. Elements are found in similar form in the *Kaddish* (e.g., the exaltation of God) and *Amidah* (e.g., the tripartite outline of praise, petition and thanksgiving). In particular, the hallowing of God's name and the reference to the coming of God's kingdom are both central to the *Kaddish*, and the appeal for forgiveness appears prominently in the *Amidah*. In some circles, early Christians were instructed to recite the Lord's Prayer three times daily (*Didache* 8:2), as Jews were the *Amidah*. Finally, the concluding doxology of the Lord's Prayer (attested in the *Didache*, though not in Matthew or Luke) is a praise of God common in the Hebrew Bible (especially the Psalms) and other early New Testament texts (e.g., Rom. 11:33–6); doxologies are also found in central Jewish prayers such as the *Shema* and *Kaddish*. In short, despite its fame as a Christian symbol, the Lord's Prayer is by far the most Jewish of all Christian prayers.

Bibliography

Clark, David, *On Earth as in Heaven: The Lord's Prayer from Jewish Prayer to Christian Ritual* (Minneapolis: Fortress, 2017).

Hart, David Bentley, 'A Prayer for the Poor', *Church Life Journal* (5 June 2018), https://churchlifejournal.nd.edu/articles/a-prayer-for-the-poor/.

Migliore, Daniel L. (ed.), *The Lord's Prayer: Perspectives for Reclaiming Christian Prayer* (Grand Rapids: Eerdmans, 1993).

Petuchowski, Jakob K., and Brocke, Michael (eds.), *The Lord's Prayer and Jewish Liturgy* (New York: Seabury, 1978).

15

Matthew 23:1–36 (late first century CE)

Text

[23:1] Then Jesus said to the crowds and to his disciples, [2] 'The scribes and the Pharisees sit on Moses's seat; [3] therefore, do whatever they teach you and follow it, but do not do as they do, for they do not practice what they teach. [4] They tie up heavy burdens, hard to bear, and lay them on the shoulders of others, but they themselves are unwilling to lift a finger to move them. [5] They do all their deeds to be seen by others, for they make their phylacteries broad and their fringes long. [6] They love to have the place of honor at banquets and the best seats in the synagogues [7] and to be greeted with respect in the marketplaces and to have people call them rabbi. [8] But you are not to be called rabbi, for you have one teacher, and you are all brothers and sisters. [9] And call no one your father on earth, for you have one Father, the one in heaven. [10] Nor are you to be called instructors, for you have one instructor, the Messiah. [11] The greatest among you will be your servant. [12] All who exalt themselves will be humbled, and all who humble themselves will be exalted.

[13] 'But woe to you, scribes and Pharisees, hypocrites! For you lock people out of the kingdom of heaven. For you do not go in yourselves, and when others are going in you stop them. [15] Woe to you, scribes and Pharisees, hypocrites! For you cross sea and land

to make a single convert, and you make the new convert twice as much a child of hell as yourselves.

[16] 'Woe to you, blind guides who say, "Whoever swears by the sanctuary is bound by nothing, but whoever swears by the gold of the sanctuary is bound by the oath." [17] You blind fools! For which is greater, the gold or the sanctuary that has made the gold sacred? [18] And you say, "Whoever swears by the altar is bound by nothing, but whoever swears by the gift that is on the altar is bound by the oath." [19] How blind you are! For which is greater, the gift or the altar that makes the gift sacred? [20] So whoever swears by the altar swears by it and by everything on it, [21] and whoever swears by the sanctuary swears by it and by the one who dwells in it, [22] and whoever swears by heaven swears by the throne of God and by the one who is seated upon it.

[23] 'Woe to you, scribes and Pharisees, hypocrites! For you tithe mint, dill, and cumin and have neglected the weightier matters of the law: justice and mercy and faith. It is these you ought to have practiced without neglecting the others. [24] You blind guides! You strain out a gnat but swallow a camel!

[25] 'Woe to you, scribes and Pharisees, hypocrites! For you clean the outside of the cup and of the plate, but inside they are full of greed and self-indulgence. [26] You blind Pharisee! First clean the inside of the cup and of the plate, so that the outside also may become clean.

[27] 'Woe to you, scribes and Pharisees, hypocrites! For you are like whitewashed tombs, which on the outside look beautiful but inside they are full of the bones of the dead and of all kinds of uncleanness. [28] So you also on the outside look righteous to others, but inside you are full of hypocrisy and lawlessness.

[29] 'Woe to you, scribes and Pharisees, hypocrites! For you build the tombs of the prophets and decorate the graves of the righteous, [30] and you say, "If we had lived in the days of our ancestors, we would not have taken part with them in shedding the blood of the prophets." [31] Thus you testify against yourselves that you are descendants of those who murdered the prophets. [32] Fill up, then, the measure of your ancestors. [33] You snakes, you brood of vipers! How can you escape the judgment of hell? [34] For this reason I send you prophets, sages, and scribes, some of whom you will kill and crucify, and some you will flog in your synagogues and pursue from town to town, [35] so that upon you may come all the righteous blood shed on earth, from the blood of righteous Abel to the blood of Zechariah son of Barachiah, whom you murdered between the sanctuary and the altar. [36] Truly I tell you, all this will come upon this generation.'

Commentary

This document, a litany of prophetic woes spoken by Jesus against the scribes and Pharisees in Matthew 23, has a dark history of Christian reception, in which some of its angriest lines ('scribes and Pharisees, hypocrites!'; 'you are like whitewashed tombs!'; 'upon you may come all the righteous blood shed on earth!') came to be recast as Christian slanders against Jews and Judaism generally. In the Gospel of Matthew, however, even this furious passage begins with an acknowledgement of the legitimate authority of the scribes and Pharisees in Galilee and Judea of the late Second Temple period: 'The scribes and the Pharisees sit on Moses's seat; therefore, do whatever they teach you and follow it.' As teachers of the law to the people, the scribes and Pharisees rightly derive their authority from Moses. This is far more than later Christian texts (or even most other New Testament texts) can bring themselves to concede.

But despite (or because of) the legitimacy of their office, Matthew's Jesus finds the scribes and Pharisees guilty of rank hypocrisy, that is, of failing to practise what they preach. They preach the commandments of Moses, as they should, but they fail to keep the commandments themselves. More specifically – so the accusation goes – they keep some commandments but not others. They offer tithes but do not maintain justice. They pray with phylacteries but do not cultivate humility. They teach at synagogue but do not give assistance to the poor. They honour the righteous dead but antagonise (those whom Matthew counts as) the righteous living, namely Jesus and his disciples. Some later anti-Jewish Christian interpreters would come to conclude that such hypocrisy was characteristic of Judaism as such, or even of the law of Moses itself. For Matthew, however, Jesus and the Pharisees agree on the principle of the sanctity of the law of Moses. The point is that Jesus, like the classical prophets before him, has to indict his contemporaries for their transgressions of the law. The closing lines of the passage, which prophesy bloodguilt for the murder of the prophets coming on the present generation, is an unsubtle hint of Matthew's post-70 CE setting and his interpretation of the destruction of Jerusalem. The bloodguilt issue arises again several chapters later in Matthew's Gospel, at the trial of Jesus, which is our next document.

Bibliography

Kampen, John, *Matthew within Sectarian Judaism* (New Haven: Yale University Press, 2019).

Runesson, Anders, *Divine Wrath and Salvation in Matthew: The Narrative World of the First Gospel* (Minneapolis: Fortress, 2016).

Saldarini, Anthony, 'Delegitimation of Leaders in Matthew 23', *Catholic Biblical Quarterly* 54 (1992), 659–80.

Yarbro Collins, Adela, 'Polemic against the Pharisees in Matthew 23', in Sievers, Joseph, and Levine, Amy-Jill (eds.), *The Pharisees* (Grand Rapids: Eerdmans, 2021), 148–69.

16

Matthew 27:15–26 (late first century CE)

Text

²⁷:¹⁵ Now at the festival the governor was accustomed to release a prisoner for the crowd, anyone whom they wanted. ¹⁶ At that time they had a notorious prisoner called Jesus Barabbas. ¹⁷ So after they had gathered, Pilate said to them, 'Whom do you want me to release for you, Jesus Barabbas or Jesus who is called the Messiah?' ¹⁸ For he realized

that it was out of jealousy that they had handed him over. [19] While he was sitting on the judgment seat, his wife sent word to him, 'Have nothing to do with that innocent man, for today I have suffered a great deal because of a dream about him.' [20] Now the chief priests and the elders persuaded the crowds to ask for Barabbas and to have Jesus killed. [21] The governor again said to them, 'Which of the two do you want me to release for you?' And they said, 'Barabbas.' [22] Pilate said to them, 'Then what should I do with Jesus who is called the Messiah?' All of them said, 'Let him be crucified!' [23] Then he asked, 'Why, what evil has he done?' But they shouted all the more, 'Let him be crucified!'

[24] So when Pilate saw that he could do nothing but rather that a riot was beginning, he took some water and washed his hands before the crowd, saying, 'I am innocent of this man's blood; see to it yourselves.' [25] Then the people as a whole answered, 'His blood be on us and on our children!' [26] So he released Barabbas for them, and after flogging Jesus he handed him over to be crucified.

Commentary

This scene – of the Roman governor Pilate releasing one of two prisoners and washing his hands of bloodguilt for the death of Jesus – is unique to Matthew's Gospel and has a sinister afterlife in the history of Christian anti-Judaism. One famous modern example: when Mel Gibson made his 2004 film *The Passion of the Christ*, he took care to include the scene of the (Jewish) crowd crying out about Jesus, 'His blood be on us and on our children!' From one quite particular interpretation of this verse comes the centuries-old Christian trope of pan-Jewish guilt for the death of Jesus, the so-called 'blood curse' of Matt. 27:25.

The Gospel-writer, who diverges from his source Mark in adding this scene, does go out of his way to read the Roman destruction of Jerusalem (after which catastrophe he is writing) as a terrible divine punishment visited upon the Jerusalemites of 30 CE and their children (*c.* 70 CE) for supposedly baying for Jesus' blood. (In another bizarre twist on this theory, Origen says that Jerusalem was destroyed as divine punishment for the murder not of Jesus but of Jesus' brother James, and says he learned this from Josephus.) Matthew's is a dark, moralising interpretation of the destruction of Jerusalem, but it is not any kind of curse upon all Jews in perpetuity. That idea is a later Christian improvisation on the text of Matthew's Gospel.

There are further layers to this story, too. Pilate's wife learns by dream divination that Jesus is an innocent man, hence Pilate asks the Jewish crowd what wrong Jesus is supposed to have done, then symbolically washes his hands so that guilt for Jesus' blood is transferred – according to the logic of the story – to the crowd. What is more, the motif of the two prisoners (both named Jesus), one put to death and the other released, could perhaps be Matthew's effort to paint Jesus as the goat sacrificed to God on Yom Kippur (cf. that idea in Hebrews 9), with the other Jesus (Barabbas) corresponding to the other goat (the so-called scapegoat or Azazel goat) released into the wilderness. In short, this story both relates Matthew's own Jewish theological interpretation of the death of Jesus and provides ample grist for the mill of later Christian anti-Jewish polemic.

Bibliography

Boys, Mary C., *Redeeming Our Sacred Story: The Death of Jesus and Relations between Jews and Christians* (New York: Paulist Press, 2013).

Buck, Erwin, 'Anti-Judaic Sentiments in the Passion Narrative According to Matthew', in Richardson, Peter (ed.), *Anti-Judaism in Early Christianity*, vol. 1 (Waterloo, ON: Wilfrid Laurier University Press, 1986), 165–80.

Moscicke, Hans M., 'Jesus, Barabbas, and the Crowd as Figures in Matthew's Day of Atonement Typology (Matthew 27:15–26)', *Journal of Biblical Literature* 139 (2020), 125–53.

Stökl Ben Ezra, Daniel, *The Impact of Yom Kippur on Early Christianity* (Tübingen: Mohr Siebeck, 2003).

17

Revelation 2:8–11, 3:7–9 (late first century CE)

Text

2:8 And to the angel of the church in Smyrna write: These are the words of the First and the Last, who was dead and came to life:

9 I know your affliction and your poverty, even though you are rich. I know the slander on the part of those who say that they are Jews and are not but are a synagogue of Satan. 10 Do not fear what you are about to suffer. Beware, the devil is about to throw some of you into prison so that you may be tested, and for ten days you will have affliction. Be faithful until death, and I will give you the crown of life. 11 Let anyone who has an ear listen to what the Spirit is saying to the churches. Whoever conquers will not be harmed by the second death […]

3:7 And to the angel of the church in Philadelphia write:

> These are the words of the Holy One, the True One,
>> who has the key of David,
>> who opens and no one will shut,
>> who shuts and no one opens:

8 I know your works. Look, I have set before you an open door that no one is able to shut. I know that you have but little power, yet you have kept my word and have not denied my name. 9 I will make those of the synagogue of Satan who say that they are Jews and are not but are lying – I will make them come and bow down before your feet, and they will learn that I have loved you.

Commentary

The Apocalypse of John, better known as the Book of Revelation, is less prominent in the history of Jewish–Christian relations than, say, the Gospels or the letters of Paul. But it is more significant, for the ancient period, at least, than its reputation might suggest, and this passage in particular has sometimes been a problem text in Jewish–Christian relations. The book is an apocalypse, a Jewish (and later also Christian) genre of revelatory literature in which a seer has visions of or takes mystical journeys to heaven, hell, the ends of the cosmos, etc. (cf. Daniel, Book of the Watchers, 4 Ezra, 2 Baruch). Revelation is written by a certain prophet called John, otherwise unknown to us (i.e., not to be identified with any other persons called John in the New Testament).

Significantly for the history of Jewish–Christian relations, in two of the brief letters that appear near the beginning of his visions (letters to Smyrna and Philadelphia, both excerpted here) John warns about certain people 'who say that they are Jews and are not but are a synagogue of Satan' (Rev. 2:9, 3:9). This is a fascinating expression, since it hints at a phenomenon which is thinly attested here and there in other ancient sources: debates over people falsely claiming the name of 'Jew'. The difficulty is that, as with many of the documents in this chapter, it is much contested who exactly our author is and what he means by this phrase. The majority interpretation to date has been that John is a Christian, of uncertain ethnicity, who here implies that he and his Christian coreligionists are the real 'Jews', while actual Jews are, in his view, only falsely so called. In fact, John supposedly avers, these actual Jews in Asia Minor are a synagogue not of God but of Satan. If this interpretation were right, then the passage would be baldly anti-Jewish and, to just that extent, an obvious problem for Jewish–Christian relations.

But as recent research has demonstrated, what clues there are in the book in fact suggest that John himself, as well as his audience, is Jewish. He and they recognise Jesus as the messiah, so we might think of them as 'Christian', but that word does not appear in the book. In John's own presentation, he and his audience are just Jews, faithful to God and to the messiah. If so, then these people 'who say they are Jews and are not' might be exactly what the phrase suggests on the surface of it, namely gentiles who try to appropriate the name 'Jew' for themselves (perhaps as godfearers or proselytes, groups well attested elsewhere in the New Testament; see documents 2, 4 and 7 above). It is quite likely, in other words, that this passage does exactly the *opposite* of what the majority interpretation has thought: it is not taking the name 'Jew' away from actual Jews; rather, it is condemning other people who do so. Revelation likely attests a religious phenomenon that was relatively common in the first century CE, but became much less so thereafter, where groups of Jews venerated Jesus alongside the Jewish God without thinking, or anyone else thinking about them, that they were 'Christian'.

Bibliography

Cohen, Shaye J. D., '"Those Who Say They Are Jews and Are Not": How Do You Know a Jew in Antiquity When You See One?', in *The Beginnings of Jewishness: Boundaries, Varieties, Uncertainties* (Berkeley: University of California Press, 1999), 25–68.

Frankfurter, David, 'Jews or Not? Reconstructing the "Other" in Rev 2:9 and 3:9', *Harvard Theological Review* 94 (2001), 403–25.

Kocar, Alexander, *Heavenly Stories: Tiered Salvation in the New Testament and Ancient Christianity* (Philadelphia: University of Pennsylvania Press, 2021), 19–43.

Marshall, John W., *Parables of War: Reading John's Jewish Apocalypse* (Waterloo, ON: Wilfrid Laurier University Press, 2001).

18

Luke 13:1–5, 31–5 (late first or early second century CE*)*

Text

^{13:1} At that very time there were some present who told Jesus about the Galileans whose blood Pilate had mingled with their sacrifices. ² He asked them, 'Do you think that because these Galileans suffered in this way they were worse sinners than all other Galileans? ³ No, I tell you, but unless you repent you will all perish as they did. ⁴ Or those eighteen who were killed when the tower of Siloam fell on them – do you think that they were worse offenders than all the other people living in Jerusalem? ⁵ No, I tell you, but unless you repent you will all perish just as they did.' […]

³¹ At that very hour some Pharisees came and said to him, 'Get away from here, for Herod wants to kill you.' ³² He said to them, 'Go and tell that fox for me, "Listen, I am casting out demons and performing cures today and tomorrow, and on the third day I finish my work. ³³ Yet today, tomorrow, and the next day I must be on my way, because it is impossible for a prophet to be killed outside of Jerusalem." ³⁴ Jerusalem, Jerusalem, the city that kills the prophets and stones those who are sent to it! How often have I desired to gather your children together as a hen gathers her brood under her wings, and you were not willing! ³⁵ See, your house is left to you. And I tell you, you will not see me until the time comes when you say, "Blessed is the one who comes in the name of the Lord."'

Commentary

The Gospel of Luke follows and makes use of Mark, certainly, and possibly also Matthew. Luke is different from its predecessors, however, in being not just a Gospel but rather a two-volume collected biography of Jesus and his apostles: Luke-plus-Acts. The Gospel of Luke and the Acts of the Apostles, although they are separated (by the Gospel of John) in the New Testament canon, were originally two volumes of a single work. Volume 2, the Acts, possibly also knew and used the works of the Jewish historian Josephus, which would push its date into the early second century.

This document, excerpted from Luke 13, is part of the long central section of the Gospel in which Jesus slowly makes his way to Jerusalem to die a prophet's death. The opening verse introduces Luke's readers to the character of Pontius Pilate (who will, of course, pull the trigger that kills Jesus at the end of the Gospel). Luke mentions in passing an episode in which Pilate murdered certain Galilean Jews who had made pilgrimage to Jerusalem to worship at the temple. This may or may not correspond to one of several incidents of Pilate's violence against Jewish festival-goers mentioned by Josephus. In Luke's Gospel, in any case, this passage establishes Pilate as an impious and murderous figure.

Later in the same chapter, in the second paragraph of our document, there is more talk of murder, when Luke reports that Herod (i.e., Herod Antipas, son of Herod the Great) is seeking to kill Jesus. This, too, foreshadows Luke's account of the trial and execution of Jesus, where Pilate and Herod appear together as co-conspirators (Luke 23:1–12, document 19 below). Herod is Jewish (or part-Jewish, according to Josephus) and Pilate Roman, but as Luke sees it, they are allied together against Jesus because of their investment in the Roman imperial rule of Judea.

Equally interesting is the fact that, here, it is certain *Pharisees* who warn Jesus to flee to safety. The Pharisees are often portrayed, in Luke as in the other Gospels, as Jesus' competitors. But here they are on his side against the murderous plotting of Herod. This episode suggests what was historically probably the case: that, on a broad map of ancient Jewish sects, Jesus was far closer to the Pharisees than he was to any other group. Some historians have argued, not implausibly, that Jesus just *was* a Pharisee. In any case, at the end of our document he speaks as a Jewish prophet, foretelling and lamenting the destruction of the holy city, very much as another Jesus, Jesus ben Ananias, did shortly before the destruction by the Romans in 70 CE (Josephus, *War* 6.300–9). Parallels like these have been a large part of the modern recovery of 'Jesus the Jew' both in historical research and in Jewish–Christian dialogue.

Bibliography

Bond, Helen K., *Pontius Pilate in History and Interpretation* (Cambridge: Cambridge University Press, 1998).

Evans, Craig A., *Jesus and His Contemporaries: Comparative Studies* (Leiden: Brill, 2001).

Schröter, Jens, 'How Close Were Jesus and the Pharisees?', in Sievers, Joseph, and Levine, Amy-Jill (eds.), *The Pharisees* (Grand Rapids: Eerdmans, 2021), 220–39.

Vermes, Geza, *Jesus the Jew* (London: Collins, 1973).

19

Luke 23:1–12 (late first or early second century CE)

Text

23:1 Then the assembly rose as a body and brought Jesus before Pilate. 2 They began to accuse him, saying, 'We found this man inciting our nation, forbidding us to pay taxes to Caesar and saying that he himself is the Messiah, a king.' 3 Then Pilate asked him, 'Are you the king of the Jews?' He answered, 'You say so.' 4 Then Pilate said to the chief priests and the crowds, 'I find no basis for an accusation against this man.' 5 But they were insistent and said, 'He stirs up the people by teaching throughout all Judea, from Galilee where he began even to this place.'

6 When Pilate heard this, he asked whether the man was a Galilean. 7 And when he learned that he was under Herod's jurisdiction, he sent him off to Herod, who was himself in Jerusalem at that time. 8 When Herod saw Jesus, he was very glad, for he had been wanting to see him for a long time because he had heard about him and was hoping to see him perform some sign. 9 He questioned him at some length, but Jesus gave him no

answer. [10] The chief priests and the scribes stood by vehemently accusing him. [11] Even Herod with his soldiers treated him with contempt and mocked him; then he put an elegant robe on him and sent him back to Pilate. [12] That same day Herod and Pilate became friends with each other; before this they had been enemies.

Commentary

Luke's account of the trial of Jesus makes explicit what Mark's account (see documents 11 and 12 above) had not, namely, that 'messiah' in the Jewish idiom can be understood to mean 'king' in the Roman idiom. Here the assembly of Jerusalem elders spells out to Pilate that he should be concerned about Jesus as a would-be king and disturber of the Roman peace. Uniquely in Luke, however, Pilate evades responsibility for the whole affair by referring it to his client ruler Herod (i.e., Herod Antipas, son of Herod the Great), tetrarch of Galilee.

The brief scene of the captive Jesus appearing before Herod occurs only here in all of the Gospels (though it is memorably recreated in Andrew Lloyd Webber's *Jesus Christ Superstar*). Luke's literary point seems to be to paint Herod as a co-conspirator with Pilate in the execution of Jesus. Luke had previously mentioned (13:1, document 18 above) that Herod had already been angling to kill Jesus. And our document ends with a remarkable report of a new friendship between the Roman governor and his client ruler, bound together by their shared resolution to rid themselves of the trouble posed by Jesus. As with the other Gospel passion narratives, one main historical lesson is how very precarious life could be for Judean and other provincial subjects under Roman imperial rule.

Even if this friendship between Herod and Pilate be judged historically implausible, it does important literary work in Luke–Acts. In Acts 4, after the resurrection of Jesus, the apostles reflect back on this moment in Luke 23 with their own midrash on Psalm 2. The apostles pray, 'Sovereign Lord, who made the heaven and the earth, the sea, and everything in them, [25] it is you who said by the Holy Spirit through our ancestor David, your servant: *"Why did the gentiles rage, and the peoples imagine vain things?* [26] *The kings of the earth took their stand, and the rulers have gathered together against the Lord and against his Messiah."* [Ps. 2:1–2] [27] For in this city, in fact, both Herod and Pontius Pilate, with the gentiles and the peoples of Israel, gathered together against your holy servant Jesus, whom you anointed [...]' (Acts 4:24–7, NRSVue). In other words, Luke takes the plural 'kings of the earth' in Ps. 2:2 to be Herod and Pilate, two 'kings' (in fact, tetrarch and prefect, respectively) who conspired together against the Lord's messiah, Jesus. Luke's interpretation is particularly significant for later Jewish–Christian relations for its assigning blame for Jesus' death not to Jews – as Matthew arguably does (document 16 above) – but rather to gentile kings. Luke's account is thus a predecessor for the conclusion of the Second Vatican Council in *Nostra aetate* (see Appendix to Part III, p. 512): 'neither all Jews indiscriminately at that time, nor Jews today, can be charged with the crimes committed during his [Jesus'] passion.'

Bibliography

Darr, John A., *Herod the Fox: Audience Criticism and Lukan Characterization* (Sheffield: Sheffield Academic, 1998).

Gaston, Lloyd, 'Anti-Judaism and the Passion Narrative in Luke and Acts', in Richardson, Peter (ed.), *Anti-Judaism in Early Christianity*, vol. 1 (Waterloo, ON: Wilfrid Laurier University Press, 1986), 127–54.

Neyrey, Jerome H., *The Passion According to Luke: A Redaction Study of Luke's Soteriology* (New York: Paulist, 1985).

20

Acts 21:17–26 (late first or early second century CE)

Text

[21:17] When we arrived in Jerusalem, the brothers welcomed us warmly. [18] The next day Paul went with us to visit James, and all the elders were present. [19] After greeting them, he related one by one the things that God had done among the gentiles through his ministry. [20] When they heard it, they praised God. Then they said to him, 'You see, brother, how many thousands of believers there are among the Jews, and they are all zealous for the law. [21] They have been told about you that you teach all the Jews living among the gentiles to forsake Moses and that you tell them not to circumcise their children or observe the customs. [22] What then is to be done? They will certainly hear that you have come. [23] So do what we tell you. We have four men who are under a vow. [24] Join these men, go through the rite of purification with them, and pay for the shaving of their heads. Thus all will know that there is nothing in what they have been told about you but that you yourself observe and guard the law. [25] But as for the gentiles who have become believers, we have sent a letter with our judgment that they should abstain from what has been sacrificed to idols and from blood and from what is strangled and from sexual immorality.' [26] Then Paul took the men, and the next day, having purified himself, he entered the temple with them, making public the completion of the days of purification when the sacrifice would be made for each of them.

Commentary

This document takes us into Luke's second volume: the Acts of the Apostles. The story is continuous with Luke's Gospel; volume 1 ends and volume 2 begins with the same scene: Jesus being taken up into heaven. The remainder of volume 2 relates the exploits of the apostles, in particular Peter and Paul. This document, excerpted from Acts 21, near the end of the book, tells the story of Paul's return to Jerusalem after his several years preaching the risen Christ to gentiles all around Asia, Macedonia and Achaia. As the story goes, it is a dangerous visit for Paul because Jews in Jerusalem think that he is actively undermining Jewish law and custom in the diaspora.

The remarkable thing, however, is that Luke presents these Jerusalemite rumours about Paul as manifestly *false*. Luke is quite precise about saying that Paul opposes proselyte circumcision for gentiles, not traditional circumcision for Jews (Acts 15:1–2, 22:3, 24:14, 25:8). (And this actually agrees exactly with what Paul says in his own letters; see documents 2, 4 and 7 above.) To underline the point, Luke narrates Paul taking part in a votive offering at the Jerusalem temple with several other Jewish Christ-believers. As for gentile Christ-believers, Luke here reiterates the rule that Paul and the other apostles had agreed to in Acts 15, namely that they must abstain from idol sacrifices, food with blood, food from a strangled animal and sexual immorality. These prohibitions are an early instance of the so-called Noahide laws of later rabbinic tradition (e.g., b.Sanh. 56a): commandments given to Noah and applicable to gentiles (in contrast to the Torah of Moses applicable to Israel alone). Jesus and the apostles, being Jews, continue to keep Torah, up to and including the priestly sacrifices in the temple.

This is all the more interesting given that Acts comes from at least the late first, possibly even the second, century. Many other Christian texts from after 70 CE adopted the view that the Christian church had replaced the Jerusalem temple as the site of God's presence in the world, and that the death of Jesus had supplanted all plant and animal sacrifices (see, for example, document 8 above). Acts, however, portrays the apostles as participating fully in the sacrificial worship of the Jewish temple in Jerusalem as, historically, they almost certainly did. (Another important scene in this connection is Acts 2:43–7, where all the Jerusalem Christ-believers are portrayed as still offering Jewish worship at the temple.) It seems not to occur to our author to think that the church supersedes the temple, even though he writes well after the temple's destruction. For the author of Acts, there is no incompatibility between preaching Christ and offering traditional Jewish sacrifices.

Bibliography

Fredriksen, *When Christians Were Jews*.

Jervell, Jacob, *Luke and the People of God: A New Look at Luke–Acts* (Minneapolis: Augsburg, 1972).

Oliver, Isaac W., *Luke's Jewish Eschatology: The National Restoration of Israel in Luke–Acts* (Oxford: Oxford University Press, 2021).

Smith, David Andrew, 'The Jewishness of Luke–Acts: Locating Lukan Christianity amidst the Parting of the Ways', *Journal of Theological Studies* 72 (2021), 738–68.

21

John 8:31–47 (late first or early second century CE)

Text

8:31 Then Jesus said to the Jews who had believed in him, 'If you continue in my word, you are truly my disciples, 32 and you will know the truth, and the truth will make you free.' 33 They answered him, 'We are descendants of Abraham and have never been slaves to anyone. What do you mean by saying, "You will be made free"?'

[34] Jesus answered them, 'Very truly, I tell you, everyone who commits sin is a slave to sin. [35] The slave does not have a permanent place in the household; the son has a place there forever. [36] So if the Son makes you free, you will be free indeed. [37] I know that you are descendants of Abraham, yet you look for an opportunity to kill me because there is no place in you for my word. [38] I declare what I have seen in the Father's presence; as for you, you should do what you have heard from the Father.'

[39] They answered him, 'Abraham is our father.' Jesus said to them, 'If you are Abraham's children, you would do what Abraham did, [40] but now you are trying to kill me, a man who has told you the truth that I heard from God. This is not what Abraham did. [41] You are indeed doing what your father does.' They said to him, 'We are not illegitimate children; we have one Father, God himself.' [42] Jesus said to them, 'If God were your Father, you would love me, for I came from God, and now I am here. I did not come on my own, but he sent me. [43] Why do you not understand what I say? It is because you cannot accept my word. [44] You are from your father the devil, and you choose to do your father's desires. He was a murderer from the beginning and does not stand in the truth because there is no truth in him. When he lies, he speaks according to his own nature, for he is a liar and the father of lies. [45] But because I tell the truth, you do not believe me. [46] Which of you convicts me of sin? If I tell the truth, why do you not believe me? [47] Whoever is from God hears the words of God. The reason you do not hear them is that you are not from God.'

Commentary

The Gospel of John is fourth in canonical order and probably also in chronology. It is strikingly literarily different from the other three (Synoptic) Gospels. The author very probably knows and uses at least Mark (the earliest of the four) and possibly also Matthew and Luke, but takes considerable liberties in his own composition. He seems to know quite a lot about Jews and Judaism, even down to rather obscure details about Judean, Galilean and Samarian customs, so that we can easily imagine that he is Jewish himself. On the other hand, however, John's rhetoric towards and about Jews is some of the harshest and most polemical in the New Testament. So if he is a Jew, he has perhaps experienced an estrangement from his own people, or alternatively he may be an exceptionally well-informed gentile Christ-follower.

This document, excerpted from a dialogue between Jesus and 'the Jews' in John 8, gives a characteristic impression of John's anti-Jewish rhetoric. Like the Synoptic Gospels, John paints scenes of conflict between Jesus and the people who oppose him. But whereas the Synoptic Gospels usually single out the Pharisees (in Galilee) or the chief priests (in Jerusalem) as Jesus' opponents, at key points in John they are just 'the Jews', full stop. The effect of this change is significant. Even though, in John's story (as in historical fact), Jesus and the disciples are also Jews, they are not so called; 'the Jews' appear as a kind of stock character over against Jesus. In our document, for example, Jesus harangues the Jews, telling them that they are children of the devil (John 8:44).

The Greek *Ioudaioi* can mean Judeans as well as 'Jews', and some well-meaning Christian interpreters have argued that John's polemic only reflects a local rivalry between Galileans and Judeans, or some such, the effect of which could be to blunt the otherwise jarring anti-Jewish rhetoric of the text. It would be nice if this were the case, but historically it seems unlikely. As Adele Reinhartz has argued, John, whoever he is – whether estranged Jew or learned gentile – probably means to say that disciples of Jesus are on the side of God, Jews on the side of the devil. (In this respect, John may provide precedent for the ugly modern Christian usage of 'the Jews' in a pejorative sense; hence the problem.) John's Gospel being part of Christian scripture, and being important to Christians for other reasons (e.g., its divine Christology, without which there would be no ecumenical creeds), this poses an ethical problem for Christian readers. The Gospel is probably here to stay, so the urgent task is for the churches to find other, more humane models for Jewish–Christian relations than this document offers them. There certainly are such models elsewhere in Christian scripture (see *passim* in this chapter), but Christian readers will need to keep their ethical wits about them.

Bibliography

Bieringer, Reimund, Pollefeyt, Dider, and Vandecasteele-Vanneuville, Frederique (eds.), *Anti-Judaism and the Fourth Gospel* (Louisville: Westminster John Knox, 2001).

Cirafesi, Wally V., *John within Judaism: Religion, Ethnicity, and the Shaping of Jesus-Oriented Jewishness in the Fourth Gospel* (Leiden: Brill, 2021).

Reinhartz, Adele, *Cast Out of the Covenant: Jews and Anti-Judaism in the Gospel of John* (Minneapolis: Fortress, 2018).

22

John 9:13–34 (late first or early second century CE*)*

Text

9:13 They brought to the Pharisees the man who had formerly been blind. 14 Now it was a Sabbath day when Jesus made the mud and opened his eyes. 15 Then the Pharisees also began to ask him how he had received his sight. He said to them, 'He put mud on my eyes. Then I washed, and now I see.' 16 Some of the Pharisees said, 'This man is not from God, for he does not observe the Sabbath.' Others said, 'How can a man who is a sinner perform such signs?' And they were divided. 17 So they said again to the blind man, 'What do you say about him? It was your eyes he opened.' He said, 'He is a prophet.'

18 The Jews did not believe that he had been blind and had received his sight until they called the parents of the man who had received his sight 19 and asked them, 'Is this your son, who you say was born blind? How then does he now see?' 20 His parents answered, 'We know that this is our son and that he was born blind, 21 but we do not know how it is that now he sees, nor do we know who opened his eyes. Ask him; he is

of age. He will speak for himself.' ²² His parents said this because they were afraid of the Jews, for the Jews had already agreed that anyone who confessed Jesus to be the Messiah would be put out of the synagogue. ²³ Therefore his parents said, 'He is of age; ask him.'

²⁴ So for the second time they called the man who had been blind, and they said to him, 'Give glory to God! We know that this man is a sinner.' ²⁵ He answered, 'I do not know whether he is a sinner. One thing I do know, that though I was blind, now I see.' ²⁶ They said to him, 'What did he do to you? How did he open your eyes?' ²⁷ He answered them, 'I have told you already, and you would not listen. Why do you want to hear it again? Do you also want to become his disciples?' ²⁸ Then they reviled him, saying, 'You are his disciple, but we are disciples of Moses. ²⁹ We know that God has spoken to Moses, but as for this man, we do not know where he comes from.' ³⁰ The man answered, 'Here is an astonishing thing! You do not know where he comes from, yet he opened my eyes. ³¹ We know that God does not listen to sinners, but he does listen to one who worships him and obeys his will. ³² Never since the world began has it been heard that anyone opened the eyes of a person born blind. ³³ If this man were not from God, he could do nothing.' ³⁴ They answered him, 'You were born entirely in sins, and are you trying to teach us?' And they drove him out.

Commentary

This fascinating document has played an unusual role in the history of Jewish–Christian relations. On its surface, it is a story about a blind Jewish man healed by Jesus and the aftermath of his healing in his synagogue community. At another level, however, it has often been read as a thinly veiled account of the so-called 'parting of the ways' between Judaism and Christianity (see Chapter 2, p. 66), perhaps even – according to these readings – in the actual experience of the author and audience of the Gospel of John (the so-called 'Johannine community' of modern scholarly hypothesis).

As the story goes, the blind man's (Jewish) parents feared to speak the truth about the incident to 'the Jews' because, John says, 'the Jews had already agreed that anyone who confessed Jesus to be the Messiah would be put out of the synagogue' (9:22). The Greek word at the end of this sentence, *aposynagogos*, 'cast out of the synagogue', is a neologism; it does not occur in any other earlier or contemporary sources. Nor, again, is there any external evidence for any such decree of 'the Jews' in this period: a legal ruling that Jews who confessed Jesus as messiah would be excommunicated from synagogue. Elsewhere in ancient Judaism, being a partisan of a particular messiah (e.g., Bar Kokhba) has no bearing on one's membership in the Jewish community. The one possible exception to this generalisation is the *Birkat ha-Minim* (see Chapter 3, p. 123), the latest clause added to the *Amidah* prayer (also called the *Shemoneh Esreh* or Eighteen Benedictions), although it does not mention messiahship, and the direct evidence for it is much later than the Gospel of John, let alone the lifetime of Jesus. The *Birkat ha-Minim*, in one well-attested ancient form preserved in manuscripts from the

Cairo Genizah (and compare t.Ber. 3:25; y.Ber. 2:4 (5a); y.Ber 4:3 (8a); b.Ber. 28b–29a), reads:

> For the apostates let there be no hope,
> and uproot the kingdom of arrogance speedily and in our days.
> May the Nazarenes (*Notzrim*) and the sectarians (*minim*) perish as in a moment.
> Let them be blotted out of the book of life,
> and not be written together with the righteous.
> You are praised, O Lord, who subdues the arrogant.

J. Louis Martyn influentially argued that this Jewish curse upon Christians dated all the way back to the time of the Gospel of John, which he coordinated with the famous early rabbinic gathering at Yavneh. And this, Martyn reasoned, explained John's anxiety about 'being cast out of the synagogue'. The problem is that Martyn's hypothesis rests on an extremely fragile foundation. We do not know what exactly happened at Yavneh, nor can we securely date the *Birkat ha-Minim* that early. Nor, in any case, is the *Birkat ha-Minim* a perfect match for the scenario John describes. John's account here is *his own* perception of a breach between the synagogue and the disciples of Jesus, which may or may not map onto any events in external history. It does, however, provide some context for John's antagonistic rhetoric about 'the Jews' (*Ioudaioi*, which can also mean simply 'Judeans', but is probably used here in a more generalising and pejorative sense), noted in document 21 above.

Bibliography

Langer, Ruth, *Cursing the Christians? A History of the Birkat HaMinim* (Oxford: Oxford University Press, 2012).

Marcus, Joel, '*Birkat ha-Minim* Revisited', *New Testament Studies* 55 (2009), 523–51.

Martyn, J. Louis, *History and Theology in the Fourth Gospel*, 3rd ed. (Louisville: Westminster John Knox, 2003).

Reinhartz, Adele, *Cast Out of the Covenant: Jews and Anti-Judaism in the Gospel of John* (Minneapolis: Fortress, 2018).

23

Josephus: Jewish Antiquities *18.63–4 (early second century* CE*)*

Text

About this time there lived Jesus, a wise man, if indeed one ought to call him a man. For he was one who wrought surprising feats and was a teacher of such people as accept the truth gladly. He won over many Jews and many of the Greeks. He was the Messiah. When Pilate, upon hearing him accused by men of the highest standing amongst us, had condemned him to be crucified, those who had in the first place come to love him did not give up their affection for him. On the third day he appeared to them restored to life, for the prophets of God had prophesied these and countless other marvellous things about him. And the tribe of the Christians, so called after him, has still to this day not disappeared.

Source

Josephus, *Jewish Antiquities, Volume VIII: Books 18–19*, trans. Louis H. Feldman, Loeb Classical Library 433 (Cambridge, MA: Harvard University Press, 1965).

Commentary

This document, traditionally called the *Testimonium Flavianum*, is unlike the others in this chapter in one key respect: it is not part of the New Testament. Like the other documents in this chapter, however, it is a Jewish text from the turn of the second century (excepting a few textual interpolations, on which more in a moment) that knows of Jesus of Nazareth. The author is Flavius Josephus, *né* Joseph ben Matthias, the son of a Judean priestly family who, after the ill-fated Jewish–Roman War of 66–70 CE, became a court historian to the Flavian emperors at Rome. He wrote two major works (as well as a couple of minor ones), the first a history of the war, the second a national history of the Jewish people from the creation of the world to the early Roman empire. Our document comes from near the end of this latter work, a single paragraph of which mentions a certain Galilean wonderworker by the name of Jesus.

The text as we have it in the manuscripts, and as printed above, looks suspiciously Christian, in particular in its claims that Jesus was more than human, was the messiah and was raised from the dead as the prophets testified. Josephus himself was a non-Christian Jew, but the text of his works was transmitted through antiquity and the Middle Ages by Christian scribes. Most likely, then, what has happened here is that an original Josephan report about Jesus has been interpolated with Christian glosses further extolling him. If we set apart the likely Christian glosses in italics, leaving the likely original text in roman type, we get the following:

> About this time there lived Jesus, a wise man, *if indeed one ought to call him a man*. For he was one who wrought surprising feats and was a teacher of such people as accept the truth gladly. He won over many Jews and many of the Greeks. *He was the Messiah*. When Pilate, upon hearing him accused by men of the highest standing amongst us, had condemned him to be crucified, those who had in the first place come to love him did not give up their affection for him. *On the third day he appeared to them restored to life, for the prophets of God had prophesied these and countless other marvellous things about him*. And the tribe of the Christians, so called after him, has still to this day not disappeared.

This passage, along with Josephus' whole oeuvre, is important in the history of Jewish–Christian relations because ancient, medieval and early modern Christians made Josephus play the role of Jewish witness to (what their supersessionist theologies said was) the end of Judaism and rise of Christianity. Josephus wrote a century before the codification of the Mishnah, so he did not live to see the ascendancy of Rabbinic Judaism. Christian readers, therefore, could choose to read him as a kind of coda to their Christian Bibles. Read in this very tendentious way, Josephus' tragic account of the horrors of the Jewish–Roman War became, for Christian writers, a vindication of the church over against the synagogue. Modern historical research has restored Josephus to his own first-century Judean and Roman contexts, but the Christian reception history of his works still casts a long shadow.

Bibliography

Carleton Paget, James, 'Some Observations on Josephus and Christianity', *Journal of Theological Studies* 52 (2001), 539–624.

Novenson, Matthew V., 'Josephus and the New Testament', in Atkinson, Kenneth (ed.), *Oxford Handbook of Josephus* (forthcoming).

Olson, K. A., 'Eusebius and the *Testimonium Flavianum*', *Catholic Biblical Quarterly* 61 (1999), 305–22.

Whealey, Alice, *Josephus on Jesus: The Testimonium Flavianum Controversy from Late Antiquity to Modern Times* (New York: Peter Lang, 2003).

2

Eastern and Western Writings up to the Ninth Century

JAMES CARLETON PAGET

INTRODUCTION

The period which is the subject of this chapter is pivotal in the history of Jewish–Christian relations. It witnesses the so-called 'parting of the ways' between Christians and Jews and so the beginnings of Jewish–Christian relations proper; it sees Christianity becoming the leading state religion in the west by the end of the fourth century, with accompanying consequences for Jews; and it also witnesses the rabbis gradually becoming the acknowledged intellectual leaders of Jews in the western and eastern diaspora. It is the period which, not least through the writings of the church fathers, moulds the character of Jewish–Christian relations as these developed in the Middle Ages and beyond – relations marked predominantly by hostility and mutual recrimination but intermittently hinting also at something more positively interactive.

In spite of its momentous character, a systematic and interconnected account of the history of Jewish–Christian relations between the middle of the second century and the end of the ninth cannot be written. The reason for this lies in the extent and character of the available sources. On the Jewish side, from approximately 100 CE, in contrast to the situation among Christians, there are no literary sources in Greek or Latin, although there continued to be a substantial population of Jews in the west, who wrote inscriptions in both languages. Instead we must rely on material in Hebrew and Aramaic, mainly connected with the rabbis, who rarely mention Christians overtly and whose writings never take the form of a history, tending rather to concern themselves with questions of exegesis and practice into which historical reminiscences occasionally intrude. Other Jewish writings exist, which are covered in Chapter 3. On the Christian side, our problem is different. There is a plethora of relevant sources in Greek, Latin and Syriac, many directed against Jews (often referred to as *adversus Judaeos* (against Jews) texts), which begin to emerge in the early part of the second century. These can take the form of tracts (e.g., Tertullian's *Adversus Judaeos*) or dialogues (e.g., Justin's *Dialogue with Trypho the Jew* and some anonymous works in Syriac). These texts appear persistently in the period under discussion and set the tone and create the themes for a tradition that was to continue among Christians until relatively recent times. Material of an anti-Jewish kind also appears in an array of literary genres, including parenesis, biblical commentary, liturgy, historiography and legal texts. The difficulty here lies in establishing, first, whether the works reflect sentiments beyond the elites who were as a rule their authors; and secondly, whether, for instance, texts which mention Jews and, in most instances, argue against them, give voice to genuine interaction or are engaged in a sophisticated form of rhetoric in which questions unrelated to Jews are being discussed. Determining this is not helped by the fact that so little is known about Jewish life and opinion for large stretches of the period under discussion. Into this complex body of evidence must be added pagan texts (at least for the first five centuries) which intermittently discuss Christians and Jews and could be seen as a helpful 'outsider' perspective.

The period under discussion witnessed the final separation of the followers of Jesus from non-Christian Jews. In one version of this history, referred to as 'the parting of the ways', Christians remain broadly a part of Judaism until about the middle of the second century, when a confluence of events conspire to shatter an increasingly fragile relationship, leading to permanent rift. The supporting pillars in this theory are the so-called *Birkat ha-Minim*, thought to be a curse on Christians, introduced into the Jewish communal prayer known as the *Amidah* (see Chapter 3, p. 123); the Jewish revolts against Roman rule of 70, 115 and 132 CE, which played up antagonisms between messianic Jewish Christians and their non-Christian compatriots; and the beginnings of the appearance of literature directed specifically against Jews, seen in *Barnabas* and Justin's *Dialogue* (see documents 1 and 3).

This account has been questioned, however. As is noted in Chapter 3, a great deal of controversy surrounds the *Birkat ha-Minim*, in terms both of its original wording and of the circumstances and date of its writing and its purpose. Others have suggested that the model of the parting is based upon a misplaced view of the early power and authority of the rabbis, or of a proto-orthodox Christianity. Once both religions are deinstitutionalised and seen as more diverse and less 'controlled', it becomes difficult, until at least the latter part of the fourth century and perhaps beyond, to talk about a uniform parting, as a result of which 'partings of the ways' has gained currency as more accurately reflecting the reality of the separation. Given what little is known about the revolts and their actual effect upon Jewish–Christian relations, establishing the degree to which they caused separation is difficult, even if the final revolt under Bar Kokhba, which led to Jerusalem becoming a pagan city, was exploited by Christian authors in an attempt to show that the Jewish people had been abandoned by God.

Against this background, generalising narratives should be avoided and the local and particular highlighted. Opponents of the 'parting' paradigm also call for a more nuanced reading of *adversus Judaeos* texts, stating that when, for instance, in the first quarter of the second century Ignatius talks about 'Judaism' and 'Christianity', or a quarter of a century later Justin writes about Jews and Christians in his *Dialogue with Trypho* as if they are separate entities, the texts in which these claims are found should be read performatively, that is, as attempts to create a situation rather than simply reflecting one which already existed. As one scholar has written: 'It is perhaps this inability to control the borderland [between Judaism and Christianity] that finally accounts for the anti-Jewish rhetoric in early Christianity' (Fonrobert 2010: 254). In this view, 'Judaism' and 'Christianity' are evolving constructs, which only become proper realities in the Constantinian era and beyond, when state power allows for a stricter definition to come into being. In this messier account of parting, evidence indicating a close interconnection between Jews and Christians is emphasised, for example texts with a strongly Jewish character like the *Pseudo-Clementine* writings (document 5) and evidence for Jesus' followers attending synagogues, practising Jewish laws or seeking Jewish advice about scriptural interpretation. In this context, texts calling for Jews and Christians to live in strictly separate ways are seen as reacting to a more complicated reality in which identities are not so starkly defined.

However we assess this critique of the 'parting' paradigm, at a minimum (1) it demonstrates that we should not assume a simple narrative of 'inevitable' separation, which can be tabulated in a strictly linear way; and (2) it should be seen as a set of admonitory observations which sensitise us to the complexities of the available evidence, even where that evidence goes well beyond the fourth century, when the landscape seems to evidence broadly separate Jewish and Christian communities. So when, in the 380s, John Chrysostom rails against Christians who enter synagogues when Jews are celebrating their most important festivals (document 11), is this exceptional behaviour, brought on by changing political circumstances, or is it the intemperate bishop's objection to such cross-dressing that is distinctive? Taking sufficient account of the critique of the parting paradigm means that such questions should be asked, even if arriving at definitive answers is difficult.

Recent questioning of the parting paradigm has impinged upon an equally contested debate, namely the level of contact we can assume between Jews and Christians and the nature of that contact. In an earlier period, some influential scholars such as Adolf von Harnack (see Chapter 6, p. 322) argued for minimal interaction by about the middle of the second century. In part this view was based upon the idea that through the centuries under discussion the Jewish community was in decline and solipsistic (the rabbis by and large concern themselves with debates internal to the Jewish community and do not really look outward) and so barely entered the consciousness of Christians, whether in the Roman empire or further east in the Sasanian empire. Additional support for this thesis is found in the contents of Christian *adversus Judaeos* material, particularly so-called dialogues depicting a Jew in polemical discussion with a Christian, which are a persistent presence through this period. These, it is said, present the Jew as a straw man, devoid of individuality, and are repetitive, with the same general themes recurring, namely the temporary character of the Jewish Torah, attacks upon biblical examples of Jewish hard-heartedness and sin, Jesus being the messiah and the gentile church being God's new people – arguments supported by copious reference to the Christian Old Testament. Many of these arguments reappear in Christian apologetic literature and elsewhere, leading some to think that *adversus Judaeos* literature was principally concerned with presenting a Christian case to gentiles who wondered about the legitimacy of Christian claims which depended heavily upon the Old Testament/Tanakh and yet were opposed by non-Christian Jews who could be thought to be the legitimate interpreters of scriptures which historically belonged to them. A similar phenomenon occurs when Christians wrote texts against Marcion, a second-century Christian who argued that there was no connection between what Christians came to call the Old Testament and the New Testament. For Marcion, the latter spoke of a different god and a different set of promises. Christians opposed to him, like Tertullian, produced works whose content was very similar to works ostensibly aimed against Jews, not least because the latter and Marcion were arguing the same case from different perspectives.

The thesis for non-contact, however, underestimates the strength of the Jewish community in both the western and eastern diaspora. Especially with reference to archaeological evidence, scholars have argued that it was a force that had to be reckoned with, particularly by those who laid claim to the set of texts which was thought to be the Jewish people's possession. Moreover, if the view that Jews were in decline and inward-looking is true, the sheer amount of anti-Jewish Christian texts is an oddity. 'Why', Marcel Simon asked, 'rail against a corpse?' Moreover, there is evidence of Christians, not least Origen and Jerome, taking an interest in Jewish opinion about the shape of the canon, issues of biblical interpretation and the problem of the text of the Bible, indicating the continuing importance of Jewish opinion in the eyes of some Christians; and such interest goes well beyond the post-Constantinian period, as witnessed, for instance, in the work of Agobard and Amolo in the ninth century. While it is difficult to find in Christian writings many parallels to Jewish traditions as evidenced in rabbinic texts (the main resource available to us), it is important to remember that the rabbis represented one aspect of Jewish thought but not all of it. So while we might question the genuineness of a figure like Trypho in Justin's *Dialogue with Trypho*, we cannot be certain, given our ignorance of Greek-speaking Jewry after 100 CE, that he was an entirely unbelievable figure. Moreover, while the rabbis might not mention Christians very often in their vast corpus of literature, on occasion they betray knowledge of Christian exegetical traditions and implicitly argue against them (see Chapter 3 and Appendix to Part I). Evidence of mutual influence has also been seen in the development of the Jewish *piyyutim* and the Christian *kontakia* from the sixth century, and in the appearance of the Jewish *midrashim* and the Christian *catenae*.

Jewish–Christian relations began to develop markedly after the Roman emperor Constantine became Christian (the situation in the east differed as Sasanian monarchs may have favoured Jews over Christians because of the Christian identity of their Roman enemies). Gradually Jews' legal situation in the west changed. Under Constantine, they were prohibited *inter alia* from persecuting Jews who had become Christians or from owning Christian slaves, which affected Jewish economic activity. Over time, laws followed banning intermarriage with Christians (under Theodosius I), and with the formation of the Theodosian Code under Theodosius II (document 14), Jews were excluded from participation in the army and, aside from the curia, in politics and the legal apparatus of the Christian state, though their status as citizens was nominally confirmed (even if the proclamation of *Cunctos populos* in 380 CE effectively reduced them to second-class citizens). While Christian emperors sought to protect Jewish synagogues from attack or destruction, Jews were prohibited from building new ones, or extending existing ones, though the evidence, especially from Palestine, showing that there was building of synagogues into the sixth century contradicts such legislation, which could on occasion be closer to what Paula Fredriksen and Oded Irshai have called moral exhortation than legal prescription. Justinian I (*r.* 527–65 CE), who saw empire and church as a single unit, failed to retain in his Code (document 18) the law found in the Theodosian Code that Judaism was a so-called permitted religion (*religio licita*) and, among other things, interfered to an unprecedented extent in Jewish synagogal activities. According to Procopius of Caesarea, Justinian brought about the forced conversion of Jews in Borion in Cyrene; and the same phenomenon was witnessed under Heraclius (r. 610–41), Leo III (in 721–2) and Basil I (in 873–4), as well as in Visigothic Spain under King Sisebut (r. 612–21), though the extent to which these policies were carried out with any consistency is unclear; and generally the church opposed coercive conversion, influenced by Augustine's thinking on this matter (King Sisenand (r. 631–6), Sisebut's successor but one, for instance, would overturn his legislation on coercive conversion). Such a caveat can also be applied to the edicts of later councils against Jews – were they carried out? And did the fact of their existence point to better relations between Jews and Christians 'on the ground', where boundaries were constantly eroded by daily intercourse (see Stroumsa 2007: 157)? Sometimes the anti-Jewish literature that continued to be written, whether in the Byzantine empire or in western Europe, could be seen as reacting to what was conceived to be more positive attitudes towards Jews on the part of the ruling authorities (one thinks here of the work of Agobard as a partial reaction to the positive views held by Carolingian monarchs regarding Jews in the first part of the ninth century) or the population at large. In considering the aims of such literature, it should also be noted that the accession of Christianity to the position of state religion in the west could be seen, paradoxically, to have made it more pressing to affirm Christian triumph over Judaism, because Jewish 'opposition' appeared to run counter to the new ideology of a universal and Christian empire. When, for instance, the last pagan emperor, Julian, threatened to rebuild the Jerusalem temple in the early 360s, Christian reaction, both contemporary and much later, indicated that the role of Jews in the Christians' symbolic world remained strikingly significant; and some of this subterranean concern can be seen in the reaction to Christian conversions to Judaism. Jews might worry about Christians when they became their rulers, but Christianity's mere existence did not raise for them the same ideological and psychological difficulties that Jews' existence raised for Christians.

The extent to which these changed circumstances weighed heavily upon Jews in the west is difficult to ascertain. From what evidence there is, many Jewish communities showed resilience, not converting in large numbers and even continuing to attract converts themselves, as might be indicated by the Aphrodisias inscription, if dated to the fifth century as some suggest, and the story of the conversion of the court cleric Bodo found in the ninth-century *Annals of St-Bertin* (document 20). There is evidence of Jewish resistance mainly in the form of writings such as the *Toledot Yeshu* (see Chapter 3, p. 118) and liturgical poems, known as *piyyutim*, mentioned above, probably originating from the sixth century, in which the Christian empire is sometimes attacked. But the status of Jews in the lands of the old Roman empire gradually declined and there must have been a sense, which would not have prevailed before Constantine, that their communities' political and social situation was precarious, dependent upon the whim of a local ruler and particular circumstances.

The documents selected for this chapter reflect a number of features in this developing relationship. Some seek to illustrate the content and tone of the polemic involved in the argument between Christians and Jews. So the chapter presents the earliest (probably second-century) evidence for a Jewish–Christian dialogue (documents 2 (i) and (ii)), a genre which would become important in Christian anti-Jewish polemic, as well as a number of excerpts from a variety of other anti-Jewish works which span the whole of the period and are witnessed in Greek, Latin and Syriac traditions (e.g., documents 1, 4, 8, 10, 11 and 17), with the last of these from the Sasanian empire where, in contrast to the west, Jews and Christians were both minority communities. One document concerns the much less well evidenced subject of anti-Christian Jewish polemic (document 6). The polemical exclusivism of these texts is contrasted with a remarkable passage from a work that was still very popular in the fourth century and beyond, where the ways of Moses and Jesus are seen as legitimately separate routes for apprehending what is ethically correct (document 5). Following on from this, some of the passages discussed reflect a much less separatist picture than is implied by the polemical ones, whether this concerns evidence for Jewish converts to Christianity who continued to observe Jewish laws after their conversion or Christians who asked Jews to bless their marriages or sought to attend the synagogue at particular moments in the Jewish calendar (e.g., documents 3, 9 and 11). Contact of a different kind is seen in passages which touch upon some Christians' interest in seeking Jewish opinion about matters relating to scriptural interpretation, the Hebrew Bible and the learning of Hebrew (e.g., documents 7, 12 and 15). Others come from more formal documents, either the Theodosian Code or the Justinian *Novellae* (documents 14 and 18), or the Fourth Council of Toledo (document 19), which highlight Christian attempts both to control violent and coercive behaviour towards Jews but also to intervene in and control their lives. The ambivalence and complexity of these texts is reflected in Augustine's backhanded defence of the importance of Jews' ongoing presence in the empire in a passage from his *City of God* (document 13). Also discussed are an inscription and a passage which touch more generally on the issue of conversion both from Judaism to Christianity and vice versa (documents 16 and 20).

Bibliography

Becker, Adam, and Reed, A. Y. (eds.), *The Ways That Never Parted: Jews and Christians in Late Antiquity and the Early Middle Ages* (Tübingen: Mohr Siebeck, 2003).

Blumenkranz, Bernard, *Juifs et Chrétiens dans le monde Occidental, 430–1096* (Paris: Mouton, 1960).

Bonfil, Robert, Stroumsa, Guy, Irshai, Oded, and Talgam, Rina (eds.), *The Jews of Byzantium: Dialectics of Majority and Minority Cultures* (Leiden: Brill, 2012).

de Lange, Nicholas, 'Jews in the Age of Justinian', in Maas, Michael (ed.), *The Cambridge Companion to the Age of Justinian* (Cambridge: Cambridge University Press, 2005), 401–26.

Elukin, Jonathan, *Living Together, Living Apart: Rethinking Jewish–Christian Relations in the Middle Ages* (Princeton: Princeton University Press, 2007).

Fonrobert, Charlotte Elisheva, 'Jewish Christians, Judaizers, and Christian anti-Judaism', in Burrus, Virginia (ed.), *A People's History of Christianity*, Vol. 2: *Late Ancient Christianity* (Minneapolis: Fortress Press, 2010), 234–54.

Fredriksen, Paula, and Irshai, Oded, 'Christian Anti-Judaism: Polemics and Policies', in Katz, Steven T. (ed.), *The Cambridge History of Judaism*, Vol. 4: *The Late Roman Rabbinic Period* (Cambridge: Cambridge University Press, 2006), 977–1034.

Horbury, William, *Jews and Christians in Contact and Controversy* (Edinburgh: T&T Clark, 1998).

Kraemer, Ross, *The Mediterranean Diaspora in Late Antiquity: What Christianity Cost the Jews* (New York: Oxford University Press, 2020).

Lieu, Judith, *Image and Reality: The Jews in the World of the Christians in the Second Century* (Edinburgh: T&T Clark, 1996).

Malkiel, David, 'Jewish–Christian Relations in Europe, 840–1096', *Journal of Medieval History* 29 (2003), 55–83.

Parkes, James, *The Conflict of the Church and the Synagogue: A Study in the Origins of Anti-Semitism* (London: Soncino, 1934).

Reed, Annette Yoshiko, *Jewish-Christianity and the History of Judaism* (Minneapolis: Fortress Press, 2022).

Ruether, Rosemary Radford, *Faith and Fratricide: The Theological Roots of Anti-Semitism* (London and New York: Seabury Press, 1974).

Simon, Marcel, *Verus Israel: A Study of the Relations between Christians and Jews in the Roman Empire, AD 135–425* (Oxford: publ. for the Littmann Library of Jewish Civilization by Oxford University Press, 1986).

Stroumsa, Guy G., 'Religious Dynamics between Christians and Jews in Late Antiquity', in Casiday, Augustin, and Norris, Frederick W. (eds.), *The Cambridge History of Christianity*, Vol. 2: *Constantine to c. 600* (Cambridge: Cambridge University Press, 2007), 151–72.

DOCUMENTS

I

Epistle of Barnabas *13 (late first to early second century)*

Text

Now let us see whether this people or the former people is the heir, and whether the covenant is for us or for them. Hear, then, what the scripture says about 'the people': 'And Isaac prayed for Rebecca his wife, for she was barren; and she conceived. Then Rebecca went off to consult the Lord. And the Lord said to her, "Two nations are in your womb, and two peoples in your belly; one people will dominate the other, and the greater will serve the lesser."' You ought to understand who Isaac represents, and who Rebecca, and concerning whom he has shown that this people is greater than that one. And in another prophecy Jacob speaks more clearly to Joseph, his son, saying 'Behold, the Lord has not deprived me of your presence; bring your sons to me, so that I may bless them.' And he brought Ephraim and Manasseh, intending that Manasseh, because he was the older, should be blessed, for he brought him to the right hand of his father Jacob. But Jacob saw in the Spirit a symbol of the people to come. And what does he say? 'And Jacob crossed his hands and placed his right hand on the head of Ephraim, the second and younger, and blessed him. And Joseph said to Jacob, "Transfer your right hand to the head of Manasseh, for he is my firstborn son." And Jacob said to Joseph, "I know, my child, I know; but the greater will serve the lesser. Yet this one too shall be blessed."' Observe how by these means he has ordained that this people should be first, and heir of the covenant. Now if in addition to this the same point is also made through Abraham, we add the final touch to our knowledge. What, then, does he say to Abraham, when he alone believed and was established in righteousness? 'Behold, I have established you, Abraham, as the father of the nations who believe in God without being circumcised.'

Source

Holmes, Michael (ed. and trans.), *The Apostolic Fathers: Greek Texts and English Translations*, 3rd ed. (Grand Rapids: Baker Academic, 2007), 423.

Commentary

The *Epistle of Barnabas* was probably written in Alexandria sometime between 95 and 130 CE. It was not written by Barnabas, the companion of St Paul, and the letter may not originally have been attributed to him (his name does not occur in the letter itself). The work is thought to be an early form of the Christian genre known as *adversus Judaeos* literature because it contains themes which came to be associated with works with that title, namely scriptural proof that Jesus was the messiah, that the need to observe distinctive Jewish laws such as circumcision, sacrifice, food and sabbath had ceased with the coming of Christ and that the followers of Christ, rather than Israel, are now the rightful covenantal people.

The passage cited deals with the last of these themes, the ownership of the covenant, a point made explicit in the first sentence. It focuses on the interpretation of Gen. 25:19–25, the story of the birth to Rebecca of Jacob and Esau, and Gen. 48, the story of Jacob's blessing of Joseph's two sons Manasseh and Ephraim. In both passages (the combination of which in Christian writing we otherwise find only in Philo of Alexandria) the issue of inheritance is raised and in particular inheritance of the younger son over the older. The first passage serves Barnabas' purposes better than the second, especially because of the quotation from Gen. 25:11–13, in which it is stated that one people will dominate over the other. The latter passage, describing Jacob's blessing of his grandchildren, is carefully edited so that there is no reference to the fact that Manasseh and Ephraim are both being blessed and emphasis is placed on the younger brother being greater than the older. Through his interpretation, Barnabas shows that the displacement of the Jewish people (here referred to as 'the former people') by the followers of Jesus was predicted in scripture, even to the point that Jacob indulges in his actions because he was able to foresee that future superiority. An additional point is then made through a mixed citation of Gen. 15:6 and 17:4–5 in which Abraham is presented as the father of the uncircumcised, that is, the gentiles. Barnabas might allude to Rom. 4:11, where Paul uses the same passages from Genesis in a similar way, though he affirms the inheritance of the circumcised (Rom. 4:12), a point denied by Barnabas. As is the case throughout the epistle, Barnabas does not use the words for Jew or Christian, which has led some to think that he has only a muted view of the parting of the ways. The reference, however, to the inheritance of the uncircumcised makes this less likely. The passage exemplifies a significant theme in ancient Christian *adversus Judaeos* literature, namely the question of the true identity of the people of God, seen in terms of the supersession of the followers of Jesus. This theme, which was to have a long history, had the effect of denying the right of Jews to exist.

Bibliography

Hvalvik, Reidar, 'The Epistle of Barnabas', in Bird, Michael F., and Harrower, Scott D. (eds.), *The Cambridge Companion to the Apostolic Fathers* (Cambridge: Cambridge University Press, 2021), 268–89.

Kok, Michael, 'The True Covenant People: Ethnic Reasoning in the Epistle of Barnabas', *Studies in Religion/Sciences Religieuses* 40 (2011), 81–97.

Lookadoo, Jonathan, *The Epistle of Barnabas: A Commentary* (Eugene: Cascade, 2022).

2

The Dialogue of Jason and Papiscus *(second century)*

Text

(i) Origen: Contra Celsum *4.52*

Nevertheless, I could wish that everyone who hears Celsus' clever rhetoric asserting that the book entitled 'A Controversy between Jason and Papiscus about Christ' deserves not laughter but hatred, were to take the little book into his hands and have *the patience and endurance to give his attention* to its contents. He would then at once condemn Celsus, for he would find nothing in the book deserving of hatred. If anyone reads it impartially he will find that the book does not even move him to laughter. In it a Christian is described as disputing with a Jew from the Jewish scriptures and as showing that the prophecies about the Messiah fit Jesus; and the reply with which the other man opposes the argument is at least neither vulgar nor unsuitable to the character of a Jew.

Source

Chadwick, Henry (trans.), *Origen: Contra Celsum* (Cambridge: Cambridge University Press, 1953), 227.

(ii) Celsus: Ad Vigilium *8*

Now let me be quiet about the souls of an impious people which were once hardened and were converted to fear of the Lord thanks to the Lord himself who was spreading the Gospel; and let me fall silent about the people full of believers multiplied throughout the whole world when his apostles were preaching; and let me come to that memorable, eminent and famous instance of a dispute between Jason the Hebrew Christian and Papiscus the Alexandrian Jew, where one sees the stubborn and obstinate heart of the Jew softened by the exhortation and sweet reproaches of the Hebrew; and the teaching professed by Jason under the inspiration of the Holy Spirit and leading Papiscus, admitted to an understanding of the truth and prepared thanks to the mercy of the Lord himself, to fear the Lord, to believe that Jesus is the Christ the Son of God to plead with Jason to receive the seal. The text of this debate proves this as they contend with each other, Papiscus as the opponent of the truth and Jason who was asserting and defending the dispensation and fulfilment of Christ; it was written down in a work in the Greek language.

Source

Ciccolini, Laetitia, 'La *Controverse de Jason et Papiscus*: le témoignage de l'*Ad Vigilium episcopum de Iudaica incredulitate* faussement attribué à Cyprien de Carthage', in Morlet, Sébastien, Munnich, Olivier, and Pouderon, Bernard (eds.), *Les Dialogues ADVERSVS IVDAEOS: Permanences et mutations d'une tradition polémique* (Paris: Institut d'Études Augustiniennes, 2013), 163. Author's own translation from the French.

Commentary

These passages are two of at least six references to a no longer extant work entitled *The Dialogue of Jason and Papiscus*, generally believed to be the earliest evidence of a dialogue between a Christian and a Jew written by a Christian. The first reference is found in Origen's *Contra Celsum* (*Against Celsus*). In this work the third-century church father, at the behest of his patron Ambrosius, responds to an anti-Christian work called *The True Word* attributed to a man called Celsus, written possibly in the 180s some sixty years before Origen's response and only known through citation in Origen's work. In the passage, Origen responds to negative remarks made by Celsus about the *Dialogue of Jason and Papiscus*. The second passage is taken from a possibly fifth-century letter written by another Celsus, the Christian Celsus Africanus, to someone called Vigilius, summarising a Latin translation of the dialogue.

Little is known about the *Dialogue of Jason and Papiscus*. Writing in the sixth century, John of Scythopolis attributes it to Ariston of Pella, who is thought to have been active in the 130s and 140s, probably in Palestine. Elsewhere the work is attributed to Luke the evangelist, including in recently discovered fragments attributed to the sixth-century writer Sophronius (see below), but the attribution to Ariston is thought more likely. Where Origen describes it as a dispute between a Christian and a Jew, Celsus Africanus is more detailed, describing Papiscus as an Alexandrian Jew and Jason as a Hebrew Christian, and mentioning that the work ends in the former's conversion. Neither author quotes from the *Dialogue*. Origen agrees with Celsus about the work's unimpressive style, explained implicitly by the fact that it is written for the masses, and asserts that it attempts to prove by the use of biblical passages that Jesus is the messiah, a point that is not found in the second passage. The fragments copied by Sophronius indicate that the work concentrated on passages from the Pentateuch, in this instance a Christologically oriented interpretation of the eighth day seen as the first of sabbaths (Sunday) and recalling the new creation brought about by 'the Logos which came forth from God'. In this involved piece of exegesis we may gain a sense of an allegorical reading of scripture, of which Origen's opponent, Celsus, was so scornful.

Christian adoption of the dialogical form reflected pagan practice, not least in the second century when *Jason and Papiscus* was probably written. The dialogical form was to become a popular vehicle for presenting ancient Christian disputation with Jews. Determining the purpose of such works is difficult. Some think the fact that they sometimes end in the conversion of the Jew, as may have been the case in *Jason and Papiscus*, points to a missionary aim, that is, a desire to convert non-Christian Jews, though evidence that Jews read such texts is difficult to demonstrate. Others, however, think that they sought to bolster

Christian faith in various ways and were internally directed, a point Origen suggests when he talks about a less well educated audience, which he implies is Christian. Origen's claim that the character of the Jew seems authentic indicates that some thought such works to be artificial constructions which failed to reflect actual discussion between Jew and Christian. The *Dialogue of Jason and Papiscus*, being the earliest evidence of a literary form which would become typical of the Christian way of presenting such interaction, is therefore potentially of considerable significance in the history of Jewish–Christian relations.

Bibliography

Bovon, François, and Duffy, John M., 'A New Fragment from Ariston of Pella's *Dialogue of Jason and Papiscus*', *Harvard Theological Review* 105 (2012), 457–65.

Cameron, Averil, *Dialoguing in Late Antiquity*, Hellenic Studies 65 (Washington, DC: Center for Hellenic Studies, 2014).

Lahey, Lawrence, 'Evidence for Jewish Believers in Christian–Jewish Dialogues through the Sixth Century', in Hvalvik, Reidar, and Skarsaune, Oskar (eds.), *Jewish Believers in Jesus: The Early Centuries* (Peabody: Hendrickson, 2007), 585–91.

Tolley, Harry, 'The Jewish–Christian Dialogue *Jason and Papiscus* in Light of the Sinaiticus Fragment', *Harvard Theological Review* 114 (2021), 1–26.

3

Justin: Dialogue with Trypho *47 (150s CE)*

Text

Dialogue 47

And Trypho again inquired, 'But if some one, knowing that this is so, after he recognises that this man is Christ, and has believed in and obeys Him, wishes, however, to observe these [institutions], will he be saved?'

I said, 'In my opinion, Trypho, such an one will be saved, if he does not strive in every way to persuade other men, – I mean those Gentiles who have been circumcised from error by Christ, to observe the same things as himself, telling them that they will not be saved unless they do so. This you did yourself at the commencement of the discourse, when you declared that I would not be saved unless I observe these institutions.'

Then he replied, 'Why then have you said, "In my opinion, such an one will be saved," unless there are some who affirm that such will not be saved?'

'There are such people, Trypho,' I answered; 'and these do not venture to have any intercourse with or to extend hospitality to such persons; but I do not agree with them. But if some, through weak-mindedness, wish to observe such institutions as were given by Moses, from which they expect some virtue, but which we believe were appointed by reason of the hardness of the people's hearts, along with their hope in this Christ, and [wish to perform] the eternal and natural acts of righteousness and piety, yet choose to live with the Christians and the faithful, as I said before, not inducing them either to be circumcised like themselves, or to keep the Sabbath, or to observe any other such ceremonies, then I hold that we ought to join ourselves to such, and associate with them in all things as kinsmen and brethren. But if, Trypho,' I continued, 'some of your race, who say they believe in this Christ, compel those Gentiles who believe in this Christ to live in all respects according to the law given by Moses, or choose not to associate so intimately with them, I in like manner do not approve of them. But I believe that even those, who have been persuaded by them to observe the legal dispensation along with their confession of God in Christ, shall probably be saved. And I hold, further, that such as have confessed and known this man to be Christ, yet who have gone back from some cause to the legal dispensation, and have denied that this man is Christ, and have repented not before death, shall by no means be saved. Further, I hold that those of the seed of Abraham who live according to the law, and do not believe in this Christ before death, shall likewise not be saved, and especially those who have anathematized and do anathematize this very Christ in the synagogues, and everything by which they might obtain salvation and escape the vengeance of fire. For the goodness and the loving-kindness of God, and His boundless riches, hold righteous and sinless the man who, as Ezekiel tells, repents of sins; and reckons sinful, unrighteous, and impious the man who falls away from piety and righteousness to unrighteousness and ungodliness. Wherefore also our Lord Jesus Christ said, "In whatsoever things I shall take you, in these I shall judge you."'

Source

Roberts, Alexander, and Donaldson, James (eds.), *The Ante-Nicene Fathers: Translations of the Writings of the Fathers Down to A. D. 325*, vol. 1 (Edinburgh: T&T Clark, 1996), 218–19. (Square-bracketed words are part of the original.)

Commentary

This passage is taken from the first fully preserved Christian–Jewish dialogue, *The Dialogue of Trypho*, written by the Christian author Justin, often referred to as Justin Martyr. Its contents relate to a discussion between the latter and a Jew called Trypho, sometimes, though probably erroneously, identified with the figure known from rabbinic literature as Tarfon. Although the debate is presented as taking place in Ephesus a very short time after the Bar Kokhba revolt, most scholars date it to the 150s and place it in Rome.

As the two participants conclude their discussion of the Jewish law, focusing on Jewish identity markers such as circumcision, sabbath and food laws, Trypho asks Justin whether Jewish converts to Christianity who continue to observe these laws when they become Christians will be saved. Justin's answer is surprising given the strong criticism he has aimed at a literal understanding of the Jewish law in the preceding chapters. He argues that, contrary to what appears to be the majority view among Christians, such individuals will be saved, and they will even be saved if they seek to persuade gentile Christians to follow their practices. They will not, however, be saved if they deny Christ or if they fail to become Christians and curse Christ in their synagogues.

This passage is interesting on a number of levels. First, it highlights the ongoing existence within the Christian community of Jewish converts to Christianity who continued to behave in distinctively Jewish ways. Often called Jewish Christians or Christian Jews by scholars (terms not used in antiquity), they came to be seen by the elite as an intolerable presence, though Justin makes clear his disagreement with this view, even though he understands it to be the majority opinion. Secondly, it implies that at the time of Justin there were different groups with distinct views concerning the relationship of Christians to the Jewish law: the first relates to law-observant Jewish Christians (mentioned by Trypho and Justin), some of whom proselytise (1) and some of whom do not (2). Then there are three groups of gentiles who have become Christians: (3) those who are hostile to any version of (1) and (2); (4) moderates who reject the law but are more accepting of non-proselytising Jewish believers (Justin would be among this group); and (5) those who are convinced by 'Jewish Christians' that they ought to observe the law. Finally there are (6) anti-Christian Jews, expressing hostility to Christians by cursing them in their synagogues, which may be a slightly misleading reference to the so-called twelfth benediction of the *Amidah*, discussed in Chapter 3 (see p. 123). Aside, then, from the groups at the extremes (1 and 6), the others indicate some level of ongoing common life between Christians and Jews, and 'no compelling reason to deny the label of either Jew or Christian to these middling groups' (Edsall 2021: 268). The passage questions the general view that by the middle of the second century Jews and Christians had parted ways, as scholars from Parkes onwards have suggested.

Bibliography

Edsall, Benjamin A., 'Justin Martyr without the "Parting" of the Ways', in Schröter, Jens, Edsall, Benjamin A., and Verheyden, Joseph (eds.), *Jews and Christians – Parting Ways in the First Two Centuries: Reflections on the Gains and Losses of a Model* (Berlin: de Gruyter, 2021), 249–72.

Lieu, Judith, 'Justin Martyr's *Dialogue with Trypho*', in *Image and Reality: The Jews in the World of the Christians in the Second Century* (London and New York: T&T Clark, 1996), 103–54.

White, B. L., 'Justin between Paul and the Heretics: The Salvation of Christian Judaizers in the *Dialogue with Trypho*', *Journal of Early Christian Studies* 26 (2018), 163–89.

4

Melito of Sardis: Peri Pascha *94–6 (late second century)*

Text

94. Listen, all *you families of the nations*, and see! An extraordinary murder has taken place in the center of Jerusalem, in the city of the law, in the city of the Hebrews, in the city of the prophets, in the city thought of as just. And who has been murdered? And who is the murderer? I am ashamed to give the answer, but I must give it. For if this murder had taken place at night, or if he had been slain in a desert place, it would be well to keep silent; but it was in the middle of the main street, in the center of the city,

[in the middle of the day] while all were looking on, that the unjust murder of this just person took place.

95. And thus he has been lifted up upon the high tree, and an inscription has been affixed identifying the one who had been murdered. Who is this man? It is burdensome to tell, but it is more dreadful not to tell. Therefore, hear and tremble because of him for whom the earth quaked.

96. The one who hung the earth in space, is himself hanged; the one who fixed the heavens in place, is himself impaled; the one who firmly fixed all things, is himself firmly fixed to the tree. The Lord is insulted, God has been murdered, the King of Israel has been destroyed by the right hand of Israel.

97. O unprecedented murder! O unprecedented crime! The Lord has been made unrecognisable by his naked body, and is not allowed a garment so that he might not be seen exposed. For this reason the stars turned and fled, and the day was darkened, in order to hide the one stripped bare hung on the tree, darkening not the body of the Lord, but the eyes of men.

98. Yes, even though the people did not tremble, the earth trembled instead; the people were not afraid, but the heavens grew frightened; the people did not tear their garments, but the angel tore his; the people did not lament, but *the Lord thundered from heaven, and the most high gave voice*.

Source

Hall, Stuart G. (ed. and trans.), *Melito of Sardis: On Pascha and Fragments* (Oxford: Clarendon Press, 1979), 53–5. (Square-bracketed words are part of the original.)

Commentary

The author of this passage, Melito, is thought to have been the bishop of Sardis, a city which boasted a large and well-established Jewish community (Jews had been in Sardis from the third century BCE) to which, amongst others, Josephus makes reference. Much less is known about the Christian community's history. The *Peri Pascha* (On the Passover) was only known in small fragments until the first half of the twentieth century and was probably written around 170 CE, or at least towards the end of the second century. The work is a homily in which the freedom from Egypt won by God for the Israelites and recorded in the book of Exodus becomes a type or a prophecy of what Melito takes to be the much greater freedom wrought by Christ's incarnation and death on the cross. Some think that the work is based upon the Jewish Passover Haggadah, though this is difficult to prove. Clearly the homily was part of a service associated with the celebration of Christ's death and the Easter period more generally. Melito belonged to that group of Christians known as the Quartodecimans, that is, those who celebrated Easter on 14 Nissan, at the same time as the Jewish Passover, on whatever day of the week that happened to fall. Such a practice was gradually to be excluded from the church, being held by some to be 'Judaising'.

The passage comes from the end of the homily as Melito, in strongly rhetorical vein, describes how the Jewish nation put Jesus to death and in so doing committed the heinous act of deicide. Melito can make this bold claim – and he is the first known Christian writer to make it – because he entertained a modalist Christology, that is, one in which no distinction is made between the 'father' and the 'son' as was to become the classical Christian trinitarian position. In making such a claim, he excludes the implications of the gospel evidence that Pilate and the Romans were directly responsible for Jesus' death.

Some have thought that Melito's extreme claim is little more than the consequence of his own 'high' Christological position, his typological exegesis, which asserts the superiority of the Christian Passover as exemplified in Christ's death on the cross, and his developed rhetorical style. Others, however, have preferred to see these words as reflecting the position of Melito's Christian community in Sardis, that is, as a group who felt threatened by the much larger and more established Jewish community of the city (Jewish people remained a strong presence in the city, as exemplified by the large synagogue they built there in the fourth century). The anti-Jewish claim, one of many in the text, is, on this argument, the *cri de coeur* of a community whose ongoing stability appears threatened by a politically stronger community. Whatever the answer – and the truth may lie in a combination of both explanations – the charge of deicide made against Jews was to infect Jewish–Christian interaction for many centuries, being adopted by, among others, the Nazis and some Arab nationalists in their anti-Zionist rhetoric.

Bibliography

Hall, Stuart G. (ed.), *Melito of Sardis: On Pascha and Fragments* (Oxford: Oxford University Press, 1979).

Lieu, Judith, 'Melito of Sardis: The *Peri Pascha*', in *Image and Reality: The Jews in the World of the Christians in the Second Century* (Edinburgh: T&T Clark, 1996), 199–240.

Stewart-Sykes, Alistair, 'Melito's Anti-Judaism', *Journal of Early Christian Studies* 5 (1997), 271–83.

5

Pseudo-Clementine Homilies *8.6–7 (second century?)*

Text

6. For on this account Jesus is concealed from the Jews, who have taken Moses as their teacher, and Moses is hidden from those who have believed Jesus. For, there being one teaching by both, God accepts him who has believed either of these. But believing a teacher is for the sake of doing the things spoken by God. And that this is so, our Lord Himself says, 'I thank thee, Father of heaven and earth, because Thou hast concealed these things from the wise and elder, and hast revealed them to sucking babes.' Thus God Himself has concealed a teacher from some, as foreknowing what they ought to do, and has revealed him to others, who are ignorant what they ought to do.

7. Neither, therefore, are the Hebrews condemned on account of their ignorance of Jesus, by reason of Him who has concealed Him, if, doing the things *commanded* by

Moses, they do not hate Him whom they do not know. Neither are those from among the Gentiles condemned, who know not Moses on account of Him who hath concealed him, provided that these also, doing the things spoken by Jesus, do not hate Him whom they do not know. And some will not be profited by calling the teachers lords, but not doing the works of servants. For on this account our Jesus Himself said to one who often called Him Lord, but did none of the things which He prescribed, 'Why call ye me Lord, Lord, and do not do the things which I say?' For it is not saying that will profit any one, but doing.

Source

Roberts, Alexander, and Donaldson, James (eds.), *The Ante-Nicene Fathers: Translations of the Writings of the Fathers Down to A.D. 325*, vol. 8 (Edinburgh: T&T Clark, 1989), 271.

Commentary

The *Pseudo-Clementine Homilies* is a religious romance arranged in twenty books which Clement, apparently an early bishop of Rome, is supposed to have sent from that city to James, the brother of Jesus. The contents concern Clement's wanderings around the Mediterranean seaboard, during which he is converted to Christianity, and his witnessing to the activity of Peter. Ever since the nineteenth century, scholars have argued that the document consists of a number of different sources, some of which could be dated to the second century, though the final version of the work (as currently extant) in which the sources are welded together goes back to the fourth century. The passage is taken from the early part of a speech Peter makes to gentiles in Tripolis.

The first part of the passage is remarkable in asserting that neither Moses nor Jesus would have had to appear if people had behaved in the right way. In such a view, both Moses and Jesus are primarily teachers, and attempts to give them an exalted status are presented as wrongheaded. No attempt is made to differentiate between their respective teaching. In fact in the second part of the passage, there is an emphasis (somehow bound up with Jesus' statement about hiding things from babes) upon the single teaching of both. Far from the Jewish people being blamed for rejecting Jesus, their rejection (to which no explicit reference is made) is explained away as rational given the purpose of Jesus' ministry and its content. Similarly, gentile ignorance of Moses is excused and the affirmation made that God accepts anyone who believes in either, so no superiority is attributed to either religion (though the terms Jew and Christian are not mentioned here). Indeed the person who is exalted is the one who knows that both Jesus and Moses preach the one doctrine.

What is striking about this passage is that its author views both dispensations as of equal value and does not distinguish between them by talking, as was customary for Christian writers, of the temporary nature of the law and the importance of affirming Jesus as a messianic saviour figure. The passage might reflect, partially, a couple of passages in the third-century medical writer Galen, where in referring to Jews and

Christians he speaks about 'the School of Moses and Christ' and of 'the followers of Moses and Christ' (*De differentiis pulsum* 2.4 and 3.3) without an apparent sense of distinction between them.

The document reflects other places in the *Homilies* and *Recognitions* where the Jewish character of Christianity is emphasised (a good example being *Hom.* 4–6, where Clement is portrayed as converting to Judaism). It is easy to see this attitude as eccentric when compared with the anti-Jewish literature written by Christians from the second century onwards. The *Pseudo-Clementine* literature was popular (we have a good deal of manuscript evidence for these writings and translations into a number of languages including Arabic and Syriac) in the fourth century, when some scholars see Christian anti-Judaism as at its strongest; and it may well witness to a more complex view of 'Christian' attitudes to 'Judaism' than would allow us to generalise as some do about the 'Jewish–Christian' encounter even as late as the fourth century. In this context it might be useful, as Annette Reed has suggested, to contrast the contents of these works with those of Eusebius, who takes a far more negative attitude to Judaism and yet writes at more or less the same time as the Homilist.

Bibliography

Carleton Paget, James, 'Pseudo-Clementine Homilies 4–6: Rare Evidence of a Jewish Literary Source from the Second Century C.E.?', in *Jews, Christians and Jewish Christians in Antiquity* (Tübingen: Mohr Siebeck, 2010), 427–92.

Reed, Annette Yoshiko, 'Historiography and Identity in the Pseudo-Clementines', in *Jewish Christianity and the History of Judaism* (Minneapolis: Fortress Press, 2022), 38–42.

Stanton, Graham, 'Jewish Christian Elements in the Pseudo-Clementine Writings', in Hvalvik, Reidar, and Skarsaune, Oskar (eds.), *Jewish Believers in Jesus: The Early Centuries* (Peabody: Hendrickson, 2007), 307–24.

6

Origen: Contra Celsum *1.28 (third century)*

Text

After this he [Celsus] represents the Jew as having a conversation with Jesus himself and refuting him on many charges, as he thinks: first, because *he fabricated the story of his birth from a virgin*; and he reproaches him because *he came from a Jewish village and from a poor country woman who earned her living by spinning*. He says that *she was driven out by her husband, who was a carpenter by trade, as she was convicted of adultery*. Then he says that *after she had been driven out by her husband and while she was wandering about in a disgraceful way she secretly gave birth to Jesus*. And he says that *because he was poor he hired himself out as a workman in Egypt, and there tried his hand at certain magical powers on which the Egyptians pride themselves; he returned full of conceit because of these powers, and on account of them gave himself the title of God*.

Source

Chadwick, Henry (trans.), *Origen: Contra Celsum* (Cambridge: Cambridge University Press, 1953), 28. Italics used by the translator to indicate quotations or thoughts attributed to Celsus' Jew.

Commentary

In his *Contra Celsum* (for its background see document 2 above), Origen cites a number of quotations, which Celsus attributed to a Jew and whom he portrayed as directing a series of accusations against Jesus and his followers in dialogic style. Whether Celsus has taken these from an anti-Christian Jewish document or made use of anti-Christian jibes he associated with Jews or invented them himself is disputed. Origen, as can be seen from this passage, thought that the last of these explanations was the most convincing, citing opinions attributed to the Jew by Celsus, which he thinks bear no similarity to Jews he knew (he calls the work a poor example of *prosopopeia*, a rhetorical exercise whereby an individual sought to write something in the style of someone else). It is in the Christian, Origen's, self-interest to make such a claim, and other scholars have argued that many of the accusations thrown at Jesus by Celsus' Jew find their parallels in known anti-Christian statements by Jews found in a variety of sources, mainly of Jewish origin, meaning that at a minimum Celsus had access to these accusations. The accusation that Jesus was born illegitimate, that his mother was a pauper and that he went to Egypt to earn his keep, by implication learning some magic and returning with an inflated view of himself, are all witnessed in such sources (see, for example, Chapter 3, pp. 146–50). Some of these claims may be very old, possibly evidenced in the Gospels in the claim that Jesus was born of a virgin (here thought to be covering up the claim that Jesus was born out of wedlock), that he was possessed by a demon and hence capable of performing miracles, as well as that he did not rise from the dead (this final accusation is not witnessed in the passage under discussion but is referred to later on by Celsus).

The passage is of interest because (1) it shows how pagans interested in undermining Christian claims used Jewish attacks upon Christianity, although Celsus is the first to do this. For pagan critics of Christianity, it was significant that the group from which they hailed (and Celsus represents them as rebelling against), and whose scriptures they used, by and large rejected the Christian message; (2) it gives us early evidence of counter-narrative traditions found among Jews, which in broad terms could be taken as inversions of traditions found in the Christian Gospels. These are found in rabbinic texts and also in the well-known traditions associated with the *Toledot Yeshu* (see Chapter 3, p. 118). Such traditions are only very rarely referred to by Christian authors (they prefer to concentrate on scriptural arguments), but some think that such evidence proves the existence from a very early stage of a continuous counter-narrative about Jesus, written by Jews. Others are more sceptical.

Bibliography

Alexander, Philip, 'Celsus' Judaism', in Carleton Paget, James, and Gathercole, Simon (eds.), *Celsus in His World: Philosophy, Polemic, and Religion in the Second Century* (Cambridge: Cambridge University Press, 2021), 327–55.

Alexander, Philip, 'Narrative and Counter-Narrative: The Jewish Anti-Gospel (The *Toledot Yeshu*) and the Christian Gospels', in Baron, Lori, Hicks-Keeton, Jill, and Thiessen, Matthew (eds.), *The Ways That Often Parted* (Atlanta: SBL Press, 2018), 377–402.

Lieu, Judith, 'The Multiple Personalities of Celsus' Jew', in Carleton Paget, James, and Gathercole, Simon (eds.), *Celsus in His World: Philosophy, Polemic, and Religion in the Second Century* (Cambridge: Cambridge University Press, 2021), 360–85.

Niehoff, Maren, 'A Jewish Critique of Christianity from Second-Century Alexandria: Revisiting the Jew Mentioned in *Contra Celsum*', *Journal of Early Christian Studies* 21 (2013), 151–75.

7

Origen: Letter to Africanus 5 (c. 240 CE)

Text

In all these cases consider whether it would not be well to remember the words, *'You shall not remove the ancient landmarks which your fathers have set.'* Nor do I say this because I shun the labour of investigating the Jewish Scriptures, and comparing them with ours, and noticing their various readings. This, if it be not arrogant to say it, I have already to a great extent done to the best of my ability, labouring hard to get at the meaning in all the editions and various readings; while I paid particular attention to the interpretation of the Seventy, lest I might be found to accredit any forgery to the Churches which are under heaven, and give an occasion to those who seek such a starting-point for gratifying their desire to slander the common brethren, and to bring some accusation against those who shine forth in our community. And I make it my endeavour not to be ignorant of their various readings, lest in my controversies with the Jews I should quote to them what is not found in their copies, and that I may make some use of what is found there, even although it should not be in our Scriptures. For if we are so prepared for them in our discussions, they will not, as is their manner, scornfully laugh at Gentile believers for their ignorance of the true reading as they have them. So far as to the History of Susanna not being found in the Hebrew.

Source

Roberts, Alexander, Donaldson, James, and Coxe, A. Cleveland (eds.), *Ante-Nicene Fathers*, vol. 4, trans. Frederick Crombie (Buffalo: Christian Literature Publishing, 1885). Rev. and ed. for New Advent by Kevin Knight, www.newadvent.org/fathers/0414.htm.

Commentary

The excerpt comes from Origen's letter to Africanus, written in about 240, and concerns the subject of the authority of the Christian Old Testament, a Greek translation of the Hebrew called the Septuagint (LXX). Africanus was a distinguished Christian bibliophile and had written to Origen to complain that he had read in one of his works a discussion of the elders disputing with Susanna as this was found in the Book of Susanna. His criticism was based on the fact that Origen, in using the latter, a part of the Septuagint, had cited a text which could not be regarded as holy scripture, first because it was not in the Hebrew Bible and secondly because its style was very different from the rest of the Book of Daniel of which it was a part.

Origen's answer to Africanus falls into two parts. In the second he deals with the technical question as to whether the Book of Susanna could have been a part of the original book of Daniel. In the first half, from which the above passage comes, he contests the principle enunciated by Africanus that the contents of the Old Testament have to have been written originally in Hebrew to be legitimate. Such a principle would lead to a great deal of the Christian Old Testament, that is, the Septuagint, being excised, Origen claims, and could lead to the accusation that Christians were submitting to the opinion of the Jewish people. Tradition must be respected, a view he supports by quoting the verse in Proverbs which is the opening part of the selected passage. Origen then explains the reason for his own detailed study of the text of the Old Testament, which had led him to produce the Hexapla, a document which contained in parallel columns the Hebrew, a transliteration of the Hebrew in Greek characters followed by versions of the Bible in Greek, including the Septuagint (and the Hebrew). This, he claims, was to facilitate discussion with Jews, who often preferred to quote from such versions as that of Aquila, knowledge of which would prevent Jews mocking Christian ignorance in exegetical discussion.

While some hold Origen's comments here to be disingenuous – in fact there are grounds for thinking that his production of the Hexapla implied a position not dissimilar to that of Africanus, given the prominence accorded to the Hebrew in that document – his comment gives evidence of the apparent importance of Jewish opinion on the biblical text and, if the passage which follows (not quoted here) is to be taken seriously, Jewish opinion more generally on the interpretation of that text. We can see evidence of this as early as Justin Martyr, especially if Jewish opinion contradicted Christian opinion. While it is easy to see textual and exegetical questions as broadly the concern of intellectuals, clearly what Jews thought on this matter counted for something, not least because these were Jewish texts. Against this background, Christian adherence to the Septuagint could appear fragile and in need of the kind of robust defence we find in the passage cited. It reveals some of the complexities of the Christian response to developing Jewish views on the authentic Jewish text in which tensions between the latter and Christian practice came to the fore.

Bibliography

de Lange, Nicholas, 'The Letter of Africanus: Origen's Recantation?', *Studia Patristica* 16, no. 2 (1985), 242–7.

De Lange, Nicholas, *Origen and the Jews* (Cambridge: Cambridge University Press, 1976).

Kamesar, Adam, *Jerome, Greek Scholarship, and the Hebrew Bible: A Study of the Quaestiones Hebraicae in Genesim* (Oxford: Clarendon Press, 1993), 4–10.

Salvesen, Alison, 'A Convergence of the Ways? The Judaizing of Christian Scripture by Origen and Jerome', in Becker, Adam, and Reed, A. Y. (eds.), *The Ways That Never Parted: Jews and Christians in Late Antiquity and the Early Middle Ages* (Tübingen: Mohr Siebeck, 2003), 233–48.

8

Martyrdom of Pionius *(third century)*

Text

4. I understand that you laughed and rejoiced at those who deserted, and considered as a joke the error of those who voluntarily offered sacrifice. Men of Greece, it behoved you to listen to your teacher Homer, who counsels that it is not a holy thing to gloat over those who are to die. And as for you, men of Judaea, Moses commands, If you should see the beast of your enemy fall down under his load, *you shall not pass by but you shall go and raise it up* [Deut. 22:4]. In like manner should you listen to Solomon: *If your enemy falls*, he says, *do not rejoice, and do not be glad when he stumbles* [Prov. 24:17].

I, at any rate, in obedience to my Master, have chosen to die rather than transgress his commands, and I make every effort not to change from the things I have learned and have myself later taught. At whom then do the Jews laugh without sympathy? For even if, as they claim, we are their enemies, we are at any rate men, and men who have been treated unjustly. They claim we have our chance to speak out. Yes, but whom have we offended? Did we murder anyone? Did we prosecute anyone? Did we force anyone to worship false gods? Or perhaps they think that their crimes are similar to those now committed by men out of fear. Rather, their sins differ as much as voluntary sins are different from indeliberate ones. Who forced the Jews to sacrifice to Beelphegor? Or partake of the sacrifices offered to the dead? Or to fornicate with the daughters of foreigners? Or to sacrifice their sons and daughters to idols? To murmur against God? To slander Moses? To be ungrateful to their benefactors? Or in their hearts to return to Egypt? Or, as Moses went up to receive the Law, to say to Aaron, Make gods for us, and then to make the calf – and all the other things they did? For they are capable of deceiving you. Then let them read to you the book of Judges, Kings, or Exodus, or all the other passages which prove them wrong.

Do they ask why was it that some, without any pressure, came to sacrifice of their own accord? But would you condemn all Christians because of these? Consider the present life as though it were a threshing-floor. Which pile is the larger, the chaff or the wheat? For when the farmer comes to clear the threshing-floor with his winnowing-fan, the chaff, being lighter, is easily carried off by the wind, whereas the wheat remains where it was.

[…]

13. I understand also that the Jews have been inviting some of you to their synagogues. Beware lest you fall into a greater, more deliberate sin, lest anyone commit the unforgivable sin of blasphemy against the Holy Spirit. Do not become with them rulers of Sodom and people of Gomorrha [*sic*], whose hands are tainted with blood. We did not slay our prophets nor did we betray Christ and crucify him. But why need I say much to you? Recall what you have heard; and now put into practice what you have learned. For you have also heard that the Jews say: Christ was a man, and he died a criminal. But let them tell us, what other criminal has filled the entire world with his disciples? What other

criminal had his disciples and others with them to die for the name of their master? By what other criminal name for so many years were devils expelled, are still expelled now, and will be in future? And so it is with all the other wonders that are done in the Catholic Church. What these people forget is that this criminal departed from life at his own choice. Again, they assert that Christ performed necromancy or spirit-divination with the cross. Yet what Scripture in their possession or in ours says this of Christ? Did any good man ever say this? Are not those who say this wicked men? How then can you believe the words of the wicked rather than those of the good?

Source

Musurillo, Herbert (ed. and trans.), *The Acts of the Christian Martyrs* (Oxford: Clarendon Press, 1972), 139–41, 153–5. (Biblical references are footnotes in the original.)

Commentary

The *Martyrdom of Pionius* tells the story of the Christian Pionius' death in Smyrna in Asia Minor during the so-called persecution of Decius. The latter, who became Roman emperor in 249, had issued an edict a year later commanding general sacrifice, which caused considerable consternation within the Christian community as individuals reacted differently. Pionius refused to sacrifice and hence was martyred. Others submitted to the command, creating an ongoing problem for the Christian community.

The passages cited come from the two speeches attributed to Pionius by the anonymous author, probably writing not long after the event. Pionius is depicted as presenting both gentiles and Jews as mocking Christians who turn to idolatry. He invokes both Homer and the witness of Solomon and Moses against the view that one should gloat over the fate of an enemy. He continues by accusing the Jewish people of what amounts to a kind of hypocrisy by citing a string of passages in the Bible where Jews commit idolatry. He compares their actions unfavourably to those of the currently *lapsi* (those Christians who have agreed to sacrifice), citing the fact that the latter, unlike the Jewish people, committed their acts of idolatry under compulsion. He concludes by justifying the fact that the Christian community contains a mixture of types (from those willing to die to avoid committing idolatry to the *lapsi*).

In the second speech Pionius accuses Jews of trying to entice Christians into their synagogues. He upbraids any Christian who is willing to submit to these pleas, making plain in brutal language that the synagogue is a wicked place in which Christ's criminality is explicitly and mendaciously asserted.

Jews are depicted in these passages in a very negative light, with the author making use of well-known themes from *adversus Judaeos* texts, not least the claim that the Jewish nation was idolatrous from a very early stage and that the Jewish people were responsible for the death of Jesus. Some think that what we have here is little more than a fabrication which does not relate to any external reality but is presented as a means of defending and reclaiming the *lapsi*. Others contend that the representation of the Jewish people is closer to reality than one might think; that it comports with the presence of a large Jewish community in Smyrna (and more generally in Asia Minor), already mentioned in a negative light by the writer of Revelation 2:9; that it shows up parallels with third-century Christian polemic witnessed elsewhere; that it depicts a realistic vision of Jews working with gentiles (here one thinks of the way in which Celsus presents himself as working with a Jewish accuser of the Christians); and that it presents a number of opinions, in particular about Jesus, witnessed elsewhere in Jewish literature.

The passage clearly raises intriguing questions about the interaction of Christian and Jewish communities in a situation of social and political tension. That members of the Jewish community acted in such a way in such circumstances should not be considered unlikely if they viewed the Christian community as competitors or wished to distance themselves from Christians. Assured reconstruction on the basis of such a polemically motivated text remains impossible, however.

Bibliography

Gibson, E. Leigh, 'Jewish Antagonism or Christian Polemic: The Case of the *Martyrdom of Pionius*', *Journal of Early Christian Studies* 9 (2001), 339–58.

Horbury, William, 'Jewish–Christian Polemic in *Martyrium Pionii*', in Friedman, David A. and Czajkowski, Kimberley (eds.), *Looking In, Looking Out: Jews and Non-Jews in Mutual Contemplation*, Supplements to the *Journal for the Study of Judaism* 212 (Leiden: Brill, 2024), 267–96.

Nicklas, Tobias, *Jews and Christians? Second Century 'Christian' Perspectives on the 'Parting of the Ways'* (Tübingen: Mohr Siebeck, 2014), 57–61.

9

Canons of the Councils of Elvira and of Laodicea (early fourth and late fourth or early fifth century)

Text

(i) Council of Elvira

16. Heretics, if they are unwilling to change over to the Catholic Church, are not to have Catholic girls [in marriage], nor shall they [the girls] be given to Jews or heretics, since there can be no community for the faithful with the unfaithful: if parents act against this prohibition, they shall be kept out for five years.

[…]

49. Landholders are warned not to allow the crops which they have received from God with an act of thanksgiving to be blessed by Jews lest they make our blessing ineffectual and weak. If anyone dares to do this after the prohibition, he shall be thrown out of the church completely.

50. If any of the clergy or the faithful eats with Jews, he shall be kept from communion in order that he be corrected, as he should.

[...]

78. If one of the faithful who is married commits adultery with a Jewish or pagan woman, he shall be cut off, but if someone else exposes him, he can share Sunday communion after five years, having completed the required penance.

(ii) Council of Laodicea

16. On the Sabbath the Gospel should be read with the other scriptures.

[...]

29. Christians must not Judaise and refrain from work on the Sabbath, but they should work on that day, rather honouring the Lord's Day; and, if they can, resting then as Christians. But if any shall be found to be Judaisers, let them be anathema from Christ.

[...]

37. One should not receive festal gifts sent from the feasts of Jews or heretics, nor feast together with them.

38. One should not receive unleavened bread from the Jews, nor be partakers of their impiety.

Source

Author's translations, based on those of Boddens Hosang, F. J. E., *Establishing Boundaries: Christian–Jewish Relations in Early Council Texts and the Writings of Church Fathers* (Leiden: Brill, 2010), 40, 45, 51, 56, 93, 99.

Commentary

The sets of canons from two different church councils, one held in Elvira in Spain in the early fourth century, the other in Laodicea in Anatolia, probably at the end of the fourth century or the beginning of the fifth, present a set of interesting insights into Jewish–Christian interaction at opposite ends of the Roman empire.

What is immediately striking about these canons (they form a small fraction of the eighty-one canons of the Council of Elvira and the sixty canons of the Council of Laodicea, which deal with an array of issues aside from those cited) is that they provide evidence of actual Jewish–Christian interaction 'on the ground' in contrast to much of the relevant Christian literary evidence, which is often highly scriptural and abstract. In this context it is interesting to note that the three so-called Cappadocian Fathers, Gregory of Nyssa, Gregory Nazianzen and Basil of Caesarea – all writing at approximately the same time as the council in the region of which Laodicea was a part and where there was a large Jewish population in the fourth century – almost never refer to activity of the kind described in these canons but do make negative reference to Jews in exegetically oriented discussion.

The levels of interaction assumed are richly varied, though in some instances the precise nature of what is being described is not clear. What, for instance, is assumed to be the activity associated with the sabbath in canons 16 and 29 of the Council of Laodicea? Are we to imagine attendance on the sabbath itself in a synagogue not dissimilar to the one at Sardis? Or simply the adoption of practices associated with the sabbath day, for example desisting from work and engaging in the reading of exclusively Old Testament texts (hence the exhortation to read the Gospels)? Some think that the reference to receiving portions from Jewish feasts in canon 37 and to unleavened bread in canon 38 make the former reading more likely. And how are we to understand the reference to 'festal gifts' in canon 37? Some think that these should be associated with the feast of Purim, to which reference is made in rabbinic literature; others suggest gifts given at Passover, a thesis supported by the reference to Passover in canon 38. Other questions could be raised, not least as to what was involved in the blessing of crops (Elvira, canon 49), which seems to pick up on the idea of Jews as closely associated with the otherworldly, and how it adversely affected Christian blessings. What is clear, however we understand individual points of interpretation within the canons, is that the latter all assume close, widespread and tenacious interaction between Jews and Christians at the level of personal relations and daily practices such as eating, agricultural customs and worship. The sometimes harsh punishment proposed for those who breach the prohibitions contained within the canons is an indication of how seriously the authorities took this blurring of identities, at least as they saw these activities, and how well-established they were.

Bibliography

Boddens Hosang, F. J. E., *Establishing Boundaries: Christian–Jewish Relations in Early Council Texts and the Writings of Church Fathers* (Leiden: Brill, 2010), 23–108.

Trebilco, Paul, 'Beyond "The Parting of the Ways" between Jews and Christians in Asia Minor to a Model of Variegated Interaction', in Schröter, Jens, Edsall, Benjamin A., and Verheyden, Joseph (eds.), *Jews and Christians – Parting Ways in the First Two Centuries CE? Reflections on the Gains and Losses of a Model* (Berlin and Boston: de Gruyter, 2021), 279–80.

Van der Horst, Pieter, 'Jews and Christians in Aphrodisias in the Light of Their Relations in Other Cities of Asia Minor', *Nederlands Teologisk Tijdskrift* 43 (1989), 106–21.

10

Aphrahat: Demonstrations *21.1–2 (344 CE)*

Text

1. I heard a reproach that greatly distressed me. The unclean say, 'This people that has been gathered from the peoples has no God.' And the wicked say, 'If they have a God, why does he not seek vengeance for his people?' The gloom thickens around me even more whenever the Jews reproach us and magnify themselves over our people. It happened one day that a man who is called a 'sage of the Jews' challenged me: 'Jesus, whom you call your teacher, wrote to you, *"If there is faith like a single mustard seed among you, you will say to this mountain, 'Move!', and it will move out of your way, and 'Be lifted up!', and it will fall into the sea and obey you."* Thus, among your whole people there is not one sage whose prayer is

heard and who petitions God so that your persecutions might end. For it is written to you in your word: *'There is nothing that you will be unable to do.'*

2. When I saw that he was blaspheming and greatly misrepresenting the Way, my mind was disturbed and I knew that he would not accept the explanation of the words that he was quoting to me. I then challenged him with words from the Law and the Prophets. I said to him, 'You believe that though you are scattered, God is with you.' He asserted, 'God is with us, since God said to Israel, *"I will not leave them in the lands of their enemies, nor have I brought an end to my covenant with them."'* And I said to him, 'What I hear from you (that God is with you) is very good, but I will speak against your words. The prophet Isaiah said to Israel, as if from the mouth of his God, *"If you pass through the sea, I am with you, and rivers will not overwhelm you. If you walk on the fire, you will not be burned and the flame will not set you on fire, because the Lord your God is with you."* Thus, there is not a single upright and good and wise man among your whole people who can pass through the sea and live and not be suffocated, or [through] a river without it overwhelming him. Let him walk on the fire and see if he is not burned, or if the flame does not set him on fire! If you bring me an interpretation, I will not be persuaded by you, just as you will not accept from me the explanation of the words with which you challenged me.'

Source

Lehto, Adam, *The Demonstrations of Aphrahat, the Persian Sage* (Piscataway: Gorgias Press, 2010), 438–9. (Square-bracketed words are part of the original.)

Commentary

Aphrahat, referred to as 'the Persian Sage', is only known from his twenty-three *Demonstrations*, written in Syriac in the Sasanian empire of Shapur II. He may have been a bishop of Mar Mattai. The first ten *Demonstrations*, written in 337, concern matters of spirituality, but the next thirteen, written in 344, are principally taken up with matters of disagreement between Jews and Christians, including discussions of circumcision, the sabbath, Pesach, dietary laws and so forth. The passage quoted comes from the end of the second section of the work and reports a conversation between a Jewish sage and Aphrahat. The former challenges the latter by asserting that if the Christians believed correctly, God would protect them; but the fact that they are victims of persecution shows that God does not protect them. Gospel verses are used to support the interpretation. Assuming that Aphrahat is reporting accurately, this indicates that his Jewish opponents may have known the Gospels and were able to use them polemically, but certitude on this matter is not possible as the assumed opponents may simply be reflecting older traditions with which they were familiar.

The wider context for the passage might be a known persecution of Christians by Shapur II following his unsuccessful campaign against the Roman empire in the early fourth century and an apparent attempt to test the loyalty of his Christian subjects, whom he held to be potentially treasonous, by calling upon them to pay an increased poll tax – a request to which the Christian bishop named Shem'on objected and for which he was executed. In one much later tradition the group that speaks out against the Christians is not the Zoroastrian priests but the Jewish people, though most believe this tradition to be unreliable. For some scholars, however, this background may provide a helpful insight into the circumstances which precipitated the second section of Aphrahat's *Demonstrations*, a situation in which Jews were making use of the political difficulties of Christians to attack them and their beliefs and in which Christians perhaps found joining the Jewish community to avoid persecution an attractive option. This remains conjectural, however, with others arguing that Aphrahat's *Demonstrations* betrays very little evidence of actual encounter with Jews or for the close proximity of Jews and Christians. The uncertainty arises in part from the fact that we know so little about Jewish and Christian communities in the Persian empire and in part from what some take to be the absence of known Jewish traditions in the *Demonstrations* (see Neusner). Yet it is worth noting that in the above passage Aphrahat refers to an actual conversation with a Jewish sage and that he cites a verse (Lev. 26:44) we know was used by both Palestinian rabbis (in relation to Babylon and Rome; see Esther Rabbah 4) and Babylonian rabbis (b.Megillah 11a) to defend the idea that God is and will continue to be with the Jewish people despite their historical situation, whether one of exile or of oppression by an enemy.

In addition to raising questions about how the genuineness of a reported discussion between a Jew and a Christian can be verified (in this case by tentative reference to passages from rabbinic sources), the passage is important in that it gives the historian potentially significant information about Jewish–Christian relations in the eastern Sasanian empire rather than in the western Roman empire from which, at least for the ancient period, most of our information on this subject comes – a relationship which may well have been affected by the very different political circumstances pertaining there.

Bibliography

Koltun-Fromm, Naomi, 'A Jewish–Christian Conversation in Fourth Century Mesopotamia', *Journal of Jewish Studies* 47 (1996), 45–63.

Nedungatt, George, *Covenant Life, Law and Ministry According to Aphrahat*, Kanonika 26 (Rome: Orientalia Christiana & Valore Italiano, 2018).

Neusner, Jacob, *Aphrahat and Judaism: The Christian–Jewish Argument in Fourth-Century Iran* (Leiden: Brill, 1972).

11

John Chrysostom: Adversus Judaeos *(386–7 CE)*

Text

1.5.2

Since there are some who think of the synagogue as a holy place, I must say a few words to them. Why do you reverence that place? Must you not despise it, hold it in abomination, run away from it? They answer that the Law and the books of the prophets are kept there. What is this? Will any place where these books are be a holy place? By no means! This is the reason above all others why I hate the synagogue and abhor it. They have the prophets but do not believe them; they read the sacred writings but reject their witness – and this is a mark of men guilty of the greatest outrage.

4.3.5–6

(5) What, then, are the questions? I will ask each one who is sick with this disease: Are you a Christian? Why, then, this zeal for Jewish practices? Are you a Jew? Why then, are you making trouble for the Church? Does not a Persian side with the Persians? Is not a barbarian eager for what concerns the barbarians? Will a man who lives in the Roman empire not follow our laws and way of life? Tell me this. If ever anyone living among us is caught in collusion siding with the barbarians, is he not immediately punished? He is given neither hearing nor examination, even if he has ten thousand arguments in his own defense. If ever anyone living among the barbarians is clearly following Roman custom and law, again, will he not suffer the same punishment? How, then, do you expect to be saved by defecting to that unlawful way of life?

(6) The difference between the Jews and us is not a small one, is it? Is the dispute between us over ordinary, everyday matters, so that you think the two religions are really one and the same? Why are you mixing what cannot be mixed? They crucified the Christ whom you adore as God. Do you see how great the difference is? How is it, then, that you keep running to those who slew Christ when you say that you worship him whom they crucified? You do not think, do you, that I am the one who brings up the law on which these charges are based, nor that I make up the form which the accusation takes? Does not the Scripture treat the Jews in this way?

Source

Harkins, Paul W. (trans.) *Saint John Chrysostom: Discourses against Judaizing Christians* (Washington, DC: Catholic University of America Press, 1979), 18–19, 78–9.

Commentary

From the beginning of the autumn of 386 John Chrysostom, the bishop of Antioch and a Christian renowned for his eloquence, delivered eight sermons over about a year, later brought together as a collection with the title *Adversus Judaeos*, though some think that this title misrepresents the homilies' content, which relates to the actions of Judaisers, that is, Christians who found themselves attracted to Judaism. Whatever the case, they contain some of the most vicious attacks upon Jews delivered by any Christian in antiquity. The immediate cause of the sermon series seems to have been the fact that at the time of the great autumnal festivals such as Yom Kippur and Rosh ha-Shana a number of Christians were attending the synagogues in Antioch, a city which at the time boasted a large and ancient Jewish community.

A number of points arise from the sections quoted, which are taken from sermons 1 and 4. Notable among them is the fact, or at least the inference, that those Chrysostom is addressing have respect for the synagogue, holding it, according to the first passage, to be a holy place (this claim appears frequently in the sermons, and on one occasion John refers to an incident in which one Christian forced another to go to the synagogue to make an oath, as if doing such a thing in that setting made it more binding). The holiness seems to be associated with the fact that the books of the Old Testament were kept there, a point which Chrysostom attacks by stating that Jews misunderstand these texts, repeating a well-known Christian anti-Jewish accusation; and elsewhere he attacks the synagogue as worse than a theatre or brothel or den of thieves. What was the mindset of these individuals who regarded the synagogue as holy and attended its services? Were they Christians who, rather than knowing that they were acting in a deviant way, simply saw no contradiction between attending synagogal services and their own Christian identity? The answer to this question may be found in the second and third passages quoted. Here John is at pains to stress the fact that there is a great gulf between Jews and Christians, as if this point was not understood by members of his flock, who appeared to entertain an unacceptable view of the permeability between church and synagogue. In this context the opening questions of 4.3.5 seem particularly pertinent, as does the opening line of 4.3.6: 'The difference between the Jews and us is not a small one, is it?' By stressing the collective guilt of the Jewish people for the crucifixion of Jesus, a standard (and misleading) trope by this time, John attempts in what follows to make plain that the difference is great.

These sermons, then, which betray barely any knowledge of actual Jews living in Antioch but rather a constructed Jew, pieced together by prejudice and polemic, prove that as late as the latter part of the fourth century the presence of divergent understandings existed among Christians about how their own identity related to that of the Jewish people, and in profusion. In this context it is striking that John never cites a rule or piece of legislation forbidding the kind of activity he so persistently highlights and brutally criticises.

The sermons, inevitably, had an unfortunate afterlife. Sections from them were excerpted into the Byzantine liturgy and later anti-Jewish writers drew heavily from them. For instance, they were translated into Russian in the eleventh century at the time of the first pogrom against Jews in Russian history under Prince Vladimir (956–1015) and were read and used polemically in medieval Europe and Byzantium. Some scholars and churchmen have disputed the idea that they are antisemitic, despite this afterlife, and argued that in various ways they reflect both the context in which Chrysostom was writing and the exaggerated rhetorical practices of the time. Whatever the answer to this technical question, their bitterness of tone and sheer nastiness are striking. The Jew is now viewed as a semi-satanic person cursed by God, whose ongoing existence is an affront.

Bibliography

Fonrobert, 'Jewish Christianity, Judaizers, and Ancient Christianity', in Burrus, *A People's History of Christianity*, 236–43.

Shepardson, Christine C., *Controlling Contested Places: Late Antique Antioch and the Spatial Politics of Religious Controversy* (Berkeley, Los Angeles and London: University of California Press, 2014), 92–117.

Wilken, Robert L., *John Chrysostom and the Jews: Rhetoric and Reality in the Late Fourth Century* (Berkeley, Los Angeles and London: University of California Press, 1983).

12

Jerome: Epistles *125 and 84 (late fourth century)*

Text

Epistle *125*

When I was a young man, though I was protected by the rampart of the lonely desert, I could not endure against the promptings of sin and the ardent heat of my nature. I tried to crush them by frequent fasting, but my mind was always in a turmoil of imagination. To subdue it I put myself in the hands of one of the brethren who had been a Hebrew before his conversion, and asked him to teach me his language. Thus, after having studied the pointed style of Quintilian, the fluency of Cicero, the weightiness of Fronto, and the gentleness of Pliny, I now began to learn the alphabet again and practise harsh and guttural words. What efforts I spent on that task, what difficulties I had to face, how often I despaired, how often I gave up and then in my eagerness to learn began again, my own knowledge can witness from personal experience and those can testify who were then living with me.

Source

Wright, F. A. (trans.), *Jerome: Select Letters*, Loeb Classical Library 262 (Cambridge, MA: Harvard University Press, 1933).

Epistle *84.3*

In my younger days I was carried away with a great passion for learning, yet I was not like some presumptuous enough to teach myself. At Antioch I frequently listened to Apollinaris of Laodicea, and attended his lectures; yet, although he instructed me in the holy scriptures, I never embraced his disputable doctrine as to their meaning. At length my head became sprinkled with gray hairs so that I looked more like a master than a disciple. Yet I went on to Alexandria and heard Didymus. And I have much to thank him for: for what I did not know I learned from him, and what I knew already I did not forget. So excellent was his teaching. Men fancied that I had now made an end of learning. Yet once more I came to Jerusalem and to Bethlehem. What trouble and expense it cost me to get Baraninas to teach me under cover of night […] If it is expedient to hate any men and to loath any race, I have a strange dislike to those of the circumcision. For up to the present day they persecute our Lord Jesus Christ in the synagogues of Satan [Revelation 2:9]. Yet can anyone find fault with me for having had a Jew as a teacher?

Source

Fremantle, W. H., Lewis, G., and Martley, W. G. (trans.), *Nicene and Post-Nicene Fathers*, 2nd series (Buffalo: Christian Literature Publishing Co., 1893). (Biblical reference is a footnote in the original.)

Commentary

Both of the passages refer to the attempts made by Jerome, the first Christian writer to attribute unambiguously maximum authority to the Hebrew text of the Bible, to learn Hebrew and the help he sought from Jews in this process. The first describes a period he spent in the desert of Chalcis, probably between 373 and 380 CE while he was staying in Antioch, and the second describes a later period after his stay in Rome when he arrived in Palestine, where he remained until his death in 419 or 420.

The passages are brief, at least as they relate to any details of how Jerome learnt Hebrew, though reference is made in *Ep.* 125 to learning the alphabet first and then its pronunciation. Most assume that this was done in Greek. It is interesting that in the passage from *Ep.* 125 he asserts that he learnt the language from a Jewish convert to Christianity but then in the second passage that he learnt it from what one assumes was a non-Christian Jew. Recently, Michael Graves has suggested that such a transition was understandable. Such were the social dynamics of Jewish–Christian relations in the fourth century, it would have been impossible to approach a Jew, ask for lessons and then receive instruction in Hebrew. Once Jerome had engaged in this initial period of intensive study, it would have been easy enough to approach a non-Christian Jew 'to develop what had already been learned'. This seems speculative, as it is very difficult to surmise anything about the character of the teaching from either passage, and the second passage about Baraninas implies that there were still difficulties for Jerome in learning Hebrew from a Jew after his experience in Chalcis (hence the need for him to approach the figure at night). It's certainly true that Jerome seems to have continued to consult Jews about the biblical text (aside from the nameless Christian Jew in Chalcis, to whom he makes reference quite regularly, he cites five other teachers including Baraninas) and its translation and interpretation; and that from 391 he had become convinced that the Old Testament should be translated into Latin from the Hebrew and not from the Greek Septuagint or any other Greek version, though this was probably a decision he had arrived at himself and independent of Jewish influence.

Jerome's harsh statement in *Ep.* 84 that he loathes the Jews but that no one should begrudge him his urge to learn from them shows up further the contradictory attitude of Christians to their non-Christian Jewish neighbours. They are a source of information, so should be sought out, as Jerome sought them out when seeking to learn Hebrew, but their attitude towards Christianity inspires hatred. Jerome was especially sensitive about this matter as his decision to supplant the Septuagint with the Hebrew Bible was a controversial one and could be seen as Judaising.

Bibliography

Graves, Michael, *Jerome's Hebrew Philology: A Study* (Leiden: Brill, 2007), 76–92.

Kamesar, Adam, 'Jerome', in Carleton Paget, James, and Schaper, Joachim (eds.), *The New Cambridge History of the Bible*, Vol. 1: *From the Beginnings to 600* (Cambridge: Cambridge University Press, 2013), 653–75.

Salvesen, Alison, 'A Convergence of the Ways? The Judaizing of Christian Scripture by Origen and Jerome', in Becker, Adam, and Reed, A. Y. (eds.), *The Ways That Never Parted* (Tübingen: Mohr Siebeck, 2003), 233–48.

13

Augustine: City of God *18.4.6 (426 CE)*

Text

But the Jews, who killed him and would not believe in him, because he must needs die and rise again, were ravaged still more miserably by the Romans, and were utterly uprooted from their kingdom, where they had already been ruled by foreign-born rulers; and they were scattered throughout the lands […] and so by means of their own Scriptures they bear witness on our behalf that we have not forged the prophecies about Christ. Very many of them, considering these prophecies both before his passion and still more after his resurrection, believed on him. Of them it was predicted: 'Though the number of the sons of Israel be as the sand of the sea, the remnant shall be saved.' But the rest were blinded; of them it was predicted: 'Let their table be a trap in their presence and a retribution and a stumbling-block; let their eyes be darkened, that they may not see; and do thou bow down their backs always.' Therefore, when they do not believe in our Scriptures, their own Scriptures, to which they are blind when they read, are fulfilled in them. Unless indeed any one says that the Christians forged the prophecies about Christ that are quoted under the name of a Sibyl or of others, if there be any, which have no connection with the Jewish people. For us, to be sure, those suffice which are quoted from the books of our enemies, for we see and know that it is in order to bear this witness, – which they involuntarily supply on our behalf by possessing and preserving these same books, – that they themselves are scattered among all peoples, in whatever direction the church of Christ expands.

For a prophecy about this thing was given in advance, in the Psalms which they, too, read, where it is written: 'My God, his mercy shall go before me; my God has shown me concerning my enemies, that you are not to slay them, lest they some day forget your law; scatter them by your might.' So God has shown the church the grace of his mercy in the case of her enemies the Jews, since, as the Apostle says: 'Their sin is the salvation of the Gentiles.' For this reason he did not slay them (that is, he did not put an end to their being Jews, although they were conquered and oppressed by the Romans), lest through forgetting the law of God they should bear no effective witness on this point that we are concerned with. So it was not enough for him to say: 'You are not to slay them, lest they some day forget your law,' without also adding: 'Scatter them.' For if they dwelt with that testimony of their Scriptures in their own land only, and not everywhere, then the church, which is everywhere, could not have them at hand among all the Gentiles as witnesses to those prophecies that were given in advance concerning Christ.

Source

Greene, William Chase (trans.), *Augustine: City of God, Volume VI: Books 18.36–20*, Loeb Classical Library 416 (Cambridge, MA: Harvard University Press, 1960).

Commentary

Augustine of Hippo in North Africa, the greatest Christian theologian of the ancient church, wrote *The City of God* in 426 CE as a partial response to the sacking of Rome by the Visigoths in 410. The massive work covers an array of topics ranging from natural theology to the philosophy of history. In the passage quoted, Augustine gives voice to ideas which he had been developing for some time about the Jewish people and their place within a Christocentric conception of history, echoing well-known Christian anti-Jewish sentiments: responsibility for the killing of Jesus; a metaphorical blindness associated with their failure to understand the scriptures; evidence of divine punishment in their scattering among the nations of the earth and the destruction of Jerusalem. In contradistinction to many other Christian writers, however, he presents an argument for the ongoing significance of the Jewish people which upholds the integrity of their identity. In Augustine's vision the Jewish people become the unwitting witnesses to Christian truth. As the bearers of the scriptures, and as an ancient nation, they give evidence of the antiquity of the Christian message, and the fact that they are hostile to that message makes them more convincing witnesses to its truth, for the message can be shown not to have been constructed by those who were naturally favourable to the gospel. Indeed the blindness of Jews, their failure to believe in Christ, gives further proof of the scriptures' truthfulness, for that blindness is predicted in those same scriptures. Augustine quotes from Psalm 59:12, applying the words 'Do not slay them' to Jews. By 'slay' he understands not literal slaying ('that is, he did not put an end to their being Jews, although they were conquered and oppressed by the Romans') but the denial to Jews of the right to be Jews. To slay them would be to deny evidence of the truth of the Christian message (for the reasons stated above) and would have prevented their scattering beyond the borders of Palestine, which would in turn have prevented the news of Christianity reaching as wide an audience as possible. Elsewhere Augustine states that the scattering of the Jewish people is also an enacted parable in which the consequences of not believing in Jesus are made plain.

Augustine's defence of the right of the Jewish people to remain Jewish in a Christian setting and his concomitant opposition to forced conversion, briefly summarised in the quoted passage, which derives more from theological concerns than from contact with actual Jews known to him, can seem backhanded precisely because it is based upon a particular understanding (which Augustine endorses) of a well-known set of anti-Jewish sentiments found among ancient Christians. However, in the context in which it was forged, and against the background of Christian anti-Judaism as it existed at the time, his carefully thought-through justification of the continuing existence of the Jewish people, combined with other comments he made about the Jewish law, constitutes an advance in that they both oppose forced conversion and doggedly deny the right of Christians to perform acts of violence against the Jewish people, and they often do this in a way that can appear strikingly affirmative of Jews. Augustine's view was broadly to prevail in the Middle Ages – one notes in particular Gregory the Great's famous letter of 598 CE entitled *Sicut Judeis*, where, in the face of a call to destroy a synagogue in Palermo, the bishop invoked Augustine's principles or, almost 600 years later, Bernard of Clairvaux's invocation of the same principles in an attempt to protect Jews from physical attack during the Second Crusade (see Chapter 4, p. 186) – even if its legacy was ambivalent, a point which Jeremy Cohen in particular seeks to emphasise.

Bibliography

Cohen, Jeremy, 'Revisiting Augustine's Doctrine of Jewish Witness', *Journal of Religion* 89, no. 4 (Oct. 2009), 564–78, esp. 578.

Cohen, Jeremy, '"Slay them not": Augustine and the Jews in Modern Scholarship', *Medieval Encounters* 4 (1998), 78–92.

Fredriksen, Paula, *Augustine and the Jews: A Christian Defense of Jews and Judaism* (New York and London: Doubleday, 2008).

Fredriksen and Irshai, 'Christian Anti-Judaism', 977–1034, esp. 1014–20.

14

Codex Theodosianus *16.8.25 (429–38 CE)*

Text

It seems right that in the future none of the synagogues of the Jews shall either be indiscriminately seized or put on fire. If there are some synagogues that were seized or vindicated to churches or indeed consecrated to the venerable mysteries in a recent undertaking and after the law was passed, they shall be given in exchange new places, on which they could build, that is, to the measure of the synagogues taken. Votive offerings as well, if they are in fact seized, shall be returned to them provided that they have not yet been dedicated to the sacred mysteries; but if a venerable consecration does not permit their restitution, they shall be given the exact price for them. No [new] synagogue shall be constructed from now on, and the old ones shall remain in their state.

Source

Linder, Amnon (ed. and trans.), *The Jews in Roman Imperial Legislation* (Detroit: Wayne State University Press, 1987), 288.

Commentary

The Theodosian Code was a compilation which attempted to gather together in a coherent form laws made since the time of Constantine but also from much earlier. The process of codification was begun under the emperor Theodosius II in 429 CE and brought to completion in 438 CE.

The law under discussion, given in the name of Theodosius II and his uncle the emperor Honorius and addressed to Asklepiodotus, Prefect of the East, is dated to 423 CE. A number of points emerge from it. First, the law seems to codify something which had been imperial policy, namely the protection of synagogues. This is seen, for instance, in the so-called Callinicum incident from the reign of Theodosius I in which the emperor demanded that a synagogue that had been burnt down by Christians in the city of Callinicum on the banks of the Euphrates in 388 CE be rebuilt, and this despite strong objections by the well-known Christian bishop and theologian Ambrose. The spirit of Theodosius' response seems to be contained in a law found in *Cod. Theod.* 16.8.20, dating from 412 CE. Secondly, the legislation was necessary because such incidents probably occurred all too frequently (one thinks in particular of the treatment of the Jewish people of Minorca in 418, recorded in the *Letter of Severus*, and stories associated with the Christian monk Barsauma), though it should be noted that this law is the first to refer to the tactic of the occupation of synagogues by Christians. Thirdly, while the law seeks to support restitution of damage in the form of replacement buildings, it explicitly forbids the building of new synagogues. So Christian emperors were willing to protect Jewish synagogues but were not keen to see any expansion of Jewish synagogue-building; Jews were, after all, stubborn rejectors of the Christian message and their presence was a reminder of an alternative understanding of texts held dear by Christians.

There is evidence from the Syriac version of the *Life of Simeon Stylites* that a group of zealous Christians objected strongly to this law and were supported by Simeon. The source claims that Jewish people put pressure on the authorities at the same time and even used bribes. Whatever the circumstances, the rule was not rescinded as Simeon and his followers desired but was reaffirmed a few months later on 9 April 423.

Some scholars doubt the effectiveness of these laws protecting synagogues, citing elements of the Code of Justinian (see document 18) which point to a lifting of such protections: it is striking that the latter did not retain this particular law and that a law of 535 states, 'But neither do we grant that their synagogues may stand, but rather we wish that they be refashioned into the form of churches'. Others maintain that, as can be seen from sixth-century evidence in Palestine, new synagogues continued to be built in spite of the laws, giving more evidence of their ineffectiveness.

Bibliography

Kraemar, *The Mediterranean Diaspora in Late Antiquity*, 241–2, 245–6.

Levine, Lee, *Visual Judaism and Late Antiquity: Historical Contexts of Jewish Art* (New Haven: Yale University Press), 187–93.

Linder, Amnon (ed. and trans.), *The Jews in Roman Imperial Legislation* (Detroit: Wayne State University Press, 1987), 287–9.

15
Isidore of Pelusium: Letter *1882 (IV.17) (first half of fifth century)*

Text

Although I could show from all the scriptures that Judaism has come to an end and will never revive, it is from this same phrase on the basis of which the Jew who opposes you is bound to believe in a Jewish restoration, that I shall attempt to demonstrate its complete disappearance. How, therefore, should we understand this phrase by which he puts so much store? Scripture states: 'The latter splendour of this house shall be greater than the former.' Before coming to an interpretation, I do not know whether I should charge him [the Jew] with a lack of education or simply hate his misdeed, for it is necessary to instruct the ignorant but to accuse the wrongdoer. But since this will be at one and the same time an interpretation and an instruction for the ignorant, and an accusation for the wrongdoer, let us debate the phrase itself.

I therefore say that after Solomon had raised the temple, the Babylonian destroyed it and took the Jews into captivity. After their return, as they were about to rebuild it but had insufficient resources to do so, God, seeking to retain their best hopes, in order that they might undertake the work, said: 'The silver is mine and the gold is mine. The latter splendour of this house shall be greater than the former.' And at this point pay particular attention to me. Zerubbavel began the second construction and this oracle was spoken about him: 'The hands of Zerubbavel have laid the foundation of this house and his hands shall also complete it.' The verb 'laid the foundation' describes on the one hand the complete desolation left by the Babylonians, and on the other the second building. When the temple was raised up and exceeded the glorious appearance of the first, the Jews again made a mistake in putting Christ to death and so it was delivered into the hands of the Romans, who razed it to the ground. If he were about to raise it up again, then it should have read: 'the second house will exceed the glory of the first'. But in fact it reads 'the final glory will exceed the first', thus revealing that the second is the last. For just as there is nothing before the first, so there is nothing after the last. Indeed if one had said 'the second exceeds the first', it would be reasonable to envisage a third, but since the second is called the last, every route to their impudence is blocked off.

Source

Évieux, Pierre, with Vinel, Nicolas (ed. and trans.), *Isidore de Péluse. Lettres*, Tome III: *Lettres 1701–2000*, Sources chrétiennes 586 (Paris: Éditions du Cerf, 2017), 263–5. Author's own translation.

Commentary

Isidore of Pelusium (d. *c.* 450 CE), a city located at the mouth of the Nile not far from Alexandria, was a Christian ascetic and exegete who advised Cyril of Alexandria amongst others and was a friend of John Chrysostom. His only writings to survive are a collection of some 2,000 letters, brought together posthumously in Constantinople. They concern many different subjects, primarily of an internal Christian kind. They also include references to disputes between Jews and Christians on a range of issues, some of which relate to Christian practice, for instance the Christian Eucharist, others to matters of doctrine such as the incarnation and many to the interpretation of Old Testament passages such as Deut. 18:15. In the current passage, attempts to show how Haggai 2:7–8, used by an anonymous Jew to prove to another Isidore, a bishop, that the Jerusalem temple would be rebuilt, prove precisely the opposite, namely that the temple will never be rebuilt, for the reference in the passage to 'the second house', *pace* Isidore, refers to the Second Temple and not to some projected new temple to be built later.

The passage is interesting on a number of levels. First, it seems to show the ongoing importance, probably in Egypt, of Jewish opinion on scripture. Bishop Isidore, who has reported his discussion with a Jew to Isidore of Pelusium, is troubled by the Jewish understanding of a scriptural passage and its implications for Christian belief (here we see themes that we have already noted in our comments on Origen's *Letter to Africanus*; document 7) and there are many places in Isidore's letters where he reports such conversations. Secondly, the passage reveals the importance of the temple as a central element of polemic in ongoing Jewish–Christian interaction and in the symbolic worlds of both groups. Especially since the Bar Kokhba revolt, when the prospect of a rebuilt temple seemed to have evaporated in the wake of the creation by the emperor Hadrian of a new pagan city called Aelia Capitolina, Christians had exploited the fact of the destroyed temple (and that Palestine was no longer a Jewish land) to prove that God had rejected the Jewish people, in part because of their guilt as the 'killers' of Jesus. The claim that Jesus had predicted such an event, found in a number of Gospel passages, merely added to the importance of the fact of its destruction. The significance of the subject for Christian self-understanding is seen in Christian responses to the emperor Julian's failed attempt to rebuild the temple in 363, which led to an outpouring of polemic both at the time and well after the decision itself. Jews persisted in their hope that the temple would be rebuilt, as we can see in the fourteenth benediction of the *Amidah*, the importance attributed to issues relating to temple practice in rabbinic literature and expressions of the hope of a rebuilt temple in other Jewish texts. The passage quoted becomes further evidence of this aspiration and of Christian sensitivities to its implications, sensitivities which endured long after the temple had been destroyed and Jerusalem ceased to be a Jewish city.

Bibliography

Millar, Fergus, 'Christian Emperors, Christian Church and the Jews of the Diaspora in the Greek East', in *Empire, Church and Society in the Late Roman Near East: Greeks, Jews and Saracens (Collected Studies, 2004–2014)* (Leuven: Peeters, 2015), 476–7.

Millar, Fergus, 'Rebuilding the Temple: Pagan, Jewish and Christian Conceptions', in *Empire, Church and Society in the Late Roman Near East: Greeks, Jews and Saracens (Collected Studies, 2004–2014)* (Leuven: Peeters, 2015), 121–46.

Walker, P. W. L., *Holy City, Holy Places?* (Oxford: Oxford University Press, 1990).

Wilken, Robert L., *Judaism and the Early Christian Mind: A Study of Cyril of Alexandria's Exegesis and Theology* (New Haven: Yale University Press, 1971), 50–3.

Wilken, Robert L., *The Land Called Holy: Palestine in Christian History and Thought* (New Haven: Yale University Press, 1992), esp. 131–5 and 153–8.

16

Jewish Inscription (first half of fifth century)

Text

Here rests Petrus, also called Papario, son of Olympius the Jew, and the only one of his race, who deserved to reach the grace of Christ. In this holy building he was buried worthily […].

Source

Noy, David (ed.), *The Jewish Inscriptions of Western Europe*, Vol. 1: *Italy (Excluding the City of Rome), Spain and Gaul* (Cambridge: Cambridge University Press, 1993), 13.

Commentary

The inscription comes from a decorated mosaic panel found underground in the central nave of the duomo or cathedral of the northern Italian town of Grado. A good case can be made for dating it to the first half of the fifth century, and it may originally have been in a Christian chapel. It is almost the only inscription from antiquity which mentions a convert to Christianity from Judaism during the period under discussion. To some, this is unsurprising. One might wonder why anyone would wish to refer to their Jewishness, especially given that some Christian writers believed that Jewishness inhered in an individual as a kind of malevolent power. It may well have been the case also that, in spite of advantages accruing to Jews if they converted to Christianity (in this context one could refer to a body of restrictions on participation in civic life, the holding of slaves and evidence of such financial incentives as tax and rent relief) and the occasional use of coercion, few Jews did in fact convert, at least until the seventh century, when it is recorded that the emperor Heraclius ordered the forcible conversion of large numbers of Jews. This may in part have been because such converts faced ostracism and even violence from their former community (some early Christian legislation prohibits such action on the part of the Jewish community). We do, of course, hear of individual conversions (Joseph of Tiberias, for instance, mentioned by the fourth-century Christian writer Epiphanius) and there are stories of mass conversions in Minorca in 418, Crete in about 431, Clermont in 576 and elsewhere; but these stories are unreliable. Interestingly, Sozomen, writing in the first part of the fifth century, begins his *History* by referring to the infrequency of Jewish conversion.

The inscription is relevant to this issue. Petrus, the Jewish convert's baptismal name ('deserved to reach the grace of God' is a circumlocution for baptism), is described in the original Latin as the only member of his *gens* to convert. If *gens* is understood as race, as it is in the translation above, rather than 'family', as some have contended (at this time *genus* is the more normal word for family), it implies the rarity of the conversion of Jews, probably in this particular town (it is unlikely that Petrus was the only Jew to convert from his nation more generally). It is possible that the reference to deserving the grace of God, in addition to its baptismal significance, emphasises the meritorious act of Petrus' conversion, given that he was the only one to convert either from his family or from the group of Jews in his town or wider district.

The inscription's importance lies in the fact that (1) it witnesses to that rarest of things, epigraphic reference to a converted Jew; and (2) it touches upon wider issues relating to the (in)frequency of such conversions. Jewish communities, in spite of attempts, direct or indirect, to convert them to Christianity, often remained resiliently Jewish in this period.

Bibliography

Kraemar, *The Mediterranean Diaspora in Late Antiquity*, 273–5.

Noy, David (ed.), *The Jewish Inscriptions of Western Europe*, Vol. 1: *Italy (Excluding the City of Rome), Spain and Gaul* (Cambridge: Cambridge University Press, 1993), 13–16.

17

Anonymous Syriac Poem: 'Synagogue and Church' (late fifth to early sixth century)

Text

CHURCH: Living water has the Son given me
and those who drink of it never die;
a great fountain from His side has He opened up:
enjoy it with me; I do not begrudge you.

SYNAGOGUE: All the Prophets give me honour,
the Patriarchs love me;
the Levites as well escort me,
for I am the beloved daughter.

CHURCH: The Prophets were stoned by your scribes,
those sent were slain by your priests;
the Lord of the Prophets you hung on the wood:
sheathe your sword, murderess.

SYNAGOGUE: Moses, who wrote out my bridal contract, is witness
that the finger of the Father has sealed it.
The Father has entrusted me with His House
for I am the heiress.

CHURCH: Moses whom you invoke is indeed witness,
for he saw your adultery and broke the tablets:

seeing that the adulteresses do not inherit,
your marriage deed is annulled, so why do you dispute?

SYNAGOGUE: Peoples and kings before me He routed
and I entered in and inherited their realm;
high walls before me He overthrew.
who like me is resplendent?

CHURCH: The Father indeed routed the Peoples, but He bade you
not to worship their gods.
Because you did not listen to Him, He has dispersed you,
and invited the Peoples to come and worship Him.

SYNAGOGUE: Open up the Scriptures and read therein
my lofty and glorious history.
All the Prophets give me honour,
whereas you, how is it you dispute with me?

CHURCH: I did indeed open and read them, and I understood:
I saw your adultery in every book!
The Scriptures are full of your great shame;
how can you speak thus unabashed?

SYNAGOGUE: Statues and images were cast by you;
it was you who made all the idols.
I have never known anyone
but the Father, for it is He who has loved me.

CHURCH: That odious statue that was cast,
with four faces – who made that?
These four faces testify
that your adultery is manifest, yet you do not stay silent.

SYNAGOGUE: In the presence of Righteousness show us
how and in what way are you boasting?
What have you got to be proud of, that you contend
with the resplendent daughter of Jacob?

CHURCH: In the presence of the Father I tell you
that my pride is in His Son;
He whom you crucified has caused me to return
and it is of Him that I proudly speak.

SYNAGOGUE: Great is your shame, if only you knew it:
I crucified him because he led me astray,
whereas you have accepted him and give him worship:
he is leading you astray and you do not discern it.

CHURCH: Great is your woe; who is it you have crucified?
Great is your sickness; for whom are you so full of hate?

> You have denied the Image of the Father's glory;
> because you are blind, you do not test the matter out.

SYNAGOGUE: Keep silent in your words, if you are willing,
for the Father is hidden and cannot be seen;
it is unheard of that He should have a son:
it was the son of Joseph who was crucified.

CHURCH: Listen to the Scriptures, if you are willing,
how they testify that the Father has a Son.
Because you crucified Him you are disputing,
saying He does not exist, when He manifestly does.

SYNAGOGUE: I am amazed at how much in error you are,
worshipping a human being;
if he had the power, he would not have been crucified,
but now that he has been crucified, why do you worship him?

CHURCH: I am amazed at how you fail to believe
that He is God as well, even though crucified:
on His cross He slew very death.
Why then do you not believe?

Source

Brock, Sebastian P. (ed. and trans.), *The People and the Peoples: Syriac Dialogue Poems from Late Antiquity* (Oxford: Oxford Centre for Hebrew and Jewish Studies, 2019), 47–51.

Commentary

Syriac literature provides a number of little-known examples of dialogue poems between personifications of the Christian church and the synagogue. The form of dialogue poem goes back at least 4,000 years and is witnessed in Akkadian and Sumerian literature. It is found in the later Jewish Aramaic tradition and is first represented in the Syriac tradition by Ephrem (306–73). The poems often take the form of an alphabetic acrostic, as is the case in the example quoted, and usually contain a narrative introduction, with the verses which follow alternating between the two parties.

The anonymous poem excerpted above (the title is provided by its translator, Brock) may have been written anywhere between the latter part of the fifth century and the early sixth. The first four stanzas present the two combatants taking their case to court, where Righteousness will adjudicate. The subject is the question of who is the true heir to the House of God. At the point at which we join the dialogue, the synagogue has engaged in a lengthy discussion of the various signs of favour accorded her by God and witnessed to in scripture. The church refutes each of these by citing events which point in the opposite direction, and in our passage the discussion continues in a not dissimilar vein as the church boasts of its inheritance through Christ and the synagogue cites biblical examples of her own divine favour. Further broadly Christological exchanges focus on elements of Christian binitarian belief, with the church concluding the dialogue by expressing amazement that the synagogue cannot accept the Christian message of the cross with its affirmation of the destruction of death. Interestingly, and in contradistinction to other poems of this type, there is no explicit assertion as to who wins the contest.

The passage, like the piece taken from Aphrahat's *Demonstrations* (document 10), represents a contribution to the Jewish–Christian debate from the rich and sometimes fiercely polemical Syriac Christian tradition (one thinks in particular of works associated with Ephrem and Jacob of Serugh). It highlights both the biblical character of the debate (note in particular the almost antiphonal exchanges on what the Old Testament proves about the question of inheritance as between the church and the synagogue) and the importance of Christological questions, seen here at the end of the piece where the synagogue emphasises the impossibility of the incarnation on a number of grounds. Some, however, have argued for the existence of an internal Christian subtext in these stanzas, in which the supposed Christological position of eastern Christians is attacked as being dangerously 'dyophysite' (that is, making such a sharp distinction between the divine and the human in Jesus, for fear of attributing suffering to God, that the accusation could be made that they were man-worshippers). This would then explain the reference in the penultimate stanza to the church as worshipping a human being, though some might question the polemical logic of this accusation being made by the synagogue. The debate touches upon the important question of the purpose of anti-Jewish Christian literature and the way in which it could be used to address inner-Christian questions rather than ones straightforwardly pertinent to any mooted Jewish–Christian dialogue. One assumes that this poem's primary audience was Christians, which may well explain why no explicit adjudication is given by Righteousness, though some manuscripts add verses indicating that the church is the victor of the contest.

Bibliography

Brock, Sebastian P. (ed. and trans.), *The People and the Peoples: Syriac Dialogue Poems from Late Antiquity* (Oxford: Oxford Centre for Hebrew and Jewish Studies, 2019).
Cerbelaud, Dominique, 'Les pères syriaques et les juifs', in Auwers, Jean-Marie, Burnet, Régis, and Luciani, Didier (eds.), *L'antijudaïsme des pères. Mythe et/ou réalité?* (Paris: Beauchesne, 2017), 183–96.
Shepardson, Christine, *Anti-Judaism and Christian Orthodoxy: Ephrem's Hymns in Fourth-Century Syria* (Washington, DC: Catholic University of America Press, 2008).

18

Justinian: Novella *146 (553* CE*)*

Text

We have learnt from their petitions, which they have addressed to us, that while some maintain the Hebrew language only and want to use it in reading the Holy Books others consider it right to admit Greek as well, and they have already been quarreling among themselves about this for a long time. Having therefore studied this matter we decided that the better case is that of those who want to use also Greek in reading the Holy Books, and generally in any language that is the more suited and the better known to the hearers in each locality. [...]

We decree, therefore, that it shall be permitted to those Hebrews who want it to read the Holy Books in their synagogues and, in general, in any place where there are Hebrews, in the Greek language before those assembled and comprehending [...] We also order that there shall be no license to the commentators they have, who employ the Hebrew language to falsify it at their will, covering their own malignity by the ignorance of the many. Furthermore, those who read in Greek shall use the Septuagint tradition, which is more accurate than all the others [...] Apart from these [certain qualities of the Septuagint translation], who will not be amazed by this thing about these men, who lived a long time before the saving revelation of the great God and our Saviour Jesus Christ yet carried out the translation of the Holy Books as if they saw that this revelation was to happen in future, and as if illuminated by a prophetic grace? Let all use mainly this translation; but in order that we shall not appear to prohibit them all the other translations, we give permission to use also Akilas' translation, although he was gentile and in some readings differs not a little from the Septuagint. What they call Mishnah [*deuterōsis* in the Greek], on the other hand, we prohibit entirely, for it is not included among the Holy Books, nor was it handed down from above by the prophets, but it is an invention of men in their chatter, exclusively of earthly origin and having in it nothing of the divine.

Source

Linder, Amnon (ed. and trans.), *The Jews in Roman Imperial Legislation* (Detroit: Wayne State University Press, 1987), 408–9.

Commentary

This law or *novella* (the *Novellae Constitutiones*, diverse laws enacted after 534 CE, are considered one of the four major units of Roman law instituted during Justinian's reign), dated to February 553 CE, was addressed to Areobindus, Prefect of the East. Ostensibly, the emperor appears to have been approached by some Jews and asked to adjudicate a case relating to the role of Hebrew and Greek in the synagogue. Justinian states that there should be freedom of usage with regard to language, but that if Greek is used, which would appear to be his preference, it should ideally be the Septuagint, though he concedes that Aquila, a much more literal version of the Hebrew, can also be used. He prohibits use of what he calls the *deuterōsis*, possibly rabbinic traditions of some sort (which some scholars associate with the Mishnah, as in the translation above). Corporal punishment is invoked as a consequence for breaking any of the stated prohibitions.

The meaning of every part of this piece of legislation has been disputed. Is it likely that the Jewish community would have appealed to an emperor like Justinian to resolve a strictly internal issue? If the answer is yes, is it the supporters of Hebrew who are appealing to the emperor or the supporters of Greek? What was the situation which brought about the appeal? And why might the traditions, whatever these are, be banned?

Some see Justinian's intervention as oppressive (an attempt to do away with reading in Hebrew altogether), though this is unlikely as Hebrew is not banned in the *novella*. Others see it as opportunistic, a chance to assert the authority of the Greek version of the Old Testament, namely the Septuagint, which was predominant among Christians, in the hope that this would give Jews a better opportunity to see the validity of Christian interpretation of their own scriptures (a point supported by some statements in the passage) for these were based on the Septuagint rather than the Hebrew. The banning of the so-called *deuterōsis* points to something more oppressive though, given the obscurity of the term, it is difficult to know why such a ban was deemed necessary. Some suggest a tradition of interpretation inimical to Christianity, such as Sadducean denials of the resurrection, but this is little more than a guess. However the passage is interpreted, it gives voice to a political reality which had not been witnessed before in the pagan Roman empire, namely the involvement of an emperor, whether or not at the behest of the Jewish community, in matters relating to Jewish worship in the synagogue.

Bibliography

de Lange, Nicholas, *Japheth in the Tents of Shem: Greek Bible Translations in Byzantine Judaism* (Tübingen: Mohr Siebeck, 2015), 60–7.

Kraemar, *The Mediterranean Diaspora in Late Antiquity*, 308–14.

Levine, Lee, *Visual Judaism and Late Antiquity: Historical Contexts of Jewish Art* (New Haven: Yale University Press, 2012), 183–5.

Linder, Amnon (ed. and trans.), *The Jews in Roman Imperial Legislation* (Detroit: Wayne State University Press, 1987), 402–11.

Rutgers, Leonard, 'Justinian's *Novella* 146 between Jews and Christians', in Kalmin, Richard, and Schwartz, Seth (eds.), *Jewish Culture and Society under the Christian Roman Empire* (Leuven: Peeters, 2002), 381–403.

19

Fourth Council of Toledo, Canons 57 and 59 (633 CE)

Text

57. On the Jews, however, thus did the Holy Synod order, that no one should henceforth be forced to believe, *God hath mercy on whom he will and whom he will he hardeneth* [Rom. 9.18]; such men should not be saved unwillingly but willingly, in order that the procedure of justice should be complete; for just as man perished obedient to the serpent out of his own free will, so will any man be saved – when called by the divine grace – by believing and in converting his own mind. They should be persuaded to convert, therefore, of their own free choice, rather than forced by violence. Those, however, who were formerly forced to come to Christianity

(as was done in the days of the most religious prince Sisebut), since it is clear that they have been associated in the divine sacraments, received the grace of baptism, were anointed with chrism, and partook of the body and blood of the Lord, it is proper that they should be forced to keep the faith even though they had undertaken it under duress, lest the name of the Lord be blasphemed and the faith they had undertaken be treated as vile and contemptible.

59. Many who were formerly elevated from being Jews to the Christian faith are now blaspheming Christ, not only by being known to be practicing Jewish rites but even by daring to operate abominable circumcisions; concerning these men, the Holy Council decreed as follows, with the advice of the most pious and the most religious prince our lord Sisenand the King, namely, that such transgressors should be reformed and recalled to the veneration of the Christian dogma by the episcopal authority, in order that the priestly chastisement should correct those, whom their proper will shall not amend. Those, however, whom they will circumcise, if they are their sons, they shall be separated from their parents' company, and if slaves, they shall be given liberty in return for the injury done to their body.

Source

Linder, Amnon (ed. and trans.), *The Jews in the Legal Sources of the Early Middle Ages* (Detroit: Wayne State University Press, 1997), 486–8. (Biblical reference is a footnote in the original.)

Commentary

The Fourth Council of Toledo was convoked by the Visigothic king Sisenand on 5 December 633. Sixty-two bishops participated – under the leadership of Isidore of Seville – and seventy-five canons emerged, ten dealing with Jews, of which two are cited here.

King Sisenand's predecessor but one, Sisebut, had ordered the compulsory conversion of Jews to Christianity in 615/16 and stated that failure to convert would lead to exile. Sisebut's ruling was apparently overturned by his successor, Swinthila, who ordered Jews back from exile and allowed those who had been converted and relapsed to Judaism to do so openly. In the two canons quoted above, King Sisenand appears to be 'mopping up' the difficulties caused by this prehistory. So first of all it is made clear, here in refutation of the actions of Sisebut, that compulsory conversions are not to be permitted. However, those who had been coerced into conversion are required to remain converted in part because of the binding effect of baptism. Canon 59 further discusses the position of those who had been converted under coercion, noting how many continue their Jewish practices after their Christian initiation and so blaspheme.

A number of points arise from these passages. First, it would seem that the legislation of Sisebut had had an effect, leading to a number of conversions to Christianity, the consequences of which the legislation addresses. Secondly, the church in Spain, in spite of Sisebut, remained wedded to the idea that forced conversions should be avoided. In this context one can see the perduring character of the principles enunciated by Augustine, though the arguments we find in the latter, at least as these relate to the idea of the importance of the witness of the Jews, are not referred to (instead we have a quotation from Romans 9, which invokes the principle of providence, though no reference is made to Rom. 11, where the hope is expressed that Jews will be converted in the end time). Thirdly, in spite of the general view that forced conversions were wrong, Christians remained intent upon forcing Jews coerced to be baptised to remain in that state, and this regardless of the fact that many appeared to continue their Jewish practices. This, it seems, is the first time that the presence of such individuals was highlighted in church legislation and it foreshadows the well-known phenomenon of *marranos* in medieval Spain (see Chapter 4, p. 232). The removal of children who had been circumcised by their 'lapsed' parents appears an extreme measure, and another canon goes on to note that such children would be placed in the care of monasteries or godfearing Christian men and women (here assuming that *Iudaei* refers to those who had been baptised rather than to unbaptised Jews). In a further canon (Canon 60), converted Jews are forbidden from consorting with unconverted Jews, and such activity will lead to their enslavement and the punishment of those they have mixed with. Such legislation shows the ambivalent attitude of the church to Jewish conversion. While the conversion of Jews implied the superiority of Christianity to Judaism, and so the supersession of the former over the latter, converts, especially those who were forced and persisted in their old practices, could cause others to Judaise and by their return to Judaism could 'appear as an affront to the integrity of Christendom' (Abulafia 2018: 33). It is striking that Canon 57 was one of the most-cited canons in canonical collections from 906 to 1141.

Bibliography

Abulafia, Anna Sapir, 'Medieval Church Doctrines and Policies', in Chazan, Robert (ed.), *The Cambridge History of Judaism*, Vol. 6: *The Middle Ages: The Christian World* (Cambridge: Cambridge University Press, 2018), 32–53, esp. 33–4.

Bronisch, Alexander, *Die Judengesetzgebung im katholischen West-gotenreich von Toledo* (Hanover: Hahnsche Buchhandlung, 2005).

Linder, Amnon (ed. and trans.), *The Jews in the Legal Sources of the Early Middle Ages* (Detroit: Wayne State University Press, 1997), 485–91.

Parkes, *The Conflict of the Church and the Synagogue*, 347–59.

20

Annals of St-Bertin *(ninth century)*

Text

Meanwhile something very distressing happened, something to be bewailed by all the children of the Catholic Church. Rumour spread the news and the Emperor found out that the deacon Bodo, an Aleman by birth and deeply imbued from his earliest childhood in the Christian religion with the scholarship of the court clergy and with sacred and secular learning, a man who only the previous year had requested permission from the Emperor and the Empress to go on pilgrimage to Rome and had been granted this permission and been loaded with many gifts: this man seduced by the enemy of the human race had abandoned Christianity and converted to Judaism. First he entered into discussion about apostasy and his own perdition with some Jews whom he had brought with him to sell to the pagans. He was not afraid to make his cunning plans and having let these Jews be taken away and kept only one companion with him, a man rumoured to be his nephew, he renounced the Christian faith – we weep to say it – and professed himself a Jew. Thus he was circumcised, let his hair and beard grow and adopted – or rather usurped – the name of Eleazar. He assumed a warrior's gear, married a Jew's daughter and forced his nephew mentioned earlier also to convert to Judaism. Finally, overcome by the most despicable avarice, he entered the Spanish town of Zaragoza in mid-August along with some Jews. It was only with difficulty that the Emperor could be persuaded to believe this news at all, which clearly showed to everyone what a very distressing episode this was for the Emperor and Empress and indeed for all those redeemed through the grace of the Christian faith […]

Bodo, who some years earlier had abandoned the truth of a Christian and gone over to the perfidy of the Jews, made such further progress in evil that he devoted himself to urging all the Christians living in Spain under the king and people of the Saracens that they should abandon Christianity and convert to the insanity of the Jews or the madness of the Saracens, or, said Bodo, they would all certainly be killed. A tearful petition was sent about him by all the Christians of that realm, to King Charles, and the bishops and other clergy in his kingdom, requesting them to demand the apostate Bodo to stop presenting the Christians who lived down there with such a choice between persecution or death.

Source

Nelson, Janet L. (ed. and trans.), *The Annals of St-Bertin: Ninth Century Histories*, vol. 1 (Manchester: Manchester University Press, 1991), 41–2.

Commentary

Bodo, the subject of the passage cited, entered the Benedictine Monastery of Reichenau in approximately 820 at the age of six. After a thorough education he was sent to the Carolingian court of Louis the Pious, where he appears to have come under the influence of Judith, the consort of Louis, a woman with a controversial reputation thought to have fostered good relations with the Jewish people. In circumstances which are difficult to reconstruct, possibly while on a pilgrimage to Rome, Bodo converted to Judaism, fleeing initially to Zaragoza and ending up in Córdoba, in the part of Spain under Muslim control known as al-Andalus. He was to remain there until his death.

The passage quoted comes from the *Annals of St-Bertin*, so called because the first manuscript of this work (a year-by-year account of events) was preserved at the monastery of Saint-Bertin in Saint-Omer. The author of the section, probably Prudentius, later bishop of Troyes, gives the reader a polemical account of Bodo's conversion. It makes clear that Bodo was very well connected and expresses considerable surprise at his conversion, but gives hardly any information as to why he converted (neither Prudentius nor any of the other sources which refer to Bodo seeks to unravel matters of a private or spiritual kind). Some scholars have pointed to Bodo's intellectual formation in an atmosphere of intense engagement with the Old Testament, where interest in the *hebraica veritas* and Jewish traditions formed a part of study directed at achieving a truly Christian (as opposed to Jewish) self-understanding of the origins of the Christian faith. The intellectually curious Bodo may also have been provided with further opportunities to reflect on the Jewish–Christian argument by the activities and anti-Jewish writings of Agobard, archbishop of Lyon (especially *On the Superstition and Errors of the Jews*, which stood out from other *adversus Judaeos* works of the time for its knowledge of actual Jewish lives), and of Amolo, which were written in reaction to what were perceived as the positive attitudes towards Jews entertained by Charlemagne and his son Louis the Pious and actuated by a desire to accentuate a sense of the Jew as an enemy of Christendom. All this is guesswork. It should be noted, however, that in the early 840s Bodo, now with the 'Jewish' name Eleazar, engaged in a correspondence with a Christian called Álvaro, also from Córdoba, and while Bodo's own contribution to the exchange is only partially preserved, what remains, not least the responses of Álvaro, indicate Bodo's formidable ability to argue scripturally.

The story of Bodo gives evidence of the ongoing reality of Christian conversion to Judaism, which was to continue throughout the medieval period, not least amongst some learned churchmen (for example, Wecelin in 1005, who had been a priest in the house of Duke Conrad of Carinthia; the monk Johannes of Dreux, mentioned in the Cairo Genizah; and possibly Nestor the Priest, the author of *Sefer ha-komer*), though our records of such conversions probably do not reflect the reality as many may have happened in secret or simply not been recorded. The vehemence of the passage quoted shows how such conversions could cause consternation in the Christian community, not least when the converts were learned, like Bodo, and in this instance may have inspired some of the anti-Jewish measures proposed at the council of Paris-Meaux in 845–6 CE.

Bibliography

Albert, Bat-Sheva, '*Adversus Iudaeos* in the Carolingian Empire', in Limor, Ora, and Stroumsa, Guy (eds.), *Contra Iudaeos: Ancient and Medieval Polemics between Christians and Jews* (Tübingen: Mohr Siebeck, 1996), 119–42.
Cabaniss, Allen, 'Bodo/Eleazar: A Famous Jewish Convert', *Jewish Quarterly Review* 43 (1953), 313–28.
Malkiel, 'Jewish–Christian Relations in Europe, 840–1096'.
Riess, Frank, *The Journey of Deacon Bodo from the Rhine to the Guadalquivir: Apostasy and Conversion to Judaism in Early Medieval Europe* (New York: Peter Lang, 2019).
Tartakoff, Paola, *Conversion, Circumcision, and Ritual Murder in Medieval Europe* (Philadelphia: University of Pennsylvania Press, 2020), esp. ch. 3.

3

Classic Rabbinic Literature up to the Ninth Century

PHILIP ALEXANDER

INTRODUCTION

Classic rabbinic literature is the literature generated by the rabbinic movement in Eretz Israel (the land of Israel) and Babylonia (modern-day Iraq) in late antiquity (first to ninth century CE). At its core lies the Mishnah, a codification of rabbinic rulings on all aspects of life which was compiled around 210 CE in the Galilee by Judah ha-Nasi. This was supplemented by a parallel code, compiled around a century later and known as the Tosefta (supplement). The Mishnah became the basic text studied in the rabbinical schools of Eretz Israel and Babylonia, and over the centuries two great commentaries on it accumulated, one in Eretz Israel, the other in Babylonia, which in the end crystallised respectively into the Palestinian or Yerushalmi Talmud (largely completed around 400 CE) and the Babylonian Talmud (largely completed around 500 CE). The Mishnah, Tosefta and two Talmuds became authoritative for later Judaism, and what they say on any subject, including Christianity, remains hugely important. Other texts created in this period also carry weight. Most notable of these is a series of biblical commentaries known as Midrashim, mainly on the Torah (the Pentateuch), which aim, broadly speaking, to ground the rabbinic world view in scripture and, at the same time, implicitly or explicitly refute Christian use of biblical texts. Towards the end of our timespan other texts emerge which are important for our present purposes. Among these is a series of apocalyptic writings (such as the *Book of Zerubbavel*; see document 10 below) which define Jewish eschatology over against Christian eschatology, and established the contours of Jewish eschatology down to the present day. In the ninth century we also see the beginnings of a more theological/philosophical articulation of Judaism in the writings of Saadia Gaon (see document 16). This sharpens in philosophical language the differences between Judaism and Christianity, for example on the doctrine of God.

    The rabbinic movement is of particular importance for Jewish–Christian relations because it laid the foundations for Judaism as we know it today, and its writings retain great authority for all major current forms of Judaism. The attitudes it took vis-à-vis Christianity were highly influential in all subsequent Jewish–Christian encounters. Tension between the rabbinic movement and nascent Christianity goes right back to the beginning. The rabbis acknowledged the pre-70 CE Pharisees as their spiritual forebears, and it is clear from the Gospels that the Pharisees were among the most vocal opponents of Jesus and his followers. After the destruction of the Jerusalem temple in 70 CE the rabbinic movement made a concerted effort to offer spiritual leadership to the Jewish people, initially in Eretz Israel. Their acceptance and influence grew over the next century and a half till by the third century their authority was probably acknowledged by the majority of Jews in the region.

Down to the third century the synagogues in Palestine would have wielded greater social, economic and political influence than the small Christian churches, and there is evidence (mainly but not entirely from Christian sources) that they did what they could to suppress the Christian movement, at times involving the local Roman courts to this end. But in the fourth century the balance of political power began to shift decisively in the Christians' favour. The turning-point was the conversion of Constantine and the establishment of Christianity as the state religion of the Roman empire. This led rapidly to an aggressive Christian 'colonisation' of Palestine – the building of magnificent churches, which raised the profile of Christianity in the area and redefined the Holy Land as *Christian* sacred space. The legal position of Jews steadily worsened and all sorts of restrictions were placed on their life and worship. That the Jewish communities by and large successfully resisted this pressure is due in no small measure to the intellectual vitality of the rabbinic movement and the spiritual leadership it offered.

Rabbinic Judaism spread beyond Palestine. It was carried to the Aramaic-speaking diaspora in Babylonia by students who had studied with Judah ha-Nasi in Palestine. Rabbinic Houses of Study (*batei midrash*) were established in which the Mishnah of Judah became the basic 'textbook'. Over the next few centuries the Babylonian rabbinate flourished till it challenged in prestige and authority its counterpart in Eretz Israel. Its enduring monument was the Babylonian Talmud, which, after the Torah, became the most authoritative text in Judaism. The Jewish communities in Babylonia did not face the Christian political and cultural onslaught endured by their coreligionists in Eretz Israel, but the region in which they lived nevertheless became increasingly Christianised, and it is evident that Jewish and Christian communities lived side by side and interacted on a daily basis. The Babylonian Talmud, directly and indirectly, shows considerable interest in Jesus and Christianity, and contains evidence of Jewish–Christian debate, but the context here was different, in that Babylonian Jews were living in a non-Christian state (Zoroastrian down to the arrival of Islam, Islamic thereafter) and so could express themselves with more freedom vis-à-vis Christianity than their fellow Jews in Eretz Israel.

The penetration of Rabbinic Judaism into the Greek-speaking diaspora to the west was more fitful and slow, and it was probably not till towards the end of our period that significant numbers of Jews in the west would have acknowledged the authority of the rabbinate, whether of Eretz Israel or Babylonia. The relationships between the Jewish and Christian communities in the west followed a similar pattern to Eretz Israel. In the early period it was the synagogue which had the upper hand and from time to time persecuted the church, but from Constantine onwards the church had the upper hand and persecuted the synagogue. For knowledge of this conflict we rely heavily on Christian sources, supplemented by inscriptional and archaeological evidence. The pressure on the Jewish communities must have been intense. They were aliens, who had to live with native anti-immigrant and indeed specifically anti-Jewish prejudice, *as well as* Christian *odium theologicum* (theological hatred). Some have suggested that, lacking rabbinic leadership for much of the period, there may have been numerous conversions to Christianity, but there is little evidence for this. The non-rabbinic, traditional synagogal Judaism of the western diaspora seems to have had enough resilience – organisational, spiritual and intellectual – to withstand Christian pressure, without much rabbinic help.

The reconstruction of rabbinic attitudes towards Christianity is bedevilled by the fact that there are surprisingly few explicit references to Christians and Christianity in the vast rabbinic corpus. Some have taken this at face value and argued that in fact there was little day-to-day contact between Christians and Rabbinic Jews, and that the latter carried on their lives with little reference to the growing power and presence of the church in the wider world. However, there is an emerging consensus that Christianity was a more pervasive influence on Rabbinic Judaism than we might suppose at first sight and that the rabbis are often tacitly defining their positions in ways that are intended to counter Christian claims. This is particularly plausible in the case of Bible interpretation. Indeed, it has been argued that a major impetus towards the development of Midrash was the need to counter Christian exegetical appropriation of the Tanakh (the Christian Old Testament). The general silence about Christianity may have been a 'loud silence' – a deliberate ploy to deny Christianity the oxygen of publicity within the Jewish community. At the same time, this silence makes the point that Judaism has no need to take note of Christianity because it is the older faith and so represents the true continuation of the covenant at Sinai, as opposed to Christianity, which was an upstart sect that had strayed into serious error. Whatever the reason for the lack of explicit mention of Christianity in normative Jewish texts such as the Talmud, the more frequent and negative references to Jews and Judaism in Christian sources suggest that Jews and Judaism play a more significant role in Christian self-understanding and identity than Christianity does in Judaism.

Jesus is mentioned by name a number of times in the rabbinic literature. The form of his name used is Yeshu or, more fully, Yeshu ha-Notzri (Yeshu the Nazarene). Yeshu is also found on one ancient ossuary. It is a shortened form of Yeshua[c], which is in turn a form of Yehoshua[c] (Joshua). In Jewish tradition, however, Yeshu was taken as an acronym of *Yimmaḥ shemo ve-zikhrono*, 'May his name and memory be wiped out'. He is also referred to as Ben Pandera/Pandira/Pantiri (see documents 4, 5, 12 (i) and (ii)) or by denigratory sobriquets such as 'The Hanged One' (*Ha-Talui*). The most precise and unambiguous name for Christians was *Notzrim* (Nazarenes), but it is very seldom used in classic rabbinic literature. Instead, Christians are most often referred to as *minim*. The common translation of this is 'heretics'. It seems to have been a distinctive rabbinic coinage to denote any Jew who in the opinion of the rabbis had deviated seriously from orthodox faith and practice, and signalled a growing claim on the part of the rabbis to be the custodians of Jewish orthodoxy. There has been considerable debate as to the precise reference of the term, and it could, in principle, designate any Jew or Jewish group whom the rabbis decided had strayed from the true path, but in many cases (particularly in later traditions) it clearly denotes Christians. All Christians were *minim*, but not all *minim* were necessarily Christians.

Piecing together the various references to Christians in classic rabbinic literature, it becomes clear that the rabbis came to the view that Christianity constituted an existential threat to the Jewish people, and so had to be vigorously countered (document 1). To do this they deployed a two-pronged strategy. First, they adopted a series of practical measures aimed at excluding Christians from Jewish communities and minimising contact with them (document 2). Given that Christians were expected to preach their faith and to make converts, the dangers flowing from free contact would have been seen as very real. A key move was to exclude Christians from the synagogue. If this could be achieved, the consequences were considerable, because the synagogue was the centre of not only the religious but the social life of the Jewish community. To expel Jewish Christians from the synagogue was at least to marginalise them, if not exclude them altogether from the Jewish community. A mechanism for doing this was found by introducing a cursing of the Christians into the daily prayer now known as the *Amidah*. It is still found as Benediction 12 of the *Amidah* (or Eighteen Benedictions) and is widely known as the *Birkat ha-Minim* (see documents 3 (i), (ii) and (iii)). That Christians are in view is generally agreed, and indeed for *minim* (heretics) the old Palestinian form of the prayer has *Notzrim* (Christians). The rabbis went further and discouraged Jews from having business or social contact of any sort with Christians. They recounted cautionary tales about rabbis who had got into difficulties of various kinds due to associating with Christians (documents 4, 5). In a rabbinically oriented community these measures aimed at ostracising Christians would have made life very difficult for them and effectively driven them out. It is impossible to say how widely they would have been followed.

The second prong of the rabbinic anti-Christian strategy was to refute the key claims of Christianity, to refute Christian doctrine. Rabbinic anti-Christian polemic in our period took three main forms. The first was counter-exegesis. Jews and Christians shared the same scriptures: the Christian Old Testament was the Jewish Tanakh. And it was fundamental to Christianity that its teachings were rooted in those scriptures. Christians assembled a formidable array of proof-texts (*testimonia*) which they alleged made good this claim. The rabbis argued that the texts did not, and tried to demonstrate that the Christian exegesis was flawed (documents 6, 7 (i) and (ii)). That counter-exegesis is going on is not always obvious, in that the rabbinic interpreters often do not openly identify the views they are attacking as Christian or refute them point-blank. It is only when we set the rabbinic and the Christian exegesis side by side that it becomes clear that the rabbinic interpretation is framed in a way designed to counter the Christian reading of the text (see also Appendix to Part I). Close analysis of Midrash time and again suggests that the rabbinic knowledge of the Christian position was deeper than one might at first think. There were a number of key points of contention between Judaism and Christianity, and when we come across Midrashim relating to these points it is worth considering whether the Midrash is angled in such a way as to refute Christian interpretation of the passage under review, even when Christianity is not explicitly mentioned. Among these issues are:

(1) The identity of the messiah. Christian thinkers assembled a battery of Old Testament *testimonia* to demonstrate that Jesus was the promised messiah of Israel. When any of these *testimonia* are being discussed in Midrash, the chances of counter-exegesis are high (documents 10, 11).

(2) The unity of God. Christianity regarded Christ as divine. The rabbis opposed this idea because they held that it compromised their fundamental belief in the unity of God: they defined this as the question of whether there were 'two powers in heaven'. There may have been other non-Christian groups they would also have seen as guilty of this heresy (perhaps groups who accorded to high archangels powers close to God's), but there is no doubt that Christianity would have fallen under their condemnation, and the exegetical arguments that they developed against two powers could be used against Christianity (as for example in b.Sanh. 38b).

(3) The abrogation of the Torah. Christianity claimed that the Torah had been abrogated by the new revelation in Christ. This idea could be expressed in stronger or weaker forms. Some preferred to use the language of 'fulfilment' rather than 'replacement'. Mainstream Christianity in the end took the view that it was only the ritual laws of the Torah that had been abrogated. The moral laws (as summarised in the Ten Commandments) remained eternally valid. Whether in a weaker or stronger form, the rabbis opposed any suggestion that the Torah given to Israel at Sinai would in whole or in part be abrogated (documents 9 (i), (ii) and (iii)).

(4) The election of Israel. Christians argued that the old Israel of the Sinai Covenant had been replaced in the purposes of God by the new Israel, the church, which Christ had brought into being by his death and resurrection. Again, this view could be expressed in harder or softer forms. The softer forms spoke in terms of 'fulfilment' rather than 'replacement', but once more the rabbis failed to accept the distinction and opposed any suggestion that Israel had been rejected by God or taken up into a greater reality, the church. For them, for all Israel's failings, the covenant with God at Sinai was eternal, and the relationship forged then would endure forever. The debate on all these points was conducted primarily in terms of exegesis of verses of scripture, and this made counter-exegesis – the refutation of Christian readings of the Tanakh – the primary mode of rabbinic anti-Christian polemic in late antiquity (document 8).

But counter-exegesis was not the only way the rabbis tackled Christian claims. They also engaged in counter-narrative. This involved taking stories about Jesus and the early church and narrating them in such a way as to subvert the claims which Christians based upon them. The narratives of Jesus' birth, ministry, death, resurrection and ascension, and the establishing of the church at Pentecost, as contained in the Gospels and Acts, were foundational to Christianity. But suppose those stories were not entirely true? Suppose the Gospels and Acts were concealing what really happened? These Jewish counter-narratives focused on the birth of Jesus (he was born out of wedlock: documents 12 (i) and (ii)), his ministry (his miracles were produced by magic: documents 13, 14), and his death and resurrection (he did not rise from the dead; his body was temporarily moved elsewhere and that is why the tomb was empty: document 15). Many of these stories were circulating in the Jewish communities from the founding of Christianity and are clearly reflected in the Gospels, which at various points seem cast to counter-narrate *them*. They were later to crystallise into a collection of Jewish anti-gospels referred to collectively today as the *Toledot Yeshu* (Generations/History of Jesus; see documents 12 (ii), 15). These gospels in the forms in which we now have them are medieval or early modern, but the tradition on which they draw can be traced back into late antiquity, and indeed, as already suggested, the birth of the tradition is coeval with the birth of Christianity.

The final tactic used by the rabbis is counter-argument, whereby the positions adopted and defended by Christians were subjected to analysis, and an attempt was made to show that they were self-contradictory or irrational. This is essentially a philosophical approach, and it comes to the fore at the end of our period in an Islamic milieu, when Rabbinic Judaism fell under the spell of the philosophical/theological movement in Islam known as the Qalam. This attempted to state the doctrines of the faith in philosophically acceptable ways, an approach not unknown in earlier times. It can be traced back to pagan *philosophical* critiques of Christianity (and, indeed, sometimes of Judaism as well), and echoes of it can be found even in the New Testament. The second-century pagan philosopher Celsus deployed it in his anti-Christian polemic, as did the unnamed Jew whom he quotes at length (see Chapter 2, p. 81). Counter-argument took a number of forms. Sometimes it argued that the Christian scriptures – the New Testament – were internally contradictory: they do not constitute a consistent and coherent body of teaching (document 17). At other times it argued that key Christian doctrines were incoherent and contrary to reason. The doctrine that most obviously laid itself open to such philosophical attack was the orthodox Christian doctrine of the Trinity, and here the Jewish polemicists found useful allies in Muslim thinkers.

It is very difficult to write a strictly chronological history of Jewish–Christian relations on the basis of the classic rabbinic texts, and that is why a broadly thematic approach has been adopted here. There are two reasons for this. First, the traditions themselves are hard to date. There are more or less agreed dates for the key documents in which they are found. So anything in the Mishnah can usually be assumed to be no later than roughly the early third century CE, in the Tosefta no later than roughly 300 CE, in the Yerushalmi Talmud no later than roughly 400 CE, in the Bavli (Babylonian) Talmud no later than roughly 500 CE and in the classic Midrashim no later than roughly 800 CE, but in all these works there are cases where traditions much earlier than their 'final' editing are recorded. Pseudepigraphy (i.e., the attribution of a tradition to a prominent earlier scholar in order to give it greater authority) seems to have been widespread in rabbinic literary culture. And we should also remember that later traditions (sometimes much later) have been interpolated into all these works.

The second reason why it is difficult to write a genuine history of Jewish–Christian relations on the basis of classic rabbinic sources is that we cannot always be sure that, when there *are* references to encounters with Christians in these, they ever actually took place. Anti-Christian polemic in the Talmud and related literature is as much aimed at internal consumption as it is at external. It is intended as much, if not more so, to strengthen the faith of *Jews* as it is to influence *Christians* and prove to them the error of their ways. Nevertheless, encounters did unquestionably take place, and we can be reasonably confident that the rabbinic evidence depicts accurately enough *the terms* on which they took place, even if the historicity of a specific incident may be open to question. We should also bear in mind that particularly in the earlier period (third to fourth century) the rabbis' Christian opponents are by and large *Jewish* Christians (i.e., Jewish believers in Jesus). These were seen as the real threat, in that they remained socially within the Jewish communities. From the fourth century onwards, however, Jewish Christianity went into serious decline, ground down between the upper millstone of triumphant gentile Christianity and the lower millstone of triumphant rabbinism (though it seems to have made a relatively short-lived comeback in the early Islamic period, seventh to eighth century). Later references to Christianity in rabbinic sources are more likely to relate to gentile Christianity.

Bibliography

Alexander, Philip, 'Types of Jewish Anti-Christian Polemic in Late Antiquity and the Middle Ages, and Their Historical-Social Setting', in Morlet, Sébastien (ed.), *Jewish–Christian Disputations in Late Antiquity and the Middle Ages: Fictions and Realities* (Leuven: Peeters, 2020), 215–28.

Avi-Yonah, Michael, *The Jews under Roman and Byzantine Rule: A Political History from the Bar Kokhba War to the Arab Conquest* (Jerusalem: Magnes Press, 1984).

Becker, Adam H., and Reed, Annette Y. (eds.), *The Ways That Never Parted: Jews and Christians in Late Antiquity and the Early Middle Ages* (Minneapolis: Fortress Press, 2007).

Boyarin, Daniel, *Border Lines: The Partition of Judaeo-Christianity* (Philadelphia: University of Pennsylvania Press, 2006).

Dunn, James D. G. (ed.), *Jews and Christians: The Parting of the Ways, A. D. 70 to 135* (Tübingen: Mohr Siebeck, 1992).

Goodman, Martin, *Rome and Jerusalem: The Clash of Ancient Civilizations* (London: Allen Lane, 2007).

Goodman, Martin, and Alexander, Philip (eds.), *Rabbinic Texts and the History of Late Roman Palestine* (Oxford: Oxford University Press, 2010).

Herford, R. Travers, *Christianity in Talmud and Midrash* (London: Williams and Norgate, 1903).

Katz, Steven T. (ed.), *Cambridge History of Judaism*, Vol. 4: *The Late-Roman Rabbinic Period* (Cambridge: Cambridge University Press, 2006).

Lazarus-Yafeh, Hava, Cohen, Mark R., Somekh, Sasson, and Griffith, Sidney H. (eds.), *The Majlis: Interreligious Encounters in Medieval Islam* (Wiesbaden: Harrasowitz, 1999).

Lieberman, Philip I. (ed.), *Cambridge History of Judaism*, Vol. 5: *Jews in the Medieval Islamic World*, (Cambridge: Cambridge University Press, 2021).

Neusner, Jacob, *A History of the Jews in Babylonia*, 5 vols (Leiden: Brill, 1965–70).

Yuval, Israel, *Two Nations in Your Womb: Perceptions of Jews and Christians in Late Antiquity and the Middle Ages* (Berkeley: University of California Press, 2006).

DOCUMENTS

All the documents in this chapter appear in the author's own translations, with the exception of documents 16 and 17.

I

b.Gittin 56b–57a: Jesus' Punishment in Hell

Text

Onqelos the son of Qaloniqos, the son of the sister of Titus, wanted to convert to Judaism. He went and brought up Titus [from the other world] by necromancy and asked him: 'Who is most important in that world?' Titus replied, 'Israel!' Onqelos asked: 'What, then, about joining them [here in this world]?' Titus replied: 'Their commandments are many, and you will not be able to fulfil them. [Rather,] go and fight against them in that world [on earth], and you will become the head, as it is written, *Her adversaries have become the head* (Lam. 1:5). Anyone who oppresses Israel will become the head.' Onqelos asked: 'What is the punishment of that man [= Titus] [in the other world]?' Titus replied: 'What he decreed against himself: every day his ashes are collected and they judge him, and they burn him, and they scatter his ashes [again] over the seven seas.'

Onqelos went and brought up Balaam by necromancy and asked him: 'Who is most important in that world?' Balaam replied: 'Israel!' Onqelos asked: 'What, then, about joining them?' Balaam replied: *'You shall not seek their peace nor their prosperity all the days'* (Deut. 23:7). Onqelos asked: 'What is the punishment of that man [= Balaam]?' Balaam replied: 'With boiling semen.'

Onqelos went and brought up Yeshu ha-Notzri by necromancy and asked him: 'Who is most important in that world?' Yeshu replied: 'Israel!' Onqelos asked: 'What, then, about joining them?' Yeshu replied: 'Seek their welfare, seek not their harm. Whoever touches them is as though he touches the apple of [God's] eye!' (cf. Zech. 2:8) Onqelos asked: 'What is the punishment of that man [= Yeshu]?' Yeshu replied: 'With boiling excrement.'

For the master has said: Whoever mocks the words of the Sages is punished with boiling excrement.

Come and see the difference between the sinners of Israel and the prophets of the nations!

Commentary

This text is found only in the Babylonian Talmud, and may date from the fifth century. Onqelos, the nephew of the Roman emperor Titus, contemplating conversion to Judaism, decides to conjure up three individuals from the other world to ask them about the status of Jews there. Clearly the status of Jews in this world is not high, but maybe it is different in the next? The three individuals were all great enemies of the Jewish people: Titus destroyed the Jerusalem temple in 70 CE; Balaam, the pagan prophet, tried to curse Israel

(Num. 22–4); and Jesus mocked the words of the sages. So their testimony to the exalted status of Israel in the afterlife is particularly impressive. In some printed editions the name Jesus is systematically replaced by 'sinners of Israel' – a secondary reading which arose through self-censorship in a Christian environment. The language is coarse and deliberately shocking: Christians claimed that Jesus was sitting in glory at God's right hand in heaven (Luke 24:51, etc.); here he is sitting in boiling excrement in hell.

The idea that the punishment of the damned in hell matches their sins is a commonplace of Jewish tours of hell literature (cf. Dante's *Inferno*), but whether this applies here and, if it does, what the correlation is, is not stated. Balaam was accused of leading the Israelites into sexual relations with Moabite women, and so into idolatry (Num. 25:1–3, 31:16), so the boiling semen in his case may be appropriate. b.Eruv. 21b threatens disrespectful students with being boiled in excrement, and on the basis of this a glossator here has identified Jesus' sin as mocking the words of the sages. In the Jewish anti-Gospel, the *Toledot Yeshu*, Jesus is represented as a precocious student who was disrespectful to the sages – an allusion, probably, to the Gospel story of the boy Jesus in the temple (Luke 2:41–52), but elsewhere he is accused of the more serious charge of performing magic and using it to lead the people into idolatry (document 13).

The Talmud comments with some surprise that Jesus advised seeking the welfare of Israel, though he was a sinner, and contrasts his attitude with that of Balaam, who was a pagan prophet. Balaam, of course, actually *blessed* Israel, but he was regarded in ancient Judaism as a singularly wicked man (cf. Rev. 2:14).

Bibliography

Babylonian Talmud Gittin: text and alternative translation available online at www.sefaria.org/Gittin.56b.18?lang=bi&with=all&lang2=en.

Himmelfarb, Martha, *Tours of Hell: An Apocalyptic Form in Jewish and Christian Literature* (Philadelphia: University of Pennsylvania Press, 1983).

Murcia, Thierry, *Jésus dans le Talmud et la littérature rabbinique ancienne* (Turnhout: Brepols, 2014), 577–610.

Schäfer, Peter, *Jesus in the Talmud* (Princeton and Oxford: Princeton University Press, 2007), 82–94.

2

t.Ḥull. 2:20–1: Social and Economic Ostracism of the Minim

Text

If meat is found in the hand of a gentile, it is permitted to derive benefit from it, but if it is found in the hand of a heretic (*min*), it is forbidden to derive benefit from it.

That which comes out of a house of idolatry [i.e., a pagan temple] – this is meat of 'sacrifices to the dead' (Ps. 106:28).

For they said: The slaughtering (*sheḥitah*) of the heretic (*min*) is idolatry; their bread is the bread of a Samaritan; their wine is the wine of libation; their fruits are untithed; their books are the books of diviners; and their children are tainted (*mamzerim*).

We do not sell to them, nor do we buy from them. We do not take from them, nor do we give to them. We do not teach their sons a craft. We are not healed by them, neither healing of property nor healing of life.

Commentary

This tradition comes from the Tosefta, a code of law compiled in the fourth century, but the situation it envisages should probably be dated to some time in the third, when pagan temples and sacrifices were still flourishing. Though the reasons for a number of the rulings are obscure, their general thrust is clear: they are intended to ostracise *minim* from Jewish society. That the *minim* were understood to include Christians is shown by the continuation of this passage (quoted as document 5 below), which relates an attempted healing in the name of Jesus, to illustrate the ruling 'We are not healed by them.'

Jewish Christians and Jews who acknowledged rabbinic authority lived cheek by jowl in the Galilee and some other parts of Palestine in the third century. They spoke the same language (Aramaic) and one would have expected the normal sorts of social and commercial relationships to have developed between them. The rabbis tried to prevent these, presumably because they were afraid that Christians might corrupt the community and lead them astray. With little power to expel them *by force*, the rabbis had to rely on putting them under a ban (*ḥerem*) – in other words, persuading Jews to boycott them – in the hope of making life so intolerable for Christians that they would be driven out of the neighbourhood. That the rabbis do not appeal to the tradition of zeal for the law within Judaism, which sanctioned individuals to use violence against Torah-breakers (cf. the action of Phinehas in Num. 25:6–13), may reflect the growing political power of Christianity.

The ban is comprehensive. As well as rejecting healing from Christians, it also covers eating with them, marrying them (their children are tainted – *mamzerim*), reading Christian books (which should be treated like books of magic, which is forbidden in Torah; see Deut. 18:9–14), engaging in commercial transactions with them, and accepting Christians' sons as apprentices (which would probably have involved them living in Jewish houses). In other words, Rabbinical Jews should have nothing whatsoever to do with Christians.

Where eating is concerned, the stress is on Jews not *accepting* Christian hospitality rather than offering food to them, though the latter may be implicit. That Christians did not keep *kashrut* (the Jewish food laws) to the level demanded by the rabbis is understandable. Thus, they would not have separated from their produce the priestly portion: this is duly mentioned with regard to 'fruit' ('their fruits are untithed'). It is also not hard to envisage a problem with bread, for example because of ingredients, unkosher conditions of preparation or failure to separate the priestly dough: Christian bread was supposed to be treated like the bread of a Samaritan (i.e., someone who would have claimed to be doing things correctly, but whose rigour was always, from a rabbinic perspective, viewed as suspect). Or was the issue that it might have been drawn from a batch from which communion bread had also been drawn? This may also have been the problem with Christian wine, though what is said about it and Christian meat remains rather more puzzling. While the problem with the latter has fundamentally to do with ritual slaughter (*sheḥitah*), the argument as it is presented here may be no more than a rhetorical flourish making the point that Christians should be treated with even greater suspicion than idolators.

Whatever the problems of interpretation, the general thrust of the ruling is clear: Jews should not eat or drink with Christians, and therefore that most basic form of social intercourse – commensality – is forbidden.

Bibliography

Tosefta Ḥullin: text and alternative translation available at www.sefaria.org/Tosefta_ Chullin.2.6?lang=bi (where the reference is given as Tosefta Chullin 2.6).

Alexander, Philip S., 'Jewish Believers in Early Rabbinic Literature', in Skarsaune, Oskar, and Hvalvik, Reidar (eds.), *Jewish Believers in Jesus: The Early Centuries* (Peabody: Hendrickson, 2007), 659–709.

Cheung, Alex T., *Idol Food in Corinth: Jewish Background and Pauline Legacy* (Sheffield: Sheffield Academic Press, 1999), esp. 39–81.

Schremer, Adiel, *Brothers Estranged: Heresy, Christianity and Jewish Identity in Late Antiquity* (New York: Oxford University Press, 2010).

3

The Benediction against the Heretics

Text

*(i) b.Ber. 28b–29a: The Origins of the Benediction against the Heretics (*Birkat ha-Minim*)*

Our Rabbis taught: Shimᶜon ha-Paqoli arranged the Eighteen Benedictions in order before Rabban Gamaliel at Yavneh. Rabban Gamaliel said to the Sages: 'Is there no one who knows how to compose a benediction against the heretics (*minim*)?' Shmu'el ha-Qatan stood up and composed it […].

(ii) A Palestinian Recension of the Benediction against the Heretics

For apostates (*meshummadim*) may there be no hope, and the arrogant kingdom (*malkhut zadon*) uproot speedily in our days. May the Christians (*Notzrim*) and the heretics (*minim*) perish in an instant. *May they be blotted out of the book of the living, and may they not be written with the righteous* (Ps. 69:29). Blessed are you, O Lord, who humbles the arrogant.

Source

Ehrlich, Uri, and Langer, Ruth, 'The Earliest Texts of the *Birkat Haminim*', *Hebrew Union College Annual* 76 (2005), 63–112 (esp. 99–100).

(iii) The Authorised Daily Prayer Book Recension of the Benediction against the Heretics

For slanderers (*malshinim*) may there be no hope. May all wickedness perish in an instant. May all your enemies be swiftly cut off. Uproot, smash, overthrow and humble swiftly in our days the arrogant kingdom. Blessed are you, O Lord, who breaks the enemies and humbles the arrogant.

Source

Singer, S. (trans.), *The Authorised Daily Prayer Book of the United Hebrew Congregations of the Commonwealth*, Centenary Edition (Cambridge: Press Syndicate of Cambridge University, 1992), 81. The translation is the author's.

Commentary

The twelfth benediction (known as the *Birkat ha-Minim*, the Benediction against the Heretics) of the statutory daily prayer, the Eighteen Benedictions or *Amidah*, has played a central role in Jewish–Christian relations, because it has been widely interpreted as marking a decisive moment in the parting of the ways between the two faiths. Its introduction has been seen as an attempt by the Jewish authorities (and specifically the rabbis) to exclude Christians from public worship in the synagogue. Every aspect of it has been subjected to intense scholarly debate. There can be no doubt that the text was seen within Jewish tradition as aimed at Christians, and they are explicitly mentioned (*Notzrim* = Nazarenes) in a Palestinian version of it (document 3 (ii)), alongside 'apostates' (*meshummadim*) and 'heretics' (*minim*). Whether the latter are synonyms for *Notzrim* in this setting or we have a broad category of unacceptable persons of whom 'apostates', 'Christians' and 'heretics' are subcategories is a moot point, but Christians are very definitely included. The much less specific term 'slanderers' (*malshinim*) in the Authorised Daily Prayer Book (document 3 (iii)) is a later innovation probably introduced to blur the anti-Christian references in earlier versions of the prayer. Christian censors enforced changes to the prayer from at least as early as the mid-sixteenth century, and many modern Jewish versions omit references to *minim*.

The benediction certainly originated in the Talmudic period, but when exactly is a matter of dispute. Talmudic tradition (document 3 (i)) claims it was introduced into the *Amidah* in the late first century CE, in the time of Gamaliel II, the grandson of Gamaliel I, with whom the apostle Paul is said to have studied (Acts 22:3; cf. 5:34). The context of its composition appears to be an attempt by the rabbis to reform Jewish prayer in the wake of the destruction of the temple and Jerusalem by the Romans in 70 CE. Elements of the *Amidah* can be traced back to the pre-70 period, but others are clearly post-destruction. The tradition of its origin only emerges in rabbinic literature hundreds of years after the events it is supposed to describe, but it is recorded as a tradition dating from before 200 CE, and the very obscurity of the otherwise unknown Shimᶜon ha-Paqoli (Simeon the Flax-dealer) and Shemu'el ha-Qatan (Samuel the Less), to whom it attributes the reform, rather speaks in favour of its antiquity. Someone making the story up would surely have chosen better-known names, and there were plenty to choose from in the Mishnah.

Certainly, aspects of the benediction would fit the late first century CE. The execration of Rome, under the title 'the arrogant kingdom', could reflect the widespread animosity towards Rome among Jews in the wake of the destruction of Jerusalem and the temple. There was an apocalyptic revival in Judaism at the end of the first century and early in the second. Apocalypses of the period, such as 4 Ezra, 2 Baruch and Sibylline Oracles 5, execrate Rome in language reminiscent of the *Birkat ha-Minim* and look forward to its imminent overthrow and the restoration of Jerusalem and the temple. But there is one aspect of the text which arguably does not fit this period, and that is its bundling up of the heretics with Rome as apparently *joint* objects of execration. This would certainly fit the fourth century onwards, when, to use a rabbinic phrase, 'the empire went over to heresy (*minut*)' and Christianity became closely identified with the Roman state, but it makes little sense in the late first century. Christians at that time were just as vehemently opposed to Rome as were Jews (see the blistering condemnation of Rome in Rev. 17–18). Perhaps we should resist the urge to see any link between the 'heretics' and 'the arrogant kingdom', other than that both are enemies of God.

The *Amidah* was a statutory prayer prayed both privately and with the congregation. The effect of introducing the revised version, with the additional Benediction against the Heretics, into public worship would have been dramatic. It would have made it impossible for those against whom it was targeted to take part in the service: they could hardly have said 'Amen' to a benediction which was meant to call down divine judgement on their heads. A possible way this might have worked is as follows. The public recitation of the *Amidah* would have been led by the prayer-leader (the *sheliah ha-tzibbur*). If he did not introduce the new benediction, rabbis and their supporters in the congregation would have interrupted him and refused to let the prayers continue till he did. The fact that the rabbis had to use such an oblique mechanism to influence the synagogue would fit with the early period, when their authority was still very limited. It also presupposes a time when Christians were still attending synagogues in some numbers – a situation which, at least in Palestine, had probably come to an end by the Bar Kokhba war (132–5). In some places in the Greek-speaking diaspora it continued much longer (see Chapter 2, p. 92). In the end, the recitation of the rabbinic form of the prayer became universal, both in public and in private, and served powerfully to police the boundaries between Judaism and 'heresy'. It is unclear whether the references in the Gospel of John (from the end of the first century; see Chapter 1, p. 60) to followers of Christ being 'put out of the synagogue' (9:22, 12:42, 16:2) might reflect the introduction of the *Birkat ha-Minim*, or simply the decision of individual *archisynagogoi* (synagogue leaders) who were opposed to the followers of Jesus. Early Christian writers (Justin Martyr, *c.* 100–*c.* 165; Epiphanius, 315–403; and Jerome, 342–420) appear to allude to the *Birkat ha-Minim*.

Bibliography

Bavli Berakhot: text and alternative translation available at www.sefaria.org/Berakhot.29a.2?lang=bi.

Langer, Ruth, *Cursing the Christians? A History of the Birkat Haminim* (Oxford: Oxford University Press, 2012).

Reif, Stefan C., *Judaism and Hebrew Prayer: New Perspectives on Jewish Liturgical History* (Cambridge: Cambridge University Press, 1993).

4

t.Ḥull. 2:24: Rabbi Eliezer Is Charged with Heresy

Text

It once happened that Rabbi Eliezer was arrested for words of heresy (*minut*). They brought him to the tribunal (*bēma*) for judgement. The magistrate (*hēgemōn*) said to him, 'Does an old man like you occupy himself with such things?' He said to him: 'Trustworthy is the judge concerning me.' The magistrate supposed that he was referring to him, but he was only thinking of his Father in Heaven. The magistrate said to him: 'Since you have declared me trustworthy concerning yourself, so I will prove to be. I said, Is it possible that these academies should err in this way? *Dimissus*, behold you are discharged.'

When he had been released from the tribunal, he was troubled because he had been arrested for words of heresy. His disciples came to console him, but he would not take comfort. Rabbi Aqiva came in and said to him: 'Rabbi, can I say something which may assuage your grief?' He said to him: 'Say on.' He said to him: 'Perhaps one of the heretics (*minim*) has said to you a word of heresy, and it has pleased you.' He said: 'By Heaven, you have reminded me! Once I was walking along the main street of Sepphoris, and I met Jacob of Kefar Sikhnin, and he said to me a word of heresy in the name of Yeshu ben Pantiri, and it pleased me. And so I was arrested for words of heresy, because I transgressed the words of Torah, *Keep your way far from her, and come not near the door of her house* (Prov. 5:8), *for she has cast down many wounded* (Prov. 7:26).'

Commentary

The incident is set in early second-century CE Palestine. The tribunal before which Rabbi Eliezer is brought is Roman, as can be seen by the fact that the magistrate is given a Roman title (*hēgemōn*) and he pronounces the acquittal in Latin – *Dimissus*. The background is the fact that Judaism was a legal religion in Roman law. The period in question was one of huge political tension between Jews and the Romans, reflected in the Jewish revolts under Trajan (115–17) and the Bar Kokhba war (132–5) under Hadrian. But despite this, Judaism was never proscribed by the Romans. It remained legal to practise it. The status of Christianity in Roman law was unclear, however. This is the period when Pliny the Younger was writing from Asia Minor to get Trajan's ruling on this very question (*Letters* 10.96). If the Christians were not a *Jewish* sect, then they could not claim protection as Jews. It would have been easy for the Jewish authorities or individual Jews to denounce Christians to the Romans as a threat to the state, and there were times, it seems, when they did. They had a ready case, in that the sect had been founded by someone whom the Romans had crucified as a criminal. The book of Acts in the New Testament has Paul hauled up before the provincial Roman authorities on a number of occasions. The incident in Corinth before the proconsul Gallio in Acts 18:1–17 offers particularly interesting parallels to our case here. Unlike Gallio, the Roman magistrate here seems to take it for granted that Christianity *is* illegal, so if Rabbi Eliezer were linked with it in some way, the consequences for him could have been severe, possibly even death. It is clear that the 'heresy' here *is* Christianity because of the reference to Jesus: Yeshu ben Pantiri is a rabbinical name for Jesus (see p. 115). The implication is that Rabbi Eliezer was informed against by a fellow Jew. Informing would have been deemed unacceptable in the Jewish community, particularly at a time of high political tension, but presumably happened. The exact nature of the charge, however, is unclear. The text simply says that he was arrested 'for words of heresy' (*'al divrei minut*).

The explanation is that in the main street of the Galilean town of Sepphoris, Rabbi Eliezer met Jacob of Kefar Sikhnin (a Christian mentioned elsewhere in rabbinic heresy stories, whose identity has been much discussed: cf. Jacob of Kefar Sama in document 5), 'and', says Eliezer, 'he said to me a word of heresy in the name of Yeshu ben Pantiri, and it pleased me'. The longer version of the story in the late work Eccl.R. actually gives the 'word' which Jacob said, and it turns out to be a perfectly innocuous interpretation of Deut. 23:19, with no Christian content whatsoever (Eccl.R. 1.8 §3). Simply expressing approval for an obscure halakhic ruling of Jesus is hardly the basis for so serious a charge, so Rabbi Eliezer must be envisaged as at least *repeating* the interpretation, perhaps in the name of Jesus. The magistrate dismisses the charge on the grounds that it is *a priori* highly unlikely that someone like Eliezer, who taught in the rabbinical academies, would be spreading Christianity. He takes for granted that the rabbis are implacably opposed to Christianity. The overall moral of the story is clear: don't get involved in conversation with Christians, above all not on matters of Torah, because you risk being denounced to the Roman authorities for supporting Christianity, and losing face within the Jewish community as well.

Bibliography

Tosefta Ḥullin: text and alternative translation available at www.sefaria.org/Tosefta_ Chullin.2.6?lang=bi (where the reference is given as Tosefta Chullin 2.6).

Alexander, Loveday, 'Silent Witness: Paul's Troubles with the Roman Authorities in the Book of Acts', in Puig i Tàrrech, Armand, Barclay, John M. G., and Frey, Jörg (eds.), *The Last Years of Paul: Essays from the Tarragona Conference, June 2013* (Tübingen: Mohr Siebeck, 2015), 153–73.

Linder, Amnon (ed. and trans.), *The Jews in Roman Imperial Legislation* (Detroit: Wayne State University Press, 1987).

Neusner, Jacob, *Eliezer ben Hyrcanus: The Tradition and the Man. Part I: The Tradition* (Leiden: Brill, 1973).

Neusner, Jacob, *Eliezer ben Hyrcanus: The Tradition and the Man. Part II: Analysis of the Tradition. The Man* (Leiden: Brill, 1973).

5
t.Ḥull. 2:22–3: Healing in the Name of Jesus

Text

The case of Rabbi Eleazar ben Damah, whom a serpent bit. There came in Jacob, a man of Kefar Sama, to cure him in the name of Yeshua ben Pandira, but Rabbi Ishmael did not allow it. He said: 'You are not permitted, Ben Damah.' He [Eleazar] said: 'I will bring you a proof that he may heal me.' But he had not finished bringing a proof when he died. Rabbi Ishmael said: 'Happy are you, Ben Damah, for you have departed in peace, and have not broken through the ordinances of the Sages; for upon everyone who breaks through the fence of the wise, punishment comes at last, as it is written, *Whoso breaks a fence, a serpent shall bite him* (Eccl. 10:8).'

Commentary

This story follows on directly from document 2, and illustrates the ruling made there that Jews should not accept healing from *minim*. The same story is retold with embellishments in other rabbinic sources and was clearly seen as paradigmatic. It is set in the early second century CE. Rabbi Ishmael was one of the great sages of that time; Eleazar b. Damah is more obscure, but according to one tradition he was Ishmael's nephew. A similar story of Christian healing is found in y.Shabb. 14.4 (8) (repeated in y.AZ 2:2 (7) and Qoh.R. 10.5 §1) involving the grandson of the late third-century Rabbi Joshua b. Levi, who had a choking fit and was cured by a Christian who 'whispered to him in the name of Yeshu Pandira' – to Joshua's disapproval. These stories suggest that Christian healers were working within Jewish communities. The Jacob mentioned in our story seems to have been rather famous. He is, perhaps, the same as Jacob of Kefar Sikhnin in document 4. Jewish texts have thus, ironically, preserved the name of a Christian healer.

Healing was associated with Christianity from the very outset. Jesus was a healer, and the Gospels (and, indeed, the *Toledot Yeshu*) are full of healing miracles that he performed. But his followers could also perform healings in his name (e.g., Acts 3:6), and this ability, in a world where people were subject to numerous illnesses they did not understand and had few medical resources to combat them, may have been a significant factor in the spread of Christianity. But therein, from the rabbinic perspective, lay the danger, for these cures could be seen as validating the Christian claims about Jesus: in the *Toledot Yeshu*, Jesus uses his healing miracles to convince the people of his divinity and so lead them astray. Ishmael holds that it is better for Eleazar to die than that he should be the means of lending credence to false claims about Jesus. Interestingly, Ishmael does not question Jacob's ability to perform the healing. Rather, his actions seem predicated on the fear that Jacob's cure just might work. By engaging Eleazar in halakhic debate he not only delays the proceedings till Eleazar expires, but he delays Jacob pronouncing the crucial words and so, possibly, effecting the cure. A similar attitude to Jesus' miracles is taken in the

Toledot Yeshu: they are acknowledged as real enough and attributed to Jesus' use of the power of the Ineffable Name of God.

Not surprisingly, the rabbinic text does not dwell on how Jacob effected the cure. In the story in y.Shabb. 14, the unnamed Christian healer 'whispers' to the boy in the name of Jesus. 'Whisper' here is a technical term for reciting an incantation. This might suggest an exorcism, and many Christian healings indeed involved exorcism (i.e., the driving out of demons identified as causing the illness), but the two conditions mentioned in our rabbinic stories – snakebite and a choking fit – are not obviously demon-induced. Incantation could, however, be used in such cases as well. M.Sanh. 10.1 forbids reciting Exod. 15:28 ('I am the Lord who heals you') as an incantation over a *wound*, and one of the most common Jewish amulets from antiquity is the scorpion amulet which contained spells against scorpion stings. There was a whole world of *Jewish* magic in antiquity. The rabbis frowned upon it but were not averse at times to practising it themselves. In the end it came down to who did it and what powers were invoked. For Ishmael and Joshua the nub of the problem was the fact that a *Christian* healer was involved and that he was invoking the name of Jesus.

Bibliography

Tosefta Ḥullin: text and alternative translation available online at www.sefaria.org/Tosefta_ Chullin.2.6?lang=bi (where the reference is given as Tosefta Chullin 2.6).

Bohak, Gideon, *Ancient Jewish Magic: A History* (Cambridge: Cambridge University Press, 2008).

MacMullen, Ramsay, *Christianizing the Roman Empire* (New Haven and London: Yale University Press, 1984).

Smith, Morton, *Jesus the Magician* (New York: Harper & Row, 1978).

6

Pesiqta Rabbati 5.2: Having the Written Torah Is Not Enough

Text

Rabbi Judah son of Rabbi Simon said: '*I have made a covenant with you* (Exod. 34:27). On what basis? On the basis of *write for yourself* and on the basis of *according to the mouth of these words* (Exod. 34:27). If you preserve all that is in writing in writing, and all that is by word of mouth by word of mouth, then I have made a covenant with you, but if you change what is by word of mouth into writing and what is in writing into word of mouth, then I have not made a covenant with you.'

Rabbi Judah son of Rabbi Shallum the Levite said: 'Moses requested that the Mishnah should also be put into writing, but the Holy One foresaw that the nations of the world (*'ummot*) would one day translate the Torah and read it in Greek, [...] and would then say: "*We* are Israel. *We* are the children of the Lord." And Israel would say: "No, *we* are the children of the Lord." And the scales would be evenly balanced. Then the Holy One will say to the nations, "Why are you claiming to be my children? I do not recognise as my child anyone who does not possess my mysteries (*mistirin* = Greek *musterion*)." They will say to him, "And what are your mysteries?" He will reply, "The Mishnah'" [...]

How do we know that this differentiates between Israel and the nations? Because it says, *Had I written down the fulness of my Torah for you* [i.e., the Oral as well as the Written Torah], *you would have been accounted strangers* (Hos. 8:12).

Source

Ulmer, Rivka, *A Synoptic Edition of Pesiqta Rabbati Based upon All Extant Manuscripts and the Editio Princeps*, vol. 1 (Lanham: University Press of America, 2009), 51 (Parma Ms).

Commentary

Much of the debate between Judaism and Christianity was fought over the correct interpretation of their shared scriptures, but there was tacit recognition on both sides that exegetical arguments on their own could seldom, if ever, be decisive. Experience showed that there always seemed to be the possibility of ingenious counter-argument. In fact, neither side seems ever to have won outright *any* exegetical argument, to the extent that one openly conceded that the other was right and changed its view. Exegetical proofs from scripture served as much to reassure one's own side as to refute the opposition. In the absence of clinching arguments, both sides resorted in the end to simply *asserting* that they were right. In Rabbinic Judaism this claim was made through the doctrine of the Two Torahs. According to this, Moses received from God on Sinai the Torah in two forms – one written and one oral. The latter gave the true interpretation of the former. The Written Torah was passed down in writing, and was embodied in the Torah scroll which was read in synagogue. The Oral Torah was passed down by word of mouth from Moses through (it was claimed) a secure and unbroken line of tradents, until it was received by the rabbis.

This is the background to our document. Here it is asserted by Rabbi Judah b. Simon, a Palestinian rabbi of the early fourth century, that the maintenance of the covenant between God and Israel depends on Israel preserving the Written Torah in writing and the Oral Torah orally. Rabbi Judah b. Shallum, a slightly later Palestinian authority, explained this by arguing that the mark of the true Israel is that she possesses the Oral Torah (here represented by its foundational document, the Mishnah). Moses wanted the Mishnah also to be in writing, but God foresaw that keeping it oral would one day serve to authenticate the true Israel. Gentile Christianity, here referred to as 'the nations of the world', would acquire the Written Torah in Greek, and on this basis claim to be Israel (see also document 8). The reference is to the Septuagint translation. A new Greek version, known as Aquila, was sponsored by the rabbis in the second century to replace the Septuagint. This was part of the strategy of the rabbinic movement in Palestine to encourage the public reading of the Torah in *Hebrew* in Greek-speaking synagogues: one had not fulfilled one's duty to hear the Torah unless one had heard it in Hebrew, though it was possible to accompany the Hebrew with a simultaneous oral translation (a *targum*). It became standard for Jews to argue that Christians had been seriously misled by the Septuagint in places, for example by its rendering of the Hebrew word *ʿalmah* in Isa. 7:14 with the Greek word *parthenos* ('virgin') (cf. Matt. 1:23) when it simply denotes a young woman of child-bearing age. However, the force of this argument was somewhat blunted by the fact that the rabbinic legend of the origin of the Septuagint (b.Meg. 9a–b) seems to imply that the translation was *inspired* (cf. the *Letter of Aristeas*).

Bibliography

Braude, William G. (trans.), *Pesikta Rabbati*, 2 vols (New Haven and London: Yale University Press, 1968).

Jaffee, Martin S., *Torah in the Mouth: Writing and Oral Tradition in Palestinian Judaism 200 BCE–400 CE* (Oxford: Oxford University Press, 2001).

Marcos, Natalio Fernández, *The Septuagint in Context: Introduction to the Greek Version of the Bible* (Leiden: Brill, 2001).

Wasserstein, Abraham, and Wasserstein, David J., *The Legend of the Septuagint: From Classical Antiquity to the Present Day* (Cambridge: Cambridge University Press, 2006).

7

The Status of the Gospels

Text

(i) t.Yad. 2:13: The Gospels Do Not 'Defile the Hands'

The Gospels (*gilyonim*) and the books of the heretics (*minim*) do not defile the hands. The Book of Ben Sira, and all books that were written from then on, do not defile the hands.

(ii) t.Shabb. 13(14):5: The Gospels Are Not to Be Saved from Destruction

The Gospels (*gilyonim*) and books of heretics (*minim*) are not saved but are left where they are to burn, they and their sacred names.

Rabbi Yose ha-Gelili says: 'On a weekday one cuts out their sacred names and hides them away and burns the rest.'

Rabbi Tarfon said: 'May I bury my sons [a favourite oath of Rabbi Tarfon: see b.BM 85a], if, were they to come into my hand, I did not burn them along with their sacred names. For if a pursuer were pursuing after me, I would enter a house of idolatry rather than enter their houses, because the idolators do not acknowledge him and then deny him, but *they* do acknowledge him and then deny him. Of them Scripture says: *Behind the door and the doorpost (mezuzah) you have set up your symbol* (Isa. 57:8).'

[…]

With regard to them Scripture says: *Do I not hate them, O Lord, who hate you? Do I not strive with those who rise up against you? I hate them with a perfect hatred; I count them as my enemies* (Ps. 139:20–1).

Just as they are not saved from a fire, so they are not saved from a cave-in, nor from water, nor from anything which would destroy them.

Commentary

Mainstream Christianity accepted the canonic scriptures of Judaism as God's Word: they became its Old Testament. But it added to them a Second Testament (the New Testament), comprising the Gospels, the Epistles and other writings, which had equal if not greater authority. These Christian scriptures posed a problem for the rabbinic authorities. What was their status within Judaism? They were simply rejected as Word of God. This answer is given in document 7 (i), but in a rather odd way. The Gospels are here referred to as *gilyonim*, a cacophemistic deformation of the Greek word for 'Gospel' – *euangelion*. Linked with this, 'the books of *minim*' here are probably the rest of the authoritative early Christian writings which made up the canon of the New Testament. This text is from the fourth century, a time when the New Testament canon was more or less fixed. Denying that these Christian writings 'defile the hands' was a technical rabbinic way of saying that they were not inspired by the Holy Spirit, or spirit of prophecy, and were therefore not Word of God. For reasons that are not entirely clear, if one touched the text of a Torah scroll, one's hands became ritually unclean. To say that another text, other than a Torah scroll, 'defiled the hands' in the same way was to elevate it to the same level of authority and sanctity.

A reason is given why the Gospels and other Christian writings cannot be inspired scripture. It is not because they contain false doctrine, though the rabbis believed they did. Rather, they are rejected on a technicality, so to speak: that they were written after the time that prophecy had ceased in Israel. It was fundamental to the rabbinic world view that prophecy had departed from Israel at a particular point in the past, and authority had passed from the inspired prophets to the scribes, the authoritative interpreters of the prophetic writings. The rabbis used this principle to define their canon of scripture. Only books written before the end of prophecy could be allowed into the canon (though not every text from that period automatically became canonic: this was a necessary but not a sufficient condition). Any work written after the end of prophecy by definition could not be part of Holy Writ. The rabbis were a little vague about when prophecy had ceased. Some defined it externally as the time of Alexander the Great, so in the fourth century BCE. Here it is defined by an internal event – the appearance of the *Wisdom of Ben Sira* (Ecclesiasticus), which was written in the second century BCE. What was very clear was that the Gospels and other early Christian writings fell well after the end of prophecy and so could not, contrary to Christian claims, be accepted as Word of God.

But that was not the end of the matter. The Christian scriptures contained extensive quotations from the Jewish scriptures, and those quotations could have contained the names of God. Didn't that mean that they had to be treated with a certain care and reverence? This is the problem that underlies document 7 (ii). It poses the question in terms of what one should do if copies of these Christian writings were in danger of being destroyed – say by a fire, the collapse of a house, a flood or some other natural disaster. If a Torah scroll were put in such jeopardy one should be prepared to risk one's life to save it, but not so a copy of the Gospels: one should allow it to be destroyed, sacred names and all. If the Gospels were to come into one's possession, then Rabbi Tarfon says they should be burned. Rabbi Yosei ha-Galili offers a variation on this: one should cut out their sacred names and hide them away to rot of their own accord (this was allowed), but burn the rest. But, of course, one should only do this on a weekday, because cutting and burning are not allowed on the sabbath.

These arguments are more rhetorical than practical, because sacred names were sacred only if written in Hebrew, and Christians actually do not seem to have written their scriptures in Hebrew. There are traditions that the Gospel of Matthew was originally in Hebrew, but the other Gospels were composed in Greek, and the native Christian communities of Palestine and Syria seem to have read their Bible – both Old and New Testament – in Aramaic. Deep hostility towards Christians comes out in the quotation of Ps. 139:20–1 and in Rabbi Tarfon's statement that he would rather take refuge in a pagan temple than a church because pagans don't pretend to worship the God of Israel, whereas Christians do. They are worse than idolators because they are more likely to lead Jews astray. Their churches look innocent enough. It is only when you go inside them that you see the Christian symbols. Isa. 57:8 is quoted elsewhere in rabbinic literature to denote people who conceal their idolatrous practices behind closed doors. One would naturally take the 'symbol/memorial' here as a reference to a cross.

Bibliography

Tosefta Yadayim: text (only) available at www.sefaria.org/tsefta_yadayim.2.5?lang=bi (where the reference is given as Tosefta Yadayim 2:5).

Tosefta Shabbat: text (only) available at www.sefaria.org/Tosefta_Shabbat.14.4?lang=bi (where the reference is given as Tosefta Shabbat 14:4).

Alexander, Philip S., and Kaestli, Jean-Daniel (eds.), *The Canon of Scripture in Jewish and Christian Tradition. Le canon des Écritures dans les traditions juive et chrétienne* (Lausanne: Éditions du Zèbre, 2007).

Cook, L. Stephen, *On the Question of the 'Cessation of Prophecy' in Ancient Judaism* (Tübingen: Mohr Siebeck, 2011).

Leiman, Sid Z., *The Canonization of Hebrew Scripture: The Talmudic and Midrashic Evidence* (Hamden: Archon Books, 1976).

8

Sifrei Deuteronomy 312 (Deut. 32:9) and Sifrei Deuteronomy 308 (Deut. 32:5): God's Choice of Israel Is Not Negated by Israel's Sin

Text

(312) *For the portion of the Lord is his people* (Deut. 32:9). A parable: A king had a field which he gave to tenant farmers. The tenants began stealing from it, so he took it away from them and gave it to their sons. But they began to behave worse than their fathers, so he took it from the sons and gave it to the sons of the sons. But these behaved even worse than their

forebears. When a son was born to him, he said to them, 'Get out of my property! You can't stay here. Give me back my portion, so that I may acknowledge it as my own.'

So, when Abraham our father came into the world, dross [i.e., unworthy offspring] issued from him – Ishmael and all the sons of Keturah. When Isaac came into the world, dross issued from him – Esau and all the princes of Edom. And they became worse than their forebears. But when Jacob came into the world, he did not produce dross; rather all the sons born to him were worthy, as it is said, *And Jacob was a perfect man, dwelling in tents* (Gen. 25:27).

When did God acknowledge his portion as his own? From Jacob onwards, as it is said, *For the portion of the Lord is his people, Jacob the lot of his inheritance* (Deut. 32:9); and it also says, *For the Lord has chosen Jacob unto Himself* (Ps. 135:4).

(308) *Is corruption God's? No, to his sons belongs the blemish* (Deut. 32:5). Even though they are full of blemishes, they are still called 'sons', as it is said, *To his sons belongs the blemish*. This is the opinion of Rabbi Meir, but Rabbi Judah says: 'They have no blemishes, as it is said, *His sons have no blemish* [Deut. 32:5 read differently].'

So too, Scripture says, *A seed of evil-doers, sons who deal corruptly* (Isa. 1:4). If they are still called 'sons' when they deal corruptly, how much more so, if they did not deal corruptly.

Similarly, *They are wise to do evil* (Jer. 4:22). Is there not an argument *a fortiori* here? If they are still called 'wise' when they do evil, how much more so, if they did good.

Similarly, *They are stupid sons* (Jer. 4:22): if they are still called 'sons' when they are stupid, how much more so, if they were understanding.

Similarly, *And they come to you as a people comes, and sit before you as my people, and hear your words* (Ezek. 33:31), and lest you think that they both hear and do them, the text goes on to say, *but do them not*. Is there not an argument *a fortiori* here? If they are still called 'my people' when they hear but do not do, how much more so if they heard and did.

Commentary

Neither of these passages explicitly mentions Christianity, but close reading shows that they have Christianity in view, and specifically its claim to be the true Israel and the spiritual heir of the promises to Abraham. No other group at this time would have been questioning the right of the Jewish people to be the heir of these promises. As we noted in the Introduction to this chapter (see p. 115), this obliqueness, this refusal to name the opponent and so give him the oxygen of publicity, is typical of the rabbinic dialogue with Christianity. Both passages come from Sifrei to Deuteronomy, a composite, exegetical midrash on large portions of the biblical book of Deuteronomy, both the legal and the non-legal. The text in the manuscripts is rather unstable and it is difficult to assign a precise date to any given unit, but it is probably safe to assume that the two units quoted here are no later than the third century CE. They reflect a growing awareness among the rabbis of Christian attempts to appropriate the status of the true Israel and to prove that claim from scripture.

The doctrine that those who believed in Christ (whether Jew or gentile) were the heirs of the promises to Abraham and that they constituted the true Israel, the Israel of God, was adumbrated by Paul in Gal. 3 (see Chapter 1, p. 23) and more fully worked out in Rom. 4 in relation to God's promise to make Abraham a 'father of many nations' (Rom. 4:16f) and in Rom. 9 (see Chapter 1, p. 29). It formed the cornerstone of the supersessionist claims of the church and is developed in the *Epistle of Barnabas* (see Chapter 2, p. 71), Justin Martyr (see Chapter 2, p. 75) and other early Christian apologists. It is this teaching that the midrash has in mind. It argues its point through a parable – a typical mode of teaching for the rabbis, as it was for Jesus. The argument in the first passage (312) takes as its starting-point Deut. 32:9, *the portion of the Lord is his people*, and it raises the question of when Israel became the Lord's 'portion' (i.e., his chosen people). It concludes that this happened in the time of Jacob, not in the time of Isaac or Abraham. Only Jacob is recognised as God's son, and so worthy to inherit the field on a permanent basis. Abraham and Isaac were only tenants, who forfeited their tenancy because they produced unworthy offspring. The argument is somewhat startling, and risky, in a rabbinic context – a sign, perhaps, that it is being dictated by polemic concerns – but the basic point was important to the rabbis: God's sons are the descendants of Jacob, not the sons of Abraham, whether literal or spiritual.

The second passage (308) deploys a series of arguments *a fortiori* – a mode of argument much used by the rabbis. They are based on the simple observation that even in those passages of scripture where the Israelites are being castigated for their sins, God still refers to them as his 'sons' or his 'people': if when they hear the Torah and do *not* do it, they are still called God's people, *how much more* are they his people when they hear and do! The implication is that Israel's sin cannot finally break the bond of the covenant and lead to Israel's rejection, as Christians argued it did. For Christians the ultimate sin was the rejection of Jesus as the messiah.

Bibliography

Sifrei Deuteronomy (Devarim): text and alternative translation available at www.sefaria.org/ sifrei_devarim.312.1?lang=bi (first passage) and www.sefaria.org/sifrei_devarim.308.1?lang=bi (second passage).

Hammer, Reuven (trans.), *Sifre: A Tannaitic Commentary on the Book of Deuteronomy* (New Haven and London: Yale University Press, 1986).

Mihaly, Eugene, 'A Rabbinic Defense of the Election of Israel: An Analysis of Sifre Deuteronomy 32:9, Pisqa 312', *Hebrew Union College Annual* 35 (1964), 103–43.

Simon, Marcel, *Verus Israel: A Study of the Relations between Christians and Jews in the Roman Empire, AD 135–425* (London: publ. for the Littmann Library of Jewish Civilization by Oxford University Press, 1996).

9

The Status of the Torah

Text

(i) Targums to Deut. 5:22 (19): God Did Not Cease Speaking at Sinai

Onqelos: 'These words the Lord spoke to all your assembly on the mountain, from the midst of the fire, the cloud and the mist, in a mighty voice, and he ceased not. And he wrote them on two tablets of stone and gave them to me.'

Neofiti 1: 'These words the Lord spoke to all your assembly on the mountain, from the midst of the flames of fire, from the cloud and the darkness, in a mighty voice, and he ceased not. And he wrote them on two tablets of stone, and he gave them to me.'

Pseudo-Jonathan: 'These words the Lord spoke to all your assembly on the mountain, from the midst of the fire, the cloud and the mist, in a mighty voice, that did not cease. And that which the Dibbur (the Divine Word) spoke was found written on two tablets of marble, and he gave them to me.'

(ii) Song of Songs Rabbah 5:14 §2: The Special Laws Were on the Two Tablets

Hananiah the son of the brother of Rabbi Joshua said: 'Between every two commandments [on the Two Tablets of the Law] were written the sections and details of the Torah.' Rabbi Yoḥanan, when he was studying Scripture and he came to this verse, *Set with beryl* (Song 5:14), he used to say: 'Well did the son of the brother of Rabbi Joshua teach me this: Just as with the waves of the sea, between every two large waves there are small waves, so between every two commandments [on the Two Tablets] the sections and details of the Torah were written.'

(iii) y.Ber. 1:5 (4): The Decalogue Removed from the Liturgy to Avoid Misunderstanding

Rav Mattanah and Rabbi Samuel bar Naḥman used to say: 'It would have been proper to recite the Ten Commandments every day. So why does one not recite them? Because of the claim of the heretics (*minim*) – so that they should not say, "These alone were given to Moses on Sinai."'

Commentary

Mainstream Christianity was determined to appropriate as its own the scriptures of Israel, and it was therefore important that it could prove that those scriptures foretold the coming of Jesus and the fuller revelation he brought, that the new covenant in Christ was the realisation – 'fulfilment' was a favoured term (see, e.g., Mark 14:49; Matt. 5:17; Luke 24:44; John 13:18) – of the promises of the old covenant to Israel. The rabbis would have none of this: the Torah, given to Israel at Sinai through the mediation of Moses, was given for all time: it would never be superseded or abrogated. These competing claims involved Judaism and Christianity in a profound exegetical controversy, as each side tried to justify their contradictory readings of their shared scripture from scripture itself. Central to this debate was the status of the Torah of Moses. Christianity claimed that it had been abrogated (see, e.g., Heb. 8:7–13). Radical, antinomian Christianity (e.g., Marcionism and other forms of Gnosticism) argued that it had been *totally* abrogated. Some even argued that the God of the Old Testament was a lesser divine being and not the God and father of Jesus Christ. But orthodox Christianity came down firmly, in the end, in favour of identifying the God of the old and the God of the new covenants. It also rejected total abrogation. It drew a distinction between the moral laws and the ritual laws of the Torah of

Moses. The former, which Christians identified with the Ten Commandments, remained eternally valid; it was the latter, which included all the laws regulating the Levitical system of priesthood and sacrifice, that had been abolished (see Irenaeus, *Against Heresies* 4.16, and Chapters 1 and 2).

One rather telling exegetical argument which the Christians deployed turned on Deut. 5:22 ('These words the LORD spoke with a loud voice to your whole assembly at the mountain, out of the fire, the cloud, and the thick darkness, and he added no more. He wrote them on two stone tablets and gave them to me' (NRSVue)), which they read as saying that only the Ten Commandments were actually spoken to Israel directly by God, in his own voice. The rest were spoken to Moses, who then mediated them to Israel. But if only the Ten Commandments were spoken in God's own voice directly to the people, this, argued the Christians, set them apart from the other commandments, and the difference was that they were eternal, whereas the others were transitory. This view was rejected by the early Jewish Aramaic translations of the Bible, known as the Targums. These were used during our period to render simultaneously the Torah lections in the synagogue, which were read in the original Hebrew, into the vernacular Aramaic. All the Targums read the crucial words 'and he added no more' as 'and he did not cease [speaking]' (document 9 (i)). In other words, the remaining commandments were also said by God, only they were no longer conveyed directly to the people. The fact that all three Targums agree on this point shows the interpretation was widespread and very old.

This raised the question of the relationship between the Ten Commandments (the Decalogue) and the remaining commandments of the Torah. One solution was to see the Decalogue as a summary of the general moral principles that lay behind the specific laws. This was the position adopted by the first-century CE Alexandrian Jewish philosopher Philo (in his treatise *On the Decalogue*). He regarded the Ten Commandments as summaries (*kephalaia*) of what he called 'the special laws' (i.e., the non-Decalogue commandments of the Torah) and he tried to show how each special law was a practical outworking of one of the Ten Commandments. A similar view is taken by document 9 (ii), which is found in the eighth-century Midrash on the Song of Songs. There it is claimed that if one had looked closely at the Two Tablets of the Law (on which the Ten Commandments were inscribed) one would have found 'the sections and details of the Torah' (= Philo's special laws) written in small letters between them. It was like the waves of the sea: just as between one large wave and the next there are many small ripples, so between the large lines of the Decalogue were the smaller lines of the remaining laws. The integration and unity of the Decalogue and the Special Laws, which Christians tried to force apart, could not be asserted in more graphic terms.

The rabbis were sufficiently worried by the attempt to suggest that the Decalogue was the true, eternal Law, whereas the Special Laws (which included all the ritual laws) had a lesser status, that they forbade the venerable practice of reciting the Ten Commandments as part of the daily prayers. The reason given for discontinuing it deserves careful parsing: 'so that they [the *minim*] should not say, "These alone were given to Moses on Sinai."'

The language, if pressed, seems to imply that the special laws were *not* given to Moses on Sinai, but that he made them up! The people heard the Ten Commandments for themselves and so could verify that they came from God. But they did not hear the remaining commandments, and so could not be sure that Moses had not fabricated or doctored them. And this is precisely the charge that the Midrash lays at the door of Korah, who rebelled against Moses in the wilderness (Num. 16:1–35). In one midrash he says to Moses: 'When the Ten Commandments were given to us, every one of us was imbibing [directly] from Mount Sinai. But about dough-offering, heave-offering, tithes and fringes we have heard only from yourself. You have spoken in order to establish rulership for yourself and glory for Aaron your brother' (Yelammedenu Midrash published by Grünhut in *Sefer Liqqutim*; cf. y.Sanh. 10:1 (17); Num.R. 18:3; Midrash Proverbs to Prov. 11:27). Now this is a more radical position even than the standard Christian view. The latter would have accepted that the special laws *were* given by God, but that they were transitory and belonged to the old dispensation. What remained was the eternal, moral law of the Decalogue. The position reflected in document 9 (iii) and the Yelammedenu Midrash is more compatible with the views of antinomian, 'liberal' Jews, who wanted to ditch the ritual laws and live by the Ten Commandments alone, and who took the radical line that the ritual laws were *never* given by God. This might suggest that in *minim* here, Christians are not primarily in view. However, the Christians agreed with these *minim* in making a distinction between the Decalogue and the Special Laws, and the arguments which the rabbis deployed against the *minim* would have applied equally to them. And it is not impossible that some *Gnostic* Christians would have taken the more radical line adopted by the *minim* here. This would be a second case where controversy with the *minim* forced a significant change in the liturgy, the other being the insertion into the daily prayer of the Benediction against the Heretics (see documents 3 (i), (ii) and (iii)).

Bibliography

The texts of the Targums are available online on the website of the *Comprehensive Aramaic Lexicon*: https://cal.huc.edu.

The Targums are also translated with notes in the *Aramaic Bible*, ed. Martin J. McNamara, 22 vols. (Collegeville: Liturgical Press, 1990–2007).

Song of Songs (Shir HaShirim) Rabbah: text and alternative translation available at www.sefaria.org/Shir_HaShirim_Rabbah.5.14.2?lang=bi&with=all&lang2=en.

Jerusalem Talmud Berakhot: text and alternative translation available at www.sefaria.org/jerusalem_talmud_berakhot.1.5.4?lang=bi&with=all&lang2=en.

Flesher, Paul V. M., and Chilton, Bruce, *The Targums: A Critical Introduction* (Waco: Baylor University Press, 2011).

Heinemann, Isaac, *Reasons for the Commandments in Jewish Thought: From the Bible to the Renaissance*, trans. Leonard Levin (Brighton, MA: Academic Studies Press, 2008).

Urbach, Ephraim E., 'The Role of the Ten Commandments in Jewish Worship', in *Collected Writings in Jewish Studies*, ed. Robert Brody and Moshe D. Herr (Jerusalem: Magnes Press, 1999), 289–317.

Vermes, Geza, 'The Decalogue and the Minim', in *Post-Biblical Jewish Studies* (Leiden: Brill, 1975), 169–77.

10

Book of Zerubbavel (Sefer Zerubbavel): *Armilos and the Messiah ben David*

Text

There I continued to ask about the prince of the holy covenant (Dan. 11:22). He [Metatron/ Michael] held me fast, and brought me to a house of disgrace and scorn. He showed me there a marble stone in the shape of a virgin, and her appearance and form were fair, and most beautiful to behold. [I asked him, 'Tell me who is this?'] He answered and said to me, 'This stone is the wife of Belial. Satan will come and lie with her, and a son named Armilos will come forth from her (which means [in Greek] "Desolator of People", and in Hebrew […]). [?] He will rule over all, and his dominion will reach from one end of the earth to the other. Ten letters will be in his hand. He will worship foreign gods […] No one will be able to stand before him. Anyone who does not believe in him he will slay by the sword […] He will attack the people of the holy ones of the Most High (Dan. 7:27), and there will be with him ten kings, wielding force and great power. He will wage war on the holy ones and destroy them. He will slay the Messiah son of Joseph, that is Neḥemiah b. Ḥushi'el, and sixteen righteous men will be slain with him. They will exile Israel to the wilderness in three companies. But Hephzibah, the mother of Menaḥem b. ᶜAmmi'el, will stand at the eastern gate [of Jerusalem] so that the Wicked One may not enter there, in order to fulfil that which is written: *"But the rest of the people will not be cut off from the city"* (Zech. 14:2).

'This war will take place in the month of Av, and there will be distress in Israel such as was never before. They will flee to castles, mountains and caves, but they will not be able to hide from Armilos. All the nations of the world will go astray after him, except for Israel, who will not believe in him. All Israel will mourn Neḥemiah b. Ḥushi'el for forty days. His corpse will be thrown down mangled before the gates of Jerusalem, but no wild beast, nor bird nor animal will desecrate it. Then the Children of Israel will cry out to the Lord on account of the great oppression and deep distress, and the Lord will answer them.' […]

I continued to question him, saying to him, 'My Lord Metatron, when will the light of Israel come?' […] And Michael, who is Metatron, said to me, '[…] Menaḥem b. ᶜAmmi'el will come suddenly in the first month, the month of Nisan, on the fourteenth day of the month, and he will stand in the valley of Arbel, which belongs to Joshua b. Jehozadak the high priest. All the Sages of Israel who survive – for only a few will survive the onslaught and plunder of Gog and Armilos, and of the plunderers who despoiled them – will go out to him. Menaḥem b. ᶜAmmi'el will say to the Elders and Sages, "I am the Messiah of the Lord, who has sent me to bring you good tidings, and to save you from the hand of these your foes". But the Elders will look at him and despise him, for they will see a contemptible person in worn-out clothes, and they will despise him just as you did. Then the Messiah's anger will burn within him, and garments of vengeance will he don as his dress, and wrap himself in a mantle of zeal (Isa. 59:17).

'Then he will go to the gates of Jerusalem, [and Elijah the prophet will come with him, and they will awaken and revive Nehemiah b. Hushi'el who is being mourned at the gates of Jerusalem]. Then Hephzibah, the mother of the Messiah, will come and hand over to him the staff with which the signs are performed. All the Elders of Israel will go and the Children of Israel will see that Nehemiah is alive and standing on his feet. At once they will believe in the Messiah. [...]

'Then the Lord's Messiah, that is, Menahem b. ʿAmmi'el, will come, and he will breathe on Armilos' face and slay him (Isa. 42:13). ... There will be a helmet of salvation on his head (Isa. 59:17) and he will don armour to make war against Gog and Magog and the forces of Armilos. They will all fall dead in the Valley of Arbel [...]

'After all this, Menahem b. ʿAmmi'el will come, and Nehemiah b. Hushi'el and all Israel with him. All the dead will come back to life, and Elijah the prophet will be with them. They will go up to Jerusalem, and in the month of Av, during which they mourned Nehemiah and in which Jerusalem was laid waste, there will be great joy for Israel. They will offer sacrifices to the Lord, and the Lord will accept them. The offering of Israel will be as pleasing to the Lord as it was before, in ancient times (Mal. 3:4). The Lord will smell the sweet savour of his people Israel's sacrifices, and rejoice greatly. Then the Lord will bring down to earth the Temple [literally, 'the House'] that is built above, and the pillar of fire and the cloud of incense will ascend to heaven. The Messiah will go forth, and all Israel after him on foot, to the gates of Jerusalem. And the holy God will stand on the Mount of Olives. His awe and his glory will rest upon the heavens and the heavens of heavens, upon the whole earth and the depths beneath it, upon walls and buildings to their very foundations. All will hold their breath when the Lord God reveals himself before them on the Mount of Olives. The Mount of Olives will split beneath him (Zech. 14:4). The exiles of Jerusalem will ascend the Mount of Olives, and Zion and Jerusalem will see and say, "Who begot these for us? And where have these been?" (Isa. 49:21). Then Nehemiah and Zerubbavel will answer Jerusalem and say to her, "Behold your children whom you bore, but who went into exile from you. Rejoice greatly, daughter of Zion!"'

Source

Bodleian Library, Oxford, Ms Heb.d.11 (2797), with emendations.

Commentary

Judaism and Christianity share a similar view of historical time. They both believe that history is moving forward under God's providential guidance to a grand climax in which God's purpose in creation will be finally realised, God's kingdom will come. This idea, first adumbrated by the ancient Hebrew prophets, was elaborated by the apocalyptic writers of the late Second Temple period, around the time of the Maccabean Revolt (which began 167 BCE). They drew up complex scenarios of the end of history and the coming of the kingdom. Christianity was born in this apocalyptic milieu, and took over its key ideas.

Jesus came preaching the imminent arrival of the kingdom (Mark 1:15; Matt. 3:2, 4:17, 10:7, 12:28; Luke 10:9, 17:21, 21:31) and was regarded by his followers as the messiah, the Christ, God's special agent for bringing the kingdom in. Jesus was crucified, but that did not falsify his messiahship. Rather, Christians claimed, his death was God's paradoxical way of inaugurating the kingdom. He rose from the dead, ascended to heaven, leaving behind the church to continue his mission. From heaven he would descend at the end of time to complete the work of establishing God's kingdom on earth. Judaism also retained the apocalyptic vision of Second Temple times, and looked forward to and prayed for the coming of a messiah who would establish God's kingdom on earth. There was, then, a high degree of general convergence between the eschatological hopes of Christianity and Judaism. But there were also irreconcilable differences in detail. The most fundamental of these was the identity of the messiah. Christians believed that Jesus of Nazareth was the messiah, who had come and would come again. Jews vehemently denied this: the messiah would be someone else, who was yet to come.

Numerous visions of the end have been developed within Judaism, but a sort of standard scenario began to emerge in the sixth to eighth centuries CE. This was a period of intense eschatological speculation not only in Judaism, but also in Christianity, in Zoroastrianism and in the newly emergent Islam. People believed that they were living at the end of history, that the end of the world was at hand. The key Jewish eschatological text of this period is the *Book of Zerubbavel*, an apocalypse in Hebrew probably composed in the early seventh century CE. It was supposedly revealed by the archangel Metatron to Zerubbavel, the leader of the Jews who returned to Judea after the decree of Cyrus in 538 BCE, which ended the Babylonian exile. The text as we now have it has been reworked over time, and this has resulted in a certain amount of muddle, repetition and confusion. What is most remarkable about it is how little it owes to the earlier Jewish apocalyptic tradition (apart from some broad, framework ideas). Close reading suggests that it has been strongly influenced by Christian apocalyptic of the Byzantine era. It has been constructed to counter-narrate key elements of the Christian eschatological scenario of that period. So, it introduces into Jewish apocalyptic for the first time the figure of Armilos. He is clearly a sort of antichrist figure. His miraculous birth from a statue of the Virgin Mary and the Devil clearly parodies the Virgin Birth of Christ, but he is not Christ. Rather he corresponds to the figure of the last Roman emperor who plays a key role in contemporary Christian apocalyptic (see, e.g., the Apocalypse of Pseudo-Methodius). This claimed that at the end of history there would arise one last, great Christian Roman emperor who would conquer the whole world, but then, in Jerusalem, solemnly hand his empire over to Christ. Armilos in the *Book of Zerubbavel* is the enemy of the true messiah and the true messiah will in the end destroy him.

Another striking innovation in the *Book of Zerubbavel* is the figure of Hephzibah, the mother of the true messiah. She is modelled on the Virgin Mary, who in Byzantine tradition was seen as the defender of Constantinople, in the way that Hephzibah defends Jerusalem in our excerpt. The *Book of Zerubbavel* has two messiahs – the messiah son of Joseph, who is given the precise name of Nehemiah son of Ḥushi'el, and the messiah son of David, who has the name Menaḥem son of ᶜAmmi'el. The idea of a messiah son of Joseph alongside a messiah son of David goes back to earlier Jewish tradition, but how far back it goes is much debated. In the *Book of Zerubbavel* the messiah son of Joseph is killed by Armilos, but then the messiah son of David kills Armilos and resurrects the messiah son of Joseph. The two messiahs go up and restore Jerusalem and its Temple, and the Jewish exiles are gathered in.

Eschatology has played an important role in Jewish–Christian relations down the centuries. The elements of convergence between the two eschatologies have led to some remarkable instances of collaboration. For example, in modern times Jews and Christians have cooperated in philanthropic and political causes because each saw themselves as having a shared duty to work to bring in God's kingdom of justice and peace on earth. Jews traditionally believed that the prophecies of the ancient Hebrew prophets envisaged that one day the Jewish people would come back from exile and refound a sovereign state of Israel in their old homeland. Christians traditionally regarded those prophecies as being fulfilled *spiritually*, not literally, in the Christian church, the New Israel. But in modern times some Christians, known as Christian Zionists (see Chapters 6 and 9), have taken these promises literally, and this has led them to offer strong support to the present-day State of Israel, seen as 'the beginning of the redemption', if not the redemption itself. But by and large Jewish and Christian eschatologies have been competitive, with one firmly negating the other.

Bibliography

Text of *Sefer Zerubbavel*: Lévi, Israel, 'L'apocalypse de Zorobabel et le roi de Perse Siroès', *Revue des Études Juives* 68 (1914), 129–60; 69 (1915), 108–21; 71 (1920), 57–65.

Alternative translation of *Sefer Zerubbavel*: Reeves, John C., *Trajectories in Near Eastern Apocalyptic: A Postrabbinic Jewish Apocalypse Reader* (Atlanta: Society of Biblical Literature, 2005), 40–66.

Alexander, Philip, 'Eschatology in the Apocalyptic Revival in Judaism (Sixth to Ninth Centuries CE) in Its Historical Context', in Marlow, Hilary, Pollmann, Karla, and Van Noorden, Helen (eds.), *Eschatology in Antiquity: Forms and Functions* (London and New York: Routledge, 2021), 576–88.

Amirav, Hagit, Grypeou, Emmanouela, and Stroumsa, Guy (eds.), *Apocalypticism and Eschatology in Late Antiquity: Encounters in the Abrahamic Religions, 6th–8th Centuries* (Leuven: Peeters, 2017).

Himmelfarb, Martha, *Jewish Messiahs in a Christian Empire: A History of the Book of Zerubbabel* (Cambridge, MA: Harvard University Press, 2017).

11

Pesiqta Rabbati 36–7: The Suffering Messiah

Text

36. What is meant by, *In your light shall we see light* (Ps. 36:10)? What is the light that the congregation of Israel looks for? It is the light of the Messiah, as it is written, *And God saw the light that it was good* (Gen. 1:4). This teaches that the Holy One, blessed be he, foresaw

the Messiah and his works before the world was created, and hid away the Messiah and his generation beneath his Throne.

Satan said before the Holy One: 'Master of the World, for whom is the light which has been hidden beneath your Throne of Glory?' He said: 'For him who will turn you back and put you to shame.' Satan said: 'Master of the World, show him to me!' He said to him: 'Come and see him.' When he saw him, Satan trembled and fell upon his face and said: 'Surely this is the Messiah who will cause me and all the angelic princes of the nations of the world to fall into Gehinnom!' [...]

The Holy One, blessed be he, told the Messiah what would befall him [if the world were created. He said]: 'Those souls that are hidden away with you [beneath my Throne] – it is their sins that will put a yoke of iron round your neck, and make you like a calf whose eyes grow dim, and choke your spirit with a yoke, and because of their sins, *your tongue will cleave to the roof of your mouth* (Ps. 22:15). Are you willing to endure this?'

The Messiah said before him: 'Will my suffering last many years?' The Holy One said to him: 'By your life and the life of my head, a period of seven years have I decreed for you, but if your soul is sad, behold I am banishing these souls at once.'

The Messiah said: 'Master of the World, with joyful soul and glad heart I take upon myself this task, provided that not one person in Israel perish; that not only those who are alive will be saved in my days, but also those who are dead, who died from the days of the first Adam up to the time of the redemption; and that not only these be saved in my days, but also those who died as miscarriages; and that not only these be saved in my days, but also those whom you thought to create but were not created. This is what I desire, this is what I am taking upon myself.' In that hour the Holy One, blessed be he, was appointing him four Living Creatures who were bearing up the throne of glory of the Messiah [...]

During the seven years in which the Son of David comes, iron beams will be brought and loaded upon his neck until he is bent double. Then he will cry and weep, and his voice will rise up to the height of heaven, and he will say before God: 'Master of the World, how can my strength endure? How much can my spirit endure? How much can my limbs suffer? Am I not flesh and blood?' [...]

The Holy One, blessed be he, will say to him: 'Ephraim, my Righteous Messiah (*Meshiah Tzidqi*), long ago, ever since the six days of creation, you took this ordeal upon yourself. Now your pain will be like my pain. For from the days that the wicked Nebuchadnezzar came up and destroyed my House and burned my Temple and banished my children among the nations of the world, by your life and the life of my own head I have not gone in to my throne. And if you do not believe me, see the dew has fallen on my head, as it is written, *My head is filled with dew, my locks with the drops of the night* (Song 5:2).'

In that hour the Messiah will say before him: 'Now my mind is set at rest, on the grounds that a servant should be like his master.'

37. The Fathers of the World (the Patriarchs) will rise and say to the Messiah: 'Ephraim, our Righteous Messiah (*Meshiah Tzidqenu*), even though we are your ancestors, you are greater than we, because you bore the sins of our children, and terrible ordeals befell you, such as did not befall earlier or later generations; you became a laughing stock and

a mockery among the nations of the earth for the sake of Israel; and you sat in darkness and gloom, and your eyes saw no light, and your skin cleaved to your bones, and your body was as dry as a stick; and your eyes grew dim from fasting, and your strength dried up like a potsherd – all these on account of the sins of our children. It was your desire that our children should benefit from that goodness which the Holy One, blessed be he, has bestowed abundantly upon Israel. Yet, perhaps because of the anguish which you have suffered on their account, the more so because they chained you in prison, you are displeased with them!'

He will reply: 'O Fathers of the World, all that I have done, I have done only for your sake and for the sake of your children, for your glory and the glory of your children, so that they might benefit from the goodness which the Holy One, blessed be he, is bestowing abundantly upon Israel.'

The Fathers of the World will say to him: 'Ephraim, our true Messiah, be content with what you have done, for you have made content the mind of your Maker and our minds also.'

Source

Ulmer, Rivka, *A Synoptic Edition of Pesiqta Rabbati Based upon All Extant Manuscripts and the Editio Princeps*, vol. 2 (Lanham: University Press of America, 2009), 830–45.

Commentary

Pisqas 34 and 36–7 of the Midrash known as Pesiqta Rabbati, which was probably composed in Palestine in the fifth or sixth century, contain some of the most remarkable passages on the messiah to be found in the whole of rabbinic literature. They offer a very different account of his person and role from that found in the *Amidah* (for which see documents 3 (ii) and (iii)), in *The Book of Beliefs and Opinions* of the great rabbinic theologian Saadia Gaon (document 16) or in the *Book of Zerubbavel* quoted above (document 10). The latter offer what might be called the standard Jewish view of the messiah. According to this the messiah is a political figure, who will appear on earth at the end of history, defeat the enemies of Israel, gather in the dispersed exiles to the Holy Land, raise the dead, re-establish the ancient state of Israel and preside over a period of universal peace, justice and prosperity. According to PesR 34 and 36–7 his work will be much more spiritual – to come into the world and by his suffering atone for human sin. The three chapters do not agree exactly as to their doctrine of the messiah, nor are they always clear and consistent (there are gaps in their theological thinking), but they share a core of ideas. For present purposes the following points are worthy of note:

(1) God had foreknowledge of human sin, and devised a plan to redeem humanity when it sinned. That plan turned on the advance agreement of the (pre-existing) messiah to atone for sin. Without that agreement God would not have created humankind. The messiah entered into the agreement willingly and joyfully.

(2) The messiah's work of atonement will be effected through suffering. Part of that suffering involves rejection by Israel, the very people whom, above all, he will come to save.

(3) How precisely the suffering atones for sin is not very clearly expressed but it seems to involve a transfer of merit. Through his obedience to God, the messiah will acquire merit which will be transferred to cover Israel's sin.

(4) In virtue of his future work, God has elevated the messiah and assigned to him a throne, attended by Living Creatures (Ḥayyot), like his own Throne of Glory.

The parallels with Christian ideas on the work of the messiah, though not exact, are startling and have often been noticed. How to explain them has occasioned much debate. Some have argued that these Pisqas are strongly influenced by Christology. Others that they are explicable as an inner-Jewish theological development which could have been derived from reflection on Psalm 22 and Isaiah 53 as messianic texts – texts which had a profound influence also on Christian understanding of the sufferings and death of Jesus. These ideas are somewhat marginal within Jewish messianism, though the suffering and atoning messiah re-emerges in other Jewish texts such as the Zohar (see Zohar 2:212a quoting Isa. 53:5, though elsewhere in the Zohar, e.g., 3:217b–218a, it is the righteous in every generation who perform this role). PesR's view does intersect with normative messianism in that the messiah's atoning work leads to the manifestation of God's kingdom on earth, with Israel's triumph over her enemies, in what looks like, though it is truncated and allusive, a rather traditional scenario. The outcome in the end is broadly the same as in political messianism. What is remarkable about PesR is the focus it puts on the idea that sin must be dealt with before the kingdom of God can come, and it will be dealt with by the sufferings of the messiah.

If there is Christian influence on PesR 34 and 36–7, then it is a striking example of the continuing intense (if often hidden) interaction between Judaism and Christianity – the ability of the one to significantly influence the other, long after the parting of the ways, on points of belief where they might be thought to be implacably opposed. (See also Appendix to Part I.) If there is *no* Christian influence, then this case at least alerts us to the complexity of the messianic idea in Judaism, and warns us not to create too binary a distinction between the political messiah of Judaism and the spiritual/mystical messiah of Christianity.

Bibliography

Alternative translation of Pesiqta Rabbati: Braude, William G., *Pesikta Rabbati: Discourses for Feasts, Fasts and Special Sabbaths*, 2 vols (New Haven: Yale University Press, 1968).

Alexander, Philip, 'The Mourners for Zion and the Suffering Messiah: Pesikta Rabati 34 – Structure, Theology, and Context', in Fishbane, Michael, and Weinberg, Joanna (eds.), *Midrash Unbound: Transformations and Innovations* (Oxford: Littman Library of Jewish Civilization, 2013), 137–57.

Alexander, Philip, 'Towards a Taxonomy of Jewish Messianisms', in Ashton, John F. (ed.), *Revealed Wisdom: Studies in Apocalyptic in Honour of Christopher Rowland* (Leiden: Brill, 2014), 52–72.

12

Counter-Narratives

Text

(i) *b.Shabb. 104b: Confusion over Jesus' Parents*

He who makes scratches on his flesh. It was taught: Rabbi Eliezer said to the Sages, 'Did not Ben Stada bring spells out of Egypt in a scratching on his flesh?' They said to him: 'He was a fool, and one does not bring proof from [the behaviour of] fools.'

'Ben Stada'? But wasn't he Ben Pandira? Rav Ḥisda said: 'The husband was Stada, the paramour Pandira.' But wasn't the husband Pappus ben Judah? Rather it was his mother who was Stada. But his mother was Miriam, who plaited women's hair. Rather as they say in Pumbeditha: 'This one was unfaithful (*setat da*) to her husband.'

(ii) Toledot Yeshu: *Joseph Pandera Rapes Mary*

One time, Yoḥanan went to Miriam his fiancée on Sabbath eve [Friday evening], and he stayed with her. She said to him, 'Don't touch me for I have my period.' And he did not touch her. During the Sabbath [Saturday], Joseph Pandera made three feasts for Yoḥanan, and he gave him plenty to eat and good wine to drink. And he drank with him – or rather he pretended to drink, but he did not drink. He only gave Yoḥanan to drink, until Yoḥanan was drunk, and he lay down and slept overnight there through the night after the Sabbath [Saturday night]. During that night there was rain, hail, thunder and lightning. Joseph went to Miriam's house, and said, 'Open the door for me, for the rain is heavy.' She said, 'Who are you?' He said, 'I am Yoḥanan, your fiancé.' She opened the door to him, and he recited the Shema with great devotion. The night was pitch black. Then he went to the bed where Miriam was lying, and lay with her. She said to him, 'Yesterday, didn't I tell you that I have my period?' He said, 'But a new ruling has been taught in the House of Study, that it is permitted for a fiancé to lie with his betrothed even when she has her period.' She assumed it was Yoḥanan her fiancé, and he lay with her. And it came to pass in the morning that he slept with her again. She said to him, 'Why do you add sin to rebellion by coming to me twice?' He paid no attention to her, but did as he pleased and went on his way.

And it came to pass on the Sunday that Yoḥanan went to his fiancée, and she sat beside him and touched him. Yoḥanan said to her, 'Didn't you tell me you have your period?' She said to him, 'You are a pious fool! At night you came to me twice, and you lay with me. And you said that a new ruling had been taught in the House of Study, that it is permitted for a fiancé to lie with his betrothed even when she has her period. Now you don't want to touch me!' Yoḥanan trembled greatly and said, 'God forbid that I touched you, with even my little finger! I wasn't even with you last night.' At once she thought of Joseph Pandera. He too thought of Joseph Pandera. She said to him, 'Didn't I tell you you shouldn't befriend a bad man, but you didn't listen to me.' They both cried, and Yoḥanan left with a broken heart. And it came to pass after about three months that Yoḥanan was told, 'Behold, your fiancée is pregnant.' [...] Yoḥanan said, 'Now people will say that she is pregnant by me.' And from great shame and disgrace, he left the Land of Israel, and went to Babylonia, and stayed there.

Miriam gave birth, and she called his name Joshua after her uncle, the brother of her mother. The lad grew, and his mother hired him a teacher, and his name was Elḥanan. And he taught the lad, who was highly intelligent.

Source

Harvard Houghton Library Ms Heb. 57, 22r–v.

Commentary

Document 12 (ii) offers a classic Jewish counter-narration of the Gospel story of the Virgin Birth of Christ. It is taken from one of the versions of the Jewish anti-gospel which goes under the title *Toledot Yeshu*. Christianity claimed, in fulfilment of Isa. 7:14, that Jesus was miraculously born of a virgin. Jewish tradition claimed that he was born out of wedlock, either because Mary consented to illicit sex or because she was raped, the implication being that the story of the Virgin Birth was concocted to cover up the scandal. The version of the story in our text, which startlingly sets the events in the reign of the Hasmonean king Jannaeus (103–76 BCE), 'King Yannai' (cf. document 13), is rather sympathetic to Mary. She lives in Bethlehem with her mother Elinah, who betroths her to a modest and pious young man called Yoḥanan. Nearby lives a womanising scoundrel called Joseph Pandera, a sort of Judean Don Juan. He lusts after Miriam. In our excerpt he invites Yoḥanan to dine with him, gets him blind drunk, and, while Yoḥanan is sleeping off his excesses overnight, tricks his way into Mary's house pretending to be Yoḥanan and has sex with her. His trickery is discovered when Yoḥanan comes to visit Mary. Both Mary and Yoḥanan are devastated. Mary falls pregnant and gives birth to Jesus. Yoḥanan, disgraced, goes off to Babylonia, never to return.

This version of the story is modern, but in some shape or form it can be traced back to antiquity. The second-century pagan philosopher Celsus refers to a version of it which he got from an unnamed Jewish polemicist against Christianity, and again Celsus' version has Panther (= Pandera), a Roman soldier, as the natural father of Jesus (Origen, *Cels.* 1.28, 32). Panther is a known Roman name of the period, popular among soldiers, and, indeed, some have sensationally claimed that a first-century Roman soldier, whose tombstone was discovered at Bingerbrück on the Rhine, may actually have been Jesus' father! The story of the Virgin Birth comes late in the Gospel tradition, and is found only in Matthew and Luke. Some have argued that *it* may be a counter-narration to some version of the *Toledot Yeshu* story.

That stories of this kind were known to Jews in Talmudic times is demonstrated by document 12 (i). This forms part of a discussion of what constitutes work forbidden on sabbath. Writing can fall into the category of forbidden work, but what form of writing?

Would tattooing letters on one's skin be prohibited? This might seem an improbable case, but Rabbi Eliezer cites an example of it. Someone called Ben Stada brought magical spells out of Egypt tattooed on his skin. The sages seem to recognise the individual, and say he was a fool, and one cannot set a precedent from the behaviour of a madman. Though Jesus is not mentioned by name, the rest of the tradition presupposes that he is the fool. But surely Jesus was Ben Pandera, not Ben Stada? The first attempt to explain this discrepancy suggests that Jesus was born out of wedlock and that Pandera was his natural father, Stada his foster father, Mary's husband. But, it is objected, his foster father was Pappos ben Judah. So, it is proposed that Stada was his *mother's* name, but that surely runs counter to the tradition that his mother was Miriam the hairdresser. This objection is overcome by claiming that Stada was Miriam's *nickname*, and an etymology of it is proposed that alludes to her unfaithfulness to her husband. There is clearly a great deal of muddle and confusion here. The transmission of the tradition in the manuscripts shows many minor variants, and it was totally excised by Christian censors, who recognised the reference is to Jesus, but it shows that stories about Jesus were circulating among Jews in our period, and that these included the claim that he was born out of wedlock to someone called Pandera and that he was a magician. What we have here is only the tip of the iceberg. The idea that Jesus (Ben Stada) was a magician is picked up in document 13.

Bibliography

Babylonian Talmud Sabbath: text and alternative translation available at www.sefaria.org/Shabbat.104b.5?lang=bi&with=all&lang2=en.

Toledot Yeshu: texts and translations in Meerson, Michael, and Schäfer, Peter (eds. and trans.) *Toledot Yeshu: The Life Story of Jesus*, 2 vols. (Tübingen: Mohr Siebeck, 2014).

Alexander, Philip, 'Jesus and His Mother in the Jewish Anti-Gospel (the Toledot Yeshu)', in Chivaz, Claire, Dettweiler, Andreas, Devillers, Luc, and Norell, Enrico (eds.), *Infancy Gospels: Stories and Identities* (Tübingen: Mohr Siebeck, 2011), 588–616.

Murcia, Thierry, *Jésus dans le Talmud et la littérature rabbinique ancienne* (Turnhout: Brepols, 2014), 321–75.

Schäfer, Peter, *Jesus in the Talmud* (Princeton and Oxford: Princeton University Press, 2007), 15–24.

13

b.Sanh. 107b: Jesus as a Wayward Disciple of Joshua b. Peraḥiah

Text

Our Rabbis taught: Always have the left hand push [sinners] away but the right hand draw [them] near! [...] Not as Joshua b. Peraḥiah did, who pushed Yeshu ha-Notzri away with both hands [...]

What was the incident involving Joshua b. Peraḥiah? When King Yannai killed the Rabbis, Rabbi Joshua b. Peraḥiah and Yeshu fled to Alexandria in Egypt. When there was peace [between the King and the Rabbis], Shimᶜon b. Shetaḥ sent to Joshua the following message: 'From me, Jerusalem, the Holy City, to you, Alexandria in Egypt. O my sister, my husband resides in your midst, while I remain desolate!'

Joshua arose, went and found himself at a certain inn. They treated him with great honour. He said: 'How beautiful is this inn/innkeeper (*akhsanya*)!' Yeshu said: 'But, Rabbi, she is cross-eyed!' Joshua replied: 'Wicked one, do you occupy yourself with such a thought?!' He sounded 400 Shofar blasts and excommunicated him.

Yeshu came before Joshua several times and said to him: 'Receive me back!', but Joshua ignored him. One day, while Joshua was reciting the Shema, Yeshu came again before him. [This time] Joshua wanted to receive him back. He made a sign with his hand, but Yeshu thought he was driving him away [again]. He went off, set up a brick and worshipped it. Joshua said to him: 'Repent!', but he replied: 'Thus have I learned from you: Whoever sins and causes the masses to sin, is deprived of the power of repentance.'

The master said: 'Yeshu ha-Notzri practised magic (*kishshef*), and incited (*hesit*), and impelled (*hiddiaḥ*) Israel [into idolatry].'

Commentary

This document, which comes from the Babylonian Talmud and so dates to late antiquity, contains a charge already found in the Gospels. Interestingly, there was no denial that Jesus' miracles were genuine, in the sense that genuine effects were achieved: they were not achieved by pure trickery. Rather what was questioned was the agency by which they were done. In the Gospels the Jewish claim is that demons were involved rather than the power of God (Mark 3:22–8; Matt. 12:22–30; Luke 11:14–23). Magic in itself is a capital offence in the Torah (Exod. 22:18; Lev. 19:31, 20:6, 20:27; Deut. 18:9–14), but it is here linked with the equally serious offence of deceiving the Jewish people and leading them into idolatry (Deut. 13:6–18). Jesus used magic to convince the people that he was the son of God. 'Leading Israel astray' is added because it is the charge that is easier to make stick. The accusation of magic on its own is problematic. The miracles of Jesus were miracles of healing and deliverance: if the lame walked, the blind regained their sight, the dead were raised and demons exorcised, what could be wrong with that? Surely this was evidence that *God* was at work. Moreover, Jews themselves, and even rabbis, performed magic. Where was the difference? The rabbinic answer was that rabbis did these things by the power of God, whereas Jesus did them with the help of demons. But that is precisely the point: the outcome is the same, and it is a good outcome, so how can you differentiate between legitimate and illegitimate magic? It boils down in the end to *who* does the deed. Rabbis can be trusted. Jesus cannot, and that is shown in the fact that he used these miracles to validate his false claims and his false teaching, and so lead Israel into sin.

This is the background to the concluding summary statement of our text. The rest of the text, however, makes a rather unexpected point: that the rabbis by their uncompromising attitude had left no chance for Jesus to repent and be received back – they had pushed him away with both hands – and so were to some extent responsible for the harm he did. This is illustrated by a story about Joshua b. Peraḥiah and an erring student. This story was probably not originally about Jesus, but about an *unnamed* student. Here, however, in context, the student has been identified with Jesus. This is chronologically absurd because it makes Jesus the student of Joshua b. Peraḥiah, who lived, according to this tradition, back in the days of the Hasmonean King Alexander Jannaeus ('King Yannai'). We have already seen how document 12 (ii) also dates Jesus to the time of Jannaeus, perhaps relying on this tradition. That Jesus is the student chimes with the Christian tradition of the flight into Egypt (though he goes there as an infant: Matt. 2:13–15, 19–23) and with the widespread belief at the time that Egypt was the great fountainhead of magic. If Jesus was a magician, what better place for him to learn magic than there?

The story, which is typically told with extreme economy, seems to be as follows. The great Rabbi Joshua b. Peraḥiah, summoned back to Palestine after fleeing persecution there, checks into an inn with Jesus, one of his students, and in praising it uses the word *akhsanya*, which could mean both 'an inn' and 'a (female) innkeeper'. Jesus takes it in the latter sense, and Joshua, enraged that he is wasting his time ogling the waitress, excommunicates him. The student's attempts to make up with the rabbi fail, and he falls into idolatry. When Joshua finally calls on him to repent, it is too late: he has committed an unforgiveable sin and led others to do the same. Note the echo here of the charge against Jesus of leading Israel astray – an echo that is drawn out in the concluding summary statement.

There is a surprising wistfulness about this story, a sense of deep regret. Maybe if the rabbis had treated Jesus and the early Christians less harshly – less uncompromisingly – they could have drawn them back into the fold, and all the harm that was done to Israel could have been avoided.

Bibliography

Babylonian Talmud Sanhedrin: text and alternative translation available at www.sefaria.org/Sanhedrin.107b.8?lang=bi&with=all&lang2=en.

Alexander, Philip, 'The Talmudic Concept of Conjuring (*'Aḥizat 'Einayim*) and the Problem of the Definition of Magic (*Kishuf*)', in Elior, Rachel, and Schäfer, Peter (eds.), *Creation and Recreation in Jewish Thought: Festschrift in Honor of Joseph Dan on the Occasion of his Seventieth Birthday* (Tübingen: Mohr Siebeck, 2005), 7–20.

Murcia, Thierry, *Jésus dans le Talmud et la littérature rabbinique ancienne* (Turnhout: Brepols, 2014), 377–422.

Schäfer, Peter, *Jesus in the Talmud* (Princeton and Oxford: Princeton University Press, 2007), 34–40.

14

b.Sanh. 43a: The Trial of Jesus

Text

Abaye said: 'The herald must also say: On such and such a day, at such and such an hour, and in such and such a place the crime was committed [and so and so are the witnesses against him]. Perhaps some know [grounds for acquittal]. Let them come forward and prove the witnesses false.'

And a herald goes before him: before him, but not beforehand. But it was taught (*tanya*): On Sabbath eve and the eve of Passover Yeshu ha-Notzri was hanged. And a herald went forth before him for forty days, proclaiming: Yeshu ha-Notzri is going forth to be stoned, because he practised magic (*kishshef*) and incited (*hesit*) and impelled (*hiddiah*) Israel [to idolatry]. Whoever knows anything in his defence, let him come and state it. But since they did not find anything in his defence, they hanged him on Sabbath eve and the eve of Passover.

Ulla said: 'Do you suppose that Yeshu ha-Notzri was one for whom a defence could be made? He was a *mesit* [someone who incites a Jew to idolatry], concerning whom the Merciful One says: *Show him no compassion and do not shield him* (Deut. 13:8).'

Yeshu ha-Notzri was different, for he was close to the government (*malkhut*).

Commentary

This comment on the trial and death of Jesus comes in incidentally to a discussion in the Talmud on the death penalty. As the condemned was led to the place of execution, a herald went before him proclaiming his crime and inviting any member of the public who knew anything that contradicted the testimony of the original witnesses on which he had been found guilty to come forward and declare it. The procedure was a last-minute fail-safe to try and ensure a miscarriage of justice was not committed.

It is noted that this procedure is enacted on the day of execution itself, not earlier. But then an early tradition is cited that for *forty days* before Jesus was executed the herald made his proclamation. Doesn't this create a precedent? The tradition summarises the charge on which Jesus is being executed and it is the now-familiar claim that he practised magic and led Israel into idolatry. There is a twofold response to this tradition. The scholar Ulla questions its accuracy on the grounds that the charge (leading Israel into idolatry) was so serious that no attempt to defend it was allowed. The second response is to claim that extra care was taken in the case of Jesus, because he was 'close to the government'. In other words this procedure was adopted for specific political reasons, and did not constitute a precedent. The idea that Jesus was close to the government (i.e., to the Roman authorities) is, of course, historically absurd: he was executed *by the Romans* as a criminal. Jews did not have the *ius gladii* at the time – the right to administer capital punishment. The suggestion here reflects the situation of its author's day, when Rome had become Christian.

This lack of a grasp of historical realities is typical of the *Toledot Yeshu* tradition. The Romans are written out of the picture, despite the fact that they are so prominent in the passion narratives of the Gospels (though they are there egged on by the Jewish authorities; see Chapter 1, p. 43). Jesus undergoes a Jewish trial, and is executed by a Jewish method of capital punishment – stoning, not the Roman method of crucifixion. There was hanging involved in the death by stoning, in that the condemned, when dead, was hoisted on a stake and publicly displayed. Jews were not reluctant to accept responsibility for the death of Jesus. In their view he was a criminal who had been rightly tried and executed according to Jewish law.

Bibliography

Babylonian Talmud Sanhedrin: text and alternative translation available at www.sefaria.org/
    Sanhedrin.43a.19?lang=bi&with=all&lang2=en.

Murcia, Thierry, *Jésus dans le Talmud et la littérature rabbinique ancienne* (Turnhout: Brepols, 2014),
    423–73.

Schäfer, Peter, *Jesus in the Talmud* (Princeton and Oxford: Princeton University Press, 2007), 63–74.

15

Toledot Yeshu: *The Hiding of Jesus' Body*

Text

And it came to pass in the evening that the Sages said, 'It is not right to annul a single letter of the Torah on account of this bastard, even though he was leading people astray. Let us do for him according to the stipulation of Torah.' So they buried that bastard in the place where he had been stoned. And it came to pass at midnight that his disciples came and sat by his tomb, and wept bitterly and made lamentation for him. Judah saw this matter, and he took the corpse and buried it in his garden, in a place where there was a channel full of water. For he diverted the water, but after he had buried the body he restored the water as it had been at the first, so that it covered over the place of burial. And it came to pass when the disciples came the next day, and sat and wept, that Judah said to them, 'Why are you weeping? Seek and see the man who was buried.' So they searched but did not find him in his tomb. His band of villains shouted out, 'He is not in his tomb, but has ascended to heaven. For thus he prophesied concerning himself while he was still alive, and said, *For he shall take me. Selah!* (Ps. 49:16).'

The queen heard of these matters and sent for the Sages of Israel. They came before the queen, and she said to them, 'The man whom you said was a magician, and led the people astray, what did you do with him?' They said to her, 'We buried him according to the stipulation of Torah'. She said to them, 'Bring him to me'. They went and searched for him in his tomb, but they did not find him. They came before the queen and said, 'We do not know who took him from his tomb'. The queen answered them and said, 'He is the Son of God, and has ascended to his Father who is in heaven. For thus he prophesied concerning himself, *For he shall take me. Selah!* (Ps. 49:16)!' They answered her, 'Do not let such things enter your heart, for he was a magician. Moreover, the Sages have testified concerning him that he was a bastard, the son of a menstruating woman.' The queen answered, 'What more can I say to you? Yet if you bring him, I will not hold it against you; but if not, I will not leave among you *a remnant or a survivor* (Josh. 8:22; Jer. 42:17).' All of them answered and said, 'Give us time till we know how the matter will fall out. Perhaps we will find him there. If not, do as is good in your eyes.' She gave them three days.

The Sages and the Hasidim (the Pious) went out from the queen with a heavy heart, and they mourned, for they did not know what to do. They decreed a fast. And it came to pass, when the deadline drew near and they had not found him, that many left Jerusalem to flee from the queen. And there went out also a certain elder, and his name was Rabbi Tanḥuma. He was walking around in the fields hither and thither because of his great anguish, when he saw Judah sitting in his garden eating. Rabbi Tanḥuma said to him, 'What is this Judah? How is it that you are eating, yet all Israel is fasting and wallowing in misery?' Judah trembled and said, 'Why so, sir, on what account are they fasting?' And Rabbi Tanḥuma said to him, 'On account of that bastard that was hanged. They buried him at the place of stoning, but he has gone missing, and it is not known who took him from his grave. His band of villains say he has ascended to heaven, and the queen plans to kill all the haters of Israel if they do not find him.' Judah answered and said, 'If that bastard son of a menstruating woman is found, would there be deliverance for Israel?' Rabbi Tanḥuma said to him, 'Of course – if he is found, there will be deliverance for Israel!' Judah said, 'Come and I will show you the man whom you seek, for I stole that bastard from his tomb, for I was afraid his band of villains would steal him from his tomb. I buried him in my garden, and I passed a water channel over him.'

Rabbi Tanḥuma hurried and went and told the matter to the Sages of Israel, and all of them came as one man. They tied him to the tail of a horse, and they dragged him and threw him down before the queen. They said, 'Behold, this is the man whom you said had ascended to heaven!' The queen saw and was ashamed, for she did not know what to answer. And as they brought him, they pulled him along, and they tore out the hair of his head. And this is why Christian monks (*gallaḥim*, literally 'shaved ones') shave the hair from the middle of their heads, as a memorial of what happened to Yeshu.

Source

Harvard Houghton Library Ms Heb. 57, 25v–26r

Commentary

Jewish tradition denied that Jesus was raised from the dead, and a classic way that it did so was by counter-narrating the Gospel stories of the resurrection (Mark 15:42–16:8; Matt. 27:5–28:15; Luke 23:50–24:12; John 19:3–20:18). This document contains one such retelling from the *Toledot Yeshu*. As elsewhere in Jewish tradition, it assumes that Jesus' death was by stoning. Judah is Judas Iscariot, who in the *Toledot* is portrayed as an ally of the sages. In other versions of the story he is concerned not just that the disciples would steal the body, but that they would then proclaim that Jesus had risen.

The queen in question is Helena of Adiabene, a member of the Parthian royal family who converted to Judaism around 30 CE, around the time of Jesus' death, and took up residence in Jerusalem. She died in the early 50s CE. She is mentioned in rabbinic literature and plays a prominent role in some versions of the *Toledot Yeshu*. She is not mentioned in the Gospels, and her historical involvement in Jesus' trial and death is highly unlikely.

The story is corroborated by alleging that the Christian practice of the tonsure commemorates the fact that when Jesus was dragged by his hair before the queen, lumps of it were pulled out. The Roman tonsure used in the west, which involved shaving the *centre* of the head, is most probably in view.

The language of the *Toledot* is offensively coarse. It shows no regard whatsoever for Christian sensibilities. It parodies, burlesques and ridicules Christian tradition, with a view to making it less attractive in the eyes of potential Jewish converts. Nevertheless, it picks up elements of the Gospel tradition. Already in the Gospels the idea is floated that the Jewish authorities were worried by the possibility that Jesus' disciples would steal his body, and then proclaim that he had risen from the dead. So they begged Pilate to be allowed to put a guard on his tomb (Matt. 27:62–6). It looks as if this Gospel account was constructed to counter the story that the tomb was empty because Jesus' body had been moved. The soldiers were introduced to refute the idea that the disciples could have been responsible for its removal.

Bibliography

See bibliography to document 12.

Alexander, Philip, 'Narrative and Counternarrative: The Jewish Antigospel (The *Toledot Yeshu*) and the Christian Gospels', in Baron, Lori, Hicks-Keeton, Jill, and Thiessen, Matthew (eds.), *The Ways That Often Parted: Essays in Honor of Joel Marcus* (Atlanta: SBL Press, 2018), 377–402.

16

Saadia Gaon, Book of Beliefs and Opinions II, 5: A Refutation of the Doctrine of the Trinity

Text

Furthermore, let me say that in this matter the Christians erred when they assumed the existence of distinction in God's personality which led them to make of Him a trinity and to deviate from the orthodox belief [literally, go forth to heresy]. I shall, therefore, take occasion here to make note of what refutation of their doctrine is offered by reason, invoking the aid of the truly One and His uniqueness.

Now I do not have in mind when I present this refutation the uneducated among them who profess only a crass materialistic trinity. For I would not have my book occupy itself with answering people like that, since what that answer must be is quite clear and the task simple. It is rather my intention to reply to their elite, who maintain that they adopted their belief in the trinity as a result of rational speculation and subtle understanding, and that it was thus that they arrived at these three attributes and adhered to them. Declaring that only a thing that is living and omniscient is capable of creating, they recognized God's vitality and omniscience as two things distinct from His essence, with the result that these became for them a trinity.

Now the first point that their rebuttal reveals is that they have only the following two alternatives: either they believe (a) that God is a physical being or (b) that He is not a physical being. But if they believe that He is a physical being, then they are on a par with the common herd of their people and are accordingly subject to whatever refutation has been presented of the view of those who anthropomorphize God. If, on the other hand, they do not believe God to be a physical being, their allegation of the existence within His essence of distinction, with the result that one attribute is not identical with the other, is equivalent to an allegation on their part that He is really a physical being. They merely used another term to express the same thought. For anything that harbors distinction within itself is unquestionably a physical being.

We have, then, established the fact that these three matters constitute one attribute. It is only impossible for a human being to combine them in speech as the mind does by means of its cognition. One might cite as an analogy to the above the case of him who says that he does not worship the fire but the thing that burns and gives light and rises upward, which is in reality nothing else than fire.

Next we demand of the proponents [of the doctrine of the triune nature of God] that they declare explicitly that He is a physical being. For if they refuse to do that, asserting, 'We cannot say that He is a physical being because every physical being is created,' they would by the same token be compelled to deny that God's vitality and omniscience are things distinct from His essence, since any being whose vitality and knowledge are distinct from its essence is created. Those who hold this view are, therefore, may God have mercy on thee, ignorant of the methods of logical proof.

What I mean is that the reason why we, the community of monotheists, believe that the life of a human being is distinct from his essence is because we sometimes see him alive and sometimes dead. Therefrom we infer that there is something in him by virtue of which he lives and which, if it is removed from him, causes him to die. Likewise do we believe that man's knowledge is distinct from his essence because we note that he sometimes knows and he sometimes does not, whence we infer that there is something in him by virtue of which he possesses knowledge and which, if removed from him, causes him to be ignorant. Were it not for our personal observation apropos of these two traits in man, we would have assumed that man is essentially endowed with life and knowledge. Since, however, it is really out of the question that there be found a time in which the Creator of the universe is not living nor endowed with knowledge, as is true in the case of man, it follows of necessity, without any doubt, that He is intrinsically alive and possessed of knowledge. The course that these people followed [in theology], therefore, becomes nullified from its very root.

Moreover, the advocates of the doctrine [of the trinity] did not really pursue their theory to its logical conclusion. They namely mentioned only God's essence and His vitality and omniscience, but failed to speak of his omnipotence, as well as of the fact that He is the one that hears and sees. On the other hand, if their allegation that God is alive makes it unnecessary for them to assert that He possesses power and their allegation that He is omniscient renders it unnecessary to state that He sees and hears, then their allegation that He is omniscient should also make it unnecessary for them to assert that He is alive, since only one that is alive can know anything. Dost thou not see that they are not consistent with their own system and that they do not even follow their own logic? They merely make up this artificial thesis in order to uphold what they have been told [by their teachers].

Furthermore I say that if even a single change were to be allowed in the case of God, every change in the world would have to be granted as possible in Him. For scientific inquiry appertains to the generality of things and their species, not to the individuals and the particulars thereof. Hence, if these people base their proof on rational considerations, the unsoundness of their view has been clearly demonstrated by us.

Source

Rosenblatt, Samuel (trans.), *Saadia Gaon: The Book of Beliefs and Opinions*, Yale Judaica Series 1 (New Haven: Yale University Press, 1948), 103–5. Copyright, 1948, by Yale University Press. All rights reserved. Reproduced with permission of the Licensor through PLSclear. (Square-bracketed words are part of the original; '[literally, go forth to heresy]' is part of a footnote.)

Commentary

Saadia Gaon (882–942) spent the latter part of his life in Baghdad as the head (*gaon*) of the great rabbinical seminary of Sura. He was in Baghdad at the time of the renaissance of scholarship and thought which began under the Abbasid Caliph Harun al-Rashid (786–809) and he absorbed much from his intellectual environment. He marks a decisive turn within the rabbinic movement to philosophy, using contemporary Islamic philosophical theology (Qalam) in his masterpiece *The Book of Beliefs and Opinions* to systematise and reformulate the doctrines of Judaism in ways that would be acceptable to contemporary thought. This philosophical turn engendered a new approach to Christianity. Now the stress was on a rational critique. Christianity was rejected because it was philosophically incoherent and contrary to reason. The Christian doctrine in view here is the orthodox doctrine of the Trinity. Mainstream Christianity vehemently maintained that it believed in only one God, maker of heaven and earth, yet it held that the Godhead embraced three distinct divine 'persons' – the Father, the Son and the Holy Spirit. The unity of God was a complex unity, and orthodox theologians attempted to reconcile this claim with monotheism by subtle and complex arguments. This looked like an open goal to Jewish and Muslim polemicists, who argued that at best the Christian position was incoherent and at worst equivalent to tritheism.

Saadia does not use the language of 'persons' to define the three members of the Trinity. One should not assume that this indicates a certain ignorance of Christian doctrine on his part, for although 'persons' was the language frequently used by Greek-speaking Christian thinkers, Arabic-speaking Christianity spoke in terms of 'attributes' or 'properties' of a single self. They did so in order to accommodate the doctrine of the Trinity to contemporary debate within Islam on the attributes of God. It is this Christian Arabic formulation that Saadia reflects. So Christian theologians writing in Arabic distinguished between God's essence, his vitality and his omniscience. Essence, vitality and omniscience – hence God exists as a trinity.

Saadia is, then, well informed about the Christian position and attempts to refute it rationally. He can do so because his opponents share with him the principles of the Qalam: they embrace the same presuppositions and modes of argument. His target, he says clearly, is the Christian elite, the theologians, not ordinary Christians, who understand the Trinity in a crudely materialistic way which amounts to tritheism.

Put very simply, Saadia's philosophical refutations amount to the claim that if the attributes are fundamentally different, and do not involve simply saying the same thing in different ways, then such distinction is only possible if God is a material body, since only material bodies are capable of division. (He is invoking here a cardinal doctrine of Aristotle, which was hugely influential in medieval philosophy, that 'all things that are many in number have matter': *Metaphysics* 12.8, 1074a.33–4.) But if God has a material body, then he must have been created, since all material bodies must have come into existence at some point in time. And so the elite are no better than the ignorant masses of Christians. Moreover, God has, surely, many more attributes than the three listed (e.g., omnipotence). So why stop at a trinity?

The validity of Saadia's arguments need not detain us here. It is not clear how well they would work against a western formulation of the doctrine of the Trinity in terms of 'persons', rather than attributes. Moreover, not all Christians were trinitarians. How effective would they be against Arianism? More important for our present purposes is the cool, objective tone of the argument, and the deep knowledge it displays of the Christian position.

Bibliography

Brody, Robert, *The Geonim of Babylonia and the Shaping of Medieval Jewish Culture* (New Haven: Yale University Press, 1998).

Husseini, Sara Leila, *Early Christian–Muslim Debate on the Unity of God: Three Christian Scholars and their Engagement with Islamic Thought (9th Century C.E.)* (Leiden: Brill, 2014).

Lasker, Daniel J., *Jewish Philosophical Polemics against Christianity in the Middle Ages* (Portland: Littman Library of Jewish Civilization, 2007), 61–72.

Wolfson, Harry A., 'Saadia on the Trinity and Incarnation', in *Studies in the History of Philosophy and Religion*, ed. Isadore Twersky and George H. Williams, vol. 2 (Cambridge, MA: Harvard University Press, 1977), 393–414.

17

The Account of the Disputation of the Priest (Qiṣṣat Mujādalat al Usquf) 33–6: The Incoherence of Christianity

Text

You claim that God is Christ and that Christ is God, and that Christ descended upon earth, and that he hid himself from the eyes of humans, in order to guide people and to save them from the error of Iblīs [the Devil]. Tell me now: when he descended in order to guide them, did he guide them with his own law or with someone else's law? If you say,

'Someone else's law,' then woe to you because of [your belief in a] God who requires the law of someone else: how can he be worshipped?! And if you say, 'In his own law,' then you deny your Gospel, for Christ says [in the Gospel]: 'I have not come to abolish the Torah of Moses [cf. Matt. 5:17].'

Tell me also this: a person who follows the tradition of Christ, is he to be considered as well-guided or as someone who has gone astray? If you say, 'He is well-guided,' then you yourself have gone astray, since you do not observe his law, nor do you follow his guidance, for you have reversed everything he ordered you to do. And if you say, 'Whoever observes his [i.e., Christ's] law has gone astray,' then you disbelieve Christ, and in his brothers, the apostles.

Is it not true that Christ said in the Gospel, 'I have not come to abolish the Torah of Moses, nor to deny the prophets, but I have come to fulfil it. Truly I say to you now: the heavens and the earth will change and Moses' Torah will not change, but rather, it will be fulfilled in the true works. And whoever abolishes any of its true commandments and performs other commandments will be called "deficient" in the Kingdom of Heaven [cf. Matt. 5:17–19; Mark 13:31].'

This is what is found in the Gospel concerning anyone who rejects the law of Moses son of Amram. Now only one of two things is true in your case: Either your Gospel and your Christ are false, and because you realize this, you hold as true the contrary of what [Jesus] had said, and you abrogate the commandments of Moses, peace be on him, such as the Sabbath and circumcision and the like. Or you hold the words of Christ and the Gospel to be true, but you do the opposite, spitefully and intentionally; if this is the case, you will quickly bring upon yourself curses, both in this world and in the next, and become deficient in the Kingdom of Heaven.

Source

Lasker, Daniel J., and Stroumsa, Sarah, *The Polemic of Nestor the Priest: Qiṣṣat Mujādalat al-Usquf and Sefer Nestor Ha-Komer*, vol. 1 (Jerusalem: Ben-Zvi Institute, 1996), 58–9. (All square-bracketed words except '[the Devil]' are part of the original; '[Cf. Matt. 5:17]' and '[cf. Matt. 5:17–19; Mark 13:31]' are footnotes.)

Commentary

Among the earliest surviving polemical treatises against Christianity by a Jewish author is the *Qiṣṣat Mujādalat al-Usquf (Account of the Disputation of the Priest)*. This is cast in the form of a letter to a former coreligionist from a Christian priest who has converted to Judaism, pointing out to him the errors of the Christian faith. Originally written in Judeo-Arabic (a Jewish dialect of Arabic written in Hebrew script), it was adapted into Hebrew, and the Hebrew version circulated in Byzantium and the Latin west in the Middle Ages usually under the title of *Sefer Nestor ha-Komer (The Book of Nestor the Priest)*. It was composed in the Islamic world, possibly in Egypt in the late eighth century. Its numerous extant versions and the complexity of its textual transmission testify to its popularity. In the Judeo-Arabic version the author is not named, but in the Hebrew adaptation he is called Nestor. The reference is to Nestorius, the famous archbishop of Constantinople from 428 to 431, who was condemned for heresy by the Council of Ephesus in 431 and deposed from his see. Any link between the work and the historical Nestorius can be firmly ruled out, though the possibility that its attack on the doctrine of the Incarnation may owe something to Nestorian Christology should not be discounted. There may be an element of mischief-making here. Just as some of the *Toledot Yeshu* traditions presented Peter, the disciple of Jesus and the first pope, as a crypto-Jew and an agent of the rabbinic sages, so the famous Christian theologian Nestorius, it was alleged, was actually a convert to Judaism.

The *Disputation* attacks as irrational the divinity of Jesus and the doctrines of the Trinity and the Incarnation, but it is, perhaps, most noteworthy for the fact that it is the first work from a Jewish milieu to contain extensive and generally accurate quotations from the canonical Christian Gospels. The *Toledot Yeshu* shows knowledge of Gospel stories, both canonical and apocryphal, but little *direct* knowledge of Christian texts. Though the language of the *Disputation* can be somewhat coarse and vituperative, like that of the *Toledot*, its ethos is very different. Its author has attempted to read the Gospels and engage with them directly, and not simply through hearsay. There is evidence from the Cairo Genizah that from around the ninth century Jews in Egypt were reading the New Testament in Arabic, and this might be a reason for locating the composition in Egypt. Their engagement, however, remained superficial in that it concentrated heavily on alleged contradictions in the Gospels – the sort of contradiction which an untutored, hostile outsider who read the texts on his own would come up with. It betrays little or no engagement with actual Christian understanding of the New Testament, nor with the wider context of the verses quoted. Indeed, from the odd reference system the author uses it looks as if he was quoting from an *anthology* of Gospel extracts, divorced from their context, created probably by a Jew for polemic purposes. The appeal to reason as the arbiter of truth puts the text firmly within the tradition of rational, philosophical polemic that is characteristic of the early Islamic period.

Our excerpt is typical of the *Disputation*. It deploys its favourite mode of argument – the dilemma. This starts out from a statement which the opponent will not deny. It then claims that this position entails either *x* or *y*, where *x* and *y* are diametric opposites, only one of which can be true. If the opponent asserts *x* then certain (for him) unacceptable consequences follow, but if he asserts *y* the consequences are equally unacceptable. Our text addresses two such dilemmas: (1) Did Christ teach according to his own law or the law of another? and (2) When Christ asserted that the Torah of Moses is the eternal and unchangeable law of God, were his words true or false? The arguments are hardly profound, and had the author cared to put them to a knowledgeable Christian, he would have found ready answers, but at least he is trying to engage Christians on an objective and rational basis, accepted by both sides.

Bibliography

Alexander, Philip, and Butbul, Sagit, 'Rylands Gaster Heb. Ms. 1623/3 and the *Qiṣṣat Mujādalat al-Usquf*', in Smithuis, Renate, and Alexander, Philip (eds.), *From Cairo to Manchester: Studies in the Rylands Genizah Fragments* (Oxford: Oxford University Press, 2013), 249–89.

Lasker, Daniel J., 'The Jewish Critique of Christianity: In Search of a New Narrative', *Studies in Christian–Jewish Relations* 6 (2011), 1–9.

Niessen, Friedrich, 'New Testament Translations from the Cairo Genizah', *Collectanea Christiana Orientalia* 6 (2009), 201–22.

Szilági, Krisztina, 'Christian Books in Jewish Libraries: Fragments of Christian Arabic Writings from the Cairo Genizah', *Ginzei Qedem* 2 (2006), 107–62.

Appendix to Part I
Exegetical Encounters

EDWARD KESSLER

INTRODUCTION

Chapters 2 and 3 have presented a range of Christian perspectives of Jews and Judaism and Jewish perspectives of Christians and Christianity in the first millennium of the Common Era. For the most part they are a collection of negative accounts of the 'other', but this appendix shows a different side to the Jewish–Christian relationship, demonstrating an exegetical encounter between Jewish and Christian biblical commentators. This encounter suggests that relations were closer than the polemical texts imply.

The use of biblical interpretation as a means to better understand Jewish–Christian relations in this period is a result of the reawakening of modern scholarship to the Jewish origins of Christianity, a trend which became increasingly noticeable from the first half of the twentieth century onwards (see chapters 7 to 9). Such an awakening, it became more and more apparent, was essential for a proper understanding of the development of the early church as well as for overcoming the prejudices of those for whom Rabbinic Judaism was a form of barren legalism. Its ramifications were manifold: notably, the recognition that Jesus was born, lived and died a Jew; that the first Christians were Jews; and that (for most if not all scholars) the New Testament was a collection of Jewish writings.

These developments had significance for Jews as well as Christians. Like their Christian counterparts, European Jewish scholars began to challenge their coreligionists in the first half of the twentieth century, in their case positively reassessing Christianity, reminding Jews, for example, that Jesus was a fellow Jew – their 'great brother' as Martin Buber described him (see Chapter 8, p. 405).

Most significant for this appendix is the fact that in the latter part of the twentieth century interest began to be directed to the significance of post-biblical writings, not just those produced in the New Testament. In 2001, for example, the Pontifical Biblical Commission called for greater collaboration between Jewish and Christian scholars, noting that 'the Jewish reading of the Bible is a possible one, in continuity with the Jewish Sacred Scriptures […], a reading analogous to the Christian reading which developed in parallel fashion' (*The Jewish People and Their Sacred Scriptures in the Christian Bible*; see Appendix to Part III, p. 528). On the Jewish side, *Dabru Emet*, published a year earlier (see Appendix to Part III, p. 525), asserted that 'Jews and Christians seek authority from the same book – the Bible (what Jews call "Tanakh" and Christians call the "Old Testament")'.

It has also become apparent in the last few decades that exegetical encounters in the patristic and rabbinic periods not only shed light on historic relations between Christians and Jews but also inform the ongoing encounter, because contemporary Jewish and Christian biblical interpretation is partly based on and is a reaction to interpretations from the first millennium of the Common Era.

In Chapters 2 and 3 we saw that while Jews and Christians shared many of the same scriptures, they read them in dramatically different ways. Chapter 2 showed that Christian writers were astonished at what they considered to be Jewish 'blindness': their failure to see and comprehend the truth that was proclaimed in their own sacred texts. For their part, as Chapter 3 demonstrated, Jewish writers mocked Christian interpretations that abandoned the simple meaning of Hebrew words in favour of other significance or removed them from their historical and textual context. Although polemic existed in abundance, this appendix tells another story, narrating a more constructive and mutually beneficial encounter between Christians and Jews during these formative centuries. It betrays awareness of each other's interpretations and implies not only a shared sacred text but a shared common exegetical tradition.

One might argue against the existence of a shared sacred text because the Jewish canon consists of the twofold Torah (the Written and the Oral Torah). The rabbinic writings, alongside the Hebrew scriptures (and especially the Pentateuch), make up this canon, while the two Testaments make up the Christian canon. While this might seem to raise the question of whether the study of a common exegetical tradition is possible in the absence of an agreed shared scriptural text, the fact remains that an overlap existed although Jews and Christians possessed distinct literatures. Indeed, this overlap continues today, both in terms of sharing some of the same scriptures and, consequently, in the area of biblical interpretation.

The case studies presented in this appendix show that although there are differences between Jewish and Christian scriptures and the rabbis and the church fathers developed their own distinctive literary methods, their approaches did not prevent particular interpretations from being understood in both communities. Simply put, much of the discussion between Christians and Jews over nearly two millennia has centred upon the interpretation of the same biblical narrative (albeit in different translations), leading to the occurrence of exegetical encounters from the formative period onwards.

Of course, limitations exist. For instance, it is unlikely that a Christian in third-century CE Galilee would be familiar with the halakhic sensibilities of Rabbinic Judaism; nor would a Jew have understood the Christological debates at the Council of Nicaea and elsewhere. However, as Chapter 2 stated, the rabbis 'betray knowledge of Christian exegetical traditions', and the same can also be applied to Christian knowledge of Jewish exegesis. This is possible because the biblical narrative is shared by both, even though for Christians the Old Testament is understood with reference to the life and death of Christ, whereas for Jews the Hebrew Bible is generally read alongside the rabbinic literature.

Thus, even though Jewish and Christian interpretations are put to different uses, some demonstrate mutual awareness, influence and encounter, as our four case studies will show. The term 'exegetical encounter' refers to a Jewish interpretation influencing, or being influenced by, a Christian interpretation and vice versa. It does not imply that

Jewish and Christian exegetes met to discuss their interpretations (although this might not be ruled out: Palestinian rabbis and *minim*, a term meaning 'heretics', a category which Chapter 3 explains can include Christians, are sometimes portrayed in discussions that typically revolved around the interpretation of scripture). Rather, it has a broader meaning indicating awareness and influence by one exegete of the exegetical tradition of another, revealed in the interpretation.

The focus is on the writings of the Greek church fathers and the Palestinian rabbis (primarily before the Islamic conquest of Palestine in the mid-seventh century CE, to avoid the complications of the possible influence of Islam). It is here that exegetical encounters are to be discovered, because many of the Jews who produced the Palestinian writings either inhabited the same cities as Christians or visited areas in which there was a significant Christian presence.

Both Chapters 2 and 3 considered the problems in demonstrating exegetical contact, including the interest of Jews and Christians in different books of the Old Testament (such as Christian interest in the prophetical writings in contrast to Jewish interest in the Pentateuch). Jews and Christians also possessed different texts: Christian interpretation depended on the Septuagint (LXX), a Greek translation from the second century BCE, while the rabbis relied on the Hebrew Masoretic text. The Septuagint was used originally by Jews living in the diaspora but was taken over by the early church.

There is also a danger of overreliance on parallels, which do not in themselves prove the existence of an exegetical encounter as they might have resulted from earlier writings, such as those of Philo and Josephus, or from applying similar methods in the interpretation of the same biblical text. Another difficulty is the issue of dating. The historical background of a text – primarily the rabbinic text – is often unknown, as a consequence of a complicated process of redaction, as well as censorship.

In response, a series of criteria are applied to identify the existence of an exegetical encounter. Although, individually, none conclusively proves its existence, their occurrence at the very least suggests its possibility. Indeed, as the number of criteria fulfilled increases, the likelihood of an exegetical encounter likewise increases. They are not dependent on parallels or on dating but are applied to interpretations of a text which is of interest to both Jews and Christians and is also similar in the Septuagint and in the Masoretic text.

These similarities exist because Jews and Christians lived (and continue to live) in a biblically oriented culture. They include an insistence on the harmony of scripture and an emphasis on the sanctity of the text. Indeed, the church fathers and rabbis sometimes asked the same questions of the biblical text, as both were close readers and interested in detail. This is illustrated by the third-century Christian writer Origen, who commended his community to 'observe each detail of Scripture, which has been written. For, if one knows how to dig into the depth, he will find a treasure in the details, and perhaps also the precious jewels of the mystery lie hidden where they are not esteemed' (*Homilies on Genesis* 8:1). Origen's use of the metaphor of 'digging' beneath a text also aptly describes the rabbinic approach to scripture, which likewise seeks to derive meaning from each detail. Origen is again representative of both exegetical traditions when he writes that 'the wisdom of God pervades every divinely inspired writing, reaching out to each single letter' (*On Psalms* 1.4, PG 12 1081A). Similarly, Rabbi Ben Bag Bag, who lived in the first century CE, writes for the church fathers as well as the rabbis when he says, 'Turn it, and turn it again; and meditate therein; for all things are in it' (*Mishnah Avot* 5:22).[1]

There are a number of ways to identify an encounter between biblical commentators. Firstly, an explicit reference to a source, especially to an opposing view. This is often (although not always) found in Christian literature and especially in the *adversus Judaeos* writings. However, there is a danger that, as indicated in Chapter 2, Christian references to Jews and Judaism were simply part of a literary genre. We therefore need to show caution even in cases where a church father explicitly refers to a Jewish source. Nevertheless, patristic references to Jewish teachers and exegesis or rabbinic references to the *minim* should be taken seriously, particularly if they exist alongside other criteria. In addition, if the *adversus Judaeos* literature were directed either internally towards Christians or externally towards pagans, one would expect little or no evidence of Jewish interest. If, however, Jewish interpretations demonstrate an awareness of the Christian polemic, delivering a response was but a small step.

The second indication of an exegetical encounter is Jewish and Christian exegetes referring to the same scriptural quotation in the course of their interpretations. Although it is possible that they may have chosen the same quotation separately, the choice is unlikely to have been purely coincidental.

A third sign is the use of the same words, symbols and images, especially if the interpretations share the same extra-biblical descriptions.

A fourth indication is Jewish and Christian exegetes reaching the same or opposite conclusions (when those conclusions are not dependent upon the literal meaning of the text). It can be argued, of course, that exegetes may reach the same conclusion by separate means, but this criterion becomes particularly applicable when found alongside other criteria.

Finally, and probably most importantly, an exegetical encounter may be indicated by a reference to a well-known subject of controversy. Chapter 3 identified four subjects, all of which can be found in the four case studies that follow: (1) the identity of the messiah; (2) the unity of God; (3) the abrogation of the Torah; (4) the election of Israel.

This appendix offers examples of exegetical encounters from interpretations examining four biblical passages: (1) Genesis 1:26; (2) Genesis 22; (3) Genesis 49:8–12; (4) Song of Songs 1:1–4. Each consists of commentaries on a well-known biblical passage with few differences between the various Greek translations and the Hebrew text: Jews and Christians read the same story, often word for word, whether in Hebrew or Greek. Thus, Jewish and Christian exegetes started with a common text and encounters emerge from their interpretations and shed light on their relationship.

---

[1] Oesterley, W. O. E. (trans.), *The Sayings of the Jewish Fathers (Pirke Aboth)* (London: SPCK, 1919), 74.

Genesis 1:26: The phrase 'Let us make humans' is an unsurprising source of controversy. Christian commentators used the verse as a proof-text, emphasising the significance of the first person plural, which they applied to Christ. Sometimes they explicitly mentioned Jewish exegesis. For their part, Jewish commentators sought to mitigate Christian teaching through their own interpretations.

Genesis 22: The sacrifice of Isaac, known in rabbinic Judaism as the *Akedah*, the Binding of Isaac, was a source of debate between Jewish and Christian exegetes. For the latter, Isaac is interpreted typologically and seen as a figure of Christ. For Jewish commentators, he becomes a figure who was willing to give up his life for the Jewish people. Controversial themes found among the interpretations include the fulfilment of scripture and the election of Israel.

Genesis 49:8–12: Interpretation of Jacob's textually problematic blessing of Judah is a source of fascination to both Christian and Jewish commentators. The former read these verses as a prophecy of the coming of Jesus and justification for supersessionism, while the latter acknowledged the messianic prophecy of the blessing but applied it to the people of Israel and in particular the Davidic messiah, who is yet to come.

Song of Songs 1:1–4: Both Jewish and Christian exegetes gave the Song of Songs a mystical meaning: for the rabbis, it is an allegory about the relationship between God and Israel; for the church fathers, God and Israel are replaced by Christ and the church.

Bibliography

Grypeou, Emmanouela, and Spurling, Helen, *The Book of Genesis in Late Antiquity: Encounters between Jewish and Christian Exegesis* (Leiden: Brill, 2013).

Grypeou, Emmanouela, and Spurling, Helen (eds.), *The Exegetical Encounter between Jews and Christians in Late Antiquity* (Leiden: Brill, 2009).

Hirshman, Marc, *A Rivalry of Genius: Jewish and Christian Biblical Interpretation*, trans. Batya Stein (Albany: State University of New York Press, 1996).

Janowski, Bernd, and Stuhlmacher, Peter (eds.), *The Suffering Servant: Isaiah 53 in Jewish and Christian Sources*, trans. Daniel P. Bailey (Grand Rapids: Eerdmans Publishing Co., 2004).

Kugel, James L., *The Bible as It Was* (Cambridge, MA and London: Belknap, Harvard University Press, 1997).

Saebo, Magne (ed.), *Hebrew Bible/Old Testament* (Göttingen: Vandenhoeck and Ruprecht, 2000).

Seidman, Naomi, *Faithful Renderings: Jewish–Christian Difference and the Politics of Translation* (Chicago: University of Chicago Press, 2006).

CASE STUDIES

In contrast to the other chapters in this book, where each document is followed by an authorial commentary and the source reference for each document is given at the end of the document itself, this chapter consists of four case studies of Old Testament documents, based on a wide range of commentaries from the second to the ninth century CE. The source references for the commentaries are given in footnotes; translations are the author's own unless specified otherwise in the references. The Scripture quotations contained herein are from the New Revised Standard Version, Updated Edition Bible, copyright © 1989, 2021 by the Division of Christian Education of the National Council of the Churches of Christ in the U.S.A., and are used by permission. All rights reserved.

I

Genesis 1:26

^{1:26} Then God said, 'Let us make humans in our image, according to our likeness [...]'.

The first (and shortest) case study examines Jewish and Christian interpretations of one part of one biblical verse. As we shall see, Christian commentators were aware of the problems raised by these words for their Jewish counterparts, as illustrated by the interpretation of the second-century CE Christian writer Justin Martyr, as well as by Jewish commentators who appear to quote verses from the New Testament.

For the rabbis, the problem in the biblical text lay in its use of the first person plural: '*Let us* make humans'. Who was God speaking to? *Targum Pseudo-Jonathan* suggests God spoke to the ministering angels:

> And God said to *the angels who minister before him, who were created on the second day of the creation of the world*, 'Let us make man in our image, in our likeness.' (*Targum Pseudo-Jonathan*, Gen. 1:26)[2]

Genesis Rabbah, one of the best known and oldest *midrashim*, suggested that God spoke either to his advisors or to himself:

> 'And God said, let us make man ...'. With whom did He take counsel? Rabbi Joshua ben Levi said, 'He took counsel with the works of heaven and earth, like a king who had two advisors without whose knowledge he did nothing whatsoever [...].' Rabbi Ammi said, 'He took counsel with His own heart.' It may be compared to a king who had a palace built by an architect. (Gen. Rab. 8.3)[3]

Jewish commentators, therefore, approached Genesis 1:26 with some caution. On the one hand, they could explain that God consulted his heavenly court (such as the angels) while creating humankind, but on the other, they needed to demonstrate that God was the sole creator of the universe and that the act of creation was solely his work, not that of others. In the context of the encounter with Christianity (or the Gnostics, who believed in 'two powers') it was important to reject the possibility of any non-monotheistic contribution to the act of creation.

---

[2] Maher, Michael (trans. and ed.), *Targum Pseudo-Jonathan: Genesis*, The Aramaic Bible 1B (Edinburgh: T&T Clark, 1992), 19–20.

[3] Freedman, H., and Simon, Maurice (trans. and eds.), *Midrash Rabbah: Translated into English* (London: Soncino, 1961). Speech marks added.

Justin Martyr is aware of these Jewish sensibilities and even quotes them in his interpretation of the same verse:

> You may not, by changing the words already quoted, say what your teachers say, either that God said to Himself, 'Let us make ...' as we also, when we are about to make anything, often say, 'Let us make' to ourselves; or that God said, 'Let us make ...' to the elements, namely the earth and such like, out of which we understood that man has come into being. (*Dialogue with Trypho*, ch. 62)[4]

As we saw in Chapter 2 (see p. 75), Justin is an important historical source for the study of Jewish–Christian relations in the early patristic period primarily because of his work *Dialogue with Trypho*, which recounts a debate between himself and the eponymous Jew and from which this passage is excerpted. While scholars disagree as to whether there actually existed a Jew called Trypho, the passage indicates that Justin recorded a real debate. His knowledge of contemporary Judaism, perhaps obtained from personal encounters with Jews in Samaria, where he lived, seemed sufficient to respond to rabbinic exegesis. Justin's interpretation was repeated and sometimes developed in the writings of later church fathers, such as Theodoret of Cyrus, who rejected the rabbinic interpretation that 'the God of the universe addresses himself' and explained that God 'uses plural forms to bring out the distinction of number of the persons of the Trinity'.[5]

There is also an intriguing passage from the Jerusalem Talmud, compiled in the late fourth century, which also seems to be evidence of a Jewish–Christian debate:

> A. The heretics asked R. Simlai, How many gods created the world? He answered them, Me you're asking? Let's ask Adam, as it is said, *For ask now of the days that are past, which were before you, since the day that God created Adam ...* (Deuteronomy 4:32). It is not written, since gods created (pl.) Adam, but *since the day that God created (sing.) Adam*.
>
> B. They said to him, But it is written, *In the beginning God* [*elohim* appears to be a masculine plural] *created* (Genesis 1:1). He said to them, Is *created* written [as a plural]? What is written here is *created* [in the singular].
>
> C. R. Simlai stated, Every place that the heretics rend [a verse from context to make their point] has the appropriate [textual] response right next to it.
>
> D. They returned to ask him, What of this verse, *Let us make man in our image, after our likeness* (Genesis 1:26) [the subject, verb and objects appear to be plurals]. He answered them, It is not written, So God created (pl.) man in his image (pl.), but, *So God created (sing.) man in his own image* (Genesis 1:27). His disciples said to him, Those you pushed off with but a straw, but what shall you answer us?

4 Justin Martyr, *The Dialogue with Trypho*, trans. and ed. A. Lukyn Williams (London: SPCK; New York: Macmillan, 1930), 129.

5 Theodoret of Cyrus, *The Questions on the Octateuch*, Vol. 1: *On Genesis and Exodus*, trans. and ed. Robert C. Hill (Washington, DC: Catholic University of America Press, 2007), 47.

He told them, In the past, Adam was created from the dust, while Eve was created from Adam. From Adam onward, *In our image, after our likeness* (Genesis 1:26); it is impossible for there to be man independent of woman, nor is it possible for there to be woman independent of man, neither is it possible for both of them to be independent of the Shekhina. (*Berakot*, 12d–13a; cf. Gen. Rab. 8:9)[6]

This text has been the subject of recent scholarly debate, but little consensus has been reached as to whether the third-century Palestinian rabbi Simlai is responding to Christianity or to other *minim* such as Gnostics. In the debate with his disciples, he is using Genesis 1:26, among other biblical texts, to reject the heretical view that there is more than one God or, if his interpretation is a response to Christianity, to reject Christian interpretations which apply the biblical text to Christ.

Rabbi Simlai's interpretation seeks to safeguard the oneness and unity of God but is also an example of the intricacy of the exegetical relationship between Jewish and Christian commentators, strikingly illustrated by echoes of Paul's first Letter to the Corinthians 11:3–12:

> [11:3] I want you to understand that Christ is the head of every man, and the man is the head of the woman, and God is the head of Christ [...] [8] Indeed, man was not made from woman but woman from man. [9] Neither was man created for the sake of woman but woman for the sake of man [...] [11] in the Lord woman is not independent of man or man independent of woman. [12] For just as woman came from man, so man comes through woman, but all things come from God.

The parallel between Rabbi Simlai's interpretation and that of Paul is clear. There is nothing to prevent the conclusion that their writings are connected, illustrating that Jews and Christians lived in a biblically oriented culture, sharing not only sacred texts but sometimes even each other's biblical interpretations.

Bibliography

Visotzky, Burton L., *Fathers of the World: Essays in Rabbinic and Patristic Literatures* (Tübingen: Mohr Siebeck, 1995), 61–74.

2

Genesis 22

The sacrifice, or binding, of Isaac has been an important biblical passage in Jewish–Christian relations from at least the third century CE, when it started being read on Rosh ha-Shana, the Jewish New Year, and also mentioned by Christians in Eucharist prayers

---

[6] Visotzky, Burton L., *Fathers of the World: Essays in Rabbinic and Patristic Literatures* (Tübingen: Mohr Siebeck, 1995), 65. (Square-bracketed phrases are part of the original, '[*elohim* ... plural]' and '[the subject ... plurals]' as footnotes.)

as well as read in the period leading up to Easter. It is still read in this way in synagogues and churches today. The focus of the story is traditionally understood as Abraham's relationship with God and how his faith in and commitment to God was demonstrated by a willingness to sacrifice his long-awaited son at God's command. Interpretation has concentrated on verses 1–2 and 6–12. Verses 1–2 read:

> [22:1] After these things God tested Abraham. He said to him, 'Abraham!' And he said, 'Here I am.' [2] He said, 'Take your son, your only son Isaac, whom you love, and go to the land of Moriah and offer him there as a burnt offering on one of the mountains that I shall show you.'

The church fathers and rabbis shared a number of interpretations that discussed the reasons for the test, which provides evidence for a common exegetical framework. Examples include agreement that the purpose of the test was to exalt Abraham. *Midrash Tanhuma* stated that the *Akedah* made 'known to the peoples of the world that I [God] did not choose you [Abraham] without a reason' (*TanB Ve-year* 46).[7] Similarly, Cyril of Alexandria explained that it was 'necessary, however, for that righteous man to have such splendid repute not in the knowledge of God only, but also for his most excellent glory to be magnified and for all to know that through this act of testing, his glory is attested as being above all virtues' (*Glaphyrorum in Genesim*, PG 69 144D).[8]

Jewish and Christian commentators were also interested in God's choice of the words 'your son, your only son Isaac, whom you love'. They asked the same question (why did God not simply say 'Isaac'?) and came to the same conclusion: the purpose of the drawn-out description was to increase Abraham's affection for his son. According to the rabbis, God's words not only indicated the extent of Abraham's love for Isaac but made the test more severe by making 'Isaac more beloved in his eyes' (Gen. Rab. 55:7; cf. PesR 40:6). The fourth-century church father Gregory of Nyssa offered a similar interpretation, stating, 'through [the repetition of] these names, the affection towards him [Isaac] is brought to the boil' (*De deitate*, PG 46 568B–C).

They both even created a dialogue between Abraham and God. The church fathers imagined what Abraham might have said, but did not; while the rabbis constructed a conversation that Abraham did have with God. This is the imaginary dialogue of Gregory:

> Why do You command these things, O Lord? On account of this You made me a father so that I could become a childkiller? On account of this You made me taste the sweet gift so that I could become a story for the world? With my own hands will I slaughter my child and pour an offering of the blood of my family to You? Do You call for such things and do You delight in such sacrifices? Do I kill my son by whom I expected to be buried? Is this the marriage

---

[7] Townsend, John T. (trans. and ed.), *Midrash Tanhuma, Translated into English with Introduction, Indices and Brief Notes (S. Buber Recension)* (Hoboken: Ktav Publishing House, 1989).

[8] St Cyril of Alexandria, *Glaphyra on the Pentateuch, Volume 1: Genesis*, trans. Nicholas P. Lunn (Washington, DC: Catholic University of America Press, 2018).

chamber I prepare for him? Is this the feast of marriage that I prepare for him? Will I not light a marriage torch for him but rather a funeral pyre? Will I crown him in addition to these things? Is this how I will be a 'father of the nations' – one who has not produced a child?

Did Abraham say any such word, or think it? Not at all! (*De deitate*, PG 46 568D)

The rabbis also used dialogue and, like Gregory, developed an element of theatre, as their account of a conversation between God and Abraham shows:

> *And He* [God] *said: Take now thy son*
> [Abraham said] 'which one?'
> *Thine only son.'*
> 'Each is the only one of his mother?'
> *'Whom thou lovest.'*
> 'I love them both: are there limits to one's emotions?'
> Said He to him: *'Even Isaac.'* (Gen. Rab. 39:9 and 55:7)[9]

While the conclusion of each is different, both commentators used the same hermeneutical method – conversation – as a framework for their interpretation.

Another focus of interpretation is Genesis 22:6–12, which reads:

> [6] Abraham took the wood of the burnt offering and laid it on his son Isaac, and he himself carried the fire and the knife. And the two of them walked on together. [7] Isaac said to his father Abraham, 'Father!' And he said, 'Here I am, my son.' He said, 'The fire and the wood are here, but where is the lamb for a burnt offering?' [8] Abraham said, 'God himself will provide the lamb for a burnt offering, my son.' And the two of them walked on together.
> [9] When they came to the place that God had shown him, Abraham built an altar there and laid the wood in order. He bound his son Isaac and laid him on the altar on top of the wood. [10] Then Abraham reached out his hand and took the knife to kill his son. [11] But the angel of the LORD called to him from heaven and said, 'Abraham, Abraham!' And he said, 'Here I am.' [12] He said, 'Do not lay your hand on the boy or do anything to him [...]'.

Isaac's age is another area of mutual interest. Two strands of thought are found among Christian interpreters. In the first, Isaac is a child and in the second, a young man who has not yet reached adulthood. According to the fourth-century church father Cyril of Alexandria, Isaac was 'small and lying in the breast of his own father' (*Glaph. in Gen.*, PG 69 140D), while John Chrysostom described him as more mature: 'Isaac had come of age and was in fact in the very bloom of youth' (*Homilies on Genesis*, PG 54 429).[10]

---

[9] Freedman and Simon, *Midrash Rabbah*. Lineation and speech marks added.
[10] John Chrysostom, *Homilies on Genesis 46–67*, trans. Robert C. Hill (Washington, DC: Catholic University of America Press, 1992), 15.

The rabbinic position was significantly different, suggesting he was a grown man, and describes Isaac as stating: 'I am now thirty-seven years old, yet if God desired of me that I be slaughtered, I would not refuse' (Gen. Rab. 55:4, 56:8).[11] Another interpretation gave his age as twenty-six (Gen. Rab. 56:8) and a third proposed thirty-six years (*Targum Pseudo-Jonathan*). Unlike the biblical text, the rabbis consistently portray Isaac as an adult.

Jewish and Christian interpretations of Isaac extend beyond a common exegetical framework, and it is here we uncover an encounter. Not only was his age of mutual interest, but exegetes also explored the significance of his carrying the wood. Unsurprisingly, the church fathers viewed this as a model of Jesus carrying the cross. Evidence can be seen as early as the second century CE, as illustrated by Melito, bishop of Sardis, who lived among one of the most established Jewish communities of Asia Minor. In his commentary, he wrote:

> For as a ram he was bound [...],
>   and *as a lamb* he was shorn,
>   *and as a sheep he was led to slaughter,*
>   and as a lamb he was crucified;
> and he carried the wood on his shoulders
>   as he was led up to be slain like Isaac by his Father.
> But Christ suffered, whereas Isaac did not suffer;
>   for he was a model of the Christ who was going to suffer.
> But by being merely the model of Christ
>   he caused astonishment and fear among men.
> For it was a strange mystery to behold,
>   a son led by his father to a mountain for slaughter,
>   whose feet he bound and whom he put on the wood of the offering,
>   preparing with zeal the things for his slaughter [...]
>   and Abraham stood by and held the sword unsheathed,
>   not ashamed to put to death his son. (*Fragment* 9)[12]

For Melito, the unfulfilled sacrifice foreshadowed the complete sacrifice. He pointed to parallels between Isaac and Jesus: Isaac carrying the wood was like Christ carrying the cross; Isaac was the model of Christ; both Isaac and Jesus were bound (note his adoption of the rabbinic description – binding – rarely mentioned in the patristic writings); both were led to the sacrifice by their father; neither was sorrowful.

Although Abraham remains the model of faith (cf. Hebrews 11:17–19), Isaac becomes the model of Christ. Thus, Barnabas' brief reference to Genesis 22 is to Isaac, not Abraham, since Jesus 'fulfilled the type' that was established in Isaac (*Ep. Barnabas* 7:3). Origen similarly commented that 'Isaac who carries on himself the wood for the sacrifice is a figure, because Christ also himself carried his own cross' (*Hom. Gen.*, 8:6).

---

[11] Freedman and Simon, *Midrash Rabbah*.
[12] Hall, S. G. (trans. and ed.), *Melito of Sardis: On Pascha and Fragments* (Oxford: Clarendon Press, 1979), 75.

This typological approach provided not only parallels between Isaac and Christ but also contrasts, or anti-types. Isaac points forward to the even more amazing deed in the sacrifice of Christ. What is important is that Isaac was not sacrificed, did not suffer and remained only the model, waiting to be fulfilled. Isaac was a child and represented an outline, an immature image of what lay ahead. The child (Isaac) was to be fulfilled by the adult (Christ).

Cyril of Alexandria is one of a number of church fathers who emphasised that Isaac, like Jesus, was not forced by human hand to carry the cross but carried it freely:

> As for the boy, Isaac, the wood for the burnt offering was laid upon him by his father, and he carried it until he came to the place where the sacrifice would be made. So Christ, carrying his own cross upon his shoulder, suffered outside the gate. It was not by human strength that he was forced to suffer, but it was of his own will and the will of God the Father. (*Glaph. in Gen.*, PG 69 141D–144A)[13]

The rabbis also commented on Isaac carrying the wood, as stated in verse 6. Genesis Rabbah appropriated and modified a Christian interpretation, providing evidence of an exegetical encounter:

> 'And Abraham placed the wood of the burnt-offering [and laid it on his son Isaac].' Like one who carries his cross (*zaluvo*) on his shoulder. (Gen. Rab. 56:3)

The use of the word 'cross' is a near-explicit reference to Christianity, and it is noticeable that Jewish translations still avoid using 'cross', preferring 'stake' or something similar. Evidence of Christian influence on rabbinic exegesis is also found elsewhere. By depicting Isaac as an adult, the rabbis wanted to emphasise his willingness to be sacrificed, to suffer and to offer himself to his father. Isaac was not forced but willingly gave himself to Abraham. In this midrash from Lamentations Rabbah, Isaac is depicted speaking to God, as follows:

> Sovereign of the Universe, when my father said to me, *'God will provide Himself the lamb for a burnt-offering, my son'* (Gen. XXII, 8), I raised no objection to the carrying out of Thy words, and I willingly let myself be bound on the top of the altar and stretched out my neck beneath the knife. (Lam. Rab. Pr 24)[14]

Isaac's willingness to give up his life appears to be a rabbinic response to the Christian teaching that Christ was willing to give up his. Indeed, Isaac was informed in advance of the sacrifice and continued the journey with Abraham. 'One to bind and the other to be bound, one to slaughter and one to be slaughtered' (Gen. Rab. 56:3).[15] This is why the rabbis associated Genesis 22 with Isaac rather than with Abraham. They suggested that

---

[13] Cyril of Alexandria, *Glaphyra on the Pentateuch*, 156.
[14] Freedman and Simon, *Midrash Rabbah*.
[15] Freedman and Simon, *Midrash Rabbah*.

because Isaac was an adult, unlike his father who was an old man, he must have meta-phorically 'bound himself' for, had he so desired, he could have prevented an elderly man binding him. Thus, the self-offering of the adult Isaac provided benefit to Isaac's children (the Jewish people) in future generations.

In the rabbis' view, so willing was Isaac to give up his life that they described the *Akedah* in terms such as 'the blood of the binding of Isaac' or 'the ashes of Isaac' (e.g., Gen. Rab. 49:11, 94:5; Lev. Rab. 36:5; Num. Rab. 17:2). This is startling, because the biblical account explicitly states that the angel stopped Abraham from harming his son, commanding him 'not to do anything' to Isaac. As the *Mekhilta de Rabbi Ishmael* stated:

> 'And when I see the blood, I will pass over you' (Exodus 13:12 and 25) – I see the blood of the Binding of Isaac. For it is said, 'And Abraham called the name of that place the Lord will see'. Likewise it says in another passage, 'And as He was about to destroy, the Lord beheld and repented Him' (I Chronicles 21:15). What did He behold? He beheld the blood of the Binding of Isaac, as it is said, 'God will for Himself see to the lamb.' (*Mekhilta de Rabbi Ishmael* Pisha 7; cf. 11)[16]

The rabbinic suggestion that Isaac's blood was shed was repeated elsewhere, and there is even a midrash that Isaac was sacrificed, died and experienced resurrection. According to the eighth-century CE *Pirkei de Rabbi Eliezer*:

> When the blade touched his neck, the soul of Isaac fled and departed, (but) when he heard His voice from between the two Cherubim, saying (to Abraham), 'Lay not thine hand upon the lad' (Gen. xxii. 12), his soul returned to his body, and (Abraham) set him free, and Isaac stood upon his feet. And Isaac knew that in this manner the dead in the future will be quickened. He opened (his mouth), and said: Blessed art thou, O Lord, who quickeneth the dead. (*Pirkei de Rabbi Eliezer*, ch. 31)[17]

The interpretation in *Pirkei de Rabbi Eliezer* is further evidence that rabbinic interpreta-tions depicting the death and resurrection of Isaac demonstrate Christian influence on Jewish exegesis and the existence of an exegetical encounter.

It is worth ending this case study with the following polemical passage from a later rabbinic text, the eighth-century *Aggadat Bereshit*, which is clearly a Jewish response to Christian teaching about Christ:

> Foolish is the heart of the liars who say that the Holy One has a son. Now con-cerning the son of Abraham: when he saw that he came to slaughter him, he could not see him in pain, but immediately cried, 'do not lay your hand on the

---

[16] Author's translation based on Lauterbach, Jacob Z. (trans. and ed.), *Mekilta de-Rabbi Ishmael* (Philadelphia: Jewish Publication Society of America, 1961), 57, 87–8.

[17] Friedlander, G. (trans. and ed.), *Pirkê de Rabbi Eliezer* (London: Kegan Paul, Trench, Trubner & Co.; New York: Bloch Publishing Co., 1916), 228.

boy'. Had he had a son, would he have abandoned him, and would he not have overturned the world and turned it into chaos [*tohu v'bohu* Gen 1:2]? (*Aggadat Bereshit*, ch. 31)[18]

Bibliography

De Andrado, Paba Nidhani, '"A Model of Christ": Melito's Re-Vision of Jewish Akedah Exegeses', *Studies in Christian–Jewish Relations* 12, no. 1 (2017), https://doi.org/10.6017/scjr.v12i1.10032.

Kessler, Edward, *Bound by the Bible: Jews, Christians and the Sacrifice of Isaac* (Cambridge: Cambridge University Press, 2004).

Moberly, R. W. L., *The Bible, Theology and Faith: A Study of Abraham and Jesus* (Cambridge: Cambridge University Press, 2000).

Spiegel, Shalom, *The Last Trial: On the Legends and Lore of the Command to Abraham to Offer Isaac as a Sacrifice, The Akedah* (New York: Schocken, 1967).

3

Genesis 49:8–12

The context of this passage is that Jacob is nearing death (Gen. 48:1) and blessing each of his sons. In Genesis 49:8–12 he blesses Judah and proclaims that his tribe will produce not merely conquerors, but also kings (and one king in particular). These verses were interpreted by both Jews and Christians as messianic prophecies from an early period:

> 49:8 Judah, your brothers shall praise you;
>> your hand shall be on the neck of your enemies;
>> your father's sons shall bow down before you.
> 9 Judah is a lion's whelp;
>> from the prey, my son, you have gone up.
> He crouches down, he stretches out like a lion,
>> like a lioness – who dares rouse him up?
> 10 The scepter shall not depart from Judah,
>> nor the ruler's staff from between his feet,
> until tribute comes to him,
>> and the obedience of the peoples is his.
> 11 Binding his foal to the vine
>> and his donkey's colt to the choice vine,
> he washes his garments in wine
>> and his robe in the blood of grapes;
> 12 his eyes are darker than wine,
>> and his teeth whiter than milk.

---

[18] Teugels, Lieve M. (trans. and ed.), *Aggadat Bereshit* (Leiden: Brill, 2001), 100.

The Dead Sea Scrolls provide evidence of the early nature of this tradition, describing two messiahs (king and priest) and identifying the Davidic messiah as a fulfilment of the prophecy. As the second-century CE *Targum Onkelos* on 49:10 states, 'The ruler shall never depart from the House of Judah, nor the scribe from his children's children for evermore – until the Messiah comes, whose is the kingdom, and him shall the nations obey.'[19]

The biblical text is problematic, as demonstrated by the Hebrew words in verse 10, *ad ki ya-vo shilo*, the meaning of which is unclear but which are generally understood as a reference to the messiah. The phrase has prompted numerous translations – including 'until Shiloh comes', 'until he comes to Shiloh' or (with the Syriac version of the Old Testament) 'until he comes to whom it belongs' and (the Jewish Publication Society translation) 'as long as men come to Shiloh' – and many more interpretations, some of which illustrate an exegetical encounter. While Christian commentators read these verses as prophecy regarding the coming of Jesus, described as 'the Lion of the tribe of Judah, the Root of David' (Rev. 5:5), Jews associated them with the messiah who had yet to arrive.

However, both Jews and Christians interpreted the text to indicate that the messiah would come from the line of Judah, based on a common understanding of the phrase 'until Shiloh comes' (or 'until he comes to Shiloh' or, as the NRSVue has it, 'until tribute comes to him'). They both also referred to Psalm 45:6–7:

> [6] Your throne, O God, endures forever and ever.
>> Your royal scepter is a scepter of equity;
> [7] you love righteousness and hate wickedness.
> Therefore God, your God, has anointed you
>> with the oil of gladness beyond your companions.

For example, in Lamentations Rabbah (1:16), 'The Messiah's name is Shiloh, as it is stated, "Until Shiloh come" (Gen. 49:10), where the word is spelled *shlh* [send].'[20]

Although Eusebius uses the Septuagint translation, he is also familiar with this interpretation:

> For Siloam means *sent*. And this would be God the Word, sent by the Father, of whom Moses also says, *a ruler shall not fail from Judah, nor a prince from his loins, until he comes for whom it is stored up, and he is the expectation of nations* [Septuagint]. For instead of *for whom it is stored up*, the Hebrew has Siloam, the word of prophecy using the same word Siloam there and here, which means *the one that is sent*. (*Demonstratio Evangelica* 7.1)[21]

It is also worth mentioning that the figure of Jacob represents the people of Israel in rabbinic and patristic writings and that both Jews and Christians claimed to be his

---

[19] Aberbach, Moses, and Grossfeld, Bernard (trans. and eds.), *Targum Onkelos to Genesis* (Denver: Ktav/Center for Judaic Studies, University of Denver, 1982), 284.

[20] Freedman and Simon, *Midrash Rabbah*.

[21] Ferrar, W. J., *The Proof of the Gospel: Being the Demonstratio Evangelica of Eusebius of Caesarea*, vol. 2 (London: SPCK, 1920), 70.

(authentic) descendants. Not only was Jacob also named Israel, but the Bible recounts that his mother Rebecca was told, 'Two nations are in your womb, and [...] the elder shall serve the younger' (Gen. 25:23, NRSVue). Thus, the elder, Esau, represented the people of Edom and oppression, while the younger, Jacob, was a synonym for Israel and chosenness. Not only did both Jews and Christians claim Jacob as their ancestor, but both also identified Esau with the ancestor of the other.

For Jewish commentators, Esau/Edom is also identified with Rome and then, later, from the fourth century CE onwards if not earlier, with Christianity (b.Megilla 6a). They even describe the reconciliation of the brothers in Genesis 32 as an act of deception on the part of Esau (Gen. Rab. 78:9). For the church fathers, Christians are represented by the younger brother who receives the divine blessings instead of the older brother (representing Jews). As the second-century theologian Irenaeus of Lyon stated, 'the latter people (the gentiles) has snatched away the blessings of the former (the Jews) [...] just as Jacob took away the blessing from Esau' (*Against Heresies* 4.21).

A focus of interest is the correct interpretation of 'The scepter shall not depart from Judah, nor the ruler's staff from between his feet'. A sceptre is a staff – the parallelism in the biblical text implies equivalence – which symbolises the power a ruler had at his command and a sign of his authority. According to Genesis 49:10, this symbolic rulership will never leave the tribe of Judah. Each king from the genealogy of Judah (poetically phrased as 'between his feet') was associated with King David, whose 'throne shall be established forever' (2 Samuel 7:16, NRSVue) and from whom the messiah would be descended. Christian commentators applied the symbol of royal power, the sceptre, to Jesus, explaining that Jewish rule (Judah) had come to an end, as demonstrated by Jewish exile after the destruction of the Jerusalem temple. Since the biblical text indicates that Judah will only retain power until the messiah (Shiloh) arrives, and since Judah (Jews) no longer possesses any power, the messiah (Jesus) must have already arrived.

In response, Jewish commentators acknowledged that Jews no longer had political power but suggested this started with the destruction of the temple in 587 BCE and the Babylonian exile (followed by Persian, Greek and Roman rule). Although political independence came to an end in the sixth century BCE, Jacob's prophecy remained valid. Indeed, the sceptre had still not departed, since many subsequent leaders of Israel came from the tribe of Judah.

Other examples of exegetical encounters can be found in interpretations of these verses. For example, the rabbis and church fathers understood the praise of Judah by his brothers in the same way. Ephrem the Syrian (a fourth-century church father from Nisibis in what is now Turkey) and the fifth-century Genesis Rabbah both explain that Judah saved his brothers from being condemned for the killing of Joseph. While their interpretations may have been a logical understanding of the biblical text and may have arrived at the same conclusion independently, recent scholarship has uncovered Ephrem's literary dependence on Jewish exegesis and his proficiency in applying Jewish literary tradition (Narinskaya 2010: 77–96).

An exegetical encounter can also be uncovered in Jewish and Christian interpretations of verse 10, 'Binding his foal to the vine and his donkey's colt to the choice vine'. This verse echoes Zechariah 9:9, which is also quoted by Matthew (21:5) in his description of the entry of Jesus into Jerusalem. It is not surprising, therefore, that Christian interpreters of Genesis 49:11 make reference to Jesus. However, Ephrem the Syrian goes further in his discussion of this verse, not only bringing the church into the interpretation but also associating Jews with the vine:

> *And for Him the nations shall wait*, that is, the church of the Gentiles. *He will bind his foal to the vine and his ass's colt to the choice vine.* He calls the synagogue *the vine*, as David also did. That *He will bind his foal to the vine* is because his kingdom is bound up with and handed down through the synagogue, that is, *the sceptre will not depart from Judah until He comes to whom the kingdom belongs.* (*Commentary on Genesis* 42.5.4)[22]

Once again, Ephrem mirrors the interpretation of Genesis Rabbah 99:8, which understands the vine to be a reference to Israel. Like Christian commentators, the rabbinic text links Zechariah 9:9 to the messiah:

> Binding his foal unto the vine (49:11). This alludes to him who will gather together all Israel who are called a vine, as it says, *Thou didst pluck up a vine out of Egypt* (Ps. 80:9). And his ass's colt unto the choice vine alludes to him of whom it is written, *Lowly, and riding upon an ass, even upon a colt the foal of an ass* (Zech. 9:9). (Gen. Rab. 99:8)[23]

The fifth-century Christian biblical translator Jerome offers another interpretation, explaining that the Hebrew can be understood as 'city':

> Where we read: *binding his colt to the vine*, it is possible in the Hebrew for *his* city to be read instead of *colt*: with the same meaning in other words the Church is shown forth, concerning which is written elsewhere: *A city set on a mountain cannot be hidden*; and *The rush of the river makes glad the City of God.* (*Hebrew Questions on Genesis* 49:11)[24]

The rabbis take a similar approach. While Jerome applies the city to the church, the rabbis understand the vine to refer both to Israel and to Jerusalem (the city) as follows:

> *Vine* refers to Israel, as it is said: *Thou didst pluck up a vine out of Egypt* (Ps. 80:9). Binding his foal (*'iroh*) alludes to the Holy City (*'ir ha-kodesh*). *Unto the choice vine* refers to Israel, as is said: *Yes, I have planted thee a choice vine* (Jer. 2:21). (*Tanḥuma V'yehi* 10; cf. Gen. Rab. 98:9)[25]

---

[22] St Ephrem the Syrian, *Selected Prose Works*, trans. Edward G. Mathews and Joseph P. Amar, ed. Kathleen McVey (Washington, DC: Catholic University of America Press, 1994), 204.

[23] Freedman and Simon, *Midrash Rabbah*.

[24] Hayward, C. T. R. (trans. and ed.), *Saint Jerome's Hebrew Questions on Genesis* (Oxford: Clarendon Press, 1995), 84.

[25] Townsend, *Midrash Tanḥuma*.

A final example of exegetical contact can be seen in the interpretations of Theodoret of Cyrus, who was born in Antioch and lived in Cyrus, eighty miles away, a region that was inhabited by Jews and Christians (and where he would have encountered Jews and Jewish interpretations). His *Interpretations of Genesis* is dated to the same period as the compilation of Genesis Rabbah, and both reflect on the meaning of the words 'and his teeth whiter than milk' in verse 12, associating them with the clarity of their respective teachings.

For the rabbis, 'his teeth whiter than milk' alludes to the Sanhedrin, 'who sit and discuss the words of the Torah with their teeth [mouth] until they bring them forth as pure [clear] as milk' (Gen. Rab. 98:10).[26] Theodoret likened the 'gleaming white teeth' to the 'perfect clarity of the teaching of the disciples' who were sent into the world to bring salvation to believers.[27]

Bibliography

Hayward, C. T. R. (ed. and trans.), *Saint Jerome's Hebrew Questions on Genesis – Translated with Introduction and Commentary* (Oxford: Clarendon Press, 1995).

Kimmelman, R., 'Rabbi Yochanan and Origen on the Song of Songs', *Harvard Theological Review* 73 (1980), 567–95.

Narinskaya, Elena, *Ephrem, a 'Jewish' Sage: A Comparison of the Exegetical Writings of St. Ephrem the Syrian and Jewish Traditions* (Turnhout: Brepols, 2010).

4
Song of Songs 1:1–4

As noted in Chapters 2 and 3, the border between Christianity and Judaism remained fluid for centuries until each had absorbed or rejected groups which overlapped in their views and practice. As well as the existence of Jewish–Christian groups, it was not uncommon for 'mainstream' Jewish and Christian communities to live in the same areas, such as the Galilee, or cities such as Caesarea, in both of which we find centres of Palestinian Christianity as well as rabbinic academies. Indeed, Caesarea serves as a locus for the following discussion on the Song of Songs.

The interpretations below demonstrate similar exegetical interests as well as evidence that some Jews and Christians knew of and responded to each other's interpretations. Jewish and Christian interpreters understood the Song of Songs mystically: for the rabbis, it was an allegory about the relationship between God and Israel; for the church fathers, God and Israel were replaced by Christ and the church. The Song begins:

> [1] The song of songs, which is Solomon's.
> [2] Let him kiss me with the kisses of his mouth!
> For your love is better than wine [*yyn*].

---

[26] Freedman and Simon, *Midrash Rabbah*.
[27] Theodoret of Cyrus, *Questions on the Octateuch*, 215.

(An alternative reading of the third line is 'for your breasts': since Hebrew had no vowels until they were added in the tenth century CE, the noun could be read either as *dodim*, 'love' (the common translation), or *daddayim*, 'breasts' (derived from the same Hebrew letters). The Septuagint offers 'breasts' (*mastoi*), which is followed by Jerome (*ubera*) in the Vulgate.

Concern about the sexual and dangerous nature of the text was shared by Jewish and Christian commentators. For example, the third-century theologian Origen, who lived and delivered sermons in Caesarea, a city which was also home to a rabbinic academy, warned: 'I advise and counsel everyone who is not yet rid of the vexations of flesh and blood and has not ceased to feel the passion of his bodily nature, to refrain completely from reading this little book' (Prologue 1.1).[28] Similarly, the rabbis were suspicious of how the Song of Songs might be used, and Rabbi Akiva, who lived around 100 CE, offered the following warning: 'He who sings the Song of Songs in wine taverns, treating it as if it were a vulgar song, forfeits his share in the world to come' (*Tosefta Sanhedrin* 12.1).[29] While the presence of such similar responses does not prove the existence of an exegetical encounter, joint disquiet is a reminder of the shared approach to the biblical text.

As we saw in Chapter 2, Origen mentioned frequent disputes with Jews, some of whom he described as 'wise', a term often used in rabbinic literature as a synonym for the rabbis themselves (e.g., *Cels.* 1.55–6), and even recorded rabbinic views, notably those of his contemporary Rabbi Yohanan, who was known for visiting Caesarea. For example, Origen repeated Yohanan's view that 'as a result of the scattering of Jews, many among them become proselytes' (*Cels.* 1.55; b.Pesah 87b).[30] For his part, Yohanan expressed awareness of Christianity, explaining for example that Jews did not practise fasting on Sundays 'on account of the *Notzrim*' (b.Ta'anit 27b). It was also reported that a *min* attended Yohanan's synagogue sermons.

The traditional Christian interpretation of verse 2 can be found in the writings of Theodoret of Cyrus:

> The bride, then, longs to be kissed by the bridegroom, as if to say to his Father, 'Send me your only-begotten Son, O Lord and Father [...] I have been waiting for him for ages, longing for him for ages; I was distressed to receive his letters through patriarchs, through lawgivers, through prophets. I can no longer bear the flame of love; it is a fire burning and flaming in my innards. In all the prophets he makes a pledge to me to come, and to this day he has been unwilling to redeem his pledge. He made the pledge to me to come in David, in Jeremiah, in Isaiah, in Ezekiel, in Zechariah, in Daniel and in all the other prophets, and to consummate the marriage. I do not know why he delays, and why he spurns me in my longing [...] [E]ach day I am expectant in my longing

---

[28] Lawson, R. P. (trans.), *Origen: The Song of Songs: Commentary and Homilies*, Ancient Christian Writers 26 (Westminster, MD: The Newman Press; London: Longmans, Green and Co., 1957), 23.

[29] Phipps, William E., 'The Plight of the Song of Songs', *Journal of the American Academy of Religion* 42, no. 1 (March 1974), 85.

[30] Chadwick, Henry (ed. and trans.), *Origen: Contra Celsum* (Cambridge: Cambridge University Press, 1953).

to attain what is promised.' This is what is implied in her saying, *Let him kiss me with kisses of his mouth.* (Commentary on the Song of Songs 1:2)[31]

Theodoret focuses on the bride's desire to be kissed by the bridegroom, interpreted in terms of Jesus' fulfilment of the biblical promises made by the prophets. Indeed, the latter were no longer needed, indicating they had been rendered obsolete by the revelation in Christ. This interpretation is an example of replacement theology, commonly found among the *adversus Judaeos* writings of the church fathers (see Chapter 2, p. 65).

Does the prominence accorded to the Oral Torah in the late (perhaps seventh-century CE?) Targum of the opening verse demonstrate, implicitly at least, a response?

> Solomon the prophet said: 'Blessed be the name of the Lord who gave us the Torah at the hands of Moses, the Great Scribe, [both the Torah] written on the two tablets of stone, and the Six Orders of the Mishnah and Talmud by oral tradition, and [who] spoke with us face to face as a man kisses his friend, out of the abundance of the love wherewith He loved us more than the seventy nations.' (*Targum of Canticles* 1:2)[32]

The Targum implicitly rejects Christian claims by emphasising the significance of both the Written and Oral Torah. Jews received revelation directly from God ('He would speak with us face to face') and are superior to the 'seventy nations', a euphemism for gentiles (seventy being the numerical value of the Hebrew word for wine, *yyn*).

A remark by Yohanan in Song of Songs Rabbah goes further and explains that the Oral Torah is even superior to the Written Torah:

> The injunctions of the Scribes are more beloved than those of the Torah, as it says: *For thy love* [*dodecha*] *is better than wine* [Alternative reading: *For thy breasts (dadacha) are better than wine*]. (Song Rab. 1.2.2)[33]

It is noteworthy that both readings, ('thy love' and 'thy breasts') are offered, alongside the assertion that the Oral Torah (the 'injunctions of the Scribes') is more significant than the Written. Yohanan is likely to have had Christian exegesis in mind when he included the alternative reading offered by the Septuagint (and followed by the church fathers) and his interpretation should be viewed in the context of the Jewish–Christian encounter, as the following passage from the fifth-century Pesiqta Rabbati demonstrates:

> R. Judah the son of Shalum was of the opinion that when the Holy One, blessed be He, said to Moses *Write thou*, Moses wanted to write the Mishnah as well. However, the Holy One, blessed be He, foresaw that ultimately the nations of the world would translate the Torah into the Greek language and would claim: 'We are the Israelites.'

---

[31] Theodoret of Cyrus, *Questions on the Octateuch*, 37–8.
[32] Alexander, Philip S., *The Targum of Canticles, Translated with a Critical Introduction, Apparatus, and Notes*, The Aramaic Bible 17A (Collegeville: Liturgical Press, 2003), 78–9. (Square-bracketed words are part of the original.)
[33] Simon, Maurice (trans. and ed.), *Midrash Rabbah: The Song of Songs* (London: Soncino, 1961), 32.

> Now the scales are balanced (as to who are His people). The Holy One,
> blessed be He, can say to the nations of the world: You claim that you are My
> children, but I know that only those who know My secrets are My children.
> Where are His secrets (to be found)? In the Mishnah, which was given orally,
> and from which everything can be derived. (PesR 14b)[34]

Debate between Jews and Christians over the significance of the Oral Torah represents a
theme of the exegetical encounter. For his part, Origen explained in his commentary on
the Song of Songs:

> By wine is meant the ordinances and teachings which the Bride has been
> wont to receive through the Law and Prophets before the Bridegroom
> came. But when she now reflects upon the teaching that flows forth from the
> Bridegroom's breasts, she is amazed and marvels: she sees that it is far super-
> ior to that with which she has been gladdened as with spiritual wine served to
> her by the holy fathers and prophets, before the Bridegroom came. (*Song of
> Songs Commentary* 1.2)[35]

Both Yohanan and Origen agree that the wine refers to the 'Law and Prophets' and that
the bridegroom's breasts are superior to wine. For Origen, however, the breasts represent
the teaching of Christ, which replaces the previous revelation; for Yohanan, they represent the Oral Torah, which is superior to the Written.

Another topic in the exegetical encounter concerns the role of intermediaries. For
Origen, with the coming of Christ there is no longer any need for prophetic or angelic
intermediaries (as depicted in the Old Testament). The bridegroom (Christ) takes his
bride (the church) and no longer wants his friends (the prophets) to sing to her:

> What are the songs in relation to which this song is called 'The Song of
> Songs'[?] I think they are the songs that were sung of old by prophets or by
> angels. For the Law is said to have been *ordained by angels in the hand of a medi-
> ator* [Gal 3:19]. All those, then, that were uttered by them, were the introduc-
> tory songs sung by the Bridegroom's friends; but this unique song is that which
> the Bridegroom himself was to sing as His marriage-hymn, when about to take
> His Bride; in which same song the Bride no longer wants the Bridegroom's
> friends to sing to her, but longs to hear her Spouse who now is with her, speak
> with His own lips; wherefore she says: *Let Him kiss me with the kisses of His
> mouth*. (*Song of Songs Commentary* Prologue 1.4)[36]

Origen's allegorical interpretation of the bride, bridegroom and friends makes reference
to Galatians 3:19 which, he explains, makes clear that there is no longer any need for a

---

[34] Berman, Samuel A. (trans. and ed.), *Midrash Tanḥuma-Yelammedenu: An English Translation of Genesis and
Exodus* (Hoboken: Ktav, 1996).
[35] Lawson, *Origen: The Song of Songs*, 65.
[36] Lawson, *Origen: The Song of Songs*, 46–7. (Biblical reference is a footnote in the original.)

mediator, implying the obsolescence of the Torah. It is not coincidental that Yohanan deals with the same issue when he interprets the same verse as applying to Israel at Mount Sinai:

> It was as if a king wanted to marry a wife of good and noble family, so he sent an envoy to speak with her. She said, 'I am not worthy to be his handmaid, but all the same I desire to hear from his own mouth.' When the envoy returned to the king, he was full of smiles, but he would give no clear report to the king. The king, who was very discerning, said: 'This man is full of smiles, which would show that she consented, and he does not give any clear report, which would seem to show that she said that she wants to hear from my own mouth.' So Israel is the woman of good family, Moses is the envoy, and the king is the Holy One, blessed be He. (Song Rab. 1.2.3)[37]

Yohanan faced a problem because he could not deny that Moses was given an intermediary role. Like Origen, he also used allegory but sought to minimise the significance of Moses: the king (God) sends an envoy (Moses) to seek a bridegroom (Israel). When the envoy returns to the king, he smiles but says nothing, which is interpreted by Yohanan to mean that the king realises he needs to speak directly to his bride. Thus, Moses is merely a facilitator – a matchmaker, not an intermediary – which allows Yohanan to argue that the covenant was given directly by God to Israel and not through a mediator. This enables him to respond to Origen's position and argue that God spoke directly to Israel, who remained chosen.

Rabbi Isaac's interpretation, which is recorded in the same midrash, clarifies Yohanan's approach:

> It is as if a king was distributing largesse to his soldiers through his generals, officers and commanders, but when his son came, he gave him with his own hand. R. Isaac said: It is as if a king was eating sweetmeats, and when his son came he gave him from his own hand. (Song Rab. 1.2.5)[38]

Thus, the rabbinic interpretations of the opening verses of the Song of Songs provided a counter-narrative to Christian claims that Christ and the church replace the election of the Jewish people. While it is not possible to prove in which direction the encounter took place, Origen's and Yohanan's interpretations (as well as the supporting evidence from the patristic and rabbinic writings more widely) demonstrate the existence of an exegetical encounter.

Bibliography

de Lange, N. R. M., *Origen and the Jews: Studies in Jewish–Christian Relations in Third-Century Palestine* (Cambridge: Cambridge University Press, 1976).

Kimmelman, R., 'Rabbi Yochanan and Origen on the Song of Songs', *Harvard Theological Review* 73 (1980), 567–95.

Lieber, Laura S., *A Vocabulary of Desire: The Song of Songs in the Early Synagogue* (Leiden: Brill, 2014).

---

[37] Simon, *Midrash Rabbah*.
[38] Simon, *Midrash Rabbah*.

PART II

900 to 1800

4

The Medieval Period
The Tenth to the Fifteenth Century

MARC SAPERSTEIN AND EDWARD KESSLER

INTRODUCTION

It is tempting to consider Jewish–Christian relations from the tenth to the fifteenth century simply as 500 years of Christian oppression of Jews and mutual loathing on either side of the Jewish–Christian divide. However, as will already have become apparent, the Jewish–Christian encounter is not so straightforward, especially when evaluating relations over half a millennium. The popular assumption that the history of medieval Jewish–Christian relations is one of unmitigated Jewish suffering, a narrative that is sometimes magnified when considered through a post-Holocaust lens, needs considerable nuancing if we are to achieve a historically accurate understanding of the medieval Jewish–Christian encounter.

Our period begins with the legacy of Augustinian toleration of Jews and a more unified church which had, for the most part, overcome heresies and extinguished paganism. Attitudes towards Jews were more tolerant than those towards pagans and heretics because the church decreed that Jews should be preserved, if only to witness Christian truth. Beginning with Gregory I's statement *Sicut Judeis* in 598 (see Chapter 2, p. 98), a succession of popes had promulgated edicts whose purpose was both to limit and protect Jews, for example by forbidding forced baptism, violence against Jews and interference with Jewish worship – a tradition which would be continued between the twelfth and the fifteenth century by, among others, popes Callixtus II (*r.* 1119–24), Innocent III (see document 4 below) and Gregory X (see document 8). By the beginning of the second millennium, Jews who had settled in England, France and Germany were interacting socially with their Christian neighbours and developing networks across Europe. In Spain they were highly integrated with Christians and Muslims, as illustrated by the esteem in which Christians held the philosopher and poet Solomon ibn Gabirol (*c.* 1020–*c.* 1057), known in Latin as Avicebron. Jews owned land and engaged in a wide range of professions and occupations without noticeable Christian antipathy. In the eleventh century, then, the Jewish communities in Christian Europe were small but thriving, with papal and secular protection enshrined in law.

However, the First Crusade demonstrated that tolerant statements were no guarantee of tolerant behaviour, which came to an abrupt halt in 1096, a year which serves as a demarcation for the beginning of a new era. Although there is no evidence that Pope Urban II included anti-Jewish remarks in his call for a crusade, the Jews of the Rhineland were more accessible, vulnerable and familiar as villains from Christian scripture than Muslims in the east. Jews were not defenceless, nor were they without allies, but however much Christian leaders tried to protect them, deep Christian hostility burst the dam. Our first documents, one Christian and one Jewish, describe the anti-Jewish violence in Mainz (see documents 1 (i) and (ii)), and such crusader attacks were repeated throughout northern Europe. Regardless of secular or ecclesiastical protection, the violence was widespread. The trauma of 1096 was not easily dissipated and augured heightened tensions ahead.

Nevertheless, fifty years later, when the Second Crusade began (1146), the theologian and preacher Bernard of Clairvaux (1090–1153) intervened to protect German Jewry from attacks, a move which, combined with other Christian interventions, resulted in fewer outbreaks of anti-Jewish violence and a concurrent rise in Jewish learning. This coincided with what historians have called the 'twelfth-century renaissance', a period when Christian scholars were actively learning from Jews. Andrew of St Victor (d. 1175), a biblical exegete, engaged with contemporary Jewish commentators such as Rashi (Rabbi Solomon ben Isaac of Troyes, 1040–1105), whose emphasis on a literal approach to scriptural interpretation was adopted by the Parisian scholars of the St Victor Priory, commonly known as Victorines. As a result, Rashi's influence on Christian interpretation can be found among later Christian commentaries, such as those of Nicholas de Lyra (c. 1270–1349) and through him Martin Luther.

In general, however, Jews were regarded by the church as outsiders, and their position was one of isolation and of facing restrictive laws. In 1215, for example, the Fourth Lateran Council renewed some existing laws, such as those forbidding Jews from appearing in public during Easter, and created new ones, such as those which compelled them to wear distinctive dress (to avoid 'prohibited intercourse') and barred them from holding public office (see document 5).

Yet there is also a different story to tell, as demonstrated by church concern with Christians working in Jewish homes, a practice prohibited by the Second Lateran Council of 1179 and regularly afterwards. This implies that there was considerable and amicable contact between Jews and their Christian neighbours. Jewish texts also indicate that Christians provided a range of services to Jews, such as working in Jewish households.

Jewish religious leaders, like their Christian counterparts, sought to maintain boundaries between the communities. They followed the Talmudic position on Christianity as *avodah zarah* ('foreign worship'), a designation for an idolatrous religion. They applied Talmudic rules intended to minimise interaction, but scholars suggest that Christians and Jews came into regular daily contact, for instance through trade. Rabbenu Jacob Tam (d. 1171) illustrates this in his ruling that commercial relations between Christians and Jews were acceptable unless the goods involved were being used for Christian worship.

Just as there was more social interaction between Jews and Christians than the restrictions enacted by religious authorities might imply, a similar development can be noted in theological and philosophical encounters. This was partly because Judaism and Christianity faced similar philosophical difficulties, as illustrated by the views of Maimonides (1135–1204) and Aquinas (c. 1225–74): both found anthropomorphism problematic and argued that biblical images capture the human experience of God, not how God is. (Aquinas was familiar with Maimonides' writings, referring respectfully to 'Rabbi Moses the Egyptian'.)

The excerpts selected from Aquinas (documents 7 (i), (ii) and (iii)) are taken from two biblical commentaries. They show that he held to traditional *adversus Judaeos* positions (see Chapter 2, p. 65) such as that Christianity was the true Israel (*verus Israel*) and the value of Judaism lay in preparation for the coming of Christ. Yet in his commentary on Romans he suggests that the election of Judaism remains in the present and that while Jews will eventually recognise the truth of the Christian message, they still have a positive role to play.

A similar holding of conflicting views in tension is found in the excerpts from Maimonides (documents 3 (i) and (ii)). Since Judaism was a minority faith in Christendom (and the Islamic world), Jews naturally considered the question of why God allowed these other faiths to flourish. Maimonides, who lived his entire life in Muslim countries, nuanced the Talmudic view that Christianity was a form of idolatry by explaining that Christianity (and Islam) providentially spread scripture throughout the world, preparing the way for nations to worship the God of Israel. The philosopher Menachem ha-Me'iri (1249–1315) built on Maimonides' work and, although his was a minority opinion, argued that Christianity should be understood as a form of monotheism and coined the phrase 'nations bound by the ways of religion' to relax certain rabbinic laws and facilitate a more fruitful interaction.

Of course, one key difference between Jews and Christians concerned power. Christian authorities had the power to govern tolerantly or intolerantly, while the relatively power-less Jewish minority did not need to confront the practicalities of governing a minority. While the medieval writings of Jews and Christians include mutual condemnations and impute multiple failings to the other, only one group had the power to implement laws.

Another relevant factor is that, apart from in Spain, Jews were the only significant non-Christian community, which in and of itself constituted a problematic situation. Living as a unique 'other' was fraught with danger, made worse by the Christian identification of contemporary Jews as hostile Pharisees, responsible for the death of Christ: they remained opponents of Jesus, regarded, under the influence of contemporary interpretations of the Gospels, as a threat to Christian well-being.

Popular myths also contributed to Christian hostility, notably the infamous 'ritual murder' or 'blood libel' accusation. It is difficult today to realise the impression this made on the medieval mind. The first such accusation was made in England around 1150, when Thomas of Monmouth developed the accusation that local Jews had murdered the twelve-year-old William of Norwich in 1144 (see document 2). Other accusations followed elsewhere in England and on the European continent, spreading from one city to another. They were an expression of a popular Christian conviction that Jews were pawns of the devil.

Another common accusation was desecration of the eucharistic host, which was first made in Paris in 1290. Other Christian symbols, such as the crucifix and holy images, were also seen as targets of Jewish attacks. Jews began to be blamed for many of the ills of the period, and confession of Jewish involvement was not hard to uncover under torture. Soon it was the Jewish people as a whole and not individual Jews who came to be blamed, as epitomised by fears of well-poisoning and charges of responsibility for the Black Death in 1348 (see document 11).

Nevertheless, these accusations, which today we would call conspiracy theories, were rejected by successive popes as well as by secular authorities. Papal disavowal was especially strong, as was rejection of the charge that Jewish well-poisoning caused the plague, though on occasion local bishops encouraged cults emerging around the alleged victims of Jews, even against papal and royal policies.

Conspiracy theories also entered the world of art and literature. Medieval English texts often depicted Jews as responsible for the death of Christ or as killers of children. Geoffrey Chaucer's (c. 1342/3–1400) *The Prioress's Tale*, for example, recounts the story of a Christian boy murdered by Jews at the instigation of Satan; the blood of the Christian child cried out and Jews were punished. Representations in the visual arts also played a role, depicting Jews with forked beards, distorted facial features (e.g., hooked noses) or physical deformities. Medieval Christian artists also fashioned a pair of female figures called Ecclesia/Synagoga to represent Christianity's relationship to Judaism: a triumphant Ecclesia and defeated Synagoga can still be seen among the thirteenth-century statuary of the cathedrals of Notre Dame in Paris and Strasbourg, the proud Ecclesia standing tall, in contrast to the bowed, blindfolded figure of Synagoga. As the centuries passed, these images became more extreme in depicting the difference between the female figures.

While ecclesiastical law stipulated that Jews should enjoy the right to safety and security within Christian society (see document 4) and church leaders regularly articulated tolerance for Jews, reproofs and condemnation were commonly issued – a difficult combination to absorb. Christians were to hear of Jewish wickedness and be strengthened in their Christian identity thereby. They were not, however, to act on any feelings of outrage. Unsurprisingly, the people of medieval European towns failed, repeatedly, to meet this demand.

While the papacy taught toleration for Jews, states also provided protection, expecting Jews to contribute to the economy and political stability. Examples of secular protectors include William I the Conqueror (c. 1028–87), who established the first Jewish community in England in 1066; Henry IV, Holy Roman Emperor and King of Germany (1056–1106), who allowed baptised Jews to revert to Judaism after the First Crusade and asked Bishop Rüdiger Huzmann (d. 1090) to invite Jews to live in Speyer; and Emperor Frederick II (1194–1250), who investigated and rejected the blood libel accusation.

The desire of secular rulers to attract Jews to their territories and protect them in the imperial cities was based on Jews' status as 'servants of the crown' and so part of imperial fiscal policy. In effect, they were the ruler's property. While church doctrine forbade the taking of interest beyond the principal of the loan, secular rulers realised that the practice was an economic necessity to foster urban growth and the commercialisation of the European economy.

As well as setting interest rates, they supported Jewish moneylending, which became a feature of Jewish life, especially in northern Europe, but these transactions brought Jews into contact with the poorer sections of urban societies, which generated popular resentment.

By the end of the thirteenth century the growth of anti-Jewish sentiment became unstoppable, as illustrated by a wave of expulsions, most significantly from England in 1290 (see document 10). King Edward I of England (*r.* 1272–1307) initially used Jews as a source of funds, particularly for his crusades and to support the *Domus Conversorum* (House of Conversion), home to Jews who had converted to Christianity (only abolished in 1891). When Jews did not convert *en masse*, and their financial contribution to the throne dwindled through fiscal exploitation, Edward expelled the entire community.

Elsewhere, in southern Europe and especially in the Iberian Peninsula, Jews were living in a more tolerant environment, either alongside Christians under Muslim rule or, as Christianity regained Spanish territory, with Muslims under Christian rule. The relatively easy coexistence of Jews, Christians and Muslims commonly called the *convivencia* ('coexistence') continued until the late fourteenth century, although it is important not to romanticise this relationship.

It was also during this time that Christians came to realise that Judaism had produced new holy books, such as the Talmud, which challenged the view that the biblical heritage provided by Jews could bear witness to Christian truth (*testimonium Veritatis*). Were Jews no longer carrying, in the words of Augustine, the books of the Old Testament but instead the Talmud? If they were not really the Jews Augustine had referred to, did they have a legitimate place in Christendom as preservers of, and witnesses to, scripture? Public disputations between Christian and Jewish protagonists pioneered a new line of Christian argumentation, grounded in rabbinic literature: Christian interlocutors either proposed the Talmud contained evidence that post-biblical Jewish writings proved the truth of Christianity or was itself blasphemous and should be destroyed. Charges against the Talmud can be found as early as 1236, resulting in cartloads being burned in Paris after the disputation of 1240. The best-known disputation took place between Nachmanides and Pablo Christiani in Barcelona in 1263 (see document 6).

A feature of the examination of the rabbinic writings was the Christian desire to convert Jews, which required Jewish protagonists to listen to Christian arguments but allowed them to attempt rebuttal. Jewish failure to accept the Christian message was troubling: while rationalised as Jewish blindness, and while Christians were assured that at the end time Jews would recognise Christ, the ongoing intransigence of contemporary Jews caused deep concern. One response was for the church to force Jews to hear Christian preachers delivering sermons, usually in synagogues, for the purpose of their conversion.

We also find evidence of Jewish responses between 1000 and 1500, as Chapters 2 and 3 also show for the preceding period. Just as there was Christian anti-Jewish polemic, so our period contains Jewish anti-Christian polemic. Meir bar Simon of Narbonne (d. 1239), for example, gathered together a wide range of Jewish polemical claims against Christianity, and the anonymous *Nizzahon Vetus* (document 9) portrayed Jesus as irrational and immoral. These works helped sustain medieval Jewry through adversity, emphasising that

Jews were superior to their Christian aggressors. Even suffering was a sign of chosenness because of its unique capacity to sanctify the divine name through martyrdom.

Not only martyrdom but forced conversions were a consequence of outbursts of anti-Jewish violence. The effects of such violence in Spain from the late fourteenth century were longer-lasting than those of the First Crusade and, as Hasdai Crescas' letter to the community of Avignon shows, devastating (document 12). Many Jews chose conversion rather than death, which raised problems for both Judaism and Christianity. While the church condemned forced conversions, there was disagreement about whether such baptisms were valid or not. Some, of course, were insincere, leading to so-called 'crypto-Jews' developing a clandestine religion, passed on from generation to generation, before seeking a return to practising Judaism openly (see document 13). Others were genuine in their conversion to Christianity and, once converted, found society open, leading to social and economic progress accompanied by rapid integration.

During the course of the fifteenth century the church became aware of the growth in the number of such 'new Christians' (*cristianos nuevos*), who soon faced restrictions and then subjection to the newly created Inquisition. One consequence was the rooting out of crypto-Jews, which, combined with an increasingly strident Christianity and the concept of *limpieza de sangre* (literally, 'cleanliness of blood') and its 'blood purity' tendency, eventually led to the expulsion of Jews from Spain in 1492 and from Portugal in 1497 (see documents 14 and 15).

Where these Jews found refuge and the implications for the future history of Jewish–Christian relations must be left to the next chapter.

Bibliography

Abulafia, Anna Sapir, *Christians and Jews in the Twelfth-Century Renaissance* (London: Routledge, 1995).

Adams, Jonathan, and Hanska, Jussi (eds.), *The Jewish–Christian Encounter in Medieval Preaching* (London: Routledge, 2014).

Chazan, Robert, *Reassessing Jewish Life in Medieval Europe* (Cambridge: Cambridge University Press, 2010).

Cohen, Mark R., *Under Crescent and Cross: The Jews in the Middle Ages* (Princeton: Princeton University Press, 2008).

Elukin, Jonathan M., *Living Together, Living Apart: Rethinking Jewish–Christian Relations in the Middle Ages* (Princeton: Princeton University Press, 2007).

Frassetto, Michael (ed.), *Christian Attitudes toward the Jews in the Middle Ages: A Casebook* (New York and London: Routledge, 2007).

Katz, Jacob, *Exclusiveness and Tolerance: Studies in Jewish–Gentile Relations in Medieval and Modern Times* (London: Oxford University Press, 1961).

Rist, Rebecca, *Popes and Jews 1095–1291* (Oxford: Oxford University Press, 2016).

Saperstein, Marc, *Jewish Preaching, 1200–1800: An Anthology* (New Haven: Yale University Press, 1989).

Tartakoff, Paola, *Conversion, Circumcision, and Ritual Murder in Medieval Europe* (Philadelphia: University of Pennsylvania Press, 2020).

Yuval, Israel Jacob, *Two Nations in Your Womb: Perceptions of Jews and Christians in Late Antiquity and the Middle Ages*, trans. Barbara Harshav and Jonathan Chipman (Berkeley: University of California Press, 2006).

DOCUMENTS

I

Christian and Jewish Accounts of the First Crusade (c. 1120 and 1140)

Text

(i) Albert of Aix: History of the Journey to Jerusalem *(Historia Ierosolimitana) (c. 1120)*

[I]n the same year in which Peter [the Hermit], and Gottschalk, after collecting an army, had set out, there assembled in like fashion a large and innumerable host of Christians from diverse kingdoms and lands; namely, from the realms of France, England, Flanders, and Lorraine …. I know not whether by a judgment of the Lord, or by some error of mind, they rose in a spirit of cruelty against the Jewish people scattered throughout these cities and slaughtered them without mercy, especially in the Kingdom of Lorraine, asserting it to be the beginning of their expedition and their duty against the enemies of the Christian faith. This slaughter of Jews was done first by citizens of Cologne. These suddenly fell upon a small band of Jews and severely wounded and killed many; they destroyed the houses and synagogues of the Jews and divided among themselves a very large amount of money. When the Jews saw this cruelty, about two hundred in the silence of the night began flight by boat to Neuss. The pilgrims and crusaders discovered them, and after taking away all their possessions, inflicted on them similar slaughter, leaving not even one alive.

Not long after this, they started upon their journey, as they had vowed, and arrived in a great multitude at the city of Mainz. There Count Emico, a nobleman, a very mighty man in this region, was awaiting, with a large band of Teutons, the arrival of the pilgrims who were coming thither from diverse lands by the King's highway.

The Jews of this city, knowing of the slaughter of their brethren, and that they themselves could not escape the hands of so many, fled in hope of safety to Bishop Rothard [Ruthard]. They put an infinite treasure in his guard and trust, having much faith in his protection, because he was Bishop of the city. Then that excellent Bishop of the city cautiously set aside the incredible amount of money received from them. He placed the Jews in the very spacious hall of his own house, away from the sight of Count Emico and his followers, that they might remain safe and sound in a very secure and strong place.

But Emico and the rest of his band held a council and, after sunrise, attacked the Jews in the hall with arrows and lances. Breaking the bolts and doors, they killed the Jews, about seven hundred in number, who in vain resisted the force and attack of so many thousands. They killed the women, also, and with their swords pierced tender children of whatever age and sex. The Jews, seeing that their Christian enemies were attacking them and their children, and that they were sparing no age, likewise fell upon one another, brother, children, wives, and sisters, and thus they perished at each other's hands. Horrible to say, mothers cut the throats of nursing children with knives and stabbed others, preferring them to perish thus by their own hands rather than to be killed by the weapons of the uncircumcised.

From this cruel slaughter of the Jews a few escaped; and a few because of fear, rather than because of love of the Christian faith, were baptized. With very great spoils taken from these people, Count Emico, Clarebold, Thomas, and all that intolerable company of men and women then continued on their way to Jerusalem, directing their course towards the Kingdom of Hungary, where passage along the royal highway was usually not denied the pilgrims. But on arriving at *Wieselburg*, the fortress of the King, which the rivers Danube and Leytha protect with marshes, the bridge and gate of the fortress were found closed by command of the King of Hungary, for great fear had entered all the Hungarians because of the slaughter which had happened to their brethren ....

But while almost everything had turned out favorably for the Christians, and while they had penetrated the walls with great openings, by some chance or misfortune, I know not what, such great fear entered the whole army that they turned in flight [...]

Emico and some of his followers continued in their flight along the way by which they had come. Thomas, Clarebold, and several of their men escaped in flight toward Carinthia and Italy. So the hand of the Lord is believed to have been against the pilgrims, who had sinned by excessive impurity and fornication, and who had slaughtered the exiled Jews through greed of money, rather than for the sake of God's justice, although the Jews were opposed to Christ. The Lord is a just judge and orders no one unwillingly, or under compulsion, to come under the yoke of the Catholic faith.

Source

Krey, August C., *The First Crusade: The Accounts of Eye-Witnesses and Participants* (Princeton: Princeton University Press; London: Humphrey Milford, Oxford University Press, 1921), 54–6.

(ii) Solomon bar Samson: Jewish Account of the First Crusade (1140)

It came to pass at midday that the wicked Emicho, persecutor of the Jews, came – he and all his army – to the gate. The burghers opened the gate to him. Then the enemies of the Lord said to one another: 'Behold the gate has been opened before us. Now let us avenge the blood of the Crucified.'

[...] They then came in battalions and companies, sweeping down like a river, until Mainz was filled completely. The enemy Emicho made an announcement to the citizenry that they surrender and remove the enemy [the Jews] from the city. 'A great panic from the Lord fell upon them.' [Zech. 14:13] The men of Israel strapped on their weapons in the innermost courtyard of the archbishop and all of them approached the gate [of the courtyard] to do battle with the crusaders and the burghers. They did battle against one another at the gate. Our sins brought it about that the enemy overcame them and captured the gate. 'The hand of the Lord lay heavy' [1 Sam. 5:6] upon His people. Then all the gentiles gathered against the Jews in the courtyard, in order to destroy them totally. The hands of our people wavered, when they saw that the hand of wicked Edom had overcome them. Indeed the men of the archbishop, who had promised to help them, fled immediately, in order to turn them over to their enemies, for they were 'splintered reeds' [II Kings 18:21, Isa. 36:6]. Even the archbishop himself fled from his church, for they intended to kill him as well, since he had spoken up on behalf of Israel.

[…]

When the children of the sacred covenant saw that the decree had been enacted and that the enemy had overcome them, they entered the courtyard and all cried out together – elders, young men and young women, children, menservants and maidservants – to their Father in heaven. They wept for themselves and their lives. They accepted upon themselves the judgment of heaven. They said to one another: 'Let us be strong and suffer the yoke of the sacred awe. For the moment the enemy will kill us, but the easiest of the four deaths is by sword. We shall, however, remain alive; our souls [shall be] in paradise, in the radiance of the great light forever.' […] Then they all cried out loudly, saying in unison: 'Now let us tarry no longer, for the enemy has already come upon us. Let us go quickly and sacrifice ourselves before the Lord. Anyone who has a knife should inspect it, that it not be defective. Then he should come and slaughter us for the sanctification of the unique [God] who lives forever. Subsequently he should slaughter himself by his throat or should thrust the knife into his belly.'

[…] 'Why did the heavens not darken? Why did the stars not withdraw their brightness?' […] when one thousand one hundred holy souls were killed and slaughtered on one day, on the third day of Sivan, a Tuesday – infants and sucklings who never transgressed and never sinned and poor and innocent souls? 'At such things will you restrain yourself, O Lord?' [Isa. 64:11] 'For Your sake they were killed' [Ps. 44:23] – innumerable souls. 'Avenge the blood of your servants that has been spilled' [Ps. 79:10] in our days and before our eyes speedily. Amen.

[…]

'Who has seen anything like this; who has heard anything' like that which the saintly and pious woman, Rachel, daughter of R. Isaac ben R. Asher, wife of R. Judah, did? She said to her companions: 'I have four children. On them as well have no mercy, lest these uncircumcised come and seize them alive and they remain in their pseudo-faith. With them as well you must sanctify the Name of the holy God.' […] The father wailed and cried out when he saw the death of his four children, 'comely and beautiful' [Gen. 39:6]. He went and threw himself on the sword in his hand. His innards flowed forth and he writhed in blood on the roadway along with those who had been killed, who had been convulsing and writhing in their blood. The enemy killed all those that remained in the chamber and stripped them naked. 'See, O Lord, and behold, how abject I have become' [Lam. 1:11].

Then the crusaders began to exult in the name of the crucified, for they had done their will upon all those found in the chambers of the archbishop, and there remained not a remnant.

Source

Chazan, Robert, *European Jewry and the First Crusade* (Berkeley: University of California Press, 1987), 252–54, 256, 258–60. (Square-bracketed phrases are part of the original, the biblical references as footnotes.)

Commentary

These two documents, by a Christian and a Jewish writer respectively, relate to events which took place during the First Crusade in 1095–6, when Pope Urban II sought support to recover Jerusalem from the Saracens, and crusaders, led by lords and inspired by preachers, set out for the Holy Land. The Crusades, which lasted until the sixteenth century, were a significant blow to contemporary Jewish life in France and, especially, in Germany, and have had a continuing impact on Jewish–Christian relations.

Until then Jews had been living fairly comfortably, as illustrated by the fact that in his charter of 1084 (issued at the request of the Holy Roman Emperor Henry IV) Bishop Rüdiger of Speyer indicates his belief that the economic advancement of his home town would be significantly enhanced by inviting and convincing Jews to settle there; while the contribution anticipated from these Jewish settlers was primarily economic, the underlying theme is that Jews and Christians could flourish together. Less than a dozen years later, however, the situation in northern Europe had changed dramatically. Despite Jewish appeals to local lords and bishops and the promise of protection by Henry IV, crusaders who passed through Germany on their way to Jerusalem killed thousands of 'infidel' Jews in the larger cities such as Speyer, Worms, Mayence (Mainz) and Cologne.

It is not easy to find details and original sources of crusader attacks. There are no known contemporary Christian accounts of the anti-Jewish violence of the First Crusade, but several important Christian documents were written a generation later. Albert, canon of the church of Aachen/Aix-la-Chapelle, wrote a lengthy chronicle, *Historia Ierosolimitana* (*History of the Journey to Jerusalem*), which focuses primarily on the crusaders in the Holy Land but in a brief prelude narrates anti-Jewish violence, using the testimony of participants as well as some hearsay material (document 1 (i)). It is generally accepted as an accurate record.

Albert criticises the Christian slaughter of Jews in Cologne and, more extensively, in Mainz, describing the attack on the city's Jews led by Emicho, a German minor noble, and the response by Bishop Ruthard of Mainz on behalf of the local Jewish community. According to Albert's account, the bishop made a sincere effort to protect Jews, refusing their offer of money and placing them in a spacious hall of his own house, assuming that they would be safe. Despite his condemnation, however, soldiers broke in and killed them – men, women and children. Without explaining the exact source of his information, Albert writes that when the Jewish men realised they could not escape they decided to kill themselves. His graphic account is especially moving in that the information must have come from other Christians, and is noteworthy for the author's contempt for the actions of Emicho's army, his sympathy for the victimised Jews and his confirmation of the chilling actions *in extremis* by the Jewish male victims.

Albert's responses to the killings represent something of a departure in Christian–Jewish relations but leave unanswered the question of why the Crusades to the Holy Land inspired Christian attacks on German Jews. One explanation may be that, although Pope Urban II's call for a crusade in response to the reports of Muslim persecutions of Christians in the east did not mention Jews, the desire to respond made it difficult for many Christians to postpone any reaction during months of travel to a distant land. The strong emphasis on Christian identity that was the basis of their lengthy journey led them to think of Jews in the same category as the distant Muslims. Nevertheless, as both our documents suggest, local bishops and archbishops tried, unsuccessfully, to prevent anti-Jewish violence in their cities in pursuit of their commitment to maintaining public order and official church policy (which did not permit Jews to be attacked or forcibly converted).

As with Christian accounts, no known Jewish texts were written at the time of the disaster or even shortly afterwards. Several Jewish texts written in the middle of the twelfth century, including document 1 (ii) by Solomon bar Samson (about whom little is known), apparently reveal access to reports from survivors of the catastrophe, but are filled with direct quotations attributed to the individuals involved which were obviously the creation of subsequent Jewish writers. While such documents remain valuable primary sources, scholars remain divided on the extent to which they contain reliable testimony.

Solomon's account shows marked similarities with Albert's in its graphic description of the devastating attacks on Jews in Mainz on 27 May 1096, recording how crusaders forced their way into the archiepiscopal palace where Jews had taken refuge with the permission of the archbishop, who spoke on their behalf. Solomon describes the slaughter and suicide of Jews in this palace with all the attendant horror: many were killed or forcibly baptised; others chose to die by their own hands as martyrs, sanctifying God's name (*Kiddush ha-Shem*), shouting their contempt for Christianity and affirming their faith in God.

While for the crusaders attacks such as this were merely preparation for claiming the Holy Land for Christendom, these events continued to influence Jewish suspicion of Christians in the following centuries: even today the word 'crusade', commonly used to denote a righteous endeavour, conjures up for Jews (and Muslims) the image of unjust religious persecution. However, although both documents show how vulnerable Jews' position was at times of heightened Christian fervour, it is important to note that the First Crusade did not lead to the decimation of northern Europe's Jewish population. Communities continued to develop during the twelfth and thirteenth centuries, and crusading hostility against Jews was only one factor among many which determined medieval Christian–Jewish relations.

Bibliography

Abulafia, Anna Sapir, 'The Interrelationship between the Hebrew Chronicles of the First Crusade', *Journal of Semitic Studies* 27 (1982), 22–39.

Chazan, Robert, 'The Facticity of Medieval Narrative: A Case Study of the Hebrew First Crusade Narratives', *AJS Review* (Spring–Autumn, 1991), 31–56.

Chazan, Robert, *In the Year 1096: The First Crusade and the Jews* (Philadelphia: The Jewish Publication Society, 1996).

Marcus, Ivan, 'From Politics to Martyrdom: Shifting Paradigms in the Hebrew Narratives of the 1096 Crusade Riots', *Prooftexts* 2 (1982), 40–52.

Riley-Smith, Jonathan, 'Christian Violence and the Crusades', in Abulafia, Anna Sapir (ed.), *Religious Violence between Christians and Jews* (Basingstoke: Palgrave, 2002), 3–20.

2

Thomas of Monmouth: The Life and Passion of William of Norwich (c. *1150–73)*

Text

Following daybreak, which was their *pascha* that year, after the appropriate chants of the day were finished in the synagogue, the leaders of the Jews met in the house of the aforementioned Jew, and while the boy William was eating, fearing no treachery, they suddenly seized him and humiliated him in various wretched ways […] And so, while the enemies of the Christian name ran riot around the boy in such a spirit of evil, there were others among them who, in mockery of the Passion of the Cross, sentenced him to be crucified […] They said, 'Just as we have condemned Christ to a most shameful death, so we condemn a Christian, so that we punish both the Lord and his servant in the punishment of reproach; that which they ascribe to us we will inflict on them.' And so, conspiring to execute such execrable malice, they next seized the innocent victim with bloody hands and raised him from the ground. He was put upon the cross and they competed among themselves in rivalry to kill him.

And when we were enquiring carefully into the affair, we found the house and in it most definite and clear signs of the affair. Moreover, there was, as rumour has it, stretched out as a cross a post between two others and a wooden beam in the middle, attached on either side to the two other posts. And, similarly, we later discovered truly the traces made by the wounds and the chains. On the right, the right hand and foot tightly bound by chains; but on the left, the left hand and foot both pierced by a nail. And they did this with such care, of course, that if he was at any time found with nails fixed into him from this side and that, it would not be indicated that he had been killed by Jews, but rather by Christians. But while they did so, they added to the painful wounds other pains and wounds, since they could not extinguish their mad cruelty, nor satisfy their inborn hatred of the Christian name. Truly, after so great and so many sufferings of tortures, they inflicted a grievous wound to his left side, up into his heart and, as if bringing the affair to an end, they extinguished the mortal life that still remained within him. And since several rivers of blood flowed from the whole of his body, both in order to staunch the blood and to wash and close the wounds, they poured boiling water from his head downwards.

And so the glorious boy and martyr of Christ, William, dying in this world the disgrace of the death of the Lord, was crowned with the blood of glorious martyrdom and achieved the kingdom of eternal glory, alive for eternity. His soul is exalted joyfully in heaven among the illustrious host of saints; and his body works wonders gloriously on earth by the omnipotence of divine mercy [...]

Because we know for sure that they perpetrated this as an insult to the Passion of the Lord and to the shame of Christian law, we will prove the truth of the matter with several proofs [...]

FIFTH PROOF: We also interpose as an argument of faith and truth what we have heard told by Theobald, a person who was once a Jew and later one of our monks. He told us that in the ancient writings of their ancestors it was written that Jews could not achieve their freedom or ever return to the lands of their fathers without the shedding of human blood. Hence it was decided by them a long time ago that every year, to the shame and affront of Christ, a Christian somewhere on earth be sacrificed to the highest God, and so they take revenge for the injuries of Him, whose death is the reason for their exclusion from their fatherland and their exile as slaves in foreign lands.

Therefore, the leaders and rabbis of the Jews who dwell in Spain, at Narbonne, where the seed of kings and their glory flourishes greatly, meet together, and cast lots of all the regions where Jews lived. Whichever region was chosen by lot, its capital city had to apply that lot to the other cities and towns, and the one whose name comes up will carry out that business, as decreed. In that year, however, when William, the glorious martyr of God, was killed, it so happened that the lot fell on the men of Norwich, and all the communities of the Jews of England offered their consent by letters or by messengers for the crime to be performed at Norwich. 'I was at the time in Cambridge,' [said Theobald,] 'a Jew among Jews, and the crime of the action performed was not hidden from me. With the passage of time, when I learned of the glorious greatness of miracles which by divine virtue happened through the merits of the blessed martyr William, I was greatly afraid and, consulting my conscience, I left Judaism and converted to the faith of Christ.' These words, indeed, of the Jewish convert we believe to be all the truer for having learned them from a converted enemy, revealed by someone privy to the secrets of the enemies.

Source

From *The Life and Passion of William of Norwich* by Thomas of Monmouth, translated by Miri Rubin, published by Penguin Classics. Translation copyright © Miri Rubin 2014. Reprinted by permission of Penguin Books Limited. Text quoted from 16–18, 58, 61–2.

Commentary

The event in this passage was alleged to have happened in 1144 and concerns the death of a twelve-year-old boy, William of Norwich. There was a Jewish community living in Norwich in England, and the Jews were accused, first by William's uncle, of being responsible. The charge, which resulted in no action at the time, was later linked to an elaborate claim that not only did Jews murder Christian children, but they did so in a carefully plotted manner: every year there is an international council of Jews at which they choose the country in which a Christian child will be killed during Easter. This child murder accusation helped fuel a 'blood libel' tradition in later decades, which had spread throughout Europe by the seventeenth century (see also document 8).

The most important figure in this passage is Theobald, a Jew who became a Christian monk after hearing reports of the murder. Theobald, whose supposed knowledge of Jewish affairs was accepted because of his Jewish upbringing, reported that long ago it had been determined that every year a Christian child must be murdered by Jews as a response to their current life as slaves in foreign countries. Theobald later communicated with the author, Thomas of Monmouth, who was responsible for writing a full record of the murderous event; there is a debate among historians about when his book was completed, but it was probably sometime between 1150 and 1173. Needless to say, no proof or explanation is provided to connect the murder of William to the elaborate annual decision-making process Thomas alleges.

William's death provides the earliest direct evidence of the blood libel accusation in its child-murder form. Other cases can be found in Gloucester (1168), Bury (1181) and Bristol (1183), as well as in France, for example at Blois, and Chaucer's *Prioress's Tale* testifies to the accusation's currency in the late fourteenth century. Despite official secular and ecclesiastical investigations in the thirteenth century by Emperor Frederick II (r. 1215–50) and Pope Innocent IV (r. 1243–54) which denied any possibility that Jews used human blood, accusations continued into the twentieth century (see, for example, the Mendel Beilis case; Chapter 6, p. 337). The Nazis revived the charges that Jews killed children and used their blood, and often drew on early woodcuts to inspire their own visual representations of such imagined atrocities.

A shrine to William attracted pilgrims to Norwich Cathedral, where today a notice in the Chapel of the Holy Innocents explains the history of the case; the chapel is now dedicated to remembrance of the sufferings of all innocent victims, particularly the young, and to reconciliation between people of different faiths, especially Jewish victims of Christian persecution.

Bibliography

Langmuir, Gavin, 'Thomas of Monmouth: Detector of Ritual Murder', *Speculum* 59, no. 4 (1984), 820–46.

McColloh, John M., 'William of Norwich, Thomas of Monmouth, and the Early Dissemination of the Myth', *Speculum* 72, no. 3 (1997), 698–740.

Rose, E. M., *The Murder of William of Norwich: The Origins of Blood Libel in Medieval Europe* (Oxford: Oxford University Press, 2015).

Thomas of Monmouth, *The Life and Passion of William of Norwich*, trans. and ed. Miri Rubin (London: Penguin, 2014).

3

Maimonides: Code of Jewish Law *(Mishneh Torah)* *and 'Epistle to Yemen' (1170–80)*

Text

(i) Mishneh Torah, Book 14, Chapter 11: Judges, Kings and Wars (1170–80)

King Messiah will arise and restore the kingdom of David to its former state and original sovereignty. He will rebuild the sanctuary and gather the dispersed of Israel. All the ancient laws will be reinstituted in his days; sacrifices will again be offered; the Sabbatical and Jubilee years will again be observed in accordance with the commandments set forth in the Law.

[...]

The following is the uncensored version of the end of Kings, ch. XI.

But if he does not meet with full success, or is slain, it is obvious that he is not the Messiah promised in the Torah. He is to be regarded like all the other wholehearted and worthy kings of the House of David who died and who the Holy One, blessed be He, raised up to test the multitude, as it is written, 'And some of them that are wise shall stumble, to refine among them, and to purify, and to make white, even to the time of the end; for it is yet for the time appointed' (Dan. 11:35).

Even of Jesus of Nazareth, who imagined that he was the Messiah, but was put to death by the court, Daniel had prophesied, as it is written, 'And the children of the violent among your people shall lift themselves up to establish the vision; but they shall stumble' (Dan. 11:14). For has there ever been a greater stumbling than this? All the prophets affirmed that the Messiah would redeem Israel, save them, gather their dispersed, and confirm the commandments. But he caused Israel to be destroyed by the sword, their remnant to be dispersed and humiliated. He was instrumental in changing the Torah and causing the world to err and serve another besides God.

But it is beyond the human mind to fathom the designs of the Creator; for our ways are not His ways, neither are our thoughts His thoughts. All these matters relating to Jesus of Nazareth and the Ishmaelite (Mohammed) who came after him, only served to clear the way for King Messiah, to prepare the whole world to worship God with one accord, as it is written, 'For then will I turn to the peoples a pure language, that they may all call upon the name of the Lord to serve Him with one consent' (Zeph. 3:9). Thus the Messianic hope, the Torah, and the commandments have become familiar topics – topics of conversation (among the inhabitants) of the far isles and many peoples, uncircumcised of heart and flesh. Some say, 'Those commandments were true, but have lost their validity and are no longer binding'; others declare that they had an esoteric meaning and were not intended to be taken literally; that the Messiah has already come and revealed their occult significance. But when the true King Messiah will appear and succeed, be exalted and lifted up, they will forthwith recant and realize that they have inherited naught but lies from their fathers, that their prophets and forebears led them astray.

Source

Twersky, Isadore (ed.), *A Maimonides Reader* (New York: Behrman House, 1972), 222, 226–7.

(ii) 'Epistle to Yemen' (1173/4)

The first one to have adopted this plan was Jesus the Nazarene, may his bones be ground to dust. He was a Jew because his mother was a Jewess, although his father was a Gentile. For in accordance with the principles of our law, a child born of a Jewess and a Gentile, or of a Jewess and a slave, is legitimate (Yevamot 45a). Jesus is only figuratively termed an illegitimate child. He impelled people to believe that he was a prophet sent by God to clarify perplexities in the Torah, and that he was the Messiah that was predicted by each and every seer. He interpreted the Torah and its precepts in such a fashion as to lead to their total annulment, to the abolition of all its commandments and to the violation of its prohibitions. The sages, of blessed memory, having become aware of his plans before his reputation spread among our people, meted out fitting punishment to him.

Daniel had already alluded to him when he presaged the downfall of a wicked one and a heretic among the Jews who would endeavor to destroy the Law, claim prophecy for himself, make pretenses to miracles, and allege that he is the Messiah, as it is written, 'Also the children of the impudent among your people shall make bold to claim prophecy, but they shall fall' (Dan. 11:14).

Source

Twersky, Isadore (ed.), *A Maimonides Reader* (New York: Behrman House, 1972), 441.

Commentary

Maimonides (Moses ben Maimon, 1135–1204) was a Jewish physician, philosopher and legal authority who lived under Muslim rule in Spain, Morocco and Egypt. Known for his universalist and rationalist approach to Judaism, he wrote the *Guide for the Perplexed*, which was read by Scholastic philosophers including Thomas Aquinas (see documents 7 (i), (ii) and (iii)). Although he rarely wrote about Christianity, his views on it are found in his legal writings, profoundly influencing Jewish attitudes to Christianity over hundreds of years and continuing to influence Orthodox Jews today.

Most of Maimonides' statements about Christianity are unequivocally negative. The doctrine of the Trinity, for example, is dismissed as nonsense (*Guide* 1, 50). Christianity, unlike Islam, is depicted as idolatrous, leading him to insist that Talmudic laws limiting Jewish interaction with gentiles applied to contemporary Christians. Subsequent Jewish thinkers, such as Meiri a hundred years later, modified this view, applying Maimonides' statement that 'The pious of the Gentile nations have a share in the world to come' (*Code*, Laws of Kings 8, 11) as evidence of inclusiveness, although it is unclear whether Maimonides, who excluded idolators from eligibility, meant to include pious Christians.

Our first excerpt (document 3 (i)) comes from a discussion at the conclusion of the *Code of Jewish Law* (*Mishneh Torah*), which discusses the messianic era when the whole world will unite in the worship of the God of Israel. Maimonides states that the messiah would not be killed and the Christian claim that Jesus was the messiah is therefore false, insisting that Jesus only imagined he was the messiah but instead of improving the lot of the Jewish people made it incomparably worse. This passage was eliminated from printed versions of the text by Christian censors.

In the second excerpt, from the 'Epistle to Yemen' (document 3 (ii)), we find even more trenchant polemic. The accusation about Jesus' illegitimacy and the reference to his punishment are taken from the Talmud. Maimonides' main concern is to undermine the church's teaching that Jesus abrogated the Torah.

Maimonides' criticisms of Christianity for embracing a false messianic pretender run in parallel to Christian condemnation of Jews for failing to recognise Jesus as the true messiah. Yet Maimonides was not consistent in his condemnation. For him, Christianity prepared the way for nations to worship the God of Israel and for redemption, thus explaining why, since Judaism was a minority in both the Islamic world and Christendom, God allowed these faiths to flourish. (In this he mirrored Aquinas, whose commentary on Romans (documents 7 (ii) and (iii)) allowed for contemporary Jews to have a positive role, even though Judaism had been superseded by Christianity.) Maimonides' view was that Christianity, along with Islam, was providentially spreading knowledge of God and scripture throughout the world. There is thus, to a limited extent, a positive role for Jesus, and also for Mohammed: despite the negative aspects of both, they are part of the ultimate divine plan for the diffusion of monotheism, as well as preparing the nations for the king-messiah. It is *not* that all people will convert to Judaism but that, partly through the consequences of their actions, all will recognise the one true God of Israel.

Bibliography

Davidson, Herbert A., *Moses Maimonides: The Man and His Works* (Oxford: Oxford University Press, 2005).
Diamond, James A., *Converts, Heretics and Lepers: Maimonides and the Outsider* (Notre Dame: University of Notre Dame Press, 2007).
Haberman, Jacob, *Maimonides and Aquinas: A Contemporary Appraisal* (New York: KTAV, 1979).
Novak, David, *The Image of the Non-Jew in Judaism: The Idea of Noahide Law* (Oxford: Littman Library of Jewish Civilization, 2011), 153–75.

4

Pope Innocent III: Constitutio pro Judeis *(An Edict in Favour of the Jews) (15 September 1199)*

Text

Although the Jewish perfidy is in every way worthy of condemnation, nevertheless, because through them the truth of our own Faith is proved, they are not to be severely oppressed by the faithful. Thus the Prophet says, 'Thou shalt not kill them, lest at any time they forget thy law,' or more clearly stated, thou shalt not destroy the Jews completely, so that the Christians should never by any chance be able to forget Thy Law, which, though they themselves fail to understand it, they display in their book to those who do understand.

Therefore, just as license ought not to be granted the Jews to presume to do in their synagogues more than the law permits them, just so ought they not to suffer curtailment in those (privileges) which have been conceded them. That is why, although they prefer to remain hardened in their obstinacy rather than acknowledge the prophetic words – and the eternal secrets of their own scriptures, that they might thus arrive at the understanding of Christianity and Salvation, nevertheless, in view of the fact that they begged for our protection and our aid, and in accordance with the clemency that Christian piety imposes, we, following in the footprints of our predecessors of happy memory, the popes Calixtus, Eugene, Alexander, Clement, and Coelestine, grant their petition and offer them the shield of our protection.

We decree that no Christian shall use violence to force them to be baptized as long as they are unwilling and refuse, but that if anyone of them seeks refuge among the Christians of his own free will and by reason of his faith, (only then,) after his willingness has become quite clear, shall he be made a Christian without subjecting himself to any calumny. For surely none can be believed to possess the true faith of a Christian who is known to have come to Christian baptism not willingly, and even against his wishes.

Moreover, without the judgment of the authority of the land, no Christian shall presume to wound their persons, or kill (them) or rob them of their money, or change the good customs which they have thus far enjoyed in the place where they live. Furthermore, while they celebrate their festivals, no one shall disturb them in any way by means of sticks or stones, nor exact from any of them forced service, except that which they have been accustomed to perform from ancient times. In opposition to the wickedness and avarice of evil men in these matters, we decree that no one shall presume to desecrate or reduce the cemetery of the Jews, or, with the object of extorting money to exhume bodies there buried. If any one, however, after being acquainted with the contents of this decree, should presume to act in defiance of it (which God forbid), he shall suffer loss of honor and office, or he shall be restrained by the penalty of excommunication, unless he shall have made proper amends for his presumption.

We wish, however, to place under the protection of this decree only those (Jews) who have not presumed to plot against the Christian Faith.

Source

Grayzel, Solomon, *The Church and the Jews in the XIIIth Century: A Study of Their Relations during the Years 1198–1254, Based on the Papal Letters and the Conciliar Decrees of the Period* (New York: Hermon Press, 1966), 93, 95.

Commentary

The efforts of medieval popes to articulate a message that – despite condemning Judaism – insisted that Jews have the right to live in Christian society without persecution goes back to the early Middle Ages. Gregory I (*r.* 590–604) frequently acted to condemn anti-Jewish violence and interference with synagogues and Jewish religious practices; in his famous statement of 598, known from its opening as *Sicut Judeis*, he proclaimed: 'just as license ought not to be granted the Jews to presume to do in their synagogues more than the law permits them, just so ought they not to suffer curtailment in those (privileges) which have been conceded them'.

Our document is one in a long line of similar decrees, issued by successive popes. Following the crusader massacres of Jews in Christian Europe (see documents 1 (i) and (ii) above), popes of the twelfth to fifteenth centuries, starting with Callixtus II in 1119, began to assert their support for Jewish rights on a regular basis. Gregory's statement, a kind of constitution for the Jews, was reissued by six popes in the twelfth century. At first it applied only to the Jews of Rome, but starting with Alexander III (1159–81) it was applied more widely, to Jews in France and in England. Ten popes issued and reissued the document in the thirteenth century, four in the fourteenth century, and three in the fifteenth. Several statements were expanded to prohibit accusations of ritual murder by Jews, or to oppose false accusations of blasphemy. Iterations of *Sicut Judeis* also endorsed safeguards similar to provisions in the charters issued by kings and emperors, though not quite as generously.

Innocent III's statement has been chosen here because he added a new introduction to the established text, providing a theological basis for protecting Jews but in highly negative terms, drawing on Psalm 59 as biblical support. While its purpose, like earlier decrees, was to protect Jews against Christian violence, the document reflects the depth of Christian ambivalence, as illustrated by the opening assertion that Jews were 'worthy of condemnation'. Nevertheless, *Constitutio pro Judeis* explicitly forbids forced baptism and condemns such crimes as the wounding, killing or robbing of Jews. It also forbids Christians from interfering with Jewish worship and festival celebrations.

That the *Constitutio* is one text in a long and frequently issued list testifies to its limited success in containing anti-Jewish violence. Nevertheless, for centuries it represented the official church attitude towards the Jewish community, upholding a traditional papal policy of broad toleration. Jews should continue to live under established custom, the document states, although popes themselves, including Innocent III, modified the rules under which Jews could practise their religion, for example by the introduction of the Jewish badge at the Fourth Lateran Council in 1215 (see document 5).

While the *Constitutio* depicted Jews as undermining Christian belief, and their inferior status was an important reminder of the truth of Christianity, their survival was part of the divine plan, which should not be undermined by violence. As a consequence, church leaders tried (albeit mostly unsuccessfully) to prevent, or to offer protection during, outbursts of anti-Jewish violence and to reject conspiracy theories such as allegations of ritual murder (see document 2).

Bibliography

Chazan, Robert, 'Pope Innocent III and the Jews', in Moore, John (ed.), *Pope Innocent III and His World* (London: Routledge, 1999), 187–204.

Grayzel, Solomon, 'The Papal Bull *Sicut Judaeis*', in Ben-Horin, Meir, Weinryb, Bernard D., and Zeitlin, Solomon (eds.), *Studies and Essays in Honor of Abraham A. Neuman* (Leiden: E. J. Brill for the Dropsie College, Philadelphia, 1962), 243–80.

5

Decrees of the Fourth Lateran Council (1215)

Text

Canon 67

The more the Christians are restrained from the practice of usury, the more are they oppressed in this matter by the treachery of the Jews, so that in a short time they exhaust the resources of the Christians. Wishing, therefore, in this matter to protect the Christians against cruel oppression by the Jews, we ordain in this decree that if in the future under any pretext Jews extort from Christians oppressive and immoderate interest, the partnership of the Christians shall be denied them till they have made suitable satisfaction for their excesses. The Christians also, every appeal being set aside, shall, if necessary, be compelled by ecclesiastical censure to abstain from all commercial intercourse with them. We command the princes not to be hostile to the Christians on this account, but rather to strive to hinder the Jews from practicing such excesses. Lastly, we decree that the Jews be compelled by the same punishment […] to make satisfaction for the tithes and offerings due to the churches, which the Christians were accustomed to supply from their houses and other possessions before these properties, under whatever title, fell into the hands of the Jews, that thus the churches may be safeguarded against loss.

Canon 68

In some provinces a difference of dress distinguishes the Jews and Saracens from the Christians, but in others confusion has developed to such a degree that no difference is discernible. Whence it happens sometimes through error that Christians mingle with the women of Jews and Saracens, and, on the other hand, Jews and Saracens mingle with those of the Christians. Therefore, that such ruinous commingling through error of this kind may not serve as a refuge for further excuse for excesses, we decree that such people of both sexes […] in every Christian province and at all times be distinguished in public from other people by a difference of dress, since this was also enjoined on them by Moses. On the days of the Lamentations and on Passion Sunday they may not appear in public, because some of them, as we understand, on those days are not ashamed to show themselves more ornately attired and do not fear to amuse themselves at the expense of the Christians, who in memory of the sacred passion go about attired in robes of mourning.

Canon 69

Since it is absurd that a blasphemer of Christ exercise authority over Christians, we on account of the boldness of transgressors renew in this general council what the Synod of Toledo (589) wisely enacted in this matter, prohibiting Jews from being given preference in the matter of public offices, since in such capacity they are most troublesome to the Christians. But if anyone should commit such an office to them, let him, after previous warning, be restrained by such punishment as seems proper by the provincial synod which we command to be celebrated every year. The official, however, shall be denied the commercial and other intercourse of the Christians, till in the judgment of the bishop all that he acquired from the Christians from the time he assumed office be restored for the needs of the Christian poor, and the office that he irreverently assumed let him lose with shame. The same we extend also to pagans.

Canon 70

Some (Jews), we understand, who voluntarily approached the waters of holy baptism, do not entirely cast off the old man that they may more perfectly put on the new one, because, retaining remnants of the former rite, they obscure by such a mixture the beauty of the Christian religion. But since it is written: 'Accursed is the man that goeth on the two ways' (Ecclus. 2:14), and 'a garment that is woven together of woolen and linen' (Deut. 22:11) ought not to be put on, we decree that such persons be in every way restrained by the prelates from the observance of the former rite, that, having given themselves of their own free will to the Christian religion, salutary coercive action may preserve them in its observance, since not to know the way of the Lord is a lesser evil than to retrace one's steps after it is known.

A Series of Decrees Dealing with the Preparation of a Crusade to the Holy Land

In the case of crusaders who are bound under oath to pay interest, we command that their creditors be compelled to cancel the oath given and to cease exacting interest. Should any creditor force the payment of interest, we command that he be similarly forced to make restitution. We command also that Jews be compelled by the secular power to cancel interest, and, till they have done so, intercourse with them must be absolutely denied them by all Christians under penalty of excommunication. For those who cannot before their departure pay their debts to the Jews, the secular princes shall provide such a delay that from the time of their departure till their return or till their death is known, they shall not be embarrassed with the inconvenience of paying interest. If a Jew has received security […] for such a debt, he must, after deducting his own expenses, pay to the owner the income from such security. Prelates who manifest negligence in obtaining justice for the crusaders and their servants, shall be subject to severe penalty.

Source

Schroeder, Henry Joseph, *Disciplinary Decrees of the General Councils: Text, Translation, and Commentary* (St. Louis: B. Herder, 1937), 289–92, 294. Summaries of Canons omitted from headings.

Commentary

These passages come at the end of an extremely lengthy text completed under the leadership of Pope Innocent III (*r.* 1198–1216). The Fourth Lateran Council, with seventy-one archbishops, 400 bishops and 800 abbots, is considered to be the greatest until the Council of Trent in the mid-sixteenth century (see Chapter 5, p. 244) and placed new restrictions on Jews.

The first sixty-six canons are focused purely on internal Christian themes, including the immunity of the church against officials and governors and others who seek to oppress the churches, and the insistence on one universal church outside of which there can be no salvation, not only for Jews and Muslims but for Christians as well. Canons 67–70, in which Jews are discussed, seem almost like an appendix. Nevertheless they provide interesting details of perceived problems with the contemporary interaction of Jews and Christians from an ecclesiastical point of view, and by reaffirming some existing regulations – such as that converts from Judaism must be constrained from observing any of their former Jewish practices ('remnants of the former rite') – and extending others, resulted in a significant undermining of Jewish status.

While leaders of the church would have preferred a prohibition of all interest paid by Christians to Jews, other forces in Christian society, especially secular princes and town leaders, compelled an abandoning of this goal, and the church now focused on protecting Christians from 'oppressive and immoderate interest'. There is a striking assertion that Christians must not enter into any business relationship with Jews, which suggests that Jews and Christians were working together on an assumption of mutual benefit, if not of equality, a practice deemed inappropriate by the church.

Most influential were the decrees obliging Jews (as well as Muslims) to distinguish themselves from Christians in the way they dressed. Requiring a religious minority to wear a distinctive vestment or emblem originated in Islam, which imposed dress restrictions on both Jews and Christians from the time of Caliph 'Umar II (r. 717–20). The Fourth Lateran Council's discriminatory dress regulations, which publicly identified Jews, discouraged intercourse, particularly sexual relations, between Jews and Christians. While such stipulations were consonant with contemporary expectations that the legally defined categories to which individuals belonged should be identifiable by dress, they were nonetheless generally perceived by Jews as mandating a 'badge of shame' – a concept that would have a long afterlife in Jewish–Christian relations. (In reality, Jews often paid for exemptions from this duty.) Jews were also forbidden to wear beautiful clothing on Good Friday, when Christians wore mourning.

At the end of the Council, the contemporary Crusades raised significant problems relating to Jews. What should be the status of crusaders heading for the Holy Land who had borrowed money from Jews? We can imagine an argument that crusaders on the sacred task of freeing the Holy Land should be freed from all debt. Instead, it was decided that while crusaders who owed money to Jews would no longer need to pay interest to them, the debts would not be cancelled; rather, all payments would be deferred as supported by secular authorities.

Bibliography

Champagne, Marie-Thérèse, and Resnick, Irven M. (eds.), *Jews and Muslims under the Fourth Lateran Council* (Turnhout: Brepols, 2018).

Chazan, Robert, *The Jews of Medieval Western Christendom, 1000–1500* (Cambridge: Cambridge University Press, 2006).

Wayno, Jeffrey M., 'Rethinking the Fourth Lateran Council of 1215', *Speculum* 93, no. 3 (2018), 611–37.

6

Nachmanides and Pablo Christiani: Barcelona Disputation (1263)

Text

[Nachmanides:] Our lord the king commanded me to debate with Friar Paul in his palace, in his presence and that of his advisors, in Barcelona.

I responded and said, 'I shall do according to the dictate of my lord the king, if you give me permission to speak as I will. I request in this regard the permission of the king and the permission of Friar Raymond of Penyafort and his associates who are here.'

Friar Raymond of Penyafort replied: 'So long as you do not speak deprecatingly.'

I said to them: 'I do not wish to run afoul of your laws in this matter. But I must speak freely with respect to the debate, just as you speak freely. I have the good sense to speak properly with respect to the debate, as you have said, but it must be according to my will.'

They all gave me permission to speak freely.

[…]

The heart of the case and the dispute between Jews and Christians lie with the fact that you attribute to the essence of the divinity something most unpalatable. You, our lord the king, are a Christian son of a Christian man and woman. You have heard all your life priests and Franciscans and Dominicans speaking of the birth of Jesus. They have filled your brain and the marrow of your bones with this doctrine. [This doctrine] has been ingrained in you as a result of this habituation. However, that which you believe – and indeed it is the cornerstone of your faith – reason cannot accept and nature does not permit, and the prophets never said such a thing. Even the miraculous cannot be extended to apply to this doctrine, as I shall prove with thorough proofs at the proper place and time. [This unacceptable doctrine is] that the Creator of heaven and earth and everything in it returned and passed into the womb of a certain Jewess and grew in it for seven months and was then born tiny. Subsequently he grew and was then turned over into the hands of his enemies, who judged him to death and killed him. You say that subsequently he lived and returned to his former place. [All this] cannot be borne by the thinking of a Jew or of any person. Vainly and pointlessly you make your claims, for this is the heart of our disagreement.

[…]

When I serve my Creator under your jurisdiction in exile and in suffering and subjugation and in the obloquy of the nations, who revile me endlessly, then my reward will be rich, for I make an offering to God of my body. For this I shall merit the life of the world to come more and more. However, when there will be a Jewish king of my faith ruling all the nations, and when I shall be forced to observe the law of the Jews, then my reward will not be so extensive.

[…]

[Friar Paul Christian/Pablo Christiani:] Friar Paul proposed to the said rabbi that, with the aid of God, he would prove from writings shared and accepted by the Jews the following contentions, in order: that the messiah, who is called Christ, whom the Jews anticipate, has surely come already; also that the messiah, as prophesied, should be divine and human; also that he suffered and was killed for the salvation of mankind; also that the laws and ceremonials ceased and should have ceased after the advent of the said messiah.

[…]

It was then proved to him clearly, both through authoritative texts of the law and the prophets, as well as through the Talmud, that Christ has truly come, as Christians believe and preach. Since he was unable to respond, vanquished by proper proofs and authoritative texts, he conceded that Christ or the messiah had been born in Bethlehem a thousand years ago and had subsequently appeared in Rome to some.

[…]

Then our lord the king responded: 'If he [the messiah] was born on the day of the destruction of the Temple, from which more than a thousand years have elapsed, and he has not yet come, then how can he yet come. For it is not in the nature of man to live for a thousand years.'

I said to him, 'The conditions were that I would not dispute with you and that you would not intervene in the disputation. However, there were already among the early humans Adam and Methuselah [who lived] close to a thousand years, and Elijah and Enoch more than that. For life [lies in the hands] of God.'

Source

Chazan, Robert, *Barcelona and Beyond: The Disputation of 1263 and Its Aftermath* (Berkeley: University of California Press, 1992), 94–5, 48–9, 130, 59, 58, 118. (Square-bracketed interpolations are part of the original, with the exception of '[Nachmanides:]' and '[Friar Paul Christian/Pablo Christiani:]'. Footnotes omitted.)

Commentary

Following the rise of the mendicant orders – initiated by the Franciscans and Dominicans – in the thirteenth century, Jews were sometimes compelled to engage in public disputations, the most famous being in Paris (1240), Barcelona (1263) and Tortosa (1413–14). Christian speakers, often baptised Jews, included in their argument passages not only from the Bible but also from the Talmud, which they depicted as blasphemous to Christianity and a stumbling block to Jewish conversion. Today, the medieval concept of a disputation may seem odd, but at the time such events could result in very real consequences for Jews, who were always foretold to be the losers. The Paris disputation of 1240, for example, led to the burning of wagonloads of the Talmud and other Jewish manuscripts.

In Barcelona, Rabbi Moses ben Nahman ('Nachmanides', 1194–1270) was summoned by King James I of Aragón (r. 1231–76) to engage with Pablo Christiani ('Paul the Christian', d. 1274), a Jewish convert. There are two main accounts of the disputation, which lasted six days. According to Nachmanides' Hebrew account, the king awarded him a prize, but due to Dominican pressure, he fled to France (before moving to Palestine in 1267). Pablo's Latin narrative contradicts this account, but scholars view Nachmanides' version as the more reliable.

The Barcelona disputation was a freer debate than that in Paris owing to the presence of King James, the fame of Nachmanides and the social circumstances of the Spanish Jewish community. The king, who had previously shown a desire to convert Jews, issuing an edict in 1240 requiring them (and Muslims) to listen to Christian sermons, had an apparently warm relationship with Nachmanides, guaranteed his protection and the freedom to speak openly, and attended the disputation and asked questions. While the position of Jews had begun to deteriorate during the early years of the Inquisition, their confidence remained, as demonstrated in the excerpts by sweeping Jewish criticism of Christian messianic claims.

The disputation centred on whether the messiah had actually appeared on earth, or whether it remained a future event; whether he was to be considered as divine or as a man born of human parents; and whether Jews or Christians possessed the true faith.

Pablo Christiani, like Nicolas Donin, the Jewish convert and speaker in the Paris disputation, sought to prove the truth of Christianity with reference to the Talmud. Soon after the 1263 disputation, Pablo convinced Pope Clement XIV to require that copies of the Talmud be submitted for Christian examination and interceded with King Louis IX of France to enforce a canonical edict that required Jews to wear a badge of identification. In the disputation itself, he argued that the Talmud, especially haggadic passages (rabbinic tales and parables), demonstrated that the messiah had already appeared, while Nachmanides responded by explaining that haggadic material should not be understood literally.

One of the features of medieval disputations, as exemplified by that of Barcelona, is the use of the Talmud, which demonstrates a growing recognition among Christians that Jews not only claimed the Old Testament as sacred scripture but had developed new texts (such as the Talmud) which they also regarded as holy.

Bibliography

Caputo, Nina, *Nahmanides in Medieval Catalonia: History, Community, & Messianism* (Notre Dame: University of Notre Dame Press, 2007), 99–129.

Klepper, Deeana C., 'The Encounter between Christian Authority and Jewish Authority over Scriptural Truth: The Barcelona Disputation 1263', in Potestà, Gian Luca (ed.), *Autorität und Wahrheit: kirchliche Vorstellungen, Normen und Verfahren (13.–15. Jahrhundert)* (Munich: R. Oldenburg, 2012), 1–19.

7

Thomas Aquinas: Commentaries on Hebrews and Romans (1265–74)

Text

(i) Commentary on the Epistle to the Hebrews 7:11–19 (1265–8)

349. [...] The priesthood of Christ does away with the Levitical.

350. [...] It also does away with the law which was administered by it. He states this when he says, ***for the priesthood being translated, it is necessary that a translation also be made of the law***. For the law was under the administration of the priesthood; therefore, the priesthood being translated, it is necessary that the law be changed [...] just as a person who changes his mind about traveling by water, changes his mind about finding a ship. [...]

351. [...] Jeremiah speaks of change when he says: *behold, the days shall come, says the Lord, and I will make a new covenant with the house of Israel and with the house of Judah, not according to the covenant I made with your fathers* (Jer 31:31); *for the law of the spirit of life in Christ Jesus has delivered me from the law of sin and of death* (Rom 8:2). For the old law is called the law of sin and of death, because it did not confer grace *ex opere operato* [by the work worked], as the sacraments of the new law do.

352. But the Manicheans raise an objection here: if the old law was given by divine providence, which is immutable, the law itself should be immutable; consequently, it should not be changed. Therefore, since it was changed, it was not given by divine providence.

I answer, as Augustine says *Against Faustus*, that just as a wide dispenser by one and the same arrangement and providence gives different laws according as times and persons differ, one law for summer and another for winter, one for children and one for adults, one for perfect and another for imperfect, and yet is the same providence; so with divine providence remaining unchanged, the law was changed to fit the times; because before the coming of Christ precepts were given to prefigure his coming, but after his coming, precepts were given to signify that he had come. Furthermore, the precepts were given to them as to children, but in the new law as to the perfect. Hence, the law is called a pedagogue, which is strictly for children. Therefore, if something given in the law suggests perpetuity, this is by reason of the one prefigured.

[...]

361. Then when he says, ***there is indeed a setting aside,*** he lays down two consequents: first, in regard to the voiding of the Old Testament; second, the institution of the New, at ***but a bringing in of a better hope***.

362. The first consequent is that the Old Testament came about by the ***law of a carnal commandment***, and the other is then introduced. The first, therefore, is changed: and this is what he says, namely, there is a setting aside of the former commandment.

But nothing is set aside except what is evil: *that he may know how to refuse the evil* (Isa 7:15). But the commandment is not evil: *the law indeed is holy, and the commandment holy and just and good* (Rom 7:12).

I answer that it was not evil in itself, but inasmuch as it was unsuited to the time. For the things of the Old Testament are not to be kept in the New Testament: *sacrifice and oblation you did not desire: then said I: behold, I come* (Ps 40:7–8).

[...]

But he shows why it is weak and useless when he says, **for the law brought nothing to perfection** in regard to justice or eternal life. Hence, it was imperfect, but it was made perfect by Christ.

Source

Thomas Aquinas, *Commentary on the Letter of Saint Paul to the Hebrews*, trans. Fabian R. Larcher, O. P., ed. John Mortensen and Enrique Alarcón (Lander: The Aquinas Institute for the Study of Sacred Doctrine, 2012), 155–6, 158.

(ii) Commentary on Romans 9:1–5 (1270–4)

742. Then, when he [Paul] says **who are Israelites**, he shows the greatness of the Jews in order that his sadness appear reasonable on account of the ancient dignity of a deteriorating people, *for it is a weightier evil to lose greatness than never to have possessed it*, as the Gloss says, and not as though it arose solely from worldly love.

743. But he shows their greatness in three ways.

First, from their race when he says, **who are Israelites**, i.e., descending from the stock of Jacob who was called Israel (Gen 32:28). This pertains to their greatness, for it is said: *neither is there any nation so great as to have their gods coming to them* (Deut 4:7).

744. Second, he shows the greatness of that race from God's blessings: first, the spiritual blessings, one of which refers to the present: **to whom belongs the adoption of sons of God**. Hence it says in Exodus: *Israel is my son, my firstborn* (Exod 4:22). This refers to the spiritual men who arose among that people: but as to worldly men he stated above that they received the spirit of slavery in fear (Rom 8:15). Another spiritual blessing refers to the future when he says, **the glory**, namely, of the sons of God promised to them. A reference to this is found in Exodus: *the glory of the Lord filled the tabernacle* (Exod 40:32).

Then he sets out other, figural benefits, of which three are figures of present spiritual benefit. The first of these is the **testament**, i.e., the pact of circumcision given to Abraham, as is recorded in Genesis 17, although this could be referred to the new covenant preached first to the Jews. Hence, the Lord himself said: *I was sent only to the lost sheep of the house of Israel* (Matt 15:24); and Jeremiah: *I will make a new covenant with the house of Israel* (Jer 31:31) [...]

745. Third, he describes the Jews' dignity by their origin, when he says, **whose fathers**, because they were begotten according to the flesh by those ancestors who were especially acceptable to God: *I love your fathers and chose their descendants after them* (Deut 4:37).

Source

Thomas Aquinas, *Commentary on the Letter of Saint Paul to the Romans*, trans. Fabian R. Larcher, O. P., ed. John Mortensen and Enrique Alarcón (Lander: The Aquinas Institute for the Study of Sacred Doctrine, 2012), 248–9.

(iii) Commentary on Romans 11:25–32 (1270–4)

924. Then when he [Paul] says, ***for the gifts and the calling***, he excludes an objection.

For someone might claim that even though the Jews were formerly beloved on account of their forefathers, nevertheless the hostility they exert against the Gospel prevents them from being saved in the future. But the Apostle asserts that this is false, saying: ***for the gifts and calling of God are without repentance***. As if to say: that God gives something to certain ones or calls certain ones is ***without repentance***, because God does not change his mind: *the triumpher in Israel will not spare, and will not be moved to repentance* (1 Sam 15:29); *the Lord has sworn and will not change his mind* (Ps 110:4).

[…]

930. Then when he says, ***for as you also***, he gives the reason for the future salvation of the Jews after their unbelief. […]

931. First, therefore, he says: so I say that Israel will be saved, although they are now enemies. ***For as you also***, gentiles, ***in times past did not believe God***: *you were once without God in the world* (Eph 2:12); ***but now have obtained mercy: the gentiles are to glorify God for his mercy*** (Rom 15:9); *I will have mercy on him who was without mercy* (Hos 2:23). And this was ***through their unbelief***, which was the occasion of your salvation, as was said above.

So these also, i.e., the Jews, ***now***, i.e., in the time of grace, ***have not believed***, namely, in Christ: *why do you not believe in me?* (John 8:46). And this is what he adds: ***for your mercy***, i.e., in Christ's grace, by which you have obtained mercy: *you have saved us according to your mercy* (Titus 3:5). Or they ***have not believed*** so that they might enter into your mercy. Or they ***have not believed***, which turned out to be the occasion of the mercy shown to you, ***that they also*** at some time ***may obtain mercy***: *the Lord will have compassion on Jacob* (Isa 14:1).

932. Then, when he says ***for God has concluded***, he assigns the reason for this similarity, namely that God has willed to have mercy on all. And this is what he adds, ***for God has concluded***, i.e., permitted to be concluded, ***all***, i.e., every race of men, both Jews and gentiles, ***in unbelief***, as in a certain bond of error: *all were fettered with the bonds of darkness* (Wis 17:2). ***That he may have mercy on all***, i.e., that he may have mercy on every race of men: *but you have mercy upon all* (Wis 17:24).

Source

Thomas Aquinas, *Commentary on the Letter of Saint Paul to the Romans*, trans. Fabian R. Larcher, O. P., ed. John Mortensen and Enrique Alarcón (Lander: The Aquinas Institute for the Study of Sacred Doctrine, 2012), 315, 317.

Commentary

The Dominican Thomas Aquinas (*c.* 1225–74) systematised Christian theology by offering it a consistent philosophical underpinning. He was influenced by Maimonides' *Guide for the Perplexed*, translated into Latin in the mid-1220s, in which the biblical commandments were rationally justified. While he accepted Maimonides' view that the law was divine and rational, this was insufficient for Aquinas. Rather, the law was a necessary precondition for the coming of Christ. Each commandment, Aquinas explained, had a symbolic as well as a literal meaning, serving as preparation for the coming of Christ.

In document 7 (i), a commentary on Hebrews, Aquinas argues that observance of the ceremonial law after Christ is a sin since the eternal priesthood of Christ fulfils the old law in totality. Observance of the ceremonial law had once played an important role – prefiguring the eternal priesthood of Christ – but was 'unsuited to the time' since Christ had rendered it void. Indeed, the ceremonial law had become harmful and should be renounced.

Aquinas understood Jewish history as falling into two periods, which he described as 'under the law' and 'after the law', with Christ marking the point between. Under the law, Jewish life was a sign of God's righteousness and a symbol of what was to come. In rejecting Jesus, however, Jews fulfilled the words of the prophets and effected the sacrifice of Christ, making possible the salvation of the gentiles. Judaism was no longer valid and Christianity became the *verus Israel* ('true Israel').

In Aquinas' commentary on Romans (documents 7 (ii) and (iii)), there is a more positive view of Judaism. Although Jewish history is a chronicle of decline (Jews are 'a deteriorating people'), their dignity remains in the present and is great, based on their being Israelites according to the flesh, selected by God in the present and benefiting from spiritual blessings received as the firstborn, such as circumcision. The church is also described as a union of Jews and gentiles.

Of course, like all medieval theologians, Aquinas believed the death of Christ meant the end of Judaism, because Judaism prefigured Christ, and Jews should be viewed as preparation for his coming. Those who rejected Christ were condemned, but Aquinas could not completely sever the ties between contemporary Christians and Jews. For him, Jews were cursed, but Paul's authority made it impossible for him to adopt a wholly negative attitude: Jews were both holy and sinful, rejected and beloved. Elsewhere in the Romans commentary Aquinas explained that if the Jews' prerogative were removed because of the unbelief of some, it would follow logically that human unbelief could nullify God's faithfulness, which he described as 'an unacceptable conclusion' (*Comm. ad Rom.* 3:253).

Some scholars, such as Matthew Tapie, argue that the Romans commentary contains an affirmation of Jewish observance after Christ because of Aquinas' emphasis on Paul's adoption of the present tense, even in the face of unbelief. While Tapie suggests this challenges Hebrews' supersessionism and even looks forward to *Nostra aetate* (see Appendix to Part III, p. 512), others, such as John Hood, argue it is less clear-cut.

When read together, Aquinas' commentaries on Romans and Hebrews are distinct if not conflicting, and the theological tensions they reveal can also be seen in more modern Christian writings on the role of post-biblical Judaism.

Bibliography

Hood, John Y. B., *Aquinas and the Jews* (Philadelphia: University of Pennsylvania Press, 1995).
Soulen, R. Kendall, *The God of Israel and Christian Theology* (Minneapolis: Fortress Press, 1996).

Tapie, Matthew A., *Aquinas on Israel and the Church: The Question of Supercessionism in the Theology of Thomas Aquinas* (Eugene: Pickwick, 2015).

Wyschogrod, Michael, 'A Jewish Reading of St Thomas Aquinas', in Thoma, Clemens, and Wyschogrod, Michael (eds.), *Understanding Scripture: Explorations of Jewish and Christian Traditions of Interpretations* (Mahwah: Paulist Press, 1987), 125–40.

8

Pope Gregory X: Papal Bull (1272)

Text

Gregory, bishop, servant of the servants of God, extends greetings and the apostolic benediction to the beloved sons in Christ, the faithful Christians, to those here now and to those in the future.

[…]

Inasmuch as the Jews are not able to bear witness against the Christians, we decree furthermore that the testimony of Christians alone against Jews shall not be valid unless there is among these Christians some Jew who is there for the purpose of offering testimony. Since it happens occasionally that some Christians lose their Christian children, the Jews are accused by their enemies of secretly carrying off and killing these same Christian children and of making sacrifices of the heart and blood of these very children. It happens, too, that the parents of these children or some other Christian enemies of these Jews, secretly hide these very children in order that they may be able to injure these Jews, and in order that they may be able to extort from them a certain amount of money by redeeming them from their straits.

And most falsely do these Christians claim that the Jews have secretly and furtively carried away these children and killed them, and that the Jews offer sacrifice from the heart and the blood of these children, since their law in this matter precisely and expressly forbids Jews to sacrifice, eat, or drink the blood, or to eat the flesh of animals having claws. This has been demonstrated many times at our court by Jews converted to the Christian faith; nevertheless very many Jews are often seized and detained unjustly because of this.

We decree, therefore, that Christians need not be obeyed against Jews in a case or situation of this type, and we order that Jews seized under such a foolish pretext be freed from imprisonment, and that they shall not be arrested henceforth on such a miserable pretext, unless – which we do not believe – they be caught in the commission of the crime. We decree that no Christian shall stir up anything new against them, but that they should be maintained in that status and position in which they were in the time of our predecessors, from antiquity till now.

We decree, in order to stop the wickedness and avarice of bad men, that no one shall dare to devastate or to destroy a cemetery of the Jews or to dig up human bodies for the sake of getting money.

Moreover, if anyone, after having known the content of this decree, should – which we hope will not happen – attempt audaciously to act contrary to it, then let him suffer punishment in his rank and position, or let him be punished by the penalty of excommunication, unless he makes amends for his boldness by proper recompense. Moreover, we wish that only those Jews who have not attempted to contrive anything toward the destruction of the Christian faith be fortified by the support of such protection.

Source

Marcus, Jacob Rader, and Saperstein, Marc, *The Jews in Christian Europe: A Source Book, 315–1791* (Pittsburgh: Hebrew Union College Press/University of Pittsburgh Press, 2015), 149–51, 664: 23.1. Reproduced by permission of the Hebrew Union College Press. © 2015 Hebrew Union College Press.

Commentary

Gregory X became pope in September 1271 after years of wrangling between rival Christian groups from France and Italy. Selected as a compromise candidate, he was pope for only four and a half years before his death in 1276. Nevertheless, he is considered one of the most important medieval popes as regards Jewish history because of the papal bull that he published within the first year of his papacy.

There was of course a long tradition that every new pope would repeat a standard document in order to show the continuity which was central to Christian doctrine. Regarding Jews, there was already an established tradition from his predecessors (see document 4): there must be no forced baptisms of Jews; Christians must not attack or harm Jews or seize Jewish money inappropriately; there should be no forcing of Jewish service for Christians; and there should be no interference with Jewish festivals.

However, Gregory made several additions to this tradition. These included two striking statements. First, that while Jews may not bear witness against Christians, Christians must not condemn Jews for a sinful act without a Jewish witness to confirm the accusation. This is a significant innovation that may well have saved Jewish lives. While Jews were forbidden to bear witness against Christians (see, for example, the Justinian Code; Chapter 2, p. 106), Gregory X, in accordance with the medieval legal principle that everyone had the right to be judged by his peers (cf. Magna Carta), insisted that Jews could only be condemned if there were Jewish as well as Christian witnesses against them.

Secondly, that Jews accused of killing Christian children have a right to be protected until definitive proof can be established; that no *new* anti-Jewish calumnies will be accepted without definitive documentation; that there must be no destruction of Jewish cemeteries (a clear indication that this was an ongoing problem); and that there will be appropriate punishment for Christians who violate these rules.

Gregory further provides a vigorous refutation of the ritual murder accusation, namely that there was an ongoing practice among Jews of capturing Christian children in order to torture and murder them, take their blood and use it in their religious rituals (see document 2). He points out, properly based on Jewish traditions, that it is prohibited for Jews to drink the blood of any animal. The fact that this refutation of the so-called 'blood libel', a process begun in 1247 by Innocent IV, was repeated by various popes as late as Clement XIII (*r.* 1758–69) in 1763 might, however, suggest that it had little long-term effect in countering the accusation.

It is not surprising, nor entirely misguided, that Gregory's bull has been published in many Catholic texts as an indication of papal protection of Jews.

Bibliography

Boustan, Ra'anan S., and Champagne, Marie-Thérèse, 'Walking in the Shadows of the Past: The Jewish Experience of Rome in the Twelfth Century', *Medieval Encounters: Jewish, Christian and Muslim Culture in Confluence and Dialogue* 17, no. 4–5 (2011), 464–94.

Cohen, *Under Crescent and Cross*, 30–51.

Grayzel, Solomon, 'The Papal Bull *Sicut Judaeis*', in Ben-Horin, Meir, Weinryb, Bernard D., and Zeitlin, Solomon (eds.), *Studies and Essays in Honor of Abraham A Neuman* (Leiden: E. J. Brill for the Dropsie College, Philadelphia, 1962), 243–80.

Grayzel, Solomon, *The Church and the Jews in the XIIIth Century, Vol. II: 1254–1314*, ed. and arranged, with additional notes by Kenneth R. Stow (New York: Jewish Theological Seminary in America; Detroit: Wayne State University Press, *c.* 1989), 116–34, esp. 119–20.

9

Anonymous: Nizzahon Vetus *(thirteenth century?)*

Text

162

It is written in their books that 'Jesus was led into the wilderness where Satan tempted him. And Jesus fasted forty days and forty nights, and afterwards he was hungry. The tempter then came and said, If you are the son of God, command that these stones be made bread. But Jesus answered and said, Man shall not live by bread alone, but by every word that proceeds out of the mouth of God shall man live. Satan then took him up into the holy city, and set him on a pinnacle of the temple, and said to him, If you are the son of God, cast yourself down, for it is written, He shall give his angels charge concerning you to guard you in all your ways. Jesus answered him, Do not tempt the Lord your God. Again, Satan took him up to an exceedingly high mountain and showed him all the kingdoms of the world. He then said to him, All this will I give you if you will fall down and bow to me. Jesus said to him, You shall fear the Lord your God, and him shall you serve. Then Satan left him' [Matt. 4:1–11]. Now what was the need for relating that he fasted forty days and forty nights? What sort of praise of God is it to say that he needs food and drink? Why, all the angels of our God who serve him need no food or drink. Moreover, Moses, who was flesh and blood, was sustained by the glory of the divine presence forty days and forty nights without eating bread or drinking water, and so was Elijah. Furthermore, the Jews were unable to look upon the countenance of Moses until he placed a veil over his face because he had approached his Creator; how much more, then, should this be true of this man, who called himself God [...]

204

It is written in the Torah, 'Follow the majority' [Exod. 23:2], and this is the general custom. Now, only eleven nations have erred after the belief in Jesus, and all of them together do not equal the one nation of Ishmaelites. Thus, sixty nations including the Ishmaelites all testify that their religion is vanity, and we, the children of Israel, also testify that the hanged one was a human being born of a mother and father. Now you contend that he was the Creator, that he had mercy upon his creatures who were in hell because of Adam's sin, and that he took upon himself suffering and death to save his creatures from the judgment of hell, God forbid. If so, then he should have overridden his stern judgment in favor of his mercy – for he may do this – and caused all nations to believe in him so that they would be saved; as it is, only a minority believe in him. Thus, it is evident that their assertions are false. One can also point out that 'a matter is established by two witnesses' [Deut. 19:15], and there are two witnesses for our Torah since both you and the Ishmaelites admit that our Torah is true. However, neither we nor the Ishmaelites admit to the truth of your Torah, and neither we nor you admit to the truth of the Torah of the Ishmaelites. Consequently, there are two witnesses that our Torah is true and that our God is true and eternal. Blessed is he who chose us.

Source

Berger, David, *The Jewish–Christian Debate in the High Middle Ages: A Critical Edition of the Nizzahon Vetus with an Introduction, Translation, and Commentary* (Philadelphia: Jewish Publication Soc. of America, 1979), 176–7, 203. (Square-bracketed biblical references are part of the original.)

Commentary

Nizzahon Vetus (literally 'old book of polemic') is an anthology of northern European Jewish polemical arguments against Christianity, probably compiled in the thirteenth century. The author is unknown, although the work contains literary links to *Sefer Yosef HaMeqqaneh* by Joseph ben Nathan (fl. thirteenth century). It is an important source of Jewish anti-Christian polemic, marked by an aggressive rhetorical approach to Christian exegesis of scripture.

Its collection of refutations, including texts written in response to New Testament texts and various Christian doctrines, rituals and practices, is mocking in tone. The first excerpt illustrates its criticism of the Gospels and focuses on alleged absurdities and contradictions. It ridicules the forty-day fast of Jesus in the wilderness, pointing out that since neither Moses nor Elijah needed any sustenance over the same period it was not miraculous. One striking characteristic of *Nizzahon Vetus* is the extensive use of New Testament quotations, reflecting an intimate knowledge of the Gospels. It also shows awareness of the other books in the New Testament.

There are similarities between Jewish polemical use of the New Testament and Christian use of the Talmud in the thirteenth century. Jews and Christians shared one sacred text (albeit with slight differences) and each had a second on whose authority they differed (see also Appendix to Part I, p. 162). Previously, Jewish and Christian polemical writings had largely been restricted to different interpretations of a text whose authority both accepted (i.e., the Old Testament/Hebrew Bible). In this period, however, the New Testament began to be used by Jews and the Talmud by Christians in their contestation.

The second document demonstrates another polemical tactic used by Jews: Christianity is far from universal and does not even represent a majority, since 'only a minority believe in him [Jesus]'. The success of Islam and the power of Muslims (including the failure of the Crusades) were used to invalidate Christian claims. The twelfth and thirteenth centuries were characterised by the broadening of the horizons of Europe that took place in the wake of the Crusades. Contacts with the Muslim world provided Jewish apologists with an argument against the Christian claim that the size of Christianity proved its superiority over a religion with a small number of adherents. Jews now argued that even by the numerical test alone, Christianity would not prevail. The large numbers of Muslims (as well as the failure of the Crusades to reclaim the Holy Land) indicate that God's promise to Abraham that all nations of the world would be blessed in him and his seed has not been fulfilled through Christianity.

Nizzahon Vetus is an example of Jewish disputation at its most aggressive and represents a Jewish response to increasingly strident Christian condemnations of Judaism during a period when confrontations between Jews and Christians were on the increase and their tone became more virulent. Its appearance also paralleled the decline of Jews in France and Germany. The Crusades, combined with disputations (see, for example, document 6) and attempts to bring about large-scale Jewish conversion, such as those by King Louis IX of France (*r.* 1226–70), were significant blows for Jews in thirteenth-century northern Europe. *Nizzahon Vetus* was one response.

Bibliography

Berger, David, *Persecution, Polemic, and Dialogue: Essays in Jewish–Christian Relations* (Boston: Academic Studies Press, 2010).

Horbury, William, *Jews and Christians in Contact and Controversy* (Edinburgh: T&T Clark, 1998).

10

Edward I: Writ to the Sheriffs for the Expulsion of Jews from England (18 July 1290)

Text

Whereas the King has prefixed to all the Jews of his realm a certain time to pass out of the realm, and he wills that they shall not be treated by his ministers or others otherwise than has been customary, he orders the sheriff to cause proclamation to be made throughout his bailiwick prohibiting any one from injuring or wronging the Jews within the said time. He is ordered to cause the Jews to have safe-conduct at their cost when they, with their chattels, which the king has granted to them, direct their steps toward London in order to cross the sea, provided that before they leave they restore the pledges of Christians in their possession to those to whom they belong.

Source

Stokes, Henry P., 'Extracts from the Close Rolls, 1289–1368', *Miscellanies of the Jewish Historical Society of England* 1 (1925), x.

Commentary

The expulsion of Jews from England, Anjou and Gascony in 1290 is the best known of the expulsions at the end of the thirteenth century and the most significant until that of Spain in 1492 (see document 14). The official edict of expulsion, now lost, was issued on 18 July 1290; our document, a writ to the sheriffs issued on the same day, declared that Jews, who numbered approximately 2,000, were allowed to leave the country peaceably.

Although usury was the justification for the expulsion, Robin Mundill suggests there was another factor: King Edward I had no intention of missing the financial opportunity arising from the departure of England's Jews. By the late 1280s, Edward was under financial pressure, having run up debts waging war, and needed to negotiate a financial settlement with Parliament: in return for the expulsion, Parliament granted Edward a tax of £116,000 – the largest single tax of the Middle Ages in England. The dissolution of Jewish assets that were left behind began immediately after their departure and the king benefited from a further windfall.

The expulsion should be seen in the context of the decline of Jews in England from a position of relative prosperity in the mid-twelfth century to one of ruin and of facing an increasingly hostile church during the thirteenth. In addition, being under the protection of the crown meant that Jews were 'servants' of the king, administered by a special court: Jews in England (and elsewhere, such as in France) were categorised as *servi camerae* ('serfs of the chamber'). This allowed the monarch to transform the concept of protection into an instrument of economic and social exploitation: when Jews were no longer of value, the king's protection was no longer forthcoming.

As prince, Edward had already taxed Jews for his Crusades and to support the *Domus Conversorum* (a home for Jewish converts). Soon after he became king, the Statute of Jewry (*c*. 1275) was issued, requiring Jews to live in specific towns (such as London, Cambridge, Oxford and Winchester) and for synagogue worship to be held quietly (so that Christians could not hear it). Jews also had to attend conversionary sermons and to wear the 'Jew badge' (see document 5), were forbidden to employ Christian nurses and had to pay a three-pence tax each Easter.

An increase in anti-Jewish attitudes in England was also linked to child murder accusations, which seem to have originated in Norwich (see document 2) and resurfaced in Lincoln in 1255, and to the Crusades (see documents 1 (i) and (ii)). Outbreaks of anti-Jewish violence also occurred in London in 1189 and in York, where the Jewish community was massacred in 1190.

The expulsion of Jews from England was the climax of a century of marginalisation, and there is no evidence of resistance from the Jewish community or of violence against Jews. Unlike France, which expelled Jews only to readmit them shortly afterwards, England was unusual in the completeness of the expulsion, which was only reversed by their readmission in 1656 (see Chapter 5, p. 256).

Bibliography

Elukin, *Living Together, Living Apart.*

Mundill, Robin R., *England's Jewish Solution, 1262–1290: Experiment and Expulsion* (Cambridge: Cambridge University Press, 1998).

11

'About the Great Plague and the Burning of the Jews [of Strasbourg]' (14 February 1349)

Text

In the year 1349 there occurred the greatest epidemic that ever happened. Death went from one end of the earth to the other, on both sides of the sea, and it was even greater among the Saracens than among the Christians. In some lands everyone died so that no one was left. Ships were also found on the sea laden with wares; the crew had all died and no one guided the ship. The Bishop of Marseilles and priests and monks and more than half of all the people there died with them. In other kingdoms and cities so many people perished that it would be horrible to describe. The pope at Avignon stopped all sessions of court, locked himself in a room, allowed no one to approach him and had a fire burning before him all the time. [This last was probably intended as some sort of disinfectant.] As for the source of this epidemic, all wise teachers and physicians could say only that it was God's will. As the plague was now here, so was it in other places, and it lasted more than an entire year. This epidemic also came to Strasbourg in the summer of the aforementioned year, and it is estimated that about sixteen thousand people died.

In the matter of this plague the Jews throughout the world were reviled and accused in all lands of having caused it through the poison which they are said to have put into the water and the wells – that is what they were accused of – and for this reason the Jews were burnt all the way from the Mediterranean into Germany, but not in Avignon, for the pope protected them there.

Nevertheless they tortured a number of Jews in Berne and Zofingen [Switzerland], who then admitted that they had put poison into many wells, and they also found the poison in the wells. Thereupon they burnt the Jews in many towns and wrote of this affair to Strasbourg, Freiburg, and Basel in order that they too should burn their Jews. But the leaders in these three cities in whose hands the government lay did not believe that anything ought to be done to the Jews. However in Basel the citizens marched to the city hall and compelled the council to take an oath that they would burn the Jews, and that they would allow no Jew to enter the city for the next two hundred years. Thereupon the Jews were arrested in all these places and a conference was arranged to meet at Benfeld [Alsace, February 8, 1349].

The Bishop of Strasbourg [Berthold II], all the feudal lords of Alsace, and representatives of the three aforementioned cities came there. The deputies of the city of Strasbourg were asked what they were going to do with their Jews. They answered and said that they knew no evil of them. Then they asked the Strasbourgers why they had closed the wells and put away the buckets, and there was a great indignation and clamor against the deputies from Strasbourg. So finally the Bishop and the lords and the Imperial Cities agreed to do away with the Jews. The result was that they were burnt in many cities, and wherever they were expelled they were caught by the peasants and stabbed to death or drowned.

Source

Marcus, Jacob Rader, and Saperstein, Marc, *The Jews in Christian Europe: A Source Book, 315–1791* (Pittsburgh: Hebrew Union College Press/University of Pittsburgh Press, 2015), 155–7, 664: 24.2. Reproduced by permission of the Hebrew Union College Press. © 2015 Hebrew Union College Press. (Square-bracketed phrases are part of the original, the first as a footnote.)

Commentary

The Black Death, which swept across Europe between 1347 and 1351, marked a period of suffering and destruction for Jewish communities. The most frequently cited response to the pandemic in respect of Jewish–Christian relations is *Quamvis perfidiam*, issued by Pope Clement VI on 26 September 1348, though, as had become traditional, much of this was based on earlier papal statements. The current situation, however, appeared to be unprecedented, with Christians blaming Jews for the mass suffering and deaths of their Christian neighbours. Clement's response included a new and apparently decisive argument that most contemporary European Christians would have been unable to challenge, namely that the plague was destroying Jewish as well as Christian lives and also occurred in places where there were no Jews living at all. Christians were therefore warned by the pope that they must not murder or injure Jews, on pain of excommunication.

The current document demonstrates the limited impact of *Quamvis perfidiam* and treats specifically the destruction of the Jewish community in Strasbourg. Rumours, circulating initially in other parts of the empire and widely believed, suggested that the disease was caused by Jews poisoning the wells. Such rumours soon spread along the Rhine, reaching Germany. In Strasbourg, the bishop, together with feudal lords and members of the town council, attempted to save the Jewish community, insisting that they must not be held responsible for the plague. However, under pressure from the populace, led by the butchers' and tanners' guild and by nobles determined to do away with Jews who were their economic competitors and to whom they were indebted for loans, most of the city's Jews were killed.

Many Jewish children were baptised and forced to live the rest of their lives as Christians. All debts owed to Jews by Christians were cancelled. In Strasbourg, at least, it was not merely religious bigotry and fear of the plague but economic resentment that drove the craftsmen and nobles to attack and kill Jews. Unsurprisingly, their action did not stop the Black Death reaching the city, where 16,000 citizens perished.

Similar massacres of whole Jewish communities took place in hundreds of cities throughout the Holy Roman Empire and the Low Countries, most especially in the Rhineland, declining only with the virulence of the plague and leaving displaced Jews who in many cases were eventually allowed to resettle, as in Prague (and, according to a section of the document omitted here, Strasbourg itself in 1368). The German Jewish community went into decline and did not play an important role in Germany until the seventeenth century.

Bibliography

Barzilay, Tzafrir, *Poisoned Wells: Accusations, Persecution, and Minorities in Medieval Europe, 1321–1422* (Philadelphia: University of Pennsylvania Press, 2022).

Cohn, Samuel K., *The Black Death Transformed: Disease and Culture in Early Renaissance Europe* (London: Arnold, 2002).

Ziegler, Philip, *The Black Death* (New York: Penguin, 1982).

12

Hasdai Crescas: Letter to the Community of Avignon (1392)

Text

On the day of the New Moon of the fateful month Tammus in the year 5151 [July 1391] the Lord bent the bow of the enemies against the populous community of Seville where there were between 6,000–7,000 heads of families, and they destroyed their gates by fire and killed in that very place a great number of people; the majority, however, changed their faith. Many of them, children as well as women, were sold to the Moslems, so that the streets occupied by Jews have become empty. Many of them, sanctifying the Holy Name, endured death, but many also broke the holy Covenant.

From there the fire spread and consumed all the cedars of Lebanon [Jewish scholars, here Jews generally] in the holy community of the city of Cordova. Here, too, many changed their faith, and the community became desolate.

And on the day of misery and punishment, on which the sufferings were intensified, the wrath of the Lord was discharged on the holy city, the source of learning and the word of the Lord, namely the community of Toledo, and in the temple of the Lord the priests and the learned were murdered. In that very place the Rabbis […], together with their children and pupils, publicly sanctified the Holy Name. However, many who had not the courage to save their souls changed their faith here, too.

[…] On the 7th of the month Ab the Lord destroyed mercilessly the community of Valencia, in which there were about a thousand heads of families; about 250 men died, sanctifying the name of the Lord; the others fled into the mountain; some of these saved themselves but the majority changed their faith.

From there the plague spread over the communities of glorious Majorca, which is situated on the shore of the sea. On the day of the New Moon of Ellul, the bloodthirsty villains came there, profaned, plundered and robbed them […] There died, sanctifying the Holy Name, about 300 persons, and about 800 took refuge in the royal castle; the others changed their faith.

On the following Sabbath the Lord poured out His fury like fire, destroyed His sanctuary and profaned the crown of His teaching, namely the community of Barcelona, which was destroyed on that day. The number of murdered amounted to 250 souls; the rest fled into the castle, where they were saved. The enemies plundered all streets inhabited by Jews and set fire to some of them. The authorities of the province, however, took no part in this; instead, they endeavoured to protect the Jews with all their might. They offered food and drink to the Jews, and even set about punishing the wrongdoers, when a furious mob rose against the better classes in the country and fought against the Jews who were in the castle, with bows and missiles, and killed them in the castle itself. Amongst the many who sanctified the Name of the Lord was my only son, who was a bridegroom and whom I have offered as a faultless lamb for sacrifice […] Amongst them were many who slaughtered themselves and others who threw themselves down from the tower […] Many also came forth and sanctified the name of the Lord in the open street. All the others changed their faith, and only few found refuge in the towns of the princes […] Consequently, because of our many sins, there is none left in Barcelona today who still bears the name of Jew.

In the town of Lerida, too, many died and others changed their faith. There were only a few people who saved their lives.

In the town of Gerona, where knowledge of the Law could be found combined with humility, the Rabbis of that place sanctified the Name of the Lord publicly, and few only changed their faith. The majority of the community escaped to the houses of the citizens and are today in the castle.

In a word, in the state of Valencia not one single Jew remained, with the sole exception of the place called Murviedro. In the province of Catalonia, too, not one single Jew remained except in the towns of the princes and administrators, who nowhere attacked them.

For us, however, who are still in the country of Aragón, there is no more trouble and complaint, because the Lord has taken pity on us and has preserved the remnant of us in all these places after vehement supplication, although nothing but our bodies is left us after the distribution of our belongings. In spite of this, fear fills our hearts, and our eyes are directed towards the Father in heaven, that He may be merciful to us and may heal us of our wounds, and keep our feet from wavering.

Source

Kobler, Franz (ed.), *Letters of Jews through the Ages: From Biblical Times to the Middle of the Eighteenth Century* (London: Ararat Publishing Society/East and West Library, 1953), 272–5. (Square-bracketed phrases are part of the original.)

Commentary

Hasdai Crescas (*c.* 1340–1410), a Jewish leader from Catalonia, was a philosopher and halakhist who represented the Jewish community at the royal court of Aragón in the late fourteenth century and was, unusually for a Jew, close adviser to the king. His letter describes the 1391 anti-Jewish riots that began in Seville and spread throughout the Iberian Peninsula, marking a key moment in the decline of Spanish Jewry.

The historical context of the violence can be traced to the increasing assertiveness of the Christian kingdoms during the thirteenth and fourteenth centuries. Under Muslim rule Jews, like Christians, had become an accepted part of the religious landscape, subject to some restrictions but widely tolerated, as in Córdoba and Toledo, which became centres of Jewish learning. The term *convivencia* is used to describe this relatively easy coexistence of Jews, Christians and Muslims.

For a while, a similar openness existed in Christian Iberia, where Jews (and Muslims) were accepted as part of the fabric of society, but as Christian kingdoms such as Aragón, Catalonia and Castile began to assert their Christian identity more strongly, Jews (and Muslims) faced increasing pressure. Jews were compelled to attend conversionist sermons and participate in public disputations (see document 6). The conversion campaigns were only moderately successful until 1391, when force came into play, leading to voluntary and forced conversions (such as in Seville, where 'the majority [of Jews] changed their faith') and Córdoba. Crescas writes that in large areas of Catalonia the Jewish communities shrank almost to nothing. Thereafter, the Jewish communities in the Iberian Peninsula were divided between professing Jews and *conversos* (Jewish converts to Christianity), until the expulsion in 1492 (see document 14).

Our document was written from Zaragoza at the conclusion of the catastrophe and Crescas put together reports from the various cities. He describes how the violence began and how it quickly spread through much of the Iberian Peninsula, with devastating results for Jewish life. As well as the large numbers who converted to Christianity, many Jews fled or perished, and the *convivencia* was dealt its death blow. Those who remained faced increased marginalisation. According to Crescas, Jews viewed their suffering as God's punishment and, as in accounts of the Crusades, some even preferred acts of martyrdom.

What lay behind this anti-Jewish violence? There was increasing hostility in Christian preaching about Judaism, which was shifting from stereotypical references to Jews of antiquity to attacks against contemporary Jews. Ferrand Martinez (*c.* 1350–1419) seems to have played a key role. He delivered sermons which provoked anti-Jewish violence and inspired anti-Jewish legislation in Aragón and Castile. He also ignored calls from King John I of Castile and León (*r.* 1379–90) and Archbishop Barroso of Toledo, primate of

Spain, to cease his rabble-rousing. The deaths of both John and Barroso in 1390, leaving the eleven-year-old Henry III to rule under the regency of his mother, allowed Martinez to continue his campaign with tragic consequences.

Bibliography

Ben-Shalom, Ram, 'Hasdai Crescas: Portrait of a Leader at a Time of Crisis', in Ray, Jonathan (ed.), *The Jew in Medieval Iberia, 1100–1500* (Boston: Academic Studies Press, 2011), 309–51.

Feldman, Seymour, 'Crescas and the Crisis of 1391', in *Philosophy in a Time of Crisis: Don Isaak Abravanel Defender of the Faith* (London and New York: Routledge Curzon, 2002).

Gampel, Benjamin R., *Anti-Jewish Riots in the Crown of Aragon and the Royal Response, 1391–1392* (Cambridge: Cambridge University Press, 2016).

Lasker, Daniel J. (trans.), *The Refutation of the Christian Principles by Hasdai Crescas; Translated with an Introduction and Notes* (Albany: State University of New York, 1992).

13

Profiat Duran: 'Epistle of Lamentation, Grief and Consolation' (1393)

Text

I say that this [statement in B.T. *Menaḥot* 53b] alludes to that part of the seed of Abraham who were forced publicly to deny their faith, upon whom the decree of apostasy fell in this great region …. Some of them have been lax with regard to repentance …. It is therefore thought that this group has left the category of the Jewish people, which God has chosen as His legacy …. The answer that comes … means that the salvation and redemption that we await encompass the seed of Abraham, both those upon whom the decree of apostasy has fallen, who were 'broken, trapped, and taken captive' (Isa. 8:15) and those 'who subscribe by hand to the Lord, and are called by the name of Israel' (Isa. 44:5).

This matter in the present exile is just like that in previous ones. In the Egyptian exile, the people stumbled in idolatry, willingly …, yet this did not remove them from the category of the seed of Abraham. In the Babylonian exile, all of them stumbled in idolatry under duress except for a few individuals such as Hananiah and his companions, yet this did not remove them from the category of the seed of Abraham; no, in love and compassion God redeemed them. So it should be in this great exile of the present: if a part of the people has stumbled in a similar manner under absolute duress, because of fear for their lives, this has not removed them from the category of God's people and the seed of Abraham who loved Him [cf. Isa. 41:8], for God knows the secrets of their hearts, and He will redeem them with the rest of their brothers.

Source

Saperstein, Marc, 'A Sermon on the Akedah from the Generation of the Expulsion and Its Implications for 1391', in Mirsky, Aharon, Grossman, Avraham, and Kaplan, Yosef (eds.), *Exile and Diaspora – Studies in the History of the Jewish People: Presented to Professor Haim Beinart*

(Jerusalem: Ben-Zvi Institute of Yad Izhak Ben-Zvi and the Hebrew University of Jerusalem; Madrid: Consejo Superior de Investigaciones Científicas, 1991), 113–14. (Square-bracketed phrases are part of the original.)

Commentary

Profiat Duran (*c.* 1350–*c.* 1415), also known as the Ephodi, was a Jewish apologist, grammarian and philosopher who converted to Christianity following the 1391 anti-Jewish riots that swept through the Iberian Peninsula. He appears in official records under his *converso* Christian name, Honoratus de Bonafide, but continued to practise Judaism secretly before fleeing Spain and returning to open practice. Only then did he publish a number of Hebrew writings that he had produced previously, including polemics against Christianity.

Our document is a sermon delivered on Rosh ha-Shana (the Jewish New Year) in 1393 and deals with the problem raised by the desire of forced (or willing) converts to return to Judaism. What was their status? Should they be freely accepted back? The traditional Jewish view mirrored the Christian: conversion was deemed apostasy and condemned. This position was easier to hold with regard to individuals but became more difficult when it concerned groups or an entire population of converted Jews. Even when large numbers were involved, as in mass forced conversions during the Crusades (especially in northern France and the Rhineland), the problem lasted only for a limited period, whereas the *conversos* of Spain and Portugal lived as outwardly Christian, sometimes over many generations and hundreds of years, before seeking readmittance to Jewish communities and living openly Jewish lives.

Our passage is an excerpt from Profiat Duran's sermon on Genesis 22, known to Jews as the *Akedah* or Binding of Isaac (see Appendix to Part I, p. 168), traditionally read on Rosh ha-Shana. Duran explores Abraham's willingness to sacrifice his son, comparing it to the sacrifice by fathers of their children during the 1391 riots. We know from his contemporary Hasdai Crescas and other testimonies that some Jewish children were killed by their fathers and others by the mob; indeed, Crescas was one of many fathers who extolled the death of their sons killed in the 1391 attacks (see document 12).

Yet as many Jews converted as were killed, including Duran himself. It seems Duran is responding to Crescas' view that apostasy under duress is not a legitimate action. Saperstein has shown in his critical edition (from which our document is excerpted) that Duran was responding to Crescas' interpretation of the *Akedah* in which he argued that Abraham's willingness to sacrifice his son was a paradigm for Jews who should sacrifice their sons if threatened with forced conversion during anti-Jewish violence. Duran takes a categorically different position, arguing in his sermon that forced conversion 'did not remove them from the category of the seed of Abraham'.

How to relate to those who had accepted baptism in order to save their lives was a critical issue in Jewish–Christian relations following the violent rampages. Christian doctrine considered baptism to be permanent, and all Jews who had been baptised were expected to observe Christian doctrines and traditions. Profiat Duran is an example of a Jew who was considered by the church to have converted to Christianity (and outwardly followed the necessary Christian practices) but not only continued to think of himself as a Jew but interpreted events in biblical times as supporting the Jewishness of those who were forced to lead (publicly at least) non-Jewish lives.

Bibliography

Kriegel, Maurice, 'Paul de Burgos et Profiat Duran Déchiffrent 1391', in Clemens, Lukas, and Cluse, Christoph (eds.), *The Jews of Europe around 1400: Disruption, Crisis, and Resilience* (Wiesbaden: Harrassowitz Verlag, 2018), 235–58.

Yisraeli, Yosi, 'Constructing and Undermining Converso Jewishness: Profiat Duran and Pablo de Santa María', in Katznelson, Ira, and Rubin, Miri (eds.), *Religious Conversion: History, Experience and Meaning* (London: Routledge, 2014), 185–216.

14

Ferdinand II and Isabella I: The Edict of Expulsion, Granada (31 March 1492)

Text

You know well […] that because we were informed that in our realms there were some bad Christians who Judaized and apostatized from our holy Catholic faith, whereof the chief cause was the communication between the Christians and the Jews; in the Cortes which we convened in the city of Toledo in the past year of one thousand four hundred and eighty years, we ordained that the said Jews should be set apart in all the cities, boroughs, and places of our realms and dominions and to give them Jewish quarters and separate places where they might dwell, hoping that with this separation [the matter] would be corrected; and in addition we […] gave an order whereby inquiries should be made in our said realms and dominions, […] and by it many offenders have been revealed, […] as we are informed, by the Inquisitors and many other religious persons […] Thereby it is established and made manifest the great damage to the Christians which has resulted and results from the participation, conversation, communication which they have held and do hold with the Jews, of whom it is proved that they always attempt by whatever ways and means they can to subvert and detract faithful Christians from our holy Catholic faith and separate them from it and attract and pervert them to their cursed belief and opinion […] And although most of this was known to us even before, and we knew that the true remedy for all this harm and damage was to separate the said Jews from all communication with the Christians and to expel them from our kingdom, it was our wish to be content with ordering them to leave all the cities, boroughs, and places in Andalusia, where it appeared that they had caused the most damage […] And whereas we are informed that neither that nor the punishments that have been given to some of those said Jews, who were discovered to be great offenders in these sins and transgressions against our holy Catholic faith, are sufficient as an entire remedy, […] because every day it is discovered and made manifest that the said Jews continue ever more active in their evil and harmful purpose in every place where they dwell and have dealings, and so that there may be no place for further offence against our holy faith, both in those whom until now God has chosen to preserve, and in those who have stumbled, fallen into sin and removed themselves from the Holy Mother Church, which because of the weakness of our human character and the diabolical cunning and subterfuge which constantly makes war against us, could easily happen unless the principal reason for it is not removed, [...] we order that this our edict be given by which we order all Jews and Jewesses of whatever age they may be who live and dwell and are in our said realms and dominions, as well the native-born among them as those not native-born who in any manner and for any reason have come and are in them, that by the end of the next month of July [...] they shall leave all our said realms and dominions, with their sons and daughters and servants and maidservants and Jewish followers, as well the great as the small, [...] and that they do not dare to return to them or to be in them or in any part of them, whether dwelling or in transit or in any other manner, under the penalty that if they do not do so and comply, and are found to be in our said realms and dominions or to come to them in any manner, they incur the punishment of death and the confiscation of all their property to our exchequer and treasury [...]

[...] And so that the said Jews and Jewesses during the said time until the end of the said month of July may better dispose of themselves and of their possessions and effects, for the present we take them and place them under our security and royal protection and defence, and we assure them, to them and to their possessions, so that during the time until the said day at the end of the said month of July, they may go and be safe and may enter and sell and trade and transfer all their property moveable and immoveable, and dispose thereof in accordance with their wish, and that during the said time no one may do them evil or damage nor injustice to their persons nor to their possessions [...], under the penalty to which are subject those who trespass against our royal security.

Source

Beinart, Haim, *The Expulsion of the Jews from Spain*, trans. Jeffrey M. Green (Oxford: Littman Library of Jewish Civilization, 2002), 49–53. (Square-bracketed words are part of the original.)

Commentary

Following their expulsion of Jews from Andalusia in 1483 and their conquest of the last Muslim kingdom, Granada, in 1492, King Ferdinand (1452–1516) and Queen Isabella (1451–1504) expelled all Jews from Spain, putting an abrupt end to the largest and most distinguished Jewish community in Europe.

The Edict justifies the expulsion by accusing Jews of seeking to influence Christians to observe Jewish practices and to bring *conversos* back to their Jewish roots. A century earlier, significant numbers of Jews had converted, some voluntarily, others under pressure, following the anti-Jewish riots of 1391 (see document 12). The term *conversos* was applied both to the converts and to their descendants, some of whom (sometimes called 'crypto-Jews') maintained secret observance of Jewish practice while others abandoned their former religion altogether. Popular opinion increasingly marginalised these 'new Christians' (i.e., those with Jewish heritage), leading to their exclusion from the universities and from high office on what can only be described as racial grounds. One example is the later development of the blood purity concept of *limpieza de sangre*, which strengthened the laws against anyone of Jewish ancestry and was promoted by, among others, the Society of Jesus (even though many of the early Jesuits were *conversos*). It was not until the late nineteenth and early twentieth century that most of the resulting anti-Jewish legislation was removed.

There is no consensus among scholars as to the primary motivation of the Edict. Ben Zion Netanyahu, for example, challenged the accusation of Jewish proselytism as the great majority of *conversos* were indeed genuine Christians and pointed to the role of the Inquisition, which began in 1483, as key to the expulsion. He is supported by Haim Beinart, who highlights the role of the Inquisitor Tomas de Torquemada (?1420–98), Dominican confessor to Ferdinand and Isabella, in convincing the king and queen (after initial reluctance, according to the text of the Edict) of the need to expel all Jews. The Inquisition, led by Franciscans and Dominicans, therefore not only responded to the rise of the grandchildren or great-grandchildren of *conversos* to positions of high influence in Spanish society but played a key role in the expulsion.

Thus the expulsion from Spain was ultimately more a religious-political than a racial matter. Scholars such as David Abulafia suggest that its purpose was as much about conversion as expulsion, a view reinforced by Samuel Usque's testimony from neighbouring Portugal (document 15). Although the Catholic clergy encouraged conversion, relatively few Spanish Jews seem to have chosen this option in preference to emigration – some to Portugal, which would seek mass conversion of or expel its Jews five years later; others to Navarre, then still an independent neighbour of Spain; most by sea to destinations including North Africa, Gallipoli and Constantinople. Like the writ to the sheriffs for the expulsion of Jews from England in 1290 (see document 10), the Edict insisted that Jews be placed under royal protection in preparation for their departure.

The expulsion from Spain was part of a wave of expulsions in the fifteenth century, including from Sicily and several German and north Italian states, which left almost all of western Europe without openly Jewish populations. As Jews moved east, countries such as Poland and cities such as Naples, and even Papal Rome, welcomed Jewish craftsmen. However, together with the earlier wave of expulsions from England and France in the late thirteenth century, its impact on Jewish–Christian relations was far-reaching.

Bibliography

Abulafia, David, *Spain and 1492: Unity and Uniformity under Ferdinand and Isabella* (Bangor: Headstart History, 1992).

Beinart, Haim, *The Expulsion of the Jews from Spain*, trans. Jeffrey M. Green (Oxford: Littman Library of Jewish Civilization, 2002).

Netanyahu, B., *The Origins of the Inquisition in Fifteenth Century Spain*, 2nd ed. (New York: New York Review Books, 2001).

Pérez, Joseph, *History of a Tragedy: The Expulsion of the Jews from Spain*, trans. Lysa Hochroth (Urbana: University of Illinois Press, *c.* 2007).

Roth, Norman, *Conversos, Inquisition, and the Expulsion of the Jews from Spain* (Madison: University of Wisconsin Press, *c.* 1995).

15

Samuel Usque: Consolation for the Tribulations of Israel (Consolaçam ás tribulaçoens de Israel) *(1553)*

Text

When death had finally carried off King John, who had persecuted me so cruelly in this world, another enemy then took the scepter in his place. Once he obtained the crown, he did not wait long to torment me. He soon [December 1496] proclaimed that all Jews in his kingdom must become Christians or leave Portugal within a stipulated period. If they did not leave, and were still found practicing Judaism, they would be allowed to remain, but their estates would be confiscated.

This proclamation greatly saddened all my children, for their hearts told them that my enemy wished to perpetrate an evil greater than exile, and they determined to leave […] But when the king realized the Jews' resolve, and how little they seemed to mind exile in preference to changing their religion, he revealed his evil intent. He commanded all Jews in the kingdom to assemble in Lisbon, bruiting that he would there provide them with ships. But as soon as they had gathered them, he had them herded into large buildings called *Os Estãos* [the States]. And when he had corralled them, like sheep prepared for the slaughter, he at last exposed his venomous character, and announced that all were to become Christians; and that they should do out of love what they would otherwise have to do by compulsion.

These threats were not sufficient to make my children turn their backs to their God; instead they answered resolutely that they would not comply with his request.

The king, seeing that greater force was required to jog them, consulted his advisers. They decreed that all the Jewish youth up to the age of twenty-five should be separated from their elders […]

After the young people were removed from their families, the advisors spoke to them persuasively, covering their venomous thoughts with treacle and promising them many favors if they converted wholeheartedly. But even this was insufficient to budge them from their constancy.

Finding the children as resolute as their parents, the agents of my temptation attacked them furiously. Dragging some by their legs and arms and others by their hair and beards, they carried them forcibly into the churches, where they threw their baptismal water upon them; it touched some of them but barely reached others. Further, they imposed

Christian names on them and placed them in the custody of Old Christians, who were to submit them to their new religion and keep them from their own faith.

No sooner had they completed this violence than they turned to the parents, who clung in anguish to the life they abhorred, and dealt them another mortal blow. They told them that their children had now converted to Christianity and urged them to do the same if they wished to live in their company. But this did not move them. Finally the king commanded that food and drink be withheld from them for three days to try them with the anguish of hunger, but this they likewise courageously endured.

The king realized that even this was insufficient to change them, and that if he starved them any longer, they would perish. He therefore determined to use the violence he had employed with their children. Dragging some by their legs and others by their hair and beards, punching and mauling them, his men brought them to the churches, where the waters of baptism were thrown upon them. Many resisted valiantly: one father covered his six sons with their prayer-shawls, exhorted them sagely to die for their faith, and killed them one by one, taking his own life last. One couple hanged themselves, and those who tried to take their bodies away for burial were slain by the enemies' spears.

Source

Cohen, Martin A. (trans.), *Samuel Usque's Consolation for the Tribulations of Israel (Consolaçam ás tribulaçoens de Israel)* (Philadelphia: Jewish Publication Society of America, 1965), 202–4.

Commentary

Little is known of Samuel Usque other than that he lived for some time in Ferrara in the 1540s and later went to Safed, in the Land of Israel, governed at that time by the Ottomans. Our excerpt comes from the second edition of his *Consolaçam ás tribulaçoens de Israel* (*Consolation for the Tribulations of Israel*), which was published in 1553 and deals with events in 1497. It provides a graphic account of mass forced conversions early in the reign of King Manuel I of Portugal (*r.* 1496–1521). The king's name is not mentioned in Usque's text, an indication perhaps of the intense dislike still felt towards him fifty-six years later, and it is probably not coincidental that there is no evidence for serious popular anti-Jewish sentiment in Portugal before his rule.

In December 1496, Manuel I promulgated a decree requiring Jews (and Muslims) to convert to Christianity or leave the country by the end of 1497, perhaps the result of pressure from Spain, many of whose Jews had taken refuge in Portugal after their expulsion in 1492 (see document 14). Soon afterwards, they were prevented from leaving and forcibly converted to Christianity. The importance of the document lies less in the brutality of the baptism and more in the consequences of the mass conversion, which was accompanied by a promise not to establish the Inquisition in Portugal for a generation. This meant that it was more straightforward to maintain Jewish practice and observance there than in Spain, although 'open' Judaism was only possible in the Portuguese Jewish diaspora (in Amsterdam, London, Hamburg and the Caribbean).

The terms 'new Christian', *converso*, 'crypto-Jew' and *marrano* (Muslim converts were called *moriscos*) are key. As we have seen, the term *converso* (or 'new Christian') refers to Jews who adopted Christianity, voluntarily or under pressure, and to their descendants. It is used to distinguish converted Jews from 'old Christians' (mentioned in the document), a term which refers to those who are Christian by birth with no Jewish affiliation or lineage. Jews who embraced Christianity remained under constant suspicion, fearing denunciation simply because of their Jewish lineage. *Marrano* (literally 'swine' or those who 'mar', i.e., 'damage', the Christian faith) is a derogatory term and subcategory of *converso*. All these Jews, although outwardly Christian converts, continued to observe certain Jewish practices or were accused of doing so; another term for this phenomenon is 'crypto-Judaism', because of the underground or covert nature of the religious practice involved.

Because of fear and persecution, many Jews sought refuge in other parts of Europe and the New World, where it was easier to lead a Jewish life. A massacre of the crypto-Jews of Lisbon in 1506 and the establishment of the Portuguese Inquisition in 1530 led to greater efforts to escape from Portugal and many found refuge in the Ottoman empire, where they returned to practising Jewish observance openly.

In the early seventeenth century, after Amsterdam became independent of Spanish rule, some Portuguese *conversos* who had secretly retained their Jewish identity for more than a century left Portugal and returned to Judaism in a Dutch environment. Two of the most famous were Baruch Spinoza, whose father was a Portuguese Jewish merchant, and Menasseh ben Israel, whose parents were *marranos* (see Chapter 5, pages 256 and 253). When in 1701 Jews established the Bevis Marks synagogue in London, the oldest synagogue building in continuous use in the UK, they were called the 'Spanish and Portuguese congregation'.

Bibliography

Guerrini, Maria Teresa, 'New Documents on Samuel Usque, the Author of the *Consolaçam ás tribulaçoens de Israel*', *Sefarad* 61, no. 1 (2000), 83–9.

Soyer, François, *The Persecution of the Jews and Muslims of Portugal: King Manuel I and the End of Religious Tolerance, 1496–7* (Leiden and Boston: Brill, 2007).

5

From the Reformation to the Enlightenment
The Sixteenth to the Eighteenth Century

PAUL KERRY

INTRODUCTION

The period 1500–1800 witnessed two significant movements which had a major impact on the history of Jewish–Christian relations. First, the Reformation, the series of reform movements fuelled mightily by Martin Luther that resulted in the splintering of European Christendom, was one of the greatest revolutions in the history of western thought and broke the religious monopoly of the Roman Catholic Church. Emerging Protestant groups would struggle to engage with Jews after expectations of conversion were disappointed, while the Roman Catholic Church began to redefine its doctrine and thereby – eventually – its relationship to Judaism. Similarly, Jews splintered into many religious groupings, including messianists, religious rationalists, mystics and reformers. They also engaged with secular philosophy and by the end of our period many were assimilating or converting to Christianity, for various reasons. In combination, these changes in the make-up of both Judaism and Christianity fostered new encounters and conversations.

The rediscovery of the ancient world which was a defining characteristic of Renaissance humanism, with its emphasis on return to original sources (*ad fontes*), had seen a marked development of Hebrew scholarship, which by the beginning of our period was becoming an established element in the training of biblical scholars in European universities. Reformers tended to have a high regard for the Hebrew language and emphasised its importance for understanding scripture (which became one of many subjects of dispute between Protestants and Catholics). John Calvin (1509–64), for example, stressed the unity of the Old and New Testaments, insisting that Christians should learn from Jews in order to understand the Old Testament.

Second, the Enlightenment, variegated as it was in different locations and often seen as representing the beginning of modernity, challenged the intellectual assumptions of the traditional religious and political role of the church and religious authority in general. Modernity not only witnessed the emancipation of Jews and the eventual granting of equal rights, but also the denigration of Jews and Judaism, rooted in a new form of political and social thinking. This latter phenomenon would be given the epithet 'antisemitism' in the nineteenth century (and is therefore discussed in more detail in Chapter 6), but it would be a mistake to differentiate it completely from the much older prejudice, anti-Judaism).

The Enlightenment spread the concept of religious toleration, which made it easier for Jews and Christians to meet one another and engage in conversations, while with the rise of great cities such as Amsterdam, London, Paris, Vienna and Berlin came questions about Jewish immigration and the extension of civil rights. Yet such discussions also saw Jews caught in a new dilemma: some Christians found comfort in religious retrenchment and challenged Jews for not converting, while others embraced enlightened rationalism and attacked Jews for remaining part of what they saw as a retrograde, even barbaric faith.

The documents in this chapter include pamphlets, correspondence and plays – all signs that Jewish–Christian relations were becoming less controlled by ecclesiastical authorities with their emphasis on theological reflection and more nested in political questions about immigration, emancipation and integration within a sociopolitical environment of expanding economies, transatlantic settlement and new conceptions of the nation state, as well as the implications of humanist philosophy.

The first document – the Christian Hebraist and humanist Johannes Reuchlin's defence of post-biblical Hebrew texts against attacks from the Dominicans (document 1) – represents a link to the period covered by Chapter 4. However, while the attempt to ban and/or destroy Hebrew books is a legacy of previous centuries, Reuchlin's letter represents a new willingness on the part of Christian defenders to advance the argument that post-biblical Jewish writings could prove the truth of Christianity and thus help persuade Jews to convert.

The desire for Jewish conversion was also salient to the writings of the German Reformer Martin Luther, who initially believed that a gentler approach to Judaism than that of the Roman Catholic Church would achieve this end. His 1523 pamphlet *That Jesus Christ Was Born a Jew* (document 2 (i)) was written in the wake of the remarkable early success of Protestantism. Luther's hope that Jews might see the true light in his purified presentation of the gospel and convert was disappointed, and twenty years later, in *On the Jews and Their Lies* (document 2 (ii)), he condemned their stubbornness in adhering to Jewish traditions. His harsh judgement would fuel burning synagogues for centuries and was instrumentalised by the Nazis in precisely this way during Kristallnacht in 1938. The two approaches taken by Luther – mild persuasion and aggressive polemic – would continue to inform and animate how Protestants would treat Jews over the next three hundred years.

The challenge of the Reformation led to self-examination on the part of Roman Catholicism and to what became known as the Counter-Reformation, as illustrated by the Council of Trent, which met occasionally over almost twenty years and sought not only to address questions arising from the faithful but also criticisms from Reformers. The Council produced a new Catechism (document 3) that would be used in parishes throughout the Roman Catholic Church. This modified the charge of deicide, common in the *adversus Judaeos* writings (see Chapter 2, p. 65), that accused Jews of killing God by crucifying Christ. This key change in teaching spread slowly, however: not until the 1980s, for example, did the Oberammergau Passion Play begin to engage in Jewish–Christian dialogue to examine and reform its text. *The Catechism of the Council of Trent* continues to be influential today, as witnessed by *Nostra aetate* (see Appendix to Part III, p. 512) and the contemporary Roman Catholic Catechism.

What the Council of Trent did not change was the prohibition against usury and the negative stereotyping of Jews as moneylenders. Shakespeare's *The Merchant of Venice* (document 4) highlights such stereotypes in popular culture, though Shakespeare, whose personal knowledge of Jews (who had been expelled from England in 1290) was likely to have been minimal, portrays both Jews and Christians ambivalently. The play's reception and performance history reflect changes in characterisation and audience expectations over the centuries, providing an alternative lens on developments in the Jewish–Christian relationship to those provided by ecclesiastical or political documents, and it continues to be used today as an introduction to discussions about that relationship in schools and colleges.

Peter Stuyvesant used similar stereotypes in his attempt to expel from New Amsterdam (modern-day Lower Manhattan) a group of Jews who had fled Brazil after the Spanish Inquisition reached it (document 5). The threat of expulsion failed, partly for economic reasons – Jewish investors in Holland interceded on behalf of their coreligionists – and partly due to the Dutch West India Company's decision to act humanely. The document also illustrates the globalisation of Jewish–Christian relations, which has continued ever since.

The consequences of the Inquisition (see Chapter 4, p. 229) also provide the context to document 6, a request by a rabbi whose Portuguese family had fled to Amsterdam. Menasseh ben Israel, who was advocating for the return of Jews to England, delivered his *Humble Addresses* to the Lord Protector Oliver Cromwell in 1655. Drawing on millenarian thinking about the gathering of Israel, this document represents a new way for Jews to connect with Christians: shared eschatological thinking. The return of some Jews to England in 1656 had wider practical consequences overseas as Jews also began to settle in England's North American colonies, such as Rhode Island.

The Enlightenment's emphasis on reason, individualism and public discourse, including what we today might call dialogue, generated new intellectual movements. Although the realities of power relations meant that the direction of most public conversations between Jews and Christians went from the top down, as illustrated by the edicts of Joseph II (document 11) and Napoleon (see Chapter 6, p. 294), personal letter exchanges were another way for Jews and Christians to express different views based on reason. This was not always a discussion between equal points of view, however. Christian correspondents often expected Jews to explain why they were not persuaded to become Christians, as illustrated by the letter from Baruch Spinoza (document 7), itself a response to Albert Burgh. Spinoza invited Burgh to use reason to examine his own decision to convert to Catholicism, a method that would, in theory, allow Jews and Christians to communicate in a more equal way, namely as philosophers.

Similarly, John Toland's 1714 pamphlet *Reasons for Naturalizing the Jews in Great Britain and Ireland* (document 8) provided not theological justifications but rather philosophical arguments, founded in the writings of John Locke, for the new concept of toleration and its application to Jews. As a Protestant convert from Catholicism and an Irishman living in Hanoverian England, where naturalisation of foreigners was a major question of the day, Toland was empathetic with the plight of Jews and argued for the extension of full citizenship, focusing on their civic contributions. This shift in thinking would inform Jewish–Christian relations from Berlin to Philadelphia.

The letter exchange between Isaac de Pinto and Voltaire (document 9) provides a litmus test for the extent to which reason would guide European thinkers. Voltaire, seen by some scholars as laying the foundations for modern antisemitism, exemplified the ambivalence of the Enlightenment. He is derisive of all religions, but to Jews he suggests that the worst stereotypes are fixed parts of Jewish character. De Pinto pushed back against these views.

The Lutheran pastor Johann Gottfried Herder carried on the humanistic tradition of historicising the Bible and drawing on biblical criticism (document 12) and proposed that Jewish–Christian relations could flourish if Christians remembered that Christianity emerged from Judaism and appreciated the cultural and theological debt owed to Jews. Nevertheless, there was another and contradictory strand in Herder's thought as he outlined the irreconcilable alienness of Jews in Christian society. Herder's views on cultural particularism have led him to be seen by some as giving rise to cultural nationalism in Germany, and his writings were exploited in later generations by antisemites.

Another letter exchange took place in 1769–70 in Berlin when Moses Mendelssohn was challenged publicly by the Swiss pastor Johann Kaspar Lavater to explain on philosophical grounds why he had not converted to Christianity. Christian intellectuals argued that Christianity should be equated with the highest form of enlightened religion. The response of Mendelssohn, the leading Jewish philosopher of his generation, demonstrates that Jews still needed to defend their existence as Jews. In *Jerusalem* (document 13), he argued that Jews and Christians could get along in civil society without having to surrender religious distinctiveness and doctrinal differences and could thus avoid a union of faiths.

A similar question about religious supremacy arises in the play *Nathan the Wise* (document 10), Gotthold Ephraim Lessing's masterpiece, in which the main protagonist is modelled on Mendelssohn. The play has nothing of Shakespeare's ambivalence about Jews but proposes an optimistic vision of interfaith relations from an Enlightenment perspective in which theological truth is deferred and religious differences are minimised in favour of a shared humanity. Written in 1779 and first performed in Frederick II's Berlin in 1783, it illustrates in popular form that Jewish–Christian relations were part of the public discourse in the late eighteenth-century Prussian capital. Frederick had announced his own set of toleration policies, including for Jews, and Berlin became a seedbed for ideas on the status of Jews. Historian and son of a Lutheran pastor Christian Wilhelm Dohm had published *Concerning the Amelioration of the Civil Status of the Jews* there in 1781 (a work which caught Mendelssohn's attention), countering Christian prejudices and arguing for full emancipation, holding that political equality was key to improving the condition of Jews. Similar Enlightenment notions were put into practice by the reforming emperor Joseph II in Habsburg lands through his 1782 Edict of Toleration (document 11), which began to lift civil liabilities so that Jews would become more useful to the state.

The Enlightenment not only led to Jewish emancipation – that is, to Jews gaining civil rights on a more or less equal footing with other citizens of the countries in which they lived – but also the emancipation of women, slaves and other religious minorities (Protestant groups in some countries, Catholics in England). It also generated a Jewish equivalent, the Haskalah (from the Hebrew *sekhel*, 'reason' or 'intellect'), of which Mendelssohn is often seen as the father figure. It was generally assumed that there was one universal truth, attainable by reason, in which all might share, whether Christian or Jewish. Only the truths of reason, for instance in science, mathematics and ethics, were certain, and these were open to all.

Although emancipation resulted in political freedom for individual Jews, it did not for the Jewish people as a community. So long as Jews identified themselves primarily as individual citizens they were accorded civil rights, but their communal identity remained restricted. Thus, many Christians during this period expected Jews to convert to Christianity, and significant numbers did indeed do so (or assimilate), indicating something of the pressure on Jews to conform, at least outwardly, to the dominant faith.

Freedom of religion was also being debated across the Atlantic, in the United States. In 1783, the same year that Mendelssohn's *Jerusalem* was published, a Philadelphia synagogue put forward a petition (document 14) requesting that Jews not be required to take a religious test necessitating their affirmation of the Christian Bible in order to become civic officeholders and be placed on an equal political footing with Christians in the city. In the same year that the test was revoked, 1790, George Washington, as the newly elected President of the United States, anchored nationwide Jewish–Christian relations in the recently ratified United States Constitution's First Amendment guarantee of religious freedom when he confirmed to the Jewish community in Newport, Rhode Island, that their right to worship would continue to be protected and held inviolate, a move that affirmed the full equality of Jews with Christians in the new republic (document 15).

The three centuries covered in this chapter thus consisted of increasing conversations between Christians and Jews as Europe, transformed through the Reformation, developed into a group of states. The title of Simon Schama's volume on this period of Jewish history and interactions with Christians is 'Belonging', and amid the continued persecutions and outbursts of violence against Jews, one could perhaps characterise the years 1500–1800 as the Jewish search for belonging and acceptance in Christian communities. As European powers began to explore the globe, Jews would participate in the colonial process and begin to find their place in the Atlantic world. The emergence of Enlightenment ideas of toleration, liberty of conscience and religious freedom fostered a sense of religious equality, albeit a fragile one, between Christians and Jews. Such developments laid the foundations for the emancipation of Jews and full civil rights; however, they also occurred at a time when Jews were beginning to be perceived more along racial than religious lines.

Bibliography

de Greef, Wulfert, *Of One Tree: Calvin on Jews and Christians in the Context of the Late Middle Ages*, trans. Lyle D. Bierma (Göttingen: Vandenhoeck & Ruprecht, 2021).

Feiner, Shmuel, *The Jewish Eighteenth Century: A European Biography, 1700–1750*, trans. Jeffrey M. Green (Bloomington: Indiana University Press, 2020).

Feiner, Shmuel, *The Jewish Enlightenment*, trans. Chaya Naor (Philadelphia: University of Pennsylvania Press, 2003).

Gilman, Sander L., and Zipes, Jack (eds.), *Yale Companion to Jewish Writing and Thought in German Culture, 1096–1996* (New Haven: Yale University Press, 1997).

Guibbory, Achsah, *Christian Identity, Jews, and Israel in Seventeenth-Century England* (Oxford: Oxford University Press, 2010).

Katz, David S., *The Jews in the History of England, 1485–1850* (Oxford: Oxford University Press, 1994).

Manuel, Frank E., *The Broken Staff: Judaism through Christian Eyes* (Cambridge, MA: Harvard University Press 1992).

Oberman, Heiko A., *The Roots of Antisemitism in the Age of Renaissance and Reformation*, trans. James I. Porter (Philadelphia: Fortress Press, 1984).

Ruderman, David B., *Early Modern Jewry: A New Cultural History* (Princeton: Princeton University Press, 2010).

Schama, Simon, *The Story of the Jews: Belonging, Vol. 2: 1492–1900* (New York: HarperCollins, 2017).

Sorkin, David, *Jewish Emancipation: A History across Five Centuries* (Princeton: Princeton University Press, 2019).

Sorkin, David, *The Religious Enlightenment: Protestants, Jews, and Catholics from London to Vienna* (Princeton: Princeton University Press, 2011).

Sutcliffe, Adam, *Judaism and Enlightenment* (Cambridge: Cambridge University Press, 2003).

Teter, Magda, *Sinners on Trial: Jews and Sacrilege after the Reformation* (Cambridge, MA: Harvard University Press, 2011).

Vital, David, *A People Apart: The Jews in Europe, 1789–1939* (Oxford: Oxford University Press, 1999).

DOCUMENTS

I

Johannes Reuchlin: Letter to Bonetto de Lattes (1513)

Text

These [Dominican] theologians all came together, frightened and excited, groaning and weeping, and cried aloud: 'Help, O King and Emperor. There is a certain people, scattered and dispersed through your realm, whose laws are different from those of every other people [echoing Esth. 3:8], and this is because of the talmudic works they possess. For in those books there are written a great many reproaches and blasphemies and curses and prayers against our faith and the leaders of our religion [...]

In addition there is another great evil that we must bear in mind: if these books did not exist, there would be but one religion, and everyone would believe in Jesus, our messiah. It is those books alone that push them off the right road. Therefore "it is not in the King's interest to tolerate them" (Esth. 3:8). Bearing in mind the interests of our religion and our churches, we advise and warn, if it seem good to the Emperor, that an order be issued to seize and turn over all the books of the Jews to the treasuries of the Emperor and King, through an officer appointed for this purpose. All of them should then be burnt, except for the biblical books, because they are the basic works of our religion.

All talmudic works, however, should be burnt in a blazing fire so that they may not have any ground to curse you, our King, O Emperor our lord, nor any of our compatriots, nor to reproach nor blaspheme our God and our churches [...'.]

The one who has compassed and done all this is a certain one of your people [Pfefferkorn] who deserted your religion [...]

And this apostate, *meshummad* as you say in your language, had a number of letters from princes and bishops and particularly from a certain nun, the sister of our lord, the Emperor [...]

[...]

[... A]s a result of such admonitions, requests, and supplications, the Emperor commanded that those [classical rabbinic] books be confiscated and brought to the storehouses of the king, and they were. After this the Emperor said that he wished to secure advice as to what to do with these works, and he did. After he had been advised he sent me an official letter and adjured me by the imperial and royal decree that I should examine, search, and investigate whether such things are found in these books or not [...]

[...] I examined them, and I wrote [October, 1510] and responded to the command of the King to the effect that I did not know nor had I heard of such things in the talmudic writings. The talmudic works are divided into laws, statutes, and legends, and whoever wishes to believe them may believe them. And if such things of which this *meshummad* speaks should be found, that particular book or books should be burnt; but there are a great many kabbalistic and other important writings whose destruction would be a great loss. Everything that this *meshummad* has said, he has said only in order to provoke and to cause trouble.

After our lord, the Emperor, read my opinion and my ideas on the subject he commanded that those books that had been seized should be returned to the hands of their owners. And indeed, sir, when that *meshummad* and the scholars of Cologne University saw that it was through my advice that their plan had come to naught, they complained bitterly, saying that I was a heretic – not believing in our religion and denying its central principles [...]

[...]

[... I]nasmuch as I fear that they will summon me to appear in court outside my own town and province, and this would entail a huge expense, I would entreat your gracious favor. I have heard that your Excellency is daily at the papal quarters and that the body of his Holiness is in your skilled care. Therefore I would beg of your Excellency that you influence his Holiness, our lord, the pope, and that they should have no power or permission to compel me to appear before any other judge except the judges of my province, as is provided for by our statutes and laws. And if after this they wish to appear before his Holiness, our lord, the pope, I am ready for anything: to answer them and to straighten out the matter properly.

Source

Marcus, Jacob Rader, and Saperstein, Marc, *The Jews in Christian Europe: A Source Book, 315–1791* (Pittsburgh: Hebrew Union College Press/University of Pittsburgh Press, 2015), 206–9, 665–6: 32.1. Reproduced by permission of the Hebrew Union College Press. © 2015 Hebrew Union College Press. (Square-bracketed phrases are part of the original.)

Commentary

Johannes Reuchlin (1455–1522), a German lawyer and Christian Hebraist, was involved in a bitter controversy with Dominicans owing to his opposition to their attempt to ban post-biblical Jewish writings, such as the Talmud. The Dominicans, leading figures in the battle against heresy, were especially suspicious of humanists who valued Latin, Greek and Hebrew. In 1509, at the prompting of the Franciscan order, Johann Pfefferkorn (1469–1522), a Jewish convert to Christianity, sought and received the approval of the German emperor Maximilian I (d. 1519) to confiscate all Hebrew books (except the Bible). One of Pfefferkorn's motivations was missionary: 'take the path of books away from them. Burn the books. Then it will be much easier to bring them to the path of truth', he wrote in an anti-Jewish tract, *Mirror of the Jews* (1507). Another was to defend the church from these Jewish texts, in which 'are written a great many reproaches and blasphemies and curses'. The following year, 1510, Reuchlin was commissioned to offer an opinion on the rabbinic writings and whether they should be destroyed. He decided in favour of the Jewish works, but in doing so aroused anger, especially from the Dominican friars in Cologne.

Our document consists of an excerpt from Reuchlin's letter to the Jewish physician to Pope Leo X, Bonetto de Lattes, in which he explained the context to the controversy and asked for help, as he feared he would be summoned to trial for heresy for his book *Augenspiegel* ('Eye-Glass' or 'Ophthalmoscope'), which condemned Pfefferkorn. In particular, Reuchlin was keen that the case be kept away from the Cologne friars, but he expressed willingness to appear in his own diocese or in a papal Court of Appeal. (He was actually tried in 1514 in his own diocese, where the bishop of Speyer acquitted him.)

The controversy demonstrates the success of Christian Hebraists in defending post-biblical Jewish writings from destruction, a trend that had begun a couple of centuries earlier (see, for example, the Barcelona disputation of 1263; Chapter 4, p. 207). Although Christian hostility continued and the Dominican Inquisitor-General Cardinal Caraffa burnt all copies of the Talmud in Italy in 1559, Hebrew began to gain recognition as one of the historic languages of the west, and by 1546 chairs of Hebrew had been established in the major European universities. Pope Leo X even permitted a Christian, Daniel Bomberg, to publish the first printed edition of the Talmud in 1520.

Since Reuchlin was trained as a lawyer, he based his argument as much on civil law as on humanist values, pointing out, for example, that Jewish writings were licensed by papal as well as imperial law. The controversy marked the development of Hebrew scholarship among Christians, which profoundly affected Jewish–Christian relations. Reuchlin, who himself had a Jewish teacher, was one of many who promoted the concept of *ad fontes* (return to the original sources) and, like his Italian contemporary Pico della Mirandola (1463–94), believed that Jewish books would benefit Christianity and Christian scholarship. For Christian Hebraists, fundamental Christian truths were to be found in post-biblical Jewish writings, including mystical texts such as the Zohar.

Bibliography

Adams, Jonathan, and Hess, Cordelia (eds.), *Revealing the Secrets of the Jews: Johannes Pfefferkorn and Christian Writings about Jewish Life and Literature in Early Modern Europe* (Berlin and Boston: De Gruyter, 2017).

Dan, Joseph (ed.), *The Christian Kabbalah: Jewish Mystical Books and Their Christian Interpreters* (Cambridge, MA: Harvard College Library, 1997).

Price, David H., *Johannes Reuchlin and the Campaign to Destroy Jewish Books* (Oxford: Oxford University Press, 2011).

Rummel, Erika, *The Case against Johann Reuchlin: Religious and Social Controversy in Sixteenth-Century Germany* (Toronto: University of Toronto Press, 2002).

2

Martin Luther: That Jesus Christ Was Born a Jew *and* On the Jews and Their Lies *(1523 and 1543)*

Text

(i) That Jesus Christ Was Born a Jew *(1523)*

I will cite from Scripture the reasons that move me to believe that Christ was a Jew born of a virgin, that I might perhaps also win some Jews to the Christian faith. Our fools, the popes, bishops, sophists, and monks – the crude asses' heads – have hitherto so treated the Jews that anyone who wished to be a good Christian would almost have had to become a Jew. If I had been a Jew and had seen such dolts and blockheads govern and teach the Christian faith, I would sooner have become a hog than a Christian.

They have dealt with the Jews as if they were dogs rather than human beings; they have done little else than deride them and seize their property. When they baptize them they show them nothing of Christian doctrine or life, but only subject them to popishness and monkery. When the Jews then see that Judaism has such strong support in Scripture, and that Christianity has become a mere babble without reliance on Scripture, how can they possibly compose themselves and become right good Christians? I have myself heard from pious baptized Jews that if they had not in our day heard the gospel they would have remained Jews under the cloak of Christianity for the rest of their days. For they acknowledge that they have never yet heard anything about Christ from those who baptized and taught them.

I hope that if one deals in a kindly way with the Jews and instructs them carefully from Holy Scripture, many of them will become genuine Christians and turn again to the faith of their fathers, the prophets and patriarchs. They will only be frightened further away from it if their Judaism is so utterly rejected that nothing is allowed to remain, and they are treated only with arrogance and scorn. If the apostles, who also were Jews, had dealt with us Gentiles as we Gentiles deal with the Jews, there would never have been a Christian among the Gentiles. Since they dealt with us Gentiles in such brotherly fashion, we in our turn ought to treat the Jews in a brotherly manner in order that we might convert some of them. For even we ourselves are not yet all very far along, not to speak of having arrived.

[…]

If the Jews should take offense because we confess our Jesus to be a man, and yet true God, we will deal forcefully with that from Scripture in due time. But this is too harsh for a beginning. Let them first be suckled with milk, and begin by recognizing this man Jesus as the true Messiah; after that they may drink wine, and learn also that he is true God. For they have been led astray so long and so far that one must deal gently with them, as people who have been all too strongly indoctrinated to believe that God cannot be man.

Therefore, I would request and advise that one deal gently with them and instruct them from Scripture; then some of them may come along. Instead of this we are trying only to drive them by force, slandering them, accusing them of having Christian blood if they don't stink, and I know not what other foolishness. So long as we thus treat them like dogs, how can we expect to work any good among them?

Source

Luther, Martin, *Luther's Works, Vol. 45: The Christian in Society II*, ed. and trans. W. I. Brandt (Philadelphia: Muhlenberg Press, 1962), 200–1, 229.

(ii) On the Jews and Their Lies (1543)

What shall we Christians do with this rejected and condemned people, the Jews? Since they live among us, we dare not tolerate their conduct, now that we are aware of their lying and reviling and blaspheming. If we do, we become sharers in their lies, cursing, and blasphemy. Thus we cannot extinguish the unquenchable fire of divine wrath, of which the prophets speak, nor can we convert the Jews. With prayer and the fear of God we must practice a sharp mercy to see whether we might save at least a few from the glowing flames. We dare not avenge ourselves. Vengeance a thousand times worse than we could wish them already has them by the throat. I shall give you my sincere advice:

First, to set fire to their synagogues or schools and to bury and cover with dirt whatever will not burn, so that no man will ever again see a stone or cinder of them. This is to be done in honor of our Lord and of Christendom, so that God might see that we are Christians, and do not condone or knowingly tolerate such public lying, cursing, and blaspheming of his Son and of his Christians [...]

Second, I advise that their houses also be razed and destroyed. For they pursue in them the same aims as in their synagogues. Instead they might be lodged under a roof or in a barn, like the gypsies. This will bring home to them the fact that they are not masters in our country, as they boast, but that they are living in exile and in captivity, as they incessantly wail and lament about us before God.

Third, I advise that all their prayer books and Talmudic writings, in which such idolatry, lies, cursing, and blasphemy are taught, be taken from them.

Fourth, I advise that their rabbis be forbidden to teach henceforth on pain of loss of life and limb [...]

We cannot help it that they do not share our belief. It is impossible to force anyone to believe. However, we must avoid confirming them in their wanton lying, slandering, cursing, and defaming. Nor dare we make ourselves partners in their devilish ranting and raving by shielding and protecting them, by giving them food, drink, and shelter, or by other neighborly acts, especially since they boast so proudly and despicably when we do help and serve them that God has ordained them as lords and us as servants [...]

But if the authorities are reluctant to use force and restrain the Jews' devilish wantonness, the latter should, as we said, be expelled from the country and be told to return to their land and their possessions in Jerusalem, where they may lie, curse, blaspheme, defame, murder, steal, rob, practice usury, mock, and indulge in all those infamous abominations which they practice among us, and leave us our government, our country, our life, and our property, much more leave our Lord the Messiah, our faith, and our church undefiled and uncontaminated with their devilish tyranny and malice.

Source

Luther, Martin, *Luther's Works, Vol. 47: The Christian in Society IV*, trans. M. H. Bertram (Philadelphia: Fortress Press, 1971), 268–9, 274–6.

Commentary

Martin Luther (1483–1546) was a theologian, biblical scholar and an initiator of the Reformation. He perpetuated with medieval crudity of language the church fathers' view of Jews as enemies of God. His writings about Jews should not be seen as separate from his denunciations of the pope, false Christians and the Turks (Muslims), yet he saw Jews as unique deniers of Christ and, though his hostility was not racial, they remained the negative element in the bedrock of his theology.

The first document, *That Jesus Christ Was Born a Jew*, is from his earlier writings (1523) and chastised the Roman Catholic Church for its treatment of Jews while at the same time expressing hope for Jewish conversion under a new, gentler approach. Both Luther and Calvin called for an improvement in the Christian treatment of Jews, which they expected would result in their conversion. Luther acknowledged that Jesus was a Jew, born of the seed of Abraham but begotten by means of a miracle. He makes an appeal to deal more kindly with Jews, concluding (in a section not included in the excerpt above): 'here I will let the matter rest for the present, until I see what I have accomplished'. This conclusion clarifies the purpose of the treatise: it was a missionary tract, aimed at converting Jews. Luther was just starting to experience the incredible success of the early years of the Reformation and perhaps believed himself to be an instrument of God, destined to reveal the purified gospel. He believed that time was needed for the renewed gospel to do its work and called for patience and charity.

The second document, *On the Jews and Their Lies*, was written in 1543 by an older, bitterer Luther, but while his later words are much more brutal, they cannot be divorced from the earlier ones, as reflecting a consistent belief that truth allowed no room for tolerance. In addition, the anticipated conversion of Jews had failed to materialise and the Judaising tendencies of some reforming sects had become more apparent. Luther reacted savagely against all who differed with his theology, especially reformers such as the Sabbatarians, who, like Jews, observed the sabbath on Saturday; each opponent – Christian as well as Jew – was regarded as a manifestation of the devil. The document is the most infamous of a trilogy of anti-Jewish works in which Luther called for forcible conversion and advised rulers to confiscate rabbinic texts, forbade the rabbis to teach and called for the burning of synagogues and Jews' homes. The older Luther was deeply disappointed and indignant at Jews' refusal to accept the newly cleansed gospel completely. For him, the best strategy seemed to be that which Ferdinand and Isabella of Spain and Manuel I of Portugal had adopted less than fifty years previously – expel the Jews of the German-speaking lands forever (see Chapter 4, pages 227 and 230).

Excerpts from Luther's anti-Jewish writings provided sanction for later antisemitic movements, including Nazism, but were formally repudiated by Lutheran Church bodies from 1983 when the Missouri Synod issued a major resolution calling his antisemitic claims 'deplorable' (but also 'uncharacteristic'). A 1994 disavowal of Luther's 'anti-Judaic diatribes', the 'Declaration of the Evangelical Lutheran Church in America to the Jewish Community', was reaffirmed in revised form in 2021.

Bibliography

Kaufmann, Thomas, *Luther's Jews: A Journey into Anti-Semitism* (Oxford: Oxford University Press, 2017).

Laver, Mary Sweetland, *Calvin, Jews and Intra-Christian Polemic* (Ann Arbor: University Microfilms International, 1987).

Probst, Christopher J., *Demonizing the Jews: Luther and the Protestant Church in Nazi Germany* (Bloomington: Indiana University Press, c. 2012).

Sherman, Franklin, *Luther and the Jews: A Fateful Legacy* (Allentown: IJCU/Baltimore: ICJS, 1995).

3

The Catechism of the Council of Trent (1566)

Text

Part I: The Creed

Article IV: 'Suffered under Pontius Pilate, was crucified, dead, and buried'

Question I. Necessity of Knowing the Fourth Article, and Its Import

How great is the necessity of knowing this article, and how diligently the parish-priest should take care, that the faithful very frequently revolve in mind the remembrance of our Lord's passion, the Apostle teaches when he declares that he knows nothing 'but Jesus Christ, and him crucified.' In treating this subject, therefore, the greatest zeal and industry are to be employed, in order that it may be elucidated as much as possible, and that the faithful, excited by the commemoration of so great a benefit, may turn themselves wholly to the contemplation of the love and goodness of God towards us […]

[...]

Question XI. Reasons Why Christ Vouchsafed to Suffer Death, and What Is to Be Thought of Those, Who, Professing Christianity, Wallow in Sin

Besides, what adds to the dignity of this matter, Christ not only suffered for sinners, but sinners were also the authors and ministers of all the torments which he endured. Of this the Apostle reminds us, writing thus to the Hebrews: 'Think, diligently, upon him who endured such opposition from sinners against himself; that you be not wearied, fainting in your minds.' In this guilt we must deem all those to be involved, who fall frequently into sin; for, as our sins impelled Christ the Lord to undergo the death of the cross, certainly those who wallow in sins and iniquities, as far as in them lies, 'crucify again to themselves the Son of God, and make a mockery of him.' In us such guilt may indeed seem deeper than it was in the Jews, in as much as, according to the same Apostle, 'if they had known it, they never would have crucified the Lord of Glory'; whereas we both profess to have known him, and yet, denying him by our 'works,' seem in some sort to lay violent hands on him.

[...]

Question XIII. Christ Truly Felt, in Body and Mind, the Bitterness of His Torments

That, however, Christ the Lord underwent the most intense sufferings both of mind and body is certain. In the first place, then, there was no part of his body that did not experience the most excruciating tortures; for his hands and feet were fastened with nails to the cross; his head was pierced with thorns, and smitten with a reed; his face was befouled with spittle, and buffeted with blows; his whole body was covered with stripes. Men too of all sorts and conditions 'met together against the Lord and against his Christ.' For Jews and Gentiles were the advisers, the authors, the ministers, of his passion. Judas betrayed him: Peter denied him: the rest abandoned him [...].

Part IV: The Lord's Prayer

[...]

Question III. It Is Shown That We Must Do the Same for Our Enemies and the Foes of the Church

The Lord has commanded us, besides, to 'pray for them that persecute and calumniate' us. It is also well known from the testimony of St. Augustine, that it has been a practice received from the Apostles, to offer prayers and sighs for those, who are outside the pale of the Church; that faith may be given to infidels; that idolaters may be liberated from the errors of impiety; that Jews, their mental darkness being dissipated, may receive the light of truth; that heretics, returning to soundness, may be instructed in the precepts of the Catholic doctrine; that schismatics, linked by the bond of true charity, may be reunited to the communion of our most holy mother the Church, from whom they have separated.

Source

Donovan, Jeremy (trans.), *The Catechism of the Council of Trent* (Manchester: Isaac Slater, 1855), 47, 53–5, 57, 479–80.

Commentary

The Council of Trent was an ecumenical (or worldwide) council of the Catholic Church, a convening of bishops that met between 1545 and 1563 in Trento, northern Italy. It is regarded as a key moment in the Counter-Reformation as its purpose was to respond to Protestant doctrinal challenges that had come to the fore during the Reformation. The Council addressed a wide array of ecclesiastical topics and authorised the creation of an official manual, in Latin and vulgar languages, of fundamental church doctrine that would be used in the instruction of the faithful, known as the *Catechism of the Council of Trent*. The importance of the Council was that it set the policy of the Roman Catholic Church for 400 years, and papal absolutism emerged undisputed.

A catechism is designed for the instruction of parish priests, and the Trent *Catechism* extended the official doctrine of Roman Catholicism into the local units of the church, seeking to create a unity of the faith and the faithful. It includes traditional *adversus Judaeos* teachings, such as supersessionism and Jewish blindness and the expectation that 'Jews, their mental darkness being dissipated, may receive the light of truth'.

However, a new and positive development, which has influenced Jewish–Christian relations through to modern times, can also be noted. The church traditionally blamed Jews for the death of Christ, even labelling them 'Christ-killers' (see Melito of Sardis; Chapter 2, page 77) but the Catechism taught that 'In us [Christians] such guilt may indeed seem deeper than it was in the Jews.' This can be taken to suggest that, from the mid-sixteenth century, the Catholic Church taught that the collectivity of sinful humanity was responsible for the death of Jesus, not only Jews.

This change has had far-reaching consequences. French-Jewish historian Jules Isaac (see Chapter 8, p. 402) drew attention to the Council of Trent in his writings and in his audience with Pope John XXIII in 1960. The seventh of the *Ten Points of Seelisberg* (see Appendix to Part III, p. 510) drew out its implications, stating that 'the Christian message has always been that it was the sins of mankind which were exemplified by those Jews and the sins in which all men share that brought Christ to the Cross'. This teaching was adopted by the churches, as exemplified by the Pontifical Commission on Religious Relations with the Jews which in 1985 published *Notes on the Correct Way to Present the Jews and Judaism in Preaching and Catechesis in the Roman Catholic Church*.

The influence of the Trent *Catechism* can be seen in today's Roman Catholic catechism which states that:

> The Church has never forgotten that 'sinners were the authors and the ministers of all the sufferings that the divine Redeemer endured'. Taking into account the fact that our sins affect Christ himself, the Church does not

hesitate to impute to Christians the gravest responsibility for the torments inflicted upon Jesus, a responsibility with which they have all too often burdened the Jews alone […] And it can be seen that our crime in this case is greater in us than in the Jews. (para. 598)

Bibliography

Fisher, Eugene J., 'Reflections on the Catechism of the Catholic Church', *SIDIC* 27, no. 2 (1994), 2–8.

François, Wim, and Soen, Violet (eds.), *The Council of Trent: Reform and Controversy in Europe and Beyond (1545–1700)*, 3 vols (Göttingen: Vandenhoeck & Ruprecht, 2018).

Jedin, Hubert, *A History of the Council of Trent*, trans. Ernest Graf, 2 vols (St Louis, MO: Herder, 1957).

O'Malley, John W., *Trent: What Happened at the Council* (Cambridge, MA: Harvard University Press, 2013).

4

William Shakespeare: The Merchant of Venice (c. 1596–8)

Text

(I.iii.32–52)

BASSANIO: If it please you to dine with us.

SHYLOCK: Yes, to smell pork, to eat of the habitation which your prophet the Nazarite conjur'd the devil into. I will buy with you, sell with you, talk with you, walk with you, and so following; but I will not eat with you, drink with you, nor pray with you. What news on the Rialto? Who is he comes here?

Enter ANTONIO.

BASSANIO: This is Signior Antonio.

SHYLOCK: [*Aside*.] How like a fawning publican he looks!
I hate him for he is a Christian;
But more, for that in low simplicity
He lends out money gratis, and brings down
The rate of usance here with us in Venice.
If I can catch him once upon the hip,
I will feed fat the ancient grudge I bear him.
He hates our sacred nation, and he rails
Even there where merchants most do congregate
On me, my bargains, and my well-won thrift,
Which he calls interest. Cursed be my tribe
If I forgive him!

(III.i.54–73)

SHYLOCK: He hath disgrac'd me, and hind'red me half a million, laugh'd at my losses, mock'd at my gains, scorn'd my nation, thwarted my bargains, cool'd my friends, heated mine enemies; and what's his reason? I am a Jew. Hath not a Jew eyes? Hath not a Jew hands, organs, dimensions, senses, affections, passions; fed with the same food, hurt with the same weapons, subject to the same diseases, heal'd by the same means, warm'd and cool'd by the same winter and summer, as a Christian is? If you prick us, do we not bleed? If you tickle us, do we not laugh? If you poison us, do we not die? And if you wrong us, shall we not revenge? If we are like you in the rest, we will resemble you in that. If a Jew wrong a Christian, what is his humility? Revenge. If a Christian wrong a Jew, what should his sufferance be by Christian example? Why, revenge. The villainy you teach me, I will execute, and it shall go hard but I will better the instruction.

(IV.i.184–207)

PORTIA: The quality of mercy is not strain'd,
It droppeth as the gentle rain from heaven
Upon the place beneath. It is twice blest:
It blesseth him that gives and him that takes.
'Tis mightiest in the mightiest, it becomes
The throned monarch better than his crown,
His sceptre shows the force of temporal power,
The attribute to awe and majesty,
Wherein doth sit the dread and fear of kings;
But mercy is above this sceptred sway,
It is enthroned in the hearts of kings,
It is an attribute to God himself;
And earthly power doth then show likest God's
When mercy seasons justice. Therefore, Jew,
Though justice be thy plea, consider this,
That in the course of justice, none of us
Should see salvation. We do pray for mercy,
And that same prayer doth teach us all to render
The deeds of mercy. I have spoke thus much
To mitigate the justice of thy plea,
Which if thou follow, this strict court of Venice
Must needs give sentence 'gainst the merchant there.

SHYLOCK: My deeds upon my head! I crave the law,
The penalty and forfeit of my bond.

Source

Shakespeare, William, *The Riverside Shakespeare: The Complete Works*, 2nd ed. (Boston: Houghton Mifflin, 1997), 302, 309–11.

Commentary

William Shakespeare's *The Merchant of Venice* (*c.* 1596–8), one of his most studied and performed plays, contains perhaps the most famous portrayal of a Jewish character on the English-speaking stage and is a familiar lens through which Jewish–Christian relations have been scrutinised. That the work continues to resonate more than four centuries after it was written is testimony to its complex characterisation. Although it is tempting to reduce it to a set of binaries with, for example, Christians, mercy and generosity on one side and Jews, the law and miserliness on the other, Shakespeare offers a nuanced and complex representation of Jewish and Christian identities, although the former serve the interests of the latter (such as Jessica, who happily converts to Christianity and represents a proto-Christian, and Shylock as the Jewish enemy).

Informed by Christopher Marlowe's *The Jew of Malta* (first performed around 1590), *The Merchant of Venice* similarly draws on infamous stereotypes of unscrupulous Jews, although Shylock, the principal Jewish character, is both villain and victim. A greedy, hard-hearted and malevolent moneylender and a Christian-hater who demands a pound of flesh from merchant Antonio in payment of a debt (IV.i.89–100), he is also humanised as a heartbroken widower who becomes a wronged father, a politically powerless and socially marginalised man held in contempt by the elite society of Venice.

Shakespeare's depiction presents both divergence and convergence between Jews and Christians. The former is illustrated by Shylock's hatred of Antonio because 'he is a Christian [… and] hates our sacred nation'; the latter by Shylock's assertion that they have physical and emotional similarities: 'Hath not a Jew hands, organs, dimensions, senses, affections, passions; fed with the same food […] as a Christian is?' Jews and Christians even share the motive of vengeance. If *Merchant* portrays Jews as greedy and prejudiced in the character of Shylock, so it does Christians in Antonio, who treats Shylock and Judaism with profound disrespect, while Portia is a far cry from the embodiment of mercy and compassion she preaches as a judge, and when Shylock falls foul of the Venetian authorities, loses half his property and is subject to forced conversion to Christianity, she and others rejoice at his suffering.

Shakespeare's intentions and sources are not always easy to determine. After the expulsion of Jews from England in 1290 (see Chapter 4, p. 218), some crypto-Jews – Jews from the Iberian Peninsula who had outwardly converted to Christianity – seem to have come to England during late medieval and Tudor times, and Shylock was perhaps modelled on one of them, an oft-cited candidate being Elizabeth I's physician Roderigo Lopez, who was executed in 1594.

In its stagings and adaptations, as well as in its literary legacy, *The Merchant of Venice* has both reflected and shaped subsequent Jewish–Christian relations through to the modern day, whether in the use of 'Shylock' as a term of abuse or in differing levels of sympathy in the representation of Jewish figures in later fiction (including Dickens' Fagin and George Eliot's Daniel Deronda; see Chapter 6, p. 311) and of Shylock in productions of the play itself.

Bibliography

Kaplan, Lindsay, 'The Merchant of Venice, Jews, and Christians', in Hamlin, Hannibal (ed.), *The Cambridge Companion to Shakespeare and Religion* (Cambridge: Cambridge University Press, 2019), 168–83.

Nahshon, Edna, and Shapiro, Michael, *Wrestling with Shylock: Jewish Responses to The Merchant of Venice* (Cambridge: Cambridge University Press, 2017).

Shapiro, James, *Shakespeare and the Jews* (New York: Columbia University Press, 1996).

Yaffe, Martin D., *Shylock and the Jewish Question* (Baltimore: Johns Hopkins University Press, 1997).

5

Peter Stuyvesant's Attempt to Expel Jews from New Amsterdam (1654–5)

Text

(i) Peter Stuyvesant's Attempt to Expel Jews from New Amsterdam

Extract from a certain letter from Director Peter Stuyvesant to the Amsterdam Chamber, dated Manhattan, September 22, 1654

The Jews who have arrived would nearly all like to remain here, but learning that they (with their customary usury and deceitful trading with the Christians) were very repugnant to the inferior magistrates, as also to the people having the most affection for you; the Deaconry also fearing that owing to their present indigence they might become a charge in the coming winter, we have, for the benefit of this weak and newly developing place and the land in general, deemed it useful to require them in a friendly way to depart; praying also most seriously in this connection, for ourselves as also for the general community of your worships, that the deceitful race – such hateful enemies and blasphemers of the name of Christ – be not allowed further to infect and trouble this new colony, to the detraction of your worships and the dissatisfaction of your worships' most affectionate subjects.

(ii) Amsterdam Jewry's Successful Intercession for the Manhattan Immigrants

1655, January Petition of the Jewish Nation

[…] The merchants of the Portuguese nation residing in this City respectfully remonstrate to your Honors that it has come to their knowledge that your Honors raise obstacles to the giving of permits or passports to the Portuguese Jews to travel and to go to reside in New Netherland, which if persisted in will result to the great disadvantage of the Jewish nation. It also can be of no advantage to the general Company but rather damaging.

There are many of the nation who have lost their possessions at Pernambuco and have arrived from there in great poverty, and part of them have been dispersed here and there […] And as they cannot go to Spain or Portugal because of the Inquisition, a great part of the aforesaid people must in time be obliged to depart for other territories of their High Mightinesses the States-General and their Companies, in order there, through their labor and efforts, to be able to exist under the protection of the administrators of your Honorable Directors, observing and obeying your Honors' orders and commands.

It is well known to your Honors that the Jewish nation in Brazil have at all times been faithful and have striven to guard and maintain that place, risking for that purpose their possessions and their blood [...]

Your Honors should also consider that the Honorable Lords, the Burgomasters of the City and the Honorable High Illustrious Mighty Lords, the States-General, have in political matters always protected and considered the Jewish nation as upon the same footing as all the inhabitants and burghers. Also it is conditioned in the treaty of perpetual peace with the King of Spain that the Jewish nation shall also enjoy the same liberty as all other inhabitants of these lands.

Your Honors should also please consider that many of the Jewish nation are principal shareholders in the Company [...]

The Company has by a general resolution consented that those who wish to populate the Colony shall enjoy certain districts of land gratis. Why should now certain subjects of this State not be allowed to travel thither and live there? The French consent that the Portuguese Jews may traffic and live in Martinique, Christopher and others of their territories, whither also some have gone from here, as your Honors know. The English also consent at the present time that the Portuguese and Jewish nation may go from London and settle at Barbados, whither also some have gone.

As foreign nations consent that the Jewish nation may go to live and trade in their territories, how can your Honors forbid the same and refuse transportation to this Portuguese nation who reside here and have been settled here well on to about sixty years, many also being born here and confirmed burghers, and this to a land that needs people for its increase?

Therefore the petitioners request, for the reasons given above [...], that your Honors be pleased not to exclude but to grant the Jewish nation passage to and residence in that country; otherwise this would result in a great prejudice to their reputation. Also that by an Apostille and Act the Jewish nation be permitted, together with other inhabitants, to travel, live and traffic there, and with them enjoy liberty on condition of contributing like others, &c. [...]

(iii) The Answer of the West India Company to Stuyvesant, 26 April 1655

We would have liked to effectuate and fulfill your wishes and request that the new territories should no more be allowed to be infected by people of the Jewish nation, for we foresee therefrom the same difficulties which you fear, but after having further weighed and considered the matter, we observe that this would be somewhat unreasonable and unfair, especially because of the considerable loss sustained by this nation, with others, in the taking of Brazil, as also because of the large amount of capital which they still have invested in the shares of this company. Therefore after many deliberations we have finally decided and resolved to apostille upon a certain petition presented by said Portuguese Jews that these people may travel and trade to and in New Netherland and live and remain there, provided the poor among them shall not become a burden to the company or to the community, but be supported by their own nation. You will now govern yourself accordingly.

Source

Oppenheim, Samuel, 'The Early History of the Jews in New York, 1654–1664: Some New Matter on the Subject', *Publications of the American Jewish Historical Society* 18 (1909): 4–5, 8–11.

Commentary

The historical context of this exchange of letters highlights the transatlantic and globalising growth of Jewish–Christian relations in the seventeenth century as Jews became involved in European colonial aspirations and conflicts in the New World. Subject to the Spanish Inquisition and expelled from the Iberian Peninsula (see Chapter 4, p. 232), many Jews fled to the Netherlands (then embroiled in the Eighty Years' War, largely with Spain), where they hoped to find greater religious toleration. Throwing in their lot with the Dutch, Jews in far-flung overseas Dutch colonies were caught in the vortex of clashing European powers and sought to avoid the Inquisition in the New World as it followed the victorious Portuguese military there.

The Dutch took control of the colony of Recife from the Portuguese in 1624, and many Jews, who had been *conversos*, returned to open Jewish practice. However, thirty years later, the colony reverted to the Portuguese with the fall of the Dutch stronghold of Pernambuco, and its Jews were forced to leave. Sixteen ships sailed for Holland, but one was captured by a French ship, which transported the twenty-three Jews on board to New Amsterdam (lower Manhattan island today), the seat of the Dutch colonial government of New Netherland. The French captain, Jacques de la Mothe, claimed he was owed payment for passage and, since the Jewish refugees were unable to pay, he appealed to the Dutch governor, Peter Stuyvesant (1592–1672). Stuyvesant agreed with de la Mothe, made the Jewish group destitute by selling their belongings to raise funds, wrote to the Dutch West India Company in Amsterdam asking for permission to expel them all from the settlement and ordered two to be held in prison as collateral. In his letter (document 5 (i)) he employed a number of economic and religious stereotypes and described the refugees as 'repugnant' to their Christian hosts.

At the same time, the Jewish group wrote to friends and family in the Netherlands, some of whom were investors in the Dutch West India Company, who interceded on their behalf, arguing that the laws in Holland allowing Jewish settlement should also apply in the Dutch colonies (document 5 (ii)). They reminded the company of Jewish loyalty and investment, both in the Netherlands and in defending the overseas colony, and called on it to be humane given that these loyal subjects were now impoverished owing to their defence of Dutch interests. The company's board of directors responded to Stuyvesant (document 5 (iii)) expressing sympathy with his desire to ensure that 'the deceitful race

[…] be not allowed further to infect and trouble this new colony', but emphasised Jews' economic usefulness (not least as shareholders of the company) and determined that they should remain so long as they did not 'become a burden' on the settlement.

This series of letters demonstrates a wider pattern in Jewish–Christian relations of the time, namely that Jews found themselves in a weak position if their usefulness was jeopardised. Nevertheless, Stuyvesant's failure enabled twenty-three Jewish refugees to make new lives for themselves and to establish the first synagogue in North America, a Sephardi congregation called Shearith Israel (Remnant of Israel) which still exists today.

Bibliography

Finkleman, Paul, 'The Roots of Religious Freedom in Early America: Religious Toleration and Religious Diversity in New Netherland and Colonial New York', *Nanzan Review of American Studies* 34 (2012), 1–26.

Marcus, Jacob Rader, *The Colonial American Jew, 1492–1776*, vol. 1 (Detroit: Wayne State University Press, 1970), 215–48.

Moore, Deborah Dash, Gurock, Jeffrey S., Polland, Annie, Rock, Howard B., and Soyer, Daniel, *Jewish New York: The Remarkable Story of a City and a People* (New York: New York University Press, 2017).

Wiznitzer, Arnold, 'The Exodus from Brazil and Arrival in New Amsterdam of the Jewish Pilgrim Fathers, 1654', *Publications of the American Jewish Historical Society* 44, no. 2 (1954), 80–97.

6

Menasseh ben Israel: The Humble Addresses *(1655)*

Text

To His Highnesse the Lord Protector of the Common-wealth of England, Scotland, and Ireland.

The Humble Addresses of Menasseh Ben Israel, *a Divine, and Doctor of Physick, in behalfe of the Jewish Nation.*

[…] I, one of the least among the *Hebrews*, since by experience I have found, that through Gods great bounty toward us, many considerable and eminent persons both for Piety and Power, are moved with sincere and inward pitty and compassion towards us, and do comfort us concerning the approaching deliverance of *Israel*, could not but for my self, and in the behalf of my Countrey men, make this my humble addresse to your Highness, and beseech you for Gods sake, that ye would, according to that Piety and Power wherein you are eminent beyond others, vouchsafe to grant, that the Great and Glorious Name of the Lord our God may be extolled, and solemnly worshiped and praised by us through all the bounds of this Common-wealth; and to grant us place in your Countrey, that we may have our Synagogues, and free exercise of our Religion […] For our people did in their owne mindes presage, that the Kingly Government being now changed into that of a Common-wealth, the antient hatred towards them, would also be changed into good-will: that those rigorous Laws (if any there be yet extant, made under Kings) against so innocent a people, would happily be repealed. So that we hope now for better from your gentleness, & goodness, since, from the beginning of your Government of this Common-wealth, your Highnesse hath professed much respect, and favour towards us. Wherefore I humbly entreat your Highnesse, that you would with a gracious eye have regard unto us, and our Petition, and grant unto us, as you have done unto others, free exercise of our Religion, that we may have our Synagogues, and keep our own publick worship, as our brethren doe in *Italy*, *Germany*, *Poland*, and many other places, and we shall pray for the happinesse and Peace of this your much renowned and puissant Common-wealth.

[…]

[…] And to the end all Men may know the true Motives and Intent of this my coming [to England], I shall briefly comprehend and deliver them in these particulars.

First and formost, my Intention is to try, if by Gods good hand over me, I may obtaine here for my Nation the Liberty of a free and publick Synagogue, wherein we may daily call upon the Lord our God, that once he may be pleased to remember his Mercies and Promises done to our Fore fathers, forgiving our trespasses, and restoring us once againe into our fathers Inheritance; and besides to sue also for a blessing upon this Nation, and People of *England*, for receiving us into their bosomes, and comforting *Sion* in her distresse.

My *second* Motive is, because the opinion of many Christians and mine doe concurre herein, that we both believe that the restoring time of our Nation into their Native Countrey, is very neer at hand; I believing more particularly, that this restauration cannot be, before these words of *Daniel, Chap*. 12. *Ver*. 7. be first accomplished, when he saith, *And when the dispersion of the Holy people shall be compleated in all places, then shall all these things be compleated*: signifying therewith, that before all be fulfilled, the People of God must be first dispersed into all places & Countreyes of the World. Now we know, how our Nation at the present is spread all about, and hath its seat and dwelling in the most flourishing parts of all the Kingdomes, and Countreys of the World, as well in *America*, as in the other three parts thereof; except onely in this considerable and mighty Island. And therefore this remains onely in my judgement, before the *MESSIA* come and restore our Nation, that first we must have our seat here likewise.

My *third* Motive is grounded on the profit that I conceive this Common wealth is to reap, if it shall vouchsafe to receive us; for thence, I hope, there will follow a great blessing from God upon them, and a very abundant trading into, and from all parts of the World, not onely without prejudice to the English Nation, but for their profit, both in Importation, and Exportation of goods […]

The *fourth* Motive of my coming hither, is, my sincere affection to this Common wealth, by reason of so many Worthy Learned, and Pious men in this Nation, whose loving kindnesse and Piety I have experience of […] I perswade my selfe they will be mindfull of that Command of the Lord our God, who so highly recommends unto all men the *love of strangers* […] For this I desire all may be confident of, that I am not come to make any disturbance, or to move any disputes about matters of Religion; but only to live with my

Nation in the feare of the Lord, under the shadow of your protection, whiles we expect with you the *hope of Israel* to be revealed.

Source

Wolf, Lucien (ed.), *Menasseh ben Israel's Mission to Oliver Cromwell: Being a Reprint of the Pamphlets Published by Menasseh ben Israel to Promote the Re-Admission of the Jews to England, 1649–1656* (London: Macmillan, 1901), 75–81.

Commentary

Menasseh ben Israel, or Manoel Dias Soeiro (1604–57), was a Portuguese rabbi and printer who lived in Amsterdam. Spurred on by biblical prophecies of the dispersal and gathering of Israel, he dedicated his efforts to the return of Jews to England, from which they had been expelled in 1290 (see Chapter 4, p. 218)

Menasseh's *Humble Addresses* to Oliver Cromwell in his role as Lord Protector mount a set of arguments for the readmission of Jews. They should be seen in light of the millenarian thinking of the day and of the exegetical efforts made by Christians to explain the signs of the Second Coming of Jesus Christ, which millenarians believed would occur imminently; the British writer Mary Cary (*c.* 1621–after 1653), for example, proposed 1655–6, a date accepted by leading English and Dutch millenarians.

Menasseh tapped into ideas about the lost biblical Israel and grasped how they played into Christian eschatological thinking ('we both believe that the restoring time of our Nation into their Native Countrey, is very neer at hand'). The document is significant in highlighting how Jews understood and could draw on their knowledge of Christian thinking to bring about social and political change, in this case readmission to England. Appeals by a rabbi to Christian millenarian beliefs played into Christian supersessionist prejudices about both perceived Jewish wisdom (as the chosen people of the Old Testament) and the displacement of Jews by the finality of the Second Coming.

Although it is impossible to tell how deeply Menasseh believed in his own interpretations, he is acutely aware of his Christian audience. He deploys that awareness to leverage the disparity of power between himself and them, furnishing Christians with a route towards reconciling otherwise disparate aims and providing Cromwell with an idiom that would allow him to communicate with his wider audience. Cromwell might envy the economic success of Amsterdam and attribute some of this to Jews and their global trade network (indeed, Menasseh expresses the hope that 'very abundant trading into, and from all parts of the World, not onely without prejudice to the English Nation, but for their profit' would follow when Jews were granted permission to live in England), but he could only secure Jewish inventiveness and industry for England by pointing to supposedly higher reasons for their readmission.

Menasseh decries previous injustices done to Jews, including expulsions and such stereotypical myths as the blood libel (see Chapter 4, pages 229 and 196). He situates himself with other Puritans who saw a theological possibility for reconciliation between Christians and Jews and bases his plea for the readmittance of Jews to England on both material and spiritual grounds.

His arguments helped bring about a major conference of leading stakeholders in London in December 1655. Jews were not readmitted *en masse*, but small numbers were permitted to return to England to rent property for use as a synagogue and to purchase land for a cemetery. Although Menasseh ben Israel died believing he had failed, his advocacy led to a *de facto* toleration of Jews living openly on British soil, a concept – toleration – that would be developed further in the following centuries.

Bibliography

Kaplan, Yosef, Méchoulan, Henry, and Popkin, Richard H. (eds.), *Menasseh ben Israel and His World* (Leiden: Brill, 1989).

Katz, David S., *Philo-Semitism and the Readmission of the Jews to England, 1603–1655* (Oxford: Oxford University Press, 1992).

Morrill, John (ed.), *Oliver Cromwell and the English Revolution* (London: Longman, 1990).

Nadler, Steven, 'The English Mission', in *Menasseh Ben Israel: Rabbi of Amsterdam* (New Haven: Yale University Press, 2018), 159–202.

7

Baruch Spinoza: Letter to Albert Burgh (1675)

Text

That, which I could scarcely believe when told me by others, I learn at last from your own letter; not only have you been made a member of the Romish Church, but you are become a very keen champion of the same, and have already learned wantonly to insult and rail against your opponents.

At first I resolved to leave your letter unanswered, thinking that time and experience will assuredly be of more avail than reasoning, to restore you to yourself and your friends; not to mention other arguments, which won your approval formerly, when we were discussing the case of Steno, in whose steps you are now following. But some of my friends, who like myself had formed great hopes from your superior talents, strenuously urge me not to fail in the offices of a friend, but to consider what you lately were, rather than what you are, with other arguments of the like nature. I have thus been induced to write you this short reply, which I earnestly beg you will think worthy of calm perusal.

I will not imitate those adversaries of Romanism, who would set forth the vices of priests and popes with a view to kindling your aversion […] I will even admit, that more men of learning and of blameless life are found in the Romish Church than in any other Christian body; for, as it contains more members, so will every type of character be more largely represented in it. You cannot possibly deny, unless you have lost your memory as well as your reason, that in every Church there are thoroughly honourable men, who worship God with justice and charity. We have known many such among the Lutherans, the Reformed Church, the Mennonites, and the Enthusiasts […] In fact, you must admit, that personal holiness is not peculiar to the Romish Church, but common to all Churches.

[…]

But I return to your letter, which you begin, by lamenting that I allow myself to be ensnared by the prince of evil spirits. Pray take heart, and recollect yourself. When you had the use of your faculties, you were wont, if I mistake not, to worship an Infinite God, by Whose efficacy all things absolutely come to pass and are preserved; now you dream of a prince, God's enemy, who against God's will ensnares and deceives very many men (rarely good ones, to be sure), whom God thereupon hands over to this master of wickedness to be tortured eternally. The Divine justice therefore allows the devil to deceive men and remain unpunished; but it by no means allows to remain unpunished the men, who have been by that self-same devil miserably deceived and ensnared.

These absurdities might so far be tolerated, if you worshipped a God infinite and eternal; not one of whom Chastillon, in the town which the Dutch call Tienen, gave with impunity to horses to be eaten [while performing the Eucharist]. And, poor wretch, you bewail me? My philosophy, which you never beheld, you style a chimera? O youth deprived of understanding, who has bewitched you into believing, that the Supreme and Eternal is eaten by you, and held in your intestines?

Yet you seem to wish to employ reason, and ask me, '*How I know that my philosophy is the best among all that have ever been taught in the world, or are being taught, or ever will be taught?*' a question which I might with much greater right ask you; for I do not presume that I have found the best philosophy, I know that I understand the true philosophy […]

[…]

[… Y]ou will say, that you acquiesce in the inward testimony of the Spirit of God, while the rest of mankind are ensnared and deceived by the prince of evil spirits. But all those outside the pale of the Romish Church can with equal right proclaim of their own creed what you proclaim of yours.

As to what you add of the common consent of myriads of men and the uninterrupted ecclesiastical succession, this is the very catch-word of the Pharisees. They with no less confidence than the devotees of Rome bring forward their myriad witnesses, who as pertinaciously as the Roman witnesses repeat what they have heard, as though it were their personal experience. Further, they carry back their line to Adam. They boast with equal arrogance, that their Church has continued to this day unmoved and unimpaired in spite of the hatred of Christians and heathen. They more than any other sect are supported by antiquity. They exclaim with one voice, that they have received their traditions from God Himself, and that they alone preserve the Word of God both written and unwritten. That all heresies have issued from them, and that they have remained constant through thousands of years under no constraint of temporal dominion, but by the sole efficacy of their superstition, no one can deny. The miracles they tell of would tire a thousand tongues. But their chief boast is, that they count a far greater number of martyrs than any other nation, a number which is daily increased by those who suffer with singular constancy for the faith they profess; nor is their boasting false. I myself knew among others of a certain Judah called the faithful, who in the midst of the flames, when he was already thought to be dead, lifted his voice to sing the hymn beginning, 'To Thee, O God, I offer up my soul,' and so singing perished.

The organization of the Roman Church, which you so greatly praise, I confess to be politic, and to many lucrative. I should believe that there was no other more convenient for deceiving the people and keeping men's minds in check, if it were not for the organization of the Mahometan Church, which far surpasses it. For from the time when this superstition arose, there has been no schism in its Church.

[…]

[…] If you will […] examine the history of the Church (of which I see you are completely ignorant), in order to see how false, in many respects, is Papal tradition, and by what course of events and with what cunning the Pope of Rome six hundred years after Christ obtained supremacy over the Church, I do not doubt that you will eventually return to your senses. That this result may come to pass I, for your sake, heartily wish. Farewell, &c.

Source

Spinoza, Benedict de, *The Chief Works of Benedict de Spinoza, Vol. 2: De Intellectus Emendatione – Ethica (Select Letters)*, trans. R. H. M. Elwes, 3rd ed. (London: George Bell & Sons, 1889), 414–15, 416, 417–18, 419.

Commentary

Baruch Spinoza (1632–77) was a philosopher who at twenty-three was excommunicated from the Amsterdam Portuguese-Jewish community, established by Jews who had fled the Inquisition, for views on such matters as free will, the personal nature of God and the divine origins of the Hebrew Bible, all of which he rejected. After his expulsion, Spinoza did not convert to Christianity but opted for secularism at a time when the concept had not yet been formalised.

Our document consists of an excerpt from a letter responding to Albert Burgh, who had been a friend and admirer and in 1675 had converted to Catholicism. Burgh asked Spinoza why he had not yet himself converted, outlining a view of Christian history as a series of providential events, miracles as self-positing proofs and doctrinal statements as fixed moral law. The document highlights the difficulties that Jews, already marginalised, faced when they stood accused of ignoring what appeared self-evident to their Christian correspondents: if they did not defend themselves, it might suggest that they were overwhelmed by the Christian correspondent's argument; if they did respond, it could be perceived as an attack.

Spinoza acknowledges Burgh's claim that 'more men of learning and of blameless life are found in the [Roman Catholic] Church than in any other Christian body', but this is only because there are more Catholics than Protestants and 'in every Church there are thoroughly honourable men'. He takes a similar approach to Burgh's argument that the superior wisdom of Catholic teaching is witnessed by the many thousands of people who believe it to be true. Spinoza points out that this argument is used equally by Jews on behalf of Judaism: 'They with no less confidence than the devotees of Rome bring forward their myriad witnesses [and] carry back their line to Adam.'

Elsewhere in the letter Spinoza goes on the offensive, condemning all organised religion, characterising Roman Catholicism as a 'pernicious' superstition but applying the same description to Judaism and Islam. Differences of tradition exist between Christianity and Judaism, but for Spinoza reason stands in judgement of both and he deprecates what he sees as Burgh's incapacity to exercise his own reason (which has been 'bewitched').

Spinoza's approach would, in subsequent years, be deplored by clerics but hailed by Enlightenment philosophers, many facets of whose thinking it prefigures. Rather than solely decrying priestcraft and the abuse of religious authority, Spinoza acknowledges that all religions produce moral as well as immoral people, thus universalising both religion and his own critique. It is not so much the virtue of a faith that counts in these matters, but the number of its members: the more adherents a faith has, the greater the variety of behaviours it will capture. Such an approach obviates questions about the veracity of rituals or miracles and allows reason to judge the ethical influence of any faith. Spinoza's contention that all people of faith may make similar truth claims based on spiritual experiences, and are therefore indistinguishable from one another as to claims of inward testimonials, levels not only Christianity and Judaism but all faiths.

Bibliography

Curley, Edwin, 'Spinoza's Exchange with Albert Burgh', in Melamed, Yitzhak Y., and Rosenthal, Michael A. (eds.), *Spinoza's 'Theological-Political Treatise': A Critical Guide* (Cambridge: Cambridge University Press, 2010), 11–28.

Israel, Jonathan I., *Radical Enlightenment: Philosophy and the Making of Modernity 1650–1750* (Oxford: Oxford University Press, 2001), 224–9.

Nadler, Steven M., *Spinoza: A Life* (Cambridge: Cambridge University Press, 1999).

Schwartz, Daniel B., *The First Modern Jew: Spinoza and the History of an Image* (Princeton: Princeton University Press, 2012).

8

John Toland: Reasons for Naturalizing the Jews in Great Britain and Ireland *(1714)*

Text

Tis manifest almost at first sight, that the common reasons for a GENERAL NATURALIZATION, are as strong in behalf of the *Jews*, as of any other people whatsoever. They encrease the number of hands for labor and defence, of bellies and backs for consumption of food and raiment, and of brains for invention and contrivance, no less than any other nation. We all know that numbers of people are the true riches and power of any country, and we have been often told, that this is the reason, why *Spain* (since the expulsion of the *Jews* and *Moors*) [...] is grown so prodigiously weak and poor: wheras, tho *Holland has comparatively but few native Inhabitants, and lends great numbers yearly to the East-Indies*, yet allowing an unlimited LIBERTY OF CONSCIENCE, and receiving all nations to the right of citizens, the country is ever well stockt with people, and consequently both rich and powerful to an eminent degree [...]

My purpose at present then, is to prove, that the *Jews* are so farr from being an Excresence or Spunge (as some wou'd have it) and a useless member in the Commonwealth, or being ill subjects, and a dangerous people on any account, that they are as obedient, peaceable, useful, and advantageous as any; and even more so than many others [... I]n the first place, it is evident, that by receiving of the *Jews*, no body needs be afraid that any religious Party in the nation will thereby be weaken'd or enforc'd. The *Protestant Dissenters* have no reason to be jealous, that they shou'd join with the *National Church* to oppress them, since they have an equal Interest to preserve LIBERTY OF CONSCIENCE [...] There's as little danger they shou'd ever join with any particular Body of *Dissenters* against the *National Church*, since they can expect no more favor from the one, than the other; and that it is always their interest to preserve the legal Establishment, on which their own Security is grounded. For this reason likewise, they'll never join with any Party in civil Affairs, but that which patronizes LIBERTY OF CONSCIENCE and the NATURALIZATION, which will ever be the side of Liberty and the Constitution [...]

[...] [T]he *Jews* may properly be said to be the Brokers of [Trade], who, whithersoever they come, create business as well as manage it. Yet it is neither by any National Institution or Inclination (as many ignorantly believe) that they do now almost entirely betake themselves to business of Exchange, Insurances, and improving of money upon Security; but they are driven to this way of Livelihood by mere Necessity: for being excluded every where in *Europe*, from publick Employments in the State, as they are from following Handycraft-trades in most places, and in almost all, from purchasing immoveable Inheritances, this does [...] force 'em to Trade and Usury, since otherwise they cou'd not possibly live. Yet let 'em once be put upon an equal foot with others [...] and then I doubt not, but they'll insensibly betake themselves to Building, Farming, and all sorts of Improvement like other people [...]

[...]

There are among the *Jews*, to be sure, sordid wretches, sharpers, extortioners, villains of all sorts and degrees: and where is that happy nation, where is that religious profession, of which the same may not be as truly affirm'd? They have likewise their men of probity and worth, persons of courage and conduct, of liberal and generous spirits. But one rule of life, which is [...] pleaded by all Societies in their own case (tho miserably neglected in that of others) is, *not to impute the faults of a few to the whole number* [...] The *Jews* therefore are both in their origine and progress, not otherwise to be regarded, than under the common circumstances of human nature. The *Romans* were not less esteem'd for being descended from Shepherds and Fugitives (which original they had in common with the *Jews*), than are the *English* for being the progeny of barbarous pyrates [...]

The vulgar, I confess, are seldom pleas'd in any country with the coming in of Foreners among 'em: which proceeds, first, from their ignorance, that at the beginning they were such themselves; secondly, from their grudging at more persons sharing the same trades or business with them, which they call *taking the bread out of their mouths*; and thirdly, from their being deluded to this aversion by the artifice of those who design any change in the Government. But as wise Magistrates will prevent the last, and are sensible of the first, so they know the second cause of the people's hatred, to be the true cause of the land's felicity; and therfore, not minding those, who mind nothing but their selfish projects, they'll ever highly encourage a confluence of strangers.

Source

Toland, John, *Reasons for Naturalizing the Jews in Great Britain and Ireland, On the Same Foot with All Other Nations. Containing Also, A Defence of the Jews against All Vulgar Prejudices in All Countries* (Dublin: The Manuscript Publisher, 2013), 8, 11–15, 18–19, 32–3, 37.

Commentary

John Toland (1670–1722) was an Irish philosopher and freethinker. His anonymous 1714 pamphlet *Reasons for Naturalizing the Jews in Great Britain and Ireland*, from which these excerpts are drawn, is among the first to plead the case for comprehensive toleration of Jews in civil society in Great Britain. In it Toland brings together common stereotypes advanced against accepting Jews and his own counter-arguments.

Toland's thoughts are cut from the same cloth as John Locke's in his 1689 *Letter on Toleration* and emphasise reasonableness in religious toleration, but Toland goes beyond this in advocating not only Jewish immigration but full citizenship with its concomitant rights. The substance and clarity of Toland's arguments laid the foundations for later calls for the civil emancipation of Jews in the United Kingdom. Indeed, Jews themselves would make this argument, for example in the Petition of the Philadelphia Synagogue to the Council of Censors of Pennsylvania (see document 14).

The long history of the expulsion of Jews from European countries provided Toland with a set of case studies. By citing the economic decline of Spain after the expulsion of Jews (see Chapter 4, p. 227) and the success of the Netherlands after taking Jews in, Toland sets the stage for contemporaries to see Jews as useful citizens who would help the nation to prosper. The civic and economic usefulness of a religious minority was a typical contemporary measure of utility (and therefore value), employed by figures as diverse as Benjamin Franklin and Holy Roman Emperor Joseph II (see document 11). The notion that Jews would flourish in any area from which they were not barred not only dismantles stereotypes but places the burden of the civil emancipation of Jews on the shoulders of Christians: Christians must overcome their xenophobia and at least consider Jewish immigration on its merits. The argument that Jews could make contributions to a host community was a powerful one and would be repeated throughout the eighteenth century.

Toland acknowledges that there are 'villains of all sorts and degrees' among the Jewish people, but in this as in other respects, Jews and Christians are on an equal footing. Seeing Jews as sharing a common humanity, in concert with ventilation of facts about the condition of Jews, would be a central fixture of the Enlightenment reasoning that would lead eventually to Jewish emancipation and would be essential to the future course of Jewish–Christian relations.

Perhaps the most original feature of Toland's pamphlet, and one that would be reflected in George Washington's letter to the Hebrew Congregation of Newport, Rhode Island, later in the century (document 15), is his emphasis on the key British value of liberty of conscience. Rather than apologising for Jews, Toland argues that freedom of religion would allow them, and all faiths, to exist, and coexist, on their own terms.

Bibliography

Bernardini, Paolo L., and Lucci, Diego, 'From Toleration to Naturalization: John Toland and the Jews', in *The Jews, Instructions for Use: Four Eighteenth-Century Projects for the Emancipation of European Jews* (Boston: Academic Press, 2012), 35–88.

Champion, Justin, 'Toleration and Citizenship in Enlightenment England: John Toland and the Naturalization of the Jews', in Grell, Ole Peter, and Porter, Roy (eds.), *Toleration in Enlightenment Europe* (Cambridge: Cambridge University Press, 2000), 133–56.

Leask, Ian, 'Only Natural: John Toland and the Jewish Question', *Intellectual History Review* 28, no. 4 (2018), 516–28.

Lurbe, Pierre, 'John Toland and the Naturalization of the Jews', *Eighteenth-Century Ireland/Iris an dá chultúr* 14 (1999), 37–48.

9

Correspondence between Isaac de Pinto and Voltaire (1762)

Text

[Isaac de Pinto to Voltaire]

Sir, –Were I addressing any other but you I should be in some difficulty. I am sending you Critical Reflections on a part of your immortal writings; I who am their greatest admirer, I who ought to read and study them in silence. But as I respect the author more than I regard the work, I presume his magnanimity will pardon me this piece of criticism in favor of the truth which is so dear to him, and from which, perhaps, he has never swerved but in this single instance. I expect at least that he will think me less unworthy of pardon on this account, that I am acting in favor of a whole nation to which I belong [...]

[Excerpt from de Pinto's Critical Reflections]

But why does M. Voltaire, who was born to enlighten the world, add to that cloud of popular prejudices which have been heaped upon the professors of this religion to the scandal of humanity? How could this great man, in despite of his understanding and his heart, in contempt of reason and truth, fall into such an absence of mind? For what more gentle term can I use, when I see the enemy of prejudices, yielding up his pen to the blindest prepossession, that common tool of calumny, a monster which he has so often felled to the ground! We cannot refrain from the use of this term, especially when we see him conclude this chapter by such horrid expressions: *In short, you will find nothing amongst them* (that is the Jews) *but an ignorant and barbarous people, who have joined, for a long time, the basest avarice to the most detestable superstition, and the most violent hatred for all those nations which tolerate and enrich them: we must not, however,* (he says, in his tender mercy,) *burn them!*

I shall say modestly to M. Voltaire that many of those whom he treats so cruelly, would rather suffer the pains of fire than to merit these undeserved imputations. It would, perhaps, be easy to shew that the Jews are not more ignorant, barbarous or superstitious than other nations, and that the rich among them are more inclined to profuseness than to avarice, which is not the case among other people; but no other proof is necessary than an appeal to the public, to be informed that the Jews adopt so strongly the patriot spirit of the nations among which they live, that they push it farther even than the natives themselves. The Jews are jealous to an excess of the glory of those nations who receive them, and which they enrich. If M. Voltaire will allow himself a little time to review the subject, (for to his own tribunal I appeal,) he will see the necessity of making reparation for what he has said of the Jewish nation, to truth, to the age he lives in, but, above all, to posterity, who may plead his authority.

[…]

This people, says M. Voltaire, *was never famous for any art.*

[…]

The Jews, says M. Voltaire, *never were natural Philosophers, Geometricians, or Astronomers.*

[…]

M. Voltaire […] seems again to upbraid the Jews with the manner in which they exterminated some colonies of Canaanites, and ascribes to this action […] the ancient hatred of nations.

[…]

Might they [the Jewish people] not say to the whole Christian world what M. Montesquieu puts into the mouth of a young Jewess, who was arraigned before the tribunal of the Inquisition. We need alter but one word. *You despise, you hate us, who believe the same things you do, because we do not believe everything you do. We profess a religion which you know formerly was the favorite of God: we think that God still loves it, and because you think that He loves it no longer, you despise those who are fallen into so pardonable an error, as to believe that He still loves what he loved formerly. If you have been so much favored by heaven, as to have been shown the truth, you should be thankful; but ought the children who have entered into their father's inheritance, to hate those who have been deprived of it? – The Jewish religion,* (says the same author) *is an ancient trunk of a tree which has produced two branches that cover the earth.* Let then this sacred source be respected, and let those be pitied who have such great sacrifices to make to this old law […] The Jews are not less worthy of praise for having firmness and constancy of mind sufficient to remain in that religion which is proscribed and reviled.

[Voltaire to Isaac de Pinto]

SIR, – The lines you complain of are cruel and unjust. There are among you very learned and respectable persons. Your letter is a sufficient evidence of this. I shall take care to insert a cancel-leaf in the new edition. When a man is in the wrong he should make reparation for it; and I was wrong in attributing to a whole nation the vices of some individuals.

I shall tell you as frankly, that there are many who cannot endure your laws, your books, or your superstitions. They say that your nation has done, in every age, much hurt to itself and to the human race. If you are a philosopher, as you seem to be, you will think as those gentlemen do, but you will not say it. Superstition is the most dreadful scourge of the earth; it is superstition that in every age has caused so many Jews and Christians to be slaughtered; 'tis superstition that still sends you Jews to the stake among nations praise-worthy in other respects. There are certain aspects in which human nature is infernal nature; but genteel people, when they are passing by the place of execution where they break men on the wheel, order their coachmen to drive on quickly to the opera house, in order to divert their attention from this horrid sight on the way.

I might enter into a dispute with you about the knowledge you ascribe to the ancient Jews […] But perhaps I should provoke you to anger, and you seem to be too worthy a man to deserve provocation. As you are a Jew remain so. You will never cut the throats of 42,000 men because they pronounced the word Shibboleth wrong, nor destroy 24,000 men for having lain with the Midianite women. But be a philosopher. This is my best wish to you in this short life.

Source

Guénée, Antoine, *Letters of Certain Jews to Monsieur Voltaire: Containing an Apology for their own People and for the Old Testament*, trans. Philip Lefanu (Dublin: William Watson, 1777).

Commentary

In 1762, Isaac de Pinto (1717–87), a Dutch financier, philosopher and leader of the Dutch Sephardi Jewish community, entered into a correspondence with Voltaire (François-Marie Arouet, 1694–1778). Voltaire had published 'The Jews' in 1756, and it was subsequently included as an article in his influential *Philosophical Dictionary* of 1764. In it he decried what he perceived as the fanaticism, superstition and violence of the Hebrew people in the Old Testament. In 1762 De Pinto published his *Apologie pour la nation juive, ou Réflexions critiques* (*Apology for the Jewish Nation, or Critical Reflections*), an essay on Voltaire's work, and sent it to Voltaire with the introductory letter which provides the first paragraph of our excerpt. Although de Pinto set out to defend Jews against the 'calumnies' Voltaire levelled against them, his admiration was evident and he expressed his objections with deference, using reason, not theology, to combat Voltaire's attack and measuring Jews against Enlightenment standards, which he suggested they met. Although Pinto's tone is one of reverential politeness, the document serves as a window into the growing confidence of some Jews in Christian countries, especially in the west. De Pinto's preparedness to write a corrective to someone as renowned as Voltaire demonstrates courage, depth of learning and the literary skill necessary to engage with one of Europe's leading social critics and writers.

One of a sequence of open exchanges between Christians and Jews during the Enlightenment – of which that between Moses Mendelssohn and the Zurich theologian Johann Kaspar Lavater is a celebrated example (1769–70) – the correspondence between Voltaire and de Pinto is distinctive in that the usual motivation of the Christian to convert his Jewish correspondent is absent. Like John Toland (document 8), de Pinto argues that Jews are no better and certainly no worse than other peoples in behaviour or judgement and seeks to demonstrate their patriotism and economic utility to nations that accept them. Similarly, in claiming that the character of Jews is a result of persecution, stereotyping and civil disabilities, de Pinto shifts some responsibility for the civic improvement of Jews onto Christians. He also points out the double standard Voltaire uses in comparing Jews to their forebears in ways he does not with Christians.

In his brief reply Voltaire apologises for impugning all Jews for the actions of some and suggests that he may revise a part of his writing in future (which he did not). He affirms that there are learned Jews but also implies that Jews have brought hatred and recrimination upon themselves, identifying superstition as the root of both Jewish and Christian fanaticism and contending that it is their superstition that continues to fuel contemporary Christian hatred of Jews.

Voltaire's legacy is a complex one for Jewish–Christian relations, with some critics, such as Arthur Hertzberg, tracing a line from his views to modern racial antisemitism. Voltaire was the most vociferous of the *philosophe* critics of Jews in France in the eighteenth century, but is also famous for his call for religious tolerance (elsewhere he argued that the first Christians did not distinguish themselves from Jews). Yet he presents de Pinto with a challenge: to demonstrate the wisdom of a philosopher it is necessary to reject 'your laws, your books, […] your superstitions'. In other words, for Voltaire, Jews can be philosophers, but only after they have freed themselves from Jewish superstition.

Bibliography

Hertzberg, Arthur, *The French Enlightenment and the Jews: The Origins of Modern Anti-Semitism* (New York: Columbia University Press, 1990).

Mitchell, Harvey, *Voltaire's Jews and Modern Jewish Identity: Rethinking the Enlightenment* (Leiden: Brill, 2012).

Piazza, Marco, *Voltaire against the Jews, or The Limits of Toleration* (London: Palgrave Macmillan, 2023).

10

Gotthold Ephraim Lessing: Nathan the Wise *(1779)*

Text

Act III

NATHAN.   In days of yore, there dwelt in east a man
Who from a valued hand received a ring
Of endless worth: the stone of it an opal,
That shot an ever-changing tint: moreover,
It had the hidden virtue him to render
Of God and man beloved, who in this view,
And this persuasion, wore it. Was it strange
The eastern man ne'er drew it off his finger,
And studiously provided to secure it
For ever to his house. Thus – He bequeathed it;
First, to the *most beloved* of his sons,
Ordained that he again should leave the ring
To the *most dear* among his children – and
That without heeding birth, the *favourite* son,
In virtue of the ring alone, should always
Remain the lord o' th' house – You hear me, Sultan?

SALADIN.   I understand thee – on.

NATHAN.   From son to son,
At length this ring descended to a father,
Who had three sons, alike obedient to him;
Whom therefore he could not but love alike.
At times seemed this, now that, at times the third,
(Accordingly as each apart received
The overflowings of his heart) most worthy
To heir the ring, which with good-natured weakness
He privately to each in turn had promised.
This went on for a while. But death approached,
And the good father grew embarrassed. So
To disappoint two sons, who trust his promise,
He could not bear. What's to be done. He sends
In secret to a jeweller, of whom,
Upon the model of the real ring,
He might bespeak two others, and commanded
To spare nor cost nor pains to make them like,
Quite like the true one. This the artist managed.

The rings were brought, and e'en the father's eye
Could not distinguish which had been the model.
Quite overjoyed he summons all his sons,
Takes leave of each apart, on each bestows
His blessing and his ring, and dies – Thou hearest me?

SALADIN.　I hear, I hear, come finish with thy tale;
Is it soon ended?

NATHAN.　It is ended, Sultan,
For all that follows may be guessed of course.
Scarce is the father dead, each with his ring
Appears, and claims to be the lord o' th' house.
Comes question, strife, complaint – all to no end;
For the true ring could no more be distinguished
Than now can – the true faith.

SALADIN.　How, how, is that
To be the answer to my query?

NATHAN.　No,
But it may serve as my apology;
If I can't venture to decide between
Rings, which the father got expressly made,
That they might not be known from one another.

SALADIN.　The rings – don't trifle with me; I must think
That the religions which I named can be
Distinguished, e'en to raiment, drink and food,

NATHAN.　And only not as to their grounds of proof.
Are not all built alike on history,
Traditional, or written. History
Must be received on trust – is it not so?
In whom now are we likeliest to put trust?
In our own people surely, in those men
Whose blood we are, in them, who from our childhood
Have given us proofs of love, who ne'er deceived us,
Unless 'twere wholesomer to be deceived.
How can I less believe in my forefathers
Than thou in thine. How can I ask of thee
To own that thy forefathers falsified
In order to yield mine the praise of truth.
The like of Christians.

SALADIN.　By the living God,
The man is in the right, I must be silent.

NATHAN.   Now let us to our rings return once more.
As said, the sons complained. Each to the judge
Swore from his father's hand immediately
To have received the ring, as was the case;
After he had long obtained the father's promise,
One day to have the ring, as also was.
The father, each asserted, could to him
Not have been false, rather than so suspect
Of such a father, willing as he might be
With charity to judge his brethren, he
Of treacherous forgery was bold t' accuse them.

SALADIN.   Well, and the judge, I'm eager now to hear
What thou wilt make him say. Go on, go on.

NATHAN.   The judge said, If ye summon not the father
Before my seat, I cannot give a sentence.
Am I to guess enigmas? Or expect ye
That the true ring should here unseal its lips?
But hold – you tell me that the real ring
Enjoys the hidden power to make the wearer
Of God and man beloved; let that decide.
Which of you do two brothers love the best?
You're silent. Do these love-exciting rings
Act inward only, not without? Does each
Love but himself? Ye're all deceived deceivers,
None of your rings is true. The real ring
Perhaps is gone. To hide or to supply
Its loss, your father ordered three for one.

SALADIN.   O charming, charming!

NATHAN.   And (the judge continued)
If you will take advice in lieu of sentence,
This is my counsel to you, to take up
The matter where it stands. If each of you
Has had a ring presented by his father,
Let each believe his own the real ring.
'Tis possible the father chose no longer
To tolerate the one ring's tyranny;
And certainly, as he much loved you all,
And loved you all alike, it could not please him
By favouring one to be of two the oppressor.
Let each feel honoured by this free affection.
Unwarped of prejudice; let each endeavour

To vie with both his brothers in displaying
The virtue of his ring; assist its might
With gentleness, benevolence, forbearance,
With inward resignation to the godhead,
And if the virtues of the ring continue
To show themselves among your children's children,
After a thousand thousand years, appear
Before this judgment-seat – a greater one
Than I shall sit upon it, and decide.
So spake the modest judge.

SALADIN. God!

NATHAN. Saladin,
Feel'st thou thyself this wiser, promised man?

SALADIN. I dust, I nothing, God!
[*Precipitates himself upon Nathan, and takes hold of his hand, which he does not quit the remainder of the scene.*]

Source

Lessing, Gotthold Ephraim, *Nathan the Wise: A Dramatic Poem in Five Acts, Translated by W. Taylor. Emilia Galotti: A Tragedy in Five Acts, translated by Charles Lee Lewes*, ed. Henry Morley (London: Sampson Low, Marston, Searle & Rivington, 1868), 89–93.

Commentary

There is no play of the modern era that articulates the Enlightenment hope of interfaith harmony better than *Nathan the Wise* (1779). Written by the German dramatist, critic and philosopher Gotthold Ephraim Lessing (1729–81), whose early play *Die Juden* (*The Jews*) (1749) focused on Jews' marginal position in society, *Nathan the Wise* is set in Jerusalem at the time of the Third Crusade (1189–92) but conceived in a place and period – the Berlin of Frederick II – of intense discussion about how Jews and Christians should relate. Lessing is said to have modelled the figure of Nathan on his friend, the German philosopher and man of letters Moses Mendelssohn, often regarded as the father of the Jewish Enlightenment (see document 13).

The most important scene of the story sees the Sultan Saladin ask Nathan, a Jewish merchant, a shocking question, namely: which of the three Abrahamic faiths, Judaism, Islam or Christianity, is true? The imbalance of power and the nature of Saladin's question, given that Nathan is Jewish and the sultan Muslim, adds tension to the scene, as does the fact that the sultan is at war with Christian crusaders. Nathan senses the precariousness of his position and devises a parable – the so-called parable of the three rings – to serve as an answer to the sultan's question.

The parable posits a ring of great power, the power to be beloved by God and one's fellow humans. This ring is passed down patriarchally from father to son until a father with three sons inherits it and cannot decide which of them ought to inherit it from him. He decides to have two other identical rings crafted and in due course tells each son that he is going to inherit the ring. Upon his death, each son comes forward and shows his ring.

Unable to decide who has the true ring, the sons come before a judge who pronounces that all three sons are deceived and that the true ring is lost, perhaps because the father could not abide the tyranny of one ring. Yet the judge suggests that if the power of the ring is indeed to make one beloved by God and others, this will, after millennia, determine who has the true one. In other words, since there is no way to tell which son has the true ring, it must be discerned according to different criteria.

Lessing, in a dynamic Enlightenment move, insists that religions turn from a competition of dogma to deeds, from truth claims to good actions that contribute to human flourishing. This approach negates the futility of the older-style Christian–Jewish *disputatio* (see Chapter 4, p. 207) and also had the potential productively to harness for social purposes the religious energy that resulted not only in internecine warfare in the Holy Land – *Nathan the Wise* is meant to be a fruitful anachronism – but in such brutal eighteenth-century developments as the Revocation of the Edict of Nantes and the Expulsion of the Salzburg Protestants, and the later mass restriction of Jews to the Russian Pale of Settlement.

There is of course a humanistic element at the heart of this enterprise. *Nathan the Wise* summons Christian and Jewish faith communities to seek the roots of their identity first and foremost in a common humanity within a shared environment.

Bibliography

Eckardt, Jo-Jacqueline, *Lessing's Nathan the Wise and the Critics: 1779–1991* (Columbia, SC: Camden House, 1993).

Hess, Jonathan, 'Lessing and German-Jewish Culture: A Reappraisal' and Sutcliffe, Adam, 'Lessing and Toleration', in Robertson, Ritchie (ed.), *Lessing and the German Enlightenment* (Oxford: Voltaire Foundation, 2013).

Nisbet, Hugh B., '*Nathan the Wise*', in *Gotthold Ephraim Lessing: His Life, Works, and Thought* (Oxford: Oxford University Press, 2013), 601–23.

Yasukata, Toshimasa, *Lessing's Philosophy of Religion and the German Enlightenment* (Oxford: Oxford University Press, 2002).

II

Joseph II: Edict of Toleration (2 January 1782)

Text

From the ascension to Our reign We have directed Our most preeminent attention to the end that all Our subjects without distinction of nationality and religion, once they have been admitted and tolerated in Our States, shall participate in common in public welfare, the increase of which is Our care, shall enjoy legal freedom and not find any obstacles in any honest ways of gaining their livelihood and of increasing general industriousness […]

As it is Our goal to make the Jewish nation useful and serviceable to the State, mainly through better education and enlightenment of its youth as well as by directing them to the sciences, the arts and the crafts, We hereby grant and order:

1. It certainly is not at all our supreme wish herewith to grant the Jews residing in Vienna an expansion [of rights] with respect to external tolerance [*Duldung*]. On the contrary, in the future it will remain that they do not constitute an actual community under a designated leader from their own nation, but as hitherto each family, considered separately, will serenely enjoy the protection of the laws of the land in accordance with the tolerance [*Duldung*] specifically given it by Our government of Lower Austria. Further, as hitherto they will not be allowed public religious worship or public synagogues; they will not be permitted to establish their own press for the printing of prayer books and other Hebrew books, but when necessary they are to turn to available printing presses in Bohemia; should they wish to import Jewish books from foreign lands, which in general is forbidden, they are accordingly obligated in each such instance, to apply for permission and, like all other subjects, to submit imported books to the censor […]

7. As in the past, it is forbidden for Jews to live in rural regions of Lower Austria, except if they wish to establish a factory or pursue a useful trade in some village, in one of the market towns, in a provincial city, or perhaps in a desolate area. In such an instance, they must request permission of the government, but after they receive it their rights and freedoms will be the same as their co-religionists in the capital city [Vienna …]

8. Graciously, that the tolerated Jews may send their children in such places where they have no German schools of their own, to the Christian primary and secondary schools so that they have at least the opportunity to learn reading, writing, and counting. And although they do not have a proper synagogue in Our residence, still We hereby permit them to establish for their children at their own expense their own school, organized in the standard way with teachers appointed from amongst their co-religionists […]

9. With regard to schools of higher degrees which were never forbidden to Jewish co-religionists, We hereby merely renew and confirm this permission.

10. In order to facilitate their future means of support and to prepare the necessary ways of gaining a livelihood, We hereby most graciously permit them from now to learn all kinds of crafts or trades here as well as elsewhere from Christian masters, certainly also amongst themselves, and to this end to apprentice themselves to Christian masters or to work as their journeymen, and the latter (the Christian craftsmen) may accept them without hesitation […]

11. We hereby further grant to the Jewish nation the general license to carry on all kinds of trade, without however the right of citizenship and mastership from which they remain excluded, to be carried on by them freely, only consequently as it is usual here and even then not before having obtained permission, same as Christians do, from the *Magistrat* in this city and from the government of Lower Austria [...]

12. [...] Painting, sculpture and the practice of the other free arts are granted them as to Christians; and We further grant to the Jewish co-religionists the completely free choice of all non-civic branches of commerce [...]

13. Since the investment in factories and manufacture has always been permitted them, We only use this opportunity to renew this permission in order to encourage them openly to such undertakings that benefit the public [...]

15. Considering the numerous openings in trades and manifold contacts with Christians resulting therefrom, the care for maintaining common confidence requires that the Hebrew and the so-called Jewish language and writing of Hebrew intermixed with German be abolished .... We therefore explicitly forbid their use in all public transactions in and out of the courts; in the future the vernacular of the land is to be used [...]

16. In order to facilitate the tolerated Jews in their trades also with regard to the question of servants, it shall be permitted to them from now on to employ as many Jewish as well as Christian servants as their business requires [...]

19. No less do We hereby completely abolish the head-toll hitherto levied on foreign Jews and permit them to enter Our residence from time to time in order to carry on their business.

20. Since we have already announced that We do not wish to increase the number of Jewish families residing here, any foreign Jew who comes here, must immediately upon his arrival register with the government of Lower Austria, and indicate the business [that has brought him to Vienna] and the time required in order to complete it, to wait for the approval, or in any case an answer from the appropriate office. When this period of time is over, they must either leave [Vienna] or request from the government an extension. All those who hide or stay here without the required license or stay beyond the time allotted them, will be sought out, arrested and evicted from here. We, therefore, impose upon Our government in Lower Austria the explicit task constantly to keep a watchful eye through the police that these foreign Jews will depart [at the appointed time]. To facilitate this surveillance, We also order those Christians and [tolerated] Jews at whose homes alien Jews may be lodging to report this to the authorities, which they are in any case required to do, immediately [...]

25. Since by these favors We almost place the Jewish nation on an equal level with adherents of other religious associations in respect to trade and enjoyment of civil and domestic facilities, We hereby earnestly advise them

to observe scrupulously all political, civil and judicial laws of the country to which they are bound same as all other inhabitants, just as they remain subject with respect to all political and legal matters to the provincial and municipal authorities within their jurisdiction and pertinent activities.

Source

Preamble, paras 8–11, 16, 19, 25: Mahler, Raphael (ed. and trans.), *Jewish Emancipation: A Selection of Documents*, Pamphlet Series, Jews and the Post-War World 1 (New York: American Jewish Committee, 1941), 18–20.

Paras 1, 7, 12–13, 15, 20: Mendes-Flohr, Paul, and Reinharz, Jehuda (eds.), 'Joseph II: Edict of Tolerance (January 2, 1782)', in *The Jew in the Modern World: A Documentary History*, 3rd ed. (New York: Oxford University Press, 2011), 42, 43, 44–5. (Square-bracketed phrases are part of the original.)

Commentary

Joseph II (1741–90), the Habsburg Holy Roman Emperor who ruled from Vienna from 1765 to his death, issued an Edict of Toleration in 1782, by which time the Jewish population of the Habsburg empire had more than doubled to around 350,000 with the partition of Poland and the acquisition of Galicia (a region that straddles what is now Poland and Ukraine) a decade earlier. The Edict applied to Jews in Lower Austria, which included Vienna and surrounding areas, and followed on from a law promulgated the previous year which lifted some of the civil disabilities faced by non-Catholics and moved towards greater religious liberty. The 1782 Edict regulated the status and rights of Jews in the Habsburg lands and was widely welcomed by leaders of the *Haskalah* or Jewish Enlightenment, although traditionalist Jews were concerned that it would lead to assimilation and threaten the existing communal leadership structure, since Jews would not 'constitute an actual community under a designated leader from their own nation'. Joseph II wanted to make Jews useful to the state; however, this document differs from other similar efforts, such as those outlined in John Toland's pamphlet (document 8), in that the emperor had the power to implement his reforms.

Throughout his reign, Joseph sought to centralise his realm and bring his territories into alignment with his legal, social, political and ecclesiastical reforms. Not only did this enterprise meet with resistance from territories from the Austrian Netherlands to Hungary, but the kinds of integration Joseph sought to impose also raised new questions in Jewish–Christian relations. For example, while elementary coeducation with Christian children was to be made available for Jewish children, this effort at social inclusion and raising the educational level of the empire's inhabitants could also be seen as diluting and ultimately undermining a particular kind of Jewish culture and identity. With new privileges came new obligations, such as having to use German since Yiddish and Hebrew were prohibited as public and legal languages and limited to the religious realm.

Yet full integration was not the goal of the Edict and some civil disabilities remained: the Edict stated, 'We *almost* place the Jewish nation on an equal level with adherents of other religious associations' (emphasis added). The numbers of Jews in the capital of the empire would be closely regulated; there were no public synagogues for Jews in Vienna; and there would be no private Jewish press to publish prayer books, which would have to be purchased from pre-existing presses in the empire. Later measures abolished rabbinical jurisdiction (1784) and forced Jews to adopt German names (1787). The message seemed clear: Jews would be allowed to coexist with their Christian neighbours, learn trades and have freedom to worship privately, and in those ways to participate in Joseph II's enlightened project, but were otherwise to keep any cultural or religious distinctiveness to themselves.

Although the Edict did not confer citizenship or equality (full equality was granted in Austria and Hungary in 1867), it did reflect a desire to integrate Jews into society, both economically and culturally.

Bibliography

Beales, Derek, 'Toleration of Protestants, Greek Orthodox and Jews', in *Joseph II*, Vol. 2: *Against the World, 1780–1790* (Cambridge: Cambridge University Press, 2009), 168–213.

Judson, Pieter M., 'Servants and Citizens, Empire and Fatherland, 1780–1815', in *The Habsburg Empire: A New History* (Cambridge, MA: Harvard University Press, 2016), 51–102.

Silber, Michael K., 'The Making of Habsburg Jewry in the Long Eighteenth Century', in Karp, Jonathan, and Sutcliffe, Adam (eds.), *The Cambridge History of Judaism*, Vol. 7: *The Early Modern World, 1500–1815* (Cambridge: Cambridge University Press, 2017), 763–97.

12

Johann Gottfried Herder: On the Spirit of Hebrew Poetry *(1782–3) and* Ideas on the Philosophy of the History of Mankind *(1784–91)*

Text

(i) On the Spirit of Hebrew Poetry *(1782–3)*

The basis of theology is the Bible, and the foundation of the New Testament is the Old. It is impossible to understand the former rightly without understanding the latter: Christianity emerged out of Judaism, the genius of the language is the same in both books. And the genius of the language we cannot study better, that is, more truly, deeply, with more breadth and pleasure than through poetry, and especially in the most ancient poetry of the same. It is wrong and misleading when one promotes the New Testament to young theologians to the exclusion of the Old; without this, the other cannot even be understood in a learned manner. In addition, the Old Testament contains such a rich variety of stories, images, characters and scenes: in it, we see the multicoloured dawn, the beautiful rising of the sun. In the New Testament the sun stands at the highest point in the sky, and everyone knows which time of day is the most revitalising and fortifying to the natural eye. If one studies the Old Testament with interest and affection, even as simply a human book full of ancient poetry, then the New Testament will reveal itself to us in its purity, its supernal splendour and celestial beauty. Gather the riches of the Old Testament on its own terms, and then one will not become an empty, undiscerning, even desecrating windbag about the New Testament.

Source

Herder, Johann Gottfried, *Werke in zehn Bänden*, ed. Günter Arnold et al. (Frankfurt am Main: Deutscher Klassiker Verlag, 1985–2000); vol. 5 (1993), ed. Rudolf Smend, *Vom Geist der Ebräischen Poesie*, 669–70. Author's own translation.

(ii) Ideas on the Philosophy of the History of Mankind *(1784–91)*

The *Jews* we consider here only as parasitic plants, having attached themselves to nearly all European nations and more or less drawn on their juices. After the downfall of ancient Rome, there were yet comparatively few in Europe; they came over in great numbers owing to the persecution of the Arabs and distributed themselves across the nations. That they brought leprosy into our part of the world is unlikely. It was a more annoying condition that they became moneychangers, brokers and servants of the Empire in all barbarous centuries, became base tools of usury, and thereby strengthened the proud barbarian ignorance of Europeans in commerce against their own profit. They were treated often with cruel ferocity, and what they had obtained through miserliness and deceit, or through hard work, judiciousness and order, was tyrannically forced from them; in that they were used to such encounters and had to take it into account, they had to be all the more clever and extortionate. Meanwhile, they were absolutely essential at that time and are still for many countries; it also cannot be denied that through them Hebrew literature was preserved; the science, wisdom and medical knowledge attained by the Arabs was transmitted in the dark ages and much good was cultivated for which no other than a Jew was fit. There will come a time when no one in Europe will ask any longer who is Jewish or Christian: Jews will live according to European laws and contribute to the good of the state. Only a barbaric constitution prevented Jews from doing so, or rendered their abilities injurious.

Source

Herder, Johann Gottfried, *Werke in zehn Bänden*, ed. Günter Arnold et al. (Frankfurt am Main: Deutscher Klassiker Verlag, 1985–2000); vol. 6 (1989), ed. Martin Bollacher, *Ideen zur Philosophie der Geschichte der Menschheit*, 702. Author's own translation.

(iii) Ideas on the Philosophy of the History of Mankind *(1784–91)*

[The Hebrews] through the will of fate and a series of initiatives, the causes of which are readily ascertained, [...] have had a greater impact on other peoples than any Asian nation; yes, to a certain extent, they have become, through Christianity as well as Mohammedanism, a source for the greatest proportion of the enlightenment of the world.

A remarkable distinction is already found in that the Hebrews have written chronicles of their undertakings, dating from times in which most of the now enlightened nations were still unable to write [... T]hese narratives derive singular weight from the fact that, representing a divinely inspired tribal prerogative of this nation, they have been preserved *almost* with superstitious exactitude for thousands of years, and through Christianity were delivered into the hands of nations that examined and contested, elucidated and used them with a freer spirit than the Jewish one [...]

[S]hortly before the downfall of the Jewish state, Christianity arose in the heart of it, and Christianity initially not only failed to separate from Judaism, adopting the sacred writings of the Jews, but also and especially based upon these writings the divine mission of its Messiah. Hence, it was through Christendom that the books of the Jews came into the hands of all the nations that embraced the Christian doctrine; and according to the manner in which they have been understood, and the use that has been made of them, they have had good or ill effects on all Christian centuries. Their effect was good, insofar as in them the law of Moses made the doctrine of the one God, creator of the world, the basis of all philosophy and religion, and in so many hymns and precepts throughout these writings, spoke of this God with a dignity and loftiness, with a devotion and gratitude, attained by few other human writings [... T]he writings of the Hebrews unquestionably have had an advantageous effect on the history of humankind.

With all these advantages, however, it is equally incontestable that the misinterpretation and abuse of these writings have been detrimental to the human mind in various ways, and the more so as they have operated upon it under the aspect of divinity [... P]assages of the Old Testament have been adduced to justify the contradictory design that was to turn Christianity, which is voluntary and exclusively a moral system, into a Judaic religion of state [...] The laws of Moses were to be applicable in every region of the compass, even among people of entirely different constitutions; hence, there is not one Christian nation that has formed for itself its system of laws and political constitution from the bottom up. So it is that the most sublime good, because of often false application, borders on various evils; for is it not true that even the most sacred elements of nature may turn to destructiveness, and the most effective remedies into creeping poison? [...]

[W]hen the Christians themselves oppressed the Jews, they almost everywhere gave them the opportunity to take control of internal trade, particularly the money trade; thus, the less refined nations of Europe voluntarily became the slaves of the usury of Jews [... I]t was their very insecurity in the realms of the Mohammedans and the Christians that made this invention necessary.

Source

Herder, Johann Gottfried, *On World History: An Anthology*, ed. Hans Adler and Ernest A. Menze, trans. Ernest A. Menze and Michael Palma (Armonk: M. E. Sharpe, 1997), 257–62. Menze and Palma relied on T. Churchill (trans.), *Outlines of a Philosophy of the History of Man* (London: printed for J. Johnson by Luke Hansard, 1800).

Commentary

Johann Gottfried Herder (1744–1803) possessed one of the most fertile minds of his time. His *Ideas on the Philosophy of the History of Mankind* (1784–91), from which documents 12 (ii) and (iii) come, was widely read throughout Europe, and his work as a Lutheran minister, philosopher and literary critic gave him a unique set of skills with which to think about Jewish–Christian relations. Together with his *Spirit of Hebrew Poetry* (1782–3), from which document 12 (i) is excerpted, these writings were landmarks in European culture, fostering and popularising the idea that Christianity emerged from Judaism and that the New Testament could not be understood without the Hebrew Bible. Herder was especially enamoured of the Psalms which, he wrote, contained the inner feeling of nature and the poetic consciousness of God.

This approach allowed for Jews to be appreciated rather than denigrated and for their scripture to be admired for its ethics, poetry and wisdom. In short, Herder opened up the field of the Bible as literature. Herder built on the respect for the study of biblical Hebrew and the biblical criticism that had been fostered and developed by Johann David Michaelis and his student Johann Gottfried Eichhorn at the University of Göttingen. He put forward the idea that Jews had produced a culture of their own, indeed world literature (*Weltliteratur*), a term coined by his friend Johann Wolfgang Goethe. As Herder writes in the second excerpt from Ideas above: 'to a certain extent, they have become, through Christianity as well as Mohammedanism, a source for the greatest proportion of the enlightenment of the world'.

Yet Herder's attitudes were also a product of his time. He advanced ideas of the irreconcilable strangeness of Jews in European Christian society, of their dangerous economic activities and the right to curb those activities without regard to general humanitarian principles. Our excerpts demonstrate these inconsistencies. For example, Herder considered Israel the people of God, chosen and distinguished as the cradle of monotheism, the mother of Christianity. Yet he also expressed negative views, stressing the unimportance of the Jewish people, and in his *Ideas* he twice calls Jews 'parasitic plants'.

Herder's writings were exploited in later generations by antisemites, but he is also an example of philosemitism, pointing out, for example, that European systems of law were heavily informed by the Ten Commandments and that modern notions of human dignity ultimately derive from the Hebrew Bible's monotheistic concept of God. In his *Ideas* he offered historical explanations for why Jews had become involved in commerce as merchants and moneylenders, and could thereby combat prejudice. The French political philosopher Montesquieu (1689–1755) went further in his *Spirit of the Laws* (1748) and held that Jews brought necessary and beneficial economic dynamism to Europe. Herder reminded his audience that it was often the cruelty of Christians and Muslims that contributed to the modern condition of Jews. Moreover, he took the sting out of the stereotype of usury by noting that moneylending was essential to the economic functioning of many nations of the world. Herder's observation that Jews had preserved much learning from Arabs can also be seen as a positive step in the direction of Jewish–Christian–Muslim relations.

Although Herder was influenced by the prejudices around him and did not always apply to Jews the principles of humanism he embraced in other respects, his outlook rested on a hermeneutic of historical understanding, defanging harmful prejudice and superstitions, and on appreciating the contributions that Hebrew ideas and scripture had made to European civilisation.

Bibliography

Beiser, Frederick C., 'Herder and the Jewish Question', in Waldow, Anik, and DeSouza, Nigel (eds.), *Herder: Philosophy and Anthropology* (Oxford: Oxford University Press, 2017), 240–55.

Librett, Jeffrey S., 'Ordering Chaos: The Orient in J. G. Herder's Teleological Historicism', in *Orientalism and the Figure of the Jew* (New York: Fordham University Press, 2015), 29–51.

Niekerk, Carl, 'Johann Gottfried Herder, Enlightenment Anthropology, and the Jew as a "Parasitic Plant"', *Leo Baeck Institute Year Book* 67, no. 1 (2022), 20–36.

Sikka, Sonia, *Herder on Humanity and Cultural Difference* (Cambridge: Cambridge University Press, 2011).

13

Moses Mendelssohn: Jerusalem *(1783)*

Text

'[H]ow will the prophecy come true that someday *there will be only one shepherd and one flock?*'

Dear brothers, who have the best intentions toward mankind, do not allow yourselves to be deluded! In order to be under the care of this omnipresent shepherd the entire flock need neither graze in one pasture nor enter and leave the master's house through a single door. This is neither what the shepherd wants nor advantageous to the prosperity of the flock. Is it a case of mistaking ideas or deliberately seeking to confuse them? One puts it to you that a union of faiths is the shortest way to the brotherly love and brotherly tolerance which you kindhearted people so ardently desire. There are some who want to persuade you that if only all of us had one and the same faith we would no longer hate one another for reasons of faith [...] and the happy days would arrive, of which it is said *the wolf shall dwell with the lamb* [...] The gentle souls who make this proposal are ready to go to work; they wish to meet as negotiators and make the humanitarian effort to bring about a compromise between the faiths, to bargain for truths as if they were rights, or merchandise for sale; they want to demand, offer, haggle, obtain by hook or by crook, surprise and outwit until the parties shake hands and the contract for the felicity of the human race can be written down. Many, indeed, who reject such an enterprise as chimerical and impracticable, nevertheless speak of the union of faiths as a very desirable state of affairs, and sadly pity the human race because this pinnacle of felicity cannot be reached by human powers. Beware, friends of men, of listening to such sentiments without the most careful scrutiny [...]

Brothers, if you care for true piety, let us not feign agreement where diversity is evidently the plan and purpose of Providence. None of us thinks and feels exactly like his fellow man; why then do we wish to deceive each other with delusive words? [...] Does this not amount to doing our very best to resist Providence, to frustrate, if it be possible, the purpose of creation? Is this not deliberately to contravene our calling, our destiny in this life and the next? – Rulers of the earth! If it be permitted to an insignificant fellow inhabitant thereof to lift up his voice to you: do not trust the counselors who wish to mislead you by smooth words to so harmful an undertaking [...] Our noblest treasure, the liberty to think, will be forfeited if you listen to them. For the sake of your felicity and ours, *a union of faiths is not tolerance*; it is diametrically opposed to true tolerance! [... D]o not use your powerful authority to transform some *eternal truth*, without which civil felicity can exist, into a *law*, some *religious opinion*, which is a matter of indifference to the state, into an *ordinance of the land!* Pay heed to the [right] *conduct* of men; upon this bring to bear the tribunal of wise laws, and leave us *thought and speech* which the Father of us all assigned to us as an inalienable heritage and granted to us as an immutable right [...] At least pave the way for a happy posterity toward that height of culture, toward that universal tolerance of man for which reason still sighs in vain! Reward and punish no doctrine, tempt and bribe no one to adopt any religious opinion! Let everyone be permitted to speak as he thinks, to invoke God after his own manner or that of his fathers, and to seek eternal salvation where he thinks he may find it, as long as he does not disturb public felicity and acts honestly toward the civil laws, toward you and his fellow citizens. Let no one in your states be a searcher of hearts and a judge of thoughts; let no one assume a right that the Omniscient has reserved to himself alone! If we render unto *Caesar* what is *Caesar's* then do you yourselves render unto *God what is God's! Love truth! Love peace!*

Source

Mendelssohn, Moses, *Jerusalem: Or on Religious Power and Judaism*, trans. Allan Arkush (Hanover, NH: Brandeis University Press, 1983), 135–9. (The square-bracketed '[right]' is part of the original.)

Commentary

Moses Mendelssohn (1729–86) was a German philosopher, theologian and man of letters often regarded as the father of the Jewish Enlightenment or *Haskalah*. His *Jerusalem* (1783) marks a high point in the articulation of Jewish–Christian relations in this period and is notable for originating from an Orthodox Jewish point of view. When interfaith work is led by progressive thinkers, the accusation can be made that they may not take religious doctrine and practice seriously: Mendelssohn was an observant and practising Jew who reminds readers in this acclaimed work that it is not in coming to a unity of belief that Jewish–Christian or any interfaith work resides, but in finding ways to respect each other's distinctive beliefs and practices and thus generating, in the words of the contemporary Jewish leader Jonathan Sacks (1948–2020), a dignity of difference.

At the time of publication of *Jerusalem* Mendelssohn – whose open correspondence (1769–70) with the Zurich theologian Johann Kaspar Lavater (1741–1801) contrasted

Christian dogma, which is dependent upon belief, with Jewish principles, which are in accordance with reason – was highly respected in leading philosophical circles in Berlin for his emphasis on rationality, and was esteemed by such luminaries as Kant and Lessing (see document 10). *Jerusalem* was published as Mendelssohn worked on translations of the Pentateuch and Psalms and reveals his sensitivity to the two valences that defined the philosophical relationship between Christians and Jews during the late eighteenth century, namely the claim of the Mosaic law to be the defining element of Judaism and the literary-cultural heritage of the Hebrew Bible that was taken very seriously by learned Christian Germans such as Michaelis, Eichhorn and Herder (see document 12).

Our excerpt demonstrates that Mendelssohn was deeply concerned by talk in Prussia of a union of faiths (a project which came to partial fruition for Protestants in 1817). A formal dialogue between faiths had been a thesis put forward in one way or another by thinkers of the *Aufklärung* (German Enlightenment) such as Herder and Goethe, who conceived of a parliament of world religions. Mendelssohn was aware that, while dialogue between Jews and Christians could lead to increased understanding, abolishing differences would limit freedom of conscience and worship, hence his insistence that Jews be able to maintain not only their beliefs, but also their distinctive practices: 'Let everyone be permitted to speak as he thinks, to invoke God after his own manner or that of his fathers.'

His argument that 'diversity is evidently the plan and purpose of Providence' was ignored by many Jews in later generations who assimilated or converted to Christianity, not least several members of Mendelssohn's own family, including his son Abraham and his grandchildren the composers Fanny and Felix Mendelssohn (see Chapter 6, p. 302).

Interestingly, and perhaps fittingly, Berlin, the city where Moses Mendelssohn spent much of his life, is the site of the House of One, a single edifice that houses three different places of worship side by side: a church, a mosque and a synagogue.

Bibliography

Altmann, Alexander, 'Turning Point: The Lavater Affair', in *Moses Mendelssohn: A Biographical Study* (Liverpool: Liverpool University Press, 1984), 194–263.

Feiner, Shmuel, 'Affront and Sickness: The Lavater Affair', in *Moses Mendelssohn: Sage of Modernity*, trans. Anthony Berris (New Haven: Yale University Press, 2010), 83–106.

Gottlieb, Michah, *Faith and Freedom: Moses Mendelssohn's Theological-Political Thought* (Oxford: Oxford University Press, 2011).

14

Petition of the Philadelphia Synagogue to the Council of Censors of Pennsylvania (23 December 1783)

Text

To the honourable the COUNCIL of CENSORS, assembled agreeable to the Constitution of the State of Pennsylvania. The Memorial of Rabbi Ger. Seixas of the Synagogue of the Jews at Philadelphia [...]

Most respectfully showeth,

That by the tenth section of the Frame of Government of this Commonwealth, it is ordered that each member of the general assembly of representatives of the freemen of Pennsylvania, before he takes his seat, shall make and subscribe a declaration, which ends in these words, 'I do acknowledge the Scriptures of the old and new Testament to be given by divine inspiration,' to which is added an assurance, that 'no further or other religious test shall ever hereafter be required of any civil officer or magistrate in this state.'

Your memorialists beg leave to observe, that this clause seems to limit the civil rights of your citizens to one very special article of the creed; whereas by the second paragraph of the declaration of the rights of the inhabitants, it is asserted without any other limitation than the professing the existence of God, in plain words, 'that no man who acknowledges the being of a God can be justly deprived or abridged of any civil rights as a citizen on account of his religious sentiments.' But certainly this religious test deprives the Jews of the most eminent rights of freemen, solemnly ascertained to all men who are not professed Atheists.

May it please your Honors,

Although the Jews in Pennsylvania are but few in number, yet liberty of the people in one country, and the declaration of the government thereof, that these liberties are the rights of the people, may prove a powerful attractive to men, who live under restraints in another country. Holland and England have made valuable acquisitions of men, who for their religious sentiments, were distressed in their own countries. – And if Jews in Europe or elsewhere, should incline to transport themselves to America, and would, for reason of some certain advantage of the soil, climate, or the trade of Pennsylvania, rather become inhabitants thereof, than of any other State; yet the disability of Jews to take seat among the representatives of the people, as worded by the said religious test, might determine their free choice to go to New York, or to any other of the United States of America, where there is no such like restraint laid upon the nation and religion of the Jews, as in Pennsylvania. – Your memorialists cannot say that the Jews are particularly fond of being representatives of the people in assembly or civil officers and magistrates in the State; but with great submission they apprehend that a clause in the constitution, which disables them to be elected by their fellow citizens to represent them in assembly, is a stigma upon their nation and religion, and it is inconsonant with the second paragraph of the said bill of rights; otherwise Jews are as fond of liberty as their religious societies can be, and it must create in them a displeasure, when they perceive that for their professed dissent to doctrine, which is inconsistent with their religious sentiments, they should be excluded from the most important and honourable part of the rights of a free citizen.

Your memorialists beg further leave to represent, that in the religious books of the Jews […] there are no such doctrines or principles established as are inconsistent with the safety and happiness of the people of Pennsylvania, and that the conduct and behaviour of the Jews in this and the neighbouring States, has always tallied with the great design of the Revolution; that the Jews of Charlestown, New York, New-Port and other posts, occupied by the British troops, have distinguishedly suffered for their attachment to the Revolution principles [...] The Jews of Pennsylvania in proportion to the number of their members, can count with any religious society whatsoever [...]; they have served some of them in the Continental army; some went out in the militia to fight the common enemy; all of them have cheerfully contributed to the support of the militia, and of the government of this State; they have no inconsiderable property in lands and tenements, but particularly in the way of trade, some more, some less, for which they pay taxes; they have, upon every plan formed for public utility, been forward to contribute as much as their circumstances would admit of; and as a nation or a religious society, they stand unimpeached of any matter whatsoever, against the safety and happiness of the people.

And your memorialists humbly pray, that if your honours, from any consideration than the subject of this address, should think proper to call a convention for revising the constitution, you would be pleased to recommend this to the notice of that convention.

Source

The Founders' Constitution, Volume 4, Article 6, Clause 3, in Stokes, Anson Phelps, and Pfeffer, Leo (eds.), *Church and State in the United States*, vol. 1 (New York: Harper & Row, 1950), 287–9.

Commentary

This is an important petition made by Rabbi Gershom Seixas and other members of the Philadelphia congregation of the synagogue Mikveh Israel in the wake of the Treaty of Paris, which concluded the American War of Independence. Philadelphia, a leading city in the newly formed United States of America, was known to be a city of religious toleration, and Pennsylvania, the former colony of William Penn, a place of religious pluralism that impressed many European travellers. Philadelphia, where the Declaration of Independence had been drafted and announced, would be enshrined as the city of the American Founding when in 1787 delegates to a constitutional convention there produced the world's first written national constitution, which was ratified and became the law of the land in 1788. In 1789 the Bill of Rights amended the US Constitution, anchoring religious liberty in its First Amendment.

The petition dates from six years earlier, in 1783, when Pennsylvania, like some other states that grew out of the thirteen formerly British colonies, preserved the English common law tradition of imposing religious tests, in Pennsylvania's case for officeholders. This effectively barred Jews from serving in public office, since while requiring belief in God would not disqualify observant Jews (as it did atheists), requiring affirmation that the Christian Bible was given by divine inspiration certainly did. It also cast a shadow on the trustworthiness of Jews and other non-Christians who could not make the affirmation. (After the petition was submitted, Seixas returned to New York, which he had left during the British occupation of 1776 and which did not require a religious test to hold public office.)

Of particular interest for Jewish–Christian relations is the way the Jewish petitioners argued their case with the Council of Censors, a body created by the Pennsylvania constitution as a check on executive and legislative authority. They noted that the affirmation requirement was at odds with the Pennsylvania Declaration of Rights, part of the Pennsylvania constitution of 1776, and thus asked only for the standing law to be applied equally. Yet they also point out that the Jews of Pennsylvania and other former British colonies had faithfully served the cause of liberty during the war, in both arms and treasure. The implication here is that they, along with others, had some purchase on the rights gained during the conflict, including that of representing their fellow citizens. Finally, they drew on a much older tradition, one that Jewish communities had brought with them from Europe and which had helped regulate their affairs with Christian communities there: they pointed out that Jewish immigrants to the United States, some with resources to invest, would seek to go to those states where they were most welcome.

In 1790 the Pennsylvania State Constitution revoked the religious requirement that prevented Jews from holding public office. In the interim, in 1788, Mikveh Israel, on the verge of bankruptcy after many Jews left Philadelphia in the wake of the War of Independence, had sent out an appeal to non-Jews which was answered generously by Benjamin Franklin and other national luminaries, including Charles Biddle, Vice President of Pennsylvania; David Rittenhouse, first director of the US Mint; and Thomas Fitzsimmons, a signatory of the US Constitution. The synagogue continues to flourish today.

Bibliography

Marcus, Jacob Rader, *The Colonial American Jew, 1492–1776*, vol. 3 (Detroit: Wayne State University Press, 1970), 215–48.

Rezneck, Samuel, *Unrecognized Patriots: The Jews in the American Revolution* (Westport: Greenwood Press, 1975).

Rosenbach, Hyman Polock, *The Jews in Philadelphia, Prior to 1800* (Philadelphia: Edward Stern, 1883).

Wolf, Edwin, *The History of the Jews of Philadelphia from Colonial Times to the Age of Jackson* (Philadelphia: Jewish Publication Society of America, 1956).

15

George Washington: Letter to the Hebrew Congregation in Newport, Rhode Island (August 1790)

Text

Gentlemen.

While I receive, with much satisfaction, your Address replete with expressions of affection and esteem; I rejoice in the opportunity of assuring you, that I shall always retain a grateful remembrance of the cordial welcome I experienced in my visit to Newport, from all classes of Citizens.

The reflection on the days of difficulty and danger which are past is rendered the more sweet, from a consciousness that they are succeeded by days of uncommon prosperity and security. If we have wisdom to make the best use of the advantages with which we are now favored, we cannot fail, under the just administration of a good Government, to become a great and a happy people.

The Citizens of the United States of America have a right to applaud themselves for having given to mankind examples of an enlarged and liberal policy: a policy worthy of imitation. All possess alike liberty of conscience and immunities of citizenship. It is now no more that toleration is spoken of, as if it was by the indulgence of one class of people, that another enjoyed the exercise of their inherent natural rights. For happily the Government of the United States, which gives to bigotry no sanction, to persecution no assistance, requires only that they who live under its protection should demean themselves as good citizens, in giving it on all occasions their effectual support.

It would be inconsistent with the frankness of my character not to avow that I am pleased with your favorable opinion of my Administration, and fervent wishes for my felicity. May the Children of the Stock of Abraham, who dwell in this land, continue to merit and enjoy the good will of the other Inhabitants; while every one shall sit in safety under his own vine and figtree, and there shall be none to make him afraid. May the father of all mercies scatter light and not darkness in our paths, and make us all in our several vocations useful here, and in his own due time and way everlastingly happy.

Go: Washington

Source

'From George Washington to the Hebrew Congregation in Newport, Rhode Island, 18 August 1790', *Founders Online*, National Archives, https://founders.archives.gov/documents/ Washington/05-06-02-0135.
(Original source: Mastromarino, Mark A. (ed.), *The Papers of George Washington, Presidential Series*, vol. 6: *1 July 1790–30 November 1790* (Charlottesville: University Press of Virginia, 1996), 284–6.)

Commentary

George Washington (1732–99), elected the first president of the United States in 1789, commands a place of unique respect in the founding narratives of his country. In an age of demythologisation of historical heroes, his authority has proved stubbornly resistant to reduction. This document, in which Washington endorsed Jews and their right to worship, set the tone for the future course of Christian–Jewish relations in the young country. Widely published at the time, it continues to be referenced today in US Jewish–Christian relations, especially by Jewish scholars such as Jonathan Sarna.

Rhode Island was the last of the thirteen states to ratify the United States Constitution, on 29 July 1790, and Washington arrived in Newport, with an entourage including Secretary of State Thomas Jefferson, on 17 August. The next day he visited the city's synagogue, established by Sephardi Jews in 1763, and was presented with an address in the form of an open letter signed by the warden of the synagogue, Moses Seixas (brother of Gershom Seixas of New York; see document 14 above), in which 'the Hebrew Congregation in Newport' sought assurances of religious freedom.

In his letter of reply, Washington, who responded to at least fifteen such letters from religious groups between 1789 and 1791, contrasted the universal possession of 'liberty of conscience and immunities of citizenship' with the model of 'toleration' under which monarchical and papal decrees tolerated Jewish presence in particular territories – see, for example, Pope Gregory X (Chapter 4, p. 214) and Joseph II (document 11 above) – and demonstrated his awareness of the Jewish experience of persecution in Europe in his assertion that the government would give 'to bigotry no sanction, to persecution no assistance' (itself an echo of the letter of the Hebrew Congregation). Jews' freedom to worship in a majority Christian country thus serves as a quintessential marker of the move from tolerance to acceptance as a natural right, which was a central element in Washington's political thought, though scholarly debate continues over the degree of conditionality in the requirement to 'demean themselves as good citizens'.

Washington used his considerable personal prestige as well as the moral and political authority of the presidential office to show Christians, the vast majority in the newly founded republic, that the foundational principle of 'liberty of conscience' anchored in the First Amendment of the Bill of Rights ('Congress shall make no law respecting an establishment of religion, or prohibiting the free exercise thereof') applied to all and that Jews would be equal partakers of the protection and plurality of values that the new nation would guarantee to uphold in its Constitution.

Bibliography

Dalin, David G., *Jews and American Public Life: Essays on American Jewish History and Politics* (Boston: Academic Studies Press 2022), 2–45.

Diner, Hasia R., *The Jews of the United States, 1654 to 2000* (Berkeley: University of California Press, 2004), 13–41.

Sarna, Jonathan D., *Coming to Terms with America: Essays on Jewish History, Religion, Culture* (Lincoln, NE: University of Nebraska Press/Jewish Publication Society, 2021).

Sarna, Jonathan D., and Dalin, David G., *Religion and State in the American Jewish Experience* (Notre Dame: University of Notre Dame Press, 1997).

PART III

1800 to the Present Day

6

The Rise of Antisemitism to Early Zionism
1800–1914

EDWARD KESSLER

INTRODUCTION

While the walls of the ghetto – a term that refers to an enclosed Jewish quarter designed to minimise Jewish contact with Christians – began to crumble before 1800 during the early years of the emancipation of Jews, our period witnessed a dramatic increase in encounters between Jews and Christians. Significant numbers of Jews now began to benefit from improved conditions, especially economic, political, religious and social. Between the turn of the nineteenth century and the outbreak of World War I, in most Christian countries, and notably in the Habsburg empire, liberal changes allowed Jews to engage more actively in Christian society.

Antisemitism remained common, however, and in the Russian empire, pervasive. This geographical area held 45 per cent of the world's Jewish population, a consequence of the Russian conquest of eastern Poland during the reign of Catherine II (*r.* 1762–96). By 1900, 5 million Jews lived in Russia, most of them isolated from the Orthodox Christian population and required to live in the Pale of Settlement in western Russia (Ukraine). Towards the end of the century, after outbreaks of violence against Jews following the assassination of Tsar Alexander II in 1881, significant numbers fled, the largest cohort finding refuge in the United States. By the outbreak of World War I, a third of the 4 million Jews who left had reached American shores, where some experienced traditional prejudice (although in a less potent form than in Europe) and others more positive relations with Christians, as illustrated by the correspondence between Rachel Mordecai Lazarus and the novelist Maria Edgeworth (see document 2). In particular, among US (and European) Reform and Liberal synagogues and mainstream churches, friendships between Jewish and Christian clergy were no longer the exception. Indeed, similar styles of preaching could be found in their respective pulpits; German Reform preaching, for example, was modelled on the German Protestant edificatory sermon.

The years 1800–1914 thus witnessed the growth of a new order which projected a more liberal mindset on the part of Christian authorities, but Jews were expected to demonstrate a new kind of loyalty to the nation state and to possess a more exclusive identity as Austrians, Germans, French, etc. The period therefore saw a narrowing of identity for Jews and Christians which impacted on their relationship, sometimes prompting new forms of Christian intolerance of Jews, as well as secular attacks on Judaism and Christianity (and on all religious belief).

As a disparate collection of small communities, Jews represented the only major non-Christian community in Christian society, and their dissenting presence aroused concern. While the church fostered anti-Jewish animosity and pressed for limitations on Jewish practice, its basic position also included safeguards for life and property and a recognition of the right to observe Judaism within the Christian world. As for the imperial and secular authorities, they also offered protection but for different reasons, which were less about theology and more about pragmatism: political stability and economic progress.

Antisemitism, both theological and racial, increased in intensity during these years. At the same time, albeit to a lesser extent, encounters between Christians and Jews also led to genuine Christian–Jewish dialogue and a recognition of a positive and shared heritage, as illustrated in some Victorian novels (for example, *Daniel Deronda*; document 7), as well as in the writings of progressive Christian and Jewish theologians such as Claude Montefiore (document 15). Christian restorationists in particular embraced early forms of modern Zionism (even though most Zionists were secular), seeing the movement through a millennial and even messianic lens.

The emancipation of Jews in France is the theme of our earliest documents (documents 1 (i) and (ii)). Although Jewish emancipation can be traced to 1789, it was expanded by Napoleon Bonaparte from 1806 onwards, his establishment of the Grand Sanhedrin making Judaism an official religion of France alongside Roman Catholicism, Lutheranism and Calvinism. His goal was to make Jews full French citizens but also to fix the boundaries between religion – a personal choice – and the nation state. Tensions between Jews and the nation state are found throughout this period in France (and elsewhere), as witnessed by the Dreyfus affair (1894–9) in which the French Jewish captain Alfred Dreyfus (1859–1935) was found guilty of treason by antisemitic army officers on the basis of forged documents. French Protestants tended to support Dreyfus and Catholics to oppose him, and the affair split the country, with Dreyfus becoming a symbol either of the eternal Jewish traitor or of the denial of justice. The French Jewish community kept very quiet.

The benefits of emancipation were enjoyed by Jews throughout central and western Europe, including in Sweden, Prussia and Great Britain. In Sweden, intermittently from 1838, Jewish disabilities began to be removed; in Prussia more liberal attitudes followed the issue of an Edict of Emancipation in 1812; and in Great Britain the first Jewish Member of Parliament, Lionel de Rothschild (1808–79), was elected in 1847, three decades after civil disabilities against Catholics were removed (though he was only able to take his seat a decade later, when the Jewish Disabilities Bill was passed in 1858).

Our documents are excerpted from theological writings, political tracts, newspaper articles and advertising, from diaries, sermons, letters, novels (and correspondence between author and reader), as well as from conference proceedings. They demonstrate that in what is today called the Global North, Jews desired to be accepted in Christian society. From a few cultured and 'protected' Jews who emerged in the previous century (as epitomised by Moses Mendelssohn; see Chapter 5, p. 278), greater numbers followed who sought to participate fully in the Christian culture around them and to combine observance of Judaism with loyalty to the Christian state in which they lived. This led to a dramatic increase in assimilation, particularly in cities such as Berlin, Vienna and Budapest, which were the cultural and political centres of their respective empires. This is exemplified by the Hungarian government, which on the eve of World War I had five Jewish-born ministers – all by then Christian converts – and by Benjamin Disraeli, twice prime minister of the United Kingdom (1868 and 1874–80), who was born Jewish but was baptised into the Church of England at the age of twelve.

Another consequence of emancipation, albeit to a lesser extent, was philosemitism and a desire among Christians to understand 'the people of the Bible'. This feature of Christian–Jewish relations was found especially among restorationists and early Christian Zionists, who emphasised the importance of a shared Old Testament as well as of biblical prophecy. The support of Protestant ministers such as William Hechler (1845–1931), who attended the first World Zionist Conference in 1897, was key to securing Christian support for what was primarily a secular Jewish movement. Theodor Herzl, the Budapest-born father of political Zionism, benefited from the support of Christian Zionists, who facilitated meetings with European leaders, including with Pope Pius X in 1904 (see document 13).

Amid the fundamental changes to society during the nineteenth century, none had a greater impact on Jewish–Christian relations than the integration of Jews, especially in western and central Europe. Notably, the Habsburgs began a policy of welcoming Jewish immigrants, primarily from Galicia and the Russian Pale of Settlement, to help foster economic growth. The Jewish population increased from 120,000 in 1800 to 430,000 by 1860 (50 per cent of whom lived in Pest), and Jews adopted the local culture and language, praying in Magyar and at national holidays decorating synagogues with the Hungarian national flag. Jews became agents of modernisation and by the end of our period were acknowledged as leaders of the new capitalism in Hungary in an era of extraordinary expansion. While Jews constituted only 8 per cent of Hungary's population according to the 1910 census, 25 per cent of Budapest's inhabitants were Jewish – the second largest urban Jewish population in Europe after Warsaw (36 per cent). Jews provided half of Budapest's doctors and lawyers, a third of its engineers, and a quarter of its artists and writers. A similar pattern was found in other European cities.

A consequence of Jewish integration into Christian society was that substantial numbers converted to Christianity, including many prominent figures, such as the poet Heinrich Heine (1797–1856), who called his adoption of Christianity a 'ticket of admission to European culture'; others, like Abraham Mendelssohn (document 3), brought up their children as Christians, and many changed their surnames to make them sound more indigenous, or at least less Jewish.

The integration of Jews in a period of urbanisation meant that commerce provided the working environment for Jews, and mass consumption resulted in buying and selling being more profitable than toiling in a field or workshop. Jews now found themselves in a stronger economic position than in earlier centuries when they had been restricted to a narrow range of occupations by Christian statutes. In many places they were still forbidden from owning land but, paradoxically, this proved an advantage because their capital was not tied down in property. Nevertheless, they were still dependent upon the patronage and protection of the Christian authorities, subscribing to an unwritten contract: economic benefit for the rulers and rapid integration for Jews. It did not take much for such a contract to unravel, and the Hungarian poet Endre Ady (1877–1917) likened the relationship to an Aboriginal dance called Korrobori:

> Here two nationalities, equally foreign and devoid of pedigree, are making love to each other according to the rules of the dance. The Jews take their place here with their musical instruments, copied from already established cultures. And we, who call ourselves Hungarians, are filled with a mixture of hatred and longing … Here in our mutual love-strangle, we will either create a new nation – or after us, the deluge. (Sebestyen 2022: 173)

For the poor, in particular, Jews were easily perceived as the face of exploitation and oppression, the middlemen between Christian rulers and the Christian impoverished. This contributed to Jews being seen as a 'problem' which needed a 'solution', and growing opposition to their becoming citizens of the states in which they lived. Their distinctiveness – economic, religious and social – became the subject of public debate about their fate and their future, the so-called 'Jewish question' (*die Judenfrage*, sometimes translated and understood as 'the Jewish problem'). Discussions took place in salons and political arenas (see the excerpts from Bruno Bauer and Karl Marx; documents 5 (i) and (ii)). Although it was not uncommon for antisemitic right-wing secularists to join forces with conservative Christian traditionalists in a joint condemnation of Judaism, the debate often led to attacks on the church and on religion as a whole. The attitudes towards Jews of Christian leaders and state authorities were not monolithic, however, and Vladimir Soloviev (document 9) is an example of an Orthodox Christian thinker who contributed to the 'Jewish question' debate by defending Jews.

This period also saw the rise of demagogic antisemitism, as illustrated by the writings of Richard Wagner (document 6) and the career of Karl Lueger (1844–1910), mayor of Vienna in the 1890s and leader of the Christian Social Party, who dubbed Budapest 'Judapest'. Antisemitism was as deep-rooted in the Austro-Hungarian empire as Budapest was one of the most welcoming cities in Europe. Jews faced not only traditional forms of (mainly theologically based) antisemitism but also new forms based on pseudo-scientific racism, economic stereotyping and conspiracy theories, the latter epitomised by the *Protocols of the Elders of Zion* (1903), which purported to be a series of lectures given by an 'elder of Zion' to people to whom he could openly reveal the Jewish plot to take over the world by overthrowing its rulers. The *Protocols* were based upon *Dialogue aux enfers entre Machiavel et Montesquieu*, a satire by Maurice Joly (1829–78) on the grandiose ambitions of Napoleon III (emperor of France, 1852–70); the authors of the *Protocols* simply substituted 'the Elders of Zion' for Napoleon III. All types of antisemitism were forms of othering, and while antisemitism acquired a modern complexion, it was sustained by premodern prejudice (as for example in the sermons of John Creagh; document 12).

Violent attacks on Jews in Russia known as pogroms (*pogrom* is the Russian word for 'devastation') dramatically increased after the assassination of Tsar Alexander II in 1881. They were prompted by social and economic factors, but the accusation of ritual murder against Jews (killing Christian children at Passover to use their blood for *matzah* (unleavened bread)) was also a factor. These blood libel accusations continued throughout the period, one of the best known being in Damascus in 1840 when Jews were falsely accused of the ritual murder of a Catholic priest. The Anglo-Jewish leader Moses Montefiore (1784–1885) visited and successfully intervened on behalf of the imprisoned Jews, who were later released. (See also the excerpts from *La Civiltà Cattolica* and coverage of the Mendel Beilis trial; documents 8 and 17 (i), (ii) and (iii)).

Antisemitism and pogroms in the Russian empire also led to significant Jewish emigration to Palestine. The Kishinev pogrom of 1903, for example, led Hayyim Bialik (1873–1934) to compose two poems, 'On the Slaughter' and 'In the City of Slaughter', and he, like tens of thousands of Jews from eastern Europe, decided to leave for Palestine, at that time under the control of the Ottomans. From the latter part of the nineteenth century, Protestant, Catholic and Orthodox states competed for influence in Palestine, seeing Jerusalem especially as a potential jewel in their colonial crowns. Victorian tours of the Holy Land, archaeological excavations and investment in the local infrastructure followed: an Italian hospital was modelled on Florence's Renaissance city hall, a French complex was built to house 1,600 Catholic pilgrims, the British built the Anglican Saint George's Cathedral, and in 1898 Kaiser Wilhelm II (r. 1888–1918) dedicated the Lutheran Church in the Old City, saying, 'From Jerusalem came the light in splendour from which the German nation became great and glorious.' With the decline of the Muslim Ottomans and the limited (albeit growing) presence of Jews, Christian colonial aspirations fostered a volatile brew of religion and politics, which was to shape the region as well as the encounter with Jews and Muslims for the next century.

The nineteenth century also witnessed a notable increase in Christian missionary activity and preaching of the gospel, including to Jews, particularly by Protestants. In 1809 the Church of England established the London Society for Promoting Christianity amongst the Jews (later called the Church's Ministry among Jewish People), with the support of leading evangelicals, including William Wilberforce (1759–1833). Some missionaries expressed considerable sympathy for the desire of some Jews to return to the Holy Land (see for example Lord Shaftesbury's 1840 notice in *The Times*; document 4), while others were active not only in seeking to bring the gospel to the Jewish people but also in protesting against the persecution of Jews in Russia and elsewhere (see for example the World Missionary Conference; document 16). Other conversionist activity was more forced, as illustrated by Tsar Alexander I's 1817 edict which readily granted Jews permission to leave the Pale of Settlement if they chose to be baptised.

Christian missionary pressure was countered by Jewish polemical and apologetic writings. In late nineteenth-century Britain, both Orthodox and Reform rabbis, such as Hermann Adler (1829–1911) and David Woolf Marks (1811–1909), published works defending Judaism against missionary argument and activity or responded to the scholarly discipline of biblical criticism (see also Heinrich Graetz; document 10). For many centuries, Christian theologians sought to define the Christian relationship with Judaism in terms of replacement. In the late nineteenth century, German Protestant Liberal scholars in particular, such as Adolf von Harnack (document 11), depicted the Judaism of the first century CE and the preceding few centuries as having lost vitality, becoming a fossilised, pedantic remnant of a once-eloquent vision. Jesus was described as radically different from his fellow Jews, overcoming 'the Law' and representing a fundamental break from Judaism. Jewish scholars such as Leo Baeck (document 14) responded by producing apologetic writings of their own, stereotyping Christianity as reliant on correct doctrine rather than right action and describing Judaism as the higher form of religion.

In sum, the tumultuous years 1800–1914 consisted of a dramatic increase in encounters between Jews and Christians. The foundations of greater understanding were laid and the seeds of genuine Jewish–Christian dialogue were planted. However, both trends were overshadowed and undermined by the growth of virulent antisemitism and the looming threat of war.

Bibliography

Bakker, Arjen F., Bloch, René, Fisch, Yael, Fredriksen, Paula and Najman, Hindy (eds.), *Protestant Bible Scholarship: Anti-Semitism, Philo-Semitism and Anti-Judaism*, Supplements to the *Journal for the Study of Judaism* 200 (Leiden and Boston: Brill, 2022).

Beller, Steven, *Vienna and the Jews 1867–1938: A Cultural History* (Cambridge: Cambridge University Press, 1989).

Burns, M., *Dreyfus: A Family Affair 1789–1945* (New York: HarperCollins, 1991).

Feldman, David, *Englishmen and Jews: Social Relations and Political Culture 1840–1914* (New Haven and London: Yale University Press, 1994).

Liedtke, Rainer, and Wendehorst, Stephan (eds.), *The Emancipation of Catholics, Jews and Protestants: Minorities and the Nation State in Nineteenth-Century Europe* (Manchester: Manchester University Press, 1999).

Sebestyen, Victor, *Budapest: Between East and West* (London: Weidenfeld & Nicolson, 2022).

Smith, Helmut Walser (ed.), *Protestants, Catholics and Jews in Germany, 1800–1914* (Oxford: Berg, 2001).

Tal, Uriel, *Christians and Jews in Germany: Religion, Politics, and Ideology in the Second Reich, 1870–1914*, trans. Noah Jonathan Jacobs (Ithaca: Cornell University Press, 1975).

DOCUMENTS

1

Napoleon's Instructions to the Assembly of Jewish Notables and the Assembly of Jewish Notables' Answers to Napoleon (1806)

Text

(i) Napoleon's Instructions to the Assembly of Jewish Notables (29 July 1806)

The laws which have been imposed on individuals of your religion have been different in the several parts of the world: often they have been dictated by the interest of the day. But, as an assembly like the present, has no precedent in the annals of Christianity, so will you be judged, for the first time, with justice, and you will see your fate irrevocably fixed by a Christian Prince. The wish of His Majesty is, that you should be Frenchmen; it remains with you to accept of the proffered title, without forgetting that, to prove unworthy of it, would be renouncing it altogether.

(ii) The Assembly of Jewish Notables, Answers to Napoleon (1806)

First question: *Is it lawful for Jews to marry more than one wife?*

Answer: It is not lawful for Jews to marry more than one wife: in all European countries they conform to the general practice of marrying only one [...]

Second question: *Is divorce allowed by the Jewish Religion? Is divorce valid when not pronounced by Courts of Justice by Virtue of Laws in Contradiction with those of the French Code?*

Answer: Repudiation is allowed by the law of Moses; but it is not valid if not previously pronounced by the French code.

In the eyes of every Israelite, without exception, submission to the prince is the first of duties. It is a principle generally acknowledged among them, that, in every thing relating to civil or political interests, the law of the state is the supreme law [...]

Third question: *Can a Jewess marry a Christian, and a Jew a Christian woman? Or does the law allow the Jews to intermarry only among themselves?*

Answer: The law does not say that a Jewess cannot marry a Christian, nor a Jew a Christian woman; nor does it state that the Jews can only intermarry among themselves.

The only marriages expressly forbidden by the law, are those with the seven Canaanean nations [...] but we cannot dissemble that the opinion of the Rabbies [*sic*] is against these marriages [...]

In general they would be no more inclined to bless the union of a Jewess with a Christian, or of a Jew with a Christian woman, than Catholic priests themselves would be disposed to sanction unions of this kind. The Rabbies acknowledge, however, that a Jew, who marries a Christian woman, does not cease on that account, to be considered as a Jew by his brethren, any more than if he had married a Jewess *civilly* and not *religiously*.

[...]

Fourth question: *In the eyes of Jews, are Frenchmen considered as their brethren? Or are they considered as strangers?*

Answer: In the eyes of Jews Frenchmen are their brethren, and are not strangers.

The true spirit of the law of Moses is consonant to this mode of considering Frenchmen [...]

And how could they consider them otherwise when they inhabit the same land, when they are ruled and protected by the same government, and by the same laws? When they enjoy the same rights, and have the same duties to fulfil? There exists, even between the Jew and Christian, a tie which abundantly compensates for religion – it is the tie of gratitude [...] Yes, France is our country; all Frenchmen are our brethren, and this glorious title, by raising us in our own esteem, becomes a sure pledge that we shall never cease to be worthy of it.

> Fifth question: *In either case, what line of conduct does their law prescribe towards Frenchmen not of their religion?*
> Answer: The line of conduct prescribed towards Frenchmen not of our religion, is the same as that prescribed between Jews themselves; we admit of no difference but that of worshipping the Supreme Being, every one in his own way [...]

[...]

> Eighth question: *What police jurisdiction do Rabbies exercise among the Jews? What judicial power do they enjoy among them?*
> Answer: The Rabbies exercise no manner of Police Jurisdiction among the Jews [...]

Sometimes [...] a Rabbi and two other doctors formed a kind of tribunal, named *Bethin*, that is, House of Justice; the Rabbi fulfilled the functions of judge, and the other two those of his assessors.

The attributes, and even the existence of these tribunals, have, to this day, always depended on the will of governments under which the Jews have lived, and on the degree of tolerance they have enjoyed. Since the revolution these rabbinical tribunals are totally suppressed in France, and in Italy [...]

[...]

> Twelfth question: *Does it* [the law] *forbid, or does it allow* [Jews] *to take usury from strangers?*
> Answer: [... T]he prohibition of usury, considered as the smallest interest, was a maxim of charity and of benevolence, rather than a commercial regulation. In this point of view, it is equally condemned by the law of Moses and by the Talmud; we are generally forbidden, always on the score of charity, to lend upon interest to our fellow-citizens of different persuasions, as well as to our fellow-Jews.

The disposition of the law, which allows to take interest from the stranger, evidently refers only to nations in commercial intercourse with us; otherwise there would be an evident contradiction between this passage and twenty others of the sacred writings [...]

But if there are some not over-nice in this particular, is it just to accuse one hundred thousand individuals of this vice? Would it not be deemed an injustice to lay the same imputation on all Christians because some of them are guilty of usury?

Source

Tama, M. Diogene, *Transactions of the Parisian Sanhedrim*, trans. F. D. Kirwan (London: Charles Taylor, 1807), 131–2, 150–2, 154–6, 176, 179–80, 193–5, 201–2, 207.

Commentary

Napoleon Bonaparte (1769–1821) was emperor of France between 1804 and 1814/15, having seized power initially in 1799, ten years after the French National Assembly's Declaration of the Rights of Man and of the Citizen, which asserted that 'all men are born and remain free and equal in rights'. Although anti-Jewish laws began to be repealed in the 1780s, it was the French Revolution that granted Jews citizenship (with an emphasis on individual Jews rather than the Jewish community), as illustrated by the Assembly's statement in 1791 which annulled 'all adjournments, restrictions, and exceptions, contained in the preceding decrees, affecting individuals of the Jewish persuasion, who shall take the civic oath'.

However, Napoleon's actions also represented a key moment in the emancipation of the Jews of France. Our excerpts are taken from the proceedings of the Assembly of Jewish Notables in Paris in 1806, which Napoleon convened to ask twelve questions of the Jewish community, some of which related to the interaction between Jews and their Christian neighbours (e.g., question 3) while others addressed their relationship with the nation (e.g., questions 4 and 5). Napoleon desired that Jews 'should be Frenchmen' and his goal was to assimilate Jews into French society and culture.

A year later, Napoleon established a Grand Sanhedrin, modelled after its rabbinic predecessor, which agreed a set of religiously binding decisions to reinforce the Assembly's answers. The Sanhedrin generated considerable publicity, including condemnation from the Lutheran Church in Prussia and from Tsar Alexander I, who described Napoleon as the 'Anti-Christ and the enemy of God' because of his support for Jewish emancipation.

One consequence was widespread Jewish assimilation in France and some conversions to Christianity (mainly for social advancement). Another was state control over Jewish life by the establishment of a Central Consistory – a term borrowed from Protestants. Judaism was consequently defined as a Christian-like religion and organised hierarchically. Napoleon considered Jews 'a nation within a nation', and this Jewish communal structure, sanctioned by the state, made Judaism a recognised religion and placed it under government control.

It is worth noting that Napoleon also restored the Catholic Church to France by the Concordat of 1801 with the papacy but also formally recognised the Lutheran and Reformed Churches. Anti-Jewish legislation was also abolished in countries conquered by Napoleon, such as the papal states, resulting, among other things, in the abandonment of ghettos and the lifting of restrictions on rights to property, worship and Jewish dress.

After Napoleon's defeat, many of these changes were abandoned, and in contrast to the position with Protestants, whose freedom was maintained by Louis XVIII, discriminatory anti-Jewish measures were restored. This provided a seedbed for the growth of antisemitism some decades later; it was in this atmosphere that the Dreyfus affair, a key motivation for the Zionism of Theodor Herzl (see document 13), would unfold.

Although the Assembly of Jewish Notables and the Sanhedrin were failures and their rulings ignored by most European Jews, their legacy was the establishment of boundaries between religion and the state, and the tensions therein continue to play a role in France today, with ongoing debates and controversy about the role of *laïcité* ('secularism').

Bibliography

Schwarzfuchs, Simon, *Napoleon, the Jews and the Sanhedrin* (Oxford: Oxford University Press, 1984).

2

Correspondence between Rachel Mordecai Lazarus and Maria Edgeworth (1815–21)

Text

Warrenton, North Carolina
U.S. of America
August 7th, 1815

Relying on the good sense and candour of Miss Edgeworth I would ask, how it can be that she, who on all other subjects shows such justice and liberality, should on one alone appear biased by prejudice: should even instill that prejudice into the minds of youth! Can my allusion be mistaken? It is to the species of character which wherever a *Jew* is introduced is invariably attached to him. Can it be believed that this race of men are by nature mean, avaricious, and unprincipled? Forbid it, mercy. Yet this is more than insinuated by the stigma usually affixed to the *name*. In those parts of the world where these people are oppressed and made continually the subject of scorn and derision, they may in many instances deserve censure; but in this happy country, where religious distinctions are scarcely known, where character and talents are all sufficient to attain advancement, we find the Jews to form a respectable part of the community. They are in most instances liberally educated, many following the honourable professions of the Law, and Physick, with credit and ability, and associating with the best society our country affords. The penetration of Miss Edgeworth has already conjectured that it is a Jewess who addresses her; it is so, but one who thinks she does not flatter herself in believing that were she not, her opinion on this subject would be exactly what it is now. Living in a small village, her father's the only family of Israelites who reside in or near it, all her juvenile friendships and attachments have been formed with those of persuasions different from her own; yet each has looked upon the variations of the other as things of course – differences which take place in every society [...]

> With sentiments of admiration, esteem, and gratitude,
> Miss Edgeworth's most respectful and obedient servant
> Rachel Mordecai

Edgeworthstown, Ireland

Dear Madam,

Your polite, benevolent and touching letter has given me much pleasure, and much pain. As to the pain I hope you will sometime see that it has excited me to make all the atonement and reparation in my power for the past. It was impossible to remonstrate with more gentleness or in a more convincing as well as persuasive manner than you have done. Your own letter is the very best evidence that could have been offered of the truth of all you urge in favor of those of your own religious persuasion. And the candor and spirit of tolerance and benevolence you shew, you have a right to expect from others.

Will you be so kind to tell me how I can send you what I am now preparing for the press? It probably will not be published till the end of the year, so that I shall have time for your answer […]

I am Dear Madam
Your obliged and grateful
Maria Edgeworth

Warrenton, October 28th, 1817

A few days since I had the pleasure of receiving the packet of books, for which I am indebted to the attentive kindness of Miss Edgeworth […]

The portrait of Mr. Montenero is rendered the more gratifying by its contrast with even the very few of those Israelites who have, in fictitious writings, been represented as estimable. I have met with none, that I recollect, but Cumberland's Shever. And in Shever, tho' we find much to approve, there is still a want of respectability. He was a benevolent man; but in the profession of a *userer* [*sic*], there is something against which correct principle revolts. Mr. Montenero is a good man, a man of science, and a gentleman whose acquaintance and intimacy anyone may covet. It is difficult duly to appreciate the greatness of mind which can relinquish opinions long indulged and avowed, and which has courage to recant when convinced that justice calls for recantation. The passage, page 30, beginning, 'I have met with authors, professing candour and toleration, etc.,' I read with peculiar satisfaction; such an instance of the candour, the superiority of Miss Edgeworth's mind and heart, I dwell on with a degree of pleasure, I may venture to say it, nearly equal to that which the reflection of having written it must yield herself. Many other remarks on this volume present themselves, but if I attempt to tell of all I found in it to give me pleasure, I shall say both too much and too little. Let me therefore, without dwelling longer on its many excellences, confess with frankness that in one event I was disappointed. Berenice was not a Jewess. I have endeavoured to discover Miss Edgeworth's motive for not suffering her to remain such; it appeared that there must be another, besides that of the obstacle it presented to her union with Harrington; and I have at length adopted an opinion suggested by my dear father, that this circumstance was intended as an additional proof of the united liberality and firmness of Mr. Montenero's principles. He had married a lady of different religious persuasion, without being inclined to swerve in the least from his own; and he had brought up his daughter in the belief of her mother, but with an equal regard for both religions; inculcating thereby the principle that, provided the heart is sincere in its adoration, the conduct governed by justice, benevolence, and morality, the modes of faith and forms of worship are immaterial; all equally acceptable to that Almighty Being, who looks down on all his creatures with an eye of mercy and forgiveness. It is not wonderful that I should, in the present instance, have adopted this opinion, for it is that in which all my father's children have been educated: we regard our own faith as sacred, but we respect that of others, and believe it equally capable of conducting them to the Throne of Grace. It would be gratifying to us to know how far our impressions respecting Berenice are correct [...]

With every wish for Miss Edgeworth's prosperity and happiness, I have the honour of subscribing myself, her very grateful friend and servant.

R. Mordecai

June 21st, 1821
Edgeworthstown, Ireland

[...] I have never, I believe, written to you since I received a very kind letter from you about Harrington and Ormond. It came to my hands when I was so unhappy that I could not write any answer. The feeling that my Father would have been so much gratified by it and that it came when he could no longer sympathise with me as he had done for so many happy years was dreadful. I have since read your letter again lately, after an interval of near four years, and feel grateful now for not having thanked you. I wish you would thank your kindhearted father for the reason he gave for my making Berenice turn out to be a Christian. It was a better reason than I own I had ever thought up [...]

Believe me, Dear Madam, your grateful
Maria Edgeworth

Source

From *The Education of the Heart: The Correspondence of Rachel Mordecai Lazarus and Maria Edgeworth* edited by Edgar E. MacDonald. Copyright © 1977 by the University of North Carolina Press. Used by permission of the publisher. www.uncpress.org. Text quoted from pp. 6–9, 13–18, 23.

Commentary

This document consists of excerpts from correspondence between Maria Edgeworth (1768–1849), a prolific Anglo-Irish novelist, and Rachel Mordecai Lazarus (1788–1838), an American teacher. Rachel worked at a girls' school established by her father Jacob in Wincanton, North Carolina, and was an avid reader of Maria's writings. Brought up in

England, Maria moved to Ireland to join her father Richard in managing the family estate. Rachel (and Jacob) admired Maria and Richard for their humanitarian approach to children's education.

One of Edgeworth's most popular novels, *The Absentee*, was published in 1812. It contained numerous antisemitic tropes, particularly relating to the main Jewish character, also called Mordecai. In her first letter (1815) Rachel expresses admiration for the Edgeworth family, but asks why Maria would write of Jews in a derogatory manner and voices disappointment that her family name has been given to an unscrupulous character. Her letter represents an appeal against the anti-Jewish prejudice not uncommon in British works of literature, Shakespeare's *The Merchant of Venice* (see Chapter 5, p. 247) and Dickens' *Oliver Twist* (1838) being prominent examples. In her experience, Rachel points out, positive relations between Jews and Christians in the US are common, 'religious distinctions are scarcely known [… and] we find the Jews to form a respectable part of the community'.

Edgeworth replied apologetically, and her subsequent novel, *Harrington* (1817), was partly a response to this criticism, as she and her father acknowledged in the preface, citing 'an extremely well written letter' from one of her American readers, 'a Jewish lady, complaining of the illiberality with which the Jewish nation had been treated in some of Miss Edgeworth's works'. The novel depicts the life of Simon Harrington, whose initial anti-Jewish prejudice changes through a friendship with his Jewish servant, Jacob, and his love for Berenice, the daughter of an extremely wealthy but kind and cultured Spanish-born Jewish merchant, Mr Montenero. A key moment occurs when Harrington witnesses Berenice's dismay at a performance of *The Merchant of Venice*. He marries her, a decision his parents reluctantly accept, but Harrington's Jewish wife turns out to be an English Protestant.

However good her intentions, Edgeworth still used traditional tropes and stereotypes in her depictions of, for example, the wealth of Mr Montenero and the perpetually long-suffering Jewish figure Jacob, who literally serves, but never retorts to, his abusers: neither is a real character, rather they are straw figures representing 'good' Jews. In addition, Edgeworth 'Christianises' Berenice, unexpectedly revealing at the end of the book that she was Christian all along, suggesting that Jews were more acceptable in English society when they adopted Christianity and Christian values. The parallel with the contemporary Jewish experience in France is noticeable. In 1817, Rachel wrote to Maria again and challenged her as to why the Jewish heroine needed to become Christian. Maria admitted she had no answer but welcomed Rachel's father Jacob's suggestion that she wanted to emphasise the nobility of character of Berenice's father Mr Montenero.

Although Rachel and Maria never met, the correspondence made them, as they called themselves, 'family friends', and the families stayed in contact after their deaths.

It is important to view both the novels and the correspondence in their early nineteenth-century context: they represent steps towards Jewish integration and emancipation in Christian society, albeit through full acculturation and conversion. Edgeworth was influential on later novelists such as Walter Scott, whose *Ivanhoe* (1819) also sympathetically depicts a central Jewish character, Rebecca, who refuses to convert to Christianity but remains a Jew her whole life.

Bibliography

Anderson, Emily Hodgson, 'Autobiographical Interpolations in Maria Edgeworth's *Harrington*', *ELH* 76, no. 1 (Spring 2009), 1–18.

Del Balzo, Angelina, '"The Feelings of Others": Sympathy and Anti-Semitism in Maria Edgeworth's *Harrington*', *Eighteenth-Century Fiction* 31, no. 4 (Summer 2019), 685–704.

MacDonald, Edgar E. (ed.), *The Education of the Heart: The Correspondence of Rachel Mordecai Lazarus and Maria Edgeworth* (Chapel Hill: University of North Carolina Press, 1977).

Page, Judith W., 'Maria Edgeworth's *Harrington*: From Shylock to Shadowy Peddlers', *The Wordsworth Circle* 32, no. 1 (January 2001), 9–13.

3

Abraham Mendelssohn Bartholdy: Letter to His Daughter Fanny (July 1820)

Text

My dear Daughter,

You have taken an important step, and in sending you my best wishes for the day and for your future happiness, I have it at heart to speak seriously to you on subjects hitherto not touched upon [...]

The outward form of religion your teacher has given you is historical, and changeable like all human ordinances. Some thousands of years ago, the Jewish form was the reigning one, then the heathen form, and now it is the Christian. We, your mother and I, were born and brought up by our parents as Jews, and without being obliged to change the form of our religion have been able to follow the divine instinct in us and in our conscience. We have educated you and your brothers and sister in the Christian faith, because it is the creed of most civilised people, and contains nothing that can lead you away from what is good, and much that guides you to love, obedience, tolerance, and resignation, even if it offered nothing but the example of its Founder, understood by so few, and followed by still fewer.

By pronouncing your confession of faith you have fulfilled the claims of *society* on you, and obtained the *name* of a Christian. Now *be* what your duty as a human being demands of you, *true*, *faithful*, *good*; obedient and devoted till death to your mother, and I may also say to your father, unremittingly attentive to the voice of your conscience, which may be suppressed but never silenced, and you will gain the highest happiness that is to be found on earth, harmony and contentedness with yourself.

I embrace you with fatherly tenderness, and hope always to find in you a daughter worthy of your, of our, mother. Farewell, and remember my words.

Source

Hensel, Sebastian, *The Mendelssohn Family (1729–1847): From Letters and Journals*, vol. 1, 2nd rev. ed., trans. Carl Klingemann (London: Sampson Low, Marston, Searle, & Rivington, 1881), 79–80.

Commentary

Abraham Mendelssohn (1786–1835) was the son of the philosopher Moses and father of the composer Felix. Our excerpt, taken from a letter to his daughter Fanny at her confirmation, deals with the theme of Jewish assimilation and conversion to Christianity, which had increased dramatically in the nineteenth century, having been foreshadowed by the Answers of the French Notables to Napoleon (see document 1 (ii)). While Moses Mendelssohn called for assimilation into German society (see Chapter 5, p. 278), he remained Jewish, but four of his six children converted, two becoming Catholic and two, including Abraham, Protestant.

In line with Moses' ideas, Abraham had a liberal education. He became one of the founding members of the Jewish liberal society Gesellschaft der Freunde (1792) and the Sing-Akademie zu Berlin (1793) and was elected a Berlin town councillor (1825). In his view, Judaism was once 'reigning' but, since Christianity had become dominant, he and his wife Lea decided not to have their sons Felix and Paul circumcised. Although his children were initially brought up without religious education, they were baptised in 1816, followed by Abraham and Lea in 1822.

Abraham also added the name Bartholdy to the family surname, at the suggestion of his brother-in-law, Jacob Levin Salomon, who had taken this name when he converted to Christianity. As Abraham wrote to Felix in 1829, 'a name is like a garment; it has to be appropriate for the time, the use, and the rank, if it is not to become a hindrance and a laughing-stock […] There can no more be a Christian Mendelssohn than there can be a Jewish Confucius. If Mendelssohn is your name, you are ipso facto a Jew' (Warner 1955: 555–6).

Despite their conversion and that of several family members, the Mendelssohns were always known as Jews, experiencing the antisemitism common at the time (and afterwards), notably in the 'Hep-Hep' riots of 1819, during which anti-Jewish violence swept through Germany following the end of the Napoleonic Wars, the Congress of Berlin (1815) and the famine of 1816–17.

Abraham's letter to Fanny illustrated a common desire, especially among European Jews, to assure the next generation a life free from the restrictions imposed on them by the prevailing law and culture. He concluded that conversion suited the family's practical and philosophical needs. Becoming Lutheran offered the best future for his children and represented a quick emancipation at a time when nationalist intellectuals were emphasising a patriotism based on Lutheranism and restored anti-Jewish discrimination, such as the exclusion of Jews from academic posts (1822). Like Heinrich Heine, Abraham saw conversion as the 'ticket of admission into European culture'. Thus he explains the decision to raise his children as Christian on the grounds that 'it is the creed of most civilised people today'. There is no evidence of a spiritual impulse.

Jewish assimilation into Christian society (as well as conversion) remains a controversial topic in Jewish–Christian relations, although today this is likely to be the result less of a desire to gain social acceptance than of intermarriage and the rise of secularism, which, ironically perhaps, now represent challenges to both traditions.

Bibliography

Hertz, Deborah, *How Jews Became Germans* (New Haven: Yale University Press, 2007).

Mack, Michael, *German Idealism and the Jew: The Inner Anti-Semitism of Philosophy and German Jewish Responses* (Chicago: University of Chicago Press, 2003).

Warner, Eric, 'New Light on the Family of Felix Mendelssohn', *Hebrew Union College Annual* 26 (1955), 543–65, esp. 555–6.

4

Lord Shaftesbury: Notice in The Times *(9 March 1840)*

Text

RESTORATION OF THE JEWS – A memorandum has been addressed to the Protestant monarchs of Europe on the subject of the restoration of the Jewish people to the land of Palestine. The document in question, dictated by the peculiar conjuncture of affairs in the East, and the other striking 'signs of the times,' reverts to the original covenant which secures that land to the descendants of Abraham, and urges upon the consideration of the powers addressed what may be the probable line of duty on the part of Protestant Christendom to the Jewish people in the present controversy in the East.

Source

Lord Shaftesbury, 'Restoration of the Jews', *The Times* (9 March 1840).

Commentary

Anthony Ashley Cooper, 7th Earl of Shaftesbury (1801–85), was a politician, renowned social reformer and influential early voice in Christian Zionism, sometimes known as 'restorationism', the belief that it is God's will that Jews should move to Palestine and thus facilitate Christ's Second Coming. Shaftesbury was influenced by Church of England evangelicals, as well as by Jewish converts to Christianity, both which groups believed that restorationism would lead to the conversion of Jews; Shaftesbury himself was president of the London Society for Promoting Christianity amongst the Jews from 1848 to his death. Shaftesbury's notice in *The Times* expresses his restorationist belief that God would restore His people Israel and return them to the Promised Land.

The origins of restorationism can be traced to the Puritans of the seventeenth century, when there was a desire to study the scriptures in their original language. While there was an abundance of Greek and Latin scholars, few knew Hebrew, and Puritans turned to Dutch rabbis for their Hebrew education. They soon rejected traditional replacement theology, reassessing the covenant and attitudes towards the Holy Land, concluding it was the home of the Jewish people and that God would ensure their return. Among the considerable consequences was the return of Jews to England in 1656 following the 1290 expulsion (see Chapter 4, p. 218).

The year before the *Times* notice, Shaftesbury had outlined his restorationist views in an article published in the *Quarterly Review* in which he discussed the relationship between Europe's Jews and Palestine. It is striking that the article makes no mention of the Muslim inhabitants of Palestine. Indeed, in a later diary note, dated 17 May 1854, Shaftesbury wrote of Palestine that 'there is a country without a nation; and God now, in his wisdom and mercy, directs us to a nation without a country', identifying the latter as 'His own loved, nay, still loved people, the sons of Abraham, Isaac and Jacob'. The phrase 'conjuncture of affairs' in the *Times* notice refers to the realignment of political power in the period before the outbreak of the Crimean War in 1854: Palestine was controlled by Muhammad Ali of Egypt, nominally reporting to the Sublime Porte, the central government of the Ottoman empire, but as pressure on the Ottomans grew and the end of their empire seemed to be approaching, advocacy of restorationism increased.

Although Shaftesbury supported the hopes of the Jewish people to return to Palestine and had a high personal regard for Jews, he opposed their admission to Parliament because of his commitment to Britain as a Christian nation. Nevertheless, he supported their admission to other civil offices that did not compromise Britain's profession of Christianity. Shaftesbury also argued that a Jewish return to Palestine would provide political and economic advantages to Britain and he persuaded Foreign Minister Palmerston (his father-in-law) to send a British consul to Jerusalem in 1838. Shaftesbury's hopes of enshrining the Jewish return in government policy were fulfilled in the Balfour Declaration in 1917, thirty-two years after his death (see Chapter 7, p. 337).

Bibliography

Clark, Victoria, *Allies for Armageddon* (New Haven: Yale University Press, 2007).
Endelman, Todd M., and Kushner, Tony (eds.), *Disraeli's Jewishness* (London: Vallentine Mitchell, 2002).
Lewis, Donald M., *The Origins of Christian Zionism* (Cambridge: Cambridge University Press, 2010).

5

The Jewish Question

Text

(i) Bruno Bauer: Die Judenfrage (The Jewish Question) (1843)

In history nothing stands outside the law of causality, least of all the Jews. With a stubbornness which their advocates themselves praise and admire they have clung to their nationality and resisted the movements and changes of history. The will of history is evolution, new forms, progress, change; the Jews want to stay forever what they are, therefore they fought against the first law of history – does this not prove that by pressing against this mighty spring they provoked counter-pressure? They were oppressed because they first pressed by placing themselves against the wheel of history.

Had the Jews been outside this action of the law of causality, had they been entirely passive, had they not from their side strained against the Christian world, there would not be any tie to connect them with history. They could never have entered into the new development of history and have influenced it. Then their cause would be quite lost.

Therefore, give the Jews the honor that they were to blame for the oppression which they suffered, that the hardening of their character caused by this oppression was their own fault [...]

Like the community of the believers, Israel boasts of a special privilege. Therefore, one privilege confronts another: one excludes the other. The Christian state is under the obligation to respect privileges, to protect them, to base its organization upon them. The Jew regards his special character as a privilege. Therefore, his only possible position in the Christian state is that of a privileged one, the Jews can only exist as a special corporation [...]

It had to happen, this epoch had to become a time of general suffering. The error had been that one thought emancipation possible while the privileges of the religious barriers remained standing, even acknowledged in the emancipation itself. The Jew received concessions as Jew, was allowed to continue to exist as a being segregated from all others, and this in itself made true emancipation impossible. Everybody still lacked courage to be simply a human being. Some privileges were sacrificed at that time, but the main privilege, the heavenly, god-given, supernatural privilege remained in force and this in turn must always generate all the others.

The emancipation of the Jews in a thoroughgoing, successful, safe manner will only be possible when they are emancipated not as Jews, that is as forever alien to the Christians, but as human beings who are no longer separated from their fellowmen by barriers which they wrongly consider to be all-important [...]

If the Jews want to become real – they cannot achieve it in their chimerical nationality, only in the real nations of our time living in history – then they have to give up the chimerical prerogative which will always alienate them from the other nations and history. They have to sacrifice their disbelief in the other nations and their exclusive belief in their own nationality. Only then will they be able to participate sincerely in national and state affairs.

Source

Bauer, Bruno, *The Jewish Problem*, ed. Ellis Rivkin, trans. Helen Lederer (Cincinnati: Hebrew Union College/Jewish Institute of Religion, 1958), 5–6, 61–4. (Originally published as *Die Judenfrage*, 1843.)

(ii) Karl Marx: Zur Judenfrage (On the Jewish Question) (1844)

It is on this point that [Bauer's] *one-sided* formulation of the Jewish question stands out.

It is by no means sufficient to ask: who should do the emancipating? who should be emancipated? There is a third thing that criticism has to do. It has to ask: what *sort of emancipation* is at issue? What conditions flow from the nature of the desired emancipation? [...]

[…]

The *political* emancipation of the Jews, of the Christians, of *religious* persons in general, is the *emancipation of the state* from Judaism, from Christianity, from *religion* in general. In its form, in a fashion proper to its nature, the state as *state* emancipates itself from religion in that it emancipates itself from *state religion*, i.e., in that the state as state acknowledges no religion, in that the state rather acknowledges itself as state. *Political* emancipation from religion is not the completed, contradiction-free emancipation from religion, because political emancipation is not the completed, contradiction-free form of *human* emancipation.

The restricted character of political emancipation immediately appears in the fact that the *state* can free itself of a limitation without the human being *truly* being free of it, in the fact that the state can be a *free state* without the man being *a free man* […]

[…]

Money is the jealous god of Israel, before which no other god can exist. Money humbles all of man's gods – and turns them into a commodity. Money is the universal *value* of all things, constituted for itself. It has therefore robbed the entire world, the world of man as well as nature, of their own value. Money is the estranged essence of man's labour and existence, and this estranged essence dominates him, and he worships it.

[…]

Judaism reaches its high point with the completion of civil society; but civil society first completes itself in the *Christian* world. Only under the authority of Christianity, which makes *all* national, natural, ethical, theoretical relationships *external* to man, can civil society fully separate itself from the life of the state, sunder all species-bonds of man and replace them with egoism, self-seeking need, and dissolve the world of man into a world of atomic, mutually hostile individuals.

[…]

In its completed praxis the Christian egoism of happiness is necessarily transformed into the material egoism of the Jew, heavenly need into worldly need, subjectivism into self-interest. The tenacity of the Jew is not to be explained by religion, but much rather by the human basis of his religion, by practical need and egoism.

Because the real essence of the Jew has been universally realised and secularised in civil society, civil society could not convince the Jew of the *unreality* of his *religious* essence, which is just the ideal view of practical need. Thus, not just in the Pentateuch or in the Talmud [but] in contemporary society do we find the essence of the contemporary Jew, not as an abstract but rather as a highly empirical being, not just as a limitation of the Jew but as the Jewish limitation of society.

As soon as society succeeds in abolishing the *empirical* essence of Judaism, i.e., haggling and its presuppositions, the Jew will become *impossible*, because his consciousness will no longer have an object, because the subjective basis of Judaism, practical need, will be humanised, because the conflict of individual sensuous existence with the species-existence of man will be superseded.

The *social* emancipation of the Jew is the *emancipation of society from Judaism*.

Source

O'Malley, Joseph, with Davis, Richard A. (ed. and trans.), *Marx: Early Political Writings*, Cambridge Texts in the History of Political Thought (Cambridge: Cambridge University Press, 1994), 31–2, 34, 54, 55, 56. (The square-bracketed '[but]' is part of the original.)

Commentary

Bruno Bauer (1809–82) and Karl Marx (1818–83) were two intellectuals among many who took part in discussions about *die Judenfrage*, literally 'the Jewish question' (but sometimes translated as 'the Jewish problem'). Bauer, philosopher, historian and theologian, argued in *Die Judenfrage* that Jews themselves were responsible for being persecuted and opposed the removal of anti-Jewish legal discrimination unless Jews first abandoned their religion. In *Zur Judenfrage*, his review article on Bauer's book and another of Bauer's publications, *Die Fähigkeit der heutigen Juden und Christen, frei zu werden* (*The Capacity of Contemporary Jews and Christians to Become Free*), Marx, philosopher, political theorist and revolutionary socialist, agreed with the criticism of Judaism but rejected Bauer's conclusion about Jewish emancipation. For Marx, Jewish emancipation could not take place by simply overcoming barriers of separation, which Jews themselves had erected.

These two documents were written when condescending language about Jews was commonplace, alongside renewed public interest in the 'Jewish question' prompted by the government of King Frederick William IV of Prussia (*r.* 1840–61) under which both Bauer and Marx lived at the time and which was considering the removal of civil and political restrictions. The reappearance of the ritual murder charge in Damascus in 1840 had also generated public interest and contributed to widespread antisemitic sentiment (see p. 293).

Bauer argued that state oppression of Jews was justified because Jewish practice, which he elsewhere called 'Jewish Jesuitism', meant that Jews could not coexist in the same state with another legal system. Jews must free themselves from their religion before they can claim political equality. Christianity did not fare much better in his view, although it was deemed the perfection of Judaism, demonstrating the highest stage in the development of religious consciousness. Christian universality broke with Jewish exclusiveness, which represented a 'war against humanity'. Only the complete abolition of all religious privileges, which would amount to the total revolution of religion itself, could ensure freedom and equality for Jews. The solution to *die Judenfrage* was for Jews to abandon their religion. As long as they continued Jewish practice, they were incapable of becoming free and equal citizens of the modern state.

For Marx, the key attributes of Judaism, which he portrayed using familiar antisemitic tropes, were not racial, religious or cultural but economic: it was in bourgeois society that 'the real essence of the Jew has been universally realised'. His answer to *die Judenfrage* was likewise to abolish Judaism, but he also attacked Christianity which, although originating out of Judaism, had, he argued, merged into it again. Judaism and Christianity became two sides of the same coin, which meant that the state needed to be emancipated from religion as a whole. Marx sought to secularise and abolish religion, which he famously described as 'the opium of the people'. Marx's rejection of the whole of Jewish and Christian tradition was influenced by Liberal Protestant writings which emphasised the centrality of Hellenism and non-Hebraic elements of European tradition: David Friedrich Strauss had recently published *The Life of Jesus* (1835) and Ludwig Feuerbach proposed a reversal of theological order by describing God as the creation of humankind in his *Das Wesen des Christenthums* (*Essence of Christianity*, 1841).

For both Bauer and Marx, as long as Jews insisted on maintaining a religion that claimed sovereignty, they could not gain citizenship. The idea of a chosen people ('Israel boasts of a special privilege', according to Bauer) made Judaism not only anti-social but anti-historical as well. Christianity as the majority religion could not help but oppress Jews as a foreign element in the body of the nation.

The writings of Bauer and Marx, and the discussions they provoked, led to a number of German Jews going into print, notably Abraham Geiger and Samuel Raphael Hirsch, who sought to refute views that were not only hostile to religion in general but contemptuous of Jews and Judaism in particular.

Bibliography

Leopold, David, 'The Hegelian Antisemitism of Bruno Bauer', *History of European Ideas* 25, no. 4 (1999), 179–206.

Peled, Yoav, 'From Theology to Sociology: Bruno Bauer and Karl Marx on the Question of Jewish Emancipation', *History of Political Thought* 13 (1992), 463–85.

Stedman Jones, Gareth, *Karl Marx: Greatness and Illusion* (Cambridge, MA: Harvard University Press, 2016).

6

Richard Wagner: Das Judenthum in der Musik (Judaism in Music) *(September 1850)*

Text

The Jew, who is innately incapable of enouncing himself to us artistically through either his outward appearance or his speech, and least of all through his singing, has nevertheless been able in the widest-spread of modern art-varieties, to wit in Music, to reach the rulership of public taste. – To explain to ourselves this phenomenon, let us first consider *how* it grew possible to the Jew to become a musician.

From that turning-point in our social evolution where Money, with less and less disguise, was raised to the virtual patent of nobility, the Jews – to whom money-making without actual labour, i.e., Usury, had been left as their only trade – the Jews not merely could no longer be denied the diploma of a new society that needed naught but gold, but they brought it with them in their pockets. Wherefore our modern Culture, accessible to no one but the well-to-do, remained the less a closed book to them, as it had sunk into a venal article of Luxury. Henceforward, then, the *cultured Jew* appears in our

Society; his distinction from the uncultured, the common Jew, we now have closely to observe. The cultured Jew has taken the most indicible pains to strip off all the obvious tokens of his lower co-religionists: in many a case he has even held it wise to make a Christian baptism wash away the traces of his origin. This zeal, however, has never got so far as to let him reap the hoped-for fruits: it has conducted only to his utter isolation, and to making him the most heartless of all human beings; to such a pitch, that we have been bound to lose even our earlier sympathy for the tragic history of his stock. His connexion with the former comrades in his suffering, which he arrogantly tore asunder, it has stayed impossible for him to replace by a new connexion with that society whereto he has soared up. He stands in correlation with none but those who need his money: and never yet has money thriven to the point of knitting a goodly bond 'twixt man and man. Alien and apathetic stands the educated Jew in midst of a society he does not understand, with whose tastes and aspirations he does not sympathise, whose history and evolution have always been indifferent to him.

Source

Wagner, Richard, *Judaism in Music and Other Essays*, trans. William Ashton Ellis (Lincoln, NE and London: University of Nebraska Press, 1995), 87–8.

Commentary

The German composer Richard Wagner (1813–83) was a virulent antisemite, as demonstrated by his essay *Das Judenthum in der Musik* (*Judaism in Music*), from which our document is excerpted. He argued that Jews were innately avaricious, sought world domination and were unassimilable. His writings were later adopted and promoted by the Nazis. He became known as Hitler's favourite composer, and Bayreuth, the opera house Wagner built for his own operas, was called Hitler's court theatre by the novelist Thomas Mann.

Judaism in Music was published anonymously in the music journal *Neue Zeitschrift für Musik* in 1850, but Wagner was soon rumoured to be its author and added his name to the second and expanded edition (1869). In it he condemned the Jewish composer Giacomo Meyerbeer, even though he had viewed Wagner as his protégé, and Felix Mendelssohn, despite the latter's conversion to Christianity and the fact that his compositions explored Christian themes, as for example in the oratorio *St Paul*. For Wagner, they polluted German music, their compositions were shallow and artificial, and they remained an alien presence within German society and culture.

Wagner's antisemitism was obsessive: in 1851 he wrote to the composer Franz Liszt that his hatred of Jews was 'as necessary to my nature as gall is to the blood'. He even denied that Jesus was a Jew and referred to a synagogue service as a 'nonsensical gurgling, yodeling, and cackling'. Nevertheless, he had some Jewish friends and admirers such as Angelo Neumann, who arranged for his operas to be performed in Europe, and two of the twelve pallbearers at his funeral were Jewish.

Although he lived at a time when antisemitism was common, the reason Wagner remains controversial is his connection in the public mind to the rise of Hitler and, consequently, to the Holocaust, even though both took place more than forty years after his death. There's no doubt that the Nazis adopted Wagner to give credibility to their removal of Jews from the annals of German history and culture. Yet as Jacob Katz, in the conclusion of his book *The Darker Side of Genius*, and a number of subsequent scholars have suggested, attempts to blame Wagner for Hitler are at best questionable.

Wagner's music was banned by Jews in Palestine after Kristallnacht (1938) and remains rarely played in Israel. In 1992 Daniel Barenboim announced a Wagner concert by the Israel Philharmonic, but it was cancelled after protests. The first public performance of Wagner's music in Israel was in 2000, when Holocaust survivor Mendi Rodan conducted *Siegfried Idyll* in Rishon LeZion, and in 2001 a concert conducted by Barenboim in Tel Aviv included as an encore an extract from *Tristan und Isolde*, which divided the audience between applause and protest.

Unsurprisingly, Wagner remains a subject of controversy in Jewish–Christian relations and there is still a tendency to tread carefully when his works are performed.

Bibliography

Brener, Milton E., *Richard Wagner and the Jews* (Jefferson, NC and London: McFarland & Co., 2006).

HaCohen, Ruth, *The Music Libel against the Jews* (New Haven and London: Yale University Press, 2011).

Katz, Jacob, *The Darker Side of Genius: Richard Wagner's Anti-Semitism* (Hanover, NH and London: University Press of New England for Brandeis University Press, 1986).

Weiner, Marc A., *Richard Wagner and the Anti-Semitic Imagination* (Lincoln, NE and London: University of Nebraska Press, 1997).

7

George Eliot: Daniel Deronda *(1876)*

Text

Deronda himself, with all his masculine instruction, had been roused by this apparition of Mirah to the consciousness of knowing hardly anything about modern Judaism or the inner Jewish history. The Chosen People have been commonly treated as a people chosen for the sake of somebody else; and their thinking as something (no matter exactly what) that ought to have been entirely otherwise; and Deronda, like his neighbours, had regarded Judaism as a sort of eccentric fossilized form, which an accomplished man might dispense with studying, and leave to specialists. But Mirah, with her terrified flight from one parent, and her yearning after the other, had flashed on him the hitherto neglected reality that Judaism was something still throbbing in human lives, still making for them the only conceivable vesture of the world; and in the idling excursion on which he immediately afterwards set out with Sir Hugo he began to look for the outsides of synagogues, and the titles of books about the Jews. This wakening of a new interest – this passing from the supposition that we hold the right opinions on a subject we are careless about, to a sudden care for it, and a sense that our opinions were ignorance – is an effectual remedy for *ennui*, which, unhappily cannot be secured on a physician's prescription; but Deronda had carried it with him, and endured his weeks of lounging all the better. It was on this journey that he first entered a Jewish synagogue – at Frankfort – where his party rested on a Friday […]

[Deronda said to Mirah] 'I went to the synagogue at Frankfort before I came home, and the service impressed me just as much as if I had followed the words – perhaps more.'

'Oh, was it great to you? Did it go to your heart?' said Mirah, eagerly. 'I thought none but our people would feel that. I thought it was all shut away like a river in a deep valley, where only heaven saw – I mean –' she hesitated, feeling that she could not disentangle her thought from its imagery.

'I understand,' said Deronda. 'But there is not really such a separation – deeper down, as Mrs Meyrick says. Our religion is chiefly a Hebrew religion; and since Jews are men, their religious feelings must have much in common with those of other men – just as their poetry, though in one sense peculiar, has a great deal in common with the poetry of other nations. Still it is to be expected that a Jew would feel the forms of his people's religion more than one of another race – and yet' – here Deronda hesitated in his turn – 'that is perhaps not always so.'

'Ah no,' said Mirah, sadly. 'I have seen that. I have seen them mock. Is it not like mocking your parents? – like rejoicing in your parents' shame?'

'Some minds naturally rebel against whatever they were brought up in, and like the opposite; they see the faults in what is nearest to them,' said Deronda apologetically.

'But you are not like that,' said Mirah, looking at him with unconscious fixedness.

'No, I think not,' said Deronda; 'but you know I was not brought up as a Jew.'

'Ah, I am always forgetting,' said Mirah, with a look of disappointed recollection, and slightly blushing.

Deronda also felt rather embarrassed, and there was an awkward pause, which he put an end to by saying playfully –

'Whichever way we take it, we have to tolerate each other; for if we all went in opposition to our teaching, we must end in difference, just the same.'

'To be sure. We should go on for ever in zigzags,' said Mrs Meyrick. 'I think it is very weak-minded to make your creed up by the rule of contrary. Still one may honour one's parents, without following their notions exactly, any more than the exact cut of their clothing. My father was a Scotch Calvinist and my mother was a French Calvinist; I am neither quite Scotch, nor quite French, nor two Calvinists rolled into one, yet I honour my parents' memory.'

'But I could not make myself not a Jewess,' said Mirah, insistently, 'even if I changed my belief.'

'No, my dear. But if Jews and Jewesses went on changing their religion, and making no difference between themselves and Christians, there would come a time when there would be no Jews to be seen' said Mrs Meyrick, taking that consummation very cheerfully.

'Oh, please not to say that,' said Mirah, the tears gathering. 'It is the first unkind thing you ever said. I will not begin that. I will never separate myself from my mother's people. I was forced to fly from my father; but if he came back in age and weakness and want, and needed me, should I say, "This is not my father?" [sic] If he had shame, I must share it. It was he who was given to me for my father, and not another. And so it is with my people. I will always be a Jewess. I will love Christians when they are good, like you. But I will always cling to my people. I will always worship with them.'

As Mirah had gone on speaking she had become possessed with a sorrowful passion – fervent, not violent. Holding her little hands tightly clasped and looking at Mrs Meyrick with beseeching, she seemed to Deronda a personification of that spirit which impelled men after a long inheritance of professed Catholicism to leave wealth and high place, and risk their lives in flight, that they might join their own people and say, 'I am a Jew.'

Source

Eliot, George, *Daniel Deronda* (London: William Blackwood and Sons, 1876), 291–2, 314–17.

Commentary

George Eliot (1819–80), a pseudonym for Mary Ann Evans, was a novelist raised as an evangelical, who later became a freethinker, questioning the accuracy of the Bible and the value of church doctrine. Eliot maintained a lifelong interest in Judaism, epitomised by the novel *Daniel Deronda* in which the Jewish characters are created from real-life encounters, notably her friendship with Jewish rabbinic scholar Immanuel Deutsch, who died three years before its publication.

Eliot's depiction of Jews contrasted strongly with those in other nineteenth-century novels, such as Dickens' *Oliver Twist* (1838) or George du Maurier's *Trilby* (1894), and was published during a time when restorationism had a strong following. The novel impacted some early Zionists, Jewish and Christian, and among those who acknowledged its influence were Eliezer ben-Yehudah, author of the first modern Hebrew dictionary; the American Jewish poet Emma Lazarus; Henrietta Szold, founder of Hadassah, the Women's Zionist Organization of America; and the early Christian Zionists William Hechler and Laurence Oliphant.

One of the central characters of the novel, modelled on Deutsch, is Mordecai Cohen, who advocates a Jewish return to Palestine, pre-empting Theodor Herzl (see document 13) when he states, 'Let there be another great migration, another choosing of Israel to be a nationality!' Three streets in the Israeli cities of Haifa, Tel-Aviv and Jerusalem are named after George Eliot.

Our excerpt, however, explores another topic in Jewish–Christian relations: negative Christian stereotypes of Jews. This is illustrated by Daniel Deronda himself, who moves away from the traditional view of Judaism as 'a sort of eccentric fossilized form'. As a result of his relationship with Mirah, he comes to realise that Christianity is not so different from Judaism, acknowledging that 'Our religion is chiefly a Hebrew religion', a statement that anticipated later positive Christian engagement with Jews (e.g., Marc Boegner's declaration, 'I know that the Church of Jesus Christ is the daughter of what it calls the ancient Church of Israel'; see Chapter 7, p. 362).

Daniel was raised by Sir Hugo Mallinger who, the reader assumes, was his father, and the novel explores Daniel's personal journey. He rescues Mirah Lapidoth, a young Jewish woman who has returned to London to search for her mother and brother, from an attempt to drown herself. Daniel takes Mirah to live with his friends the Meyricks, who welcome her into their home, treating her with respect and care, offering refuge and food. Hearing her story, Deronda is sympathetic and vows to help her.

During a search for her long-lost relatives, he is introduced to Judaism and Jewish practice. Mirah and Daniel grow close, and eventually Daniel meets his mother and learns that she was a Jewish opera singer whom Sir Hugo once loved and who asked Sir Hugo to raise her son as an Englishman, never to know that he was Jewish. Upon learning his origins, Daniel finally feels comfortable with his love for Mirah, and they marry.

The novel thus presents an idealised image of Jewish life, reversing the traditional plot of Jewish conversion to Christianity, at once distinguishing 'Jews' and 'Englishmen' and yet also arguing for their affinity.

Bibliography

Cheyette, Bryan, *Constructions of 'the Jew' in English Literature and Society: Racial Representations, 1875–1945* (Cambridge: Cambridge University Press, 1993), 13–54.
Himmelfarb, Gertrude, *The Jewish Odyssey of George Eliot* (New York: Encounter Books, 2009).
Shalvi, Alice, *Daniel Deronda: A Centenary Symposium* (Jerusalem: Jerusalem Academic Press, 1976).

8

La Civiltà Cattolica: *Excerpts from a Series of Articles on Jews and Blood Libel Allegations (1881–2)*

Text

Aug 20, 1881 [...]
The practice of killing children for the Paschal Feast is now very rare in the more cultivated parts of Europe, more frequent in Eastern Europe, and common, all too common, in the East properly so called. [In the West, the Jews] have now other things to think of

than to make their unleavened bread with Christian blood, occupied as they are in ruling almost like kings in finance and journalism.

Dec 3, 1881 [...]
It remains therefore generally proved ... that the sanguinary Paschal rite ... is a general law binding on the consciences of all Hebrews to make use of the blood of a Christian child, primarily for the sanctification of their souls, and also, although secondarily, to bring shame and disgrace to Christ and to Christianity.

Jan 21, 1882 [...]
Opinions of the Hebrew casuists in the Middle Ages differed, as they do now, not about the substance but about the accidents of the sanguinary Pascal rites ... Some hold that the blood of a child is essential, others, as we shall see, think that the blood of an adult is sufficient.

Feb 4, 1882 [...]
In the century which invented printing, discovered America, revived literature and science, half of Europe was full of ... Masters in Israel who bought and sold and made use of Christian blood for their piety and devotion. But now the light has been thrown on these deeds which we know even more about than our ancestors did.

Feb 18, 1882 [...]
In Hebrew Jubilee years, the fresh blood of a child is essential; in ordinary years the dried blood will do.

Mar 4, 1882 [...]
Every practising Hebrew worthy of that name is obliged even now, in conscience, to use in food, in drink, in circumcision, and in various other rites of his religious and civil life the fresh or dried blood of a Christian child, under the pain of infringing his laws and passing among his acquaintants for a bad Hebrew. How all this is still true and faithfully observed in the present century, we shall see, God willing, with all the evidence, in the next installment of our correspondence.

Source

Hay, Malcolm, *Europe and the Jews* (Chicago: Academy Chicago, 1992), 415–17.

Commentary

La Civiltà Cattolica (*Catholic Civilisation*) is a Jesuit periodical first published in 1850, soon after the restoration of the Society of Jesus in 1814. Ironically, a number of Jewish converts were among the leading figures in the restoration, but within a few decades both the Society and the journal became known for a conservative rejection of 'modernism' as well as for numerous antisemitic articles, of which our excerpt is one example. It accuses Jews of the blood libel and ritual murder as well as of controlling society (the latter hinted at by the reference to Jews 'ruling almost like kings in finance and journalism').

Our focus is on the blood libel accusations against Jews, which have a long history (although ironically early Christians were also accused of eating human flesh, as reported by Tertullian in the third century CE). Anti-Jewish accusations spread from England in the eleventh century (William of Norwich is an early example; see Chapter 4, p. 196) and were found throughout Europe by the seventeenth century, both in popular Christian imagination and in theological writings such as the antisemitic works of Johann Eisenmenger (1654–1704), whose *Entdecktes Judenthum* (*Judaism Unmasked*, 1700; translated in 1732–4 as *The Traditions of the Jews*) influenced modern 'scientific' antisemitism (see p. 292). The *La Civiltà Cattolica* documents are taken from a multipart series and, following the *adversus Judaeos* tradition, associate the blood libel with the observance of Passover and Easter. The accusation is that Jews kill a young Christian boy and use his blood in the ritual preparation of unleavened bread (*matzah*) for Passover (termed the Paschal Feast).

Despite regular rejection by both ecclesiastical leaders such as the thirteenth-century pope Innocent IV and secular rulers such as Innocent's contemporary Emperor Frederick II, ritual murder accusations remained rife, and although they began to subside in western and central Europe in the sixteenth century – perhaps partly due to the rise of Lutheranism (which rejected transubstantiation, thus undermining the theological underpinnings of the blood libel) and to the emergence of Christian scholars who could read Jewish texts in Hebrew – they continued into the modern period. The accusation held particular sway in Catholic Europe, especially in the Polish Lithuanian Commonwealth where the bulk of Europe's Jews lived in the seventeenth century. As Jews migrated eastward due to expulsions from the west, so too did the blood libel, hence the reference in our excerpt to its being 'more frequent in Eastern Europe, and common, all too common, in the East properly so called'.

Recent research highlights the way the blood libel held the imagination of Catholic clergy and laity in eastern Europe while it was in decline in the west, as illustrated by the Damascus blood libel accusation in 1840, when Jews were falsely accused of the ritual murder of a local priest, Father Thomas. As our excerpts demonstrate, during the nineteenth century ritual murder accusations experienced a resurgence in central Europe, a fact which historians attribute to the emergence of modern antisemitism. Blood libel accusations continued into more recent times, including, unsurprisingly, under the Nazis.

La Civiltà Cattolica's approach to Jewish–Christian relations has changed dramatically since the 1880s, and during Vatican II it was the German Jesuit Augustin Bea who was among the key promoters of the changes in church teaching that led to *Nostra aetate* (see Appendix to Part III, p. 512).

Bibliography

Bernauer, James, and Maryks, Robert A. (eds.), '*The Tragic Couple': Encounters between Jews and Jesuits* (Leiden and Boston: Brill, 2014).

Dundes, Alan (ed.), *The Blood Libel Legend: A Casebook in Anti-Semitic Folklore* (Madison: University of Wisconsin Press, 1991).

9

Vladimir Soloviev: 'The Jews and the Christian Question' (1884)

Text

The fortunes of the Hebrew nation, in our view, are connected chiefly with three facts of their history. The first fact is that Christ was a Jew on his Mother's side and Christianity came out of Judaism; the second fact is that the greater part of the Jewish people rejected Christ and took a decidedly hostile position with respect to Christianity; the third fact is that the chief part of the Hebrew nation and the religious center of recent Judaism is not in Western Europe, but in two Slavic countries – Russia and Poland. The first of these facts – the Incarnation of Christ in Judea – defined the *past* of Israel – its original designation as God's chosen people; the second fact – the nonacknowledgment of Christ by the Jews and their alienation from Christianity – defines the *present* situation of Judaism in the world, its temporary rejection; finally, the third fact – the population of Israel on Slavic soil among nations that have not yet spoken their piece to the world – forecasts the *future* fortunes of Judaism, the ultimate restoration of its religious significance. Former Judaism lived by faith and hope for a *promised* God-manhood; present Judaism lives in protest and enmity to the unacknowledged Messiah God-man, the *seed* of God-manhood on earth; future Judaism will live a full life when it finds and acknowledges in a renewed Christianity the image of a *perfected* God-manhood.

This hope has the firmest foundation in the word of God. Yahweh preselected Israel, concluded a covenant with it, made it a promise. Yahweh is not a man to be deceived, and not a Son of Man to repent of His promises. A part of the Israelite nation rejected the first appearance of the Messiah and for this suffers a difficult requital, but only for a time, for the word of God can not be violated; and this word of the Old Testament, which is resolutely confirmed in the New Testament through the lips of the Apostle to the Gentiles, clearly and incontestably says: *all Israel will be saved*.

The Jews who demanded the death of Christ cried: 'His blood be on us and on our children' [Mt. 27:25]. But this blood is the *blood of redemption*. And the cry of human evil is surely insufficiently powerful to silence the Divine word of remission: 'Father, forgive them, for they know not what they do' [Lk 23:34]. The bloodthirsty mob that gathered at Golgotha consisted of Jews; but Jews were also those three thousand and then five thousand people who, according to the preaching of the Apostle Peter, were baptized and comprised the original Christian church. Anna and Caiaphas were Jews, as were Joseph and Nicodemus. To one and the same people belonged both Judas, who betrayed Christ to Crucifixion, and Peter and Andrew, who themselves were crucified for Christ. Thomas, who disbelieved the Resurrection, was a Jew; he did not cease being a Jew when he believed in the Resurrected One and said to Him: 'My Lord and My God!' [Jn 20:28]. Saul, the most terrible persecutor of Christians, was a Jew, and as Paul, who, persecuted for Christianity and 'having labored more abundantly than all' [1 Cor 15:10] for it, remained a Jew among Jews. And what is greater and more important than everything else, He Himself, the God-man Christ, who was betrayed and killed by Jews, in human body and soul was the most faultless Jew.

In view of this striking fact is it not strange for us to condemn all Jewish people, to which Christ himself inalienably belongs as well – *in the name of Christ*? And is this not especially strange on the part of those among us, who, if not directly renouncing Christ, in any case do not manifest in any way their connection to Him?

If Christ is not God, then the Jews are no more guilty than the Hellenes who killed Socrates. If we acknowledge Christ as God, then it is necessary to acknowledge in the Jews a *God-generating* nation. Romans are together with Jews to blame for the death of Jesus; but His birth belongs only to God and to Israel. Jews, they say, are the constant enemies of Christianity; however, not Jews, not Semites, but those who were born Christians of the Aryan tribe stand at the head of the anti-Christian movement of the last few centuries. The denial of Christianity and the struggle against it on the part of several thinkers of Jewish descent has a more honest and more religious character than on the part of writers who came out of the midst of Christianity. Better Spinoza than Voltaire, better Joseph Salvador than Mr. Ernst Renan.

To despise Judaism is insane; to quarrel with Jews is useless; it is better to comprehend Judaism, although this is more difficult. It is difficult to comprehend Judaism because those three great facts with which its fortunes are connected do not appear as something simple, natural, and comprehensible in and of themselves. They have need of specific and complex elucidation. These three facts are at the same time three questions, three problems for resolution:

1 Why was Christ a Jew? Why take the cornerstone of the universal church from the house of Israel?
2 Why did the greater part of Israel not acknowledge its Messiah? Why did the Old Testament church not dissolve in the New Testament church? Why do the majority of Jews prefer to be entirely without a temple rather than to enter into the Christian temple?
3 Finally, why and for the sake of what have the sturdiest (in a religious sense) parts of the Jewish people been thrust into Russia and Poland, set on the border of the Greco-Slavic and Latin-Slavic world?

Let them deny and lessen the significance of this last fact. Let the haters of Jews relative to the second point as well find it natural that such an unfit and unscrupulous nation renounced and killed Christ; but then let them also explain why Christ belonged precisely to this nation. On the other hand, if one finds to the contrary the first fact – Christ belonging to the nation of Israel, predesignated and chosen for this from the beginning – to be comprehensible, then in this case how can we explain this chosen nation turning out to be unworthy of election *precisely in the purpose for which* it was chosen?

Source

Soloviev, Vladimir S., *Freedom, Faith, and Dogma: Essays by V. S. Soloviev on Christianity and Judaism*, ed. and trans. Vladimir Wozniuk (Albany: State University of New York Press, 2008), 47–9. (Square-bracketed references are part of the original.)

Commentary

Vladimir Soloviev (1853–1900) was a Russian Orthodox Christian philosopher and political thinker who wrote about Judaism and Jewish–Christian relations and studied Hebrew (biblical and Mishnaic) as well as Kabbalah. This excerpt from an 1884 article presents his reflections on the significance of the Jewishness of Jesus and the early church, in which he famously called Jews a '*God-generating* nation'. He explores reasons for the Jewish rejection of Jesus, condemns Christian antisemitic attitudes and actions, and highlights the significance of so many Jews living in Slavic lands. In his later writings ('Three Discussions' and 'A Short Story on the Anti-Christ', both 1899), he describes Jews as joining Christians in a battle against the antichrist, together with their return to the Holy Land. He was influential on later Jewish thinkers such as Simon Dubnov (1860–1941) and Abraham Kook (1865–1935), chief rabbi of Palestine, as well as Orthodox Christian philosophers Nikolai Berdyaev (1874–1948), Sergei Bulgakov (1871–1944) and even the antisemitic Vasily Rozanov (1856–1919). He also influenced modern Russian Orthodox priests actively engaged in fostering better relations with Jews and Judaism, such as Sergei Hackel (1931–2005) and Alexander Men (1935–90).

The number of Jews who lived in Russia increased significantly from the late eighteenth century – a result of the growing Russian empire, which included 1 million Jews in Belarus, Lithuania and Ukraine alone. By the beginning of the twentieth century, about 5 million Jews, half the world's Jewish population, were located in Russia, most restricted by law to the Pale of Settlement (legislation which remained in place until 1917).

Alexander II (*r*. 1855–81) reversed the harsh anti-Jewish measures of his father, and Jews began to assimilate into Russian society, a period of reform which overlapped with Soloviev's formative years. However, Alexander's assassination in 1881 led to a wave of pogroms – not by chance a Russian loanword into English – and antisemitism returned to the norm in Orthodox writings and in Russian society in general. Soloviev condemned the anti-Jewish violence as well as tropes such as 'God-killers' and 'enemies of Christ'. Jews, such as Mendel Beilis (see documents 17 (i), (ii) and (ii)), were accused of killing Christian children at Passover to use their blood for *matzah* and were also considered guilty of Christ's crucifixion, a belief reinforced by Orthodox Good Friday services. In such a milieu there was a ready welcome for the *Protocols of the Elders of Zion*, which first appeared in 1903 under Russian auspices and on Russian soil (see p. 292).

The title of Soloviev's article betrays his idea that there is no 'Jewish question' as such in Russia; rather, the failure of Russians to treat Jews fairly makes this a 'Christian Question', due to the failure of Christians to live up to the demands of Christianity. While he takes it for granted that Jewish suffering is a result of Jews' rejection of Christianity, God's selection of the Jewish people was deliberate because they attracted favour by an innate faith, intense personality and 'sacred materialism' (Rubin 2010: 32). This did not prevent Soloviev from condemning Jews who lived at the time of Jesus, but he was equally condemnatory of Russian Christians, especially Christian nationalists.

Bibliography

Halperin, Jean, 'Vladimir Soloviev Listens to Israel: The Christian Question', *Immanuel: Orthodox Christians and Jews on Continuity and Renewal* 26 (1994), 198–210.

Kornblatt Deutsch, Judith, 'Vladimir Solov'ev on Spiritual Nationhood, Russia and the Jews', *Russian Review* 56 (April 1997), 157–77.

Rubin, Dominic, *Holy Russia, Sacred Israel: Jewish–Christian Encounters in Russian Religious Thought* (Boston: Academic Studies Press, 2010).

Solovyov, Vladimir, *The Burning Bush: Writings on Jews and Judaism*, ed., trans. and with commentary by Gregory Glazov (Notre Dame: University of Notre Dame Press, 2016).

10

Heinrich Graetz: 'Judaism and Biblical Criticism' (5 August 1887)

Text

Judaism is a healthy religion and cannot be affected by the diseases that threaten Protestantism and Christianity. Its adherents need not yet look out for a new basis for their faith, as Mr. Henriques recommends, because he regards its present foundation as undermined.

I go still further and contend that so far from Judaism being capable of suffering from critical inquiries, it would gain in trustworthiness and power of conviction. It is true that if it were like Christianity in its two chief or many subsidiary forms as a belief or a dogma, then it might be endangered by the attacks of criticism, but luckily it is neither a belief nor a dogma. The fundamental dogma of Christian [*sic*] is that of a Divine man, and this rests entirely on the resurrection of Jesus. Biblical criticism showing that the proofs for this belief in the New Testament are full of contradictions, and that the Resurrection, as many Christian scholars grant, is a fact of only the slightest probability, or in other words, unhistorical, while physiology and biology have established beyond all question the law that the corpse even of the most gifted soul could not live again in a human form, the whole edifice of faith would fall together and all that remains is either *credo quia absurdum* [I believe it because it is absurd] or the most radical unbelief.

It is far otherwise with Judaism. If all the miraculous stories in the Old Testament were put down as the legendary creations of imagination or to conscious poetical fancy, still much, very much, would remain that can be regarded as truth. The essential fact remains of the recognition of the unity and lofty holiness of God; from this follows the demand for a holy life for His servants, for the love of our neighbours, and care for the stranger, the widow, and the orphan; in short, for the lofty ethics which Judaism posits as its ideal, and of which the Ten Commandments offer a short summary. This essential germ of Judaism cannot be affected by doubts as to the historic reality of the narratives in which it is embodied [...] Nor can the rites of Judaism, such as the Sabbath, festivals, dietary laws, &c., insofar as they are contained in the Biblical book, be really attacked with success by Biblical criticism [...]

But a sound and positive criticism can do much to aid it [Judaism]. Christianity possesses a uniform set of literary sources from the Gospels to Revelation. If a single one of these is proved unhistorical, the remainder fall to pieces. It is far otherwise with Judaism. Besides the Pentateuch and the historical books it has others whose genuineness and authenticity no critic dares to impugn, the Prophets from the earliest Amos to the latest Malachi, and besides these the Psalms, Proverbs, and other works. These contain references to the historic events of earlier times, and, rightly understood, fully confirm the historical narratives in the Pentateuch and other books. The deeper one penetrates into the spirit of the greater Prophets, the more-confirmed becomes the historical truth of the remaining Scriptures. We have then a wide field for Biblical criticism which produces a richer harvest the more rigidly it is exercised. Such a criticism does not destroy, it builds afresh.

Source

Graetz, Heinrich, 'Judaism and Biblical Criticism', *The Jewish Chronicle* (5 August 1887), 9.

Commentary

Heinrich Graetz (1817–91), a German-Jewish historian and Bible scholar, was one of the first to write a comprehensive modern history of the Jewish people. His eleven-volume *Geschichte der Juden von den ältesten Zeiten bis auf die Gegenwart* (1853–76), published in a condensed English version as *History of the Jews* (1891–8), was translated into many languages and generated wide interest in Jewish history among Christians as well as Jews. Graetz's emphasis on suffering perpetrated by Christians was later characterised by social historian Salo Baron (1895–1989) as a 'lachrymose conception of Jewish history'. Graetz's *History* also emphasised Jewish ethics and intellectual achievement, and he followed in the footsteps of Moses Mendelssohn (see Chapter 5, p. 278) in arguing that Judaism, unlike Christianity, was a religion of reason.

In our document, an excerpt from an article published in the *Jewish Chronicle* and therefore written primarily for a Jewish audience, Graetz discusses the discipline of biblical criticism, which was influential at the time. This consisted of lower criticism, which examined the biblical text, comparing and correcting it with ancient manuscripts, and higher criticism, which inquired into the authorship and dates of different biblical books and weighed their value as historical documents. Biblical criticism was viewed by many Christians and Jews as threatening because it appeared to undermine the authority of the Old and New Testaments.

The discipline had been used by some Christians, especially German Liberal Protestant scholars such as Julius Wellhausen (1844–1918), to direct their criticism at Judaism in particular by, for example, arguing that the latest strata of the Pentateuch reflected a degeneration of Jewish spirituality into a compulsively legalistic fixation, later abolished by Jesus. These views were taken to an extreme by some Christian scholars in the Nazi period, notably Gerhard Kittel (see Chapter 7, p. 353) and were designated the 'Higher Antisemitism' by Solomon Schechter (1847–1915), one of a number of Jews who equated biblical criticism with antisemitism. Graetz himself was a target of antisemitic attacks, including from the extreme nationalist historian Heinrich von Treitschke (1834–96), who was critical of Catholics, Poles and socialists as well as Jews. Von Treitschke accused Graetz of a hatred of Christianity.

In our document, Graetz argued that biblical criticism was more of a threat to Christianity than to Judaism because of the former's reliance on dogma and belief in the Resurrection. For Graetz, if biblical criticism successfully undermined one aspect of Christianity, the edifice of faith would collapse. Christians were correct, he implied, to be concerned about the effects of the discipline. Jews had less to worry about, although he was aware that some (epitomised by Basil Henriques, mentioned in the excerpt) were wary. Biblical criticism, he argued, was non-threatening to Judaism because it was a rational religion, the purpose of which was to disseminate ethical values to the world and to be the sole bearer of monotheism. An emphasis on the universal ethics of Judaism allowed Graetz to accept many of the results of modern biblical scholarship. In this he was followed by, among others, Claude Montefiore (see document 15).

This excerpt, and Graetz's writings as a whole, are influenced by the Enlightenment tradition and the assumption that there was one universal truth, attainable by reason, in which all might share, Jew and Christian alike. Yet, since dogma was uncertain, only the truths of reason, including ethics, were assured.

Bibliography

Barton, John, 'Jewish and Christian Approaches to Biblical Theology', in Bakker, Arjen F., Bloch, René, Fisch, Yael, Fredriksen, Paula, and Najman, Hindy (eds.), *Protestant Bible Scholarship: Anti-Semitism, Philo-Semitism and Anti-Judaism* (Leiden and Boston: Brill, 2022), 200–16.

Brenner, Michael, 'Between Religion and Nation: Graetz and His Construction of Jewish History', in *Prophets of the Past: Interpreters of Jewish History*, trans. Steven Rendall (Princeton: Princeton University Press, 2010), 53–91.

Graetz, Heinrich, *The Structure of Jewish History, and Other Essays*, ed., trans. and intro. Ismar Schorsch (New York: Jewish Theological Seminary of America, 1975).

11

Adolf von Harnack: What Is Christianity? *(1899–1900)*

Text

'What do you want with your Christ,' we are asked, principally by Jewish scholars; 'he introduced nothing new.' I answer with Wellhausen: it is quite true that what Jesus proclaimed, what John the Baptist expressed before him in his exhortation to repentance, was also to be found in the prophets, and even in the Jewish tradition of their time. The

Pharisees themselves were in possession of it; but unfortunately they were in possession of much else besides. With them it was weighted, darkened, distorted, rendered ineffective and deprived of its force, by a thousand things which they also held to be religious and every whit as important as mercy and judgment. They reduced everything to one dead level, wove everything into one fabric; the good and holy was only one woof in a broad earthly warp. You ask again, then: 'What was there that was new?' The question is out of place in a monotheistic religion. Ask rather: 'Had what was here proclaimed any strength and any vigour?' I answer: Take the people of Israel and search the whole history of their religion; take history generally, and where would you find any message about God and the good that was ever so pure and so full of strength – for purity and strength go together – as we hear and read of in the Gospels? As regards purity, the spring of holiness had, indeed, long been opened; but it was choked with sand and dirt, and its water was polluted. For the rabbis and theologians to come afterwards and distil this water, even if they were successful, makes no difference. But now the spring burst forth afresh, and broke and broke a new way for itself through the rubbish – through the rubbish which priests and theologians had heaped up so as to smother the true element in religion; for how often does it happen in history that theology is only the instrument by which religion is discarded! The other element was that of strength. Pharisaical teachers had proclaimed that everything was contained in the injunction to love God and one's neighbour. They spoke excellently; the words might have come out of Jesus' mouth. But what was the result of their language? That the nation, that in particular their own pupils, condemned the man who took the words seriously. All that they did was weak and, because weak, harmful. Words effect nothing; it is the power of the personality that stands behind them. But he 'taught as one having authority and not as the Scribes.' Such was the impression of him which his disciples received. His words became to them 'the words of life,' seeds which sprang up and bore fruit. That was what was new.

Source

Harnack, Adolf von, *What Is Christianity?*, trans. Thomas B. Saunders (London: Williams and Norgate, 1901), 47–9. (Originally published as *Das Wesen des Christentums*, 1899.)

Commentary

In 1899–1900, the renowned German Protestant theologian Adolf von Harnack (1851–1930) delivered a series of lectures which were published under the title *Das Wesen des Christentums* (literally *The Essence of Christianity*, but translated into English in 1901 as *What Is Christianity?*). Although he criticised both Catholic and Orthodox Christian teachings, neither of which, he argued, was compatible with the teachings of Jesus, his primary target was Judaism.

What Is Christianity? sought to present essential original Christianity as a liberal faith that was unrelated to contemporary Judaism. Striving to show the originality of Jesus' teachings, von Harnack denigrated the Pharisees and Second Temple Judaism as 'weighted, darkened, distorted, rendered ineffective and deprived of its force'. Such was the extent of the misrepresentation that leading Jewish figures such as Leo Baeck (see document 14), Claude Montefiore (document 15) and Solomon Schechter felt the need to respond.

The portrait of Jesus in *Das Wesen des Christentums* was highly influential at the time and remains something of a barrier in Jewish–Christian relations, since it presents a Jesus radically different from his contemporaries. In a later book on the second-century CE Christian heretic Marcion (*Marcion, das Evangelium vom fremden Gott*, 1920) von Harnack even advocated that the Old Testament should be removed from the Christian canon altogether (see also Chapter 2, p. 67).

The impact of von Harnack and other late nineteenth-century German Liberal Protestant scholars such as Emil Schurer and Julius Wellhausen on Christian attitudes towards Jews and Judaism only began to wane in the latter decades of the twentieth century. Writing in the 1970s, for example, the Catholic scholar Charlotte Klein highlighted the ongoing influence of such attitudes on post-World War II Christian writings, which continued to depict Jewish leaders in Jesus' time as in moral decline (see Chapter 8, p. 446).

Von Harnack represented a modern version of the *adversus Judaeos* tradition that, with the coming of Jesus, the covenant of the Jewish people was abrogated, a tradition epitomised by the remark that 'the spring burst forth afresh, and broke and broke a new way for itself through the rubbish'. He was one in a long line of Christian theologians who promoted replacement theology, arguing that the Jewish people had lost their election as the true Israel (*verus Israel*) and been replaced by the church, which offered the old benefits in a new and superior, humanising form, over and against what was depicted as Judaism's narrow, self-interested, particularistic concerns.

Von Harnack's view no longer represents the teaching of the mainstream churches, as Appendix to Part III demonstrates.

Bibliography

Edwards, Laurence, 'Christian Wiese. Challenging Colonial Discourse: Jewish Studies and Protestant Theology in Wilhelmine Germany', *Studies in Christian–Jewish Relations* 2, no. 2 (2008), https://doi.org/10.6017/scjr.v2i2.1437.

Kinzig, Wolfram, *Harnack, Marcion und das Judentum: nebst einer kommentierten Edition des Briefwechsels Adolf von Harnacks mit Houston Stewart Chamberlain/Wolfram Kinzig* (Leipzig: Evangelische Verlagsanstalt, 2004).

Taylor, Miriam, *Anti-Judaism and Early Christian Identity: A Critique of the Scholarly Consensus* (Leiden: Brill, 1995).

12

John Creagh: Sermon (11 January 1904)

Text

Does not the law of Our Lord Jesus Christ bind us to love all men, to look upon men as our brothers and even to do good to those who hate or persecute us? And again has not our own Irish Nation ever been distinguished by its hospitality to the stranger and for its sympathy with the oppressed. Yes; truly our Lord does bind us to love even our enemies, to do good to all, and our Nation stands pre-eminent by its hospitality and by the *caed mille failthe* [a hundred thousand welcomes] that is ever on its lips. But the law of charity never interfered with or lessened a law of nature – the law of self-preservation. Individual self-sacrifice is permitted and even necessary at times. The common good and welfare of the community can never be sacrificed, but must be guarded and defended, and when a common danger is pointed out, all are bound to do their utmost to avert it and preserve themselves. It would be madness for a man to nourish in his own breast a viper that might at any moment slay its benefactor with its poisonous bite. So, too, is it madness for a people to allow an evil to grow in their midst that will eventually cause them pain […] The Jews were once the chosen people of God. God's mercy and favours towards them were boundless. They were the people of whom was born the Messiah, Jesus Christ, Our Lord and Master. But they rejected Jesus – they crucified Him – they called down the curse of His precious blood upon their own heads – 'His blood be upon us and our children' they cried and that curse came upon them […]

Twenty years ago and less Jews were known only by name and evil repute in Limerick. They were sucking the blood of other nations, but those nations rose up and turned them out. And they came to our land to fasten themselves on us like leeches and to draw our blood when they had been forced away from other countries. They have, indeed, fastened themselves upon us; and now the question is whether or not we will allow them to fasten themselves still more upon us, until we and our children are the helpless victims of rapacity. The Jews came to Limerick apparently the most miserable tribe imaginable, with want on their faces, but now they had enriched themselves and could boast of very considerable house property in the city. The rags have been exchanged for silk. They have wormed themselves into every form of business. They are in the furniture trade, the mineral water trade, the milk trade, the drapery trade, and in fact into business of every description and traded even under Irish names […]

[… T]here are no greater enemies of the Catholic Church than the Jews. Yet you will see the Jew carrying through town and country pictures of our Divine Lord, crucifixes, statues, and pictures of the Blessed Virgin Mary. This very day a man told me that not long ago he saw a Jew selling pictures of Our Lord, and as he walked along, when he thought no one heard him, he was blaspheming the Holy Name of Jesus. If you want an example look to France. What is going on at present in that land? The little children are being deprived of their education. No Nun, Monk, or Priest can teach in a school. The little ones are forced to go where God's name is never mentioned – to go to Godless schools. The Jews are in league with the Freemasons in France, and have succeeded in turning out of that country all the nuns and religious orders. The Redemptorist Fathers to the number of two hundred had been turned out of France, and that is what the Jews would do in our own country if they are allowed to get into power. To say nothing of charges of immorality brought against the Jews by distributing to innocent country people indecent pictures, impure books, and aiding corruption of morals in other ways, for these things are hard to be proved, for the guilty one must carry on his unlawful practice in a manner that cannot be detected lest he might be punished by the law.

Source

Creagh, John, 'Jewish Trading, Its Growth in Limerick, Address to the Confraternity', *Munster News* (13 January 1904). Quoted in Keogh, Dermot and McCarthy, Andrew, *Limerick Boycott 1904: Anti-Semitism in Ireland* (Cork: Mercier Press, 2005), 35–6.

Commentary

Small numbers of Jews lived in Ireland from the early nineteenth century, but Irish preoccupation with British colonialism meant that the community attracted little attention or overt antisemitism until the early twentieth century. From fewer than 500 in 1881, the number of Jews increased to 3,800 within three decades, mainly due to the arrival of refugees from pogroms in eastern Europe. The Jews of Ireland were religious and ethnic outsiders at a time of hope for Irish self-rule and tension between Catholic and Protestant communities.

Born in Limerick, Father John Creagh (1870–1947) was a Redemptorist priest. He became a postulant in 1884, the year of the first anti-Jewish riot in Limerick's history, which took place on Easter Sunday. In 1902 he became director of the Holy Family Confraternity of Limerick, a Catholic lay association with 6,000 to 7,000 members in a city of 38,000. The Jewish population was sixty to seventy adults.

Our excerpt is taken from a newspaper report of the first of two consecutive sermons delivered on 11 January 1904, soon after which Jews experienced a number of violent attacks from locals as well as an economic boycott. According to Creagh, Jews represented a clear and present danger, an 'evil […] in their midst'. He was angered that they arrived as paupers but were now wealthy, having 'wormed themselves into every form of business […] and traded even under Irish names'. Creagh's theological condemnation of Jews sits alongside racial antisemitism: Jews were 'once the chosen people' but were now divinely rejected as Christ-killers. There were 'no greater enemies of the Catholic Church' than the Jewish people; in other words, they were a threat to Catholic Ireland. In concluding remarks not included in the excerpt, Creagh urged his listeners, whom he had earlier called 'slaves of Jew usurers', to extract themselves from any transactions with Jews 'and then afterwards keep far away from them', prompting the boycott of Jewish businesses and pedlars.

Creagh was probably influenced by French clerical antisemitism, which reached a climax during the Dreyfus affair of 1894–9 (see p. 290). Creagh had lived in France during the Third Republic (1870–1940), when the Catholic Church was under pressure from the state, a situation for which he blamed Freemasons and Jews. In 1902 French parochial schools were closed and all fifty-four Catholic orders, including the Redemptorists, were dissolved.

The Creagh-initiated boycott received popular support, although his sermons were condemned by the Irish political leader Michael Davitt, a popular figure who had recently travelled to Russia and reported on the persecution of Jews. Arthur Griffith, founder of Sinn Féin, spoke in support of the boycott, as did the Redemptorist hierarchy. The Limerick rabbi Elias Levin wrote to the visiting superior general of the Redemptorist order, Fr Matthias Raus, seeking an audience when he visited Limerick in July 1904, but received no response.

The boycott continued for two years, and over half of the Jewish community left the city, accelerating a general decline which by 1926 saw only thirty Jews still living there. Although the violence and economic boycott were limited to Limerick, recent research shows that across Ireland Jews were accused of taking Irish jobs, enriching themselves on Irish misery and practising unscrupulous business methods, suggesting that Jews (alongside Protestants) were generally viewed negatively by most Irish Roman Catholics.

Bibliography

Beatty, Aidan, and O'Brien, Dan (eds.), *Irish Questions and Jewish Questions: Crossovers in Culture* (Syracuse: Syracuse University Press, 2018).

Keogh, Dermot, *Jews in Twentieth-Century Ireland: Refugees, Anti-Semitism and the Holocaust* (Cork: Cork University Press, 1998).

Keogh, Dermot, and McCarthy, Andrew, *Limerick Boycott 1904: Anti-Semitism in Ireland* (Douglas Village, Cork: Mercier Press, 2005).

Oakley Kessler, Patricia, 'Jews as a Threat to Irish Society? Economic Antisemitism and the Stereotype of the "Economic Jew"', in Gannon, Seán W., and Wynn, Natalie (eds.), *The Limerick Boycott in Context* (Berlin: Peter Lang, in press, expected 2024).

13

Theodor Herzl: Audience with Pope Pius X (26 January 1904)

Text

I briefly placed my request before him. He, however, possibly annoyed by my refusal to kiss his hand, answered sternly and resolutely:

'We cannot give approval to this movement. We cannot prevent the Jews from going to Jerusalem – but we could never sanction it. The soil of Jerusalem, if it was not always sacred, has been sanctified by the life of Jesus Christ. As the head of the Church I cannot tell you anything different. The Jews have not recognized our Lord, therefore we cannot recognize the Jewish people.'

Hence the conflict between Rome, represented by him, and Jerusalem, represented by me, was once again opened up.

At the outset, to be sure, I tried to be conciliatory. I recited my little piece about extraterritorialization, *res sacrae extra commercium* [holy places removed from business]. It didn't make much of an impression. *Gerusalemme*, he said, must not get into the hands of the Jews.

'And its present status, Holy Father?'

'I know, it is not pleasant to see the Turks in possession of our Holy Places. We simply have to put up with that. But to support the Jews in the acquisition of the Holy Places, that we cannot do.'

I said that our point of departure had been solely the distress of the Jews and that we desired to avoid the religious issues.

'Yes, but we, and I as the head of the Church, cannot do this. There are two possibilities. Either the Jews will cling to their faith and continue to await the Messiah who, for us, has already appeared. In that case they will be denying the divinity of Jesus and we cannot help them. Or else they will go there without any religion, and then we can be even less favorable to them.

'The Jewish religion was the foundation of our own; but it was superseded by the teachings of Christ, and we cannot concede it any further validity. The Jews, who ought to have been the first to acknowledge Jesus Christ, have not done so to this day.' […]

[…]

'But, Holy Father, the Jews are in terrible straits. I don't know if Your Holiness is acquainted with the full extent of this sad situation. We need a land for these persecuted people.'

'Does it have to be *Gerusalemme*?'

'We are not asking for Jerusalem, but for Palestine – only the secular land.'

'We cannot be in favor of it.'

'Does Your Holiness know the situation of the Jews?'

'Yes, from my Mantua days. Jews live there. And I have always been on good terms with Jews. Only the other evening two Jews were here to see me. After all, there are other bonds than those of religion: courtesy and philanthropy. These we do not deny to the Jews. Indeed, we also pray for them: that their minds be enlightened. This very day the Church is celebrating the feast of an unbeliever who, on the road to Damascus, became miraculously converted to the true faith. And so, if you come to Palestine and settle your people there, we shall have churches and priests ready to baptize all of you.'

Count Lippay had had himself announced. The Pope permitted him to enter. The Count kneeled, kissed his hand, then joined in the conversation by telling of our 'miraculous' meeting in Bauer's Beer Hall in Venice. The miracle was that he had originally planned to spend the night in Padua. As it happened, I had expressed the wish to be allowed to kiss the Holy Father's foot.

At this the Pope made *une tête* [a long face], for I hadn't even kissed his hand. Lippay went on to say that I had expressed myself appreciatively on Jesus Christ's noble qualities. The Pope listened, now and then took a pinch of snuff, and sneezed into a big red cotton handkerchief. Actually, these peasant touches are what I like best about him and what compels my respect.

In this way Lippay wanted to account for his introducing me, perhaps to excuse it. But the Pope said: 'On the contrary, I am glad you brought me the *Signor Commendatore*.'

As to the real business, he repeated what he had told me: *Non possumus* [We can't!]

Until he dismissed us Lippay spent some time kneeling before him and couldn't seem to get his fill of kissing his hand. Then I realized that the Pope liked this sort of thing. But on parting, too, all I did was to give him a warm hand-squeeze and a low bow.

Duration of the audience: about 25 minutes.

In the Raphael *stanze* [rooms], where I spent the next hour, I saw a picture of an Emperor kneeling to let a seated Pope put the crown on his head.

That's the way Rome wants it.

Source

Herzl, Theodor, *The Complete Diaries of Theodor Herzl*, vol. 4, ed. Raphael Patai, trans. Harry Zohn (New York and London: The Herzl Press, Thomas Yoseloff, 1960), 1601–5. (Square-bracketed words are part of the original. The Italian of the second paragraph is omitted in favour of the English translation, which is also part of the original.)

Commentary

In 1904, the year after Giuseppe Sarto (1835–1914) was elected Pope Pius X, Theodor Herzl (1860–1904), the father of modern political Zionism, met him in the Vatican.

In *The Jewish State* (1896) Herzl had argued for the establishment of a Jewish state in response to the growth of antisemitism. Influenced by his work reporting on the Dreyfus affair in 1895 as a journalist for a Viennese newspaper, he believed that Jews could only be safe in their own land. In 1897 the First Zionist Congress adopted Herzl's Basel Programme, and the movement for Jewish self-determination gained strength, especially in eastern Europe.

Even though he had a secular state in mind, Herzl sought Christian support, and the Anglican priest and restorationist William Hechler (1845–1931) introduced him to high-level political contacts, helping him secure support for the Zionist movement from some European powers. Hechler was influenced by Christian rediscovery of the Holy Land as well as by dispensationalism, which viewed restoration of the Jewish people to the Land of Israel as a necessary prelude to the Parousia (the Second Coming of Christ).

Herzl held hope for papal support and was aware that Pius X had 'always been on good terms with Jews' (as the pope himself says in the excerpt). Indeed, Pius was known for maintaining good personal relationships with individual Jews from early in his ecclesiastical career. Even though the papal count and Vatican artist B. Lippay (whom Herzl had met in Venice) arranged the audience, the fact that the pope agreed to meet, understanding in advance the purpose of the visit, should not be overlooked. The excerpt is taken from Herzl's diary account of the meeting.

Herzl asked for support in bringing Jews back to the land of Israel, but was told by the pope that 'the Jews have not recognised our Lord, therefore we cannot recognise the Jewish people'. Although this document evidences unequivocal rejection, the pope nonetheless recognised that 'we cannot prevent the Jews from going to Jerusalem'. Pius X thus took a contrasting position to Christian restorationists, insisting the church could not condone the return of the Jewish people to Jerusalem, and showed himself more concerned about their conversion ('if you come to Palestine and settle your people there, we shall have churches and priests ready to baptize all of you'). Herzl died three months after the meeting.

It is not surprising that the Vatican was hostile to Zionist aspirations on doctrinal and political grounds, but when assessing Pius X's position it is worth remembering that much of contemporary Italian Jewry was also opposed to Zionism. Indeed, Herzl noted in his diary that the day before the papal audience he had met the Jewish senator Giacomo Malvano, a staunch anti-Zionist, and that a Jewish friend of the pontiff, Leone Romanin Jacur, another critic of Zionism, had refused to meet him.

The attitude of Roman Catholicism towards Zionism changed greatly in the course of the twentieth century, by the end of which the Holy See had established official diplomatic relations with the State of Israel (1994) and Pope John Paul II had made an historic visit to Jerusalem (2000) – a precedent that would be followed by his papal successors – displaying support for Herzl's Zionist aspirations which would have shocked and dismayed Pope Pius X.

Bibliography

Black, Ian, *Enemies and Neighbours: Arabs and Jews in Palestine and Israel, 1917–2017* (London: Allen Lane, 2017).
Merkley, Paul C., *The Politics of Christian Zionism 1891–1948* (London: Frank Cass, 1998).

14

Leo Baeck: The Essence of Judaism *(1905)*

Text

In the Church, the stress was laid upon faith, it was *articles of faith*, or dogmas which had to serve *there* the purpose of linking the community together, and of fitting it for resistance. It is, for instance, surely not a mere coincidence that, at the time when the secular power of the pope began to totter, and Catholicism seemed thus to be in danger, dogma should have acquired new strength as a weapon of defence in the struggle. Similarly, it was not a mere coincidence that the anxiety for those 'signs' and forms had begun to show itself most decisively in Judaism, just when an old bond was broken, and the old homeland of Judaism and the State, which had kept the individuals together, were ruined and destroyed [...]

In Judaism, and herein is expressed its innermost being, it is a *demand*, the demand for *definite* deeds, in which anxiety for the preservation of the holy community is expressed [...]

The significance which belongs to them is characteristically expressed in the Talmudic phrase which describes them as 'the fence around the Law'. They do not constitute the doctrine of Judaism, but they are a barricade for it. This distinction has been maintained;

the religion itself was not confused with these statutes, nor were the two regarded as interchangeable. One bit of evidence is clear and definite for this distinction: the performance of a ceremonial statute is never regarded as a 'good deed'; only religious and ethical action is so called [...]

If the peculiar quality of this 'fence' has unfortunately been frequently mistaken or misinterpreted, especially in the interest of a Christian construction of history, this is partly due to an old translation's misunderstanding, and partly to the error caused by old polemics [...] The polemic of Paul's epistles makes special use of this suggested implication and stresses it. Here the new covenant, as the covenant of Faith, is placed in opposition to the old one, as the covenant of Law. The Law is something lesser and lower, something temporary, which has been supplanted by something else. Judaism, the religion of law, is superseded by the religion of grace, which tells of the miracle which can happen to man, and which signifies everything, so that he has but to wait in order to receive it. Compared with this miracle, all human action and activity vanish, and are valueless in the relationship between God and man, and between man and God [...]

Judaism had to be depreciated by representing it as a legal religion, and through its legalism characterized by rigid formalism and outwardness. But it became increasingly difficult to regard the commandments about justice and love, which to Paul are also law, as law in that bad sense and construction, which the words Law and Legalism had been made to acquire. Thus the so-called 'ceremonial' commandments had to take the blame; they *were the Law*, as meaning something inferior and bad; and to the present day they serve as grounds for reproaching Judaism with being a religion of Law. Since Judaism had to be represented as essentially a *legal* religion, there remained no alternative but to regard these ceremonial statutes as the most important part of the Jewish religion: they are supposed to stand on a level of complete equality with the commandments of love and justice, if indeed they do not drive these below their own level of value and importance. The doctrine of Paul, which put morality side by side with ritual, was foisted upon Judaism. Thus, in accordance with this false equality, the Jewish Law, in the interpretation of the Church, was described as mere outward service, something which has significance and value in itself as mere mechanical deed, a kind of sacramental act. This had to be done because only by degrading their opponents could men gain a conception of the loftiness of their own creed.

On all this too is based the reproach of the 'burden of the law.' Such a burden has very seldom been felt in Judaism, incomparably less indeed than many a Christian denomination has felt the burden of its own 'law', namely *dogma*. The contrary, indeed, is the case. The history of Judaism bears witness that all these statutes were an element in the joy of life; it is even legitimate to speak of the spiritual joys which they awaken [...]

Every individual Jew becomes thus a creator of religion and of its significance, and a creator of the community. Here we have again that peculiarity of Jewish religiousness, that it both lays its commands upon man, and attributes to him the power of creation. In the Church, the individual is supported by the Church; it existed before him, and is more than he; in its faith he stands, and with and by his faith he lives. In Judaism, there is no Church; the community takes its place. The community lives in the individual; it is

331

subsequent to him, and exists through him; his duty is to support it, and only through *his* prayer is *its* prayer. Wherever there are Jews, fulfilling the commandments of religion, though their number may be small, the Jewish community exists; the whole of Judaism exists there. The Church always tries to be a Church of the many; it yields in the end to the idea of power; few 'Churches' have so far escaped this fate. The community is always a community of the few, and to each of the few the entire religion is commanded; upon each one of them it is imposed. The community is a combination of strength and of the sanctification of God's name; its genius is to be small in order to be great.

Source

Baeck, Leo, *The Essence of Judaism*, trans. Victor Grubwieser and Leonard Pearl (London: Macmillan, 1936), 269–73, 280–1. (Originally published as *Das Wesen des Judentums*, 1905.) Reproduced courtesy of James N. Dreyfus and family, the descendants of Rabbi Leo Baeck.

Commentary

Leo Baeck (1873–1956) was a German Reform leader and theologian who moved to London after the end of World War II, having survived Theresienstadt concentration camp to which he had been deported in 1943. Baeck followed in the footsteps of Reform figures such as Abraham Geiger and Stephen Wise (see Chapter 7, p. 381) who embraced the Jewishness of Jesus, and was also influenced by the Jewish philosopher Hermann Cohen, who argued that Jewish ethics were superior to Christian.

Early in his career, Baeck publicly challenged the renowned Protestant theologian and church historian Adolf von Harnack and, in particular, vehemently rejected his portrayal of Judaism in *Das Wesen des Christentums* (literally 'the essence of Christianity'; see document 11). In his 1901 review of von Harnack's book, Baeck criticised his misrepresentation of Second Temple Judaism, which Baeck argued was not only erroneous but primarily motivated by a desire to assert the originality of the teachings of Jesus.

Our excerpt comes from Baeck's *Das Wesen des Judentums* (*The Essence of Judaism*), the title of which makes clear that it is a response to Harnack, although Baeck doesn't explicitly mention him by name in the book. Baeck critiques the Christian view which, he argues, ignorantly condemned Judaism 'as a legal religion [...] characterized by rigid formalism and outwardness'. Christian dogma, Baeck suggests, overrides right action, which he contrasts with the position taken by Judaism. He extols Judaism as the highest form of religion because it demands '*definite* deeds' in order to lead an ethical life.

Baeck identified Paul, whom he regarded as the founder of Christianity, as responsible for this skewed representation of Judaism. Indeed, it is Paul, not Jesus, who is radically different from his contemporaries, a fact which led to Christians being so focused on the presence of Jewish ceremonial law that the *mitzvoth* ('good deeds') were ignored. Consequently Christians mistakenly compared the ethics of Jesus, not with the ethics of the Pharisees, but with their ritual regulations. In other writings, Baeck defined

Christianity as a 'romantic religion', centring on feelings, while Judaism was a 'classical religion' which emphasised action, based on ethics.

In his later years, Baeck became increasingly involved in Jewish–Christian dialogue on an academic and community level, and Leo Baeck College, a rabbinical college named in his honour, was established in London in 1956, the year of his death, and continues to undertake interfaith dialogue, notably with Christians and Muslims.

Bibliography

Homolka, Walter, *Jewish Identity in Modern Times: Leo Baeck and German Protestantism* (New York: Berghahn, 1995).

Rothschild, Fritz A., *Jewish Perspectives on Christianity: Leo Baeck, Martin Buber, Franz Rosenzweig, Will Herberg, and Abraham J. Heschel* (New York: Continuum, 1996).

15

Claude Montefiore: The Synoptic Gospels *(1909/10)*

Text

For Jews – so long as they are and remain Jews (i.e., members of the Jewish faith) – the great interest or value of the Synoptic Gospels lies in the *teaching* ascribed to Jesus rather than in the personality or the life. We persist in separating the one from the other, whereas to Christians they form a unity, a whole. From his childhood upwards the Jew's highest conceptions of goodness and God have never been associated with Jesus. These conceptions may have been due to an idealization of O.T. teaching, or of Rabbinic teaching or of both. Some might argue (whether wrongly or rightly) that they are partly due to an unconscious absorption and adoption of Christian and Gospel teaching. But, consciously and deliberately, his highest conceptions of goodness and God have been ever presented to the Jew, whether the orthodox or the liberal Jew, as wholly, and characteristically Jewish. Moreover, he has had it ingrained into him that there need and can be nothing – no mediator, no divine man – between himself and God. The position of Jesus, the place he fills, even in Unitarian Christianity, is impossible for the Jew, for two reasons which, at first sight, may seem somewhat irreconcilable with each other. God is too 'far'; God is too 'near'. To make Jesus as 'divine' as Christians make him seems to the Jew presumptuous and out of the question. Man is man, he says; God is God. The best man is infinitely removed from the perfect goodness of God, and the fullness of the divine righteousness can be revealed in no man's life. On the other hand, God is so near that there is no *room*, as well as no *need*, for a *tertium quid* [third thing] between man and God. The Jew, so long as he is and remains a Jew, simply cannot believe that any man was ever endowed with the fullness of every conceivable moral excellence – that any man was ever wholly sinless, and conscious of his sinlessness, the more perfect because of this consciousness, the acme and cream of goodness and love. The Jew simply cannot believe in such a being, on the one hand, and he has no room or place for him on the other. Jesus has not introduced the Jews to God in their childhood; they do not require him in order to get to God in their manhood.

But the *teaching* of Jesus abides. The unprejudiced Jew, even remaining a Jew, can find bits of his teaching which go beyond O.T. teaching, or which, at any rate, bring out occasional utterances and teachings of the O.T. more clearly and fully. Jesus links on to the Prophets, and sometimes seems to go beyond them. Let us imagine that the writings of a new Hebrew prophet, a contemporary, say, of Isaiah or Jeremiah, were brought to light. The Jewish position would not be changed but the Jews would be delighted to obtain some fresh teachings and sayings of beauty and value, and even of originality, to add to those which they already possess. So it is, or so it can be, as regards Jesus and the Gospel. But the Christian, even the Unitarian Christian, has received the highest conceptions of God and righteousness through Jesus. To the Christian, alike in his teaching and in his personality and life, Jesus reveals God. To the Christian, even to the Unitarian Christian, the N.T. is the book which tells him most truly and fully about goodness and God, and within the N.T. it is the Gospels which tell him best of all. He fits in Jesus with his purest thoughts of God; Jesus brings God near to him. Whereas, to the Jews, Jesus – or any man – would be in their way in their relations with, and in their approaches to, God, to the Christian, even to the Unitarian Christian, Jesus smooths the way to God and shortens it. He *is* the way. Without Jesus – if that fatality could for a moment be conceived – God, even to the Unitarian Christian, would be more distant and more dim; without Jesus, God, to the Jew, would be no less near and no less bright.

Source

Montefiore, Claude G., *The Synoptic Gospels*, vol. 1, 2nd ed. (London: Macmillan, 1927), xxiv–xxvi. (First edition published 1909.)

Commentary

Anglo-Jewish leader and scholar Claude Montefiore (1858–1938) was a pioneer in Jewish–Christian relations and one of the founders of Liberal Judaism in the United Kingdom. His Liberal Jewish views form the basis of his writings, which focused on four subjects: the Hebrew Bible (generally called the Old Testament by Jews and Christians alike at that time); the New Testament and Christianity; Rabbinic Judaism; and Liberal Judaism. This document is excerpted from his *The Synoptic Gospels* (1909–10), a two-volume introduction, translation and commentary on the first three Gospels.

Montefiore attempted to introduce the New Testament to Jews, and in particular 'the teaching of Jesus [which] abides', arguing that it was part of Jewish literature. His views were met with dissent within the Jewish community and provoked discussion in Christian circles. Previously, it had been the norm for Jews to look for defects in Christian works or for parallels in rabbinic writings. 'What was true could not be new and what was new could not be true' summarised the majority of contemporary Jewish attitudes towards Christianity. Montefiore took a more balanced approach. As far as Christians were concerned, he did not have to assume that Jesus was always right; with Jews, he did not feel obligated to defend Rabbinic Judaism. As a result, some Christians attacked him for being too Jewish and some Jews for being too Christian.

For Montefiore, Jesus' teaching represented a revival of prophetic Judaism, which emphasised inward goodness at the expense of outward forms (and, as he wrote elsewhere, in some respects pointed forward to Liberal Judaism). While Jesus should be viewed as a great and wise teacher, he was in no sense God, although his teachings sometimes 'go beyond' the prophets. Montefiore called on Jews to read the New Testament and to admire Jesus since both the book and its central figure were Jewish, but he was equally vocal that Christians should realise that Jews are 'no less near' to God without Jesus.

At the heart of his approach was a Liberal Jewish understanding of progressive revelation, which viewed revelation as something that existed not just in the Pentateuch but also in the prophets, writings and rabbinic literature. This was not all. Revelation could also be discovered in other religions. According to Montefiore, Liberal Judaism denied God had enabled humanity to attain religious truth exclusively through a single channel. This allowed Liberal Judaism to select the 'highest' elements of all religions as well as to omit the cruder and more primitive elements of Judaism, providing the justification for freedom to criticise both Christianity and Judaism.

Montefiore had an understanding of and appreciation for both Judaism and Christianity, giving him a distinctive fusion of their thought that led to an important position in Jewish–Christian relations and in the Jewish study of the New Testament, in the footsteps of which Geza Vermes and Amy-Jill Levine (see Chapter 9, p. 499) followed. Montefiore did not inaugurate a new era in Jewish–Christian relations, but his life and work contributed towards a more positive relationship between the two faiths and a greater understanding of the Jewishness of Jesus.

Bibliography

Diamond, Bryan, *Claude Montefiore: Jewish Scholar, Communal Leader, Philanthropist* (self-published, 2024).

Kessler, Edward, *An English Jew: The Life and Writings of Claude Montefiore* (London: Vallentine Mitchell, 1989).

Langton, Daniel, *Claude Montefiore: His Life and Thought* (London: Vallentine Mitchell, 2002).

16

World Missionary Conference: Carrying the Gospel to All the Non-Christian World *(1910)*

Text

Followers of the Lord Jesus Christ – Himself after the flesh a Jew – should give to the presentation of Christ to the Jew its rightful place in the Great Commission. It is not a task to be left to a few enthusiastic believers, but the obligation and responsibility of the whole Christian Church. The Gospel must be preached to the Jew wherever he may be found.

For centuries the Church has paid little heed to the missionary message of the Apostle to the Gentiles, 'There is no difference between the Jew and the Greek.' Both are sinners, for both have come short of the glory of God, and both need a Saviour, even the Lord Jesus Christ. Yet the Church has acted as though it believed otherwise. The attitude of the Christian to the Jew has not been merely one of neglect but of bitter hostility. Reparation is due for the contempt and injustice meted out by the Christian Church and its members to the race into which its Founder was born and out of which He drew His first disciples. Christianity was born in Judaism and owes a debt to bring the Jew home at last to the fold of Christ.

There is urgent need, therefore, that the Church should change its attitude toward an enterprise which is carrying out an essential part of our Lord's Great Commission. The spasmodic efforts to bring the Jew to Christ must be replaced by missions as strong, persistent, and sympathetic as those among other races of mankind. Many of the difficulties are of the Church's own creating; and will disappear with a deeper faith in the power of God through the Gospel and a wiser approach imbued with a true sympathy. No other methods are needed than those which have been blessed in the past among both Jews and Gentiles. The issue remains unchanged. It is still Jesus whom the Jew must accept or reject. Reform Jewish rabbis in the United States may speak of Him in flattering terms, and accept Him as one of the great prophets and teachers of mankind, but the gulf between them and Christianity remains practically as wide as that which must be crossed by the Orthodox Jew before he acknowledges the Lordship, Divinity, and Messiahship of Jesus of Nazareth.

The time to reach the Jews with the Gospel is now, when they are rapidly drifting away from the faith of their fathers and are groping for something, they know not what. The Jews are becoming more and more an integral part of Christian cities, strongly influencing and often even dominating them by their enormous and increasing wealth and by their remarkable intellectual ability. However far they may have drifted, there still remains with them that inherent religious instinct, that capacity to appreciate great moral and spiritual truths which has characterised them throughout their history, and which, consecrated to the service of Christ, will enrich and revitalise Christianity itself. 'For if the casting away of them be the reconciling of the world, what shall be the receiving of them, but life from the dead.'

Source

World Missionary Conference, *Carrying the Gospel to All the Non-Christian World* (Edinburgh: Oliphant, Anderson & Ferrier, 1910), 276–8.

Commentary

The nineteenth century saw a surge in missionary activity towards Jews with the founding of new societies for promoting the gospel to Jews, such as the London Society for Promoting Christianity amongst the Jews in 1809 (which later became the Church's Ministry among Jewish People). The 1910 World Missionary Conference, held in Edinburgh from 14 to 23 June 1910, was the third international missionary conference, following gatherings in

London (1888) and New York (1900). The Edinburgh conference has been seen both as the culmination of Protestant Christian missionary activity and as the beginning of the modern ecumenical movement (following a sequence of interdenominational meetings starting in 1854). It is not by chance that it was held in the capital of Scotland, renowned for establishing missions throughout the world and despatching missionaries such as David Livingstone to spread the gospel.

Some missionaries offered active support for the establishment of a Jewish homeland, a position today termed Christian Zionism (see also documents 4 and 13 above), and the 1,215 delegates who gathered for the first meeting were chaired by the conference president Lord Balfour, a former British foreign secretary. A few years later, in 1917, Balfour authored a letter to Lord Rothschild, a prominent English Jewish Zionist, publicly declaring the support of the British government for the Jewish claim to Palestine, a document known as the Balfour Declaration.

Carrying the Gospel to All the Non-Christian World was the outcome of one of eight commissions which took place during the conference and was partly a response to the increasing assimilation of Jews and a consequent reduction in traditional religious observance. As far as mission to the Jewish people was concerned, the document explained that the biggest barrier to Jewish conversion was antisemitism. It acknowledged that Christian attitudes were epitomised not by neglect of Jews but by 'bitter hostility'. As well as deploring antisemitism, the conference reminded Christians that Jesus himself was Jewish and exhorted the church to undertake the mission to Jews, which was proposed as the cure for antisemitism: 'The time to reach the Jews with the Gospel is now.'

Although there was optimism about the future conversion of the Jewish people, there was also recognition elsewhere in the report that 'Jewish missions are only in their infancy and we cannot conscientiously say that any part of the world field, except perhaps London, is adequately occupied'. In using terms such as 'occupied' and 'occupation', the commission deployed military metaphors to reinforce the idea of Christendom as Christ's kingdom on earth.

Bibliography

Stanley, Brian, *The World Missionary Conference, Edinburgh 1910* (Grand Rapids: William B. Eerdmans, 2009).

17
The Mendel Beilis Ritual Murder Trial (1911–13)

Text

(i) Accusation of Ritual Murder: Novoe vremia (New Times) (29 April 1911)

State Duma deputy Grigorii G. Zamyslovskii:
However, in spite of the fact that Jews, prompted by religious fanaticism, drain the blood from Christian youths, it has been established without a doubt that the government

stubbornly refuses to take measures to discover those Jewish sects that adhere to such vile and barbaric rites.

Every time when a murder or an attempted murder as a consequence of such a rite comes to light, the government confines its investigation only to the matter of the specific murder, shutting its eyes to the criminal association and religious learning that push its fellow members toward crime … Instead of taking measures to find out about the fanatical Judaic sect whose members commit murder, the investigation is wasting time by suspecting that Iushchinskii's mother tortured her son.

Source

Weinberg, Robert, *Blood Libel in Late Imperial Russia: The Ritual Murder Trial of Mendel Beilis* (Bloomington: Indiana University Press, 2014), 89. (Originally published in *Novoe vremia* 12,617 (29 April 1911), 1.)

(ii) *The Government Response:* Kievlianin *(The Kievan) (1 May 1911)*

As we know, the question about ritual murders, that is, about murders committed out of religious fanaticism, is very old and extremely controversial. In the first century the Romans accused Christians of these murders, and then in the Middle Ages similar accusations against Jews arose and called forth a series of trials that have been repeated until our time in various countries including Russia. Although courts in the Middle Ages and in much later epochs issued several guilty verdicts, all these trials were so darkened by ignorance that they did not prove the existence of special fanatical sects that engage in ritual murder. The question still remains extremely controversial. When the supposition about the possibility of ritual murder is unproven, then it remains in the realm of legend and conjecture. It is impermissible to call any mysterious murder a ritual murder when all we can say is that we do not know anything about it. Almost every mysterious (*temnoe*) crime can give rise to dozens of guesses, dozens of suggested explanations, but all of them do not have the slightest value since they are built either on fantasy or lack the basis of its conclusions.

We declare that the malicious gossip and slanderous reproaches thrown from the rostrum of the Duma were introduced by the authors of the interpellation for the sake of arousing the Christian population against the Jews and instigating a pogrom. Recognizing that the hypothesis about ritual murders is unproven, we however understand that not a small number of people absolutely and sincerely believe in the existence of such horrible acts … and absolutely and sincerely are worried. But the members of the State Duma occupy a position of responsibility that obligates them not to lend credence to ignorant rumors, guesses, and unverified idle talk and gossip.

Source

Weinberg, Robert, *Blood Libel in Late Imperial Russia: The Ritual Murder Trial of Mendel Beilis* (Bloomington: Indiana University Press, 2014), 91–2. (Originally published in *Kievlianin* 119 (1 May 1911), 2–3.)

(iii) The Verdict: The Times *(11 November 1913)*

An Ambiguous Verdict: The Kieff 'ritual murder' trial ended yesterday in a verdict acquitting Beiliss of the charge of having murdered the boy Yushchinsky, but declaring that the murder was committed in the brickyard or factory belonging to the well-known Jewish family, Zaitseff.

While satisfactory in so far as it absolves Beiliss of the monstrous charge preferred against him on the flimsiest of evidence, the verdict must be regarded as eminently calculated to perpetuate the agitation by which the trial has been accompanied. In fairness to the Russian jury, it must be noted that the questions formulated for its decision by the presiding Judge practically prescribed the verdict to be rendered. Its effect will be to remove the burden of the accusation from the shoulders of the unfortunate Beiliss, who has been kept in prison since his arrest in August, 1911, while casting suspicion on to the Jewish community as a whole.

Source

'Beiliss Acquitted. Closing Scenes of the Kieff Trial', *The Times* (11 November 1913).

Commentary

In 1911 Mendel Beilis (1874–1934), a Russian Jew, was accused in Kiev of the ritual murder of Andrei Yushchinsky, a twelve-year-old boy. At Yushchinsky's funeral, leaflets accusing Jews of blood libel were distributed by the reactionary Black Hundred organisation. The police initially suspected Andrei's mother of her son's murder but soon concluded that a violent gang associated with Vera Cheberiak, the mother of one of Andrei's friends, were guilty. Nevertheless, the minister of justice in St Petersburg, I. G. Shcheglovitov, prompted by far-right politicians such as Grigorii G. Zamyslovskii, ignored their investigation and treated the crime as ritual murder (see also Chapter 4, p. 196).

Mendel Beilis was arrested in July 1911 and imprisoned until the trial started in September 1913. The prosecution manufactured evidence, pressured witnesses and called antisemitic witnesses, such as Justin Pranaitis, a Catholic priest with a criminal record who offered 'scientific' evidence for the accusation that Jews committed ritual murder. The Beilis case combined theological and racial antisemitism, which influenced and reinforced one another, and represented an example of local authorities coordinating with far-right antisemitic groups for political ends.

During the nineteenth century, books and articles in Russia explored accusations of ritual murder, prompting public discussion about the 'Jewish question' (see documents 5 (i) and (ii)) and ensuring their close connection in the public mind. The participation of some Jews in revolutionary organisations from the 1860s onwards, culminating in the assassination of Tsar Alexander II in 1881, reinforced the authorities' belief that Jews posed a threat to Russian society. The assassination was followed by the first wave of pogroms, notably the 1903 Kishinev pogrom, which was also inspired by the blood libel accusation. Pogroms often appeared spontaneous, but were usually condoned, if not organised, by political leaders. The pogroms in Russia of 1881, 1903 and 1905 provide the context to the Beilis trial, but others took place afterwards, including in Ukraine.

The Beilis case generated great controversy. In Russia, the writer Maxim Gorky (1868–1936) supported Beilis, but Vasily Rozanov (1856–1919) wrote against him in a series of antisemitic articles. There were also church leaders, such as the Metropolitan of St Petersburg Antonii Vadkovskii (1846–1912), who condemned the blood libel and the pogroms and made efforts to prevent their recurrence. Overseas, the trial caused the same kind of public outcry as the Damascus affair in 1840, the Dreyfus affair in France in the 1890s and the lynching of Leo Frank in the United States in 1915. Unlike in France, anti-Jewish violence did not follow, nor did the Orthodox Church support the prosecution of Beilis (in contrast to the Catholic Church in France, which was actively engaged against Dreyfus).

The jury unanimously declared Beilis 'not guilty', which showed that while local politicians and right-wing groups may have assumed a successful prosecution would prove beneficial to their careers, others – notably the State Duma and the presiding judge – were not willing to trample on the rule of law and submit to 'malicious gossip and slanderous reproaches' at a time when the Tsarist regime was under intense scrutiny from foreign governments and domestic critics. Beilis and his family left Russia and settled in the United States. Bernard Malamud's novel *The Fixer* (1968) is based on the case.

Bibliography

Beilis, Jay, Garber, Jeremy S., and Stein, Mark A. (eds.), *Blood Libel: The Life and Memory of Mendel Beilis* (Chicago: Beilis Publishing, 2011).

Lindemann, Albert S., *The Jew Accused: Three Anti-Semitic Affairs (Dreyfus, Beilis, Frank), 1894–1915* (Cambridge: Cambridge University Press, 1993).

Weinberg, Robert, *Blood Libel in Late Imperial Russia: The Ritual Murder Trial of Mendel Beilis* (Bloomington and Indianapolis: Indiana University Press, 2014).

7

From World War I to the Holocaust
1914–1947
VICTORIA BARNETT

INTRODUCTION

Between 1914 and 1947, religious identities and self-understandings, theological conversations and Jewish–Christian relations were at the mercy of new political movements and agendas. Politically, economically and socially, World War I was a shattering event: empires collapsed, borders were redrawn and millions of refugees fled from one region to another. Amidst this instability extremist nationalist political movements appeared, often claiming a Christian identity. Jewish communities suffered terrible violence, and in 1933 such violence became state policy in Germany, culminating in the genocide of millions of European Jews.

Jews and Christians in Europe and North America were drawn deeply into these events. The American Jewish Joint Distribution Committee was founded in 1914 to address the needs of Jewish minority communities and refugees; the World Jewish Congress (WJC) was established in 1936 to address antisemitism and the persecution of Jews in Nazi Germany. New organisations emerged to promote interreligious understanding, such as the National Conference of Jews and Christians in the United States (founded as a subcommittee of the Federal Council of Churches (FCC) in 1928 and renamed 'the National Conference of Christians and Jews' in 1938) and the Council of Christians and Jews in Great Britain in 1942. There were a surprising number of localised Jewish–Christian initiatives in Germany, France and Great Britain. During the 1920s, the Protestant ecumenical movement in Europe and North America became involved in issues like refugee work and minority rights; during the 1930s they focused on the theological divisions in the German churches. The international political profile of the Roman Catholic leadership in Rome grew after Vatican City gained recognition as an independent state under the 1929 Italian Lateran Treaty, and the Holy See played a seminal role in questions of Palestine and in responding to the Nazi regime after 1933.

Although very much a minority within their respective communities, there were Jews and Christians involved in theological encounters. There was new critical biblical scholarship, more open Jewish critiques of Christianity and new Christian theological scholarship on Jesus and Judaism. In Germany Martin Buber's journal *Der Jude*, published from 1916 to 1928, offered a platform for Jewish and Christian authors to address public and religious developments in conversation with each other (see document 3 below).

Already in the 1920s, however, Jews felt growing alarm about rising antisemitic rhetoric and violence. The ascent to power of a National Socialist German government, with antisemitism as a core principle of its ideology and policy, marked a clear caesura in 1933, altering Jewish–Christian relations around the world.

Two interrelated issues in the interwar period – one affecting Jews, the other confronting Christians – had particular consequences after 1933 for the Jewish–Christian relationship. The first was the vulnerable status of religious and ethnic minorities after World War I, particularly those within redrawn borders. One third of the population of the newly constituted Second Polish Republic after 1918, for example, comprised national minorities, including 3 million Jews, 4 million Ukrainians and 1 million Germans.

This had humanitarian repercussions across Europe. Jewish communities in Ukraine, Poland and parts of Russia suffered horrific pogroms in the early postwar period. A network of international Jewish organisations addressed their plight, laying the foundation for subsequent refugee work after 1933 and energising the Zionist movement. Politically, the rights and citizenship of minorities were protected under the early postwar Minorities Treaties, which Jews in particular viewed as a new and promising development. Christian leaders were more focused on the status of Catholic, Orthodox and Protestant minorities and the destabilising potential of intergroup tensions.

The interwar issue of minority rights shaped subsequent Christian and Jewish understandings of events in Nazi Germany (as well as attitudes towards Zionism) in very different ways (see, e.g., document 2). During the early years of Nazi rule, many Christian leaders interpreted Nazi anti-Jewish measures as an attack on Christianity as well (their focus was on the repression of Christian opponents of Nazism), not as a specifically Jewish crisis that marked a terrible new chapter in the long history of antisemitism (see, e.g., documents 7, 13). While this perception was shaken by events such as the November 1938 pogroms (see document 13) and the 1942 confirmation of the genocide of European Jews (documents 17 (i), (ii) and (iii)), only after 1945 did Christian leaders and theologians begin to confront the ways in which Christian history and theology were deeply implicated in the centuries of antisemitic violence that led to the Holocaust (see *The Ten Points of Seelisberg*, Appendix to Part III, p. 510).

The second, related issue concerned the rise throughout Europe of antisemitic Christian pro-fascist and nationalist groups. The most infamous of these was the German Christian Faith Movement (formally established in 1932), which sought to align the German Protestant Church with the Nazi regime, but there were right-wing Protestant, Catholic and Orthodox movements in Italy, Finland, Romania, Hungary, France and the United States. Whatever their other agendas, all of these movements were antisemitic (see documents 4 (i), 6, 9, 11, 12).

Even among Jews who had been engaged in Jewish–Christian dialogue, these developments sparked a renewed distrust of Christianity and led them to question the extent to which they could depend on Christian allies (see documents 5, 14, 15). There were grave fears about the future for Jews in Europe and doubts about the very possibility of assimilation or integration, leading to a renewed commitment to Judaism and Jewish identity (see documents 3, 5, 20).

These interwar developments also strengthened the Zionist movement in the US and in Europe. While there were still very different conceptions of the ultimate goal of Zionism, Jews everywhere shared a growing realisation of the significance of a homeland. Thousands of European Jewish immigrants arrived in Palestine in the early years after 1918, and the League of Nations approved the mandate for a Jewish homeland in July 1922. Many western Christian denominations, as well as the ecumenical movement and the Holy See, had close relationships with their member churches in Palestine. The Zionist issue quickly became a charged one in Jewish–Christian relations (see documents 2, 5, 9, 15).

In 1933 the German Jewish community experienced a traumatic and unexpected transition from an era of emancipation and assimilation to persecution. The German Jewish population was quite small (600,000, in a nation of 60 million). Statistics about the number of 'assimilated' Jews (people who had converted to Christianity or had Jewish ancestry but were secular or had no ties to a Jewish community) vary widely, ranging from c. 350,000 to 900,000, but their situation compelled Catholic and Protestant leaders to take a position on the new racial laws.

In the Protestant Church, the German Christian Movement (there was no comparable group in the Catholic Church, although some 138 Catholic priests joined the Nazi Party (Spicer 2008: 239)) embraced an explicitly ethno-nationalist version of Christianity that challenged traditional Christian teachings about the relationship between the Old and New Testaments, the doctrine of Christian baptism and the Christian mission to Jews (and the very possibility of conversion). They also opposed the belief in a universal Christian church, insisting on a 'Germanic' Reich church that would reflect the will of the German nation, remain 'racially pure' and worship an 'Aryan' Jesus, creating a racialised, antisemitic Christology (see documents 4 (i), 6, 12).

In the spring and summer of 1933 the German Christians' growing strength in the German Protestant church (to which two-thirds of the German population belonged) prompted an opposition movement (see document 4 (ii)) that became the Confessing Church in 1934. In July 1933 the Nazi state called for national church elections. German Christian candidates won seats in all the regional church governments, gaining oversight of most Protestant theological faculties and the ordination of clergy.

The issue that unleashed what became known as the Protestant Church Struggle (*Kirchenkampf*) concerned the status of church members of Jewish descent – generally referred to as 'non-Aryan' Christians (which is how they were classified under Nazi racial laws). Through the introduction of a church 'Aryan paragraph' (based upon the 7 April

1933 Law for the Restoration of the Civil Service) the German Christians sought to conform church law to the newly passed state racial legislation barring Jews from the civil service. This would have led to the dismissal of affected clergy (around 100 pastors, out of *c.* 18,000 ordained clergy in 1933) and the establishment of separate congregations for affected church members.

It proved impossible to implement such church laws nationally, since each of Germany's twenty-eight regional churches had its own governance structures, but internal church debates about these questions continued throughout the 1930s. These debates reflected the intersections of racial antisemitism, theological anti-Judaism and ethno-nationalist assumptions about the 'Christian nature' of German culture (see document 4 (i)).

They also mirrored Nazi political rhetoric that portrayed Germans as the new 'chosen people' and Hitler as the leader who would lead them out of the wilderness (see document 6). Beginning with its embrace of 'positive Christianity' in its 1920 party platform, the Nazi Party skilfully wooed the Christian population, and Nazi propaganda frequently incorporated Christian imagery (in symbolic images of the female figure of Germania being crucified by Jews, for example).

Theologically, Confessing Church pastors opposed the German Christians' heretical positions, such as declaring racialised criteria for baptism or eliminating the Old Testament from Protestant Bibles. Politically, their attitudes towards the Nazi state varied considerably; there were even Confessing pastors who were Nazi Party members. Although they opposed racialised criteria for church membership, baptism and ordination, Confessing leaders still affirmed the mission to convert Jews – in fact, in their zeal to oppose the German Christian stance, some placed a new emphasis on it. There were very few in the Confessing Church who had relationships with the Jewish community or any familiarity with Judaism. Moreover, antisemitism was pervasive throughout both the Protestant and Catholic churches.

Particularly between 1933 and 1938, international Protestant responses to Nazism focused more on the ongoing battles between the German Christians and the Confessing Church, not on the plight of German Jews. Across Europe, the reality faced by Jewish communities and their traditions varied considerably country by country, and the same was true of Orthodox, Catholic and Protestant churches. One reason was chronological. In 1933 international attention was on Germany. Elsewhere, European Jews (including some who had fled Germany) were swept up in the whirlwind of Nazi violence only after war began in 1939, although they certainly suffered antisemitism within their own countries before then.

The documents in this chapter can only reflect a limited survey of different groups and locations, and they portray a wide range of theological responses to the challenges of the historical moment. All Christian churches in Europe and North America, however, bore the imprint of the long history of Christian antisemitism. This was reflected even in critiques of the Nazi persecution of Jews and the theological heresies of the German Christians, especially their rejection of the Old Testament, openly racialised scriptural interpretations and ecclesiology, and attempts to 'Nazify' Christian doctrine to serve the state (e.g., documents 4 (ii), 7, 10, 13).

Internationally, there were a few statements of clear solidarity with German Jews that acknowledged the unique bond between Judaism and Christianity, as well as the failure of Christian churches to combat antisemitism (documents 7, 10, 13). Before 1945 there were fewer Christian thinkers who explored how Christianity itself had laid the foundation for western antisemitism, both theologically and historically. Two such figures were Catholic laywoman Irene Harand and Anglican priest James Parkes (documents 8, 19). Parkes (in his 1934 *The Conflict of the Church and the Synagogue*) and Harand (in her 1937 *His Struggle*) attributed Christian antisemitism to a fundamental ignorance about Judaism and to the supersessionist denial of the eternal validity of the covenant between Israel and God. After 1945, Parkes demanded greater Christian literacy about Judaism; he was one of the few from this era whose work became useful for postwar Christian scholars as they attempted to rethink Christian theology in the wake of the Holocaust.

The difficulty of this theological task was epitomised by the thorny issue of Christian proselytisation and conversion of Jews, a matter that provoked strong emotions among Jews (see, e.g., documents 3, 5, 16, 20). Paul's letters and the call to 'preach the Gospel to all nations' (see, e.g., Matt. 24:14, Mark 13:10, Gal. 3:8) were a central component of Christian supersessionism. In defending this mission, and opposing the German Christians' racialised rejection of Jesus' Jewishness and the Jewish roots of Christianity, Christian leaders invariably offered supersessionist arguments (see, e.g., document 4 (ii)). After 1945, dismantling the theological underpinnings of supersessionism became an extensive project that required a deeper rethinking of Christianity itself. The documents in this chapter by Maritain (on the 'mystery of Israel'; document 10) and Ehrenberg (on the 'rediscovery of the Jew in Christianity'; document 18) were early attempts to acknowledge the ongoing covenant with Israel, albeit leading to very different conclusions.

Post-Holocaust Jewish–Christian conversations addressed how the Christian theological foundations of antisemitism had contributed to the genocide of millions of European Jews. The 1947 declaration *The Ten Points of Seelisberg* was predicated on this recognition as the starting point for any post-Holocaust Jewish–Christian encounter, opening the way for new theological understandings of Christianity.

Before 1945, however, most of the documents included here illustrate how Jews and Christians reacted to the immediate crises they confronted. Among Christians, this included addressing the radically ideological Christianity of the German Christians and expressing the ethical and theological imperative to stand with the persecuted Jews. The specific nature of the German Protestant Church Struggle led liberal and ecumenical Protestants to focus more on church/state issues than on Jewish–Christian issues. As we have seen, several documents in this chapter are characterised by Christian antisemitism. The texts by Harand and Parkes are early acknowledgements of Christianity's role in fostering antisemitism. Although some of the documents in this chapter expressed clear solidarity with Jews (e.g., documents 7, 10, 13, 17 (i), (ii) and (iii)), with the exception of

Maritain they did not offer much of a *theological* foundation for the dramatic rethinking of the Jewish–Christian relationship after 1945.

The Jewish documents offer a vivid portrait of the reactions of different Jewish communities in particular moments: the critique of how Christendom's alignment with power had twisted Christian teachings (document 1); the affirmation of Jewish identity and tradition (documents 3, 16, 20); and the convergence of anger at the Christian world with a renewed commitment to Zionism (documents 5, 15). These were Jewish thinkers addressing their communities and pondering their future over several decades of growing vulnerability, isolation and catastrophe.

Many of these documents are little known among scholars engaged in contemporary scholarship on Jewish–Christian relations; the statements by the FCC, the Archbishop of Canterbury and the World Council of Churches (WCC) and WJC are equally unfamiliar to many (documents 13, 17 (ii) and (iii)). This may be due to a certain lack of logical continuity with the post-Holocaust era. Just as 1933 marked a dramatic caesura with the conversations that had preceded it, the same can be said of the post-1945 world. As such, the primary significance of the documents in this chapter may be how they trace the lived theological and ethical engagement of Jews and Christians – and their understandings of one another – over the course of a violent and tragic historical era.

Bibliography

Barnett, Victoria, *For the Soul of the People: Protestant Protest against Hitler* (New York: Oxford University Press, 1992).

Bergen, Doris, *Twisted Cross: The German Christian Movement in the Third Reich*, 2nd ed. (Chapel Hill: University of North Carolina Press, 1996).

Berkowitz, Michael, *Western Jewry and the Zionist Project, 1914–1933* (Cambridge: Cambridge University Press, 1997).

Carter-Chand, Rebecca, and Spicer, Kevin (eds.), *Religion, Ethnonationalism and Antisemitism in the Era of the Two World Wars* (Montreal: McGill University Press, 2022).

Heschel, Susannah, *The Aryan Jesus: Christian Theologians and the Bible in Nazi Germany* (Princeton: Princeton University Press, 2008).

Loeffler, James, *Rooted Cosmopolitans: Jews and Human Rights in the Twentieth Century* (New Haven: Yale University Press, 2018).

Mendes-Flohr, Paul, *German Jews: A Dual Identity* (New Haven: Yale University Press, 1999).

Nirenberg, David, *Anti-Judaism: The Western Tradition* (New York: W. W. Norton, 2013).

Phayer, Michael, *The Catholic Church and the Holocaust, 1930–1965* (Bloomington: Indiana University Press, 2000).

Popa, Ion, *The Romanian Orthodox Church and the Holocaust* (Bloomington: Indiana University Press, 2017).

Snoek, Johan M., *The Grey Book: A Collection of Protests against Anti-Semitism and the Persecution of the Jews Issued by Non-Roman Catholic Churches and Church Leaders during Hitler's Rule*, intro. Uriel Tal (Assen: Van Gorcum & Co., 1969).

Solberg, Mary (ed. and trans.), *A Church Undone: Documents from the German Christian Faith Movement, 1932–1940* (Minneapolis: Fortress Press, 2015).

Spicer, Kevin, *Hitler's Priests: Catholic Clergy and National Socialism* (DeKalb: Northern Illinois University Press, 2008).

DOCUMENTS

I

Morris Joseph: 'Christmas and War' (25 December 1915)

Text

[... W]hat faithlessness to the 'Prince of Peace' can be more flagrant than that which has plunged twentieth-century Christendom into the worst horrors of war? [...] The Gospel of Peace and Goodwill, which he claimed to have been divinely chosen to preach, has been flouted, derided, falsified by its plighted adherents. Verily Christ has been slain in this war.

[...] Christmas Day, which should be the festival of peace and goodwill, falls in a time of general carnage and rapine; the birthday of the Master becomes a day of mourning at this murder.

The thought will find utterance in many a Christian pulpit this morning [...] The seeming failure of Christ! – a thousand preachers will discuss the theme. As for us, let us be just [...] Shall we not rather say that Christendom is bankrupt? What is good, and true, and mighty in the Christian religion is good, and true, and mighty still. It will bear fruit in God's good time. Why should we not acknowledge it, as great Jews, like Maimonides and Jehudah Halevi, acknowledged it? When the simple teaching of the Gospels, as distinguished from St. Paul's pagan travesty of it, triumphs, when men turn to God, the Father, and serve Him with one consent, when they practise righteousness and love towards each other all the world over, then Israel's hope, cherished through the ages with pathetic persistence, will be fulfilled. The Gentiles will have been led along the way of their own religions to the one Religion which Judaism enshrines. No; it is not Christianity – true Christianity – that has failed, but its self-styled adherents [...]

[...] Christianity, in its essence, is still a living religion [...] The old theistic and ethical ideas of its Founder are indestructible. We Jews must necessarily believe it because those ideas were derived from the Judaism in which he who taught them was born and nourished. The pagan teachings grafted upon them will perish. And it is to these later accretions that we must look for the causes of the failure of which Christianity seemingly stands convicted [...] The Church Militant [...] is the origin of half the wars that have devastated the earth. The Church has strained after earthly power and dominion even more eagerly than after spiritual supremacy. It has emphasized the religious differences of men instead of reconciling them, seeking its victories not by conciliation, but by persecution, as we Jews know to our cost, triumphing not by love, but by destruction and death. In one hand it has held the crucifix, in the other the sword [...]

But again let us be just. This conception of the character and mission of the church is old and well nigh outworn; it is fading away before the uprising of a nobler vision. In all the civilized world Religion is being regenerated by the infusion of humanitarian ideas.

Source

Joseph, Morris, *The Spirit of Judaism: Sermons Preached Chiefly at the West London Synagogue* (London: Routledge, 1930), 214–19.

Commentary

Rabbi Morris Joseph (1848–1930) was a prominent preacher in Great Britain and the author of three volumes of sermons. Delivered in the West London Synagogue one year after the 1914 Christmas Truce (during which an estimated 100,000 German and British soldiers on the Western Front in Europe briefly ceased hostilities), this sermon offered a Jewish critique of Christian complicity in the war.

Joseph began by noting the irony that Anton Lang, the German actor famous for playing Jesus in the Oberammergau Passion Play, had been killed in battle. Christian support for the war, however, was emblematic of a deeper crisis in western Christendom. Although there were a few Christian pacifists, most Christian leaders on both sides of the conflict justified the war not merely as a noble patriotic cause but as a fight on behalf of Christianity itself. In England, they emphasised 'the Church Militant', a term first used in the fifteenth century that portrayed Christianity in ongoing battle with the forces of evil in the world. Such sentiments were echoed in Germany, where ninety-three leading German intellectuals, including theological giants like Adolf von Harnack (see Chapter 6, p. 322), signed a 1914 manifesto ('Appeal to the Civilized World') defending the war as a just theological cause.

The corrective, Joseph preached, was a reorientation towards Jesus' own Jewish tradition. Addressing themes that would later define post-Holocaust literature on the Jewish–Christian relationship, he emphasised Christianity's roots in the Jewish tradition and community, the necessity of understanding Jesus' teachings as fundamentally Jewish and critiquing the 'pagan teachings' of followers like Paul who deviated from Jesus' own Judaism. These core teachings remained valid, despite the church's long history of aligning itself not with spiritual power but with state authority – leading among other things to the persecution of Jews. Joseph distinguished between 'Christendom' and the Christian faith. Only a return to Jesus' teachings, rooted in Judaism, could pull Christianity away from the temptations of worldly power.

Peeling back the layers of 'Christendom' to explore the essence of the Christian faith and its potential commonalities with Judaism, Joseph's sermon drew upon the new Jewish literature about the significance of Jesus' Jewishness, including the works of Jewish scholars like Abraham Geiger in Germany and Claude Montefiore in England (see Chapter 6, p. 333) who reflected critically on the meaning of Christianity in the modern age. Between 1918 and 1933 there was greater discussion of these questions, particularly within a small circle of German Jews and Christians, including Max Eschelbacher (document 3).

Joseph hoped that 'religion' itself might be 'regenerated' by 'humanitarian ideas' and that the war's trauma would inspire a new drive for international cooperation. It was a vision shared by some European Protestants and the interfaith movement. And a similar critique of the destructive and 'outworn' concept of Christendom began to emerge from some European Protestant theologians, notably Karl Barth, whose disillusionment with German theologians' enthusiasm for World War I led to the development of his dialectical theology (see Chapter 8, p. 410).

Bibliography

Heschel, Susannah, *Abraham Geiger and the Jewish Jesus* (Chicago: University of Chicago Press, 1998).

2

Pietro Gasparri: 'British Mandate for Palestine – Cardinal [Gasparri] Secretary of State of the Holy See, Vatican – Observations of the Holy See on This Mandate' (15 May 1922)

Text

[…] The Holy See makes no objection to the same civil rights being conferred on the Jews as are enjoyed by other nationalities and creeds, but it cannot agree:

1. that the Jews should be given a privileged and preponderating position as against the other nationalities and creeds:
2. that the rights of the Christian denominations should not be adequately safeguarded.

   […]
   [… I]t appears from the wording of the articles that there is an intention to confer a definitely preponderating influence, from an economic, administrative and political point of view, on the Jewish element as compared with the other nationalities. Thus, in the articles of the draft mandate:

(a) A Jewish agency, which is nothing less than the very influential Zionist organisation, is recognised as a public body (Article 4);
(b) This Jewish agency is given the role of cooperating with the Administration of Palestine and is endowed with very wide powers even in questions regarding 'the development of the country';
(c) The Immigration of Jews (Article 6) and the acquisition of Palestinian citizenship by Jews (Article 7) are encouraged; provision is especially made for 'close-settlement by Jews' who are even to receive grants of state lands and waste lands, (Article 6); they are also to be given preference in connection with the construction of public works (Article 11).

The effect of all these provisions of the draft tending to give the Jewish element a definitely preponderating influence over all the other races of Palestine, appears to be not only a grave injury to the established rights of other nationalities, but also to be incompatible with Article 22 of the Treaty of Versailles […]

According to the Article referred to above, a mandate is a form of protection […] for the benefit of 'peoples not yet able to stand by themselves under the strenuous conditions of the modern world', and its object is 'a sacred trust of civilization', namely, 'the well-being and development of such peoples'.

The passages just quoted are obviously incompatible with a mandate which would prove to be an instrument for the subjection of the native populations for the benefit of another nationality.

Source

United Nations Library and Archives Geneva: File R16/1/20808/2413, https://archives.ungeneva
.org/british-mandate-for-palestine-cardinal-gasparri-secretary-of-state-of-the-holy-see-
vatican-observations-of-the-holy-see-on-this-mandate.

Commentary

In 1920 the League of Nations mandated Great Britain to govern the territories of Palestinian and Transjordan; work on the Draft Mandate progressed from 1920 to 1922. A central issue concerned protections of religious freedom and independent oversight of holy places (churches, mosques, etc.). Article 14 of the Draft Mandate was a proposal for the establishment of an international commission, with representatives of the different religious communities in the region, to oversee all rights and claims pertaining to religious issues. These plans met with considerable resistance from the Vatican. Pope Benedict XV warned that it would be unacceptable 'if infidels were placed in a more prominent position' in Palestine (Chamedes 2019: 57). In February 1922 Benedict was succeeded by the equally outspoken Pius XI. This letter of 15 May 1922 from Vatican Secretary of State Pietro Cardinal Gasparri made the Vatican's concerns clear.

The Holy See opposed Article 14 because it placed Catholics and Catholic sites under the oversight of non-Catholics. But as this excerpt illustrates, Gasparri raised other issues, including the fear that the Draft Mandate gave 'the Jewish element' a privileged position that would jeopardise the rights of the 'native populations'. Gasparri objected to the Mandate's recognition of a Jewish agency as a 'public body' (which was proposed because there was no Jewish government or internationally recognised leader that could act in that capacity). Referring to the Treaty of Versailles' rationale for mandates (a protective one for endangered minority populations), Gasparri observed that the Mandate was 'incompatible' with that purpose – despite the fact that in the early 1920s Jewish minority communities throughout Europe were the target of violent pogroms.

In a letter of 1 July 1922 to the League Secretary General, the British government addressed Gasparri's concerns, stating at the outset that Gasparri had misunderstood the Draft Mandate. The legal and political parameters for the relationship between Jewish and non-Jewish populations in Palestine would guarantee that all inhabitants, of whatever religious community, would be Palestinian in citizenship, thereby enjoying the same rights. The British letter also acknowledged the 'variety of religious interests' there and assured the Secretary General 'that nothing will be done in Palestine which might be construed as negligence of or indifference to Christian sentiment'.

This 1922 exchange concerned political matters, not theological ones, and the Vatican was focused on the interests of the Catholic population of Palestine. Gasparri's criticisms of the Draft Mandate, however, were all related to the Jewish population. It is an important reminder that while Jewish–Christian relations during this period were never entirely religious or theological in nature (particularly with regard to the questions of Zionism and Palestine), distrust was never far below the surface. Formal dialogues between the Holy See and representatives of the Jewish community began only after 1945. The Holy See never agreed to Article 14, and it was never implemented. International discussions about Palestine were among the most contentious political and interreligious topics of the interwar period, and have remained so, not least in respect of Jewish–Christian relations, to the present day.

Bibliography

Chamedes, Giuliana, *A Twentieth Century Crusade: The Vatican's Battle to Remake Christian Europe* (Cambridge, MA: Harvard University Press, 2019).

'Mandate for Palestine – UK Response to Letter from Cardinal Gasparri to the League of Nations' (C.436.1922/VI, published 4 July 1922), www.un.org/unispal/document/mandate-for-palestine-uk-response-to-letter-from-the-cardinal-secretary-of-state-vatican-to-the-league-of-nations/.

Minerbi, Sergio I, *The Vatican and Zionism: Conflict and the Holy Land, 1895–1925* (New York and Oxford: Oxford University Press, 1990).

Pedersen, Susan, 'Writing the Balfour Declaration into the Mandate for Palestine', *The International History Review* 45, no. 2 (2022), 279–91.

3

Max Eschelbacher: 'The Jewish Law' (1927)

Text

[...] What is the nature and character of the Jewish religion? In these pages Dibelius sees the difference in the contrast between Grace and Law, according to which Christianity represents the concept of grace, Judaism that of law. This contrast is not entirely correctly formulated. For Judaism universally teaches about the unfulfilled nature of human beings and the necessity of divine grace, imparted to us without our having earned it [...]

The decisive expression of pure Christianity is Paul's statement: 'If I speak in the tongues of angels and of mortals, but do not have love, I am a noisy gong or a clanging cymbal' (1 Cor. 13:1) [...] The love of which Paul speaks is infinitely rare. Indeed, whoever has it does not need the commandment, for according to the words of the Talmud, the Torah was not given to the angels. What, however, is to become of the poor person who has not received it through grace? Paul renders a harsh judgement on such a person. He may begin whatever he wants, may speak with the tongues of mortals and angels, [...] may give away all his possessions and his very body to be burned, but none of this will help him. Judaism, however, is kindhearted, compassionate and filled with genuine love as it presents the basic teaching that deliverance and salvation rest in good deeds [...] 'The wages of mitzvah is the mitzvah, and the wages of sin is sin. For a mitzvah attracts a mitzvah, and a sin attracts another sin.' [...] There is a well-known old Jewish saying: 'God wants to purify Israel, which is why He gave it many teachings and commandments.' [...]

This belief in law, order, moral discipline, obedience to God, is the soul of Judaism [...] Yet the unadorned word 'law' fails to convey what Judaism understands by Torah and *mitzvoth* [...] We can often experience the remarkable power contained within the unremarkable word *mitzvah*. This word is like a battery that stores religious energy. We would forfeit one of the most powerful incentives for a higher moral life and succumb to the weaknesses of natural human beings, if we were to give up our belief in 'the law', which the Christian world views only as a form of religious regimentation [...] The law is not a dead object of externally commanded works-salvation, but rather the path to human beings' salvation. The Catholic Church has come closer to Judaism when in the sacraments, while acknowledging the difference, it created something comparable to the *mitzvoth*. *Invisibilis gratiae visibile signum ad nostrum iustificationem institutum* [invisible grace is made visible by these established signs of our justification]. This definition of the sacraments in the Roman Catechism could apply just as well to our *mitzvoth* [...]

Judaism is not young, but its power of renewal is wonderful [...] The Jew who gives up his Jewish origins surrenders the best of his nature, but even after leaving it he remains blessed through this wellspring from which he flows. Whoever is called to the Torah thanks God 'who has given us his Torah and with that planted eternal life in our midst'.

Source

Eschelbacher, Max, 'Das jüdische Gesetz', *Der Jude* 9, no. 4, special issue 'Judentum und Christentum' (1927), 58–66. Author's own translation.

Commentary

Published by Martin Buber from 1916 to 1928, *Der Jude* was an important interwar platform for Jewish scholars, and Buber invited Christian scholars into this conversation. Eschelbacher's essay appeared in a special edition on Judaism and Christianity. A prolific German legal scholar and the Chief Rabbi in Düsseldorf, Eschelbacher was responding to an article by German New Testament scholar Martin Dibelius.

Dibelius argued that Jesus had broken with the Judaism of his day in overcoming what he described as the narrow-minded legalism of the Pharisees, leading to Christianity as a new religious tradition based upon 'grace' versus Judaism's emphasis on 'law'. A common distortion of Judaism that is central to Christian supersessionism, for centuries this distinction has led to antisemitic portrayals of Jews as judgemental and vengeful (e.g., in Shakespeare's *The Merchant of Venice*; see Chapter 5, p. 247).

Eschelbacher's refutation begins with a critique of Paul's portrayal of 'love', describing it as the 'decisive expression' of a Christianity that misrepresents the Jewish understanding that the law and love are inextricably interwoven. The essence of Judaism consists of obedience to God's law, a path that keeps human beings in relationship to God, thereby opening them to acts of genuine generosity and love. Sanctification comes through following Torah and doing *mitzvoth* ('good deeds') – which is indeed a form of 'grace'. Eschelbacher offers a rich portrait of the centrality of the law to the beauty of the Jewish tradition. He also draws a striking parallel between this understanding and Catholicism's understanding of the sacraments.

Although written in response to Dibelius' caricature of Judaism, this essay is directed more towards Eschelbacher's fellow German Jews – a diverse population that included Orthodox, conservative and secular Jews – urging them to wrestle with what it meant to be Jewish in a society in which the achievements of Jewish intellectuals and artists were celebrated amidst a pervasive and growing cultural and religious antisemitism. He was also wooing secularised German Jews, particularly the younger generation, to return to their religious tradition and experience its beauty (elsewhere in the essay he wrote of young German Jews rediscovering the sabbath and the Jewish holidays). In the interwar years there was a renewed interest in Judaism among some German Jews. What did it mean to be Jewish in the modern world? What defined the Jewish community and tradition? Was there a continuity, a shared tradition, between Judaism and Christianity, which could enrich both groups? Eschelbacher sought to ensure that any such continuity did not come at the expense of an accurate appreciation of the riches of Judaism.

Bibliography

Brenner, Michael, and Penslar, Derek J., *In Search of Jewish Community: Jewish Identities in Germany and Austria, 1918–1933* (Bloomington: Indiana University Press, 1998).

4

Protestant Responses to the Nazi Aryan Laws (1933)

Text

(i) Gerhard Kittel: 'The Jewish Question' (1933)

The Seriousness of the Question

Among the questions currently arising from today's German political situation, the Jewish question is the one that engenders an intense sense of insecurity and helplessness among many serious-minded people, both domestically and internationally. It is widely felt that there is much about antisemitism that is legitimate, that in fact there has been something about the situation of the Jews and their influence in Germany that has not been quite right [...] It thus becomes a serious question whether such radical legislation against Jews is really necessary and fair – legislation that will after all inevitably have a severe impact on a very great number of honest people – whether this sort of legislation can be justified from an ethical or a Christian point of view [...]

For Christians generally a very hard question arises out of the polemic against the Old Testament and certainly from the antisemitic attacks on the Jewish aspects of New Testament religion [...] Many wrestle unsuccessfully over this point, trying to balance the ethno-national [*völkisch*] ideal and the Christian-ethical claim [...]

[...] The National Socialist German Workers Party represents a positive Christianity [...] This carries with it the unconditional claim that the fight against Judaism must also be carried out on the basis of a conscious and clear Christian conviction. It is not enough, then, to base this struggle solely on racialist views or popular religion. *The true and complete answer can only be found if the Jewish question is successfully supported in religious terms and the fight against Judaism is given a Christian frame of reference.* On this point we must also find a clear path, one that allows us to think and to act in a way *that is at the same time both German and Christian* [...]

Judaism as a Religious Problem

[...] For Jews, returning to the God of the ancestors also always means coming back to the God of history. But God's history with the Jewish people has meant, for the last two thousand years, an existence as sojourners among the nations of the world. Returning to God means for the Jews to say an obedient 'yes' to this history with God: the misery of being scattered, the pain of obedient acceptance of Israel's forced exile [...] *Real Judaism remains true to its symbolic being as a restless and homeless sojourner wandering the earth.*

So for the best of the Jews today the problem is: whether it will be possible *to awaken a living religion within a Judaism that affirms its stranger-status* [...]

The situation is, indeed, analogous to that of the Christian nations [...] We are all learning again that the ultimate questions of the peoples cannot be answered by civilization and cultural philosophy [...] but only where culture and common life are sustained by a living faith in God that grows out of the *Volkstum* [...]

Jewish Christianity

[... *T*]*he baptism of a Jew does not affect his Jewishness* [...] *becoming a Christian does not mean becoming a German. The converted Jew does not become a German, but rather a Jewish Christian*, just as the Jews of whom the New Testament reports that they accepted baptism did not become part of a different ethnic culture [*Volkstum*], but were and remained Jewish Christians and members of the Jewish people.

Source

Kittel, Gerhard, 'The Jewish Question', in Solberg, Mary (ed. and trans.), *A Church Undone: Documents from the German Christian Faith Movement, 1932–1940* (Minneapolis: Fortress Press, 2015), 204–6, 219, 222. Reproduced by permission of Augsburg Fortress. Copyright © 2015 Fortress Press. All rights reserved. (Square-bracketed words are part of the original.)

(ii) Bethel Confession (August 1933 Version)

Section 1, 'On the Holy Scriptures' (Written by Dietrich Bonhoeffer and Hermann Sasse)

We reject the false doctrine that presents the history of salvation as a parable, for example, that the election of Israel as God's chosen people can be applied to any other people, or perhaps to all peoples. This is a denial of the uniqueness and the historicity of God's revelation [...]

We reject the false doctrine that tears apart the unity of the Holy Scriptures, rejecting the Old Testament or even replacing it with non-Christian documents from the ancient pagan history of another people. For the unity of the Holy Scriptures in their entirety and *their* unity alone is Christ.

For the same reason we reject the false doctrine that recognizes the Old Testament only as the Bible of Jesus, that is, of the original Christian church, and recognizes its validity only in that context (religious antisemitism).

Section 6, 'The Church and the Jews' (Written by Swiss Theologian Wilhelm Vischer)

The church teaches that God elected Israel, from among all the earth's peoples, to be the people of God [...] Jesus, the Christ promised by the Law and the Prophets, was rejected by the high council and the Jewish people according to the Scriptures. They wanted a national Messiah who would liberate them politically and make them masters of the world. But this, Christ Jesus was not, and did not do; he died at their hands, and for their sake. Through the crucifixion and raising from the dead of Christ Jesus, the dividing wall between Jews and Gentiles has been broken down (Eph. 2). The place of the Old Testament people of the covenant has been taken not by another nation but rather by the Christian church, called out of, and within, all nations.

God glorifies his overflowing faithfulness in remaining true to Israel according to the flesh, from which Christ was born in the flesh, despite all Israel's unfaithfulness and even after the crucifixion [...] God has preserved, according to the flesh, a sacred remnant of Israel, which neither becomes absorbed into any other nation by emancipation and assimilation, nor becomes a nation among others through Zionistic or similar efforts, nor can be annihilated by measures such as those used by Pharaoh. This sacred remnant has the *character indelebilis* [indelible character] of the chosen people.

The church has received from its Lord the mission to call the Jews to conversion and to baptize those who believe in the name of Jesus Christ, for the forgiveness of sins

(Matt. 10:5–6; Acts 2:38ff.; and 3:19–26). A mission to the Jews that refuses altogether to carry out baptisms of Jews because of cultural or political considerations is refusing to obey its Lord. Christ crucified is a stumbling block to the Jews and foolishness to the Gentiles (1 Cor. 1:22ff.) [...]

The fellowship of those belonging to the church is determined not by blood nor, therefore, by race, but by the Holy Spirit and baptism.

Source

Bonhoeffer, Dietrich, 'The Bethel Confession – August Version', in Rasmussen, Larry L. (ed.), *Berlin: 1932–1933*, trans. Isabel Best and David Higgins (Minneapolis: Fortress Press, 2009), 378–9, 416–19.

Commentary

In the summer of 1933 Protestant theologians and clergy were deeply divided about implementing a church 'Aryan paragraph', corresponding to the Nazi state's new civil service laws (see pp. 343–4). These two documents exemplify the opposing positions drawn by the pro-Nazi German Christians and the group that subsequently became the Confessing Church. As a theological defence of Nazi ideological claims about the 'threat' posed by the Jews, Gerhard Kittel's essay was more openly political, aligning Christianity with the state and embracing the 'positive Christianity' affirmed in the 1920 Nazi Party programme. In contrast, the Bethel Confession avoided direct political positions, instead offering a theological critique of the German Christians' distortions of Christian theological teachings about the Old Testament and Judaism.

One of the twentieth century's leading biblical scholars, Gerhard Kittel (1888–1948) is more notorious today for his open support for National Socialism and its antisemitic policies. Ironically, during the 1920s he was a respected Christian scholar on rabbinic thought, winning the praise of Jewish dialogue partners like Rabbi Max Dienemann. As document 4 (i) illustrates, however, Kittel's scholarship was based upon an understanding of Christianity that combined Christian supersessionism, anti-Judaism and the ethno-nationalist (*völkisch*) thinking that exemplified the German Christian Faith Movement. This text is from the published version of a 1933 speech in which Kittel addressed Zionism, 'race mixing' and the international 'Jewish problem'.

Kittel's renown as a biblical scholar made him very influential in German Protestantism, offering Nazi antisemitism a semblance of theological legitimacy. Here he re-envisioned Judaism and Christianity as expressions of very different, divinely ordained national purposes. A 'true Judaism' was being called to reaffirm its 'stranger' status among the nations – the logical outcome of the political charge that Jewish assimilation 'undermined' German culture. For Kittel, the necessary political consequences included revoking German Jews' citizenship and civil rights. His essay even included a brief section on 'extermination', which he dismissed as falling short of 'mastering the task at hand'.

That 'task' was nothing less than fulfilling God's will in history, which Kittel believed was inextricably tied to Christian anti-Jewish teachings. The deicide charge and the eternal 'judgement against the Jews' constituted permanent sins that could not be resolved even through conversion. Kittel was already arguing in 1933 for separate congregations for Christians of Jewish ancestry. His essay illustrates that even the 1939 Godesberg Declaration (which did establish such separate congregations in many regional churches; see document 12) would be only a transitional phase in a larger and more terrible political process.

The Bethel Confession (document 4 (ii)) was the first attempt by a group of opposition pastors and theologians (including Martin Niemoeller and Dietrich Bonhoeffer) to address the larger theological issues at stake in the Church Struggle (see p. 343). Two drafts were written in the summer of 1933; the final document was approved in November. Neither of these passages from the August version was included in the November version, which Bonhoeffer refused to sign.

Like the subsequent Barmen Declaration in May 1934, the Bethel Confession was both a theological critique of German Christian heresies and a reaffirmation of core Christian confessional beliefs. Both documents rejected the claim that Germans represented the new 'chosen people' and the related theological revisions.

In focusing on theological orthodoxy, the second Bethel excerpt ('The Church and the Jews') failed to confront the Christian theological underpinnings of antisemitism. In the accusation against Israel of 'unfaithfulness' for its rejection of Jesus as messiah, the passage on the 'Confessing Church and the Jews' expressed traditional anti-Judaism and replacement theology, although it clearly rejected the German Christians' embrace of a racialised and nationalised Christianity.

The first Bethel excerpt ('On the Holy Scriptures') is somewhat more striking. Not only did it affirm the uniqueness of God's election of Israel; it critiqued the claim that the Old Testament can only be read from the perspective of Christian salvation as a form of 'religious antisemitism'. As we have seen, however, this was omitted from the final version of the Bethel Confession, and Bonhoeffer did not pursue the question in his theological writings. The one Confessing Church theologian who wrote at length on the relationship between Judaism and Christianity was Hans Ehrenberg (see document 18).

Bibliography

Barnett, *For the Soul of the People*.

Ericksen, Robert P., *Theologians under Hitler: Gerhard Kittel, Paul Althaus, and Emanuel Hirsch* (New Haven: Yale University Press, 1985).

Gerlach, Wolfgang, *And the Witnesses Were Silent: The Confessing Church and the Jews*, trans. Victoria J. Barnett (Lincoln: University of Nebraska Press, 2000).

Rosenhagen, Ulrich, 'Together a Step towards the Messianic Goal: Jewish Protestant Encounters in the Weimar Republic', in Kaplan, Leonard, and Koshar, Rudy (eds.), *The Weimar Moment: Liberalism, Political Theology, and the Law* (Lanham: Lexington Books, 2012), 47–72.

5

Joseph Hertz: 'A Moral Challenge to British Jewry'
(31 March 1934)

Text

I take as my text the words from the opening section of the Haggadah, 'This year we are bondmen: next year may we be free men.' [...] Alas, it is no longer necessary to travel to far-off ages [...] to find a Jewry whose agony and martyrdom bring out the full meaning of [...] 'this year we are bondmen.' The unbelievable has come to pass. Only fourteen months ago, German Jewry was on the heights – illustrious through its achievement in every walk of life, strong in religious endeavour, and rich in worldly blessings. To-day, it is hurled down from its eminence: facing misery, insult and degradation; and sinking in deep waters of intolerance and hate.

[...] Neither Jewish statesmanship, nor pro-Jewish statesmanship, nor League of Nations statesmanship has been able to stem the repeal of Jewish emancipation by the Nazi rulers [...] What is worst of all, the world is coming to accept the outlawing, for fantastic racial reasons, of 600,000 and more human beings as a normal thing, with which no outside Government has the right to interfere [...]

Several spokesmen of Anglo-Jewry have referred to it as the greatest calamity that has befallen Jews and Judaism since the destruction of the Temple, and declare it to be without parallel in the annals of Israel. Neither of these statements is correct [...] Even in our own times there have been far more bestial attempts at annihilating the Jew. In the Ukraine, in the years after the Great War, there took place 887 large and 349 small pogroms, with a toll of 60,000 slain, and over 70,000 wounded [...]

Even Nazi persecution of men and women who are merely of Jewish descent is not something novel. That policy was anticipated five hundred years ago by the forerunners and founders of the Spanish Inquisition [...] Great was the joy of all sections of the Spanish people over these Marranos, or *conversos*, as these New Christians were then called [... S]ome *conversos* were still secretly practising their Judaism [...] The cry was raised, 'The Jew has wormed his way into the Church and into Spanish society in order to undermine them from within!' No distinction was made between genuine and ungenuine converts. Thousands of men and women whose only crime was that their ancestors generations ago were Jews, were massacred.

[... W]e are to-day witnessing a striking instance of history repeating itself. For over 150 years, every kind of pressure was brought to bear upon the Jews of Germany to leave the Jewish past, to despise their Jewish tradition, to give up their Faith, and become assimilated, body and soul, with their non-Jewish environment. Such thorough-going absorption alone, they were told, would entitle to full citizenship [...]

And now it is seen that all the sacrifices that were exacted by assimilation have been in vain [...] 'The Jew has wormed his way into every sphere of German life in order to undermine it from within,' is the Nazi echo of the older Spanish cry [...]

Have all these dread happenings no message for Jews of other lands? Some Jews neither learn anything nor forget anything. They still place pathetic trust in absolute assimilation [... I]n the first sermon I preached in this country, I maintained that no people was immune against the moral plague-germs of anti-Semitism; and [...] there was no Jewry that is absolutely safe.

Source

Hertz, Joseph, *A Moral Challenge to British Jewry: A Passover Sermon by the Chief Rabbi* (London: The Central British Fund for German Jewry, 1934), 1–9.

Commentary

Rabbi Joseph Hertz (1872–1946) was an internationally prominent rabbi and scholar of Judaism. Born in Hungary and educated in the United States, he spent his early career in South Africa before becoming Chief Rabbi of the United Hebrew Congregations of the British Empire in 1913.

In the early period of Nazism, there was widespread shock and disbelief among converted Germans of Jewish descent that they were affected by the Nazi racial laws. It was this issue that sparked the Protestant Church Struggle (see p. 343). Internationally, Christian leaders portrayed this expansion of antisemitic laws as something dramatically new; ecumenical leaders warned that National Socialism represented a new racially or ethno-nationally defined 'religion'.

As Hertz noted in his Passover sermon of 1934, however, the Nazis were not doing anything new. There was ample historical precedent for the racialisation of antisemitic hatred and violence. The same thing had happened in the Spanish Inquisition, with its targeting of *conversos* and accusations that Jews were only pretending to be Christians in order to infiltrate and 'undermine' society. Then and now, he argued, those who thought they could save themselves by converting to Christianity or believed that assimilation would guarantee their civil rights were tragically mistaken. History had shown repeatedly that antisemitism was pervasive and ineradicable, that antisemitic violence could strike any Jewish community anywhere and at any time. This conviction underscored his own Zionism.

Hertz's sermon exemplified the mood of many Jews in Europe and North America. Germany had been viewed as a success story for Jewish achievement and integration. Jewish communities around the world were stunned by the rise of an openly antisemitic government and the quickness with which non-Jewish Germans abandoned and attacked their neighbours and colleagues. Hertz's sermon was a summons to Jewish solidarity (he was raising money to help German Jews emigrate), but can also be read as a call for Christian support in the fight against antisemitism. A conservative rabbi and ardent Zionist, Hertz was already involved in Jewish–Christian relations and subsequently co-founded (with the Archbishop of Canterbury William Temple; see document 17 (ii)) the British Council of Christians and Jews in 1942.

Bibliography

Berkowitz, Michael, *Zionist Culture and West European Jewry Before the First World War* (Cambridge and New York: Cambridge University Press, 1993).
Mendes-Flohr, *German Jews*.

6

Siegfried Leffler: 'Christ in Germany's Third Reich' (1935)

Text

[…] In the whole history of humankind only one people experienced itself as a people down to its blood, that spoke of God as its own God who was with them, who knew and spoke of the meaning of their existence, their mission for the world. That is the people Israel. As a people it became a Satanic curse for the world when it decided against the God of heaven and earth and crucified him in Christ his Son […]

From of old, one people refused to serve the eternal Creator, refused to open itself to his kingdom on earth. One people once turned against the Redeemer. Today, should not one people, prepared by its disposition and its history, and equipped for this calling, set an example of freedom for the world, by in its best members clearly choosing God and his Savior? Today, should not one people be selected to become the counter-people [*Gegenvolk*] to the Jews, to remove the veil of night from the cross, and to perform for the world a truly redemptive service, a service no people on earth has done until this day?

This is our belief, from which we cannot release ourselves: that after 2000 years the Eternal One has called the German people to the mission that he has been nurturing for them since time began …

The world must choose between Israel and Germany, between a people with a law that looses destructive, ruinous forces everywhere and binds the creative spirit, that struck the Lord dead, and a people with the will and the gift to bring heaven and earth into a mysterious and creative relationship, and thereby to exorcise the forces of destruction. Germany's destiny is the world's destiny […]

The Old Testament

[…] The Old Testament is the national book [*Volksbuch*] of the Jewish people […] Do we as Germans have anything to seek in this book? For the old church, and for ecclesial and religious history, it will have and retain its value and meaning. We cannot simply say that it has no value for religious life; it contains insights and words of lasting value that will be respected by all peoples at all times. I think only of a verse from Psalm 23, '… and though I walk through the valley of the shadow, I will fear no evil, for you are with me!' or the opening verses of the 90th Psalm: 'Lord, you have been our dwelling place in all genera-tions; before the mountains were brought forth, or ever you had formed the earth and the world, from everlasting to everlasting you are God.' Whether such passages have Nordic origins, whether Nordic wisdom is expressed in the writings of the prophets, is not the first question for religious life in general [...]

However, it is also understandable that serious *völkisch-* [ethno-national] and German-minded people reject the Old Testament. They say, we are doing political battle with Judaism, and at the same time we are allowing their influence to affect our people's religious life through the Old Testament. We also think that German history and faithful German people and seers are more important for the instruction and edification of German children's souls than pious Jewish history. To our mature German comrades [*Volksgenossen*] we would advise the following: Dear friend, if you are happy without the Old Testament, by all means leave it aside! But don't take away from your fellow Germans – especially if you want to be tolerant – the words and insights that they have found comforting in their hour of need [...] The judgments of a Herder, a Goethe, or a Kant, to name just these, show us how much one can learn here, with gratitude, for one's spiritual enrichment, without thereby ceasing to be a good German.

Source

Leffler, Siegfried, 'Christ in Germany's Third Reich', in Solberg, Mary (ed. and trans.), *A Church Undone: Documents from the German Christian Faith Movement, 1932–1940* (Minneapolis: Fortress Press, 2015), 347–9, 359–61. Reproduced by permission of Augsburg Fortress. Copyright © 2015 Fortress Press. All rights reserved. (The square-bracketed German terms are part of the original.)

Commentary

Siegfried Leffler (1900–83) was the German Christian leader in Thuringia and one of the founders in 1939 of the Institute for the Study and Eradication of Jewish Influence on German Religious Life.

The most controversial aspect of the German Christian Movement was its proposal to completely 'dejudaicise' Christianity by removing the Old Testament from German Bibles, as well as all references to Jews (and to Jesus' Jewishness) from Protestant hymnals, liturgies and religious educational materials. The Nazi attack on 'Jewish influence' was well underway in 1933, but most theologians and clergy still viewed removing the Old Testament from Christian tradition as heresy (see document 4 (ii)). In addition to the establishment of racialised criteria for baptism and conversion, the removal of the Old Testament provoked a backlash among many church leaders and theologians in late 1933, leading hundreds of members to resign from the movement.

Here Leffler addressed the German Christian Movement's claims about what distinguished Christianity from Judaism, revealing the overlap between Nazi political ideology and Christian anti-Judaism. Echoing Nazi propaganda, Leffler argued that God had elected the German nation as the new 'chosen people', destined to replace the Jews as the original people of Israel and rescue the world from its 'Satanic curse'. Christian theology of that era was still based upon the supersessionist claim of replacement theology (i.e., that Christianity had replaced Judaism), and assumptions about the 'Christian nature' of German culture were widespread long before the Nazis rose to power. Leffler's argument was therefore less shocking to Christians in Germany than one might think, but the shift to declaring the racially defined German *Volk* as the 'chosen people of God' who had replaced the Jewish people was a dramatic one that illustrates how far the ideological reworking of biblical scholarship had progressed beyond traditional supersessionism (see document 4 (i)). Such messianic claims were also reflected in the extreme Christology of the 'Aryan' Jesus that was compatible with Nazi ideology.

In this 1935 document Leffler cautiously acknowledged the reluctance of many churchgoers to abandon the Old Testament and urged his colleagues to be tolerant of those who still found meaning in it. By 1939 when the Institute was established, however, he and his movement were firmly committed to erasing all traces of 'Jewish influence' from Christianity.

Bibliography

Bergen, *Twisted Cross*.
Heschel, *The Aryan Jesus*.
Lehmann, Hartmut, 'The Germans as Chosen People: Old Testament Themes in German Nationalism', *German Studies Review* 14, no. 2 (May 1991), 261–73.

7

Marc Boegner: Address to a Protest Meeting in the Hall of Chopin, Paris (20 November 1935)

Text

What Christianity Owes to Judaism

Christianity [...] is essentially a universal creed. Once one believes in Christ, whatever one's denomination may be, it is impossible not to subscribe fully to the words of that Jew of olden times St. Paul, the apostle, who having plumbed the depths of Christ's thought, exclaimed: 'There is neither Jew nor Greek, there is neither bond nor free, there is neither male nor female; for ye are all one in Christ Jesus' (Gal. 3, 28).

This is the basic tenet on which, since July 1933, all preaching in the Churches of Germany has been practically proscribed.

First, I wish to state that what has shocked and appalled Christian conscience, what has provoked protests from one end of the Christian world to the other – protests which will certainly be reiterated and increased – is precisely the fact that this new gospel of racialism already has been applied to the Jews, and seems to have reached its culmination point in the Nuremberg Decrees. One cannot know whether even worse may not happen later on [...]

Christian as I am, and knowing what Christianity owes to Judaism, I know that the Church of Jesus Christ is the daughter of what it calls the ancient Church of Israel ... The Protestant in me knows what the Gospel owes to those prophets who, beginning eight centuries before Jesus Christ, have presaged the universalism which the religion of Christ would later proclaim throughout the world.

Did not Isaiah welcome the day when all nations would flow unto the mountain of the Lord? And others after him, such as Jeremiah, did they not show their people, the only people ever elected, the road by means of which they were to bring to others the revelation which had been bestowed upon them, so that all nations might come to know the true God?

The Gospel is the heritage and fulfilment of that great hope of the prophets. It is impossible for a Christian, when he sees the infamous crusades conducted against Judaism, not to be among those who declare that they are unable to forget what they owe to the Jewish people. We are among those who remember all this with deep gratitude. We believe that this gratitude, in view of the suffering of this people who are being crucified once again, ought to be shown in acts of sympathy and solidarity […]

The 'New Gospel'

It is not only through the persecution of the non-Aryans that the desire has arisen amongst many Germans to preach a new gospel, but because of a claim to meet Christ on a new basis, particularly on the basis of the glorification of the German race and blood […] Paganism has asserted itself on the fringes of the Church and its influence gradually has pervaded it. An effort even has been made […] to have the Old Testament – containing the magnificent history of the Jewish people and I even would say, of God's great acts toward the Jewish race – banned and barred from religious instruction.

Source

Reprinted by permission of the Snoek family from *The Grey Book: A Collection of Protests against Anti-Semitism and the Persecution of the Jews issued by Non-Roman Catholic Churches and Church Leaders during Hitler's Rule* by Johan M. Snoek, published by Van Gorcum & Co. Copyright © 1969 Johan M. Snoek. Text quoted from pp. 50–2.

Commentary

Marc Boegner (1881–1970) was President of the Protestant Federation of France and a leading figure in the European ecumenical movement. The French Protestant churches were a minority in Roman Catholic France, and the historical persecution of French Huguenots made Protestants sensitive to minority issues. In April 1933 Boegner wrote a letter to the Chief Rabbi of France referring to this history, assuring him of Protestant solidarity with the Jewish community. It was one of several such letters that French Protestant leaders sent to French rabbis and Jewish organisations in 1933.

His 1935 address was delivered at a large protest rally organised by French political and religious leaders in the wake of the September 1935 Nuremberg laws, the culmination of Nazi antisemitic racial legislation that (among other measures) revoked German Jews' citizenship. Most of Boegner's remarks concerned developments in the German Protestant

Church since the July 1933 church elections, including the widespread denial of Jesus' Jewishness and the promotion of a 'gospel of racialism' by the German Christians. His perspective was shared by other European and US ecumenists like Willem Visser't Hooft and Henry Smith Leiper, who believed that National Socialism represented a dangerous, destabilising ideological 'national religion' (in Boegner's words, a form of 'paganism') that was antithetical to the universality of the Christian message.

Protestant ecumenical leaders issued some of the strongest and earliest condemnations of Nazi antisemitic policies, beginning with the September 1933 declaration from an ecumenical meeting in Sofia, Bulgaria. Nonetheless, their early statements often failed to address the specifically Christian roots of antisemitism. German Christians invoked New Testament texts as theological justification for their positions and Nazi propaganda used slanders like the deicide charge to incite hatred against German Jews. In this address Boegner theologically affirmed the Jewish foundations of Christianity – particularly the prophetic books – as the living heritage that not only shaped Christian obligations to the Jewish people but were critical for understanding the true meaning of the Gospel. His claims to Christian 'universalism' and his description of Christianity as 'the fulfilment' of Isaiah's prophecies, however, still showed supersessionism.

Boegner continued to be outspoken against antisemitism throughout the 1930s. During the Nazi occupation of France he was a complex figure. A pacifist, he refused to join the Maquis resistance but worked behind the scenes to rescue French Jews. In conjunction with the CIMADE (Comité inter-mouvements auprès des évacués, a French resistance group that hid and saved hundreds of Jews) he helped several hundred French Jews reach Switzerland and was recognised by Yad Vashem as a Righteous Gentile in 1988. He was also appointed to the Vichy National Council and testified after the war on behalf of Marshal Pétain. After 1945 he continued his ecumenical engagement as an observer to the Second Vatican Council.

Bibliography

Barnett, Victoria, 'Ecumenical Protestant Responses to the Rise of Nazism, Fascism, and Antisemitism during the 1920s and 1930s', in Spicer, Kevin P. and Carter-Chand, Rebecca (eds.), *Religion, Ethnonationalism and Antisemitism in the Era of the Two World Wars* (Montreal: McGill-Queen's University Press, 2022), 356–77.

Caron, Vicki, *Uneasy Asylum: France and the Jewish Refugee Crisis, 1933–1942* (Stanford: Stanford University Press, 2002).

Visser't Hooft, Willem A., *Memoirs* (Philadelphia: Westminster Press, 1973).

8

Irene Harand: His Struggle *(1935)*

Text

Chapter 11: 'Trial Balance of the Swastika'

Every anti-Semite is a sinner. He ought to know that our Lord detests nothing more than hypocrisy, than hate, than pitilessness, than the assumption of the role of moral judge when the judge himself is not free of guilt. How heavily all these errors must weigh in the scale of justice when throughout the centuries we have tormented and persecuted our fellow-men [...]

Whoever reads this book and still remains an anti-Semite, furnishes proof of non-belief in God. I go even a step further: I know that the majority of my Christian coreligionists reject anti-Semitism. That they are content merely to reject it makes them equally responsible for the agony of our Jewish fellow-men, for the horrible physical and spiritual suffering inflicted upon them merely because they are Jews. It is not sufficient to reject anti-Semitism. It is the duty of all good Christians to take an active part against it, and by spreading truth and knowledge, remove the disgrace of the Swastika. We must realize what dreadful injustice hatred against the Jews does to our children. In school and in their daily living they will be inclined to blame the Jews for any evil that may befall them. Hatred will prevent them from seeing things as they really are; it will obscure their judgement. For anti-Semitism as a mass expression warps the normal intellectual development of humanity [...]

Chapter 12: Conclusion

What about the spiritual heritage of the Jews? They are the creators of the Bible. We, Catholics, see in the Bible a revelation of God. Can we assume that God would have chosen a most unworthy people to transmit his revelations to us? Even those who believe the Bible to be the work of men must all the more admire its creators. In addition to the Bible, the Jews have compiled the Talmud and many other religious guide books, the high ethical value of which cannot be controverted [...] I have quoted a large number of teachings contained in these writings. They testify to an admirable depth of feeling for others, to a purity of character, to an integrity of sentiment and to a rectitude in trade and conduct [...]

The Hitlerites not only rob us of reason but also despoil human sentiment. Can a German child, the silent witness of his Jewish playmate's unjust torture and humiliation, become a good person? Can a National Socialist, who beats, torments or even murders his neighbor in a concentration camp, feel any vestige of love or compassion? Will not his soul be deadened by the constant atrocities, by hatred, barbarity and lust for killing? Mankind requires for its progress not only reason but also love [...]

As it is, Christianity pioneered for Hitler when it condoned anti-Semitism. In fact, we nurtured it by hanging a religious cloak about it. We preached love of neighbor, but in our hearts we fostered envy and hatred against a group of humans who committed no wrong. We allowed the serums of Jewish physicians to cure our ills, we accepted everything created by Jewish intellect. At the same time we did everything to fan hatred of the Jews. This truth must be acknowledged if the evil is to be checked in time. It is not yet too late [...]

If we want to protect ourselves and our children from the atrocities inherent in Nazi-ism, we must do everything possible to obviate hatred of the Jews. Our children must be inoculated with the idea – even before school age – that people are equal before God, and that one must fight only evil individuals. If our children come in contact with Jewish children or adults, we must impress upon them the respect due the Jewish religion and the value of Jews as human beings.

Source

Harand, Irene, *His Struggle (An Answer to Hitler)* (Chicago: Artcraft Press, 1937), 247–8, 315–19.
(Harand self-published the original German *Sein Kampf* in Austria in 1935.)

Commentary

In 1933 the Austrian Catholic journalist Irene Harand (1900–75) founded a Viennese weekly publication, *Gerechtigkeit (Justice)*, in response to the Nazi rise to power in Germany. She also became politically active in fighting antisemitism. Neither a theologian nor a church employee, Harand's activism was shaped by her understanding of Christian ethics. She developed close ties to Austrian Catholic leaders as well as to the Viennese Jewish community (her co-editor at *Gerechtigkeit* was Moritz Zalman, a Jewish lawyer), and her activities were known in international Jewish circles.

In contrast to the ecumenical documents of this era and their focus on the racialised nature of Nazi antisemitism, especially within the German Christian Movement, she argued that the foundations of Nazi antisemitism were theological and could be traced to Christianity. For that reason it was not enough for Christians to oppose antisemitism privately; they had to fight actively against it. That included studying and condemning the long history of Christian anti-Jewish teachings and actions as well as teaching Christian children respect for the riches of Judaism. In particular, she argued, churches had a special responsibility for the moral formation of children. Antisemitism affected not only its Jewish victims; it was a rot that eroded Christians' sense of justice, love and compassion.

Like James Parkes' *The Conflict of the Church and the Synagogue* (1934), Harand's 1935 book *His Struggle* began with a detailed history of the Christian persecution of Jews over the centuries and concluded by urging her readers to study and appreciate the Jewish tradition. As historian John Connelly has observed, one thing that distinguished Harand and Parkes from other Christians of the era was that they actually had friendships and conversations with Jews, leading them to 'a new quality of solidarity' (2012: 143). Nonetheless, Harand remained relatively unknown in the postwar period.

Harand was on a lecture tour in England when Nazi Germany took over Austria in 1938 and subsequently immigrated to the United States. In 1969 Yad Vashem honoured her as one of the Righteous among the Nations.

Bibliography

Connelly, John, *From Enemy to Brother: The Revolution in Catholic Teaching on the Jews, 1933–1965* (Cambridge, MA: Harvard University Press, 2012).

'Harand Irene', Yad Vashem, https://collections.yadvashem.org/en/righteous/4015210.

'Harand, Irene (1900–1975)', in Commire, Anne (ed.), *Women in World History: A Biographical Encyclopedia* (Waterford: Yorkin Publications, 2002).

9

Miron Cristea: Statement Published with Commentary in The Churchman *(1937)*

Text

'The Jews have caused an epidemic of corruption and social unrest. They monopolize the press, which, with the aid of foreign help, permanently flays all the spiritual treasures of the Rumanians. One feels like crying with pity for the good Rumanian nation, whose very marrow has been sucked from its bones by the Jews.

To defend ourselves is a national and patriotic duty, not anti-Semitic. Lack of measures to get rid of this plague would indicate that we are lazy cowards who let ourselves be carried alive to our graves.

Why should the Jews enjoy the privilege of living like parasites on our backs? Why should we not get rid of these parasites who suck Rumanian Christian blood? It is logical and holy to react against them.

To dislocate Arabs from their homes in Palestine for the sake of the Jew is neither right nor humane.

The duty of a Christian is to love himself first and to see that his needs are satisfied. Only then can he help his neighbor if he approaches him with a clean soul and in the spirit of good neighborliness.'

[…]

The Churchman: 'Nowhere else in the world, so far as we are aware, has the leader of a Christian communion made so black a statement. At a time when in the United States Christians, both Catholic and Protestant, are working together with Jews in such organizations as the National Conference of Jews and Christians toward better understanding and cooperation, such a declaration stands out in sinister delineation. While the hands of the Christian church in America are by no means clean in respect to anti-Semitism, our recognized leaders have not as yet been guilty of any similar denunciation of our Jewish brothers, and we pray that no one of them may ever bring that guilt upon the religion they represent. If we have our pro-Fascist, anti-Semitic groups in this country […] we have as yet sanity and decency enough to condemn them as composed of a lunatic fringe which, by its activities, has sacrificed the right to be called Christian. In no one of these groups is there a leader of prominence even remotely approaching that of the Rumanian patriarch, whose fantastic statement should deprive him, among his fellow religionists throughout the world, of the right to the Christian name.'

Source

'Ecclesiastical "Christianity"', *The Churchman* 151, no. 16 (15 September 1937), 8.

Commentary

International attention during the 1930s was focused on events in Nazi Germany, but Patriarch Cristea's 1937 speech is a reminder that antisemitism was widespread in Christian Europe. Originally a bishop in the Transylvanian Orthodox Church under Hungarian rule, Cristea (1868–1939) was the first Patriarch of the Romanian Orthodox Church from 1925 to 1939 and became prime minister of Romania in 1938.

In his early career Cristea had promoted tolerance towards the Jewish community, but by the early 1930s he was an outspoken antisemite who aligned the Romanian Orthodox Church leadership with the Iron Guard. The Iron Guard (also known as the Legion of the Archangel St Michael) was a fascist antisemitic movement that had emerged in Romania during the late 1920s. Its leaders drew heavily on Orthodox mysticism and the group soon found widespread support among Orthodox priests and the laity. During Cristea's time as Patriarch and prime minister, almost a quarter of Romanian Jews were stripped of their citizenship. In November 1940 Romania joined the Axis alliance. Almost 220,000 Romanian Jews were murdered in the Holocaust; Romanian troops participated in the murders of their Jewish compatriots.

Cristea's speech offered a litany of widespread antisemitic stereotypes, including the argument that Christians had the duty to defend themselves and their countries against the purported threats from Jews. His claim that the battle against Jews was both a national and a Christian duty was echoed by other fascist movements of that era, illustrating the integration of traditional antisemitism into the more modern form of Christian ethno-nationalism. His text also included a striking anti-Zionist perspective that was evident elsewhere during the 1930s, not only among Christian fascist movements but among other sectors of the Christian church as well. As a growing number of European Jews began to seek refuge in Palestine, European and North American Christians (influenced by their historical ties to Arab churches through the missionary movement) tended to share the perspective of the Arab population (see p. 343 and document 2). Their statements about Jewish refugees and Zionism sometimes included antisemitic stereotypes.

It is striking that an Episcopal magazine in the United States chose to publish Cristea's speech, along with a strong condemnation. American church leaders and interfaith organisations like the National Conference of Christians and Jews were closely following developments in European churches and concerned about possible parallels in the United States. The threat of antisemitism and the growing number of pro-fascist movements in the United States remained a concern. This publication of Cristea's comments with the Episcopal response may well have been intended as a warning about the events unfolding in Europe and the necessity of US churches taking a clear stand against antisemitism. Although some American fascist movements were openly Christian nationalist (cf. document 11), none of the established national churches in the US developed a pro-fascist movement comparable to the Iron Guard or the German Christians. (See also document 14.)

Bibliography

Carter-Chand and Spicer, *Religion, Ethnonationalism and Antisemitism*.
Popa, *The Romanian Orthodox Church and the Holocaust*.

10

Jacques Maritain: 'Antisemitism' (1938)

Text

[... A]ccording to St. Paul, we gentile Christians have been grafted on to the predestined olive tree of Israel in place of the branches which did not recognise the Messiah foretold by the prophets. Thus we are converts to the God of Israel who is the true God, to the Father whom Israel recognised, to the Son whom it rejected. Christianity, then, is the overflowing expansion and the supernatural fulfilment of Judaism [...]

Between Israel and the world, as between the Church and the world, there is a supra-human relation. It is only by considering this triad, that one can form some idea, even enigmatically, of the mystery of Israel [...] The Church is the mystical body of Christ. Indeed, Jewish thought is itself aware that in a quite different sense and in its own way, Israel is a *corpus mysticum*, a mystical body [...] The bond which unifies Israel is not simply the bond of flesh and blood, or that of an ethico-historical community; it is a sacred and suprahistorical bond, of promise and yearning rather than of possession. In the eyes of a Christian who remembers that the promises of God are irrevocable and without repentance, Israel continues its sacred mission [...] Israel, like the Church, is in the world and not of the world [...] Thus is the mystery of Israel understood from a Christian viewpoint.

[... W]hile the Church is assigned the labour of supernatural and supratemporal redemption of the world, Israel, we believe, is assigned, on the plane and within the limits of secular history, a task of *earthly activisation* of the mass of the world [... I]t teaches the world to be discontented and restless as long as the world has not God; it stimulates the movement of history.

The Spiritual Essence of Antisemitism

It seems to me that these considerations explain something of the spiritual essence of antisemitism.

[...] If the world hates the Jews, it is because the world clearly senses that they will always be 'outsiders' in a supernatural sense, it is because the world detests their passion for the absolute and the unbearable stimulus which it inflicts. It is the vocation of Israel that the world execrates. To be hated by the world is their glory, as it is also the glory of Christians who live by faith [...]

Thus hatred of Jews and hatred of Christians spring from a common source, from the same recalcitrance of the world [...] We are good enough as we are, says the world, we have no need of grace or transfiguration, we ourselves will accomplish our own happiness in our own nature. This is neither Christian hope in a helping God, nor Jewish hope for a God on earth [...]

Jews and Christians

[...] Thence come the conflicts and the tension which, under all sorts of masks, necessarily prevail between Israel and the nations.

It is an illusion to believe that that tension can completely vanish; but it is a villainy to desire to put an end to the problem by antisemitic violence [...] The only way is to accept the state of tension and to face it [...] not with hatred, but with that concrete intelligence which love demands from each, so that he may come to an early understanding with his adversary while they travel together, and in the consciousness that 'all have sinned and need the glory of God' [...]

On the spiritual plane, the drama of love between Israel and its God, if we are to believe St. Paul, will reach a *dénouement* only with the reconciliation of the Synagogue and the Church [...]

[... I]n September, 1938 [...] the Pope said, 'Notice that Abraham is called our Patriarch, our ancestor. Antisemitism is incompatible with the thought and sublime reality expressed in this text [the words in the Catholic mass about the 'sacrifice of our father Abraham']. It is a movement in which we Christians can have no part whatsoever ... Antisemitism is unacceptable. Spiritually we are Semites.'

[... F]rom the Catholic viewpoint, antisemitism [...] seems to be a pathological phenomenon, which indicates a deterioration of Christian conscience when it becomes incapable of accepting its own historic responsibilities and of remaining existentially faithful to the high exigencies of Christian truth.

Source

Maritain, Jacques, *Antisemitism* (London: Geoffrey Bles, The Centenary Press, 1939), 16–22, 27–8. (US title: *A Christian Looks at the Jewish Question.*)

Commentary

Jacques Maritain (1882–1973) was a French philosopher whose work encompassed metaphysics, ethics, political theory and human rights. Raised a Protestant, he was a convert to Catholicism and married to a Jewish woman. Both factors gave him a critical outsider's view on the role of the Catholic Church and its theology during the Shoah. During the Nazi years he taught in the United States and Canada, but was outspoken in his condemnation of the Vichy regime and involved in helping Jewish refugees. As French ambassador to the Vatican after World War II, in 1946 Maritain famously tried to convince Pope Pius XII to denounce antisemitism and he went on to play a seminal role in the conversations leading up to the Second Vatican Council (see *Nostra aetate*, Appendix to Part III, p. 512). His writings continue to be influential in Catholic scholarship on the relationship to Judaism.

Among Christian theologians and church leaders a more systemic critical rethinking of Christian teachings about Jews only began after 1945. Up to that point, even Christians who opposed antisemitism and were horrified by the Nazified versions of Christianity in Germany usually remained supersessionist, viewing the fulfilment of Israel as necessarily bound to its acceptance of Jesus as the messiah.

In this striking 1938 speech, delivered both in Paris (on 5 February) and in New York (for the National Conference of Jews and Christians, 14 December), the basis for Maritain's later theology is clearly evident, including his foundational rethinking of the Jewish–Christian relationship. The 'mystery of Israel' leads him to recognise the 'mystery' of the church: the tension between what God intends and the human understanding of the Jewish–Christian relationship. That 'mystery' opens the way for a deeper Christian self-understanding of Christianity's place in the world, leading to his insight that there is a 'common source' for anti-Christian and anti-Jewish hatred: both communities would be hated as 'outsiders' if they were faithful to their vocation.

The multiple complexities of the historical and theological relationship between Israel and the Christian church led Maritain to recognise that Israel continued to have a mission, with the clear implication that its covenant with God had neither been superseded nor replaced. This in turn led him to reflect on the challenge of antisemitism not just as a political or even a theological problem, but very much as a deeper spiritual one. He concluded by noting Pius XI's 1938 condemnation of antisemitism, adding that antisemitism represented a 'pathological [...] deterioration of Christian conscience'. There are echoes here of Harand, Parkes and Elisabeth Schmitz (1893–1977), theologian and lay member of the Confessing Church in Berlin – all Christians in the 1930s who grasped the ineradicable damage that antisemitism was doing to Christianity (see documents 8, 19).

Bibliography

Connelly, John, *From Enemy to Brother: The Revolution in Catholic Teaching on the Jews, 1933–1965* (Cambridge, MA: Harvard University Press, 2012).

Crane, Richard, *Passion of Israel: Jacques Maritain, Catholic Conscience and the Holocaust* (Scranton: University of Scranton Press, 2010).

Kornberg, Jacques, *The Pope's Dilemma: Pius XII Faces Atrocities and Genocide in the Second World War* (Toronto: University of Toronto Press, 2015), 159–60.

11

Charles Coughlin: 'Persecution: Jewish and Christian' (20 November 1938)

Text

[...] In all countries Jews are in the minority. They have no nation of their own; they have no flag. '*The World Almanac*' states that there are only 15-million Jews in all the world and only 4-million resident in North America. Certainly they are in the minority – but a closely woven minority in their racial tendencies; a powerful minority in their influence;

a minority endowed with an aggressiveness, an initiative which, despite all obstacles, has carried their sons to the pinnacle of success in journalism, in radio, in finance and in all the sciences and arts [...]

Therefore, I say to the good Jews of America, be not indulgent with the irreligious, atheistic Jews and gentiles who promote the cause of persecution in the land of the Communists; the same ones who promote the cause of atheism in America. Yes, be not lenient with your high financiers, and politicians who assisted at the birth of the only political, social, and economic system in all civilization that adopted atheism as its religion, internationalism as its patriotism and slavery as its liberty [...]

My fellow citizens, I am not ignorant of Jewish history. I know its glories. I am acquainted with its glorious sons. I am aware of the keen intellectuality which has characterized its progress in commerce, in finance, in all the arts and sciences and, particularly, in the field of communications.

But I am also aware that every nation from time immemorial has lifted in its hand the lash of persecution to strike the back of Jewry. From Nineveh to Berlin; from ancient to modern times, a constant moan of suffering has been raised from the Weeping Wall whose structure now has encompassed the world.

Portugal and Spain, France and Germany, England and the northern countries, Italy and Russia – all, in turn, have taken their stand at the pillar of persecution to wield the leaden lash about the shoulders of Jews – for what reason I need not detail at the moment. I will satisfy myself simply by drawing to your attention that, since the time of Christ, Jewish persecution only followed after Christians first were persecuted – persecuted either by exploiters within their own ranks, as in the Middle Ages, or by enemies from without, as in our own days – the days of Communism.

Source

Coughlin, Rev. Charles E., *'Am I an Anti-Semite?': Nine Addresses on Various 'ISMS' Answering the Question, November 6, 1938–January 1, 1939* (Detroit: Condon Printing Co., 1939), 36–43.

Commentary

Charles Coughlin (1891–1979) was a Canadian-born Catholic diocesan priest who became the most notorious antisemite in the United States during the 1930s. A staunch anti-communist and populist, in 1926 Coughlin launched a weekly radio show, 'The Hour of Power', that drew a national audience of millions. Although initially focused on religious themes, Coughlin's broadcasts were soon devoted to political commentary.

In 1938 Coughlin founded the Christian Front, intended to combat the influence of 'international Jews' and communists, and he openly defended fascism and Nazism. The Christian Front organised a national 'Buy Christian' boycott of Jewish stores, and some of its members violently attacked American Jewish citizens. His political views led him to support the Axis powers in World War II, and the American government finally moved against him in 1942. Only then did his bishop, the newly appointed Edward Mooney, order him to cease his political activities. He continued to serve as priest in his Detroit church until he retired in 1966. He was never defrocked.

In this radio sermon, preached only days after the 9 November pogroms (although he never mentioned Nazi Germany), Coughlin used a number of antisemitic stereotypes to attack Jews, weaving in religious references. Noting the persecution of Jews through the ages in 'every nation', he justified it obliquely ('for what reason I need not detail at the moment') with a clear reference to the scourging of Jesus before his crucifixion ('the leaden lash across the shoulders').

Coughlin also restated a claim that appeared frequently in Christian responses at the time, even among Christians who opposed Nazi Germany (see, e.g., document 13): that the Christian churches were the ultimate targets of Nazi policies, and that Christians were already suffering. The very title of the sermon, 'Persecution: Jewish and Christian', minimised the horror of what had just occurred throughout Germany and Austria. Anti-Catholicism was indeed widespread in the United States during that era, and fears of anti-clericalism led most American Catholics to support Franco in the Spanish Civil War (putting them at odds with American Jews, who supported the loyalists). In this sermon Coughlin referred to these Catholic fears as he dismissed the widespread condemnation of the German pogroms. The Jews of Germany might be persecuted, he argued, but only because Christians had suffered all the more, often at the hands of Jews.

Bibliography

'Charles Coughlin', United States Holocaust Memorial Museum, https://encyclopedia.ushmm.org/content/en/article/charles-e-coughlin.

Gallagher, Charles, *Nazis of Copley Square: The Forgotten Story of the Christian Front* (Cambridge, MA: Harvard University Press, 2021).

12

Evangelical Church of the Old Prussian Union: The Godesberg Declaration (1939)

Text

With an unwavering determination to lead the church struggle to a resolution in accord with positive Christianity, representatives of the National Church Union of German Christians and men from various groups of Protestant pastors and laymen have come together to consult with one another. The decision was taken to engage in a loosely constituted comradely and cooperative project. The following statements are the basis for our work together:

1. With all the strength of our faith and our active life we serve the man who has led our people [*Volk*] out of servitude and misery to freedom and true greatness.

2. We battle relentlessly against all elements that disguise religion as political freedom. Part of the great religious-political struggle that in our era is coursing through our entire people is evident in the church struggle [*Kirchenkampf*]. The forms of the church struggle are degrading, the struggles for power are reprehensible, but the struggle itself we affirm as a sign of the new growth of religious life.

3. The core questions of this religious debate are the following:

a. What is the relationship between politics and religion; what is the relationship between the National Socialist worldview and the Christian faith?

To this question we respond:

In that National Socialism contests any claim on the part of the churches to political authority and makes the National Socialist worldview appropriate to the German people obligatory for everyone, it carries on Martin Luther's work in the political-philosophical realm, and in this way helps us, from a religious point of view, to return to a true understanding of the Christian faith.

b. What is the relationship between Judaism and Christianity? Is Christianity derived from Judaism and therefore its continuation and fulfillment, or does Christianity stand in contradiction to Judaism?

To this question we respond:

The Christian faith is the unbridgeable religious opposite of Judaism.

c. Is Christianity essentially supranational and international?

To this question we respond:

Supranational and international ecclesiasticism of the Roman Catholic or world-Protestant type is a political degeneration of Christianity. Genuine Christian faith develops fruitfully only within the given orders of creation.

4. On the basis of our fundamental knowledge of the tenor of the religious debate, it is self-evident that constructions, constitutions, and legislation will never move things forward. The struggle must rather be carried out internally.

5. The preconditions for such a religious debate are order and tolerance in the church. We applaud as a substantial contribution the regulations of the Protestant Church of the Prussian Union that have just appeared.

6. The stance described by these statements will be the basis for beginning our work together.

Source

Leffler, Siegfried, et al., 'The Godesberg Declaration and Responses', in Solberg, Mary (ed. and trans.), *A Church Undone: Documents from the German Christian Faith Movement, 1932–1940*

Commentary

The Godesberg Declaration marked the culmination of the German Christians' efforts to align German Protestantism – institutionally and theologically – with National Socialism. The very first sentence embraced the 'positive Christianity' that had been defined in Article 24 of the 1920 Nazi Party platform. Point 2 was a clear condemnation of the Confessing Church, which they accused of misrepresenting 'religion as political freedom' in a 'reprehensible' power struggle. Point 3.c challenged the idea that Christianity was a religion that transcended international boundaries, arguing instead that German Protestantism had to reflect the values of the German nation. This was based upon the German Christians' highly disputed interpretation of the Lutheran and Reformed doctrines of 'orders of creation' and the claim that God had created certain fixed worldly orders like the state.

The document was the logical outcome of the theological positions taken by figures like Gerhard Kittel and Siegfried Leffler (documents 4 (i) and 6). It declared the unity of National Socialism and Christianity as a task that continued Luther's legacy, leading to a 'true understanding' of Christian faith. In a full integration of antisemitism and Christian biblical theology, Judaism and Christianity were declared to be 'unbridgeable' opposites. The Godesberg Declaration effectively upended supersessionism: not only was the church 'the new Israel', but Christianity's roots in Judaism were utterly denied. Jesus of Nazareth was to be understood as an 'Ayran Jesus'.

The Declaration had two dramatic consequences. First, it provided an official foundation for a process already underway, establishing separate congregations for Christians of Jewish descent and barring them from attending regular congregations (point 5 of the Declaration refers to these regulations). With that, what little support from the church leadership remained for 'non-Aryan' members was effectively withdrawn. The full 'Aryanisation' of these regional churches was complete.

Secondly, the Declaration led to the founding of the Institute for the Study and Eradication of Jewish Influence in German Church Life in 1939 (see also Chapter 9, p. 486). Siegfried Leffler was named director and its faculty included leading German biblical scholars like Walter Grundmann. Dedicated to carrying forth the Declaration's antisemitic agenda, the Institute produced a new version of the Bible that eliminated the Old Testament, revising New Testament scriptures to 'dejudaicise' Jesus and his followers. It also published a new hymnal and liturgical material.

The Godesberg Declaration was signed by only eleven of Germany's twenty-eight regional churches (and the Protestant Church of Austria); all eleven regions had been German Christian and Nazi Party strongholds since 1933. It immediately provoked protests from the Confessing Church and the Confederation of Reformed Churches in Nazi Germany, as well as a condemnation from the nascent WCC in Geneva (until 1948 officially known as the World Council of Churches in process of formation (WCC-ipof)). While all these protests condemned the heretical theological nature of the statement and its repercussions for the future of Christianity in Nazi Germany, none of them explicitly critiqued the wider repercussions of this extreme radicalisation of the Protestant church for Jews.

Bibliography

Gerlach, Wolfgang, *And the Witnesses Were Silent: The Confessing Church and the Jews*, trans. Victoria J. Barnett (Lincoln: University of Nebraska Press, 2000).
Heschel, *The Aryan Jesus*.

13

Federal Council of Churches of the United States: 'The Christian Attitude toward Anti-Semitism' (1939)

Text

Every thoughtful Christian must gratefully acknowledge his spiritual indebtedness to the Hebrews. We Christians have inherited the ethical and religious insights of Israel. We hold them with a difference – at one point with a momentous difference – but we can never forget that the historic roots of our faith are in the Hebrew people.

From Israel we inherit the Ten Commandments, which are still our basic moral standards. From Israel we inherit the priceless treasure of the Psalms, which are an essential part of Christian worship around the world. From Israel we inherit the vision of social justice which has come to us through Amos and Isaiah and Micah. From Israel we inherit even our own unique Christian classic, the New Testament, nearly all of which (if not all) was written by Jews.

A Christian who faces the modern world must also be conscious of a present spiritual kinship with his Jewish neighbors to whom their religious heritage is still a vital force. That kinship is grounded in our common faith in the ultimate spiritual foundations of the universe. Over against those who adhere to a materialistic philosophy of life and a mechanistic conception of human destiny, we recognize ourselves as at one with the Jews in the first sublime affirmation of the Pentateuch: 'In the beginning God.' Over against current disillusionment and despair Christian and Hebrew stand together in their belief in the one Holy God Who is the Creator of all and whose righteous will gives meaning and direction to life.

A Christian who knows anything of history must also speak a word of confession. For he cannot help recalling how grievously the Jewish people have suffered at the hands of men who called themselves Christians. The record of the treatment of Jews in Europe through long centuries is one which Christians of today view with penitence and sorrow.

One has also regretfully to admit that the day of cruel treatment of the Jews by some who call themselves Christians is not yet a thing of the past. Even in our own country there are misguided groups which circulate statements that spread a poison of mistrust and hate which is antithetical to the true genius both of America and of the Christian religion. Anti-Semitism is inherently un-Christian, contrary to the plain teaching and spirit of our Lord, and it can be asserted with confidence that an intolerant attitude towards the Jews is opposed by the great body of American Christians [...]

But everything which has happened since shows that what started as a movement against the Jews turns out to be a movement against Christianity also.

Source

The Federal Council of Churches of Christ in America, 'The Christian Attitude toward Anti-Semitism', *Federal Council Bulletin* 22, no. 2 (February 1939), 3–4.

Commentary

The FCC was the ecumenical body of Protestant churches in the United States, with thirty-three member churches in 1933. During the Nazi era it actively monitored church events unfolding in Europe; its primary liaison with the European churches and ecumenical movement was Reverend Henry Smith Leiper, who was ecumenical secretary and liaison from 1929 to 1945 (in 1938 he became associate general secretary of the nascent WCC). Leiper was also supportive of Jewish–Christian relations: the National Conference of Christians and Jews began as a programme division in his office in 1928, becoming an independent organisation in 1932.

While the FCC issued some of the earliest condemnations of Nazi anti-Jewish policies that came from US church circles, its focus soon turned to the battles within German Protestantism. This changed after the November 1938 pogroms in Nazi Germany. This 1939 resolution was one of several issued by US churches that addressed the threat posed by antisemitism and acknowledged the history of Christian persecution of Jews (there were similarly strong statements by the General Assembly of the Presbyterian Church and the General Synod of the Reformed Church in America). As this FCC document illustrates, church leaders were also alarmed by growing antisemitism in the United States; that same year the FCC published a pamphlet titled 'Anti-Semitism: Un-American and Un-Christian'.

As the title of that pamphlet suggests, FCC statements tended to frame antisemitism as an attack on democratic values and the civil liberties of religious minorities. This 1939 statement marked a clear shift in its emphasis on the Jewish roots of Christianity (including the acknowledgement that the writers of the New Testament scriptures were Jews); its description of the Judaism of American Jews as a living religion (a 'vital force'), not a religion to be overcome or converted; and its recognition that antisemitism was both a historical and a continuing reality. While not deeply theological in the way that Maritain's 1938 lecture had been (document 10), it was a striking break from previous documents.

Like many of the other Christian documents in this chapter, it concluded with the warning that persecution of the Jews inevitably led to the persecution of Christians. This was a reference to the pressures on the Confessing Church in Nazi Germany, but in the context of the statement as a whole it could also be read as an expression of solidarity.

Bibliography

Barnett, 'Ecumenical Protestant Responses to the Rise of Nazism, Fascism, and Antisemitism during the 1920s and 1930s', in Carter-Chand and Spicer (eds.), *Religion, Ethnonationalism and Antisemitism*, 356–77.
Snoek, *The Grey Book*.

14

Circular Letter #341 of the Central Jewish Consistory in Bulgaria and Reply from the Holy Synod of the Bulgarian Orthodox Church (1940)

Text

Circular letter #341, Central Jewish Consistory in Bulgaria. Sofia, 15 October 1940

To the respected Jewish communities of the Kingdom

The announcements made by the Minister of the Interior regarding the proposed Law for the Defense of the Nation, which considerably restricts the rights of Jews in Bulgaria, have greatly, yet justifiably dismayed the Jewish population. This terrible blow is as much unexpected as it is undeserved. […]

Bulgarian Jewry must not fall in despair. We must not forget that the Bulgarian Jewry, integrating itself in the Bulgarian nation ever since the first days after Bulgaria's liberation and sharing with its Bulgarian brothers all the joys and sorrows brought upon the country, still has many friends among the Bulgarian people, who would never want to hurt the dignity or damage the rights of the Bulgarian Jewry. Even today, these good friends of ours are loudly and clearly voicing their disapproval of the proposed restrictions and they will keep voicing it in the future wherever and whenever they can.

Minutes #11 of the Session on 12 November 1940 of the All-Member Meeting of the Holy Synod of the Bulgarian Orthodox Church: on the letter received from the Central Consistory of Jews regarding the plight of the Jews in the country and the forthcoming entering in the National Assembly of the Bill for the Defense of the Nation (signed by the eight Metropolitans of the Holy Synod)

[…]

Metropolitan Stefan of Sofia: '[…] the Jews in our country, with small exceptions, are good, loyal and proper citizens, who possess and defend with pride and patriotism their Bulgarian citizenship. They serve as proof to the rest of the world of Bulgaria's tolerance and within the nation they behave as true patriots. They have never acted as fanatics and a good part of them have accepted voluntarily the Christian faith […] Lately, after the announcement of the creation of this Bill, [...] there is an influx of people wishing to be converted to Christianity [... T]o prevent rash actions, I gave the strict order that no priest accepts a similar request without preliminary preparations and not one of those willing to be converted to the Christian faith without my secondary and personal blessing [...] I got in touch with the police, so they can provide us with information about particular persons, who demonstrate a will to be christened [...]'

[...]

Metropolitan Kyril of Plovdiv: 'It is true that we have to distinguish between Jews, which have accepted Christianity and those, who have not done so. And if we take any actions in defence of the Jews, they must be in the first place in defence [of] the christened Jews [...].'

[...]

Metropolitan Joseph of Varna and Preslav: '[...] we, as prelates and servants of the Church, must draw all our conclusions based on the fact that we are members of the Bulgarian state and the Bulgarian nation. The question of the attitude of our Church towards the Jews, who have accepted Christianity, is complicated [... E]ach of us would admit that Jews do not share evenly the weight of public life. My conclusion is that, from the point of view of the nation and the Church, we must not publicly raise any question whatsoever in defence of the Jews.'

[...]

Metropolitan Michael of Dorostol and Cherven: '[...] The Israelite Jews must not be blamed for their origin and their faith. If the nation sees the speculative spirit of some Jews in our country as a danger to its economy, it can limit the number of the profiteers and punish them for their wrongdoings rather than for their ethnic belonging [...] Our nation – small and underprivileged – has always distinguished itself with its tolerance towards other nationalities [...] Jews in Bulgaria have never done anything against our national interests [...] We owe them fair and proper treatment. It is the duty of the Church to advocate for such treatment in front of the appropriate government officials.'

Metropolitan Paisiy of Vratza: '[...] As we all know, the religion and nationality of the Jews are so closely interwoven that without the Jewish religion, no Jews can exist [...] Other laws will most probably follow this law, with even more restrictions placed on the Jews, as we witness happening in other countries [...] If this happens, in the future there will be no opportunities for Jews to become Christians [...] The Bulgarian Orthodox Church would commit an act of high patriotism if it makes its voice heard [...]'.

Source

Taneva, Albena, and Gezenko, Ivanka (eds.), *The Power of Civil Society in a Time of Genocide: Proceedings of the Holy Synod of the Bulgarian Orthodox Church on the Rescue of the Jews in Bulgaria, 1940–1944*, trans. Alex Tanev (Sofia: Sofia University Center for Jewish Studies/ Sofia University Press, 2005), 49–59.

Commentary

In 1934 Bulgaria was a predominantly Orthodox country of 6 million citizens, with a minority Jewish population of *c.* 50,000; the Bulgarian Orthodox Church was part of the Eastern Orthodox Church. Bulgaria formed an alliance with Nazi Germany in 1935. In 1941 it joined the Axis powers and participated in the invasions of Yugoslavia and Greece. Under Bulgarian occupation more than 11,000 Yugoslavian and Greek Jews were deported to Treblinka. In 1943, leading Bulgarian intellectuals, opposition politicians and clergy (including the Orthodox Metropolitans in Sofia and Plovdiv, both quoted here) protested the governmental plans to deport Bulgarian Jews. Under this pressure the government backed down, instead expelling the Jewish population of Sofia to forced labour camps in the countryside. Most Jewish citizens of Bulgaria survived the war, although many chose to emigrate in the early postwar period.

The excerpts here document an early exchange between Jewish community leaders and the leaders of the Bulgarian Orthodox Church in response to the anti-Jewish legislation introduced in 1940. Jewish leaders sent their statement directly to the Orthodox leaders, poignantly emphasising their loyalty to the Bulgarian nation and their 'many friends' who would stand by them. The Orthodox responses, particularly by Metropolitans Stefan and Kiril (who subsequently protested the planned deportations), are all the more striking. All emphasised the priority of converted Jews (even noting that the new laws would make conversions difficult, which implies that their real concern was the church's freedom to proselytise). Several voiced antisemitic convictions and suggested that the church bore no responsibility for the Jewish community. Often portrayed as an advocate for the Bulgarian Jewish community, Metropolitan Stefan defended their patriotism. At the same time, however, he expressed concern about insincere conversions, even contacting the police to investigate potential converts.

This 1940 exchange underscores the complexity of the Bulgarian case, particularly the role played by the Orthodox Church leadership there. Most Bulgarian Jews were saved from deportation to extermination camps, and early postwar accounts lauded the church's role as heroic. The Orthodox leaders' statements of solidarity, however, were undermined by their deeper theological anti-Jewish convictions. Ultimately their support for Bulgarian Jews was ambivalent. In September 1942 Metropolitan Stefan delivered a sermon in which he condemned antisemitic violence while stating that 'God had punished the Jews for the crucifixion of Jesus' (Snoek 1969: 182).

Historian Antony Polonsky has noted that anti-Judaism was widespread throughout the various Orthodox churches in eastern Europe and Jews 'reciprocated the contempt'. The nineteenth-century process of Jewish emancipation and integration proved more contentious and fragile in some majority Orthodox societies such as Romania (see document 9), and the Jewish community remained a vulnerable minority. While this may have been less true in Bulgaria than elsewhere in the Orthodox world, the 1940 exchange reflects these realities. In contrast to Catholic and Protestant church leadership in many European countries, there have been few statements by the respective Orthodox churches addressing their own role during the Holocaust (but see those at www.ccjr.us/ dialogika-resources/documents-and-statements/e-orthodox).

Bibliography

'Bulgaria', *Holocaust Encyclopedia*, https://encyclopedia.ush m.org/en/article/bulgaria.

Polonsky, Antony, 'Relations between Jews and Non-Jews: Historical Overview', *The Yivo Encyclopedia of Jews in Eastern Europe*, https://yivoencyclopedia.org/article.aspx/ Relations_between_Jews_and_Non-Jews/Historical_Overview.

Snoek, *The Grey Book*, 180–94.

Taneva, Albena, and Gezenko, Ivanka (eds.), *The Power of Civil Society in a Time of Genocide: Proceedings of the Holy Synod of the Bulgarian Orthodox Church on the Rescue of the Jews in Bulgaria, 1940–1944*, trans. Alex Tanev (Sofia: Sofia University Center for Jewish Studies/ Sofia University Press, 2005).

15

Stephen Wise to John Haynes Holmes: Letter on Palestine (1941)

Text

I am writing at this moment to touch upon your recent letter to Emanuel Neumann of the American Palestine Committee. In it you speak of the announcement that 'the American Palestine Committee is considering giving support to the proposal that the Jewish community in Palestine put a sizeable military force in the field,' etc.

I do not, dear Holmes, consider that a fair way of putting the matter. Thanks to the perfidy of France, the Axis Powers have access, through Syria, into Palestine. 550,000 Jews live there, surrounded by one and a quarter million Arabs. Do you wonder that the Jewish community in Palestine insists upon the right to defend itself against the Axis, which will either destroy Palestine and its people or else incite the Arabs to do it? Can you, in reason, expect the Jews of Palestine, who know and have reason to feel – including one hundred thousand German refugees among them – that the purpose of Hitler is to obliterate them, to refrain from self-defence, to suffer their women to be raped and their children to be hacked to pieces? Non-resistance is an attitude which one has the right to adopt for oneself under any and all circumstances. But have we in America, who have been partly responsible for the resettlement of Jews in Palestine, the right to ask our fellow-Jews that they shall suffer the Nazis to invade and to destroy the land without defending themselves? They cannot do this. They must not be asked to do this.

I think I know what you mean. You would like Jews to set the example to the world of being what Christians profess to be in the matter of non-resistance to force. But that can only come to pass after the Christian peoples have set the example of non-resistance and of rejecting the use of force in self-defence. That we Jews should pay the price of that Christian concept without ever having had the help and inspiration of Christian example is too much. I cannot ask you to bless the efforts of Jews to save themselves, their land and their country if Hitler and his hosts invade Palestine. But I hope that you will rejoice in

Palestine being saved, if it should come to pass that with American help it can be achieved. My complaint – and I know whereof I speak – is not that England will use a military force in Palestine, but that England may deny to Jews the elementary right of self-defence in the only way in which self-defence is possible against the Axis savages, namely, through all the considerable weapons of war.

It is all a very sad and confused story. But we, who have seen the blue-prints of [the] Madagascar settlement of Jews as the next step in the proposed expulsion of Jews from Europe which they have helped to enrich and civilize for two thousand years, cannot reconcile ourselves to the ideal of non-resistance, though advocated by a Jew and studiously and systematically ignored by the nations and peoples which, far from practicing non-resistance against Jesus' people, have, for nineteen centuries, assailed and broken the Jew.

Source

Polier, Justine Wise, and Wise, James Waterman (eds.), *The Personal Letters of Stephen Wise* (Boston: The Beacon Press, 1956), 256–7.

Commentary

One of the most interesting friendships throughout this period was that between the prominent US Jewish leader Rabbi Stephen Wise (1874–1949) and the Unitarian pacifist minister John Haynes Holmes (1879–1964). Their friendship pre-dated World War I, when both had helped found the National Association for the Advancement of Colored People (NAACP), and they worked together on a number of progressive and interfaith issues. Their correspondence reflects the closeness and frankness of their friendship.

As noted in the introduction to this chapter, during this period there was considerable dissent within and between the Jewish and Christian communities about the issue of Zionism and Jewish emigration to Palestine, and a wide range of positions in both communities about what Zionism meant, particularly with respect to the establishment of a Jewish state. Holmes was a proponent of Zionism but opposed the establishment of a Jewish state. He was also a staunch pacifist who took a controversial public stand against US involvement in World War II. In the 1941 letter to which Wise was replying, Holmes had expressed criticism of a proposal to provide arms to the Jewish community in Palestine. He suggested instead that Jews explore pacifist options in dealing with their Arab neighbours.

Wise's reply addressed the political realities of that moment. It also revealed the anguish of the Jewish community in the United States as they witnessed the intensification of European persecution and the plight of vulnerable refugees, and a deeper anger about the Christian world's betrayal of European Jews. As more Jews tried to escape Europe, various schemes for the relocation of refugees were considered, including a 1940 proposal to deport European Jews to Madagascar. Wise mentioned this, with the bitter observation that European Jews were being forced to flee the continent to which they had contributed so much.

Even after they had escaped Nazi-occupied Europe, however, Jews were not out of harm's way. In 1941 the Vichy government's collaboration with the Axis powers placed Jewish emigrants to North Africa and Palestine at risk once again. American Jews were now considering sending military support to help the community defend itself, particularly if Nazi Germany gained control of Palestine.

Holmes, however, had touched a nerve that went beyond the issue of Jewish self-defence. 'That we Jews should pay the price of that Christian concept [of non-resistance] without ever having had the help and inspiration of Christian example is too much', Wise answered him, proceeding to refer to the centuries of Christian persecution of Jews.

Bibliography

Breitman, Richard, *FDR and the Jews* (Cambridge, MA: Harvard University Press, 2013).

Breitman, Richard, McDonald Stewart, Barbara, and Hochberg, Severin (eds.), *Refugees and Rescue: The Diaries and Papers of James G. McDonald, 1935–1945* (Bloomington: Indiana University Press, 2009).

16

Unknown Author: 'On the Danger of Forced Conversion' (December 1942)

Text

> 'There shall not be found among you anyone who passes his son or daughter through fire …'
> Devarim/Deuteronomy 18:10.

Dedicated to my beloved daughter Miriam Sarah that was taken from us on the day of September 5th, 1942

[…] We have reached a time unparalleled in the history of our people, though experienced and drenched in blood were our brothers and sisters.

[…] As a result, some parents resorted to handing their children to monasteries and other religious establishments, saying 'we only do this to save our Jewish children, as it is said: "the one who sustains one soul of Israel, as if he sustained a whole world." […]' […]

This raises the question: 'the body or the soul – which is more important?' The one who gives his children to be educated in a monastery, he may be saving them from the talons of the yellow beast [i.e., the Nazis]. However, at the same time, that person risks their Jewish souls, as it is well known that the education in a monastery has only one goal – to add souls to the church of Christ. It is inconceivable that when a young boy or girl is educated by priests, their soul will stay unharmed, and they will manage to maintain their Jewish identity. It is comparable to burning the soul while the body remains – who dares to say that it is a worthy thing?

Our forefathers knew that conversion out of Judaism is considered a mortal offence for it is written: 'Let him be killed rather than transgress.' Therefore they willingly and happily ascended the stake. Killed and slaughtered as martyrs – their bodies were exterminated, their souls remained unsullied, like burned parchments whose words flew away and were not desecrated. Here we wish to do the exact opposite: to desert the soul and save the body, to burn the letters but save the empty parchments, or worse – write on them other letters whose content is entirely foreign to us and to our spirit.

Whoever has the slightest knowledge about the nature, character, and ways of the clergy, understands that it is for a good reason that they accept pupils with such open arms; proselytizing has been always their way to acquire new souls; even if they now pretend that they want to educate the children in their institution out of mercy and compassion […], the main reason for that kindness is still visible: converting the students, or in other words fishing in troubled waters. They want to take advantage of the fear of the parents who worry for their beloved children, and accept the latter into their establishments with one clear goal: to convert them to Christianity.

It is clear that it is not commiseration, as it was preached and taught by that man from Nazareth, that drives the clergy to feel compassion for our children. Otherwise they would have helped not only children but also elderly people. We are yet to hear that the clergy helped those who escaped from within the ghettos, knocking on doors unanswered in their search for refuge. Likewise, we are yet to hear of clergy campaigning in favour of the Jews, calling to stop exploiting them or not to hand them to the enemy.

Generation upon generation our people fought against the influence of the foreign spirit and an entire literature was dedicated to this effort; from the days of the Maccabees to the Middle Ages, from the times of forced conversion in Russia and later, when a peril of assimilation into foreign society was present.

Are we to destroy all of this at once?

Are we to betray the eternity of Israel and sell our sons to the barren?

I am confident that if we could hold a referendum on this question, the unanimous result would be that we will not pass our sons and daughters through heathen fire.

A.H.K.

Warsaw, Chanukah, 5703 [1942]

Source

RG 15.079M, Courtesy of the Jewish Historical Institute, Warsaw/Experiencing History, United States Holocaust Memorial Museum Archives, Washington, DC.

'On the Danger of Forced Conversion', *Experiencing History: Holocaust Sources in Context*, https://perspectives.ushmm.org/item/on-the-danger-of-forced-conversion. (Readers can click on 'View this Religious Text' to see the Hebrew original.)

Commentary

This letter, written by an anonymous rabbi in the Warsaw Ghetto, is one of the most powerful documents of this period. Dedicated to his daughter, who had just been deported, and written for the community of Jews suffering in the ghetto, it addressed the questions of what Christian rescue might mean not just for the preservation of the Jewish community but for the deeper sense of Jewish identity, integrity and the survival of Jewish life itself.

In the late summer of 1942 over 265,000 Jews were deported from the Warsaw Ghetto. Emanuel Ringelblum, a Jewish historian who documented the realities of ghetto life, received word that Polish Catholic clergy were offering to shelter children (for payment, it should be noted). He brought the question to ghetto leaders. There were differences of opinion about the sincerity and motivations of the offer. Naturally the chance to rescue their children was compelling.

And yet for the Jews in the ghetto, the prospect of rescue through conversion to Christianity was a bitter pill indeed – even or especially as they faced the immediate threat of deportation and the deaths of their community and their children. Centuries of Christian persecution and antisemitism led them to suspect the intentions of the Catholics who were offering this form of rescue – was it truly to save the lives of their children or simply to add more souls to the Christian flock? And what would such a form of rescue mean for their children, who would not be accepted or respected for who they were? Suspicious of the true intentions behind this offer of rescue, the author notes that if Christians were genuinely interested in saving Jewish lives they would have spoken out and been active before then.

As a long-standing point of friction between Christians and Jews, the issue of proselytisation and conversion symbolised a much deeper and more bitter division during this period. As a path to assimilation and full civil rights it had failed, as Rabbi Hertz noted in 1934 (document 5); in the Inquisition the Catholic Church had been all too willing to betray the *conversos*. The Confessing Church vigorously protested the exclusion of baptised Christians from the church – but very few in that movement stood in solidarity with the religious Jewish community, and over time the Confessing Church abandoned even its own members affected by the racial laws (see document 18). In the late 1930s the Confessing Church's Grüber office helped about 2,000 people emigrate from Nazi Germany, but most were converts or Christians married to Jews.

Similarly to John Holmes' letter to Stephen Wise (document 15), the immediacy of the violence that threatened them exposed the Jewish community's vulnerability as well as its rage at the Christian world. Jews wanted to survive; they also wanted to save their children as Jews. This document is an important reminder of the complex realities underlying even stories of Christian rescue during this period.

Bibliography

Kassow, Samuel D., *Who Will Write Our History? Emanuel Ringelblum, the Warsaw Ghetto, and the Oyneg Shabes Archives* (Bloomington: Indiana University Press, 2007).

Paldiel, Mordecai, *Churches and the Holocaust: Unholy Teaching, Good Samaritans, and Reconciliation* (Jersey City: Ktav, 2005).

17

Responses to the Confirmation of the Genocide of European Jews (1942–3)

Text

(i) Pope Pius XII: 'The Internal Order of States and People' (Christmas Radio Address of 1942)

[…] Mankind owes that vow [see p. 388 below] to the countless dead who lie buried on the field of battle: the sacrifice of their lives in fulfillment of their duty is a holocaust offered for a new and better social order.

Mankind owes that vow to the innumerable sorrowing host of mothers, widows and orphans who have seen the light, the solace and the support of their lives wrenched from them.

Mankind owes that vow to those numberless exiles whom the hurricane of war has torn from their native land and scattered in the land of the stranger; who can make their own the lament of the Prophet: 'our inheritance is turned to aliens; our house to strangers.'

Mankind owes that vow to the hundreds of thousands of persons who, without any fault on their part, sometimes only because of their nationality or race, have been consigned to death or to a slow decline.

Mankind owes that vow to the many thousands of non-combatants, women, children, sick and aged, from whom aerial warfare – whose horrors we have from the beginning frequently denounced – has, without discrimination or through inadequate precautions, taken life, goods, health, home, charitable refuge, or house of prayer.

Mankind owes that vow to the flood of tears and bitterness, to the accumulation of sorrow and suffering, emanating from the murderous ruin of the dreadful conflict and crying to heaven to send down the Holy Spirit to liberate the world from the inundation of violence and terror.

Source

Pius XII, *1942 Christmas Message of Pope Pius XII* (Washington, DC: National Catholic Welfare Conference, 1943), 21.

(ii) William Temple, Archbishop of Canterbury: Speeches of 23 March and 8 December 1943

Speech to the House of Lords, 23 March 1943:
We are wisely advised not to limit our attention […] to the sufferers of any one race, and we must remember that there are citizens of many countries who are subject to just the same kind of monstrous persecution, and even massacre. None the less, there has been a concentration of this fury against the Jews, and it is inevitable that we should give special attention to what is being carried through […].

Speech to the Council of Christians and Jews in London, 8 December 1943:

[...] It is one of the most terrible consequences of war that the sensitiveness of people tends to become hardened [...] There is a great moral danger in the paralysis of feeling that is liable to be brought about. It is most important for our own moral health and vigor that we express horror at the persecution of the Jews [which] almost baffles imagination and leaves one horrified at the power of the evil that can show itself in human nature.

Source

Reprinted by permission of the Snoek family from *The Grey Book: A Collection of Protests against Anti-Semitism and the Persecution of the Jews issued by Non-Roman Catholic Churches and Church Leaders during Hitler's Rule* by Johan M. Snoek, published by Van Gorcum & Co. Copyright © 1969 Johan M. Snoek. Text quoted from pp. 254–5, 246.

(iii) Aide-mémoire from the Secretariats of the World Council of Churches and the World Jewish Congress, Geneva, March 1943. Sent to the League of Nations High Commissioner for Refugees and Leaders of the Governments and Jewish and Church Bodies in the United States and Great Britain

While welcoming most warmly the determination of the Allied governments to bring help to the persecuted people of all races, nationalities and religions, fleeing from Axis terror, [the Secretariats] wish to emphasise that the most urgent and acute problem which requires immediate action, is the situation of the Jewish communities under direct or indirect Nazi control.

   The Secretariats of the World Council of Churches and of the World Jewish Congress have in their possession most reliable reports indicating that the campaign of deliberate extermination of the Jews organised by the Nazi officials in nearly all countries of Europe under their control, is now at its climax. They therefore beg to call the attention of the Allied Governments to the absolute necessity of organising without delay a rescue action for the persecuted Jewish communities on the following lines:

1. Measures of immediate rescue should have priority over the study of post-war arrangements.
2. The rescue action should enable the neutral States to grant temporary asylum to the Jews who would reach their frontiers [...] Only explicit and comprehensive guarantees of reemigration of the refugees [...] can lead the neutral countries to adopt a more liberal and understanding attitude towards the Jewish refugees [...]
3. A scheme for exchange of Jews in Germany and the territories under German control for German civilians in North and South America, Palestine, and other countries, should be pressed forward by all possible means [...] We feel that in spite of the great difficulties which we do not underestimate, a workable scheme of exchanging Jews for Germans would constitute an important method of rescuing a considerable number of persecuted people from the countries under Nazi control.

Source

Reprinted by permission of the Snoek family from *The Grey Book: A Collection of Protests against Anti-Semitism and the Persecution of the Jews issued by Non-Roman Catholic Churches and Church Leaders during Hitler's Rule* by Johan M. Snoek, published by Van Gorcum & Co. Copyright © 1969 Johan M. Snoek. Text quoted from pp. 275–7.

Commentary

With the German invasion of Poland in 1939, British and US intelligence began receiving reports of widespread massacres of Jewish communities. In the late summer of 1942 a German businessman travelled to Switzerland with confirmation that Nazi Germany had begun the systematic deportation and murder of Jews, with plans to annihilate the entire Jewish population of Europe. This news was conveyed to Gerhart Riegner, head of the WJC in Geneva, who shared it with British and US diplomats as well as with Protestant ecumenical leaders in Europe, who gave it to Samuel Cavert, the head of the FCC in New York. The FCC issued a strong condemnation on 11 December 1942. Jewish communities around the world declared 2 December 1942 a day of mourning. The news also reached the Vatican.

These three statements were issued in the knowledge that the Nazis had begun the full-scale genocide of European Jews. There are striking differences between them, including the openness with which they addressed the reality of the genocide.

Pius XII began his Christmas address by describing the battlefield deaths of soldiers as a 'holocaust' (the term, of course, was not yet used to refer to the genocide of European Jews). He then included all those targeted because of 'nationality or race' and bemoaned the suffering of numerous non-combatants. Such language of course could have referred to all war victims and refugees, whether Jewish or not. In each case he solemnly affirmed humanity's 'vow' to each community that was suffering in the war – a vow perhaps referring to the church's commitment to honour and to help. He did not, however, explicitly mention the persecution of Jews. The pope's 1942 Christmas message was the one occasion on which he publicly addressed the events of the war, and his wording remains a central issue in the continuing debates about his moral leadership during the Holocaust (see also Chapter 8, pp. 424–5, and Chapter 9, p. 476).

The two other documents are more explicit. Archbishop of Canterbury William Temple issued several forthright statements in the autumn of 1942, acknowledging a special Christian responsibility to assist Jews after centuries of persecution; he also sent messages of support to British Jewish leaders. In the second excerpt here, from 1943, he warned of the 'moral danger' of ignoring the genocide. Like Pius XII, he acknowledged that many non-Jewish non-combatants were suffering in the war but argued that Jews were the particular targets of the violence. The central message of his speech, however, was that Britain had to open its doors to more refugees immediately. Temple and his predecessor, Cosmo Lang, had close relationships with the British Jewish community and this probably contributed to his clarity and sense of urgency. While his advocacy for refugees certainly had the support of some bishops and clergy in the Church of England, the focus of most other Anglican leaders was on ending the war, and there were already deep divisions about Palestine.

The March 1943 memorandum issued by the WCC and WJC was one of the rare statements issued jointly by Jews and Christians during this era. It was the product of regular cooperation, particularly on refugee issues, between the two agencies in Geneva during the war years. Gerhard Riegner, head of the WJC, met weekly with Willem Visser't Hooft at the WCC and later described this partnership as 'the light in the darkness that surrounded us' (2006: 127). The memorandum was not a theological document but a call to action. Addressing the urgent peril faced by Jewish populations in Nazi-held territory, its tone was urgent and pragmatic, arguing that Allied governments needed to move quickly on re-emigration, relocation and rescue efforts as well as broader refugee assistance. Their concrete suggestions included German prisoner exchanges for Jewish refugees.

While these three documents illustrate the extent to which major church leaders spoke out about the genocide of the Jews as it was happening, with the exception of the papal letter they are little known. Particularly in the case of Temple, Riegner and Visser't Hooft, these statements reflect the passions and convictions of these leaders, not the policies of the institutions they represented or an ongoing theological dialogue with Jews.

Bibliography

Lawson, Tom, *The Church of England and the Holocaust: Christianity, Memory, and Nazism* (Woodbridge: Boydell & Brewer, 2006).

Riegner, Gerhard, *Never Despair: Sixty Years in the Service of the Jewish People and the Cause of Human Rights*, trans. William Sayers (Chicago: Ivan R. Dee, 2006).

Ventresca, Robert, *Soldier of Christ: The Life of Pope Pius XII* (Cambridge, MA: Belknap Press of Harvard University Press, 2013).

18

Hans Ehrenberg, 'The Rediscovery of the Jew in Christianity (with Special Reference to Pascal)' (1944)

Text

[...] From the second to the seventeenth century people could see little in the Jews [...] but their guilt, their hardness of heart and their rejection of Christ. The Jew, as the murderer of Jesus Christ, was the permanent accused: but how much of the pre-Christian, pagan antagonism of the Gentiles toward the chosen people of God was at the root of this permanent accusation on the part of the Christian peoples? [... T]he Christian Church has not had an entirely quiet conscience in relation to the Jews, as is evident from the way in which practice towards them has fluctuated between protection and persecution. And so far as the Jews of the Bible are concerned, apart from their relation to the life of Christ, the Church [...] has idealized the Jews in a way that obstructed the right interpretation of the Old Testament as much as their accusation has obstructed that of the New Testament and the building up of a right tradition in the Church.

[... T]he two tendencies, to judge and to idealize the Jews, have lasted till our day. But since the age of Rationalism they have outwardly diverged, in a humanistic, philosophic direction on the one hand, and in a political, antisemitic direction on the other, the one no longer restricted by any kind of consideration of the condemnation of the Jews through the Cross, and the other no longer mitigated by the thought that God's choice of Israel as his Elect has never been revoked.

[...] If we are to find in the Christian Church a bastion to stand against Hitler's purpose of exterminating the Jews [...] we must go back before the age of the Enlightenment and of Humanism, to that peculiarly Evangelical-Catholic thinker, Pascal [...]

[... A] large section of his *Pensées* is devoted to the question of the Jews. It is as if someone has caught sight of the Jews for the first time, and calls on them to help him, with quotations from Midrash and Talmud, to give his testimony to the doctrine of original sin: the Jew of the Talmud as a fellow-witness to the Augustinian and Reformed conception of sin over against the modernism of the Pelagian Jesuits! But Pascal never forgot the irreconcilability of Judaism with Christianity [...]

[...]

In Pascal's view, the situation between Jew and Christian is clear and yet in permanent flux [...] Pascal emphasizes constantly that the Father of Jesus Christ is the God of Abraham, Isaac and Jacob and that He and not the God of the philosophers and scholars is the true God; He alone has in Jesus Christ His Son.

[...]

From that viewpoint Pascal sees Judaism in the following light:

> '[...] While all philosophers separate into different sects, there is found in one corner of the world the most ancient people in it, declaring that all the world is in error, that God has revealed to them the truth, that they will always exist on earth. In fact, all other sects come to an end, this one still endures, and has done so for four thousand years.'

[...] But is it, perhaps, only because they form the living witness of God's curse on those who crucified His Son? No [...] for, if we look back from Christ to the people of Christ, we see the messianic prophecy of the old Covenant inverted, and Christ, the very Person whose testimony it rejects, bearing witness to it, so that even Judaism becomes part of the mystery of the Faith. Its age, its durableness, its sincerity, take one's breath away. What candour in the confession of a people's own sins! [...]

[...] In its attitude to the Jews, and in its evangelistic mission to them, the Church, after more than two hundred and fifty years, has now readopted Pascal's confession of faith [...] Above all, the Church, without realizing it, has established the task of its mission to Israel, imposed upon it in *Romans* IX–XI, exactly on the arguments of Pascal. The entry of the heathen and the homecoming of Israel have still not been accomplished in the twentieth century but they have become something in which the children of light can believe and they should be written on the heart of the evangelizing Church. The Christians of the seventeenth century, the first century of the Modern Age, saw the heathen religions and the new heathenism that was appearing in Europe [...] taking shape before their eyes, and at the same time the outline of a force that would counter every sort of heathenism, namely, the Jews. From that period all three branches of the Christian mission drew the sense of purpose and vocation which we today, after our enhanced experience, are well inclined to encourage: the mission to the heathen, home missions and the mission to the Jews.

Source

Ehrenberg, Hans, 'The Rediscovery of the Jew in Christianity (with Special Reference to Pascal)', *The International Review of Mission* 33, no. 4 (1944), 400–6.

Commentary

Hans Ehrenberg (1883–1958) was a German Jewish philosopher and theologian who converted to Protestantism in 1911 and became an ordained minister. In 1933 he wrote a widely circulated critique of the German Christian attempt to create a church 'Aryan paragraph' that would correspond to Nazi racial laws (see p. 343). Titled 'Seventy-Two Theses on the Jewish–Christian Question', Ehrenberg's essay condemned antisemitism and argued that Christianity was still bound to its Jewish roots. This made him an early target of the Nazi regime and the German Christian leaders. Although he was a leading figure in the Confessing Church, its leadership gradually withdrew its support for clergy affected by the Nazi racial laws. By September 1938 he could no longer preach, and following the November 1938 pogroms he was imprisoned in Sachsenhausen concentration camp. Upon his release in March 1939 he fled to Great Britain. He returned to Germany in 1947.

Ehrenberg is often viewed today as a 'messianic Jew' (a member of an evangelical movement of converted Jews that incorporates Jewish traditions). Even in 1933 he described himself as a 'Jewish Christian' (an unusual designation in that era among converted Jews). As this 1944 essay shows, even the experiences of persecution, imprisonment and exile did not shake his conviction that Judaism and Christianity should be understood together as a single religious tradition.

In this essay he argued for a pre-Enlightenment understanding of Judaism that neither idealised it philosophically nor demonised it antisemitically. Ehrenberg affirmed many tenets, such as God's enduring covenant with Israel, that remain central to a respectful relationship between Jews and Christians today, and he condemned supersessionism. Yet he agreed with Pascal (1623–62) that the claims of the two traditions were irreconcilable. Christians indeed worship the God of Israel, who has sent the messiah in the person of Jesus Christ. In this way Judaism remains 'part of the mystery of the [Christian] Faith'. Judaism thereby constituted an indispensable part of Christianity. Ehrenberg defended the mission to Jews and conversion – more for the sake of Christianity than for Judaism.

The complexity of his theology (and his continued defence of conversion) meant that there was little room for Ehrenberg in the postwar theological landscape, including in Jewish–Christian dialogue. It is worth noting, however, that many of his theological insights echoed figures like Maritain (document 10). He had close friendships with Franz Rosenzweig (who was his cousin), Martin Buber (see Chapter 8, p. 405) and Eugen Rosenstock-Hussy, all of whom influenced his thought. In a sense, this 1944 essay was a continuation of the 1920s German conversations about the Jewish–Christian relationship that ended so abruptly in 1933.

Bibliography

Ehrenberg, Hans, *Autobiography of a German Pastor*, trans. Geraint V. Jones (London: Student Christian Movement Press, 1943).
Gerlach, Wolfgang, *And the Witnesses Were Silent: The Confessing Church and the Jews*, trans. Victoria J. Barnett (Lincoln: University of Nebraska Press, 2000).

19

James Parkes: An Enemy of the People: Antisemitism *(1945)*

Text

The main difficulty [...] is that there are not enough non-Jews who know anything about Jewish history or the actual facts of contemporary Jewish life [...] In every community in which there is a local Jewish population it ought to be the duty of a local society of Jews and Christians to see that in the municipal offices and among the municipal councillors and committees; in the educational committees, among the magistrates and police, and among the local churches there are some non-Jews who know something solid about the Jewish question.

A particular responsibility lies upon the churches. And, with many notable exceptions, their ignorance is both dishonorable and disgusting. There is nothing whatever to be said in their defense. They maintain missions to convert the Jews, while at the same time they will not spend a penny of either time or effort to see that Judaism and the story of the Jewish people are fairly presented to their congregations. This might not matter if they could ignore the Jews. But references to them are bound to crop up continually in sermons, lectures, and books; and nine-tenths of those references are ill-informed, often to the point of being definitely untrue. They don't mean to be prejudiced; they are not conscious of antisemitic feeling; but the share that they bear for providing a fertile breeding ground for every kind of antisemitic misrepresentation is an exceedingly heavy one; and a few resolutions of sympathy with the victims of Hitler's massacres do not square the account. Innumerable ministers of religion preach sermons on the Pharisees; and know nothing whatever about them. They talk of 'the Law' and they have not the slightest idea what 'Torah' (the Hebrew for Law) means to a Jew. They speak of 'the Jews' when they describe the less attractive activities of the early Israelites with complete indifference to the fact that the congregation will relate their words to the conduct of a contemporary 20th-century Jewish community. This is particularly the case in their ignorant contrasts of the 'Jewish' and 'Christian' ideas of God. I have met ministers who believed that 'love thy neighbor as thyself' was an entirely New Testament idea, and are unaware that Jesus is endorsing the teaching of Moses (Lev. xix.18), not giving original teaching Himself in the passage. With sublime indifference to the evidence of the Synoptic Gospels themselves (which contain no mention of the Pharisees in the events of the arrest, trial and death of Jesus), they lay the blame for the Crucifixion on Pharisaic shoulders. As to the post-New Testament developments of Judaism they know nothing; and they preach to their people as though the less attractive beliefs of Old or New Testament times contained the sum total of the Jewish religion for the last two thousand years. And all these things are doubly abominable when they occur in Sunday School lessons to the young.

Today humanity is spiritually as homeless as the Jewish people have been geographically homeless; we cannot go back to the world of 1939; we must go forward or perish [... A] healthy society is also a society in which men do justly one with another. And antisemitism is a giant we must slay also for the sake of the victims, for the sake of the Jews.

Source

Parkes, James, *An Enemy of the People: Antisemitism* (London: Penguin, 1945), 143–5.

Commentary

James Parkes (1886–1981) was a British Anglican clergyman whose concern about antisemitism led him to a thorough re-evaluation of Christian teachings. Although he briefly became involved in the Protestant ecumenical movement in the 1920s, by the early 1930s his focus had turned to antisemitism as the central problem in modern Christianity. He grew openly critical of the proselytisation and conversion of Jews and the antisemitic uses of traditional Christian teachings. He was also an open critic of National Socialism, and in 1935 Nazi sympathisers attempted to assassinate him in Geneva. After returning to England he wrote widely on the persecution of European Jews.

His second book, *The Conflict of the Church and the Synagogue: A Study in the Origins of Antisemitism* (1934), provided a groundbreaking analysis of the long history of Christian anti-Jewish teachings and the ways in which they had led to the pervasive antisemitism in western culture and its social and political systems. Parkes was one of the first Christians to write critically on the specific ways in which Christian teachings about Jews undergirded the fabric of broader political and cultural antisemitism.

Published soon after the end of the war in Great Britain, *An Enemy of the People* drew heavily on his 1934 book, beginning with an overview of the development of historical antisemitism in conjunction with anti-Jewish teachings. Now, however, he pleaded for greater literacy about the Jewish tradition as the very foundation of Christianity. Noting how many 'Christian' teachings in fact came from Jesus' Jewish tradition, he argued that the churches and local organisations of Jews and Christians needed to educate the wider community if antisemitism was to be eradicated.

Parkes was clearly motivated by the recent catastrophe of the Holocaust. The years since the publication of his 1934 book had proven him right, and his concluding chapter, from which this excerpt is taken, addresses the particular responsibility of the churches in what had happened. He also makes the argument that antisemitism has been a catastrophe for non-Jews – for western culture more broadly – as well. '[W]e must go forward or perish', he wrote.

As one of the few Christian theologians who had written before the Holocaust about the relationship between Christians and Jews and the particular obligation of Christians to combat antisemitism, Parkes' work became an important resource for Christian–Jewish dialogue after 1945. He helped found the Council of Christians and Jews in the UK and continued to be active in the postwar era.

Bibliography

Richmond, Colin, *Campaigner against Antisemitism: The Reverend James Parkes, 1896–1981* (London and Portland: Vallentine Mitchell, 2005).

20

Margarete Susman: The Book of Job and the Fate of the Jewish People *(1946)*

Text

Christ's relationship to death and life, time and eternity, good and evil, God and man, is the pure truth of Israel. From the origin of the people through all the miracles and events of their history, it is one single line of resistance to time and death, chaos and nothingness that leads to the life of the evangelical Christ who raises the dead and himself rises from the dead.

The only difference is that in Christ's life this relationship of summons and doctrine to the life he himself leads, and everything that up to now was prophecy and judgment, becomes the 'I' that announces itself. With the word: 'But I say to you,' with which Christ replaces the word of the prophet: 'Thus speaks the Lord,' he breaks with the forefathers, while affirming their truth [...]

And with that, everything has changed. The claim has become a new and unprecedented one. In the figure of God-become-man, Israel's basic truth has ruptured the circle of the people and split it in two at its most profound depth. It has divided it into the part that took on God's truth in the figure of Christ and carried it forth into the world in ardent disciple- and apostleship, and into the part that rejected God in the form of the human self as incompatible with the ultimate truth of Israel.

The part that accepted Christ no longer lives; it has melded with the world; the part that rejected him goes on living its dark historical fate while being rejected by the world [...]

The immense tragedy of the Jewish people can be comprehended only out of the ultimate depth of Israel, namely that, for the sake of their most profound essence, they decided against their most profound essence.

[...]

With their decision to detach themselves from the history of nations, the Jewish people retained a third element instead of grace and faith: *hope*. Hope in its essence differs from both grace and faith, yet also shares in both. Hope is the blossom of law; it springs from the law as a divine gift and as a human decision.

[...]

Hope is where everything is decided [...] Hope is the strength of the soul to embrace its own reality. Hope is where the force of reality of prophecy is proven. It is the reality of human life under the law.

[...]

Hope, and the endurance in hope for the sake of mankind united in peace is thus the ultimate test of the people. It is also their deepest distress. For it is hope that connects them ineluctably to their historical existence, and hope that causes them to be spread throughout history, and causes them to be expelled from history. In hope lies the immense tension of salvation from which springs their inability to die. In hope lies their sojourn on earth and their homelessness on earth [...]

The decision of the surviving people was made by clinging to hope.

To understand this decision as a national one would be to totally misunderstand the concept of the people of Israel. The decision was made not out of an externally defined national reality, but it was made within the *meaning* of that reality. As a people of that law that was inscribed into their hearts, they rejected the dissolution of their existence because it had been issued to them as a people, and as a people they were responsible for it. As a people of the redemption of mankind, they refuse to accept redemption in an unredeemed world [...]

[... T]he decision to continue fulfilling their mission is not a free one, any more than the decision to accept the law of Sinai [...]

Here they are completely alone with their God, enclosed with him in the mystery from which arises the certainty of Job: 'I will see him myself, and my eyes will behold him, and no stranger will behold him thus!'

[...]

The light of blessing is deeply concealed in the chaos of historical life; the darkness of the curse is exposed to the light of day.

Source

Susman, Margarete, 'Selections from *Das Buch Hiob und das Schicksal des jüdischen Volkes*', trans. Gerda Neu-Sokol, in Caspi, Mishael M., and Milstein, Sara J. (eds.) in collaboration with Gerda Neu-Sokol, *Why Hidest Thy Face: Job in Traditions and Literature* (North Richland Hills: BIBAL Press, 2004), 300–6.

Commentary

Margarete Susman (1872–1966) was a German-born Jewish writer who wrote extensively about culture, religion and philosophy. Born to a secular family, she was educated in a Protestant school and studied Judaism as an adult; she immigrated to Switzerland in 1933. In addition to publishing works on Buber, Rosenzweig and Kafka, she wrote often about the Jewish–Christian relationship in Germany, tracing the historical intersections of Jewish and German intellectual life and the rich legacy of Jewish contributions to German culture.

The Nazi years led her to question whether German Jews still had a place in the intellectual and artistic culture to which they had contributed so greatly. For Susman this was a religious, historical and philosophical question that raised painful questions about Jewish identity and destiny. Her 1946 book on Job is one of the earliest Jewish philosophical and theological reflections on the meaning of the Shoah.

In this passage Susman focuses on the 'parting of the ways' between Judaism and Christianity (see Chapter 2, p. 66). She interpreted this not as the Christian break with Judaism that took final form in the fourth century CE, but as the Jewish decision to remain faithful to the law and the prophets. In his teachings, Jesus of Nazareth affirmed the 'pure truth' of Jewish teachings and law. As the Christ, however, he represented the rejection of that tradition. Jews remained faithful to the law, and paid a terrible price: they became outcasts in the Christian world, persecuted as the symbol of guilt and God's rejection. As Susman writes elsewhere in the same chapter: 'nothing remains for them but hatred and despising, humiliation and expulsion, sickness, ugliness, and immeasurable suffering. As no other people on earth, the Jewish people thus exist […] like Job in the constant unanswerable questioning of the existence imposed upon them' (p. 282).

Susman's reading of Job is illuminating, particularly her insight into Job's faithfulness. In remaining faithful to the law, Job (and the people of Israel) experience hope as a form of grace still 'concealed in the chaos of historical life'. There are echoes here of Max Eschelbacher's 1927 essay (document 3), particularly his emphasis on the law as the grounding for Jewish identity and hope, and the presence of grace in Jewish teachings.

Although Susman and Ehrenberg each wrote early post-Holocaust reflections on the theological significance of the Jewish–Christian relationship, they drew opposite conclusions. For Ehrenberg, Jesus was the unifying bridge between Judaism and Christianity; he considered them one tradition (see document 18). This conviction shaped his understanding of Christianity's future. Susman's understanding of the break between the two traditions, and the continued faithfulness of Israel, was essential to how she interpreted the meaning of the Holocaust.

Bibliography

Klapheck, Elisa (ed.), *Margarete Susman: Religious-Political Essays on Judaism*, trans. Laura Radosh (Geneva: Palgrave Macmillan, 2021).

8

The State of Israel to the Election of Pope John Paul II
1948–1978

KARMA BEN-JOHANAN

INTRODUCTION

The period explored in this chapter, 1948–78, is one of fundamental shifts. World War II had left Europe devastated and in a state of cultural chaos. The long history of European Jews had been abruptly and violently terminated. Around 6 million Jews were murdered. Others, who were able to escape before the so-called Final Solution, or managed to survive the effort of annihilation in Europe, found new homes mostly outside the continent, especially in Mandatory Palestine and the United States.

The Christian communities who witnessed the fate of their former neighbours in Europe were now searching for a language with which to think and speak of what had happened. A particularly difficult question was how it came about that the centuries-old Christian heritage of Europe was unable to provide sufficient moral means to prevent the bloodshed which flooded such large portions of the world, and especially the unprecedented brutality of Auschwitz. Slowly and gradually, with the influence of many of the authors whose works are excerpted in this chapter, an even more tormenting question took centre stage – whether the Holocaust occurred not *despite* Christianity, but *because of* centuries of Christian anti-Jewish teaching (what the French Jewish historian Jules Isaac called 'the teaching of contempt'; see document 1) that prepared the ground for the Final Solution. The question of the connection between the Holocaust and the history of Jewish–Christian relations was the central, all-encompassing theme which arguably occupied (or burdened) every Jewish–Christian encounter, every intra-Jewish discussion of Christianity and every intra-Christian discussion of Jews and Judaism between 1948 and 1978, certainly in Europe and Israel, and with implications all over the world.

The excerpted documents in this chapter render visible a chronological line of development – complicated and not entirely linear, but a development nonetheless. With the exception of Jules Isaac, whose bold thesis called for and energised transformations which would only be dealt with in depth from the mid-1960s, the earlier texts of the period reflect, in retrospect, a liminal space between older paradigms and what would become the new framework for Jewish–Christian relations in the following two decades. In Christian texts of the period we find strong statements against antisemitism side by side with accusations of Jews' responsibility for the crucifixion of Christ (see Gerlach 2000). A salient example not included in the chapter is the Confessing Church's declaration of 1948. The authors of this declaration state that they 'realise with shame and sorrow that we have failed Israel'; yet, at the same time, they maintain that 'By crucifying the Messiah, Israel rejected its election and destiny'. Examples of such Christian ambivalence are ample in this chapter: in his conversation with the Swiss Jewish youth movement Emuna, the prominent theologian and Confessing Church leader Karl Barth renounces antisemitism, while at the same time suggesting that Jews should take pride in it, as it pronounces their election (see document 4 (iii)); Rabbi Richard Rubenstein describes his 1961 meeting with Heinrich Grüber, another Protestant leader of the Christian anti-Nazi resistance, as pointing to a theological justification of the Holocaust as willed by God (document 12). In France, too, even devout Catholics who risked their lives to save Jews during the Holocaust were involved in the infamous 'Finaly affair' of 1953 (document 3).

This state of affairs underwent a gradual, albeit dramatic change between the early 1950s and the mid-1960s, largely energised by Jewish interlocutors who engaged in dialogue with Christians while boldly expressing their unease regarding the ambivalent perceptions of their Christian counterparts. Martin Buber blamed Paul for distorting what Buber saw as Jesus' Pharisaic-Jewish faith and provoking anti-Judaism (document 2). Abraham J. Heschel protested against the Second Vatican Council's rumination on the future conversion of Jews to Catholicism in its draft document on relations with Jews, calling Christian attention to the fact that many Jews see Christian mission not only as outright offensive, but even as a spiritual extension of physical annihilation (document 13). The incommensurability of conversion with the mainstream perception of Jewish identity is evidenced also in the 1962 trial of Brother Daniel in Israel (document 6), which was concluded shortly before the opening of Vatican II. Above all, Jules Isaac's study of the Christian theological roots of modern antisemitism in a series of publications and dialogical engagements from the late 1940s onwards obliged both Catholic and Protestant communities to cast a sober gaze on the dark side of their traditions and to account for their part in the agony of Jews (document 1). Buttressed by the wide reception of Rolf Hochhuth's relentless criticism of Christian silence during the Holocaust in his historic 1963 play *The Deputy* (document 8), these Jewish intellectuals posed an enormous challenge to the church leadership, a challenge of penitence and responsibility. It is hard to decide which aspect of these Jewish positions is more stunning – the fact that they were not afraid to express to Christian ears such harsh criticisms of Christianity or the fact that they trusted Christians to listen to those criticisms from the outset and were willing to engage in dialogue with them (a willingness which was not at all obvious, as is evident in Joseph Ber Soloveitchik's reservations about Jewish engagement in Christian–Jewish dialogue (document 10)).

Yet the Christian responses were no less stunning. From high-ranking Vatican officials to independent theologians, Christian thinkers and leaders listened to the claims of their Jewish critics and used them, from around the mid-1960s, to call for an overarching revision of Christian theology. *Nostra aetate* (1965), a statement from the highest level of the Roman Catholic Church that garnered a great deal of publicity and influenced the leadership of other churches, too, denounced antisemitism, emphasised the Jewish roots of Christianity and rejected the charge of deicide (see Appendix to Part III, p. 512). Theological giant Karl Barth admitted his own antisemitic tendencies and failing to fight for the Jews during the Holocaust and openly embraced criticisms of his doctrine of Israel, as well as the new theological horizons offered by his student Friedrich-Wilhelm Marquardt. Moreover, following Isaac's lead, Christian theologians began to search for the intersections at which the Christian tradition neglected the Jewishness of its origins and became anti-Jewish: whether in Luther's reading of Paul's writings on the Law in Romans and Galatians, as Krister Stendahl argued (document 7), or the patristic *adversus Judaeos* tradition, as argued by Alice and Roy Eckardt (document 14); or even whether, as in Rosemary Radford Ruether's radical thesis (document 16), the seeds of contempt were already present in the New Testament, where anti-Judaism emerged as the 'left hand of Christology' (1974: 365). Everything was put to the test, including the foundations of Christian theology and its relation to history, as in Johann Baptist Metz's work, and the Christian perceptions of God himself, as in Dorothee Sölle's political theology (document 11). Criticism wasn't lacking among contemporary academics either, as exemplified in Sister Charlotte Klein's scrutiny of the transmission of anti-Jewish ideas through scholarly works of key biblical scholars and systematic theologians (document 17). Christian thinkers, in other words, were willing to doubt the very integrity of Christianity in the face of Auschwitz. Such a bold move is imaginable only in the context of the Holocaust's immediate aftermath, a context of immense instability in which the almost total dissolution of Europe allowed space for a radical and encompassing reconsideration of the entire Christian tradition.

The question was, and perhaps still is, whether this shift remained, profoundly, an occidental story, relevant for a specific moment in western history, or whether Jewish–Christian relations have changed forever, regardless of their specific local contexts. How, then, did Jewish–Christian relations look, during the period covered by this chapter, in other parts of the world, imprinted by different sets of cultural, political and religious memories? This question is especially salient because even if Europe remained the central *intellectual* locus for reimagining Jewish–Christian relations, a non-negligible portion of the Jewish community after the Holocaust was based elsewhere, away from the western context of Europe and North America.

The 'east', of course, can mean many things. In this chapter, for example, a unique Eastern Orthodox invitation to dialogue is excerpted from Metropolitan Damaskinos' 1972 lecture in Geneva (document 18). And yet the 'east' which stood in the midst of, and complicated, the Jewish–Christian renewal from 1948 onwards was, of course, the Middle East.

Before the dust of World War II settled, while an unstable Europe was in search of a new identity and Germany was still occupied by the western allies, the Yishuv (i.e., the body of Jewish residents in Eretz Israel) announced on 14 May 1948 the establishment of the State of Israel. Many Holocaust survivors became, in the blink of an eye, the citizens of a Jewish nation state. Yet for much of the native Arab population, British colonialism was simply replaced with a new kind of European domination in the form of Zionism (though some employed a distinctly essentialist antisemitic language to describe the State of Israel, before and after the 1967 war, as an expression of Jewish aggression). The Zionist state now set the tone for the region without the official consent of the Christian and Muslim inhabitants of Palestine or of neighbouring Arab countries.

The State of Israel was indeed established according to the model of western nation states. It received the support of the UN – not negligibly, because the world recognised, at that time more than ever before, Jews' need for a national home like other nations. Yet Israel's establishment precisely on *that* land, the Holy Land, the land of the Bible, endowed this nation state with an enormous historical and theological gravity, for Jews and for Christians alike (and for Muslims, too). Was Israel a secular political entity established for the survival, even the thriving, of a persecuted and vulnerable people, or was it theologically meaningful? And if so, what might its theological meaning be? And how should the ongoing violence in the region be dealt with by Christians within and without the Middle East? The question of how to relate to the State of Israel stood at the heart of the Jewish–Christian relationship and was second only to the issue of Christian responsibility (or lack thereof) for the Holocaust. Israel was difficult: in both the 1961 New Delhi World Council of Churches (WCC) assembly (document 5) and the Second Vatican Council's discussions, European and North American Christian representatives pushed for a maximalist theological affirmation of Jews and Judaism, while Arab representatives feared that a positive theology of Israel would imply a political affirmation of the state (see Miccoli 2003). For this reason, there were voices who advocated for separating the theological from the political, and leaving the State of Israel out of the process of Jewish–Christian reconciliation. Yet for others, such as the American Methodist minister, church historian and Holocaust scholar Franklin Littell, just as the Holocaust was 'the crucifixion of the Jews' (as Littell's famous book is titled), of Jesus' people, so the return of great numbers of Jews to Zion and their revival there were imagined as a resurrection. Friedrich-Wilhelm Marquardt, on the other hand, abstained from such a Christological imaginary and saw in Israel precisely a living Jewish reality that does not require the theological mediation of Christian theology from which to derive its own sense of meaning (document 9). Moreover, as Alice and Roy Eckardt wrote after the June War of 1967, if the 'exile' of the Jewish people had been theologically significant in the eyes of Christians for centuries, how could a Christian resistance to Israel, or even Christian indifference, derive from anything other than the Christian teaching of contempt (document 14)? This perception was indeed in line with mainstream Jewish historical consciousness, which saw the State of Israel both as a vital remedy for antisemitism and as quenching an age-old Jewish thirst for return. Yet, as surfaces in the excerpt from Metropolitan Khodr – the only Arab Christian voice included in this chapter – western Christian support for the State of Israel designed to counter antisemitism created a deep divide between western and (Middle) eastern Christianity, which was (and still is) the major part of Christianity in the region, and at the same time prob-lematised the possibility of a Christian–Muslim dialogue which was globally important and even more urgent in that specific part of the world (document 15). Israel, as seen through this prism, was largely a western import of Europe's problems into the east.

Thus the Holocaust and the State of Israel were the two overarching questions that emerged between 1948 and 1978, from which many other issues branched out. All the excerpted documents, like a variety of other important texts from the period, respond in one way or another to at least one of these questions, and in many of them the two are intertwined. The chapter explores the various ways in which these questions evolved, and the ways in which they were answered, through the prism of these excerpts, which are authored by Protestants, Catholics, Orthodox Christians, Orthodox Jews, liberal Jews and secular Jews, from Europe, the United States, the Middle East and South Asia. Some of these documents are considered today to be the new 'classics' of Jewish–Christian rela-tions, and many of them had an enormous impact on the field. Others became famous for reasons which are only indirectly related to Jewish–Christian relations (prominent exam-ples being the excerpts from Paul Bénichou's article in *Le Monde*, from Brother Daniel's trial and from Dorothee Sölle's book; documents 3, 6 and 11). These excerpts have been chosen in order to highlight the interconnectedness with Jewish–Christian relations of Jewish identity, church–state or religion–politics relations, secularism and political the-ology, since the drama of the Jewish–Christian relationship often takes place outside official dialogue and scholarly encounter – in individual cases, in political turmoil, in public debates or in mundane instances of everyday life. Lastly, excerpts are included from documents which remain almost completely unknown in the field, notwithstanding their significance in their respective religious communities and the unique perspectives from which they approach the Jewish–Christian relationship, notably the two Orthodox Christian texts from the 1970s (documents 15 and 18).

The diversity of perspectives is intensified by a diversity of genres: the chapter includes theological and scholarly works alongside a newspaper article, a trial record, a play, a speech, some reports and the protocol of a lively intra-Christian discussion. Through this polyphony the reader may sense both the seismic changes and the over-whelming effort on the part of both Christians and Jews to change things for the better, often along with the resurfacing of painful memories and suspicions, intra-Jewish and intra-Christian polemics, and a disquieting yet fascinating entanglement of theology, history and politics.

Bibliography

Adorno, Theodor W., and Tiedemann, Rolf (eds.), *Can One Live after Auschwitz? A Philosophical Reader* (Stanford: Stanford University Press, 2003).

Baum, Gregory, *Is the New Testament Anti-Semitic? A Re-Examination of the New Testament* (Glen Rock: Paulist Press, 1965).

Ben-Chorin, Schalom, *Brother Jesus: The Nazarene through Jewish Eyes*, trans. Jared S. Klein and Max Reinhart (Athens: University of Georgia Press, 2012).

Ben-Johanan, Karma, *Jacob's Younger Brother: Christian–Jewish Relations after Vatican II* (Cambridge, MA: Harvard University Press, 2022).

Connelly, John, *From Enemy to Brother: The Revolution in Catholic Teaching on the Jews, 1933–1965* (Cambridge, MA: Harvard University Press, 2012).

Gerlach, Wolfgang, *And the Witnesses Were Silent: The Confessing Church and the Persecution of the Jews*, trans. Victoria Barnett (Lincoln, NE and London: University of Nebraska Press, 2000).

Littell, Franklin H., *The Crucifixion of the Jews* (New York: Harper & Row, 1975).

Miccoli, Giovanni, 'Two Sensitive Issues: Religious Freedom and The Jews', in Alberigo, Giuseppe (ed.), *History of Vatican II, vol. IV: Church as Communion: Third Period and Intersession, September 1964–September 1965* (Maryknoll: Orbis; Louvain: Peeters, 2003), 95–193.

Ramon, Amnon, *Christianity & Christians in the Jewish State: Israeli Policy toward the Churches and Christian Communities (1948–2018)*, trans. Shaul Vardi (Jerusalem and New York: Jerusalem Institute for Policy Research/Rossing Center for Education and Dialogue, Israel Academic Press, 2021).

Ruether, Rosemary Radford, 'Anti-Semitism in Christian Theology', *Theology Today* (1974), 365–81.

Sanders, Ed Parish, *Paul and Palestinian Judaism: A Comparison of Patterns of Religion* (London: SCM, 1977).

Van Buren, Paul M., *The Burden of Freedom: Americans and the God of Israel* (New York: Seabury Press, 1976).

The author is grateful to Benedikt Skorzenski for his assistance in collecting the chapter's sources and to Michael G. Azar for his good advice with regard to the Christian Orthodox sources.

DOCUMENTS

I

Jules Isaac: Jesus and Israel *(1948)*

Text

One wonders, I myself have wondered: given the groundlessness of the Christian accusation [of deicide], how can we explain that it was accepted in this way, transmitted from generation to generation, from antiquity to our own day, almost without any contradiction?

[...]

Intentionally or not, the accusers have started from a point of confusion. Fundamental confusion. Which has been sustained from century to century. Which is still sustained and reigns over minds.

Confusion of two historical problems, two historical facts, which are entirely distinct.

The first of these problems is one we have examined: Jesus and Israel, Jesus and his people. In the apparently rather narrow Jewish sphere in which he lived, preached, spread the Gospel, Jesus found adversaries, enemies, disciples, the sympathies of the masses. These are the facts. There was neither a rejection of the Jewish people by Jesus nor a rejection of Jesus by the Jewish people.

The second problem is quite other: Judaism and Christianity. We have not broached it but have only alluded to it. It is also a fact, but later and quite other, that at a given moment, after a strong surge of conversions, the Jewish people, regrouped behind their doctors, became resistant to Christian preaching. What the Jewish people rejected at that moment was not Jesus, not even the Christ; it was the Christian faith and rule, as they were defined by the new Church. Moreover, there was a parallel and mutual rebuff, of Christianity by Judaism and of Judaism by Christianity, the two rebuffs closely related to one another. Which was cause, which effect? Let us not forget, primitive Christianity was Judeo-Christianity. From the day when it ceased to be so, when Judeo-Christianity saw itself relegated to the rank of an inferior sect, then a heresy, a breach opened between the two confessions: to ask the Jewish people to cast off a Law they venerated as dictated by God Himself, to ask them that, which Jesus had never asked, was truly to ask the impossible. The growing mutual hostility of the doctors (Christian and Jewish) and the development of Christian dogmatics did the rest: the breach became an abyss.

[...]

The German responsibility for these crimes, as overwhelming as it has been, is only a derivative responsibility, grafted like a most hideous parasite on a centuries-old tradition which is a Christian tradition. How can we forget that Christianity, especially from the eleventh century on, practiced a policy of degradation and pogroms against the Jews which has extended – among certain Christian peoples – into the contemporary era, and whose survival is observable still in Poland, with its highly Catholic history, whose Hitlerian system was merely an atrociously perfected copy?

Anti-Judaism will retain its virulence as long as the Christian Churches and peoples do not recognize their initial responsibility, as long as they do not have the heart to wipe it out. Latent anti-Semitism exists everywhere, and the contrary would be surprising: for the perennial source of this latent anti-Semitism is none other than Christian religious teaching in all its forms, the traditional and tendentious interpretation of Scripture, the interpretation which I am absolutely convinced is contrary to the truth and love of him who was the Jew Jesus. The Jewish problem is not only a temporal problem; it is first and fundamentally a spiritual problem, whose resolution can be found only in a profound spiritual and religious renewal.

I urge true Christians, and also true Israelites, to undertake this effort of renewal, of purification, this strenuous examination of conscience. Such is the aim I have envisaged. Such is the major lesson that emerges from meditation on Auschwitz, which I cannot release myself from, which no man of heart could abstain from. The glow of the Auschwitz crematorium is the beacon that lights, that guides all my thoughts. Oh, my Jewish brothers, and you as well, my Christian brothers, do you not think that it mingles with another glow, that of the Cross?

Source

Isaac, Jules, *Jesus and Israel*, ed. Claire H. Bishop, trans. Sally Gran (New York: Holt, Rinehart and Winston, 1971), 397–400. (Originally published as *Jésus et Israël*, 1948.)

Commentary

Among a number of Jewish scholars and leaders who influenced the dramatic transition in Christian approaches to Jews and Judaism in the second half of the twentieth century, a special place is reserved for French Jewish historian Jules Isaac (1880–1963). Isaac's research on Christian anti-Judaism, combined with his relentless efforts to promote Jewish–Christian dialogue and understanding, helped set the tone for the process of Jewish–Christian rapprochement. Isaac was a central driving force behind the 1947 Seelisberg Conference and its *Ten Points* (see Appendix to Part III, p. 510); he was the cofounder and president of the federation Amitié Judéo–Chrétienne de France (Christian and Jewish Friendship); and, most importantly, his historic meeting with Pope John XXIII in 1960 was crucial in raising the Jewish issue to the agenda of the Second Vatican Council.

Of special importance are Isaac's two influential books on the Christian contribution to the development of antisemitism: the first, *Jésus et Israël*, was authored as the Holocaust unfolded, to which Isaac lost his wife and daughter. *Jésus et Israël* was published in 1948 and in English translation (as *Jesus and Israel*) in 1971. Isaac's main thesis in this book is that the sources of modern antisemitism are to be found in Christian teaching, in a way that urgently calls Christians to examine their consciousness when facing the destruction of European Jewry. Nevertheless, the deeply rooted Christian hostility to Jews which has nurtured European civilisation evolved, according to Isaac, from a distorted reading of the New Testament Gospels, a reading that severely misunderstood the relationship between Jesus and Israel. The manuscript of *Jésus et Israël* was of central importance to the discussions at the Seelisberg Conference.

Isaac's other influential book, *L'Enseignement du mépris*, was first published in 1962, a year before Isaac's death and the year in which Vatican II was convened, with an English translation (*The Teaching of Contempt*) in 1964. In this book, Isaac boldly argues that the Christian root of antisemitism is first and foremost the 'deicide charge', which puts the blame for the crucifixion on the entire Jewish people, in every generation. Though such animosity appears already in certain parts of the Gospels (see, e.g., Chapter 1, p. 51), Isaac anchors it above all in Christianity's transition to becoming primarily gentile from the second century onwards, and especially in Christian post-Constantinian literature, after 'the victorious Church was allied with Empire' (1964: 33). Isaac's coinage 'the teaching of contempt' became a synonym for Christian anti-Judaism.

In sum, Isaac's scholarly and diplomatic work made an unprecedented contribution to the formation of the Vatican Council's discussion of Jews and Judaism in the fourth section of *Nostra aetate* (see Appendix to Part III, p. 512). His resonating question about the Christian sources of antisemitism and the line he drew from Europe's Christian heritage to the Holocaust, combined with his historical-critical approach to New Testament depictions of Jews and Judaism and his research on the evolution of the deicide charge, continue to be regularly cited in studies of Jewish–Christian relations.

Bibliography

Isaac, Jules, *The Teaching of Contempt: Christian Roots of Anti-Semitism*, trans. Helen Weaver
 (New York: McGraw-Hill, 1964). (Originally published as *L'Enseignement du mépris: vérité
 historique et mythes théologiques*, 1962.)
Tobias, Norman, *Jewish Conscience of the Church: Jules Isaac and the Second Vatican Council*
 (Cham, Switzerland: Palgrave Macmillan, 2017).

2

Martin Buber: Two Types of Faith *(1950)*

Text

In the comparison of the two types of faith which I have attempted in this book I confine myself principally to the primitive and early days of Christianity, and for that almost exclusively to the New Testament records on the one hand, and on the other side in the main to the sayings of the Talmud and the Midrashim, originating from the core of Pharisaism, which was to be sure influenced by Hellenism but which did not surrender to it; I draw on Hellenistic Judaism only for purposes of clarification. (The after-effects of the Old Testament always lead on to the problem of its interpretation.) It becomes evident that Jesus and central Pharisaism belong essentially to one another, just as early Christianity and Hellenistic Judaism do.

[…]

From my youth onwards I have found in Jesus my great brother. That Christianity has regarded and does regard him as God and Saviour has always appeared to me a fact of the highest importance which, for his sake and my own, I must endeavour to understand. A small part of the results of this desire to understand is recorded here. My own fraternally open relationship to him has grown ever stronger and clearer, and to-day I see him more strongly and clearly than ever before.

[…]

Paul found in his Greek Bible at this point [Gen. 15:6] something which is immersed in a different atmosphere. Abraham does not believe 'in' God, in the sense of a perseverance in Him, but he believes Him – which to be sure does not require to mean that he believed His words (such a weakening of the sentence is not in the mind of the translator), but it does denote an act of the soul in the moment described. More important still is the fact that instead of the divine consideration, deeming, ratification, there has come into being an attributing, a category in the judicial computation of items of guilt and innocence against each other, and in connexion with this instead of the proving true, a 'righteousness', the rightness of the conduct which justifies the individual before God; both are a limitation, a deflation of that original fulness of life, a limitation common to Alexandrian and contemporary Rabbinical Judaism. With its assumption by Paul however the sentence is penetrated by the principles of the Pauline faith and justification doctrine, and its import is changed: faith, as the divine activity in man, gives rise to the condition of being righteous, which the 'works', proceeding from men alone, the mere fulfilment of the 'law', are not able to bring about. The simple face-to-face relationship between God and man in the Genesis story is replaced by an interpenetration which comes about by faith and faith alone, the dialogical by the mystical situation; but this situation does not remain, as nearly always in mysticism, an end in itself; it is grasped and discussed as the situation which alone can place the individual in that state in which he can stand the judgement of God. By imparting the state of faith God Himself renders it possible as it were for Him to be gracious without detriment to His justice. When we read that sentence first in the original and then in the Septuagint we are displaced from the high-ground where God receives Abraham's attitude of faith, his persistence in Him, as proving true, to the deep valley, where the act of faith is entered in the book of judgement, as the decisive fact of the case in favour of the person judged; when we read the sentence afterwards in the context of the Pauline letters we are removed on to a rocky slope where the inner divine dialectic governs exclusively. The fundamentals of this dialectic-idea are to be found in Judaism, namely in the early Talmud, but the conception of the intercourse between the divine attributes of severity and of mercy changes here to the extreme real paradox, by which for Paul [...] even the great theme of his faith, his Christology, is supported, without it being possible to be expressed: in redeeming the world by the surrender of His son God redeems Himself from the fate of His justice, which would condemn it.

Source

Buber, Martin, *Two Types of Faith*, trans. Norman P. Goldhawk (New York: Macmillan, 1951), 11–12, 46–7. (Originally published as *Zwei Glaubensweisen*, 1950.)

Commentary

The Vienna-born Jewish thinker Martin Buber (1878–1965) is one of the most studied Jewish philosophers in the world, and in Christian circles in particular. Buber was in close and deep dialogue with Christian theologians, some of whom he knew well and held in the highest esteem. He was a reader of the New Testament and of contemporary Christian theology, from Kierkegaard to Bultmann. His own work was, in turn, read and commented on by various Christian thinkers, from Hans Urs von Balthasar to Friedrich-Wilhelm Marquardt (see document 9), from Alice and Roy Eckardt (document 14) to Pope Benedict XVI and Metropolitan Damaskinos (document 18). Buber's dialogical philosophy, especially his *I and Thou* (1923), enjoyed a global reception and became a classic of modern Jewish thought.

Buber was extremely appreciative of Jesus, whom he called a 'great brother'. Buber insisted on rooting Jesus in the Jewish, and especially the Pharisaic, tradition, rather than perceiving him as the founder of a new religion. Buber's Jesus made a decisive contribution to the growing acknowledgement of Jesus' Jewishness among Christian circles (consider, for example, Marquardt's work) and, no less importantly, as the title of Schalom Ben-Chorin's *Brother Jesus: The Nazarene through Jewish Eyes* testifies, provided inspiration for a growing body of Jewish literature on the Jewish Jesus which continues to diversify with recent projects such as Amy-Jill Levine and Marc Zvi Brettler's *The Jewish Annotated New Testament* or Paula Fredriksen's *When Christians Were Jews* (see also Chapter 9, pp. 499–501). The contextualisation of New Testament texts in the Jewish milieu in which they originally emerged is considerably indebted to Buber's initiative, even if many of Buber's insights are not compatible with biblical scholarship today.

Yet the opinions of this important mediator between Jews and Christians about the Christian faith were not all favourable. Especially in *Two Types of Faith*, it is evident that Buber's dialogue with Christianity can also take the form of polemic – 'a major attack on Christianity', as the Swiss theologian Emil Brunner (1967: 313) put it. As reflected in the excerpts, Buber's reappropriation of Jesus was in no way a reappropriation of Christianity as a whole; rather, Buber maintained that Jesus' Jewish teachings were largely distorted by Paul's teaching, which was largely inspired by Jewish Hellenism, and especially by the 'Hellenised' translation of the Hebrew Bible into Greek. It was Paul who turned Jesus from a great teacher into a proposition of faith, and faith itself from trust in God to a belief in God, a distinction which Buber made through a (semantically problematic) differentiation between the Hebrew *emuna* and the Greek *pistis*. While Buber judged Jesus favourably, as compatible with the prophetic Jewish tradition, Paul was judged as the real father of Christianity, that is, of Christianity as a different type of faith from Judaism. Buber's Paul is a dogmatist, an antinomist, a Gnostic, even an ideologue, who turned the God of Israel into a wrathful God and verged close to Marcion's contempt of both creation and the Hebrew scripture (see Chapter 2, p. 67). Though negative, Buber's depiction of Paul as an antinomist is heavily influenced by classical Protestant readings of Paul as the great rival of Jewish legalism – exactly the sort of readings that biblical scholars such as Krister Stendahl and others sought to refute in integrating Paul, along with Jesus, back into Judaism.

Bibliography

Balthasar, Hans Urs von, *Martin Buber and Christianity: A Dialogue between Israel and the Church*, trans. Alexander Dru (London: Harvill, 1961).
Brunner, Emil, 'Judaism and Christianity in Buber', in Schilpp, Paul Arthur, and Friedman, Maurice (eds.), *The Philosophy of Martin Buber* (La Salle: Open Court, 1967), 309–18.
Mendes-Flohr, Paul, *Martin Buber: A Life of Faith and Dissent* (New Haven: Yale University Press, 2019).
Schmidt, Christoph, 'Beyond the Law and Without the Cross: Martin Buber and Saint Paul as an Apostolic Competition between "Two Types of Faith"', in Berrin Shonkoff, Sam (ed.), *Martin Buber: His Intellectual and Scholarly Legacy* (Leiden: Brill, 2018), 66–77.

3

Paul Bénichou: 'Reflections on "the Affair"' (2 March 1953)

Text

Given that the debate is open, it should be taken all the way. That which we dare not say but which in fact is being said is the following: that, given the events, the Finaly children, born outside of the Catholic Church, were annexed into it; baptism tied them to the church; they must stay tied to it. The adoptive mother from whom they risk escaping if they are given back to their legal family is not Mademoiselle Brun but rather the Roman Church. This is the crux of the affair; that is how it is implicitly presented. It is as if the rights of the family, sacred in the eyes of Catholics when it comes to, for example, opposing the state school system, were subject to curious distinctions. The family is lawful when Catholic; the non-Catholic family is a sort of *de facto* grouping, provisional, without legitimacy, which baptism (even forced) of one of its members is sufficient to break. The Catholic family is sacred; the non-Catholic family is nothing: when touched by the sacrament of baptism it is pulverised. What else is signified by the flagrant violation of laws, the devious doctrinal complacency, the signs of which are manifold, the allusions to the rights of the church over baptised children, the superior considerations pitted against secular law, the mysteries of faith and conscience that accompany breaching the law, the pretence to impose a compromise between the law and some unnamed 'entity'? Is it not time to remember that law is the sole sovereign in France, that no church is imbued with legal power, that the sacraments of all religions have no civil value? It has been thus for more than 150 years, at least. We thought that this was no longer in doubt. The Finaly affair proves otherwise and it is because of this that it is a very serious matter.

We are threatened with an outburst of discontent if the clergy, complicit by their own admission in the abduction of children, continue to be questioned; hanging over our heads is the threat of Catholic indignation should justice take its course; early threats are in the process of being made. Have we considered the fact that discontent and indignation will flare up far more legitimately in support of the law than against those who violate it? We can if we want question the (possibly unstable) balance that people of good faith have wanted to establish between the Catholic Church and contemporary society. However, problems will arise once more, conflicts will be reignited, the consequences of which we might not yet measure. When public opinion understands what is at stake, which will not take long, we will probably perceive more clearly what are its true feelings and wishes in the matter.

Source

Bénichou, Paul, 'Réflexions sur "l'affaire"', *Le Monde* (2 March 1953). (Translation by Sami Everett.)

Commentary

One of the most serious postwar crises in European Jewish–Christian relations occurred in France in 1953. 'L'affaire Finaly', the Finaly affair, was defined by the *New York Times* as 'the worst religious storm of post-war France' and by many as the greatest public controversy involving Jews in France since the Dreyfus affair in the 1890s (see Chapter 6, p. 290). At the heart of the Finaly affair stood the fate of two children, Robert and Gerald Finaly, whose Jewish parents were murdered in Auschwitz and who survived the Holocaust years in the municipal nursery of Grenoble under the custody of a Roman Catholic school director, Antoinette Brun. In 1945 Mademoiselle Brun, who was given custody of the children by Mother Marie-Antonine of Notre-Dame de Sion in Grenoble, refused to return them to their Jewish family, igniting a years-long juridical struggle. The children were baptised by Brun into the Catholic faith, which provoked a clash between canon law – according to which the church is the custodian of baptised children and should take care of their Christian upbringing – and civil law, which eventually judged in favour of the children's Jewish family.

Brun did not surrender the children even after the court found her guilty of kidnapping: assisted by several priests, nuns and church officials, she managed to hide them under false names. After a long and difficult struggle, the children were handed over to the guardianship of their aunt and in June 1953 moved to Israel.

The Finaly affair caused immense public uproar in France, and involved rabbis, priests, theologians, politicians and intellectuals – Jewish, Catholic, Protestant and secular alike. The excerpt above is taken from one of the most widely read articles written at the height of this debate, authored by the French literary scholar and secular Jew Paul Bénichou. Bénichou's position is important precisely because it transfers the Finaly affair from the realm of Jewish–Christian relations to that of church–state relations, arguing that what was at stake in 1953 was, in fact, the secular authority of the state and the sovereignty of law. By this move, and by avoiding depicting it as a 'Jewish' matter, Bénichou ties the Finaly affair to the identity of the French state since the Enlightenment. Bénichou's secularist position, which developed into a debate in the pages of *Le Monde*, was mentioned in the international coverage of the affair in 1953 and later discussed in scholarly accounts of the controversy.

Other prominent figures among the many who took part in the controversy were Rabbi Jacob Kaplan, then Chief Rabbi of France, who relentlessly fought for the return of the children to their Jewish relatives; Catholic author and Nobel laureate François Mauriac, who hoped that the children themselves would come to integrate both their Catholicism and their Jewishness into their identities; and Fr Paul Démann, a priest of the Congregation of the Fathers of Our Lady of Sion and one of the period's main leaders of Jewish–Christian rapprochement, who urged the Church of France to demand the return of the children to their families.

Based on a recent examination of the newly opened Vatican archives from the pontificate of Pius XII, historians David Kertzer and Roberto Benedetti argue that the Vatican was directly involved in the effort to prevent the children's access to their relatives. This recent interest in the Finaly affair demonstrates the extent to which it still touches a raw nerve in Jewish–Christian relations.

Bibliography

Jones, Priscilla Dale, 'The Finaly Affair: Issues and Implications', *Religion* 13, no. 3 (1983), 177–203.

Kertzer, David, and Benedetti, Roberto, 'The Vatican's Role in the Finaly Children's Kidnapping Case', *SCJR* 15, no. 1 (2020), 1–21.

Lazarus, Joyce Block, *In the Shadow of Vichy: The Finaly Affair* (New York: Peter Lang, 2008).

4

Karl Barth: Church Dogmatics *and Interview with Jewish Youth (1953, 1950)*

Text

(i) Karl Barth: Church Dogmatics, *'The Jewish Jesus' (1953)*

The Word did not simply become any 'flesh,' any man humbled and suffering. It became Jewish flesh. The Church's whole doctrine of the incarnation and the atonement becomes abstract and valueless and meaningless to the extent that this comes to be regarded as something accidental and incidental. The New Testament witness to Jesus the Christ, the Son of God, stands on the soil of the Old Testament and cannot be separated from it. The pronouncements of New Testament Christology may have been shaped by a very non-Jewish environment. But they relate always to a man who is seen to be not a man in general, a neutral man, but the conclusion and sum of the history of God with the people of Israel, the One who fulfils the covenant made by God with this people. And it is as such that He is the obedient Son and servant of God, and therefore the One who essentially and necessarily suffers.

Source

Barth, Karl, *Church Dogmatics IV.1: The Doctrine of Reconciliation*, ed. G. W. Bromiley and T. F. Torrance, trans. G. W. Bromiley (New York: T&T Clark, 2009), 159. (Originally published as *Die Kirchliche Dogmatik* IV/1, 1953.)

(ii) Karl Barth: Church Dogmatics, *'The Ecclesiological Wound' (1953)*

Where the Church has taken Rom. 9–11 seriously, it has not been able to escape or explain away the fact that its unity in this sense is compromised by the existence of a Judaism which does not believe in Jesus Christ. More than anything else, this makes its own existence problematical. For it belongs to its nature and situation as the community in the world to be separated from all kinds of religions and religious communities. Its very aim as a missionary community is to call men out of these, to call them from false gods to the true God. But this being the case, the existence of the Synagogue side by side with the Church is an ontological impossibility, a wound, a gaping hole: in the body of Christ, something which is quite intolerable. For what does the Church have which the Synagogue does not also have, and long before it (Rom. 9:4–5) – especially Jesus Christ himself, who is of the Jews, who is the Jewish Messiah, and only as such the Lord of the Church? The decisive question is not what the Jewish Synagogue can be without Him, but what the Church is as long as it confronts an alien and hostile Israel?

Source

Barth, Karl, *Church Dogmatics IV.1: The Doctrine of Reconciliation*, ed. G. W. Bromiley and T. F. Torrance, trans. G. W. Bromiley (New York: T&T Clark, 2009), 159. (Originally published as *Die Kirchliche Dogmatik* IV/1, 1953.)

(iii) Jewish Youth Interview Karl Barth (1950)

The next question of special interest [...] is that of the *mission to the Jews*. From where do Christians derive the moral right to proselytise members of Judaism who represent a pure religion, while Christianity, in the eyes of the Jews, is to be regarded as a compromise of Judaism with paganism? For the time being, Professor Barth opposed any mission to the Jews, if it were understood to be missionary work as it is applied to pagans. The phrase *mission to the Jews* in his opinion is unfortunate, because it absolutely does not reflect the relationship between Israel and the Christian community. We stand together.

Especially from the perspective of Christ, we belong to the same people: Israel, the people who go towards Christ, and the Christian Church, which comes from Christ. According to Professor Barth, this is a unity that Israel does not perceive. The Christian community could not be without Israel. From the Christian point of view, being a Christian means being a right Jew, because the whole of the Old Testament has one goal, its fulfilment in Jesus Christ. It should not be a mission, because the Jews should recognise for themselves that the Old and the New Testament form a unity. Especially in regard to this issue, the discussion revealed the fundamental difference between the religious conceptions of Jews and Christians, which precludes a deep understanding of each other. One speaker stated that the focus of the Christian was on 'being redeemed' and that of the Jew was 'being obliged'.

The last problem to be discussed here is that of *antisemitism*. How does the Church explain the world's hatred of the Jews? Professor Barth's answer: True Christians have to be excluded from the world here, because true Christianity is *not compatible* with antisemitism. *Israel* is the people chosen by God. It is an historical as well as a theological miracle. As He has promised, God is faithful to His people. The *existence of Israel* is the actual proof of God. The world is unwilling to accept this because it is unwilling to accept God [...] Israel should actually be proud of antisemitism, despite all condemnation of it, because it is *proof* of Israel's being chosen and of its outstanding mission.

On the Jewish side, it was stated that this might well be correct from the evangelical-theological point of view, but that the *reality* in its full atrocious nature would not permit such a fatal notion. *Other* factors would also have to be considered here. Prof. Barth replied: The theological aspect is comprehensive. This is about an understanding that begins with God.

Source

'Jüdische Jugend befragt Karl Barth', *Freiburger Rundbrief* 7 (1950), 20. (Translation by Iris Koch.)

Commentary

Karl Barth (1886–1968), the greatest theologian of the twentieth century and arguably the most extensively read among Jewish readers, was also one of the most complicated, original and influential Christian thinkers with regard to the Jewish people. The ambiguity and density of Barth's 'doctrine of Israel' – a theology which evolved and changed during his many decades of activity – led to ambivalent evaluations. Was Barth pro-Jewish or anti-Jewish? Did his theology give room to post-crucifixion Judaism and Jewish history, and was his support of the State of Israel theologically motivated? Was he a forerunner of Jewish–Christian dialogue, or did Jewish–Christian dialogue have to supersede Barth in order to achieve true rapprochement?

These questions emerge from the complex nature of Barth's dialectical theology, from his own autobiographical notes, and from his Christian leadership more generally. Barth was an uncontested leader of the *Kirchenkampf* ('Church Struggle') under the Nazi regime (see Chapter 7, p. 343). He headed the Confessing Church's fight against the *Deutsche Christen*, in a relentless effort to prevent the merging of the churches with the Nazi state. In his resistance to the implementation of the Aryan paragraph in the churches, Barth clearly rejected racist antisemitism and advocated on behalf of converted Jews. Yet, as he himself confessed in 1967, the fate of non-converted Jews did not stand at the centre of his agenda in the same way. On the one hand, Barth declared that antisemitism was a sin against the Holy Spirit, reflected on the Jewishness of Jesus and laid the foundations for a rejection of Christian mission to Jews. On the other, as he admitted to his student Friedrich-Wilhelm Marquardt, he contended with 'a totally irrational aversion' towards individual Jews, an aversion he struggled to suppress.

This profound ambivalence of Barth's doctrine of Israel is evident in the excerpts above. The first delves into Barth's bold acknowledgement of Jesus' Jewishness, an acknowledgement whose doctrinal implications occupy scholars of Jewish–Christian relations to this day, and which strongly contradicts nineteenth- and twentieth-century theological separations of Jesus from his Jewishness. The second excerpt presents Barth's insight with regard to the ecumenical importance of Jewish–Christian reconciliation. The third excerpt summarises an actual encounter which Barth held in 1950 with Emunah, a group of young Swiss Jews, during which they discussed pending – and painful – theological questions. Barth argues here, quite counterintuitively for his time, that the party that remains severely wounded by the separation of church and synagogue is not the synagogue but the church; that is, the church needs the Jews more than the Jews need the church. This argument has far-reaching implications for the very idea that Christians should be missionising Jews – an idea that Barth was one of the first to reject. In a parallel with Rubenstein's dialogue with Grüber (document 12), Barth's suggestion that the Jews should be 'proud' of antisemitism as evidence of their election is rejected by his dialogue partners as outright cruel.

Barth's long-lasting influence on Jewish–Christian relations is evident, among other things, in the intensity of Jewish intellectuals' engagement with his theology, for example in the works of Yeshayahu Leibovich, Joseph Soloveitchik (see document 10) and Michael Wyschogrod.

Bibliography

Barnett, Victoria J., 'Karl Barth and the Early Postwar Interfaith Encounters, 1945–1950', in Hunsinger, George (ed.), *Karl Barth, the Jews, and Judaism* (Grand Rapids: Eerdmans, 2018), 103–17.

Lindsay, Mark R., *Barth, Israel and Jesus* (Aldershot and Burlington: Ashgate, 2007).

Sonderegger, Katherine, *That Jesus Christ Was Born a Jew: Karl Barth's 'Doctrine of Israel'* (University Park: Pennsylvania State University Press, 1992).

5

World Council of Churches: The New Delhi Report *(1961)*

Text

Resolution on Anti-Semitism

Upon recommendation of the Policy Reference Committee, and after amendment from the floor, it was *VOTED to adopt the following resolution:*

The Third Assembly recalls the following words which were addressed to the churches by the First Assembly of the World Council of Churches in 1948:

> *'We call upon all the churches we represent to denounce anti-semitism, no matter what its origin, as absolutely irreconcilable with the profession and practice of the Christian faith. Anti-semitism is sin against God and man. Only as we give convincing evidence to our Jewish neighbours that we seek for them the common rights and dignities which God wills for his children, can we come to such a meeting with them as would make it possible to share with them the best which God has given us in Christ.'*

The Assembly renews this plea in view of the fact that situations continue to exist in which Jews are subject to discrimination and even persecution. The Assembly urges its member churches to do all in their power to resist every form of anti-semitism. In Christian teaching the historic events which led to the Crucifixion should not be so presented as to fasten upon the Jewish people of today responsibilities which belong to our corporate humanity and not to one race or community. Jews were the first to accept Jesus and Jews are not the only ones who do not yet recognize him.

In discussion of this resolution, the following points were made:

Principal J. Russell Chandran (Church of South India) said he felt that this proposal would give a distorted picture of the World Council's social concerns since anti-semitism was only one form of social injustice, and had no peculiar significance. He asked the Assembly not to adopt the resolution in view of the fact that other actions of the Assembly had dealt with various forms of social and racial discrimination.

Bishop E. G. Gulin (Evangelical Lutheran Church of Finland) supported the resolution but proposed that the original wording of the last sentence, which read 'Jews are not the only ones to reject him', should be amended to read: 'Jews were the first to accept Jesus and Jews are not the only ones who do not yet recognize him.' Bishop Gulin urged that this formulation would prove to be more eirenic and would facilitate the right approach to the Jews.

[...]

Sir Francis Ibiam (Presbyterian Church of Nigeria) supported the resolution and especially welcomed the reference to the 'responsibilities which belong to our corporate humanity'. 'The Jew harbours no ill-will against any nation nor does he overthrow any other nation.' Any statement on anti-semitism should include reference to all governments which practise uncharitable acts. On this ground he would like to see a resolution which was addressed to the USA, Great Britain, Russia, China, the Central Africa Federation, South Africa, Ghana, France, etc.

[...]

The Rev. Christoph Schnyder (Swiss Protestant Church Federation) proposed that the last but one sentence of the draft Resolution should be ended at the words 'corporate humanity' and this new sentence inserted to follow: 'On the contrary, the Jews remain God's chosen people (cf. Rom. 9–11), for even their rejection for a time must contribute to the world's salvation.'

[...]

Fr Makary el Souriany (Coptic Orthodox Church, Egypt) said he supported the resolution as being concerned with a racial issue, not a political one. 'We agreed in Evanston and St Andrews that any theological study concerning ancient Israel in its biblical meaning must not have any bearing on the existence of Israel as a political entity. So I reject any mention of Israel in this statement.'

Professor John C. Bennett (United Church of Christ, USA) said he feared lest the discussion should result in an uncertain voice on anti-semitism, a result which would be disastrous. 'There is a mid-way position between the view of anti-semitism as merely a racial issue and that which regards it as being based on theological factors.... Anti-semitism is in part a result of the misuse of Christian teaching and Christian symbols. Religious feeling is an essential factor in its development .... We are dealing with the deposit of centuries of religious hostility, a kind of cultural memory of the West .... It is an indication of the problem that Pope John XXIII has deleted some words from the Good Friday Liturgy because they help to perpetuate religious hostility towards the Jews. Similarly, in the United States there has been a review of Christian educational curricula with the same intention.' He hoped that members of the Assembly who came from parts of the world where this 'inherited guilt' was not felt would refrain from causing the voice of this Assembly to be indecisive on the subject.

Source

World Council of Churches, *The New Delhi Report: The Third Assembly of the World Council of Churches 1961*, ed. Hooft, Willem A. Visser't (London: SCM Press, 1962), 148–50.

Commentary

The excerpts above are taken from the third assembly of the WCC, which gathered in New Delhi in 1961. The assembly's discussion on issues of Jewish–Christian relations was in many ways a continuation of the two previous assemblies of the WCC – the inaugural assembly in Amsterdam in 1948 and the second which gathered in Evanston,

Illinois, in 1954 – and focused on the issue of antisemitism. It approved the words of the Amsterdam assembly thirteen years earlier, which renounced antisemitism as 'sin against God and man'. To this previous renunciation it now added a rebuttal of the so-called 'deicide charge'.

The wording of this 1961 resolution is strikingly similar to that of section 4 of the Second Vatican Council's *Nostra aetate*, which was promulgated four years later (see Appendix to Part III, p. 512). In fact, the discussion among the WCC member churches which follows the resolution is also close in spirit to the debates which occurred among the Council fathers and the *periti* at Vatican II. In both cases, church officials from different geographical, national and cultural backgrounds approached the sensitive questions pertaining to Jewish–Christian relations rather differently and had difficulties in reaching common, universally binding conclusions. Is antisemitism merely a form of racism, or does it have a unique status, and therefore should be approached separately? Does any theological engagement with post-Christian 'Israel' necessarily entail a political judgement with regard to the (still rather new reality of the) State of Israel or can the theological be separated from the political? Should the question of Christian responsibility for the evolution of antisemitism be addressed? And finally, shouldn't a resolution against antisemitism stress also the positive theological significance of the Jewish people for Christianity, and their continuous election?

Dr Visser't Hooft, the first secretary general of the WCC, made a considerable effort to avoid these complicated questions and limit the discussion to one issue on which it seemed possible to reach a consensus – the renunciation of antisemitism. In his attempt to tame the polemics, Hooft referred back to the second WCC assembly in Evanston, where it became clear that a theological consensus on these questions was still far from reach; in Evanston, a small sub-group of delegates – all from Europe or the United States – authored a 'minority statement', which meant that the Assembly as a whole remained divided on the matter.

Christian theologians and church officials have delved deeply into each of these open questions in the decades which followed the New Delhi Report and *Nostra aetate*. Nevertheless, the specific contexts and historical consciousness from which Christian representatives think and speak are also crucial in determining their positions today. Perhaps due to the topic's sensitivity in the global setting, successive WCC discussions on Jewish–Christian relations generally refrained from probing these theological complexities and concentrated mainly on the political conflict between Israelis and Palestinians. The work of the WCC on these matters remains strongly contested within broader Jewish–Christian discourse.

Bibliography

Brockway, Allan, van Buren, Paul, Rendtorff, Rolf, and Schoon, Simon (eds.), *The Theology of the Churches and the Jewish People: Statements by the World Council of Churches and Its Member Churches* (Geneva: WCC Publications, 1988).

Marshall, David, 'The World Council of Churches and the Theology of Christian–Jewish Relations', *The Ecumenical Review* 72, no. 5 (2020), 861–94.

6

The Brother Daniel Case: Rufeisen v Minister of Interior *(1962)*

Text

(i) Excerpts from Judge Silberg

[…] The question of law before us is very simply the meaning of the expression 'Jew' as used in the Law of Return, 1950. Does it also include a Jew who has changed his religion and been baptised as a Christian but who still feels and regards himself as a Jew in spite of his conversion?

[…]

[…] And because the Law of Return is an Israel statute, originally enacted in Hebrew and not translated, the term 'Jew' must be interpreted in the sense that it is understood by Jews, for they are nearest to the subject matter of the Law, and who better than they know the essential content of the term 'Jew'?

Once more the question must be asked, what is the ordinary Jewish meaning of the term 'Jew', and does it include a Jew who has become a Christian?

[…] The answer to this question is, in my opinion, sharp and clear – a Jew who has become a Christian is *not* deemed a 'Jew'.

(ii) Excerpts from Judge Cohen

I agree […] with Silberg J. when he says that 'we do not cut ourselves off from our historic past nor do we deny our ancestral heritage.' For my part I would add that a fundamental Law such as the Law of Return which translates into reality the credo of the State must be construed, as it ought to be construed, so as not to conflict with the background and conception of the establishment of the State of Israel but to promote the fulfilment of its prophetic vision and its aims.

But I cannot agree that in giving such an interpretation to the Law of Return it is imperative or permissible to deprive the petitioner of his rights as a Jew.

[…]

Never has there been such a revolutionary event in the history of the Jewish people, scattered and dispersed amongst the nations, as the establishment of the State of Israel. In the Diaspora we were a minority, tolerated or persecuted, but in our own State we are an independent nation like all other nations. In place of our former status as a minority, whether religious, ethnic, national or racial, we have created for ourselves in our own State 'the status of a fully-privileged member of the comity of nations' (as it is expressed in the Declaration of the Establishment of the State of Israel). This revolution is not merely of a political character; it renders imperative a revision of the values which we have imbibed in our long exile […]

[…]

It is difficult not to recall those Jews who, loyal to their ancestral faith, donned the outward garb of the Christian religion so that they might continue to dwell in the lands beloved to them and harvest the fruit of their toils. How loudly they cried: 'We are Christians, open up the gates'. But had they revealed their true selves, their devotion to the religion of Israel, all gates would have been closed before them.

Times have changed and the wheel has turned full circle. There comes now to the State of Israel a man who regards Israel as his mother land and craves to find fulfilment within its borders, but his religion is Christian. Shall we therefore close the gates? Does the turning wheel of history indeed demand that we deal out measure for measure? Should the State of Israel, 'based on freedom, justice and peace as envisaged by the prophets of Israel', act towards its inhabitants and those who return as did the evil rulers of some Catholic kingdoms in the past?

(iii) Excerpts from Judge Landau

The respondent was correct in the distinction he drew, for the purpose of the Law of Return, between a Jew and a non-Jew with regard to conversion from one religion to another. Our State is based on freedom of conscience and no Jew may therefore be compelled to declare himself an adherent of the doctrines of the Jewish faith when he is a non-believer. It follows, in my opinion, that a Jew who regards himself as non-religious discharges his duty to register his religion under the Registration of Inhabitants Ordinance, 1949, by so declaring to the registration officer. But a person who attaches so much importance to religious belief as to be converted of his own free will from one religion to another – and how much more so a person like the petitioner who has placed religion at the centre of his life – creates a complete contradiction which prevents his recognition as a Jew for the purposes of the Law of Return, although in point of origin he remains a Jew.

Source

Rufeisen v Minister of the Interior (1962) 16 P.D. 2428. Published in Landau, Asher Felix (ed.),
    Selected Judgments of the Supreme Court of Israel (Jerusalem: The Ministry of Justice, 1971), 3,
    10–11, 14–16, 23.

Commentary

One of the most famous trials in the history of the State of Israel occurred in 1962, when five Israeli judges – Silberg, Landau, Berinson, Cohen and Manny – discussed the petition of Oswald Rufeisen, also known as 'Brother Daniel', to be recognised as a Jew for the purposes of naturalisation in Israel according to the Law of Return.

Rufeisen was born in 1922 to a Jewish family in Poland. He was raised Jewish and was a member of the Zionist Youth movement Bnei Akiva. Acquiring forged documents, Rufeisen survived the war under the identity of a German Pole. He served as a translator to the Gestapo in the town of Mir, Belarus, and used this position to inform fellow Jews of the Nazis' plans and equip them with weapons, saving hundreds of lives at the risk of his own. Rufeisen spent the last years of the Holocaust hiding in a convent, where he converted to Catholicism in 1942. He later joined the Carmelite order and became a priest, giving up his Polish passport in 1958 and immigrating to Israel. There Rufeisen immediately applied for citizenship under the Law of Return, which grants Jews who seek to settle in Israel the right to Israeli citizenship.

Rufeisen's remarkable biography forced the Israeli supreme court to delve into the complicated question of 'who is a Jew?' according to Israeli law. In Judge Silberg's words, cited above, does the word 'Jew' 'also include a Jew who has changed his religion and been baptised as a Christian but who feels and regards himself as a Jew in spite of his conversion?'

At the heart of the discussion stood the fact that halakhic law does indeed refer to a converted Jew as a Jew for (almost) all intents and purposes, according to the Talmudic dictum that 'A Jew, even if he has sinned, remains a Jew' (Sanhedrin 44a). Nevertheless, with the exception of Judge Chaim Cohen, all the judges agreed that, in the public opinion and cultural memory of Jews, a convert to Christianity and a Jew are contradictory terms that cannot be reconciled. It was precisely because of the secular character of the State of Israel that the judges chose to follow the commonsense perception of Israeli Jews and not halakhic law. While emphasising that they had no quarrel with the contemporary Catholic Church, the court therefore denied Brother Daniel's petition to be acknowledged as a Jew according to the Law of Return. Nonetheless, Rufeisen became a citizen of Israel by naturalisation, and lived in the Stella Maris Carmelite Monastery in Haifa until his death in 1998.

The trial revealed the great sensitivity of the question of conversion to Christianity for Jewish identity, even in the secular State of Israel. It pointed to a certain discrepancy between emerging Christian perceptions that it is not impossible to profess Christ but remain Jewish (as these were reflected, for example, in outstanding life stories such as those of Edith Stein and Jean-Marie Lustiger, as well as in the claims of messianic Jews) and common Jewish perceptions which see Christian and Jewish self-understandings as essentially contradictory.

Bibliography

Goldman, Shalom, *Jewish–Christian Difference and Modern Jewish Identity: Seven Twentieth-Century Converts* (Lanham: Lexington Books, 2015).

Polyakov, Emma O'Donnell, 'Jewish–Christian Identities in Conflict: The Cases of Fr. Daniel Rufeisen and Fr. Elias Friedman', *Religions* 12, no. 12 (2021), www.mdpi.com/2077-1444/12/12/1101.

7

Krister Stendahl: 'The Apostle Paul and the Introspective Conscience of the West' (1963)

Text

The problem we are trying to isolate could be expressed in hermeneutical terms somewhat like this: The Reformers' interpretation of Paul rests on an analogism when Pauline statements about Faith and Works, Law and Gospel, Jews and Gentiles are read in the framework of late medieval piety. The Law, the Torah, with its specific requirements of circumcision and food restrictions becomes a general principle of 'legalism' in religious matters. Where Paul was concerned about the possibility for Gentiles to be included in the messianic community, his statements are now read as answers to the quest for assurance about man's salvation out of a common human predicament.

This shift in the frame of reference affects the interpretation at many points. A good illustration can be seen in what Luther calls the Second Use of the Law, i.e., its function as a Tutor or Schoolmaster unto Christ. The crucial passage for this understanding of the Law is Gal. 3:24, a passage which the King James Version – in unconscious accord with Western tradition – renders: 'Wherefore the law was our schoolmaster (R.V. and A.S.V.: tutor) to bring us unto Christ,' but which the Revised Standard Version translates more adequately: 'So that the law was custodian until Christ came.' In his extensive argument for the possibility of Gentiles becoming Christians without circumcision etc., Paul states that the Law had not come in until 430 years after the promise to Abraham, and that it was meant to have validity only up to the time of the Messiah (Gal. 3:15–22). Hence, its function was to serve as a Custodian for the Jews until that time. Once the Messiah had come, and once the faith in Him – not 'faith' as a general religious attitude – was available as the decisive ground for salvation, the Law had done its duty as a custodian for the Jews, or as a waiting room with strong locks (vv. 22f.) Hence, it is clear that Paul's problem is how to explain why there is no reason to impose the Law on the Gentiles, who now, in God's good Messianic time, have become partakers in the fulfillment of the promises to Abraham (v. 29).

In the common interpretation of Western Christianity, the matter looks very different. One could even say that Paul's argument has been reversed into saying the opposite to his original intention. Now the Law is the Tutor *unto* Christ. Nobody attains a true faith in Christ unless his self-righteousness has been crushed by the Law. The function of the Second Use of the Law is to make man see his desperate need for a Savior. In such an interpretation, we note how Paul's distinction between Jews and Gentiles is gone. '*Our* Tutor/Custodian' is now a statement applied to man in general, not 'our' in the sense of 'I, Paul, and my fellow Jews.' Furthermore, the Law is not any more the Law of Moses which requires circumcision etc., and which has become obsolete when faith in the Messiah is a live option – it is the moral imperative as such, in the form of the will of God. And finally, Paul's argument that the Gentiles must not, and should not come to Christ *via* the Law, i.e., *via* circumcision etc., has turned into a statement according to which all men must come to Christ with consciences properly convicted by the Law and its insatiable requirements for righteousness. So drastic is the reinterpretation once the original framework of 'Jews and Gentiles' is lost, and the Western problems of conscience become its unchallenged and self-evident substitute.

Source

Stendahl, Krister, 'The Apostle Paul and the Introspective Conscience of the West', *Harvard Theological Review* 56, no. 3 (1963), 205–7.

Commentary

'The Apostle Paul and the Introspective Conscience of the West' is one of two seminal articles (the other being 'Paul among Jews and Gentiles') published in the early 1960s by prominent Swedish Lutheran theologian, New Testament scholar and Church of Sweden Bishop of Stockholm (1984–8) Krister Stendahl (1921–2008). These two articles introduced a paradigm shift in both Jewish–Christian relations and Pauline studies and put the cornerstone to a far-reaching scholarly trajectory known today as 'the new perspective on Paul'.

Stendahl proposed a radical rereading of the Pauline epistles based on their placement in the original milieux within which they were written and to which they were addressed (see Chapter 1, pp. 22–35). This, Stendahl argued, entails centring our reading of Paul on the relationship between Jews and gentiles and, more specifically, on how to include the gentiles in the promises that God made to Israel when the messiah comes. Through this prism, Paul seems to differentiate between Jews and gentiles with regard to the law rather than to establish an absolute negation of the law universally applicable to both Jews and gentiles.

What, then, was so subversive about this new focus on Paul as the 'apostle to the gentiles'? The change of focus meant, so Stendahl maintained, a break with the way in which established traditions understood Paul. For hundreds of years, we have been interpreting Paul through Luther's eyes, conflating Luther's concerns – which are embedded in his own time in the sixteenth century – with the concerns of the first-century apostle (see also Chapter 5, p. 241). Inspired by Augustine's reading of Paul, Luther interpreted him as an adversary to the law who argues that only by despairing of the self-righteous conviction that one is capable of observing the law in full may one attain true faith. The law, in this reading, has to be overcome, superseded by the individual on her way to true faith. Generations of readers have adopted this interpretation of Paul, turning him from one who sought to *include* gentiles in the promises made to Abraham to one who *excludes* Jews from those very promises, just as law and faith became contradictory terms.

Stendahl's shift of framework was adopted by leading New Testament scholars (see Chapter 9, p. 488) as well as by theologians and church officials (Stendahl's fingerprints are evident in the Commission for Religious Relations with the Jews' 2015 document *The Gifts and Calling of God Are Irrevocable*; see Appendix to Part III, p. 547) and eventually undermined the perception of Paul as the founding father of supersessionism. It also opened up a rich vein of research on Paul's own Jewish identity, as reflected in the work of E. P. Sanders, Paula Fredriksen, Marc Nanos and others. If Martin Buber adopted Protestant readings of Paul to differentiate Paul's thought from that of Judaism, contemporary Jewish studies scholars such as Daniel Boyarin use Stendahl's insights to explore the Pauline epistles as Jewish texts, which may in turn provide insights for contemporary Jewish discourses.

Bibliography

Boyarin, Daniel, *A Radical Jew: Paul and the Politics of Identity* (Berkeley: University of California Press, 1994).

Dunn, James D. G., *The New Perspective on Paul* (Grand Rapids: Eerdmans, 2008).
Gager, John G., *Reinventing Paul* (Oxford: Oxford University Press, 2002).

8

Rolf Hochhuth: The Deputy: A Christian Tragedy *(1963)*

Text

FONTANA: Your Holiness, this message,
in which not one word mentions the arrests,
cannot be construed as a reference
to the Jewish problem.

POPE (*his patience exhausted*):
Have we not spoken expressis verbis
of men *of all races*, Count Fontana?
[…]

FONTANA: Father General, as you well know,
the Holy See has other means
to command a hearing.
Your Holiness, send Hitler an ultimatum,
or even just a letter that Weizsäcker can deliver.
[…]

SCRIBE (*bows*):   If I may humbly remind Your Holiness,
Your Holiness has not yet signed.

The POPE *goes up to him and in extreme vexation reaches for the writing case which the* SCRIBE *holds out. Meanwhile* RICCARDO *takes out the yellow Star of David and pins it to his cassock. At this moment the* POPE *sees it. He is struck dumb. He reaches or rather gropes for the golden pen which the* SCRIBE *holds out to him, his gaze fixed on* RICCARDO, *intending to dip the pen into the inkwell […] Absently, he dips the pen into the ink, and as he starts to sign the* CARDINAL *speaks.*

CARDINAL (*breathless, furious*):
Minutante, now you forget yourself!
Remove – this – this thing.
How dare you, in the presence of the Holy Father.
Blasphemy – on a priest's robe – blasphemy!

FONTANA (*pleadingly*): Riccardo – please don't …

RICCARDO (*undeterred, passionately*):
Your Holiness, what you have set your name to
grants Hitler unrestricted license to go on
treating the Jews as he has always done …

While the POPE, *intensely agitated, swiftly traces his signature, the pen slips from his fingers; he smears ink over his hand and holds it out reproachfully so that the others can see.*

                       […]

POPE: In the name of the victims … this … *this*
                       arrogance as well! And this impertinence –
                       the Star of David on the habit of Christ's servants!
                       […]

RICCARDO (*readily answering the* POPE's *reproach*):
                       This star which every Jew must wear
                       as soon as he is six years old,
                       to show he is an outlaw – I shall wear it too
                       until …

POPE (*quivering with rage*): He will *not!* We forbid him –
                       forbid – on a cassock – this …

He stops, his voice failing him.

RICCARDO (*almost quietly, soberly*): I shall wear this star until
                       Your Holiness proclaims before the world
                       a curse upon the man who slaughters
                       Europe's Jews like cattle.

The POPE *is silenced by his obvious inability to check* RICCARDO *or to find his voice.*

CARDINAL: Criminal folly! Get out!

RICCARDO (*his voice rising*):
                       Folly? No, Your Holiness. The King
                       of Denmark, a defenseless man,
                       threatened Hitler that he would wear this star,
                       along with *every member* of his house,
                       if the Jews in Denmark were forced to wear it.
                       They were not forced. When will the Vatican
                       at last act so that we priests
                       can once again own without shame that we are
                       servants of that Church which holds
                       brotherly love as its first commandment!

CARDINAL: Obedience, unconditional obedience
                       is the Jesuit's first commandment, Minutante!

RICCARDO: Yes, obedience to God.

CARDINAL: Who speaks through the voice and will of
                       His Holiness, you know. Obey!

The POPE *remains ostentatiously silent.*

[…]

FONTANA: I ask permission to take my leave, Your Holiness.

POPE: Remain, Count. This son of yours
is trial enough for you. You need not pay for his folly.

FONTANA: Please, Your Holiness, permit me to go.

POPE (*with cold imperiousness*):
You stay, and that is that. You, Father General

He turns to the Father General. The SCRIBE *has entered noiselessly carrying a large brass or copper basin of water and a towel.*

will be responsible to Us: make sure that this –
this scandalous behavior stops.
Accompany the Minutante to his home.
God watch over him, he knows not what he speaks.
We have forgiven him.
Of course he cannot return to his post,
nor to Lisbon …

RICCARDO *stands by as though all this has ceased to concern him; it is impossible even to tell whether he is listening. The* SCRIBE *approaches the* POPE, *carrying the basin.* FONTANA, *crushed, falls to his knees before the* POPE […]

FONTANA: Your Holiness, please … I beg you, Holy Father …

POPE (*embarrassed*):
Fontana, do stand up, you're not to blame.
Your son's behavior cannot make a breach
between the two of us.
(*At last, with crystal clarity and hardness.*)
Non possumus.
We cannot – will not – write to Hitler.
He would – and in his accursed self
the Germans in corpore –
only be antagonized and outraged.
But we desire them, and also Roosevelt,
to see in us impartial go-betweens.
Now, that is enough. Ad acta.

As he speaks the last sentence he returns to the throne and is about to begin washing his hands in the proffered basin. RICCARDO, *already at the door, says firmly and quietly –*

RICCARDO: God shall not destroy His Church
only because a Pope shrinks from His summons.

Source

Hochhuth, Rolf, *The Deputy*, trans. Richard and Clara Winston (Baltimore: The Johns Hopkins University Press, 1997), 216–20. (Originally published as *Der Stellvertreter*, 1963.)

Commentary

Theatre often influences public debate on broad political and social issues. It is not often, however, that a single play initiates controversy on the scale of the 1963 drama *Der Stellvertreter: Ein christliches Trauerspiel*, translated into English in 1964 as *The Deputy: A Christian Tragedy*. The first play by Rolf Hochhuth, a German Protestant from Eschwege, *The Deputy* was published when he was only thirty-one years old, and helped attract the world's attention to the Holocaust.

At the heart of this semi-historical work, set in 1942 and written partly in free verse, stands the figure of Pope Pius XII, the vicar of Christ (hence 'the Deputy') and his alleged 'silence' during the destruction of European Jewry. Pius, who appears on stage in Act 4, is depicted as a calculating, cold aristocrat, fully aware of what is being done 'under his very windows', yet determined not to intervene on behalf of Jews. Willing to tolerate Nazi atrocities as the 'lesser evil' to communism, Hochhuth's pope pronounces only weak, fuzzy protests, avoiding naming the crime in unequivocal terms. At the decisive moment, Pius XII washes his hands in a gesture that recalls Pontius Pilate.

The pope's sinister figure is contrasted, in Hochhuth's rendering, with two Christian protagonists who are willing to put their own lives at risk in order to save Jews: Kurt Gerstein and Jesuit Fr Riccardo Fontana. Gerstein is a (remarkable) historical figure, a Protestant SS officer who tried, to no avail, to inform the Vatican and the Allies of the details of the Final Solution as it occurred; the fictional Fontana pins the yellow star of David on his own cassock and goes on to share the fate of the Jews in the gas chambers. Fontana was based on the figures of Bernhard Lichtenberg, a German Catholic provost who publicly protested against the persecution of Jews, and Maximilian Kolbe, a Polish Franciscan priest who volunteered to be murdered in Auschwitz instead of a fellow Pole. (Kolbe was later canonised by John Paul II; his publication activities, however, included the dissemination of antisemitic texts.)

First staged in West Berlin on 20 February 1963, Hochhuth's *Deputy* soon appeared in theatres (and was banned in others) across Europe, in the US and in Israel (Costa-Gavras' 2002 film adaptation *Amen* testifies to the play's continuing relevance). The storm around *The Deputy* hit Rome at the height of the Second Vatican Council; Pope Paul VI vehemently objected to its depiction of his predecessor, and the formulators of *Nostra aetate* pondered how to cope with the public relations disaster it caused. Together with Jules Isaac's 1962 critique of the roots of Christian antisemitism (see document 1), *The Deputy* was influential in pushing the Catholic leadership to reflect on the church's own responsibility for the fate of European Jewry.

Hochhuth's play had a powerful effect on historiography, and is credited with firing the first shot in a long 'Pius war' among historians – from the early work of Saul Friedländer in 1964 to the sensation of John Cornwell's *Hitler's Pope* in 1999 – which not only engaged a long list of scholars, including David G. Dalin, Michael Phayer, Susan Zuccotti and Robert Ventresca, but continues to hinder the church's initiative to put Pius XII forward for canonisation.

New data on Pius XII's knowledge and actions during the Holocaust has become available since Hochhuth's initial research (especially since the 2020 opening of the Vatican archives on Pius' pontificate). Nevertheless, questions about his role remain a continuing source of friction in Jewish–Catholic relations.

Bibliography

Bigsby, Christopher, *Remembering and Imagining the Holocaust: The Chain of Memory* (Cambridge: Cambridge University Press, 2006), 115–48.

Friedländer, Saul, *Pius XII and the Third Reich: A Documentation*, trans. Charles Fullman (New York: A. A. Knopf, 1966).

Ventresca, Robert, *Soldier of Christ: The Life of Pope Pius XII* (Cambridge, MA: Belknap Press of Harvard University Press, 2013).

9

Friedrich-Wilhelm Marquardt: The Significance of the Biblical Land Promise for Christians *(1964)*

Text

Hence the Christian side can only conduct the conversation (if at all, if not in utter naivety, if not still far too early) in the hope of the forgiveness of sins. This is a condition which we cannot assume and grant ourselves and which we therefore cannot disregard. Theologians in particular have to be on their guard: for knowing this condition, yet only asserting it in the sense of a notional truth, is a pitfall of the theologian's profession. In practice – under the covert assumption of the forgiveness of sins – we often take perhaps too reckless, uninhibited steps towards the common theological 'cause' that has remained with us, and do not even notice how this opens up a dimension of transgression in the Christian–Jewish counterpart that challenges our entire endeavour for truth: we too easily disregard the existence of the interlocutor (and our own existence) as the absolutely concrete, no longer abstractable basic realities of the dialogical endeavour for truth.

[...]

[...] The Jewish partner now speaks out again in the categories of biblical historical thinking that the Christian counterpart can also understand, thus contributing to the dismantling of the Christian prejudice that Judaism is merely a religious phenomenon and not a historical witness in the actual biblical sense. In addition, however, the emphatic self-awareness of the surviving Jewish community in the State of Israel is quite obviously the external and internal reason for this encounter, more so than all Christian self-reflection. Both of these factors (Israel's biblical self-interpretation and its emergence as a new historical subject) are causing Christian theology grave embarrassment.

For virtually all traditional judgements about Israel, be they negative or positive, as well as all methods of obtaining and justifying a theological judgement about Israel, are negated in view of the reality of Israel's salvation and resurgence. Salvation and the resurgence of Israel are historically inextricably linked and can only be regarded by secular reason as a single event – a 'full historical reality' which at the same time poses for us a question. Certainly, quick answers cannot be given, because Christian theology, especially in the Protestant sphere, is totally unprepared to recognise and process the history we ourselves have witnessed as God's action. Thus, the first critical basic question is whether Christian theology can perceive and appreciate eyewitness testimony at all today or whether it must act as if nothing could happen.

[…]

[…] Thus, for example, those theologians who consider Judaism to be either just a secular phenomenon or a witness of God's judgement must ask themselves how they can deny the truth to the face of the Jews who today identify and comfort themselves with the promises of the Old Testament. It is no longer good enough for Christians to define their relationship to Israel by the rejection of antisemitism, as both Christian churches in Germany and the majority of theologians have hitherto considered sufficient. Our own involvement – even if it is only our personal witnessing of Israel's and our own existence! – obliges us to ask whether the Christian tradition that teaches us to ignore Israel as a witness to the promises has 'kept its word'. In the biblical self-interpretation of Israel, so much truth of the Word has been revealed that in the Jewish–Christian relationship we should no longer set truth against untruth, but theology against theology – certainly theologies that are profoundly different from each other, yet comparable with each other because they are related to the work of the one God.

Source

Marquardt, Friedrich-Wilhelm, *Die Bedeutung der biblischen Landverheissungen für die Christen* (Munich: Christian Kaiser, 1964), 3, 4–5, 6–7. (Translation by Iris Koch.)

Commentary

A central thread in the transformation of Jewish–Christian relations after the Holocaust was Christian willingness to carve out a new place for Jews and Judaism within Christian tradition. This was, arguably, first and foremost an internal Christian task, a search, to paraphrase *Nostra aetate*, into the church's own mystery. Reaffirming the importance of biblical Judaism for Christianity was easier than considering the importance of Talmudic Judaism for Christian thought or exploring the theological reverberations of contemporary Jewish history in God's plan for humankind. In other words, transforming the internalised image of the Jew within the Christian self was often done without significant engagement with Jews in the outside world – and especially without considering the tormenting discrepancies between Jewish and Christian self-understandings.

German theologian Friedrich-Wilhelm Marquardt (1928–2002) was convinced that Jewish self-perception must be acknowledged by Christian theology, including the ways in which Jews interpret the Hebrew Bible, the Talmud and the halakhah; the way they understand the land and the State of Israel; their reluctance to participate in the Christian initiative of creating affinity and closeness; and even the Jewish grounds for the Jewish 'no' to Jesus as Christ.

Marquardt was born to a Nazi family in 1929 (he grew up with memories of his father leaving the house on Kristallnacht in SS uniform). Overwhelmed by the war, he followed the Protestant minister Martin Niemöller's sermons on German guilt with devotion. He began his theological career as a disciple of Rudolf Bultmann, moved first to Basel, where he studied with Karl Barth, and then to (West) Berlin. According to Marquardt himself, a visit to Israel in 1959, during which he visited the *kibbutzim* and met with Martin Buber and Schalom Ben-Chorin, marked his theology ever afterwards. The excerpts from Marquardt's 1964 book on the meaning of the promise of the land of Israel for Christians address the theological questions which the visit evoked in him. Most concretely, the actual encounter with Israeli Jews and the link they made between their present and the (Hebrew) Bible – which, for them, was not translated into Christological terms of any kind – at once turned Jews, for Marquardt, from a religious abstraction to a concrete reality (though a biblical reality, nonetheless).

Marquardt's doctoral dissertation, which he completed at the Free University of Berlin, reflected on Barth's 'doctrine of Israel'. Although Marquardt was appreciative of Barth's theology of Israel, he pointed to the holes in Barth's thought and to the areas where Barth's position – and especially his lack of reflection on the significance of postbiblical Judaism – verged on anti-Judaism. In a letter to Marquardt – the same letter in which he confessed his 'absolutely irrational aversion' to the Jews he encountered – Barth endorsed Marquardt's analysis and accepted his critique.

Marquardt continued to study Judaism with and from Jews throughout his entire life and persisted in his path notwithstanding the unease his theology caused among many of his more conservative colleagues. An incredibly prolific writer, he remains, though mostly untranslated, one of the most important German systematic theologians in the field of Jewish–Christian relations. Above all, his work is remembered for the boldness and originality with which he brought even neglected areas such as Talmudic and halakhic law into Protestant theological study, as well as for his emphasis on the vitality of the Jewish covenant with God and the theological implications of Jesus' Jewishness.

Bibliography

Meyer, Barbara U., *Jesus the Jew in Christian Memory: Theological and Philosophical Explorations* (Cambridge: Cambridge University Press, 2020).

Pangritz, Andreas, 'Friedrich-Wilhelm Marquardt – A Theological-Biographical Sketch', *European Judaism: A Journal for the New Europe* 38, no. 1 (Spring 2005), 17–47.

Pangritz, Andreas, and Chung, Paul S. (eds.), *Theological Audacities: Selected Essays/Friedrich-Wilhelm Marquardt*, trans. Don McCord, H. Martin Rumscheidt and Paul S. Chung (Eugene: Pickwick Publications, 2010).

10

Joseph Ber Soloveitchik: 'Confrontation' (1964)

Text

It is self-evident that a confrontation of two faith communities is possible only if it is accompanied by a clear assurance that both parties will enjoy equal rights and full religious freedom. We shall resent any attempt on the part of the community of the many to engage us in a peculiar encounter in which our confronter will command us to take a position beneath him while placing himself not alongside of but above us. A democratic confrontation certainly does not demand that we submit to an attitude of self-righteousness taken by the community of the many which, while debating whether or not to 'absolve' the community of the few of some mythical guilt, completely ignores its own historical responsibility for the suffering and martyrdom so frequently recorded in the annals of the history of the few, the weak, and the persecuted.

We are not ready for a meeting with another faith community in which we shall become an object of observation, judgment and evaluation, even though the community of the many may then condescendingly display a sense of compassion with the community of the few and advise the many not to harm or persecute the few […]

[…]

[…] We are a totally independent faith community. We do not revolve as a satellite in any orbit. Nor are we related to any other faith community as 'brethren' even though 'separated.' […]

[…]

Therefore, any intimation, overt or covert, on the part of the community of the many that it is expected of the community of the few that it shed its uniqueness and cease existing because it has fulfilled its mission by paving the way for the community of the many, must be rejected as undemocratic and contravening the very idea of religious freedom. The small community has as much right to profess its faith in the ultimate certitude concerning the doctrinal worth of its world formula and to behold its own eschatological vision as does the community of the many. I do not deny the right of the community of the many to address itself to the community of the few in its own eschatological terms. However, building a practical program upon this right is hardly consonant with religious democracy and liberalism.

[…]

[…] The confrontation should occur not at a theological, but at a mundane human level. There, all of us speak the universal language of modern man […]

[…]

[… W]e members of the community of the few should always act with tact and understanding and refrain from suggesting to the community of the many, which is both proud and prudent, changes in its ritual or emendations of its texts. If the genuinely liberal dignitaries of the faith community of the many deem some changes advisable, they will act in accordance with their convictions without any prompting on our part. It is not within our purview to advise or solicit. For it would be both impertinent and unwise for an outsider to intrude upon the most private sector of the human existential experience, namely, the way in which a faith community expresses its relationship to God [...]

[... W]e certainly have not been authorized by our history, sanctified by the martyrdom of millions, to even hint to another faith community that we are mentally ready to revise historical attitudes, to trade favors pertaining to fundamental matters of faith, and to reconcile 'some' differences. Such a suggestion would be nothing but a betrayal of our great tradition and heritage and would, furthermore, produce no practical benefits. Let us not forget that the community of the many will not be satisfied with half measures and compromises which are only indicative of a feeling of insecurity and inner emptiness. We cannot command the respect of our confronters by displaying a servile attitude. Only a candid, frank and unequivocal policy reflecting unconditional commitment to our God, a sense of dignity, pride and inner joy in being what we are, believing with great passion in the ultimate truthfulness of our views, praying fervently for and expecting confidently the fulfillment of our eschatological vision when our faith will rise from particularity to universality, will impress the peers of the other faith community among whom we have both adversaries and friends. I hope and pray that our friends in the community of the many will sustain their liberal convictions and humanitarian ideals by articulating their position on the right of the community of the few to live, create, and worship God in its own way, in freedom and with dignity.

Source

Soloveitchik, Joseph B., 'Confrontation', *Tradition* 6, no. 2 (1964), 21, 23–5.

Commentary

During the years when the Second Vatican Council's 'Jewish document' was being formulated (what later became section 4 of *Nostra aetate*; see Appendix to Part III, p. 512), the Jewish community was divided on how to react. While some Jewish leaders, such as Rabbi Abraham J. Heschel (see document 13), encouraged and engaged in dialogue with Vatican officials about the contents of the Council's declaration, others preferred to abstain from directly intervening in the debates taking place in Rome. The most famous representative of this latter approach was Rabbi Joseph B. Halevi Soloveitchik (1903–92), the undisputed leader of Modern Orthodoxy in the United States.

Soloveitchik was a great Talmudic scholar, the grandson of Reb Chaim Brisker (Chaim Soloveitchik of Brisk) and the inheritor of his well-known 'Brisker method' for studying the Talmud. Alongside his Talmudic expertise, Joseph Soloveitchik was also an expert on neo-Kantian philosophy and an existentialist writer in his own right. It is worth noting that Soloveitchik's existential work was heavily influenced by Christian thinkers such as Karl Barth, Søren Kierkegaard and Rudolf Otto. Yet his appreciation for Christian theology did not lessen his suspicion of Jewish–Christian dialogue.

Soloveitchik expresses his reservations in several places, most notably in a lecture he gave at the Rabbinical Council of America in 1964, subsequently published as an article entitled 'Confrontation' in the Orthodox journal *Tradition*. Written in existential-philosophical language, the article delineates the stakes of Jewish–Christian dialogue for Jews as threatening to compromise the singularity of the faith community. Soloveitchik then suggests limiting the involvement of Jews in any kind of theological dialogue with Christians and excluding halakhic, doctrinal and eschatological topics from interreligious discussion. These sensitive topics, he argued, would be too easily manipulated by the Christian dialogue partner, owing to the structural asymmetries between 'the community of the few' (i.e., Jews) and 'the community of the many' (i.e., Christians).

'Confrontation' was widely accepted within Orthodox communities as authoritative and largely set the tone for the Orthodox approach to Jewish–Christian dialogue in the following decades. Nevertheless, the article was interpreted in more than one way among Soloveitchik's disciples. While some saw it as a semi-halakhic obligation to refrain from all Jewish–Christian dialogue, others suggested that Soloveitchik left room for certain kinds of dialogue (for example, Meir Soloveitchik, Soloveitchik's nephew) or for certain qualified Jewish representatives to engage in it (as argued by David Hartman and David Berger, among others). Yet others (such as Michael Wyschogrod) believed that this article itself opened the door to profound theological dialogue between Christians and Jews. Soloveitchik's guidelines with regard to dialogue content were largely embraced by Israel's chief rabbinate as it came to be involved in dialogue with the Vatican, and therefore had far-reaching implications for institutional forms of dialogue which involved Jewish Orthodoxy. Interestingly, one prominent scholar of Soloveitchik's existential thought is Christian Rutishauser SJ, who continues Soloveitchik's correspondence with (mainly Protestant) Christian thinkers through his own (Catholic) engagement with Soloveitchik's work.

Bibliography

Kimelman, Reuven, 'Rabbis Joseph B. Soloveitchik and Abraham Joshua Heschel on Jewish–Christian Relations', *Modern Judaism* 24, no. 3 (2004), 251–71.

Korn, Eugene, 'The Man of Faith and Religious Dialogue: Revisiting "Confrontation"', *Modern Judaism* 25, no. 3 (2005), 290–315.

Rutishauser, Christian M., *The Human Condition and the Thought of Rabbi Joseph B. Soloveitchik*, trans. Katherine Wolfe (Jersey City: Ktav, 2013).

11

Dorothee Sölle: Christ the Representative: An Essay in Theology after the Death of God *(1965)*

Text

A Polish Jew has declared that the name 'Christ' always makes him think immediately of *pogroms*. Theology cannot disclaim its responsibility here by dismissing such considerations as lamentable lapses in practice which cannot be laid at the door of the faith itself. The story of Christian antisemitism is too ancient, too uninterrupted, and too bloody to be evaded in this way. The least we can do for its victims is to re-think our Christian faith, for their sakes and in the light of their fate.

When we do engage in such rethinking, a final Christ – a replacement who perfectly and completely secures for us the reconciling grace of God – vanishes. That this final Christ is inevitably totalitarian is shown by the story of the Church's antisemitism, with its fluctuations determined by the dogmatic and political security of the Church at any given time. When things were going well for the 'new Israel', when the 'people of God' felt strong, antisemitism flourished, drawing its confidence from the security of hardened dogmatic positions. Among the decisions of the imposing Fourth Lateran Council of 1215 (a high water mark of the triumphal Church for which the suffering synagogue had to pay) were the late mediaeval dress regulations for Jews – and the doctrine of transubstantiation. The change of the eucharistic elements of bread and wine into the real presence of the body of Christ was elevated into a dogma on the basis of which all other religious customs were held to be illegal.

[...]

For the tension between the 'now already' and the 'not yet' is the tension between Christ and us whom he himself adopts representatively. G. Scholem defines the distinction between the Jewish and Christian views of redemption as one of orientation, in the one case to the visible, in the other to the invisible. What is the focus of faith? Is it really true that the Christian faith, unlike the Jewish faith, focuses on the invisible world? Surely this distinction is set aside in the representation carried out by One who is visible for others who are not now visible? The representative – of all men, not just of a particular people – performs the invisible work of redemption, but does so in order to make it visible. For the sake of the not yet visible he representatively confirms the invisible. He effects the individual – for only in this way can it be universal – reconciliation which is as yet neither public nor visible. But he does so with a view to reconciliation which is public, visible, and universal. This is the goal in view. The Christian assertion of the Messiah who has already come serves the Jewish assertion – namely, the open future of those who now need no longer to be their own 'sole' agents and guarantors. In other words, Christ enables non-Jews to become Jews; that is to say, he enables them to live in postponement.

Source

Sölle, Dorothee, *Christ the Representative: An Essay in Theology after the Death of God*, trans. David Lewis (London: SCM Press, 1967), 109, 111. (Originally published as *Stellvertretung: Ein Kapitel Theologie nach dem 'Tode Gottes'*, in *Dorothee Sölle Werke* (Stuttgart: Kreuz, 1965).)

Commentary

Where was God during Auschwitz? And what are the implications of this question for theology? In the aftermath of the Holocaust, the classical problem of theodicy – that is, the tension between the perception of God as ultimately just and good and the evident existence of evil – became as urgent as ever. If Jews (such as Richard Rubenstein, Emil Fackenheim, Hans Jonas, Eliezer Berkowitz and Emanuel Levinas) often struggled with theodicy as subjects of the evil which was evidenced in the Holocaust, Christian thinkers were asking themselves what in their theological perceptions made so many of them complicit with such evil.

The resonance of these questions was especially strong in Germany, where theologians faced their country's recent past and the evil deeds of their ancestors and coreligionists. The Protestant theologian, feminist, mystic and political activist Dorothee Sölle (1929–2003) was among the Christian thinkers who used these questions to transform Christian theology, in terms of both content and form. Struck by the need to reorient Christianity after the catastrophe, Sölle sought to shake the Christian faith out of any indifference towards the suffering of the persecuted, the poor and the oppressed. Her theology was profoundly intertwined with her political activism: in Sölle's eyes, prayer, liberation and resistance – whether to the war in Vietnam, to capitalism or to the arms race during the Cold War – belonged together.

Two other German theologians of her generation who shared many of Sölle's sensibilities are worth mentioning in this context: like Sölle, the Protestant Jürgen Moltmann and the Catholic Johann Baptist Metz were extremely critical of the theology of their teachers (for example of Karl Rahner and Rudolf Bultmann), which they found triumphalist, bourgeois and too detached from the reality of power structures and oppression. All three thinkers often employed the catastrophe of the Jewish people as a symbol of the need to do theology differently 'in the face of Auschwitz', to quote Metz (1984: 27).

The excerpt from Sölle's *Stellvertretung* (literally 'Representation') (1965) well expresses these tendencies: Sölle reflects on the Christian faith through the eyes of the Jewish victim, critically examining the theological concepts – she mentions transubstantiation and the final redemption – which are susceptible to totalitarianism and are closely connected with antisemitism (in a way that reminds us of Ruether's later dictum that anti-Judaism is the left hand of Christology).

No less interesting is how Sölle returns to one of the core theological tensions in Jewish–Christian relations throughout the centuries – that between the Christian conviction that the messiah has already come in Jesus and the Jewish conviction that the messiah is yet to come. Sölle seeks to carve new space for the 'not yet' within Christianity, as a way to replace the triumphalist confidence of Christianity with an actual political theological work towards liberation. This emphasis on the 'not yet' of salvation as an embrace of Jewish messianic hope appears later in the work of Rosemary Radford Ruether and Roy and Alice Eckardt (documents 16 and 14) and finds its way even into official documents on Jewish–Christian relations such as the Pontifical Biblical Commission's 2001 *The Jewish People and Their Sacred Scriptures in the Christian Bible* (see Appendix to Part III, p. 528).

Bibliography

Metz, Johann Baptist, 'Facing the Jews: Christian Theology after Auschwitz', in Fiorenza, Elisabeth Schüssler, and Tracy, David (eds.), *The Holocaust as Interruption*, *Concilium* 175 (Edinburgh: T&T Clark, 1984), 26–33.

Moltmann, Jürgen, *The Crucified God: The Cross of Christ as the Foundation and Criticism of Christian Theology* (London: SCM Press, 1973).

Pinnock, Sarah (ed.), *The Theology of Dorothee Soelle* (Harrisburg: Trinity Press International, 2003).

12

Richard Rubenstein: After Auschwitz: Radical Theology and Contemporary Judaism *(1966)*

Text

Having asserted that the Jews had as much right to produce scoundrels as any other people, the Dean quickly retracted. He spoke of the ancient covenant between God and Israel and how Israel as the Chosen People of God was under a very special obligation to behave in ways that are spiritually consistent with Divine ordinance.

'I don't say this about Israel; God says this in the Bible and I believe it!' he insisted with considerable emotion.

The Dean was not the first German clergyman who had spoken to me in this vein. I had previously met a number of clergymen in Berlin and Bonn. All insisted that God and Israel have a very special providential relationship, that the history of Israel is wholly in accord with God's will. This was true, they told me, in the time of the Bible. Moreover, the *Heilsgeschichte*, the 'salvation history,' of the Jewish people continues to unfold to this very day. In fairness, it must be said that the same belief has been shared by the vast majority of religious Jews throughout history. The theological significance of the Zionist movement and the establishment of the State of Israel lay largely in the rejection of *Heilsgeschichte* and in the assertion that Jewish misfortune had been made by men and could be undone by men. For the pastors the conviction remained – nay, it was strengthened – that nowhere in the world were the fruits of God's activity in history more evident than in the history of the Jewish people. Every time I heard this view, I quickly rejoined that such thinking had as its inescapable conclusion the conviction that the Nazi slaughter of the Jews was somehow God's will, that, for His own inscrutable reasons, God really wanted the Jewish people to be exterminated by Hitler. In every instance before meeting Dr. Grüber I was met by an embarrassed withdrawal.

[…]

The same openness and lack of guile that Dean Grüber had shown from the moment I met him were again manifest in his reaction to my question concerning God's role in the death of six million Jews, a question that, I believe, is decisive for contemporary Jewish theology.

'Was it God's will that Hitler destroyed the Jews?' I repeated. 'Is this what you believe concerning the events through which we have lived?'

Probst Grüber arose from his chair, dramatically removed a Bible from a bookcase, opened it, and read: 'Um deine Willen werden wir getötet den ganzen Tag – for Thy sake are we slaughtered every day' (Ps. 44:22).

'When God desires my death, I give it to him!' he continued. 'When I started my work against the Nazis I knew that I would be killed or go to the concentration camp.

Eichmann asked me, "Why do you help these Jews? They will not thank you." I had my family; there were my wife and three children. Yet I said, "Your will be done even if You ask my death." For some reason, it was part of God's plan that the Jews died. God demands our death daily. He is the Lord, He is the Master; all is in His keeping and ordering.'

[…]

When Dean Grüber put down his Bible, it seemed as if, once having started, he could not stop himself. He looked at recent events from a thoroughly biblical perspective. In the past, the Jews had been smitten by Nebuchadnezzar and other 'rods of God's anger.' Hitler was simply another such rod. The incongruity of Hitler and Auschwitz as instruments of a righteous God never seemed to occur to him. Of course, he granted that what Hitler had done was immoral, and he insisted that Hitler's followers were now being punished by God.

'At different times,' he said, 'God uses different peoples as His whip against His own people, the Jews, but those whom He uses will be punished far worse than the people of the Lord. You see it today here in Berlin. We are now in the same situation as the Jews. My church is in the East Sector. Last Sunday (August 13, the day of the border closing) I preached on Hosea 6:1 ("Come, and let us return unto the Lord: For He hath torn, and He will heal us; He hath smitten, and He will bind us up."). God has beaten us for our terrible sins; I told our people in East Berlin that they must not lose faith that He will reunify us.'

I felt a chill at that instant. There was enormous irony in the Dean's assertion that the Germans had become like Jews. *I was listening to a German clergyman interpret German defeat as the rabbis had interpreted the Fall of Jerusalem almost two thousand years before.* For the rabbis, Jerusalem fell because of the sins of the Jewish people. For Dean Grüber, Berlin had fallen because of the sins of the German people. When he sought words of consolation with which to mollify the wounding of his imprisoned church, he turned to the very same verses from Hosea which had consoled countless generations of Israel.

Source

Rubenstein, Richard L., *After Auschwitz: History, Theology, and Contemporary Judaism*, 2nd ed. (Baltimore and London: Johns Hopkins University Press, 1992), 8–10. (First edition published as *After Auschwitz: Radical Theology and Contemporary Judaism* (Indianapolis, New York and Kansas City: Bobbs-Merrill, 1966).) Copyright © 1966, 1992 by Richard L. Rubenstein. All rights reserved. Reproduced with permission of the Licensor through PLSclear.

Commentary

In 1966, the American liberal rabbi Richard L. Rubenstein (1924–2021) published his groundbreaking *After Auschwitz*, a book considered by many as the starting point of Jewish post-Holocaust theology, that is, the discourse on the implications of the Holocaust for Jewish tradition and faith. Rubenstein advocated a radical revision of

Jewish theology in the aftermath of Auschwitz. The theological concept which he perceived as unattainable after the Holocaust was that of 'sacred history' (*Heilsgeschichte*, 'salvation history' in the excerpt), or of a God who intervenes in the history of his people by means of retribution and punishment. This traditional concept, Rubenstein argued, cannot but mean that Auschwitz was, in one way or another, connected with Israel's election – in other words that God in fact *willed* Auschwitz as a fate fitting for his chosen people.

This realisation, Rubenstein explains, struck him during a visit to Germany in 1961 when he met one of the most prominent leaders of the Confessing Church (see Chapter 7, p. 343) and of faith-motivated resistance to National Socialism, Heinrich Grüber. Dr Grüber had risked his own life, as well as that of his family, in order to save Jews during the Holocaust. He ran the 'Pastor Grüber Bureau' for the relief of non-Aryan Christians and Jews, remained a sworn fighter against antisemitism after the war ended and continued to work towards the uprooting of antisemitism from German society. He was the only German who testified in the Eichmann trial in Jerusalem. At the time of his meeting with Rubenstein, Grüber was serving as dean of the Evangelical Church in Berlin.

During their conversation, Rubenstein found, however, that his interviewee's fierce resistance to Nazi antisemitism did not mean that anti-Jewish theological principles were not deeply ingrained in his theology: Grüber was convinced that the Holocaust could not be understood without the biblical concept of election, that 'it was part of God's plan that the Jews died' and that God had indeed used the Nazis as a 'whip against His own people', the Jews. In reflecting on this realisation, Rubenstein drew a clear line from the Christian perception of Jews as uniquely placed under God's providential gaze (as both chosen people and as Christ-killers) to the election of Jews for extermination by the Nazis. Even if Nazism was anti-Christian, Rubenstein argued, it was, as he wrote elsewhere in *After Auschwitz*, 'dialectically related to Christianity' (p. 47), in the same way that a heretical ritual is bound to be a variation on an orthodox one. Nazism could not have existed without Christianity.

Due to his radical ideas, Rubenstein became associated with the 'Death of God' theologians in the 1960s, as the only Jew alongside a group of prominent Christian theologians which included Thomas J. J. Altizer, Gabriel Vahanian and Paul van Buren (see Chapter 9, p. 463).

The importance of Rubenstein's report of his encounter with Dr Grüber lay not only in its contribution to the question of the relation between modern antisemitism and Christian anti-Judaism, nor only in exposing the profoundly anti-Jewish character of some of the strongest Christian antagonists to Nazi antisemitism (as evident also in the writings of such prominent thinkers as Maritain, Bonhoeffer and Barth). It also connected Judaism and Christianity precisely as traditions which uphold the ideas of election and of divine intervention in history and are therefore inevitably exposed to abuses such as Nazi antisemitism.

Dr Grüber later denied that he had said what Rubenstein quoted.

Bibliography

Braiterman, Zachary, *(God) After Auschwitz: Tradition and Change in Post-Holocaust Jewish Thought* (Princeton: Princeton University Press, 2001).

Haynes, Stephen R., and Roth, John K., *The Death of God Movement and the Holocaust: Radical Theology Encounters the Shoah* (Westport: Greenwood Press, 1999).

Krell, Marc A., *Intersecting Pathways: Modern Jewish Theologians in Conversation with Christianity* (Oxford: Oxford University Press, 2003).

13

Abraham J. Heschel: 'No Religion Is an Island' (1966)

Text

Nazism in its very roots was a rebellion against the Bible, against the God of Abraham. Realizing that it was Christianity that implanted attachment to the God of Abraham and involvement with the Hebrew Bible in the hearts of Western man, Nazism resolved that it must both exterminate the Jews and eliminate Christianity, and bring about instead a revival of Teutonic paganism.

Nazism has suffered a defeat, but the process of eliminating the Bible from the consciousness of the western world goes on. It is on the issue of saving the radiance of the Hebrew Bible in the minds of man that Jews and Christians are called upon to work together. *None of us can do it alone.* Both of us must realize that in our age anti-Semitism is anti-Christianity and that anti-Christianity is anti-Semitism.

[...]

Our era marks the end of complacency, the end of evasion, the end of self-reliance. Jews and Christians share the perils and the fears; we stand on the brink of the abyss together [...]

[...]

Horizons are wider, dangers are greater ... *No religion is an island*. We are all involved with one another. Spiritual betrayal on the part of one of us affects the faith of all of us. Views adopted in one community have an impact on other communities. Today religious isolationism is a myth. For all the profound differences in perspective and substance, Judaism is sooner or later affected by the intellectual, moral and spiritual events within the Christian society, and vice versa.

[...]

Above all, while dogmas and forms of worship are divergent, God is the same. What unites us? A commitment to the Hebrew Bible as Holy Scripture. Faith in the Creator, the God of Abraham, commitment to many of His commandments, to justice and mercy, a sense of contrition, sensitivity to the sanctity of life and to the involvement of God in history, the conviction that without the holy the good will be defeated, prayer that history may not end before the end of days, and so much more.

[...]

Both communication and separation are necessary. We must preserve our individuality as well as foster care for one another, reverence, understanding, cooperation. In the world of economics, science and technology, cooperation exists and continues to grow. Even political states, though different in culture and competing with one another, maintain diplomatic relations and strive for coexistence. Only religions are not on speaking terms [...] Granted that Judaism and Christianity are committed to contradictory claims, is it impossible to carry on a controversy without acrimony, criticism without loss of respect, disagreement without disrespect? [...]

[...]

Judaism is the mother of the Christian faith. It has a stake in the destiny of Christianity. Should a mother ignore her child, even a wayward, rebellious one? On the other hand, the Church should acknowledge that we Jews in loyalty to our tradition have a stake in its faith, recognize our vocation to preserve and to teach the legacy of the Hebrew Scripture, accept our aid in fighting anti-Marcionite trends as an act of love.

[...]

Let there be an end to disputation and polemic, an end to disparagement. We honestly and profoundly disagree in matters of creed and dogma. Indeed, there is a deep chasm between Christians and Jews concerning, e.g., the divinity and Messiahship of Jesus. But across the chasm we can extend our hands to one another.

Religion is a means, not the end. It becomes idolatrous when regarded as an end in itself. Over and above all being stands the Creator and Lord of history, He who transcends all. To equate religion and God is idolatry.

[...]

The mission to the Jews is a call to the individual Jews to betray the fellowship, the dignity, the sacred history of their people. Very few Christians seem to comprehend what is morally and spiritually involved in supporting such activities. We are Jews as we are men. The alternative to our existence as Jews is spiritual suicide, extinction. It is not a change into something else. Judaism has allies but no substitutes.

Source

Heschel, Abraham J., 'No Religion Is an Island', *Union Seminary Quarterly Review* 21, no. 2 (January 1966), 118, 119, 122, 124, 125, 126, 128–9.

Commentary

The intellectual and activist work of Rabbi Abraham J. Heschel (1907–72), one of the best-known Jewish theologians of the twentieth century, left a long-lasting mark on both Christian and Jewish communities who searched for ways to liberate themselves from the shackles of a long history of mutual antagonism.

Heschel was raised in a Hasidic family in Warsaw and educated at the liberal Hochschule für die Wissenschaft des Judentums (Higher Institute for Jewish Studies) in Berlin. Expelled by the Nazis, he fled Germany on the eve of World War II, continuing his scholarly career at the Jewish Theological Seminary in New York. He was a fierce social activist, fighting for civil rights and against the Vietnam War, famously marching with Martin Luther King, whom he befriended, in the 1965 voter rights march from Selma to Montgomery, Alabama. Himself influenced by such Christian theologians as Niebuhr and Tillich, Heschel's own theological work has been widely read by these as by other Christian theologians, making him a significant channel of mutual theological enrichment.

Heschel's rich contribution to Jewish–Christian relations may be understood as comprising three distinct aspects: first, he was not only a sharp critic of Christian anti-Judaism; he also succeeded in mediating his criticism to Christians in an unprecedented way. Heschel is known as the man who raised Christian awareness of the profound unease that Jews often feel with regard to Christian mission and the Christian expectations of a Jewish conversion to Christianity. In 1964, an early draft of section 4 of *Nostra aetate* was leaked to the press, indicating the 'deep longing' with which 'the Church awaits' its union with the Jewish people. Heschel protested vehemently against this formulation, as expressed in his famous phrase cited in *Time* magazine: 'I am ready to go to Auschwitz any time, if faced with the alternative of conversion or death.' This public protest, together with Heschel's appeal to prominent Catholic representatives such as Cardinal Augustin Bea, is known to have contributed to the absence of any reference to future Jewish conversion from the final text of *Nostra aetate* (see Appendix to Part III, p. 512).

Secondly, Heschel gave significant backing to the engagement of Jews in Christian–Jewish theological dialogue, providing an alternative to those Jewish leaders who sought to abstain from it (most prominently Soloveitchik; see document 10). 'To refuse contact with Christian theologians is, to my mind, barbarous', Heschel maintained in a 1967 article titled 'From Mission to Dialogue?' Naturally, Heschel's reputation for success in influencing the Council's agenda strongly supported his pro-dialogue position.

Lastly, Heschel articulated a Jewish justification for interfaith dialogue. 'No Religion Is an Island', the text from which the excerpts are taken, became an Urtext for interfaith dialogue as it conceptualises interfaith relations as a crucial, unavoidable horizon for contemporary society: 'We must choose between interfaith and inter-nihilism', Heschel argued (p. 119). Isolation is no longer possible, or desirable, and the only chance for faith is through mutual, interfaith support.

Bibliography

Heschel, Abraham Joshua, 'From Mission to Dialogue?', *Conservative Judaism* 21 (Spring 1967), 1–11.

Kaplan, Edward K., *Spiritual Radical: Abraham Joshua Heschel in America, 1940–1972* (New Haven: Yale University Press, 2009).

Sherwin, Bayron L., and Kasimow, Harold, *No Religion Is an Island: Abraham Joshua Heschel and Interreligious Dialogue* (Eugene: Wipf & Stock, 2008).

14

Roy and Alice Eckardt: 'Again, Silence in the Churches' (1967)

Text

The guilt of the Christian community for its dominant silence amid the Nazi slaughters of the Jewish people has in recent years been increasingly confessed within both Catholic and Protestant circles. Yet when within past weeks the extermination of the entire nation of Israel almost occurred, once again there was silence in the churches.

The few voices that were raised merely helped to make the general stillness louder [...]

[...]

[...] Had Christendom not been in the forefront of the persecution of Jews for hundreds of years, the judgments against Israel now being heard in Christian circles would not be so disheartening. These judgments cannot be received in isolation from the age-long Christian 'teaching of contempt' (Jules Isaac), the death camps in Europe and now the unabated annihilationist intentions of Arab nations.

We submit, in sum, that the overwhelming moral force of the case for Israel makes it impossible either to explain or to justify the new silence of the churches through the contention that the evidence is either lacking or equivocal. Accordingly, we are led to seek other reasons for the silence.

[...]

It is generally recognized that many peoples of the world would feel immeasurable guilt were they to permit the Arabs to slaughter the Jews of Israel. If the neutralism of church bodies and the anti-Israel statements of Christian spokesmen are any guide, it would appear that such a concern has no great strength in the churches.

If Christian silence is the silence of the Christian god, he is better off dead. Woe unto Israel had she waited for the god of neutralism and apolitical 'love' to deliver her. Instead, she refused to die, and thus – with lesser or greater faith, with 'worldly' or 'unworldly' aspirations, with 'atheist' or 'believing' assumptions – was enabled to celebrate the living Lord of creation and the God of righteousness. Christians, with other residual pagans, may not wish to be disturbed by this God of justice who earns his living in wholly worldly ways.

Deep in Christian ideology is the insistence, on the one hand, that for various reasons the reputed people of God are barred from their land, and, on the other hand, that the dominant secularity of the State of Israel flouts divine authentication and makes Christian doctrinal recognition impossible. Perhaps the Christian community could never endure the tension of bringing together doctrine and politics in this matter. For once it acknowledged and confirmed theologically the unqualified right of Israel to live, it would be confronted not only with an ideological crisis but also with the moral necessity of casting its lot publicly with Israel, in opposition to unceasing Arab exterminationism. Should Christians be enabled to overcome the theological bias that predisposes them to sympathy with the enemies and detractors of Jews, they may come to see the overwhelming moral justice of Israel's cause and be willing to stand up for it with courage.

The moral tragedy is that the only tangible way open to us to atone for our historic crimes against original Israel is by assuming a special responsibility for the rights and welfare of Jews. The present refusal to bear this obligation may well reflect the Christian community's wish to exonerate itself from culpability for the long years of antisemitism.

Karl Barth once said: 'In order to be chosen we must, for good or ill, either be Jews or else be heart and soul on the side of the Jews.' It almost seems that the entire history of Christianity, including the churches' current response to the Middle Eastern crisis, has been an attempt to make Barth's words as irrelevant as is humanly possible. Writing as Christians who oppose that attempt, we say to our Jewish brothers: we too have been shocked by the new silence. And we are greatly saddened. But we have not been surprised. The causes of the silence lie deep in the Christian soul. Therefore we can only mourn and pray and hope.

Source

Eckardt, A. Roy, and Eckardt, Alice L., 'Again, Silence in the Churches', in Eckardt, A. Roy (ed.), *Elder and Younger Brothers* (New York: Charles Scribner's Sons, 1967), 163, 169, 176–7.

Commentary

'Again, Silence in the Churches' was published in two parts in the American mainstream Protestant magazine *The Christian Century* in the summer of 1967. The authors, Methodist theologian Roy Eckardt (1918–88) and religious studies scholar Alice Eckardt (1923–2020), were two of the most prominent Christian pioneers of post-Holocaust theology and Jewish–Christian reconciliation. In this article, subsequently republished in their book *Elder and Younger Brothers*, they considered the Arab–Israeli War of June 1967, known in Israel as the Six-Day War, from a Christian perspective.

The Eckardts harshly criticised the alleged neutrality they recognised in Christian society towards the situation in the Middle East. Already in the title of the piece, they connected what they saw as 'silence' on the part of Protestant and Catholic communities with regard to the political and military threat posed to the State of Israel on the eve of the war with the churches' silence vis-à-vis the Holocaust less than three decades earlier. At the heart of the Eckardts' argument stands the claim that Christians cannot, in fact, entertain a neutral position with regard to Jewish history; even their approach to contemporary Middle Eastern politics is bound to involve the complexity of their tradition's entanglement with Jews and Judaism.

The article, then, advocates for unabashed Christian support for the State of Israel as a religious obligation which cannot separate the political from the theological. Referring to Jules Isaac's 'teaching of contempt' (see document 1), the Eckardts claim that only a pro-Israeli position is consistent with a true rejection of Christian anti-Judaism, since the criticism of Israel's right to exist veers ever closer to one of the central anti-Jewish claims in the Christian tradition – the idea that Jews are doomed to eternal exile for not accepting Jesus as their saviour.

The Eckardts' article is an illuminating example of the centrality, and the controversiality, of the State of Israel in Jewish–Christian relations. The June War particularly, during which Israel occupied territories beyond the 1947–8 borders and unified Jerusalem under Israeli sovereignty, including the central Christian sacred sites, remains to this day a bone of contention among both Jews and Christians (as well as Muslims and people of other faiths or none around the globe). As evidenced in the Eckardts' work in general, the Christian approach to the State of Israel became, for many, a barrier in the Christian churches' attempt to make amends to Jews in light of what happened in the 1930s and 1940s.

Bibliography

Carenen, Caitlin, *The Fervent Embrace: Liberal Protestants, Evangelicals, and Israel* (New York: New York University Press, 2012).

Eckardt, Roy, and Eckardt, Alice, *Long Night's Journey into Day: Life and Faith after the Holocaust* (Detroit: Wayne State University Press, 1982).

15

George Khodr: 'Feelings and Reactions of Eastern Christians towards Issues Arising from the Palestinian Problem' (1972)

Text

Who is the Christian partner of this tripartite dialogue if it takes place in the Near East?

Twelve million Christian Arabs are immediate interlocutors of Moslems and Jews, and they are the face of the Christian Church as a whole in the region. The overwhelming majority of the Arabic speaking church belongs to the Oriental Orthodoxy. They represent a more or less equal number to that of the Jews in the world. We cannot ignore this fact and behave as if the Palestinian problem concerned only the Jews for whom it is an amendment for their misfortunes, and the Moslems who ought to suffer some misfortunes to repay the lost Crusades. For the misery of the Arab world, its internal divisions and the under-development aggravated by the armaments policy, are felt as severely by the Christian Arabs as by Moslems. And if Arab history in the brilliant epoch of Baghdad and Cordoba was more than tolerant towards the Jews, it remains that the behaviour of the Arabic-speaking Christians towards them cannot suffer the weight of a political power which has not been exerted for 14 centuries.

These Christians have been for a century in the forefront of the Arab national rebirth. All the movements of national liberation and the progress of literature are immensely indebted to them. Anti-semitism was completely unknown to them, and they feel that the Judaization of Jerusalem and the Zionization of Palestine are in particular directed against this church of the Orient which during the past three decades, has known such a remarkable rebirth. The Oriental Church as such did not engage in high biblical critique. It refers theologically and liturgically to the Septuagint. It has, since St. Ignatius of Antioch, been sensitive to the permanent danger of the Judaization of the new-testamentary Revelation. The Old Testament for these Oriental Christians is essentially adapted in its typological exegesis. Furthermore, the perennia of Israel, according to an autonomous religious status, and as if it constituted a particular and still valid economy, remains for us an extremely dangerous innovation. We must add that a certain Zionist press in particular declares the Christian Arabs to be enemies of Israel. It refers, I believe, not to a simple political feud, in which these Christians are not disunited from their non-Christian compatriots, but to their theological attitude loyal to the Patristic tradition.

The Palestinian problem shows us the fundamental divergency between many Occidental Christians and the Orthodox churches of the Orient, for whom the opposition to the Israeli fact is closely linked to the unique, new and irreplaceable character of Christ. The Glory which the Saviour held, reveals itself henceforth in the liturgy of Anastasis.

It is in the very heart of Jerusalem which is being drained of its Christian community at a dangerous pace, that the problem of the Middle East originates.

It is totally misleading to proceed from European or Western considerations concerning the Nazi persecutions or anti-semitism and elaborate an 'a posteriori' theology of the colonial fact of Israel. The context for a Western enlightened consciousness, must be that of the Christian Arab church which must testify in front of the Moslems and the Jews of the Resurrected Lord.

Source

Metropolitan George Khodr, 'Feelings and Reactions of Eastern Christians towards Issues Arising from the Palestinian Problem'. Unpublished speech (WCC Archives, 1972), 4–5.

Commentary

As is clearly evidenced in many of this chapter's other texts, the central locus of the twentieth century's transition in Jewish–Christian relations has been Europe, with an extension to the United States, and it had much to do with the Holocaust. The situation often looked – and perhaps still looks – different from a Middle Eastern perspective.

The excerpts above are taken from Metropolitan George Khodr's report on the eastern churches' perspective on the 'Palestinian problem', addressed to the WCC in 1972. This text, by a prominent Arab-Christian leader, exposes several frictions which are significant for understanding the simultaneous global tensions in Christian–Jewish relations: between west and east; between Catholic/Protestant and Orthodox Christianity; between Jewish–Christian and Muslim–Christian dialogue; and between the post-Holocaust and the postcolonial condition.

Metropolitan George Khodr, Archbishop of Byblos, Botris and Mount Lebanon, was born in Tripoli, Lebanon, in 1923, and personally experienced the Lebanese struggle for independence from French colonialism. One of the founders of the *Mouvement de la jeunesse orthodoxe* (Orthodox Youth Movement), Khodr is a prominent voice in the Orthodox renewal in Lebanon and Syria, a protagonist for Arab unity and the rejuvenation of Arab culture, and a leading figure in ecumenical Christian dialogue and Christian–Muslim dialogue.

As the excerpts from his report show, Metropolitan Khodr sees the Zionist project as related to western colonialism, which he calls 'the Judaization of Jerusalem and the Zionization of Palestine', and in this sense a western exertion of power against Arab people, as well as a western Christian dismissal of Eastern Orthodox Christianity, which is practised by a majority of the Christian population in the region. Antisemitism, Khodr implies, is a completely western phenomenon, which is not part of the Arab or of the Eastern Orthodox Christian heritage. Yet in the name of the post-Holocaust anti-antisemitic struggle, western Christians seek – perhaps in a typically colonialist move – to intervene in the Orthodox tradition of eastern churches and introduce 'an "a posteriori"' theological justification for the State of Israel. This justification has to do with the idea of a persisting particular 'autonomous religious status' for Israel, which seems to endow Jews with certain privileges in Palestine based on a non-typological reading of the Old Testament. This innovation, from Khodr's perspective, is dangerous both politically and theologically. The Arab-Orthodox opposition to the State of Israel has, according to Khodr, both political grounds, as part of an anti-colonialist struggle, and theological grounds, as a preservation of authentic patristic theology (in Khodr's words: 'the opposition to the Israeli fact is closely linked to the unique, new and irreplaceable character of Christ').

Thus the intersection of the political and the theological (which is especially evident in the Eckardts' support of the State of Israel; see document 14) expresses itself in Khodr's text from the other, anti-Zionist side of the fence.

Bibliography

Avakian, Sylvie, 'The Basics of Interreligious Dialogue in Metropolitan George Khodr's Theology. Judaism and Islam from the Perspective of an Oriental Christian', *International Journal of Orthodox Theology* 8, no. 3 (2017), 180–202.

Azar, Michael G., '"Supersessionism": The Political Origin of a Theological Neologism', *SCJR* 16, no. 1 (2021), 1–25.

16

Rosemary Radford Ruether: Faith and Fratricide: The Theological Roots of Anti-Semitism *(1974)*

Text

We have seen that the anti-Judaic myth is neither a superficial nor a secondary element in Christian thought. The foundations of anti-Judaic thought were laid in the New Testament. They were developed in the classical age of Christian theology in a way that

443

laid the basis for attitudes and practices that continually produce terrible results. Most Christians today may seem more than willing to prune back the cruder expressions of these attitudes and practices. But to get at the roots from which these grew is a much more profound problem. The wheat and the tares have grown together from the beginning, and so it may seem impossible to pull up the weed without uprooting the seed of Christian faith as well. Yet as long as Christology and anti-Judaism intertwine, one cannot be safe from a repetition of this history in new form. The end of Christendom may seem to have brought an end to the possibility of legislating theological anti-Judaism as social policy. But we witnessed in Nazism the ability of this virus to appear in even worse form in secular dress. Yet I believe that this is actually a critical moment when a deep encounter with the structures of anti-Judaism is not only necessary to atone for this history, but may be essential to revitalizing the original Christian vision itself.

The end of Christendom means Christianity now must think of itself as a Diaspora religion. On the other hand, the Jewish people, shaken by the ultimate threat to Jewish survival posed by modern anti-Semitism, have taken a giant leap against all odds and against their two thousand years of urban Diaspora culture, and founded the State of Israel. The Return to the homeland has shimmered as a messianic horizon of redemption from the exile for the Jewish people for many centuries. But Christianity dogmatically denied the very possibility of such a return, declaring that eternal exile was the historical expression of Jewish reprobation. Now this Christian myth has been made obsolete by history. But the Jewish hope that gave messianic ultimacy to the Return is also in difficulty. When viewed from the perspective of oppression in the exile, the Return to Israel is indeed a liberation movement and a salvific event for Jews. But in the Middle East conflict, it manifests its historical ambiguity. In Israel the Jewish people face seemingly irreconcilable demands: Jewish nationalism versus Palestinian nationalism, national security against equality and social justice for all. This struggle takes place in a land with a heritage of communal and imperial conflicts, from ancient times to modern colonialism and neocolonialism.

Every criticism of Israel is not to be equated with anti-Semitism. Yet there is no doubt that anti-Zionism has become, for some, a way of reviving the myth of the 'perennial evil nature of the Jews,' to refuse to the Jewish people the right to exist as a people with a homeland of its own. The threat to Jewish survival, posed in ultimate terms by Nazism and never absent as long as anti-Semitism remains in the dominant culture of the Diaspora, lends urgency to the need for the Israeli state. But the religious interpretation of Israel, as the Promised Land given by God and as a land whose restoration was regarded as a messianic event, impedes the search for that pluralism that is necessary for peaceful coexistence with indigenous Arab peoples, both Moslem and Christian. Stuck between a religious orthodoxy forged in the Diaspora and secular nationalism, Israel awaits the rebirth of that prophetic tradition that can transform Zionism into a language of self-criticism in the light of that ultimate Zion of justice and peace which is still to be achieved. In Israel, the Jewish people have tasted salvation. Yet, they must now take their stand on this, not as an ultimate but as a new historical foundation from which to continue the struggle for that final redeemed earth which still eludes both Jew and Christian. The collapse of

Christendom and the founding of Israel, then, provide Christians and Jews with a new historical situation from which to rethink their relationship.

[…] The more virulent anti-Judaic myths of the sort which most modern Christians would reject are not the problem. At the most fundamental level, the problem is the presuppositions which are still affirmed by Christian theologians as basic to Christian theology, long after they have repudiated the more fanciful mythic projections. We must be frank about the risks of this undertaking. Possibly anti-Judaism is too deeply embedded in the foundations of Christianity to be rooted out entirely without destroying the whole structure. We may have to settle for the sort of ecumenical goodwill that lives with theoretical inconsistency and opts for a modus operandi that assures practical cooperation between Christianity and Judaism. Certainly, most Jewish thinkers assume that this is the best that can be done. Nevertheless, this study has made clear that the anti-Judaic structure of Christian thought is not only a problem for Jews, but rests on forms of thought that are troubling to Christians as well. Rethinking these modes of thought has become as necessary for Christian identity as it is for improved relationship with Jews. Each of the basic antitheses which were used to vilify the Jews also appears as an antithesis that has retarded Christian theological maturation. Anti-Judaism was originally more than social polemic. It was an expression of Christian self-affirmation. So now rethinking anti-Judaism has become more than an external task. It has become an internal task of Christian theological reconstruction.

Source

Ruether, Rosemary Radford, *Faith and Fratricide: The Theological Roots of Anti-Semitism* (New York: The Seabury Press, 1979), 226–8. Copyright © 1974 by The Seabury Press Inc. Used by permission of Wipf and Stock Publishers, www.wipfandstock.com.

Commentary

American Catholic theologian Rosemary Radford Ruether (1936–2022) published her monumental book *Faith and Fratricide: The Theological Roots of Anti-Semitism* in 1974 – nine years after the promulgation of *Nostra aetate* (see Appendix to Part III, p. 512). Drawing on a vast corpus of sources spanning the New Testament, and patristic, medieval and modern Christian literature, she provided what is still one of the harshest criticisms of Christian anti-Judaism. In continuation of Jules Isaac's project to trace the beginnings of Christian anti-Judaism (see document 1) and in stark contrast to *Nostra aetate* itself – which stated that the 'teaching of contempt' is a distortion of the Christian message as encoded in the New Testament – Ruether suggested that 'Possibly anti-Judaism is too deeply embedded in the foundations of Christianity to be rooted out entirely without destroying the whole structure.'

Anti-Judaism, she argued, is not a superficial addendum to core Christian beliefs, borrowed from pre-Christian pagan culture, nor is it a later distortion of Christianity which can be easily removed. Rather, anti-Judaism was present in Christianity from its very (Jewish) beginnings: it evolved within the intra-Jewish quarrel about Jesus' messianism. Jews who saw Jesus as Israel's messiah read into the Hebrew Bible their rivalry with those who did not see him this way; side by side with interpreting biblical texts as prophesying Jesus and his crucifixion and resurrection, the early Christians identified in these very same texts their antagonists, who were perceived as the enemies of the gospel and the messiah. Ruether framed this profound exegetical antagonism with her famous dictum, 'anti-Judaism in Christian theology stands as the left hand of Christology' (1974: 365). It is therefore – as suggested in the excerpt from the book's concluding chapter – only with the revision of core Christological doctrines that Christianity can purge itself of anti-Judaism.

Ruether's book was endorsed by Fr Gregory Baum, (then) an Augustinian monk who was among the drafters of section 4 of *Nostra aetate* and a Catholic authority on Jewish–Christian dialogue. In embracing Ruether's thesis, Baum retreated from his previous conviction (voiced in *Is the New Testament Anti-Semitic?*, 1965) that the roots of Christian hostility to Judaism lay outside Christian scripture. Baum's support helped spread the word on Ruether's work, which became one of the best-known (though never orthodox) works on Jewish–Christian relations in the postconciliar era, a work with which every author in the field had to grapple (see for example Alan T. Davies' 1979 edited volume of responses to Ruether's claim).

Ruether's thought continued to evolve after *Faith and Fratricide*. In later years she became an important feminist theologian and – more importantly, for our purposes – a stringent pro-Palestinian and anti-Zionist thinker, working closely with Christian Palestinian liberation theologians. Ruether's sensitivity to questions of power and sovereignty and their relevance for theology are already present in the excerpt above, in which she stresses the historical irony evidenced in the fact that Jews founded the State of Israel and thus coupled Judaism with political power at precisely the time when Christians had to learn to give up the political power which had accompanied Christianity from the time of Constantine.

Bibliography

Baum, Gregory, 'Introduction', in Ruether, Rosemary Radford, *Faith and Fratricide: The Theological Roots of Anti-Semitism* (New York: Seabury, 1974), 1–22.
Davies, Alan T. (ed.), *Antisemitism and the Foundations of Christianity* (New York: Paulist Press, 1979).
Ruether, 'Anti-Semitism in Christian Theology'.

17

Charlotte Klein: Anti-Judaism in Christian Theology *(1975)*

Text

'From Generation to Generation'

The influence on Students of theology today of the teaching on Judaism in theological literature

A few years ago, after a special course on 'Introduction to the New Testament' in the theology department of a German university, the students, working independently during the vacation, produced a number of essays [...] The present author – who gave the lectures – was at pains to give an objective description of Judaism between the Old and New Testaments: that is, not as 'late Judaism', but as a living, evolving religion and culture. Far from succumbing to ossification and corruption, Judaism was flourishing and produced a variety of new trends [...] It seemed particularly important to explain the biblical-Jewish ideas of the Messiah from a non-Christian standpoint and in the light of this to show that a personality with the claims of Jesus of Nazareth, as these are presented in the Gospels, would in normal circumstances be unacceptable to a devout Jew and that this need not involve any sin or guilt on the part of the latter.

It was therefore with a feeling of optimism that I set the students as an essay theme: 'How do you explain the general lack of understanding for Jesus on the part of his contemporaries?' In this respect, the students, after following the lectures, might have been expected to attempt to explain that it was almost impossible for a God-fearing Jew, faithful to the Torah, in virtue of his legitimate understanding of Scripture, to see in Jesus the promised envoy of God with whom the new age was to have dawned. The point had been made in the lectures that it was a question here of completely different messianic concepts: the Jewish ideas were based on a very ancient tradition and were to some extent coloured by the situation at the time; they were not obviously applicable to Jesus' messianic claims. The students might have been expected to allow for the mental climate of the age in their attempts at an explanation and thus to get rid of the ideas of 'self-inculpated stubbornness', 'culpable blindness', 'malicious rejection of the Son of God'. It was assumed that a student in 1970 would be in a position also to think in terms of form- and redaction-criticism and thus to distinguish between Jesus' own time and the time of the definitive composition of the New Testament writings. But, on the contrary, the Gospels were understood in a fundamentalist way, as verbatim reports of events in the time of Jesus. This attitude may have changed in the course of their later exegetical studies; it seems doubtful however whether this will drastically change their view of Judaism and its attitude to Jesus and his role in the world. Their opinions, probably already settled by school and home background – the liturgy also plays a role in this respect – were most probably too firmly rooted and were merely confirmed by the books they had studied.

The students made use indiscriminately of Catholic and Protestant authors for their work. Their opinions – and this is the crucial point – they drew without exception from the books examined in the previous chapters of the present work; the lectures had practically no influence on them. It should be stressed once again that neither in the department of theology as a whole nor among the students in particular was there a sign of any inclination to anti-Semitism. The anti-Judaism which could not but be noticed in all the essays arose wholly and entirely from the works of reference which were read and extensively quoted by the students. Vatican II had exercised no influence here; on the whole the students had scarcely read the Declaration on Judaism, nor – despite all the efforts of

447

the lecturer – had they understood its background. The reasons for this state of affairs are probably complex, but the main reason seems to be that the printed work, the undisputed authority of its author – usually famous – exercised a far deeper and more lasting influence than a course of lectures on a particular occasion.

Source

Klein, Charlotte, *Anti-Judaism in Christian Theology*, trans. Edward Quinn (Philadelphia: Fortress Press, 1978), 127–9. (Originally published as *Theologie und Anti-Judaismus*, 1975.)

Commentary

In his 2012 book *From Enemy to Brother*, John Connelly suggests that without the contribution of converts the Catholic Church would not have found a language to speak about the Jewish people after the Holocaust. Raisa Maritain, John M. Oesterreicher, Gregory Baum and not a few other Catholic men and women, all converts from Judaism, had an existential understanding of the connection between Judaism and Christianity. It was often they who offered the most powerful resistance to Christian anti-Judaism, and many of them paved the way to a new paradigm. One such convert was Sister Charlotte Klein (1915–85).

Klein was born and raised in a Jewish Orthodox family in Berlin. On the eve of World War II the family fled Germany and immigrated to Palestine. In Jerusalem Klein became acquainted with the Sisters of Our Lady of Sion, converted to Catholicism and joined the Sisters in 1945.

The Sisters of Our Lady of Sion played an important role in transforming the Catholic approach to Jews and Judaism. Established by Marie-Theodore and Marie-Alphonse Ratisbonne (themselves converts) in France in the 1840s, the religious congregation of the Sisters of Our Lady of Sion was dedicated to the 'regeneration' of the Jewish people and, essentially, to their conversion. The Sisters witnessed the horrors of the Holocaust from close quarters, since many of them were actively involved in saving Jewish children and women, and in the 1950s the congregation was further shaken by its involvement in the Finaly affair (see document 2).

These events seeded a long and arduous process of self-examination among the Sisters, a process which reached its culmination during the Second Vatican Council. The Sisters of Sion were working behind the scenes of the schema of the *Decretum de Judaeis* at Vatican II, and contributed to what became section 4 of *Nostra aetate* (see Appendix to Part III, p. 512). At the same time, under the leadership of their superior general Mother Marie-Félix, they transformed their own mission from one that strove for Jewish conversion to one that sought understanding and friendship with Jews.

Charlotte Klein took part in transforming the congregation's vocation. She was a scholar and activist deeply involved in Jewish–Christian dialogue, working to familiarise Christians with Judaism, to overcome Christian prejudice, and to implement the new horizons opened by *Nostra aetate* within the Christian world. Based on her international experience in teaching theology (she taught in various settings, among them Sankt Georgen in Frankfurt and the Leo Baeck College in London), Klein wrote her most significant work, *Anti-Judaism in Christian Theology*. She shows to what extent continental theologians, and especially biblical scholars (among them Rudolf Bultmann, Joachim Jeremias and Leonhard Goppelt), continued to reproduce and disseminate anti-Jewish prejudice in their scholarly work even after 1945. These prejudices, Klein argues, are not antisemitic *per se*, but rather are informed by traditional Christian presumptions about the inferiority of Judaism to Christianity. Among these presumptions Klein includes, for example, the concept of 'Late Judaism' (*Spätjudentum*) used by biblical scholars to depict Second Temple Judaism as decadent and lifeless. Indeed, Klein's critique was partly responsible for the marginalisation of this term and its eventual replacement in theological scholarship by less pejorative alternatives.

The significance of *Anti-Judaism in Christian Theology* lies, therefore, in its highlighting of the responsibility of biblical and theological scholarship in the perpetuation of anti-Jewish prejudice, as the anti-Jewish components of this tradition are passed, even if unintentionally, by both authors and readers, 'from generation to generation'.

Bibliography

Deutsch, Celia, 'Journey to Dialogue: Sisters of Our Lady of Sion and the Writing of Nostra Aetate', *Studies in Christian–Jewish Relations* 11, no. 1 (2016), 1–36.

18

Damaskinos Papandreou: 'The Necessity of Dialogue' (1976)

Text

Despite all the separating differences, there are nevertheless profound connections which can only be established after a constructive and fruitful dialogue.

Fortunately, since the beginning of the twentieth century, the relationship between the two religions has changed, for on the part of Judaism, a discussion with Christianity has begun. Since then there has been some Jewish research on Jesus within the liberal Jewish movement. The results of this Jewish research on early Christianity are unalterable insights, for example, that the spiritual preconditions of Jesus lie in Pharisaic Judaism, that many of Jesus' traits are Jewish in character while others are unrabbinical and un-Jewish. It is also essential that an accurate picture of Pharisaism also emerged outside of Judaism; for Pharisaism is not a sign of decay, but, within certain limitations, the bearer of creative development. Thus, there certainly appears to be a mutual will to communicate, especially after the Second World War, for 'Societies for Christian–Jewish Cooperation' have emerged all over West Germany, in which dialogue between the two religions is strongly cultivated.

Only through dialogue is it possible to overcome the gulf between the two religions, which has widened and deepened over the centuries and led to a complete misunderstanding on both sides, for Christianity originated from within the Jewish religion and received certain essential elements of its faith and practice from Judaism.

As an orthodox theologian, who cannot separate theology from doxology and the life of the church, I may find a certain profound parallel in the Jewish faith, which in fact comes to life in the daily service to God, i.e., in the fulfilment of the double law, the love of God and love of one's neighbour, which ultimately underpins the individual instructions of the Torah.

If one compares Jewish worship with Christian worship, one finds that Christian worship was partly shaped by Jewish worship. The Jewish times of prayer have passed into the Christian Liturgy of the Hours: Morning Prayer into Matins and Lauds, *mincha* into Vespers, and Evening Prayer into Night Prayer. Apart from the Psalms and other biblical chants, a number of formulas have been adopted by the Christian congregation from the synagogues: 'Lord, open my lips' as the introduction to the Liturgy of the Hours; 'Truly worthy and right' as the introduction to the Eucharistic Prayer (Preface); the Quedusa as the Trisagion or Sanctus; the cry 'One is holy' as the invitational call to Communion; and the responsories Hosanna, Hallelujah and Amen. The Jewish prayers of repentance have found their echo in the Christian prayers of repentance. Above all, the Jewish blessing (*berakha*) of bread and wine at the sabbath meal has become the 'Eucharistia', the holiest sacrament of Christianity.

Today, it is recognised that dialogue is one of the most important foundations of the world community.

Source

Metropolitan Damaskinos Papandreou, *Die Absolutheitsansprüche der beiden Religionen, Christentum und Judentum und die Notwendigkeit ihres Dialoges* (1976, unpublished; from the archives of the Centre orthodoxe du Patriarcat œcuménique, Chambésy, Switzerland), 14–15. (Translation by Iris Koch.)

Commentary

The transition in Jewish–Christian relations in the aftermath of the Holocaust is often seen through a western lens and is centred, accordingly, on Protestant–Jewish and Catholic–Jewish relations. Nevertheless, during the 1970s foundations for dialogue were also laid between Orthodox Christians and Jews as they began to explore the particularities of their relationship and the parallels and relatedness of the Jewish and Orthodox traditions. The unpublished speech of Metropolitan Damaskinos Papandreou (1936–2011) from which our document is excerpted was one of the formative moments in this novel form of dialogue.

The first official meeting between Orthodox Christians and Jews was convened in New York City in 1972, led by Archbishop Iakovos of the Greek Orthodox Archdiocese of America. The initiative then moved to Europe, energised by the pan-Orthodox and ecumenical work of the Centre orthodoxe du Patriarcat œcuménique (Orthodox Centre of the Ecumenical Patriarchate) in Chambésy, Switzerland. The Swiss Society for Jewish–Christian Friendship was convened in 1976 in Zurich, where Damaskinos, who would be the first Metropolitan of Switzerland from 1982 but at the time was Metropolitan of Traianoupoli in northeastern Greece and director of the Chambésy Centre, presented a lengthy lecture on Jewish–Christian relations. Damaskinos' speech spans large swathes of both traditions: from the two Testaments to the church fathers, from the Talmud to the Barcelona disputation, from Martin Buber to Rudolf Otto, from Karl Rahner to Vatican II. As the speech's title suggests ('The Absolute Claims of the Two Religions, Christianity and Judaism, and the Necessity of Their Dialogue'), instead of highlighting the commonalities between the Christian and the Jewish traditions, as is often the case in the context of Jewish–Christian dialogue, the Metropolitan focused on the foundational differences between the two faiths and stressed the coherence and the integrity of these differences within their respective traditions. In fact, the greater part of the lecture is written from the purposely balanced, scientific point of view of a scholar of comparative religion. It is only at the end of his text, part of which is included here, that the Metropolitan stresses the necessity of Jewish–Christian dialogue and advances his own point of view specifically as an Orthodox theologian.

Although it remained unpublished, Damaskinos' speech convinced both Jewish and Christian participants of the necessity to learn more about each other's traditions and paved the way for further dialogue. In the meetings that followed, Jewish and Orthodox Christian theologians, philosophers, rabbis and priests (prominent among the Jewish participants being Gerhart Riegner, Ernst Ludwig Ehrlich, Jacob Agus and Michael Wyschogrod) discussed similarities in liturgy, approaches to the Nomos/Torah, the relationship between scripture, community and faith, and their shared geographical (and eastern) origins, which mark both traditions to this day – a discussion during which they discovered an affinity in certain respects stronger than with either their Catholic or Protestant counterparts. The eleventh international meeting between Jews and Orthodox Christians took place in 2022.

Bibliography

Azar, Michael G., 'The Bible in Orthodox Christian–Jewish Dialogue', in Pentiuc, Eugen J. (ed.), *The Oxford Handbook of the Bible in Orthodox Christianity* (Oxford: Oxford University Press, 2020), 556–74.

Kratzert, Thomas, *Wir sind wie die Juden: der griechisch-orthodoxe Beitrag zu einem ökumenischen judischchristlichen Dialog* (Berlin: Institut Kirche und Judentum, 1994), 210–13.

Pătru, Alina, 'Der bilaterale Dialog zwischen Orthodoxie und Judentum ab den 70-er Jahren', *Revista Ecumenica Sibiu* 2, no. 1 (2010), 69–81.

9

The Flourishing of Jewish–Christian Relations
1978 to the Present Day

MARY C. BOYS

INTRODUCTION

This volume offers abundant evidence of the fraught history between Jews and Christians, a history that has often led to tragic consequences for Jews and grievously marred the integrity of Christianity. The twentieth century witnessed the most catastrophic event of all – the Shoah or Holocaust – and also the slow awakening of the churches and scholars to their obligation to do justice to the Jewish people and their tradition. Timidly worded acknowledgements of Christian churches gave way to searing confessions and theological rethinking. What began in 1947 at the Emergency Conference on Antisemitism in Seelisberg, Switzerland, and was given greater prominence through Vatican II's documents, particularly *Nostra aetate* in 1965 (see Appendix to Part III, p. 512), initiated a transformative process that the decades since 1978 advanced in significant ways, especially among sectors of the population in the west.

Recognition of the widespread negative portrayal of Jews and Judaism in Christian texts has given rise to an abundant literature at both scholarly and popular levels, including the relation of Christian anti-Jewish perspectives to antisemitism, which is nevertheless resurging. Exploration of the Shoah continues in literature, the performing arts, memoirs and academic tomes; Holocaust museums draw millions of visitors and many school curricula require its study. Controversy continues concerning the role of religious leaders during the Shoah, especially that of Pope Pius XII. In some cases, decades of conflict were ultimately resolved through a protracted process of formal engagement, such as the Vatican's recognition of the State of Israel in 1993 (as promulgated in 'Fundamental Agreement between the Holy See and the State of Israel'). Others reveal the fruit of years of intense dialogue, such as the statement by an international group of leading Orthodox rabbis in 2015 that speaks of Christianity as 'our partner in world redemption' (*To Do the Will of Our Father in Heaven*; see Appendix to Part III, p. 544).

The transformation continues, albeit in ways neither widely known nor well understood. Although the public is generally not cognisant of the documents designed to further understanding of issues between Jews and Christians, these texts suggest pathways for advances that are widely available for religious leaders to pursue. While the documentary tradition plays a particularly prominent part in Roman Catholicism, it transcends its boundaries to include interreligious institutions and groups as well as a range of Protestant denominations and Jewish organisations. Texts documenting aspects of this transformation are available on websites and in the two-volume collection *Bridges: Documents of the Christian–Jewish Dialogue*.

A notable factor of this period is the role of the papacy, magnified in part by widespread news coverage. The year 1978 marked the beginning of the long papacy of John Paul II (*r.* 1978–2005) that included his visits to Auschwitz in 1979 and to Rome's Great Synagogue in 1986, and his prayer for forgiveness at the Western Wall in 2000. Also of importance were formulations in various addresses, including the oft-cited reference in his 1980 'Address to the Representatives of the West German Jewish Community' to Jews as 'the people of God of the Old Covenant, never revoked by God'. His papacy also encompassed the promulgation of documents with problematic assertions about Judaism, the church's role in the Shoah and religious pluralism (respectively, *The Catechism of the Catholic Church* in 1993; 'We Remember: A Statement on the Shoah' in 1998; and *Dominus Iesus* in 2000). It included, too, the publication of what has been the most positive statement to date on the relation of the Testaments, *The Jewish People and Their Sacred Scriptures in the Christian Bible* in 2001 (see Appendix to Part III, p. 528).

Pope John Paul II's successor, Benedict XVI (*r.* 2005–13), the principal author of *Dominus Iesus*, lacked the sensibilities that arose in part from Pope John II's lifelong friendships with Jews, but he continued the tradition of visiting Auschwitz and the Great Synagogue, as has Pope Francis (*r.* 2013–). Having established a deep bond with Rabbi Avraham Skorka, with whom he wrote *On Heaven and Earth*, when he was Archbishop of Buenos Aires, Pope Francis has manifested warm hospitality to Jews. Especially noteworthy was his announcement in 2019 that the massive Vatican archives on the papacy of Pius XII (1939–58) would open in 2020, saying, 'The church is not afraid of history' (see document 7 below).

While recognising the immense contribution of Christian and Jewish institutional leaders, this chapter focuses on the scholarship that undergirds and develops their statements in greater depth and breadth. The goal is to highlight significant scholarly literature that demonstrates the flourishing of Jewish–Christian relations across a range of significant issues, perspectives, authors and methods. In some cases, this literature flows from figures with extensive involvement in national and international dialogues; the influence of other authors lies principally in the academic realm but may be exercised in conversation with Jewish or Christian interlocutors and, on occasion, in collaborative projects with them.

Several clarifications are in order. With the intention of demonstrating the flourishing of scholarship indicative of new currents of knowledge, this chapter represents positions our ancestors in faith would have found unimaginable. The excerpted documents in this chapter reflect a new breadth and depth of knowledge. Nevertheless, the misinterpretations and erroneous understandings of Judaism that have plagued Christian thinking continue to affect the preponderance of contemporary theological work. Thus, these documents should not be regarded as representative of theological scholarship as a whole, nor as yet widely accessible to the public. Some documents, moreover, are included in this chapter because they offer important insights despite including remnants of flawed views.

Finally, a word about the terminology in the commentaries. Increasingly, scholars distinguish the followers of Christ of the first centuries from those after the imperial legislation in the late fourth century, when Christianity was recognised as the state religion. So 'Christ-followers' (or synonyms thereof) indicates the first generations of the Jesus movement; 'proto-Christian' denotes the followers from the second century, most of whom were gentiles; from the fourth century, 'Christian' is the accurate term.

In the course of working on the commentaries, it became increasingly clear that the excerpts are interconnected, sometimes by their field of study, sometimes by themes – and on occasion by both. Some of these themes and fields of study are discussed below. Readers will undoubtedly tease out further connections.

Biblical scholarship is vital for absorbing the significance of sacred texts shared in large part by Jews and Christians, albeit with differing interpretative traditions. It is also essential for reorienting how we conceptualise the genesis of the Jewish–Christian relationship. The excerpts in this chapter offer insight into how Christian readings of biblical texts furthered antipathy to Jews and Judaism. Yet these excerpts also reflect significant advances, including knowledge of Second Temple Judaism and the 'Jewish Paul', and new respect for and engagement with Jewish interpretation.

Of particular pertinence to Jewish–Christian relations is the method of reception history, which traces the consequences of interpretations; so, too, is intertextuality, which reveals the intricate play of texts in relation to one another – with particular relevance for understanding the profound relationship between the Old and New Testaments. Fundamental to this scholarship is a more nuanced understanding of the historical matrix in which Judaism and Christianity emerged through mutually formative processes, evident in the extensive discussion of the so-called 'partings of the ways', the classification of much of the New Testament as Jewish Hellenistic literature and recognition of the Apostle Paul as a Jew whose preaching was directed to gentiles.

Paula Fredriksen (document 6) reveals the protracted origins of Christian anti-Jewish teachings, situates their origins with non-Jewish disciples of the Christ in the diaspora in the early second century and the intensification of these teachings in subsequent centuries. Lacking contact with Jews, proto-Christian intellectuals viewed Judaism as an abstraction, a philosophical tradition perceived as threatening the development of a separate, superior identity. John Gager (document 12) rejects the traditional, prevailing view of Paul as an educated and fervent Jew whose experience on the road to Damascus changed him irrevocably. Gager is a prominent proponent of what is termed the 'new perspective' on Paul as the apostle to the gentiles faithful to Judaism, committed to thinking theologically about the relationship of non-Jews (gentiles) to the God of Israel as well as to Jewish followers of Jesus. Amy-Jill Levine and Marc Zvi Brettler, Jewish scholars of the New Testament and of the Jewish Bible, respectively, offer an incisive analysis of the differences in Jewish and

Christian interpretative paradigms (document 17); their book illustrates the dissimilarities by explicating commentaries on selected texts from both traditions. Paul van Buren's insistence (document 3) that Christians must learn to honour Jewish readings of their scripture serves as a prescient prelude to the Levine–Brettler excerpt. Understanding of the Old Testament in relation to the New Testament surfaces again in Naim Stifan Ateek's argument that Jesus' hermeneutic of love contrasts with the violence implicit in the tribal God of the Old Testament (document 14). The excerpt from Alain Marchadour and David Neuhaus (document 9) should be read in part as a salvo against those who would selectively draw upon biblical texts to uphold their views on the seemingly 'inexorable conflict between Israelis and Palestinians', and more specifically on the land itself. Their insistence that persons be rooted in a land resonates with aspects of Gerald McDermott's exposition of the 'New' Christian Zionism (document 13). McDermott argues that the people of Israel and their land have theological significance for the church, and he regards the return of Jews to their homeland as a 'provisional and proleptic fulfillment of the promises of the new world to come'.

Historical study bears implications for Jewish–Christian relations in numerous ways, situating Early Judaism (c. 330 BCE–200 CE) and nascent Christianity in the context of Graeco-Roman culture, grappling with the tensions with Judaism occasioned by the increasing dominance of gentiles in proto-Christianity, and the maturing of scholarship on the Shoah.

The selections include Israel Jacob Yuval's work (document 5) on the mutual (and often antagonistic) use of Passover imagery by Jews and Christ-followers in the second century – a recognition he owes to his membership of a 'generation born after the Christian–Jewish polemic in its old form had come to an end' (2006: xiii). Irving Greenberg (document 4) reflects on the imperative of Jews and Christians to confront their own historicity and use their power ethically in shaping a world conducive to human dignity. 'Reluctantly but inexorably, both religions have been forced to confront their own historicity', Greenberg writes. For Jews this confrontation with history meant principally the founding of a nation where Jews could live without fear of persecution or genocide. For Christians, however, facing their history vis-à-vis Judaism has been a more protracted struggle, largely because of the temptation to evade responsibility through misleading historiography. The failure of the churches to acknowledge the ways in which Christians succumbed to 'complicity, duplicity, rationalization, fear and ambition', as Holocaust historian Victoria Barnett documents in a recent essay (2005: 361), accounts in part for the slow awakening to the imperative to do justice to Jews and Judaism.

This reluctance to admit that even persons who are 'holy' figures are subject to human frailty bears directly on Eva Fleischner's analysis of the spirituality of Pope Pius XII (document 7). In analysing Pius' correspondence with German bishops as examples of his spirituality, Fleischner shows how his otherworldly spirituality was too narrow to meet the moment. Susannah Heschel (document 11) draws upon her previous work on the 'betrayal of the churches', especially the German Christian Movement, to argue that 'anti-Judaism' should be understood as the 'term for a discourse that expresses antisemitic views in theological language'. By implication, her contention makes a strong case for church leaders to root out anti-Jewish teachings that fuel antisemitism.

Acknowledgement of theology's contextual character is a major aspect of the turn to the human subject in contemporary Christian theology. Theology is perspectival, shaped in part by the complexities of the theologian's situatedness, including one's geographical and cultural location, race and ethnicity, religious tradition and spirituality, economic and class status, and gender and sexuality. Theological works may originate 'from the margins' or 'from the underside', often for the purposes of 'liberation'.

Several documents fall under the sub-category of liberation theology, an extraordinarily important theological emphasis originally associated with the 1971 publication of Peruvian theologian Gustavo Gutiérrez's *Teología de la liberación* (*A Theology of Liberation*, 1973). Theologians and activists across the globe have taken up Gutiérrez's clarion call to examine social structures and to conceptualise sin as social as well as personal. Yet some of the selections here reflect a shadow side of some liberation theologies that draw on outmoded understandings of Judaism.

Naim Ateek's *A Palestinian Theology of Liberation* (document 14) gives voice to his longing as a Palestinian Christian – and thus as a member of a small minority among Palestinians – for release from the yoke of Israeli occupation. Ateek's experience of the occupation has revolutionised his understanding of the Bible such that he sees the Old Testament as reflecting a 'tribal and exclusive understanding of God' and thus not suffused by the 'mind or spirit of Christ'. Vietnamese-American theologian Peter Phan's analysis of Asian liberation theology (document 8) uncovers a similar view in the work of Choan-Seng Song, a prolific Taiwanese Presbyterian writer who regards Judaism's concept of God as a 'high-voltage God', remote from his people and threatening to the common people. Phan, however, attributes the negative view of Judaism among leading Asian liberationists to the legacy of missionaries, and thus considers their anti-Jewish views 'mostly unintentional'. Nevertheless, Phan sees potential in other aspects of Song's work for connecting with post-Holocaust theologies. Argentinian rabbi Leon Klenicki (document 2) recognised the potential in liberation theology in the early years of Gustavo Gutiérrez's work but also criticised what he saw as its erasure of Judaism through its unfamiliarity with rabbinic commentary, contemporary Jewish interpretation and involvement in labour movements. Judith Plaskow (document 1) voiced a similar critique, not of liberation theology but of early Christian feminist theology, which she viewed as defective insofar as it wrenched Talmudic texts from their context and treated rabbinic opinion as monolithic. Klenicki and Plaskow were two of the earliest Jewish critics of aspects of Christian liberation and feminist theologies.

Other theological issues involve Christology, Orthodox theology, religious pluralism and racism – hardly the sum total of pertinent theological issues but indicative of the range of topics. Systematic theologians Barbara U. Meyer and Willie James Jennings reflect on the relation of Jesus to contemporary Christians, the overwhelming majority of whom are gentiles. Meyer (document 18) maintains that Jesus' 'Torah-bound' life means that he remains 'Other' and therefore challenges tendencies to domesticate him. Jennings (document 10) challenges white Christians to reconsider their identity in relation to the church's primal estrangement: its separation from Jesus' Jewish body and Judaism. Jennings' own liberation approach asserts that were white Christians to identify with their gentile ancestors and thus see themselves as outsiders, they might not be so prone to assume racial superiority. Serafim Seppälä, a monk and priest in the Orthodox Church of Finland, focuses on the role of patristic theology so significant in Orthodox traditions (document 16). Seppälä concludes that because the patristic perspectives represent outmoded understandings of Judaism, they are seriously distorted and, therefore, should be set aside. Ethicist John Pawlikowski (document 15) argues that Jewish–Christian dialogue must be integrated into the wider context of interreligious encounter, particularly beyond the west. Insights from scholarship must be brought to engagement with Hinduism, Buddhism and Islam, and the church needs to be involved 'on the ground' of dialogue with those traditions. His essay implicitly evokes comparative theology as a desideratum of continuing scholarship in Jewish–Christian relations.

Excellent sources abound for the period 1978 to the present – far more than could be excerpted here. This chapter's documents might best be seen as a foretaste of a fertile era of Jewish–Christian scholarship, including the advent of open-access journals (e.g., *Studies in Christian–Jewish Relations* and *Journal of the Early Jewish Movement in Its Jewish Setting*) that help to chart new directions. The challenge ahead lies in exerting greater influence on theological inquiry and on Jewish and Christian communities for the flourishing of humanity.

Bibliography

Barnett, Victoria, 'The Creation of Ethical "Gray Zones" in the German Protestant Church', in Petropoulos, Jonathan, and Roth, John K. (eds.), *Gray Zones: Ambiguity and Compromise in the Holocaust and Its Aftermath* (New York: Berghahn, 2005), 360–71.

Becker, Adam H., and Reed, Annette Yoshiko (eds.), *The Ways that Never Parted: Jews and Christians in Late Antiquity and the Early Middle Ages* (Minneapolis: Fortress Press, 2007).

Collins, John J., and Harlow, Daniel C. (eds.), *Early Judaism: A Comprehensive Overview* (Grand Rapids: Eerdmans, 2012).

Goldberg, Sol, Ury, Scott, and Weiser, Kalman (eds.), *Key Concepts in the Study of Antisemitism* (Cham, Switzerland: Springer International, 2021).

Hayes, Peter, and Roth, John K. (eds.), *Oxford Handbook of Holocaust Studies* (Oxford: Oxford University Press, 2010).

John Paul II, *Spiritual Pilgrimage: Texts on Jews and Judaism, 1979–1995*, ed. Eugene J. Fisher and Leon Klenicki (New York: Crossroad, 1995).

Johnson, Elizabeth A., *She Who Is: The Mystery of God in Feminist Theological Discourse* (New York: Crossroad, 1992).

Mitternach, Dieter, and Runesson, Anders, *Jesus, the New Testament, and Christian Origins* (Grand Rapids: Eerdmans, 2021).

O'Malley, John W., *What Happened at Vatican II?* (Cambridge: Belknap Press of Harvard University Press, 2008).

Sherman, Franklin (ed.), *Bridges: Documents of the Christian–Jewish Dialogue*, 2 vols (New York: Paulist, 2007–14).

Yuval, Israel Jacob, *Two Nations in Your Womb: Perceptions of Jews and Christians in Late Antiquity and the Middle Ages*, trans. Barbara Harshav and Jonathan Chipman (Berkeley: University of California Press, 2006).

Zetterholm, Magnus, *Approaches to Paul: A Student's Guide to Recent Scholarship* (Minneapolis: Fortress, 2009).

DOCUMENTS

I

Judith Plaskow: 'Christian Feminism and Anti-Judaism' (1978)

Text

There is a new myth developing in Christian feminist circles. It is a myth which tells us that the ancient Hebrews invented patriarchy: that before them the goddess reigned in matriarchal glory, and that after them Jesus tried to restore egalitarianism but was foiled by the persistence of Jewish attitudes within the Christian tradition [...] The consequence of this myth is that feminism is turned into another weapon in the Christian anti-Judaic arsenal. Christian feminism gives a new slant to the old theme of Christian superiority, a theme rooted in the New Testament and since reiterated by countless Christian theologians [...]

But many feminist accounts of Jesus' Jewish milieu suffer from three serious scholarly errors or oversights which are rooted in biased views of Jesus' Jewish origins.

First of all, a number of discussions of Jewish attitudes toward women use the Talmud or passages from it to establish the role of Jewish women in Jesus' time. The Talmud, however, is a compilation of Jewish law and argument which was not given final form until the *sixth century*. Passages in it may be much older or at least reflect reworkings of earlier material. But this can be determined only on the basis of painstaking scholarly sifting of individual original texts [...]

Secondly, it is deceptive to speak of rabbinic opinion, customs, or sayings as monolithic [...] Their treatment of Judaism is analogous to conservative Christian arguments for the subordination of women which quote only certain views from Paul [...]

The third error frequently made by feminist scholars is more subtle. It lies in comparing the words and attitudes of an itinerant preacher with laws and sayings formulated in the rarefied atmosphere of rabbinic academies. Many discrepancies between Jesus and 'the Rabbis' on the subject of women can be explained by the fact that Jesus was constantly in contact with real women, speaking to and about them in the context of concrete situations [...] Where we do have rabbinic stories of actual male/female interaction, we find that rabbis too – whatever their ideological statements – were capable of reacting to women as persons [...]

Only when Christian feminists have deepened their understanding of Judaism can they honestly evaluate the uniqueness or non-uniqueness of Jesus' attitudes toward women.

At the same time that Jesus' milieu is being reevaluated, the Talmudic rabbis ought to be compared with their true contemporaries – the Church Fathers [... W]hat is immediately striking is the similarity between the two traditions – in both, the developing association of women with sexuality and the fear of woman as temptress [...]

Christian feminist anti-Judaism, however, represents precisely the continuation of a patriarchal ethic of projection [...] It projects onto Judaism the 'backsliding' of a tradition which was to develop sexism in new and virulent directions. It thus allows the Christian feminist to avoid confronting the failure of her/his own tradition [...]

The purpose of these criticisms of feminist scholarship is not to suggest that traditional Jewish attitudes towards women are praiseworthy. Of course, they are not. But Christian attitudes are in no way essentially different. They are different in detail, and these differences are extremely interesting and worthy of study. But weighed in the feminist balance, both traditions must be found wanting – and more or less to the same degree. The real tragedy is that the feminist revolution has furnished one more occasion for the projection of Christian failure onto Judaism. It ought to provide the opportunity for transcending ancient differences in the common battle against sexism.

Source

Plaskow, Judith, 'Christian Feminism and Anti-Judaism', *Cross Currents* 28, no. 3 (1978), 306–9.

Commentary

Jewish feminist theologian Judith Plaskow (b. 1947) was among the first and most significant critics of the anti-Jewish claims of many Christian feminists in the 1970s and 1980s.

As advocacy for women's rights and feminist thought advanced in the 1960s and 1970s, Christian theologians sought to argue that the teachings of Jesus provided a corrective to the patriarchal traditions of Judaism. Among the earliest and most influential was Leonard Swidler's 1971 essay 'Jesus Was a Feminist' in *The Catholic World*. He argued that because 'the overwhelmingly negative attitude toward women in Palestine did not come through the primitive Christian communal lens', it underscored the 'clearly great religious importance Jesus attached to his positive attitude – his feminist attitude – toward women: feminism, that is, personalism extended to women, is a constitutive part of the Gospel, the Good News, of Jesus' (p. 15). Swidler's widely circulated essay contributed to the formation of a theological template in which the patriarchal culture of Judaism gave way to the liberating message of Jesus and his disciples.

Plaskow's work points out ways in which feminism 'is turned into another weapon in the Christian anti-Judaic arsenal'. The 1978 essay from which the excerpt comes identifies critical methodological misinterpretations that plagued early Christian feminism – and have yet to disappear entirely. She identifies the core problem as ignorance of the complexity and diversity of Judaism, compounded by the perennial Christian proclivity to assert its superiority: 'Only when Christian feminists have deepened their understanding of Judaism can they honestly evaluate the uniqueness or non-uniqueness of Jesus' attitudes toward women.'

Plaskow's arguments were received by leading Christian feminist theologians, who developed critiques of anti-Jewish claims among their tradition's sisters. In 1982 Bernadette Brooten published her scholarly study *Women Leaders in the Ancient Synagogue*, drawing on archaeological evidence to demonstrate that in fact women held leadership roles in early Judaism. Katharina von Kellenbach's *Anti-Judaism in Feminist Religious Writings* (1994) offered an incisive analysis of the Christian representations of Judaism as marred by antitheses, scapegoating and supersession. New Testament scholar Mary Rose D'Angelo argued persuasively that portraying Jesus as saving women from Judaism, as it were, both oversimplifies and distorts the situation of Jewish women in the first century; D'Angelo collaborated with Jewish scholar Ross Kraemer to edit *Women and Christian Origins* in 1999.

In 1991, thirteen years after her essay in *Cross Currents*, Plaskow returned to her subject in 'Feminist Anti-Judaism and the Christian God', in the *Journal of Feminist Studies in Religion*. She identified three loci of anti-Judaism among Christian feminists in relation to the question of God: (1) the persistent caricature that pitted the wrathful and jealous God of the 'Old Testament' over against the tender, loving God of the New Testament; (2) the accusation that God is responsible for the death of the Goddess; and (3) the declaration that Jesus was a feminist. As she observed: 'If we acknowledge that the Jesus movement was a movement within Judaism, however, then whatever Jesus' attitudes towards women, they represent not a victory *over* Judaism but a possibility *within* early Judaism' (p. 105). She concluded her 1991 essay by strengthening the claim she first made in 1978: 'no awareness of feminist anti-Judaism and its relation to a long history, no effort to weed it out of one's thinking and writing, no sensitivity to the power imbalance in the relations between Jews and Christians can replace knowledge of Judaism as a living religion as the best antidote to anti-Judaism' (p. 108).

Bibliography

Kraemer, Ross S., *Her Share of the Blessings: Women's Religions among Pagans, Jews, and Christians in the Greco-Roman world* (New York: Oxford University Press, 1992).

Plaskow, Judith, 'Feminist Anti-Judaism and the Christian God', *Journal of Feminist Studies in Religion* 7, no. 2 (1991), 99–108.

Schüssler Fiorenza, Elisabeth, *In Memory of Her: A Feminist Theological Reconsideration of Christian Origins* (New York: Crossroad, 1983).

Swidler, Leonard, 'Jesus Was a Feminist', *The Catholic World* (15 September 1971), 2–3, 15–17.

Von Kellenbach, Katharina, *Anti-Judaism in Feminist Religious Writings* (Atlanta: Scholars Press, 1994).

2

Leon Klenicki: 'The Theology of Liberation: A Latin American Jewish Exploration' (1983)

Text

Latin America is today one of the least understood areas of the world. A Catholic continent, it is socially and theologically silent, slow to respond to the challenges of the twentieth century and the postindustrial revolution. It is a universe of unequal social and spiritual realities, exhibiting a diversity of trends [… including] a new trend […] which has made a real contribution to Catholic thought and is being seriously discussed in academic and political centers. This is the theology of liberation, based on contemporary European thought but influenced by Latin America's spiritual and economic conditions. This trend […] deserves our attention […] in exploring the implications for the Jewish communities of Latin America.

[…] The theology of liberation was officially recognized by the deliberations of the Latin American Bishops Conference (CELAM) meeting at Medellin, Colombia, in 1968. Medellin represented an actualization, an updating of Catholic religious life and ethical concerns to the realities of a continent plagued by economic and social problems. […] The Latin American Church is beginning to play a decisive role in the defense of human rights […]

[Gustavo] Gutierrez [*sic*] develops the idea of 'theology as critical reflection on praxis.' […]

[He states] that 'theology as critical reflection thus fulfills a liberating function for man and the Christian community, preserving them from fetishism and idolatry, as well as from a pernicious and belittling narcissism. Understood in this way, theology has a necessary and permanent role in the liberation from every form of religious alienation – which is often fostered by the ecclesiastical institution itself when it impedes an authentic approach to the Word of the Lord.'

[…] Gutierrez bases his theological thought upon the Book of Exodus [… His] reading of the biblical text is christological. For him (and in this he follows Catholic theology), the creation of the world and the Exodus from Egypt are steps toward the salvific experience of Jesus. As the Jews were liberated from slavery, it is incumbent upon Christians to liberate their society from poverty and exploitation.

From a Jewish perspective, Gutierrez's interpretation of the Exodus is one-dimensional. It lacks any knowledge of rabbinic commentary or contemporary Jewish religious thought […]

The reader of liberation theology has the impression that the Jewish people disappeared after the destruction of the Temple. Neither Gutierrez nor any exponent of the theological liberation refers to the State of Israel and its struggle for liberation [… nor to] the contemporary struggle of the Jewish people and the political consequences of Zionism.

[…]

Jewish immigrants arriving in Latin America in the years 1880–1914 imported social ideas that shaped the trade union movement. Many early union leaders were Jewish, members of the Bund, the Jewish socialist party. Anti-Semitism was inflamed in Argentina in the 1910's and 1920's, when conservative groups accused Jews of being agents of Marxism and promoters of the Bolshevik revolution. Fifty years later, followers of liberation theology accuse the Jewish community of being agents of Wall Street and American imperialism.

Catholic involvement in Latin American anti-Semitism after the First World War was related to two aspects of the Christian attitude toward Jews and Judaism. One was the anti-Judaism of the Church fathers, the teaching of contempt. The other was the consequence of the close spiritual and religious relationship of local churches, especially in the Argentinian church, with French Catholicism, and especially its ideological liaisons with right-wing thought [...]

The Jewish community of Latin America thus shuns any direct dialogue with the Church and Catholicism because of these negative associations as well as recent activities of local priests engaged in fascism and anti-Semitism.

Vatican II's efforts for a reckoning of the soul concerning Jews and Judaism had practically no repercussions in South America [...]

The theology of liberation, sensitive to the economic realities of Latin American life, does not consider either Jews or the Jewish situation as part of its social concern. None of its theologians has recognized the contribution of Jewish workers in the formation of Latin American trade unions and social justice [... nor] attempted to make Latin American society conscious of the lack of pluralism and the special situation of non-Catholic groups, especially the Jews [...]

Theology of liberation needs [...] to overcome the 'teaching of contempt' that has darkened Christian-Jewish relations for centuries. The typological use and abuse of biblical texts faces Jews and Judaism with a new triumphalism, an old experience of Israel in its relationship with Christianity, a refusal to recognize the messianic meaning of Zionism and the social vocation of the Latin American Jewish communities.

Source

Klenicki, Leon, 'The Theology of Liberation: A Latin American Jewish Exploration', *American Jewish Archives* 35, no. 1 (1983), 27–30, 33–9.

Commentary

Born in 1930 to Polish parents who had immigrated to Argentina in the 1920s, Rabbi Leon Klenicki played a major role in relations between Jews and Christians in Latin America and in the United States as the Director of Interfaith Affairs of the Anti-Defamation League from 1984 to 2001. His extensive publications included Jewish liturgical texts adapted for the Latin American world, studies of Argentinian Catholic religious textbooks, commentaries on papal texts, a dictionary of Christian–Jewish dialogue, and an array of essays on Jewish–Christian relations. The excerpted document marks an early interest in what became a long-standing concern with liberation theology.

In the late 1960s, Klenicki recognised liberation theology's potential to show the connections between the gospel of Jesus and the sociopolitical order. He regarded it as a means of awakening Latin American Catholics in particular from their apathy to society's inequities and to the alliance of the church with the wealthy. A few years later Peruvian theologian Gustavo Gutiérrez's 1971 *Teología de la liberación perspectivas* (*A Theology of Liberation*) took the theological world by storm.

Yet, having experienced the antisemitism prevalent in Argentina, Klenicki was sensitive to what was in many respects the erasure of Judaism in Gutiérrez's theology and in that of many who would later write in the liberation mode. Despite the centrality given to the Exodus event, it functioned for many liberation theologians as a mere prelude to the freedom offered by Jesus; Judaism was seemingly an obsolete religious tradition, and the presence of Jews in Latin American societies overlooked. No attention was given to Zionism as a liberating movement offering a homeland to a wandering people, nor to Jewish commitment to labour and trade unions.

In the years since, and partly under Klenicki's influence, Jewish response to liberation theology has been mixed. Rabbi Daniel Cohn-Sherbok has written about the common ground that liberation theology establishes with Jewish thought, especially its emphasis on the historical reality of Jesus as a first-century Jew. Marc Ellis, an outspoken critic of Israel, published *Toward a Jewish Theology of Liberation* in 1987; Desmond Tutu and Gustavo Gutiérrez contributed the foreword to its third expanded edition. In contrast, Adam Gregerman has penned a searing critique of the way certain liberation theologians reprise anti-Jewish stereotypes and vicious images of Jews in their criticisms of Israel, concluding that liberation theology impedes serious dialogue. Much of what Judith Plaskow identified as problematic among Christian feminist theologians (see document 1 above) was similarly at issue among many liberation thinkers: outmoded understandings of Judaism.

Klenicki famously deplored Jewish sociopolitical Christian dialogue that was merely an exchange of 'tea and sympathy'. His wariness of liberation theologies revealed his commitment to speak with candour as well as compassion. His influence, however, transcended his mixed response to liberation themes and is evident in his many publications and warm friendships with church leaders and theologians, as is seen in the 2013 volume in his honour, *Toward the Future: Essays on Jewish–Catholic Relations in Memory of Rabbi León Klenicki*.

Bibliography

Deutsch, Celia, Fisher, Eugene, and Rudin, A. James (eds.), *Toward the Future: Essays on Catholic–Jewish Relations in Memory of Rabbi León Klenicki* (New York: Paulist, 2013).

Gutiérrez, Gustavo, *A Theology of Liberation: History, Politics and Salvation*, trans. Sister Caridad Inda and John Eagleson (Maryknoll: Orbis, 1973). (Originally published as *Teología de la liberación*, 1971.)

Roland, Christopher (ed.), *The Cambridge Companion to Liberation Theology* (Cambridge: Cambridge University Press, 1999).

3

Paul M. van Buren: A Christian Theology of the People Israel *(1983)*

Text

'A Christian theology of the people Israel … asks about the church's duty and ability to hear the testimony of the Jewish people to God.' […]

A Christian theology of Israel *asks*. In this undertaking the church puts questions to itself […] The presupposition of these questions […] is that Israel has something to say which the church needs to hear. The church has always believed that Israel *had* something to say worth hearing, namely, what Israel said in the Scriptures which make up our Old Testament. Here, however, we shall be raising the further question, whether living, postbiblical Israel has something more to say, either in its way of interpreting its Scriptures, or in its further reflections arising out of its continuing history in the covenant with God […]

In a Christian theology of Israel, we ask about the *duty* and *ability* of the church to hear. The question of duty precedes that of ability, on the assumption that living Israel's testimony is willed by God to be heard by the church […]

We are asking about *Israel's* testimony, not ours. That means in part to ask about the Scriptures as Israel's Scriptures, not primarily as our Old Testament; or rather, it is to ask about what can be our Old Testament only as and because it is first of all Israel's Scriptures. A Christian theology of Israel, therefore, will have to listen to Israel's *Halakhah* [law] and *Aggadah* [narrative] as Israel's exegesis of and commentary on covenant existence. It will need to listen to Jewish Rabbis, philosophers, and poets as to those who expounded God's will for this people, that they might become what he had made them: a light for the Gentiles and so for the Gentiles' church, as well as ultimately for the whole world […]

These elaborations of the definition of a Christian theology of Israel lead to perhaps the most fundamental problem for such a theology and for the church: our traditional understanding of how the New Testament is related to the Old. If the church has a duty to listen to Israel, […] it will have to reconsider its traditional view of the relationship between its New and Old Testaments. The pattern of 'promise and fulfillment,' its primary interpretive model, will need to come under the closest scrutiny. To evade this critical examination would undercut the development of a Christian theology of Israel […]

We have defined the task before us as an inquiry into that which God has to say to the church through the testimony and life of the Jewish people. This task only makes sense if Israel is indeed commissioned by God to be his witness before the world, and therefore also before the church, in its life as well as in its words. A theology of Israel would then not only make sense; it would become a necessity for the church, for the same reason that a theology of Jesus Christ is necessary. In both cases, the church would be asking about its faithfulness in listening to and obeying the word of the LORD God of Israel. If this God, the church's God, has set Israel in the world as his witness, then a Christian theology of Israel is no more optional for the church than its Christology […]

A Christian theology of Israel is necessary, […] not only because Israel lives, but because living Israel stands before the church and its universal message and says No. It says that the address of the church's message does not and cannot include Israel […] It rejects the church's 'Old Testament' as a misunderstanding of *Tanakh*, Israel's Scriptures. It rejects the church's claim that all God's promises to Israel have been fulfilled in Christ. It rejects, finally, the church's claim that Jesus of Nazareth was and is the Messiah promised to Israel […]

The fundamental meaning of the Jewish No, which the church should understand therefore, is that it was from the beginning and continues to be an act of fidelity to Torah and Torah's God [...] The theological reality which such a theology must address, then, is that Israel said No to Jesus Christ out of faithfulness to his Father, the God of Israel.

Source

van Buren, Paul M., *A Theology of the Jewish–Christian Reality, Part 2: A Christian Theology of the People Israel* (San Francisco: Harper & Row, 1983), 18–21, 33–4.

Commentary

A scholar of Karl Barth and an analytic philosopher, Paul van Buren (1924–98) came relatively late to Jewish–Christian relations, initially drawn in by the thought of Franz Rosenzweig. Contact with the Jewish world, as he wrote in the 1981 essay 'Probing the Jewish–Christian Reality' in *The Christian Century*, 'opened my eyes to something I had been looking at somewhat casually all along but had never really seen: Israel, the Jewish people, the people of God, was definitely alive'. For the first time he glimpsed 'actual Judaism, the living faith of this living people of God'. 'I was more than fascinated', he wrote: 'I was set to thinking furiously.'

Indeed, his furious thinking became an absorption as he pursued the question of what Christian theology would be if its theologians were to take 'this living people of God' into account. Five books flowed from his pursuit. Particularly noteworthy is his trilogy *A Theology of the Jewish–Christian Reality*, published over the course of nine years (1980–8). In these volumes, van Buren offers a systematic re-examination of and reorientation to a Christian theology that took Judaism seriously. The excerpt presented here is from the middle volume, characterised by his attentiveness to Jewish self-understanding.

Perhaps to contemporary readers, van Buren's insistence that a Christian theology of Israel begins by *asking* will seem commonplace, even mundane. Yet in fact for most of its history, Christian theology arose out of assumed or even imposed understandings of Judaism, building upon familiar tropes of its infidelity, legalism and obsolescence. Yes, the church did always assume Israel had something to say, but it judged Israel's Scriptures as speaking only a word of promise, not the message of fulfilment that came uniquely with Jesus and his church. The church's task now, van Buren argues, is to pay attention to how living Israel interpreted its sacred texts; in so doing, the church will adhere more closely to the 'Torah-faithful Jew Jesus' (p. 238) – a formulation that adumbrates the description of the Vatican's Commission on Religious Relations with the Jews: Jesus Christ as the 'living Torah of God' in its 2015 statement *The Gifts and the Calling of God Are Irrevocable* (see Appendix to Part III, p. 547).

Even at more than forty years' distance, van Buren's conviction that Israel's 'No' is an act of fidelity to God, the covenant and Torah will sound radical to many Christians. To ask a word from living Israel requires the church to commit to valuing the depth and breadth of Jewish interpretation of Torah. Yet from its beginnings until relatively recently, the church has not so much *engaged* Jewish interpretation as rejected or disregarded it altogether – and, consequently, erected some of the components of its Christology on the sand of misunderstanding. Volume 3 of van Buren's trilogy, subtitled *Christ in Context*, took up the task of refashioning a Christology rooted in what he learned from living Israel.

Paul van Buren's work enjoyed extensive circulation in the 1970s and 1980s, appearing not only in theological journals but in publications in liturgical studies and religious education. Today his direct influence may be seen in the work of systematic theologians such as Ellen Charry and Barbara U. Meyer (document 18). When read in the context of developments in biblical studies today, his work seems prescient (see, for example, the excerpt from Amy-Jill Levine and Marc Zvi Brettler; document 17).

Bibliography

Hartman, David, *A Living Covenant: The Innovative Spirit in Traditional Judaism* (New York: Free Press, 1985).

van Buren, Paul M., 'Probing the Jewish–Christian Reality', *The Christian Century* (17–24 June 1981), 665–8.

Williamson, Clark M., *A Guest in the House of Israel: Post-Holocaust Church Theology* (Louisville: Westminster/John Knox, 1993).

4

Irving Greenberg: For the Sake of Heaven and Earth: The New Encounter between Judaism and Christianity *(1986)*

Text

Revelation is in history [...] Reluctantly but inexorably, both religions have been forced to confront their own historicity.

[...] In the Holocaust, Jews discovered they had no choice but to go back into history. If they did not take power, they would be dead. The only way to prevent a recurrence was for Jews to go to their land, establish a state and protect themselves, and to take responsibility so that the covenant people could be kept alive [...]

Christians also have been forced back into history by the impact of this event. Those faithful Christians realized that the evil portrait of Judaism, the whole attempt to assure Christian triumphalism, had become a source of the teaching of contempt and had convicted Christianity or implicated it in a genocide in the face of which it was indifferent or silent. The Holocaust forced Jews and Christians to see that the attempt to protect faith against history was an error, and that both religions can have no credibility in a world in which evil can totally triumph [...] Just as Jews, in response, took up arms and took up the power of the state, so Christians are called simultaneously to purge themselves of the hatred that made them indifferent to others and to take up the responsibility of working in the world to bring perfection. This is the common challenge of both faiths; they can ill afford to go on focusing on the other as *the* enemy.

There is another possible implication. Destruction of the Temple meant that God was more hidden. Therefore, one had to look for God in the more 'secular' area. Living after the Holocaust, the greatest destruction of all time in Jewish history, one would have to say that God is even more hidden. Therefore, the sacred is even more present in every 'secular' area. Building a better world, freeing the slaves, curing sickness, and taking responsibility for the kind of economic perfection that is needed to make this a world of true human dignity – all these activities pose as secular. But in the profoundest sort of way, these activities are where God is most present. When God is most hidden, God is present everywhere. If when God was hidden after the destruction of the Temple, one could find God in the synagogue, then when God is hidden after Auschwitz, one must find God in the street, in the hospital, and in the bar. And that responsibility of holy secularity is the responsibility of all human beings [...]

The real question is: What was God's message when God did not stop the Holocaust? God is calling humans to take full responsibility for the achievement of the covenant. It is their obligation to take up arms against evil and to stop it.

[...] If God wants humans to grow to a final perfection, then the ultimate logic of covenant is for humans to take full responsibility. Taking full responsibility does not imply a human arrogance that dismisses God, or the human arrogance that says more human power is automatically good. 'Covenantal commitment' implies the humility of knowing that human is not God. The human is like God, but is ultimately called by God to be the partner [...] Using this covenantal understanding, one can perceive God as the Presence everywhere – suffering, sharing, participating, and calling. However, trust in God or awareness of God is necessary but not sufficient for living out faith. The awareness moderates the use of power; trust curbs power ethically. But the theological consequence is that without taking power, and without getting involved in history, one is religiously irresponsible. To pray to God as a substitute for taking power is blasphemous [...]

One might suggest that the Holocaust has its primary impact on Judaism. Nevertheless, as a Jewish theologian, I suggest that Christianity also cannot be untouched by the event. At the least, I believe that Christianity will have to enter its second stage. If we follow the Rabbis' model, this stage will be marked by greater 'worldliness' in holiness. The role of the laity would shift from being relatively passive followers in a sacramental religion to full (or fuller) participation [...]

Unless this shift toward wrestling with God takes place, those Christians who seek to correct Christianity vis-à-vis Judaism will be blocked by the fact that within the New Testament itself are hateful images of Jews. Therefore, humans must take full responsibility for repairing the breach, but not out of arrogance or idolatry. It must be done without making God into the convenient one who says what one wants to hear. Out of the fullest responsibility to its covenant partner, Christianity can undergo the renewal that I believe it must undertake.

The unfinished agenda of the Jewish-Christian dialogue is the recognition of the profound interrelationship between both [...] Humans are called in this generation to renew the covenant – a renewal that will demand openness to each other, learning from each other, and a respect for the distinctiveness of the ongoing validity of each other. Such openness puts no religious claim beyond possibility, but places the completion of total redemption at the center of the agenda.

Source

Greenberg, Irving, *For the Sake of Heaven and Earth: The New Encounter between Judaism and Christianity* (Philadelphia: The Jewish Publication Society, 2004), 158–61.

Commentary

Irving ('Yitz') Greenberg (b. 1933) has been at the forefront of dialogue with Christians for over fifty years. A Modern Orthodox rabbi with a doctorate in American history from Harvard University, Greenberg's involvement with Christianity began, ironically, with his initial immersion in Holocaust literature in 1961–2 while serving as a Fulbright lecturer at Tel Aviv University. Devastated by what he was learning and propelled by his anger at the indifference and complicity of Christians, Greenberg entered into the fledgling dialogue in the spirit of an avenging angel, only to be touched by the commitment of Christian scholars such as Alice and Roy Eckardt (see Chapter 8, p. 439), John Pawlikowski (document 15), Eva Fleischner (document 7), Franklin Littell and Krister Stendahl (Chapter 8, p. 418), among others. Thus began his relentless resolve to face the evil of the Shoah while edified by the learned passion and witness of his dialogue partners.

The essay from which the present document is excerpted appears in a volume consisting of seven essays published between 1967 and 2000, supplemented by an introductory chapter chronicling Greenberg's personal journey and a lengthy essay offering a vision of Judaism and Christianity as 'covenantal partners' in postmodernity. The theme of covenant runs throughout the volume. In this 1986 essay, Greenberg argues that God's hiddenness during the Shoah demands that humans take responsibility for their covenantal relationship by assuming a more active part in exercising power in order to advance redemption.

Both Jews and Christians must, Greenberg writes, be committed to facing their history, that is, to come to terms with their respective traditions in their contingencies and in their complacency in the face of evil. For Christians in particular, this means being shaken by the Shoah, awakened from the slumber induced by otherworldly pieties and nurtured by a sense of superiority to Judaism. As German theologian Johann Baptist

Metz wrote in *The Emergent Church*: 'Ask yourselves if the theology you are learning is such that it could remain unchanged before and after Auschwitz. If this be the case, be on your guard' (p. 28).

Greenberg also raises the necessity of Christians confronting the 'hateful images of Jews' found in the New Testament. On this matter, abundant scholarship, available in a variety of modes, testifies to the seriousness with which the interpretational mandate has been taken up. At the popular level, however, less sensitivity to the toxic effects of troubling texts is evident. Just as Greenberg summons Christians to learn from history, so too, he insists, must they be coached to *hear* the problematic claims of the New Testament writers, *situate* them in literary and historical contexts and *seek to repair* the harm resulting from sacred texts used to denigrate the Jewish people over time. The magnitude of this responsibility cannot be overemphasised.

As of 2023, Greenberg continues his advocacy of Jewish–Christian dialogue, often in collaboration with his wife, Blu Greenberg.

Bibliography

Ferzinger, Adam, Freud-Kandel, Miri, and Bayme, Steven (eds.), *Irving Greenberg and Modern Orthodoxy: The Road Not Taken* (Boston: Academic Studies Press, 2019).

Fleischner, Eva (ed.), *Auschwitz: Beginning of a New Era?* (New York: Cathedral Church of St. John the Divine, 1977).

Metz, Johann Baptist, *The Emergent Church* (London: SCM Press, 1981).

5

Israel Jacob Yuval: Two Nations in Your Womb *(1999)*

Text

While a comparative examination of explicit religious ideas tends to reveal and to emphasize the difference between the two religions, the language of symbols and ceremonies reveals the common means by which both religions were able to elucidate and refine their independent identities. This common language should not mislead us into thinking it constituted any sort of closeness between the religions. To the contrary: hostility and rivalry demand a common language for formulating diametrically opposed positions, because conflicting conceptual messages can only be conveyed through symbols understood by both sides […]

The new Passover liturgy – the story and the remembering – was created in Judaism and Christianity in parallel fashion. In both religions, the contents of the Passover night were shaped by a story that begins in 'disgrace' and ends in 'glory,' a story intended to offer consolation and hope for Redemption. The stories themselves are quite different from one another, but despite their differences, there are clear textual parallels between them […]

[… M]ore than fifty years ago, two very important Christian texts were discovered that justify a reexamination of our understanding of the relationship between the

Talmudic Passover and the Christian Easter, particularly that of the *Quartodecimani* [proto-Christians of Israel, Syria and Asia Minor who celebrated Easter on the 14th of Nisan in contrast to those of Rome and Alexandria, who celebrated Easter on Sunday]. One is the homily *Peri Pascha* by Melito of Sardis, and the other is a work of the same name by Origen [...]

[... H]istorical criticism ought to lead us to the conclusion that ancient Christianity and Mishnaic Judaism are in a certain sense two sister religions that took shape in the same period and with a common background of subjugation and destruction. Hence, there is no reason not to assume that there was at times a parallel and even common development of the two religions, during which Judaism also internalized religious ideas from its sister and rival religion. These two religions did not emerge as two separate entities with clear identities. During the second and third centuries, there were all kinds of Jews and all kinds of Christians, all of them engaged in the struggle against pagan Rome, hence their agreement on the centrality of the messianic idea and the centrality of Passover [...]

By reviewing [...] the various sections of the Haggadah [...] we find ourselves harnessing some of the central sections of the Passover Haggadah to the chariot of anti-Christian polemic [... T]ime has come to reevaluate the close and difficult struggle between the great religious reformers, both Christian and Jewish, during the generations following the Destruction [of Jerusalem in 70 CE]. Hence, the literature of the Talmudic Sages should be read not only as a source for Christian ideas and ceremonies, but also as a response to the challenge posed by Christianity to Judaism, for the Oral Torah is, in the deepest sense, a Jewish answer to the Christian Torah, the New Testament.

Source

Yuval, Israel Jacob, *Two Nations in Your Womb: Perceptions of Jews and Christians in Late Antiquity and the Middle Ages*, trans. Barbara Harshav and Jonathan Chipman (Berkeley: University of California Press, 2006), 33, 68–70, 89–90. (Hebrew original published 1999.)

Commentary

At least until the 1980s, many scholars assumed that Judaism was the 'mother' of Christianity; a related, popular metaphor is that Judaism forms the 'root' of Christianity. Israeli historian Israel Jacob Yuval (b. 1949) unsettled such assumptions through his groundbreaking 1999 study of the intricate connection between Passover and Easter. Thus, he strengthened the claim that they are 'sister' religions contending with each other during their formative process after Rome's destruction of Jerusalem in 70 CE. Since Passover also served as a key motif in the New Testament, this festival of liberation became both a common and yet a contested symbol. In the case of Judaism, however, its dispute with its sibling tradition was encoded in narrative and ritual rather than in explicit argumentation, with the Haggadah ('telling') as the major exemplar.

Yuval highlights aspects of the Haggadah, a complex, post-Second Temple composition constituting the script of the Seder meal and bearing similarity to proto-Christian texts from the second and third centuries, such as the sermon (*c.* 170 CE) of Melito, bishop of Sardis, *Peri Pascha* (*On the Passover*; see Chapter 2, p. 77). His homily – what Yuval terms a 'Christian Haggadah' – elegantly elucidates Jesus as the 'Passover of our salvation'. Figures such as Isaac, Jacob and Joseph were 'types' who prefigured Jesus, the 'lamb who was slaughtered', and for which Israel bears responsibility: 'The King of Israel is destroyed by an Israelite hand' (Melito, *Peri Pascha* 96). In the ninth-century church, Melito's refrain of an ungrateful Israel became a reproach to Jews; by the fourteenth century, the Reproaches were chanted as part of the veneration of the cross in the Roman Catholic and Byzantine rites on Good Friday: 'My people, what have I done to you? How have I offended you? Answer me! / I led you out of Egypt, from slavery to freedom, but you led your Savior to the cross.' (Since Vatican II, the Reproaches are no longer part of the official liturgy of Good Friday.)

If the community of Christ's followers considered Jews to be ungrateful, the Jewish response came encoded in song originating in the medieval period, the *Dayyenu* (or *Dayenu*, 'It would have been enough'). For example: 'If He had fed us the manna and had not given us the Shabbat; [it would have been] enough for us.'

Yuval's densely argued analysis of the fraught relationship between Jewish and proto-Christian understandings of Passover became a significant catalyst for works that show the complex interactions between the two traditions in late antiquity and the Middle Ages. By emphasising the centrality of symbol and ritual, Yuval has shown that Judaism is related to Christianity not as mother to daughter but as a sibling engaged in a 'mutual flow of ideas'.

Bibliography

Bradshaw, Paul, and Hoffman, Lawrence (eds.), *Passover and Easter: Origin and History to Modern Times* (Notre Dame: University of Notre Dame Press, 1999).

Cantalamessa, Raniero, *Easter in the Early Church: An Anthology of Jewish and Early Christian Texts*, trans. James M. Quigley and Joseph T. Lienhard (Collegeville: Liturgical Press, 1993).

6

Paula Fredriksen: 'The Birth of Christianity and the Origins of Christian Anti-Judaism' (2002)

Text

How, given Christianity's origins in Judaism, did Christianity come to be so anti-Jewish? When did this happen? Or, to address the same issues differently: When did the form of Christianity most familiar to Western culture begin? [...]

Christian antipathy toward Jews and Judaism began when Christian Hellenistic Jewish texts, such as the letters of Paul and the Gospels, began to circulate among total outsiders, that is, among Gentiles without any connection to the synagogue and without any attachment to Jewish traditions of practice and interpretation. At that point, the intra-Jewish polemics preserved in these texts began to be understood as condemnations of Judaism *tout court* ['without qualification']. The next stage intensified the process, by taking the outsider's perspective to the text of the Septuagint. By the early second century, the engagement of intellectuals enriched the controversy by putting it on a philosophical basis, thereby integrating what otherwise might have remained secondhand name-calling into comprehensive, rational, total worldviews. Christian theologies of many different sorts were thereby born.

Orthodoxy's anti-Judaism was the most strident, because orthodoxy's stance was the most complicated, both offensive (against Jewish claims to the Bible as well as against other Christian interpretations of it) and defensive (why claim the Book if they would not, in a sense, practice what they preached, and start living according to Jewish law?). But then why, by the fourth century, did imperial patronage not soften their tone? After all, by then this church had won. Its Christian competition was on the run; its communities were subsidized by government largesse; its bishops had powers that their secular counterparts [...] could only envy. What was true in the second century was still true [...] in the fourth: Jews had no temple and no territory. Why then, at this point, does the *contra Iudaeos* tradition only become worse – more strident, more comprehensive, more furious? It metastasizes through all known genres of surviving Christian literature, including systematic theologies, biblical commentaries, martyr stories, church histories, antiheretical tracts, preaching handbooks, sermons. Why?

It spread, I think, because of the Diaspora synagogue [...] Synagogues are thriving; in places like Sardis, they are monumental. Gentiles keep dropping by, cocelebrating Sabbaths and holidays, picking up the occasional Jewish practice, hearing Bible stories read and psalms sung in Greek (or, in the West, in Latin) [...] Fourth-century Gentile Christians, despite the anti-Jewish ideology of their own bishops, kept Saturdays as their day of rest, accepted gifts of matzo from Jewish friends at Passover, indeed still celebrated Easter according to when Jews kept Passover. This last was particularly aggravating to bishops, and even to emperors. Gentile Christians made the effort to take oaths in front of Torah scrolls, tended lamps for Jewish friends on the Sabbath and on Jewish holidays, had rabbis bless their fields, and let their children marry one another. Occasionally, and despite heavy penalties, these Christians even converted to Judaism. We can still hear the frustration and plaintive anger that this behavior inspired in a sermon, preached in August of 387 by the orthodox bishop of Antioch, John Chrysostom [...]

The anti-Judaism of the ideologues, the theologians and the bishops, increased in volume. Their pitch rose with their frustration. As long as Mediterranean social life [...] [and] the culture of the Hellenistic city with its long tradition of religious openness still lived – and it did live, well into the late Empire – Jews and Gentiles still mixed and mingled, saw each other at the baths and at the theaters, worked with each other on town councils, lived together, and, on Sabbaths and the holidays, occasionally heard Scripture together. When this changed, in the early Middle Ages, this tradition of civility changed too, and Christian anti-Judaism led more directly to violence, even murder [...]

How did Christian anti-Judaism happen? Gentiles interpreted the intra-Jewish disputes of the earliest Christian movement as the condemnation of all Judaism by those parties to the dispute with whom these Gentiles now identified. When did this happen? Toward the turn of the first century through the first half of the second, when warring Gentile Christian intellectuals staked out their territory and systematized their convictions into theologies. When, then, does Christianity begin? It is twice-born, once in the mid-second century, and again after Constantine, in the fourth. And in that second birth especially, orthodox Christian anti-Judaism increased in range and in intensity.

The answer to a fourth, and more important question, I leave to you: What, knowing this history, is today's Christian to do?

Source

Fredriksen, Paula, 'The Birth of Christianity and the Origins of Christian Anti-Judaism', in Fredriksen, Paula, and Reinhartz, Adele (eds.), *Jesus, Judaism, and Christian Anti-Judaism: Reading the New Testament after the Holocaust* (Louisville: Westminster John Knox, 2002), 28–30.

Commentary

Paula Fredriksen (b. 1951), an eminent historian and biblical scholar, is one of the most prolific authors writing on Jewish–Christian relations. Her influence is particularly noted in her extensive work on Augustine and on the Apostle Paul, both the subject of lengthy books and an impressive array of essays manifesting her deep knowledge of Graeco-Roman culture and biblical exegesis.

The essay from which the excerpt is taken constitutes a clear and concise account of how and why leaders of the church-in-formation articulated discipleship to Jesus Christ in a manner that denigrated Judaism. In her concluding paragraph, she challenges readers to consider the antidote to this model of binary opposition that left such a tragic legacy.

Of particular note is her recognition of the significance of a common culture – *paideia* – of the educated Graeco-Roman elite of its male citizens, a number of whom would prove significant in framing proto-Christian thinking in the second and third centuries CE. Although their arguments proceeded from different vantage points, each employed the method of comparison and contrast, caricaturing Jewish ways of practice and belief. Valentinus and his followers, for example, regarded matter as inferior. Influenced by Gnosticism, they taught that Israel missed the point of its scriptures by emphasising fleshy matters (e.g., dietary norms, circumcision) rather than Christ's true spiritual revelation. The bishop Marcion, also influenced by Gnosticism, held that the Septuagint, though sacred for Jews, bore no relevance for followers of Christ. Ultimately, Valentinus' and Marcion's perspectives did not prevail, but those of a third school of thought did.

Associated with intellectuals such as Justin Martyr, Tertullian, Irenaeus and Hippolytus, this philosophy became the orthodox church tradition. Israel's scriptures were not to be rejected but to be read spiritually. Jews, in contrast, were mired in a literal reading, thus rendering them impervious to the spiritual dimension and thereby misinterpreting their own scriptures. These early church writers judged the outcries of the prophets as an indictment of Israel's sinfulness rather than as a manifestation of Judaism's profound self-criticism (see Chapter 2).

Central to Fredriksen's argument is her insistence that orthodox theologians, lacking contact with Jewish life, had little reliable basis for their comparison-contrast. Without interacting with Jewish communities, the orthodox theologians were in effect arguing against 'hermeneutical Jews', not flesh-and-blood Jews. The irony: these intellectuals accusing Jews of misreading their scriptures were in fact misreading Judaism. It was an abstraction against which to exercise their finely honed rhetorical skills in the course of articulating a theological justification for Christianity.

Once the orthodox position became dominant, particularly after Constantine and the imperial legislation of 380, its anti-Jewish hermeneutic intensified, becoming, as Fredriksen writes, 'more strident, more comprehensive, more furious'. She attributes this increased antipathy to the reality of life on the ground: Judaism was flourishing in the diaspora, despite its loss of Jerusalem and its temple, and Christians were insufficiently observing the borderlines the orthodox theological authorities were drawing. In short, church leaders perceived Judaism as a threat to Christian identity.

How, Fredriksen asks, do contemporary Christians repair this legacy of our ancestors in faith, who in arguing for the truth of following the way of Jesus Christ, defamed Judaism? How, indeed?

Bibliography

Runesson, Anders, 'Jewish and Christian Interaction from the First to the Fifth Centuries', in Esler, Philip F. (ed.), *The Early Christian World*, vol. 1 (New York: Routledge, 2000), 244–65.

7

Eva Fleischner: 'The Spirituality of Pius XII' (2002)

Text

If Pius XII is eventually destined for sainthood in the Roman Catholic Church, I suspect that the spiritual features highlighted in this chapter will be crucial in driving the canonization process forward [...] Pius was a man of great holiness and interiority [...]

Why, then, the controversy surrounding his beatification? [... T]o beatify or canonize a person surrounded by controversy is unwise, as well as bad politics [...] In the face of one of the most brutal dictatorships the world has known, which led to the murder of millions of innocent Jews and other victims, neither Pius's personal holiness and trust in prayer nor his chosen tool of quiet diplomacy was enough.

Clearly, Pius was a sensitive man, not impervious to the sufferings of the war's victims, whether within or outside the Church. Nevertheless, the means with which he chose to fight the evil were inadequate. What was needed was a strong, prophetic voice [...]

In early April 2000, I participated in [a] King's College seminar [...] One of the scholars, Gershon Greenberg, an Orthodox Jew, [... asked]: 'There is a question I need to ask of you, especially of the Catholics present [...] Did the question of martyrdom never arise? Did the pope, and those around him, ever consider that he should perhaps be ready to be killed, if he spoke out publicly against the evil of Nazism and in defense of the Jews?'

None of us had an answer for Gershon. I know the idea had not even occurred to me. I have since asked myself, Why not? After all, some of the early popes had been martyred [...]

Oscar Romero, the [assassinated] Archbishop of San Salvador [...] was no politician. He was conservative by nature [...] But he saw and listened. And what he heard and saw radicalized him [...] It was too much for those in power, and they gave orders for his murder, which was carried out so efficiently that a single bullet [...] went through Romero's heart as he celebrated Mass. Instead of being silenced, however, his voice and example still reverberate throughout the world.

'It would be sad,' Romero said shortly before his death, 'if priests were not being killed when Salvadorans are being killed.' [...] He was an authentic martyr, not only for his Christian faith but also for justice [...]

With Gershon Greenberg's question still fresh in my mind, I began to wonder if [...] Romero's might not be the kind of witness the world has wanted – however impossibly – from Pius XII [... W]hy martyrdom, at least as a possibility, was not even considered as a viable option during the Shoah. Had the Church become too big and powerful? [...] In reading the Vatican documents published in ADSS [*Actes et documents du Saint Siège relatifs à la Seconde Guerre mondiale*], one often gets the impression that 'the Jews' are an abstraction – one group of victims among many others [...]

[... T]he impact of a Mohandas Gandhi or a Martin Luther King, Jr., continues to have power to inspire. If this is so, then no matter what we, or any number of archivists and historians, may find out about Pope Pius XII, the archival findings will come up short [...]

[...] Many women and men today find Pius's concept and embodiment of holiness [...] too narrow and other-worldly. Particularly amidst the Holocaust's shadows, they doubt its fidelity to the teaching and example of Jesus: 'Greater love than this no one has, than to lay down one's life for one's friends.'

Source

Fleischner, Eva, 'The Spirituality of Pius XII', in Rittner, Carol, and Roth, John K. (eds.), *Pope Pius XII and the Holocaust* (London: Bloomsbury Academic, 2016), 132–6. (Originally published by Continuum, 2002.)

Commentary

The many volumes written about Eugenio Pacelli/Pope Pius XII as the apostolic nuncio to Germany (1920–30), Vatican Secretary of State (1930–39) and as pope (1939–58), and especially his alleged silence during the Holocaust, reveal a contentious quest to understand this sophisticated diplomat and ecclesiastical figure (see also Chapter 8, pp. 424–5). Arguments over his role have been a source of long-standing tension between Jews and Catholics, particularly those on the right, who have mounted a vigorous defence of the pope and campaigned for his beatification, at times drawing on antisemitic stereotypes. The scrutiny will only intensify now that the Vatican has, since 2020, opened its extensive archives – some 16 million pages housed in 20,000 archival units – to scholars of the years 1939–58.

Viennese-born Eva Fleischner (1925–2020) was involved in an earlier initiative in 1999 as one of six scholars the Vatican appointed to the International Catholic–Jewish Historical Commission. Mandated to raise relevant questions and issues regarding previously released documents related to Pope Pius XII, the commission examined the eleven volumes of the *Actes et documents du Saint Siège relatifs à la Seconde Guerre mondiale* (*Acts and Documents of the Holy See Relating to the Second World War*), consisting of diplomatic correspondence, notes and memoranda from meetings with diplomats and church leaders. Fleischner and her colleagues submitted forty-seven challenging questions that remain unaddressed by the Vatican. The newly opened archives may provide answers to, or at least new perspectives on, the commission's inquiries.

Fleischner based her 2002 essay on Pius' spirituality on letters to the German bishops from 1939–44 in the second volume of the *Actes et documents*. The letters, she finds, reveal him as a prayerful person, devoted to Mary as the 'mother of Christianity', and imbued with the church's liturgical life. He understood suffering as a purifying experience and sought to help the German bishops find meaning in the suffering of the war years. He also spoke of his own suffering as one burdened by the responsibilities of the papacy and of his uncertainty regarding the best course of action vis-à-vis the Nazi regime: 'Where the pope would like to shout, he is forced to wait and keep silence; where he would act and help, he must wait patiently' (p. 131).

Fleischner, one of the first to teach Holocaust studies in higher education in the United States as well as a deeply learned and committed Catholic, concluded that Pius XII exemplified a traditional Catholic piety. He attempted to live in accord with God's will and in concert with his responsibility to safeguard the church. His piety, however, was, as she concludes, 'too narrow and other-worldly', ill-fitting the prophetic witness for which our world still yearns. Deeply moved by Gershon Greenberg's question about whether the pope's spirituality might have encompassed a willingness to be martyred, Fleischner points to the continuing inspiration of Bishop Oscar Romero's prophetic witness that led to and flows from his assassination in 1980, which ultimately led to his canonisation in 2018.

Fleischner's foray into the spiritual grounding of Pope Pius XII's faith adds a theological dimension to the historian's task: to what extent did otherworldly pieties – especially passive acceptance of suffering – cloak the obligation to counter evil? As Jews and Christians together probe more deeply into the Shoah, they must attend to theologies of suffering, including this question: in what circumstances does one's spiritual integrity require an openness to martyrdom?

Bibliography

Rittner, Carol, and Roth, John K. (eds.), *The Memory of Goodness: Eva Fleischner and Her Contributions to Holocaust Studies* (Greensburg: Seton Hill University, 2022).

Ventresca, Robert, *Soldier of Christ: The Life of Pope Pius XII* (Cambridge, MA: Harvard University Press, 2013).

8

Peter Phan: 'Jews and Judaism in Asian Theology' (2005)

Text

Despite these vestiges of mostly unintentional anti-Judaism, Asian liberation theology offers rich resources to construct a post-Holocaust theology that serves well the cause of Christian-Jewish dialogue [...]

While Orthodox Jewish theologians have generally tended to minimize the negative impact of the Holocaust on the Jewish belief in God, most Jewish and Christian Holocaust theologians maintain that the Holocaust has shattered the traditional belief in God, that is, a God who is both infinitely good and omnipotent [...]

With their reflections on the human-divine relationship, Asian liberation theologians can offer a significant contribution to the project of reconceptualizing God in a manner appropriate to our post-Holocaust time [...] Choan-Seng Song rejects the 'God of retribution' and argues for the God of compassion. Describing the compassionate God as 'the speaking God' (sometimes in anger), 'the listening God,' and 'the remembering God,' Song goes on to speak of God as 'the mute God.' Jesus' Abba-God, who has spoken, listened, and remembered throughout Jesus' life, Song suggests, became the mute God when his Son died on the cross. More precisely, the God of Jesus was shocked into silence by grief [...] Was God silent during the Holocaust, not because God had abandoned God's covenanted people or was absent from them, but because God was shocked into silence by the horror of their sufferings?

But silence, Song points out, is not necessarily a sign of weakness; it can also be a 'silence of protest.' Just as Jesus' silence before the religious authorities and the Roman court was a silence of protest, God's silence at the cross was a silence of protest: 'God did not respond to Jesus' cry, not because God had abandoned him, but because God's horror and grief must have turned into silent protest. Look! God must have been filling the air with silent grief and protest saying, "What have you human beings done to Jesus, 'my beloved Son'?" Was God not protesting with horror and grief during the Holocaust: "Look! What have you human beings, Nazis and otherwise, done to Israel, my beloved and chosen people?"'

Furthermore, God's silence is not just grief and protest. For Song, it is also 'a silence of pity (*karuna*)': 'It is not just anger. It is not simply grief. It is not merely a protest. It, above all, must be pity, *karuna*, the matrix, the womb, engaged in the creation of life and nourishment of it.' […]

… [T]he God of compassion is not an 'omnipotent' God. Song laments the fact that 'the answer of traditional theology to this world of power is a powerful God.' […] Rather, the God of compassion is the God who has 'the power to love others and to suffer with them.' […]

'A tearful God may invite our sympathy but not our trust and confidence.' What is needed is the God of powerful grace […] But this powerful grace, Song argues, is not available to us until in faith we become active participants in its working in history, until in faith we get involved in the struggle against the power that oppresses us.

Source

Phan, Peter C., 'Jews and Judaism in Asian Theology', *Gregorianum* 86, no. 4 (2005), 821–4.

Commentary

Born in Vietnam in 1946, Peter Phan (Phan Đình Cho) emigrated to the United States in 1975 as the government of South Vietnam was collapsing. Having left his homeland with virtually nothing, he took a job as a refuse collector upon his arrival in Texas. Already in the midst of completing a doctoral degree in Rome, Phan went on to acquire two more doctoral degrees and to produce a prodigious publication record, revealing wide-ranging expertise in, among other subjects, eschatology, trinitarian thought, Christology, religious pluralism and Christianity in Asia.

The excerpt begins *in medias res*, so a word of explanation is in order. Phan, acutely conscious of Christianity's theological antisemitism, opens the essay by tracing Jewish migration to Asia and documenting how seventeenth-century missionaries, steeped in European culture, transmitted anti-Jewish teachings in the course of their evangelising missions. Phan shows how disparagement of Judaism and supersessionist claims continue to persist in Asian theologies, drawing on the work of the influential Asian theologians Aloysius Pieris, a Sri Lankan Jesuit, and Choan-Seng Song, a Taiwanese Presbyterian, as cases in point. Their works are replete with conventional stereotypes of Judaism, including Song's depiction of a 'God of retribution' in contrast to the 'Abba' God of Jesus.

Phan, however, regards the theological antisemitism of Pieris and Song as 'vestiges of mostly unintentional anti-Judaism' insofar as it is a consequence of their own theological formation and lack of connection with Jewish communities, particularly because of Asia's minuscule Jewish population. Nevertheless, Phan sees Song's work as providing a possibility of meaningful dialogue between Asian liberation theology and post-Holocaust thought, especially with those for whom God can no longer be understood as omnipotent.

Later in the essay, Phan explores other connections, such as between post-Holocaust thought and the work of Korean *minjung* theologians (those attentive to the oppressed and exploited) on the concept of *han*, which means something like unresolved bitterness against an experience of injustice. Resolving one's *han* necessitates a spiritual discipline that allows solidarity with other victims; it involves a movement from self-obsession to altruism.

Well-intentioned but misguided missionaries may have exported theological anti-semitism to Asia, but Asian theologians, responsive to situations of injustice, are articulating responses ripe with possibility for dialogue with Jews. Phan's attentiveness to theological antisemitism as it has been exported by the west is an important desideratum for grasping the protean character of global antisemitism. Moreover, his knowledge of Jewish life and criticism of Christian supersessionist theologies constitute a valuable contribution to systematic and comparative theologies.

Bibliography

Phan, Peter C., *Asian Christianities: History, Theology, Practice* (Maryknoll: Orbis, 2018).
Song, Choan-Seng, *Jesus, the Crucified People* (New York: Crossroad, 1990).
Sugirtharajah, R. S. (ed.), *Asian Faces of Jesus* (Maryknoll: Orbis, 1993).

9

Alain Marchadour and David Neuhaus:
The Land, the Bible, and History *(2007)*

Text

Although the issue of the Land is profoundly rooted in the Bible, we are supremely conscious that the Bible does not offer us ready-made solutions to resolve our contemporary conflicts. The present situation in the Holy Land is the result of many of the complex political, social, economic, human, and religious factors […]

The territorial imperative and the conflicts it engenders have always been an element of the history of humankind. The situation in Israel and Palestine, then, is not unique. With regard to this Holy Land, many […] propose variant and diverse readings of the situation and sometimes even suggest solutions. For our part, we have no intention of taking the place of the politicians and political leaders who must search for possible solutions that will bring about the necessary compromise for justice and peace.

We believe, however, that the present discourse of the Church does provide possibilities and openings that might inspire Christians and all people of good faith in approaching what seems like an inextricable conflict between Israelis and Palestinians. We propose that the fundamental insights of the Apostolic Letter *Redemptionis anno*, published by the late Pope John Paul II in 1984 on Jerusalem as sacred heritage of all believers, is a coherent starting point. In its conclusion, this letter reviews all the aspects of the Land and particularly the city of Jerusalem that a Christian must take into account. These aspects include the particular status of the holy places, the situation of the local Christians in the Land, the role of the Bible in clarifying the vocation of the Holy Land, the tragic history of the Jewish people and the creation of the State of Israel, the dramatic situation of the Palestinian people with the burning issue of the refugees, the importance of Islam and the place of Muslims in the ongoing debate, and finally the requirements of justice for lasting peace. In the light of the multiple and complex claims and requirements, each observer is called to examine how his or her own reading of the situation might be partial, focusing on one element, be it, for example, the question of justice for the Palestinians or reconciliation with the Jews. Taking into account all the elements might stretch us beyond simplistic and single-minded ideologies. Remaining true to the multiple elements involved is at the root of a prophetic stance that must be the Church's as all men and women of good will continue to search for ways to bring peace and justice, pardon and reconciliation, prosperity and security for all the inhabitants of God's Land […]

Our presentation of the position of the Catholic Church is in radical opposition to this kind of fundamentalist discourse [among some Christian Zionists] that focuses on eschatological and apocalyptic themes, often ignoring the biblical values of peace, justice, and pardon […]

[… T]he Land, as it is described in the biblical narrative, takes on an exemplary value for all humanity in all times […] In many different places all over the globe, the land, instead of being a place of covenant and reconciliation, is still a place of exploitation and injustice […]

Being rooted in a land is essential for any human being; the Bible eloquently shows this in underlining the concrete dimension of a land 'that flows with milk and honey.' […] Attributing to God righteousness and justice, the Bible transforms categories of human law, equity, and justice into the very grounds of divine revelation itself. These qualities of human government on earth are sacred in the eyes of God.

Source

Marchadour, Alain, and Neuhaus, David, *The Land, the Bible, and History: Toward the Land That I Will Show You* (New York: Fordham University Press, 2007), 195–8, 200–1.

Commentary

As denizens of Israel, authors Alain Marchadour (b. 1937) and David Neuhaus (b. 1962) experience it as a 'land of breathtaking beauty and mind-boggling diversity, of troubling complexity and intense passions, of mystical attachment and blood-curdling claims of exclusivity, a fascinating land because of its history, both human and divine' (p. 5). As biblical scholars, they believe that the diverse ways scripture speaks of the Land offer wisdom for the communities who regard it as sacred. As Catholic priests, they seek to draw upon the church's modern modes of biblical interpretation that honour the socio-cultural and literary dimensions of the texts, thereby countering fundamentalist and Christian Zionist readings that tend to manipulate meaning according to the interpreter.

In the second major section of their book, Marchadour and Neuhaus draw explicitly and at some length on contemporary Catholic statements about the Land – teaching that they acknowledge may appear disjointed and overly cautious because of the complexity and political delicacy of the issues. They focus in particular on the relatively unknown 1984 apostolic letter *Redemptoris anno* by Pope John Paul II, which they believe best connects the major complexities of the church's relationship with Israel as viewed after Vatican II (1962–5).

In their analysis of *Redemptoris anno*, the authors highlight key areas that necessitate nuanced understanding. One involves the reverence for Christian attachment to the Land and the Land's sacramentality insofar as it bears witness to the covenantal tradition and the memory of Jesus. A second issue concerns interpretation of biblical texts on the Land. Interpretation requires recognition of varying contexts and the multiplicity of voices, which fundamentalist approaches miss. Third, Christians must develop sensitivity to the interreligious dimensions of the Land, including Jewish and Muslim claims as well as the situation of the Palestinian people, including its Christian minority (less than 1 per cent in the Palestinian Territories). Fourth, pursuing justice and peace in the Middle East and particularly in the Holy Land requires acknowledgement of the legitimate rights of both Israeli and Palestinian claims and fostering relationships with representatives of both peoples.

Marchadour and Neuhaus are mindful that the Catholic Church cannot assume the high moral ground when it issues statements on Israel, citing Jewish historian Pinchas Lapide's characterisation of Christian behaviour towards Jews as 'strangely ambivalent' – loving Israel in the abstract as 'the people of the Bible'/'the Old Covenant', but in the realm of flesh and blood treating Jews with hostility.

Marchadour and Neuhaus offer a reading of current ecclesial discourse they believe offers possibilities and openings that might inspire not only Christians but all persons of good faith to approach the seemingly intractable issues of the Land. Possibilities and openings are not everything. But they refute those who use the Bible to justify highly partisan positions.

Bibliography

Cunningham, Philip A., Langer, Ruth, and Svartvik, Jesper (eds.), *Enabling Dialogue about the Land: A Resource Book for Jews and Christians* (New York: Paulist, 2020).

Davies, W. D., *The Territorial Dimension of Judaism* (Berkeley: University of California Press, 1982).

van Ruiten, Jacques, and de Vos, J. Cornelius (eds.), *The Land of Israel in Bible, History and Theology* (Leiden: Brill, 2009).

10

Willie James Jennings: The Christian Imagination: Theology and the Origins of Race *(2010)*

Text

The church is always turned toward Israel by its very life. If, in fact, the church has come to be precisely through the witness of Israel to the world through Jesus, then by implication Israel by its life always witnesses the true God, a witness forever acknowledged and received by the church […]

Both church and Israel witness to the world of the one true God. The communion that constitutes Christian life and identity should echo something strangely identifiable in living Israel [...]

If Christian social imagination is ever going to be turned back toward the possibilities of communion, then it must be brought back into the original relationship – of Israel and the Gentiles. But by this return I am not simply affirming interreligious dialogue between Judaism and Christianity, although such dialogue is close to the heart of the matter. A painful hollowness characterizes much Jewish-Christian interreligious dialogue precisely because it builds on the naturalization of the racial imagination. Until we clearly reckon with the awesome power of the racial calculus deeply embedded in the theological vision of the Western world, no amount of exacting exegesis, careful theological clarification of doctrinal differences, or parsing of the connections or distinctions between Jewish and Christian historical liturgical trajectories will bring us to the deepest possibilities of communion.

The return to the original relationship of Jews and Gentiles is blocked by the advent of whiteness and its deeply embedded social performances in the pedagogical, economic, and cultural relations of the Western world. The return I envision brings us back to bodies, and the formation of racialized bodies. We must think through to the utter limits of the racial calculus to expose its deepest fault lines. We must do this in order to tear open racial identity so as to reveal the original relation – exposing it afresh to our social imaginations. If whiteness became the fascinating reality, as that form of identity inside of which all other identities could be imagined, then walking away from or renouncing or questioning existence within white identity is no simple matter. There are, however, two bodies inscribed in the racial calculus that exists in a crucial position in relation to its utter limits and its fault lines, the (racialized) Jewish body and the black body. The way forward for a renewed Christian social imagination will be greatly aided by meditating on the racialized bodies of blacks and Jews in modernity. Such a meditation would allow us to peer through the cracks of the modern racial calculus and discern fragments of the original situation of Israel and Gentiles, of Israel and a Gentile church, of the Jewish body and the Gentile body joined [...]

By carefully attending to the realities of modernity constituted around and signified by the black and Jewish body Christians might be able to gather what they are in desperate need of, namely, a clear, unobstructed view of a redemptive word spoken to Israel and the Gentiles. However, the significance of these bodies will be fully understood only as Christians allow black and Jewish situations to illumine the white body and the constructing realities of whiteness. The irony of the history of Jewish-black relations is that in the midst of sociopolitical and literary-artistic collaborations and with a parallel sense of the challenges of exilic existence, both groups have yet to reflect together about the reality of Jesus' body, why this body figures into our histories and for many of us haunts us daily. Instead, the body of another has remained at the center of our relational imagination, the body of a powerful, white, Western man, the image of self-sufficiency, social power, and self-determination. If Jewish-black relations are marked by the absence of serious reflection on the body of Jesus, then Jewish-Christian theological dialogue is marked by the absence of serious reflection on that racial body, the body of the centered white man.

Source

Jennings, Willie James, *The Christian Imagination: Theology and the Origins of Race* (New Haven: Yale University Press, 2010), 274–5, 285–6.

Commentary

In his 2020 memoir on theological education, *After Whiteness: An Education in Belonging*, Willie James Jennings (b. 1961) describes himself as being a 'listener of bodies', a 'reader of thoughts' and 'a lover of God'. As a shy and sensitive Black child growing up in Grand Rapids, Michigan, Jennings' life often depended on his ability to interpret white people's bodies; reading opened up new possibilities that, combined with loving God, drew him to theological education. His award-winning book *The Christian Imagination*, published a decade before his memoir, illuminates all three traits. This commentary highlights only a few central ideas of this dense and lengthy book.

The concept of 'social imagination' functions as a key term for Jennings. Specifically, it is a call to Christians, with their 'diseased imagination', to enlarge and reorient their world, following Jesus' way of belonging, connection and intimacy between peoples. This call begins by revisiting the primal estrangement of the church from living Israel by remembering and reclaiming identities as gentiles – as outsiders. White Christians in particular have lost sight of this outsider status – identifying, for example, with Jesus rather than with the Canaanite woman (see Matt. 15:21–8) whose passion for the healing of her daughter overcomes Jesus' initial reluctance to go beyond his call to the 'lost sheep of Israel'. It is within this gendered social and religious hierarchy, Jennings claims, that Christians might recognise the path drawing us to the Jewish body of Jesus – and the Canaanite woman in her boldness and tenacity offers a hint to the way forward by recognising that even those outside Israel may benefit from God's gifts to Israel. Instead, however, white colonisers inverted hospitality by assuming in their superiority that they were the hosts, the true believers.

Because the supersessionist Christian paradigm regards Judaism as an 'antiquated element' in divine revelation, the church must not only learn to reread Torah alongside living Israel, as Paul van Buren had exhorted in the early 1980s (see document 3), but also face the question of why Christian identity has proven so weak vis-à-vis social divisions. A major reason for this weakness, Jennings argues, is the dominance of whiteness, more specifically white, western men, in whose world view neither Blacks nor Jews fit. And, often, women.

Christians, in sum, need to find ways of living so that peoples now separated by race, violence and poverty might be brought together in communion with God. In reimagining God's vision for the world – a 'God who surprises us by a love of Difference' – they must look to Jesus' Jewish body. Grappling with Jesus as embodying otherness – also a major theme in the work of Barbara U. Meyer (see document 18) – offers a path to a revivified social imagination in which Jews and gentiles might form, metaphorically speaking, a new multiracial humanity through God's spirit.

Jennings' insight about white Christian responsibility to wrestle with the otherness of Jesus constitutes a relatively brief section of *The Christian Imagination*. Yet he complements this book, which was awarded the 2015 Grawemeyer Award in Religion, with numerous essays that develop this crucial understanding.

Bibliography

Fredrickson, George M., *Racism: A Short History* (Princeton: Princeton University Press, 2002).

Parfitt, Tudor, *Hybrid Hate: Conflations of Antisemitism and Anti-Black Racism from the Renaissance to the Third Reich* (New York: Oxford University Press, 2020).

Schorsch, Jonathan, *Jews and Blacks in the Early Modern World* (New York: Cambridge University Press, 2004).

11

Susannah Heschel: 'Historiography of Antisemitism versus Anti-Judaism: A Response to Robert Morgan' (2011)

Text

I am part of a growing number of scholars who no longer find the distinction between theological anti-Judaism and antisemitism to be helpful, particularly when studying the German Christian Movement of the Third Reich. I am aware that there are still many Christian theologians who define the distinction this way: anti-Judaism is a disparaging critique of Judaism and of Jews that allows Jews to convert to Christianity and thereby lose their objectionable characteristics. By contrast, antisemites disparage Jews on racial grounds that allow Jews no possibilities of ameliorating or escaping their degeneracy, not even through conversion to Christianity […]

The distinction between anti-Judaism and antisemitism is often thought to be chronological, based on the claim that racism and antisemitism are modern phenomena. According to this definition, antisemitism would then be limited to those who insist on the immutable nature of the negative characteristics of Jews, whereas anti-Judaism would be theological, the term applied to Christianity, since the church, it has been argued, offered the possibility of erasing the degeneracy of Jewishness through baptism, whereas racism, it is argued, views Jews and other 'others' as possessing immutable dangers. The distinction is also incorporated in official church statements claiming that antisemitism stresses abhorrent aspects of Jews' bodies, while anti-Judaism focuses on negative aspects of the religion of Judaism that lead to Jews' immoral behavior.

However, in recent decades numerous scholars from a range of disciplines, including those as diverse in their interests as the sociologist Helen Fein, the Ottomanist Bernard

Lewis and the theologian Edward Flannery, among many others, have come to use the term 'antisemitism' as hostility toward Judaism and Jews that may be expressed in a variety of ways, including through economics, politics, nationalism, religious discourse or race. Anti-Judaism then becomes the term for a discourse that expresses antisemitic views in theological language. In the view of many historians today, antisemitism cannot be confined in its descriptive applicability to the modern era, despite the term having been coined in the nineteenth century. Heiko Oberman, for example, in his study of the Renaissance and Reformation, sees the roots of the antisemitism of those periods stemming from much earlier eras [...] My colleague, the New Testament scholar Adele Reinhartz, has helpfully written to me:

> The problem is that even in the patristic and medieval eras, long before the coinage of the term antisemitism as such, it is almost impossible to distinguish between the racial and religious/ethnic elements. For many of these authors, as I've seen in my Caiaphas research, Jews were by their nature evil, and their rejection/killing of Christ is evidence of that evil nature.

[...] Let me explain why I and other historians have decided that the term 'antisemitism' more accurately defines the rhetoric of the pro-Nazi theologians I examine in my book [*The Aryan Jesus*, 2008]. First, explicitly Nazi language: words such as 'entlarvt' (unmasked or debunked) take a central role in Christian discussions of Jews and Judaism during the Third Reich, moving Christian writings from theological language to the language of Nazi antisemitism [...] Second, historians recognize that strongly negative theological statements about Jews have to be understood in the context of the era in which they were written [...] Third, 'das Judentum' is an ambiguous term in German: it can indicate Judaism, the Jews or Jewishness, so that statements about eradicating 'das Judentum' may refer to the religion, but may just as well refer to the human beings who adhere to that religion, namely the Jews, shifting meaning away from a theological polemic to a polemic against people.

Source

Heschel, Susannah, 'Historiography of Antisemitism versus Anti-Judaism: A Response to Robert Morgan', *Journal for the Study of the New Testament* 33, no. 3 (2011), 258–61.

Commentary

Denigration of Judaism and hostility to Jews both have a long history; identifying the appropriate nomenclature for this antagonism continues to be a vexed question. The perduring legacy of the *adversus Judaeos* literature of the early church gave rise to the term 'anti-Judaism' as denoting claims that Christianity superseded Judaism as the way to salvation. The language of anti-Judaism, however, typically reflects a reduction-istic view in which Judaism is solely a religion, thereby disregarding the significance of peoplehood to Jewish identity. Moreover, anti-Judaism is not a monolithic phenomenon and is freighted with inconsistency.

As Susannah Heschel (b. 1956) notes, many distinguish anti-Judaism from antisemitism, the nineteenth-century neologism coined by German journalist Wilhelm Marr. Particularly after the unspeakable horrors of the Shoah, many Christians thus differentiate anti-Judaism – highly problematic as it is – from antisemitism, which has more political and racial overtones. Marr, for example, argued that Jews were unassimilable and disproportionately powerful. Moreover, as the eugenics movement developed in the late nineteenth and early twentieth century, antisemitism became associated with race ideology.

As a keen student of modern German history, however, Heschel takes issue with this distinction. Based on her immersion in the archives of the Institute for the Study and Eradication of Jewish Influence on German Religious Life, Heschel documents the many ways the Institute, the theological engine of the German Christian Movement (*Deutsche Christen*), served to Nazify Christianity, including proclaiming an Aryan Jesus (see Chapter 7, p. 343). In her book *The Aryan Jesus*, Heschel characterises the Institute's efforts as a 'Nazi project'.

The documentation uncovered by her research, Heschel writes, convincingly demonstrates that anti-Judaism and antisemitism cannot be neatly demarcated. As the 'dejudaisation' project indicates, Christian theology has indeed functioned in ways that furthered antisemitism or at least disparaged Judaism in such a manner that Christians were more susceptible to antisemitic ideologies. Thus, Heschel argues that anti-Judaism then becomes the term for 'a discourse that expresses antisemitic views in theological language'.

Scholarship on antisemitism is multidisciplinary and prolific. One of the most widely recognised definitions is that of Helen Fein: 'a persisting latent structure of hostile beliefs toward Jews as a collectivity manifested in individuals as attitudes, and in culture as myth, ideology, folklore, and imagery, and in actions – social or legal discrimination, political mobilization against the Jews, and collective or state violence – which results in and/or is designed to distance, displace, or destroy Jews as Jews' (p. 67). Anti-Judaism finds a place in Fein's definition, which has influenced Heschel as well.

Heschel does not consider Christianity intrinsically antisemitic. There can be little doubt, however, that elements of its theological formulations are antisemitic – and thus a clarion call for the church to intensify its commitment to counter antisemitism.

Bibliography

Fein, Helen, 'Dimensions of Antisemitism: Attitudes, Collective Accusations, and Actions', in *The Persisting Question* (Berlin: De Gruyter, 1987), 67–85.

Heschel, Susannah, *The Aryan Jesus: Christian Theologians and the Bible in Nazi Germany* (Princeton: Princeton University Press, 2008).

Lindemann, Albert S., and Levy, Richard S. (eds.), *Antisemitism: A History* (Oxford and New York: Oxford University Press, 2010), available at www.holocaustremembrance.com/resources/working-definitions-charters/working-definition-antisemitism.

12

John G. Gager: Who Made Christianity? The Jewish Lives of the Apostle Paul *(2015)*

Text

What difference does it make that the 'new' Paul was a Jew; that there was no Christianity, or even any idea of Christianity in his time [...]? Does anyone really care that there was no centuries-long Jewish polemic against Paul [...]? So what that Jewish communities and synagogues did not disappear from the scene with the birth of Christianity [...] or that significant numbers of non-Jews – Gentiles and Christians – found their way to synagogues and were welcomed there by local Jews? And does it really matter – today – that Jews did not wither away under the onslaught of Christian anti-Judaism and anti-Semitism in Late Antiquity and the early Middle Ages? And what about those we call Jewish Christians, who worshiped Jesus and observed the Jewish Law? [...] In short, who cares?

Scholars certainly care. The mountain of writing about Paul proves that. But with decidedly mixed results [...]

Here it must be said, as numerous recent critics have argued, that most traditional Christian interpreters fail these texts. Their readings are anachronistic. They read back into Paul views that emerged long after his time, most notably, the very idea of Christianity and with it Christian anti-Judaism. G. F. Moore and Charlotte Klein, among others, have demonstrated with great vigor that Christian views of Paul and Judaism are deeply rooted in Christian theology. Moore's judgment [...] is worth repeating here: 'Christian interest in Jewish literature has always been apologetic or polemic rather than historical.' Thus, against the plain meaning of his letters, Paul becomes a Christian and the maker of anti-Judaism. Along with this anachronistic reading come, as E. P. Sanders and others have shown, a woeful ignorance and distortion of the Judaism in which Paul – not to mention Jesus, Matthew, the author of the Apocalypse, and numerous others – was deeply embedded [...] All too often, Christian exegetes have misread what Paul says about Jews and Judaism and then turned around to use that distorted image in their descriptions of Judaism 'as it really was.'

[...] As [Stanley] Stowers states [...] 'The more we have learned about Judaism as it actually existed rather than the Judaism of Christian imagination, the more impossible it has become to give a historical account of the traditional Paul.' Yet another consequence is the realization that translations, commentaries, dictionaries, and the like are themselves deeply permeated by traditional anti-Jewish assumptions [...]

But why has the apostle mattered so much to Jews from the fourth century to the present? Michael Wyschogrod has offered compelling answers to this question. His Jewish Paul, the one who neither converted to Christianity nor repudiated Judaism, leads him to speak of a post-supersessionist Christianity that will 'sense the overwhelming love with which God relates to his people [the Jews] and find it possible to participate in that love.' Gentile Christians will understand themselves as 'the gathering of people around the people of Israel … Through the Jew Jesus, when properly understood, the gentile enters into the covenant and becomes a member of the household, *as long as he or she does not claim that his or her entrance replaces the original children.*' […]

There can be little doubt that the discovery of the Jewish Paul, along with the Jewish gospels and the Jewish Jesus, has had a real impact on the thinking of various Christian churches and denominations […] As a result, in all of these cases, efforts to convert Jews have been largely abandoned. There is no point. Jews are already 'in.'

Source

Gager, John G., *Who Made Early Christianity? The Jewish Lives of the Apostle Paul* (New York: Columbia University Press, 2015), 139–45. (The square-bracketed interpolation '[the Jews]' is part of the original.)

Commentary

The seeds of John Gager's (b. 1937) work on Paul were planted in 1963, when Krister Stendahl published an essay that challenged the consensus that the apostle Paul's mysterious meeting with the Christ on the road to Damascus resulted in his becoming a Christian and, consequently, to his repudiation of the 'works' of the law (see Chapter 8, p. 418). Contrary to Martin Luther's depiction of Paul as burdened by the law and desperate to earn God's love, Stendahl contended that Paul had a 'robust' conscience and understood himself 'as to righteousness under the law, blameless' (Phil. 3:6, NRSVue). Further, Stendahl contended that Paul's mysterious encounter on the road to Damascus did not result in his *conversion* to Christianity but rather led to his *call* to preach to the gentiles so that they, too, could experience the salvific love of Israel's God. Stendahl proffered a new reading of Paul and the Law: Paul's preoccupation was with the ways gentiles *as non-Jews* should come to know the God of Israel. Paul had redirected his religious intensity to the gentiles; therein lay his passion. Paul had not ceased to be Jewish; his call transcended his own community.

Scholarship on Paul has proliferated in the nearly sixty years since Stendahl's initial foray into the subject. Gager has been prominent among scholars, including E. P. Sanders, Lloyd Gaston, Daniel Boyarin, Paula Fredriksen (see document 6) and Mark Nanos (albeit with variations), who have extended Stendahl's thinking, revealing in greater depth the ways in which Jesus, Paul, Matthew and others were 'deeply embedded' in Jewish life – a recognition that has not been given sufficient attention by more conventional readings. Among the most significant refinements has been the greater acknowledgement of the fact that Judaism and Christianity both emerged only in the fourth or fifth century CE through a process of conflict, conversation and collaboration. Consequently, there was no 'Christianity' in Paul's day to which he could have 'converted'. Paul remained a highly literate, Greek-speaking Jew, preoccupied not with his fellow Jews but rather with his gentile congregants. For gentiles such as those at Galatia to take on Jewish practices (e.g., circumcision, dietary laws) belied the new reality: *their salvific path lay in discipleship to Christ Jesus*, not in the following of Torah, which was the Jewish way to Israel's God (see also Chapter 1, p. 23). As Gager argues, Christian exegetes have misread Paul, and then used him to perpetuate a distorted understanding of Judaism as mired in legalism, contrasting it to the liberating love of Christ and Christianity.

It is difficult to measure the extent to which the new perspectives on Paul have permeated the churches. Certainly, *Nostra aetate* (see Appendix to Part III, p. 512) has significantly countered the once-common notion among Christians that Jews were (and remain) responsible for the death of Jesus, and its inclusion of citations from Paul hints at a Jewish Paul. Underlying Gager's work is his conviction that the church should care about the 'mountain of writing' Pauline scholars have generated since Stendahl's initial study. As he indicates, some in the church do care. The question is whether their number and learning will lead to an embrace of a Jewish Paul in the church.

Bibliography

Eisenbaum, Pamela, *Paul Was Not a Christian* (New York: Harper One, 2009).
Fredriksen, Paula, *Paul the Pagan's Apostle* (New Haven: Yale University Press, 2017).
Stendahl, Krister, 'The Apostle Paul and the Introspective Conscience of the West', *Harvard Theological Review* 56, no. 3 (1963), 199–215.

13

Gerald R. McDermott: 'What Is the New Christian Zionism?' (2016)

Text

So what do the scholars and experts [...] mean by 'the New Christian Zionism'? [...] The first is that the people and land of Israel are central to the story of the Bible. That might seem obvious. But Israel has not been central to the church's traditional way of telling the story of salvation [...] We propose that the history of salvation is ongoing: the people of Israel and their land continue to have theological significance [...]

We are also convinced that the return of Jews from all over the world to their land, and their efforts to establish a nation state after two millennia of being separated from controlling the land, is *part* of the fulfillment of biblical prophecy. Further, we believe that Jews need and deserve a homeland in Israel – not to displace others but to accept and develop what the family of nations – the United Nations – ratified in 1948 [...]

The burden of these chapters is to show *theologically* that the people of Israel *continue* to be significant for the history of redemption and that the land of Israel, which is at the heart of the covenantal promises, *continues* to be important to God's providential purposes [...]

Israel alone can point to an ancient civilization on the same land with the same religion and language [...]

No matter the character of modern nationalism, Jews have lived in the land of Israel for three thousand years, all the while thinking of themselves as Jews in the homeland of Jewish culture. This means that Jews thought of Israel as their natural home for millennia before the nineteenth century [...]

For fifteen hundred years Jews have prayed the Amidah in the morning, afternoon and night, ending with these words: 'May it be your will, Lord our God and God of our fathers, that the beit Hamikdash [holy temple] be speedily rebuilt in our days, and grant us our portion in Your Torah.' The siddur, the Jewish prayer book, is full of references like this, creating a yearning for Zion in Jewish hearts for the last fifteen centuries [...]

It is not accurate to say, then, that Zionism is a recent innovation [...]

Israel has always been a people defined by religion, even for those who don't believe. The religious identity of Israel – not their race – defines the people, even those who say they don't believe in the God of Israel but identify with the people who do [...]

Importantly, as a democracy Israel has almost two million Muslim and Christian Arabs, Druze, Bahá'ís, Circassians and other ethnic groups as citizens with full rights [...]

The New Christian Zionism asserts that the people and land of Israel represent a provisional and proleptic fulfillment of the promises of that new world to come. So Jesus brought a new era to the history of Israel but without abolishing what came before, and he predicted that his people and land would be central to that new world. This is why the New Christian Zionism speaks of fulfillment and not supersessionism [...]

In short, the New Christian Zionism hopes to alert scholars and other Christians to beware of the geographical-docetic temptation that anti-Zionism proffers. Supersessionist anti-Zionism proposes theology divorced from embodiment and physicality – a people without a land, a Jesus without his people and land and tradition, and the early church living, as it were, suspended in air above the Palestinian ground. It suggests that land, earth and territory do not matter to embodied human existence. It would not be stretching too much to say that it is ecclesiology and eschatology without incarnation.

Source

McDermott, Gerald R., 'What Is the New Christian Zionism?', in McDermott, Gerald R. (ed.), *The New Christian Zionism: Fresh Perspectives on Israel and the Land* (Downers Grove: InterVarsity Press, 2016), 11–13, 16, 19–20, 22–3, 27, 29.

Commentary

Christian Zionism is principally an influential Protestant evangelical movement encompassing a range of theological and political perspectives. Associated particularly with the work of John Nelson Darby and C. I. Scofield of the eponymous *Scofield Reference Bible* (1909) and more recently with popularisers such as Hal Lindsey and Tim LaHaye, Christian Zionism generally stresses the periodisation of history or 'dispensations' through which God's plan unfolds in history. Earlier dispensations having revealed Israel's unfaithfulness, God's covenantal love continues to be manifest in the life of

Jesus and through the gentile church. Ultimately, however, the world will experience a time of tribulation – giving rise to apocalyptic scenarios of the 'rapture' – and then culminate in the thousand-year reign of Jesus for those not left behind, such as Jews who do not convert to Christianity.

Gerald R. McDermott, an American Anglican evangelical theologian, argues for a radically revised Zionism in which Christians will no longer relegate the Old Testament to previous dispensations or regard the existence of Israel as a summons to conversion. On the contrary: Israel's experience is crucial to the church's ongoing life. Israel, both the people and the land, witnesses to God's providential plan. Biblical prophecy, he asserts, is being fulfilled in our time. Israel's existence serves as a sign of God's fidelity to eschatological fulfilment.

A prolific author and a prominent scholar of the Anglo-American preacher and philosophical theologian Jonathan Edwards (1703–58), McDermott views Israel through the lens of prophecy fulfilled rather than as the Old Testament superseded. In advocating for the centrality of Israel for the church, he asserts that Jesus 'predicted' that the land and 'his' people would be pivotal for the new world he preached and that while Israel today has its flaws, its critics wrongly condemn it as an apartheid state and as an exemplar of colonialism.

McDermott's hermeneutical stance seems to situate him in proximity to messianic Judaism; some of the contributors to the edited volume from which this essay is drawn are identified with that movement. In a concluding chapter, McDermott speaks of Christian worship of the God of Israel as leading Christians to communion with Jews: 'This begins with messianic Jews. We don't know how or when nonmessianic Jewish believers will be joined self-consciously with Israel's *Messiah*, but we believe that God will bring that about in his perfect way and time' (p. 333).

McDermott and his colleagues who situate themselves under the umbrella of the 'new' Christian Zionism have carved out a distinctive position on the Christian theological landscape. Their influence lies principally within streams of messianic Jewish and high Anglican theologies, as well as encompassing Catholic theologian Gavin D'Costa.

Bibliography

Burnett, Carol Monica (ed.), *Zionism through Christian Lenses* (Eugene: Pickwick, 2013).
Shapiro, Faydra L., *Christian Zionism: Navigating the Christian–Jewish Border* (Eugene: Cascade, 2015).

14

Naim Stifan Ateek: A Palestinian Theology of Liberation: The Bible, Justice, and the Palestine–Israel Conflict *(2017)*

Text

1. Palestinian liberation theology is a *contextual theology*. It takes the Palestinian context and situation in life seriously, and it addresses that specific context directly […]

2. It is a *liberation theology*. We seek the liberation of our people from oppression by the state of Israel and from the unjust and illegal occupation of Palestinian land, and the liberation of Israeli Jews from the sin of oppressing the Palestinians [...]

3. It is a *grassroots theology*. It developed out of Bible studies by the local community reflecting on its situation [...] through the eyes of faith.

4. It is an *inclusive theology*. It rejects exclusive concepts of God that dehumanize and subjugate people. It demands that the laws of the state accord with international law.

5. It is an *ecumenical theology* [...]

6. It is an *interfaith theology* [...] We seek to relate to one another in love and respect for the dignity of every human being, to serve one another, and to work together for justice and peace for all people.

7. It is a *humanitarian theology* that champions and respects the dignity of every human being, especially the poor and oppressed, the marginalized and disadvantaged.

8. It is a *theology of nonviolence* [...] He [Jesus] talked about peacemaking in a situation where people were living under a brutal and oppressive occupation. He taught the people to love their enemies and to pray for those who harm them.

9. It is a *prophetic theology* that demands that faithful Christians courageously speak truth to power [...]

10. It is a *christological theology* for Christians, where Jesus Christ is both the model and paradigm of faith, and where Christ is the guide and the hermeneutic that can help us discern the authentic word of God.

Most Christians are taught from childhood that the Bible is the word of God. It is important to emphasize that the conflict over Palestine has revolutionized our reading and understanding of the Bible. Frankly, the sacred position that the Bible has held for many people has been called into question due to texts that depict God as being violent [...] Most of those texts reflect a tribal and exclusive understanding of God that was critiqued and rejected by later prophetic writers. Such texts do not contain any word from God for us. They do not reflect the mind or spirit of Christ. When we apply the hermeneutic of love, they fail the test [...] They have no value for us. Therefore, we can no longer say simply that the Bible is the word of God [...] God can still speak to us through some biblical texts, but Jesus Christ must be the determining hermeneutic [...]

For Christians, Jesus Christ has shown God's true nature and character. Christ is the hermeneutic by which we can determine what pleases and displeases God [...]

So long as the government of Israel continues in the oppression of the Palestinian people and the occupation of Palestinian land, it is mandatory for all people of faith and all who believe in justice and peace to resist, using all the nonviolent methods and means that are available.

Source

Ateek, Naim Stifan, *A Palestinian Theology of Liberation: The Bible, Justice, and the Palestine–Israel Conflict* (Maryknoll: Orbis, 2017), 139–44, 146, 148.

Commentary

Palestinian theologies emerged in the 1980s as an exploration of the appropriate social and political responsibilities of local churches in light of the particularities of their context. Energised in part by the spirit of the First Intifada ('Uprising') that began in December 1987, Palestinian theologians developed various ways of doing theology contextually.

Naim Stifan Ateek (b. 1937), an Anglican priest and founder of the Sabeel Ecumenical Liberation Theology Center in 1990, is among the most prominent voices and the architect of Palestinian liberation theology. Although sharing in many of the themes of Latin American liberation theologies that grew out of Peruvian priest and theologian Gustavo Gutiérrez's *Teología de la liberación* (1971; see also document 2), Palestinian liberation theologies placed less emphasis on the critique of economic systems that dehumanise people living in poverty and more on the situation of Palestinians living in the grip of Israeli domination – many of whom are impoverished.

Ateek attributes the genesis of his liberation theology to his experience of the Nakba ('Catastrophe') of 1948 in which more than 700,000 Arab refugees fled or were expelled in the wake of Israel becoming a state. He sees the Nakba as catastrophic in three ways: as a trauma that ruptured the social fabric of Palestinian life, as a loss of social and political identity, and as a crisis of faith. Out of this crisis of faith, Ateek ascertains a fundamental question: how, in the light of what Palestinian Christians have endured, can they consider the Old Testament, as used by certain Zionists, to be the word of God?

In earlier chapters of the book excerpted here, *A Palestinian Theology of Liberation*, Ateek speaks of 'liberating the scriptures from Zionism' and accuses the Zionist 'enterprise' of treating the Bible as a mere tool for justifying Jewish possession of the land. In articulating his hermeneutical approach to the Old Testament more fully in the concluding chapter, from which the excerpt is taken, he criticises the predominantly exclusivist perspective of the Torah, contrasting it to more universalist texts such as the Book of Jonah, portions of Ezekiel and selected Psalms. These exclusionary texts and their depiction of a violent tribal God should, he argues, hold no revelatory power for Christians because they have rationalised and justified violence in the name of religion. It is the hermeneutic of love revealed in Jesus Christ in which we see the face of the God of justice, peace and mercy.

Ateek's outcry for justice for the Palestinian is here cast as contemporary prophetic denunciation of Jewish occupation. As a work of theology, however, his unfamiliarity with Jewish modes of biblical interpretation and dependence on outmoded caricatures such as the angry God of the Old Testament in contrast with the loving God of the New can be seen as undermining the resonance of his cry, particularly among those committed to Jewish–Christian relations.

Bibliography

Gregerman, Adam, 'New Wine in Old Bottles', *Journal of Ecumenical Studies* 41, no. 3 (2004), 313–40.
Marteijn, Elizabeth S., 'The Revival of Palestinian Christianity', *Exchange* 49 (2020), 257–77.
van Ruiten, Jacques, and van Bekkun, Koert (eds.), *Violence in the Hebrew Bible* (Leiden: Brill, 2020).

15

John Pawlikowski: 'The Uniqueness of the Christian–Jewish Dialogue: A Yes and a No' (2017)

Text

[N]ew developments in understanding the Jewish context in which the Christian church arose, developments which affect Christian self-understanding, need to be integrated into dialogues with Islam, Hinduism, Buddhism, and other religious traditions. We cannot present Christianity in such discussions as though the Christian-Jewish discussion has had no effect on how we perceive Christian origins today [...]

The new emphasis on the church's gradual emergence from Judaism over a period of several centuries is becoming the dominant scholarly view, thanks largely to [...] 'The Parting of the Ways' research. Christians [...] can no longer simplistically argue that Jesus established a totally new religious entity, apart from Judaism, during his own lifetime. Increasing scholarly evidence undercuts such an ecclesiological outlook [...] Such scholarship, generated to a significant extent by chapter four of Nostra Aetate, needs to be incorporated throughout global Christianity in any statement of ecclesiology. This is another example of how Nostra Aetate's section on Jews and Judaism remains in every interreligious dialogue in which the church is involved [...]

So-called 'Parting of the Ways' scholarship also affects how we present Jesus' own identity and his ministerial objectives and how and when the church took over responsibility for promulgating his message, a process that developed gradually over several centuries. Buddhists, Jains, Hindus, Muslims and other religious communities that have chosen to engage in dialogue with Christians must come to understand Christianity through this new lens. Only in this way can religious traditions outside of Christianity understand its origins and evolution as we have come to perceive Christian identity today in light of recent scholarship on the Jewish roots of the Church. Thus, the Christian-Jewish dialogue to which chapter four gave birth remains pivotal outside the North Atlantic region [...]

[... T]he Christian-Jewish dialogue cannot be isolated from the wider interreligious context. And if we are to be successful in integrating it into dialogues outside the North Atlantic area then we must modify overstated claims about its uniqueness. Christian-Jewish dialogue should be included under the generic umbrella of 'interreligious dialogue' while continuing to affirm its important distinctive features. No Jewish leader I know would define Jewish identity as centrally rooted in a bond with Christianity. Christians who make such a claim about the Jewish-Christian relationship do so largely because [...] they overemphasize Judaism as a biblical religion and give insufficient attention to the central role of post-biblical commentaries and such experiences as the Shoah and the re-establishment of the state of Israel in the forging of contemporary Jewish identities. Without question there are definitely distinctive aspects in the Christian-Jewish encounter that have no parallels in other interreligious dialogues. Christians do share a part of the Bible with the Jewish community even though we have often interpreted our common biblical texts in quite different ways. And we regard Jews as having authentic revelation from the Christian theological perspective [...]

Nonetheless, by overstressing these distinctive aspects of the Christian-Jewish dialogue in comparison with other interreligious encounters we run the risk of giving the discussion with Jews and Judaism a measure of superiority, of special privilege, which has the effect of downplaying other dialogues, leaving the impression that they are of secondary importance. But in fact in many parts of the world some of the other interreligious encounters in which the church is involved matter far more on the ground.

Source

Pawlikowski, John T., 'The Uniqueness of the Christian–Jewish Dialogue: A Yes and a No', *Studies in Christian–Jewish Relations* 12, no. 1 (2017), 3–5.

Commentary

John T. Pawlikowski (b. 1940), a Servite priest and now emeritus professor at Catholic Theological Union in Chicago, focuses his prolific writings on Jewish–Christian relations principally upon Catholic ecclesial thinking in the post-*Nostra aetate* era, Christology and the Shoah. The essay from which this excerpt is taken expands these foci to include religious pluralism, an interest indebted particularly to Pawlikowski's long involvement in the Parliament of the World's Religions.

Pawlikowski notes the tendency among many scholars to overemphasise the singularity of Christianity's relationship to Judaism. In contrast, he argues, this relation is more adequately situated within the interreligious context. Only when viewed in this larger horizon will the post-*Nostra aetate* scholarship that has reoriented Christian ecclesial identity have an effect beyond the west.

Pawlikowski attributes much of this reorientation to research categorised under the 'partings of the ways' (see also Chapter 2, p. 66), highlighting the gradual emergence of the church from Judaism over the course of several centuries in contrast to earlier perspectives that identified the beginnings of Christianity with Jesus or Paul. The category itself is problematic, however, insofar as it rests on the assumption that Judaism and Christianity – two traditions that ultimately were differentiated – had a common origin from which separations happened at various points. Yet to speak of 'Judaism' and 'Christianity' before the fourth century CE is anachronistic. Regardless of terminology, however, Pawlikowski's larger point is important: reconceptualising Christianity as 'emerging' over the course of several centuries rather than beginning with Jesus or early in the second century CE means that Christians can no longer responsibly assert that Jesus established Christianity over against Judaism. Reconceptualising development of what would ultimately become Christianity as a distinctive tradition rather than as a unique religion founded by Jesus Christ offers a promising opening for serious engagement with the wider world of interreligious exchange.

Pawlikowski is simultaneously underscoring the significance of scholarship emanating from dialogue and collaboration on Christian–Jewish issues *and* arguing for drawing upon that scholarship in extending the conversation globally. The Christological thinking grounded in the Jewish matrix of the Jesus movement and of Paul, as well as the complicated evolution from a Jewish to a dominantly gentile tradition, bear relevance not simply for dialogue with its Abrahamic partner Islam but also for Asian traditions – and, one might add, for indigenous religious traditions.

In a very real sense, Pawlikowski's vision is for the *oikumēnē*, the Greek term for the 'whole inhabited earth' from which 'ecumenical' is derived. In bringing together *Nostra aetate*'s fourth section on the church and Judaism (see Appendix to Part III, p. 512) with its first three more global sections, he reminds us that what began at Vatican II carries implications for what Pope Francis calls 'our common home' in *Laudato Si'*. Given Pawlikowski's enormous contributions to scholarship on Christian–Jewish relations over the years, his call to integrate this field into the wider realm of interreligious engagement will surely be heeded.

Bibliography

Becker and Reed, *The Ways That Never Parted*.
Lefebure, Leo (ed.), *Theology without Borders* (Washington, DC: Georgetown University Press, 2022).

16

Serafim Seppälä: 'Forsaken or Not? Patristic Argumentation on the Forsakenness of Jews Revisited' (2019)

Text

Orthodox theology and overall ethos is so organically connected with the patristic thinking and patristic authority that any updating of attitudes and teachings is much more problematic and painstaking than in the Catholic Church, not to mention Protestant ones […]

Evidently, the painful separation of Judaism and Christianity into two religions, and the subsequent construction of Christian self-formation in relation to the Other, contributed to very negative estimation of the spiritual value of Judaism in the early patristic literature […]

[M]ost of the negative views on Jews in the patristic literature are part of biblical hermeneutics and have very little to do with actual Jews or Rabbinic Judaism of post-biblical times. The flow of endless patristic remarks on the 'literal understanding' of Jews carries on the tradition of the first century conflicts and constitutes a caricature that does not correspond with the reality of Rabbinic Judaism. It is evident for anyone who opens any book on Rabbinic exegesis that it is, by and large, more imaginative and visionary – and in any case, more multi-layered – than any Christian allegorical interpretation. Thus, even the basic patristic statements and remarks about Jewishness are simply not reliable.

[...]

Most references to Jews and Judaism do not refer to actual Jews or Rabbinic Judaism, but to the Christian doctrine and its constituents, interpretative traditions and theological malfunctions. Therefore, they should not be read as definitive evaluations of Judaism at all.

Yet what we do have about Jews and Judaism in the patristic literature, seems to be thoroughly negative. The question is whether these negative views are *theologoumena* that can be updated or reconsidered, or do they constitute a case of *consensus patrum* [a consensus of the church fathers as a means of defining doctrinal positions] that should be seen irremovable from the Orthodox faith? Indeed, they are often presented in organic connection with the fundamental truth of Christianity.

[...]

Evidently, it was taken for granted that if Christianity is the new truth, the old one must be utterly rejected by God.

[...]

The rejection and forsakenness of Jews was often strongly connected with their loss of Jerusalem and the Holy Land, and the loss was presented as proof for the former [...]

[...] The Jews have been ruling the Holy Land since 1948 and the Holy City since 1967, and their presence is fully established. One weighty patristic argument has clearly proven to be false. This should encourage even the extreme supporters of *consensus patrum* to consider the option of re-orientation and reinterpretation [...]

To reach this aim [of theological reconciliation with Judaism], it seems that it would be necessary for the Orthodox to acknowledge that

1. After the *Shoah*, something has essentially changed [... T]here has to be a post-holocaust theological vision.
2. For better or worse, most of the patristic views on Jews and Judaism have accomplished their mission. They did serve to protect Christian identity formation in the first centuries, but today one may safely admit that the views were essentially one-sided, too strict, not free of hatred, and they did not correspond at all to the inner character of Judaism for which the fathers usually show no knowledge or understanding, or even interest. [...]
3. The return of Jews to their Holy Land and Holy City, and the emergence of the state of Israel is an extremely extraordinary process that no patristic author deemed possible [...]

[...] Judaism as a religion is not what the patristic authors claimed and supposed it to be, and the Jews of the 20th century achieved what the patristic authors declared impossible. Therefore, there is an evident need for a thorough reassessment of Orthodox views based on patristic legacy [...]

Of course, the practical reality of Orthodox churches is that no definitive steps in this matter are to be expected in decades, perhaps centuries [...] Meanwhile, I challenge every Orthodox theologian to read ten books by/about the spiritual masters of Judaism and to see whether or not they are worthy of our deep theological and spiritual respect.

Source

Seppälä, Serafim, 'Forsaken or Not? Patristic Argumentation on the Forsakenness of Jews Revisited', *Review of Ecumenical Studies* 11, no. 2 (2019), 182, 184–7, 193, 197–8.

Commentary

As the documents in this volume attest, the Christian tradition encompasses many works portraying Jews negatively. This phenomenon is especially evident among early church writers in the turbulent period of Christianity's identity formation, both in the Greek east and the Latin west (see Chapter 2). As noted by Serafim Seppälä (b. 1970), an ordained monk and priest in the Orthodox Church of Finland, the patristic writers' depiction of Judaism as obsolete and God-forsaken is unambiguous. Precisely because early church literature holds an exceptional status in the theology and liturgical life of Orthodox Christianity, its interpretation poses a substantial challenge.

Orthodoxy's distinctive ecclesiology adds to the complexity. Organised into various autocephalous jurisdictions, each under a patriarch, archbishop or metropolitan, the Orthodox Church has no one principal authority figure. The Ecumenical Patriarch of Constantinople may be 'first among equals', but his title is honorific. Given the autonomy of the jurisdictions, no mechanism for change comparable to Vatican Council II exists. Further, the dominant population of Orthodoxy lies in eastern Europe, where large swathes of the church have been suppressed or even persecuted by political authorities; in many cases, the churches are still recovering from the repression. Russia's invasion of Ukraine, with the support of Patriarch Kirill, primate of the Russian Orthodox Church, has further divided Orthodoxy. And because the Shoah decimated much of the Jewish population of Europe, interaction with the relatively few Jewish communities is less likely. Consequently, relations with Jews and Judaism are generally at an embryonic stage; in some jurisdictions, the process of reconciliation has barely begun, if at all.

Thus, Orthodox scholarship on Jewish–Christian relations is more limited, and no single line of argumentation may be readily identified. Seppälä, who is also a professor at Eastern Finland University, suggests one hermeneutical approach. He asserts that because the patristic writers did not possess an accurate understanding of Judaism, particularly the mode developing under rabbinic authorities in the third through seventh centuries, their claim that God had rejected the Jews can no longer be regarded as a reliable basis for theological judgements. Their literal interpretation of scripture, especially of the prophets and the passion narratives, can no longer be sustained. Further, the conclusion of the patristic writers that the Romans' destruction of the temple and Jerusalem rendered Judaism obsolete is contradicted by the existence of the State of Israel. Seppälä concludes, therefore, that Orthodoxy should relegate patristic writings on Jews to history and discover the spiritual depth of Judaism.

The distinctiveness of the Orthodox tradition means it must find its own paths to dialogue with Jews and Judaism. Seppälä offers a promising way forward. To what extent his views and those of a small number of Orthodox scholars of a similar perspective will influence their tradition is as yet unclear.

Bibliography

Azar, Michael G., *Exegeting the Jews: The Early Reception of the Johannine 'Jews'* (Leiden: Brill, 2016).

Lieu, Judith M., *Image and Reality: The Jews in the World of the Christians in the Second Century* (London: T&T Clark, 2003).

17

Amy-Jill Levine and Marc Zvi Brettler: The Bible with and without Jesus: How Jews and Christians Read the Same Stories Differently *(2020)*

Text

Although we live in a world of polemics, ever more present in social media, we must try to live in a world of possibilities, where we can affirm our own beliefs without negating the beliefs of others. [… U]nderstanding the other is not only good but also necessary for a civil society and for religious commitment […] We believe that it is crucial to understand the texts and beliefs of others – not only because we live in a multicultural society, but also because understanding others helps us better to understand ourselves.

We shall try to avoid polemics, except for one case, where we discuss the polemical position known as supersessionism or replacement theology […] We believe that this theology, which claims that the gentile church replaces the people of Israel as heirs of God's covenants and promises, is harmful for both Jews and Christians. But otherwise we do our best to present historical-critical, Jewish and Christian positions with equal sympathy and clarity.

[…]

[…] Several historical factors facilitate our sympathetic understanding of Christian biblical interpretation. These include the development of the academic study of religion; the integration into biblical studies of reception history, that is, how biblical texts were understood, variously and over time, in the postbiblical period; the rise of historical-critical study; and the recognition of ambiguity and multiple understandings of texts. Our readings are also inspired by numerous Christians who have recognized how scriptural interpretation has been used to harm Jews and who have sought alternative messages.

The Roman Catholic Church has played an essential role in encouraging the reading of the entire Christian Bible in a manner that appreciates Jewish perspectives without supersessionist assumptions […] The church has both enriched its own interpretive practices and encouraged mutual respect […]

[…] Jews and Christians are not reading the same scriptures; the church's Old Testament is not the same thing as the synagogue's Tanakh. We should acknowledge the logic to each system rather than accuse others of misreading.

It is also essential that we read together not only to see facets of our own traditions that might otherwise go unnoted but also to gain understanding of our neighbors. For example, we can learn to appreciate how different communities create a canon within a canon by highlighting particular books, chapters, and even verses […]

[...] While the church attends more to the prophetic corpus of Israel's scripture, the synagogue focuses on the Torah. The church stresses the covenant with David; the synagogue concentrates on the covenants with Abraham and Moses. Jews read the entire Torah, every word, Genesis 1 through the end of Deuteronomy; Christian churches who follow a lectionary never hear Numbers [...] proclaimed on Sunday morning, and [seldom ...] Leviticus [...] This Christian focus leads to a difference in theological emphasis, useful though oversimplifying: the church, in terms of scriptural interpretation, focuses on how Jesus fulfilled prophecy in the past and how he will come again in the future; the synagogue focuses on the present.

Indeed, a notable number of Christians are concerned with eschatology – the endtime. The book of Daniel, largely unknown within contemporary Jewish circles, is hugely important especially in conservative Christian circles. But the more the church, at least in antiquity, stressed the world to come, the kingdom of God, or getting into heaven, the more the synagogue stressed sanctification: the making holy of this world through observing the norms of the Torah.

Even when both communities share the same texts or themes, they often emphasize different aspects [...] Jews and Christians have different vocabularies, different orders to their shared scripture, and different translations. They have different cultural memories, different interpretive understandings, and different emphases. Christians and Jews are now sufficiently different, and sufficiently strong on their own ground, that they might want to think about reading together, with a generosity of spirit that the twenty-first century calls for.

Source

Levine, Amy-Jill, and Brettler, Marc Zvi, *The Bible with and without Jesus: How Jews and Christians Read the Same Stories Differently* (New York: HarperCollins, 2020), 60–6.

Commentary

'Christianity', Paula Fredriksen asserted in the edited volume *Jews, Christians, and the Roman Empire*, 'was born in an argument over how to understand Jewish texts' (p. 249). Although her claim does not fully account for the complexity of Christianity's genesis, it accentuates the polemical cast of early Christian interpretations typified by the contention that Jews failed to understand their own scriptures: 'For we believe and obey them, whereas you, though you read them, do not grasp their spirit' (Justin Martyr, *Dialogue with Trypho* 29.2; see also Chapter 2, p. 75).

Amy-Jill Levine (b. 1956) and Marc Zvi Brettler (b. 1958) offer a perspective complementing Fredriksen's in their book *The Bible with and without Jesus*. They offer insight into how two traditions each developed distinctive interpretational patterns and provide a *vade mecum* for entering into the other's interpretive process.

Levine and Brettler view Jewish interpretations as characteristically concerned with orthopraxy and Christian interpretations as aligned with belief, thereby contributing to an emphasis on orthodoxy. Among the key interpretive differences is that Christian communities – at least until recently – view the Old Testament as fore-shadowing the New. In so doing, Christians typically read their scriptures through a Christological lens.

The Levine–Brettler assertion that 'Jews and Christians are not reading the same scriptures; the church's Old Testament is not the same thing as the synagogue's Tanakh' challenges the assumptions of many, if not most, Christians. The Christian world typically considers Judaism a religion based primarily on the Old Testament; it further assumes that its Old Testament is identical to the Jewish Bible. Rather, the latter is an anthology of twenty-four books in Hebrew (with a few Aramaic passages) ordered in tripartite fashion – *Torah* (Torah), *Nevi'im* (Prophets) and *Kethuvim* (Writings), forming the acronym 'Tanakh' – that differs from the Old Testament, which follows the divisions of the Septuagint (the oldest extant Greek translation from the Hebrew, *c.* 250 BCE). The Protestant canon consists of the same books as in Tanakh but ordered differently; the Catholic and Orthodox canons include books authored later (*c.* 200 BCE–100 CE) and variously termed 'deuterocanonical' in Catholicism or 'things that are read publicly' by the Orthodox churches. Protestants regard these books as 'apocryphal', and thus not scriptural.

The distinctiveness of Tanakh, moreover, lies in the centrality accorded to rabbinic exegesis. As Levine and Brettler note, 'The Bible itself is less important in Judaism than the Bible *interpreted*' (p. 31). Over the centuries, Christians have not so much engaged Jewish interpretive traditions as debated or disregarded them – a loss that *The Bible with and without Jesus* helps to mitigate.

The asymmetries between Judaism and Christianity remain, though differences need not result in division when mutual knowledge undergirds dialogue. Moreover, some dissimilarities, such as regarding the Old Testament as preparation for the New Testament, are understood today in much more complex ways – at least among scholars in many Christian circles, with whom Levine and Brettler often collaborate: 'Both readings are bound up with the vision of their respective faiths, of which the readings are the result and expression' (see *The Jewish People and Their Sacred Scriptures in the Christian Bible*; Appendix to Part III, p. 528).

Bibliography

Berlin, Adele, and Brettler, Marc Zvi (eds.), *The Jewish Study Bible*, 2nd ed. (New York: Oxford University Press, 2014).

Dohrmann, Natalie B., and Reed, Annette Yoshiko (eds.), *Jews, Christians, and the Roman Empire: The Poetics of Power in Late Antiquity* (Philadelphia: University of Pennsylvania Press, 2013).

Fredriksen, Paula, 'Roman Christianity and the Post-Roman West: The Social Correlates of the *Contra Iudeos* Tradition', in Fredriksen, Paula, and Reinhartz, Adele (eds.), *Jews, Christians, and the Roman Empire: The Poetics of Power in Late Antiquity* (Philadelphia: University of Pennsylvania Press, 2013), 249–66.

Pontifical Biblical Commission, *The Jewish People and Their Sacred Scriptures in the Christian Bible* (Rome: Libreria Editrice Vaticana, 2002).

18

Barbara U. Meyer: Jesus the Jew in Christian Memory *(2020)*

Text

Christologies written in the context of reframing Jewish-Christian relations usually pictured the Jewishness of Jesus as a bridge between Judaism and Christianity. Difference as a structuring principle of Christology had been traditionally bound to a negative account of Judaism, with Jesus pictured as different and thus detached from his Jewish environment. 'Different,' in this Christian thought tradition, always meant better or higher, possessing deeper truth and imbued with greater spirituality. Difference, when stated positively, was used to underline Jesus' uniqueness that was likewise synonymous with superiority. Yet, seldom has 'otherness' been made a central category to a Christology committed to renewed Jewish-Christian dialogue, and seldom has the developing language of otherness been applied to talk about Jesus' Jewishness – both probably due to the previous prevailing effort of Christian theologians to embrace Jesus' Jewishness as primarily a bridge to Jews and Judaism […]

Otherness and Jewishness may be seen as interpreting each other with regard to Jesus Christ but this mutual interpretation is no simple matter. The interconnection between Jewishness and otherness belongs to a Christology of Gentiles only – but then, Gentiles are the ones in need of […] confirmation that Jesus Christ is 'like us' regarding his human nature. Christians are meant to identify with Jesus, as he is proclaimed and confessed to be 'like us.' But God sides with the otherness of Christ and continues to protect him from our efforts to domesticate him. In this dynamic, otherness needs God's protection but also protects the vitality of Jesus Christ. The human urge to approach Jesus – in devout fellowship as well as in historical scholarship – is appropriate for the Christian. Looking for Jesus in history and coveting his closeness in the present are Christian intellectual and spiritual practices. That Jesus Christ will not be defined […] is an expression of God opting for Christ's ongoing otherness. In this interpretation, otherness can function as a Christological category, sustaining the uniqueness of Jesus Christ in accordance with the early Christian creed […]

Jesus the Jew is contemporary Christians' Other mainly in the sense of his Jewish life. His being Jewish is expressed by a certain perception of time and belonging, by structuring the year according to the major feasts and pilgrimages to Jerusalem, by discussing, performing, and interpreting commandments, by knowing and studying the texts of the Pentateuch and the Prophets. All together this can be called a Torah-bound life. Christians today do not share this life of Torah, they do not share its rhythm of the year, the month, or the week, they do not practice discussion of religious laws, and they generally regard study as a secondary religious practice. Still, today's Christians are not disconnected from Torah. They know of Jesus' bond with Torah and they consider the written Torah as a part of their own holy book. Christians live with the traits of a Torah-bound life; certain texts and certain laws, such as the Ten Commandments, are central to the Christian faith. The promises of God's covenantal care as expressed in the covenant of Noah and Abraham represent core stories of the Christian heritage. Most of all, Christians know that the Torah is from God; this they know from Paul.

Source

Meyer, Barbara U., *Jesus the Jew in Christian Memory: Theological and Philosophical Explorations* (Cambridge: Cambridge University Press, 2020), 151–2, 155–7.

Commentary

In *Jesus the Jew in Christian Memory*, Barbara U. Meyer (b. 1968), a professor of religious studies at Tel Aviv University and systematic theologian in the Lutheran tradition, argues that the Jewishness of Jesus generates an otherness that expands the spiritual, ethical and intellectual horizons for non-Jewish Christians. Jesus' Jewishness – 'more declared than elaborated on or explained' (p. 7) – is a memory requiring revitalisation. Christians who remember Jesus yet neglect his relationship (and their own) with Jewish communities thereby separate themselves from the Jewish Jesus and his God. In contrast, by engaging in remembering Jesus in his Jewishness, Christians participate in a 'mending of memory'.

Meyer's Jesus was a Jew who had a 'specific practice, narrative and tradition', and thus one who had daily practices and time structures, and likely a distinctive approach to God connected to Jewish practice of the time (pp. 46–7). Jesus is thus best described as a 'halakhic Jew' who was 'knowledgeable about the written and oral Torah, observant of contemporaneous Jewish law, and an active, even passionate, participant in halakhic discussion' (p. 65).

She upends the common misconception that Jesus understood himself in contrast to the law. Following in the tradition of her mentor Friedrich Marquardt (see Chapter 8, p. 425), Meyer depicts Jesus as a 'practicing, Torah-observant and halakhically committed Jew' (pp. 51–2) – a wording close to that of Paul van Buren's 'Torah-faithful Jew'. Jesus' disputations with the Pharisees, whom many Christians misunderstand as sanctimonious hypocrites (at best), reveal him engaging in characteristically Jewish debates about how Torah should be lived out. Recent scholarly studies on the Pharisees, such as *The Pharisees* (2021), offer considerable detail complementing Meyer's observations.

In advocating for theologians to give greater prominence in Christology informed by Jewish–Christian studies, Meyer argues they should speak more 'thoughtfully and hesitantly' about Jesus and salvation but 'more intensely' about the evil of the Shoah (p. 102). In her view, many interpretations of Christian dogma overemphasise the positive aspects of Christ's death and resurrection by speaking as though salvation had been accomplished, and thus obscuring the reality of evil and glossing over the Shoah.

The excerpt here, taken from the final chapter, proposes a Christology grounded in the profound reality that precisely *as a Jew* Jesus remains other to Christians. Thus, non-Jewish Christians encounter Jesus as stranger – and it is his otherness, his strangeness, that confronts those who follow him to ponder what is entailed in walking in the way of the Jewish Jesus. Within the textual tradition of the Pentateuch and Prophets, the 'Jesus texts' give priority to the disadvantaged, especially the widow, the orphan and the stranger. The church has stressed Jesus' suffering so much that it has failed to emphasise that Christians must act to counter suffering, as did Jesus. Otherness thus becomes an important category for reflecting on the significance of Jesus Christ.

In highlighting Jesus' otherness, Meyer has launched an international conversation that offers a creative perspective for the field of Jewish–Christian relations.

Bibliography

Homolka, Walter, *Jewish Jesus Research and Its Challenge to Christology Today* (Boston: Brill, 2016).
Levine, Amy-Jill, and Sievers, Joseph (eds.), *The Pharisees* (Grand Rapids: Eerdmans, 2021).
van Buren, Paul M., *A Theology of the Jewish–Christian Reality, Part 3: Christ in Context* (San Francisco: Harper & Row, 1988).

Appendix to Part III
Institutional Statements: 1947 to the Present Day

EDWARD KESSLER

INTRODUCTION

This Appendix is devoted to the distinct documentary genre of institutional statements, which have, since the end of World War II, become a common feature of high-level and formal encounters. It begins with the 1947 *Ten Points of Seelisberg*, a declaration issued by Christian theologians which paved the way for modern institutional dialogue (document 1). The subsequent fourteen documents represent efforts from Jewish and Christian organisations and denominations to formalise relations and foster understanding within as well as between their communities. They deal with a range of themes including antisemitism and supersessionism, Zionism and the State of Israel, mission and dialogue.

The statements of official church and Jewish bodies do not usually make very interesting reading. However, on this subject they are important. First of all, they indicate, far more than the work of specific religious leaders, the thinking of an institution at a particular stage. The work of an individual theologian may be profound and far-seeing, but the attitude of a religious institution extends beyond the individual. While it is tempting to attribute more significance to statements than they warrant, some official pronouncements carry authority and have been highly influential on relations.

The institutional statements betray some of the ongoing tensions of the Jewish–Christian relationship, such as critical Christian voices about the State of Israel, as well as ongoing Jewish suspicion about Christian missionary aims, but in spite of the problems encountered they demonstrate the extent to which changes in the Jewish–Christian encounter in the last seventy years have become institutionalised.

This introduction will refer both to statements discussed in individual commentaries and to other institutional statements not included due to lack of space. Two themes arise from Christian institutional statements, each of which resulted in Jewish responses: the first theme is the realisation that Christians have made a significant contribution to anti-Judaism and antisemitism; the second theme is the reawakening among Christians to the Jewishness of Christianity.

The Jewish responses are: in light of the first theme, distrust of Christian overtures; in light of the second, defensive engagement in dialogue (in other words, for the sake of combating antisemitism).

In the last twenty-five years, a third and shared theme in institutional statements has become noticeable: recognition of a common purpose. For some of the churches this is expressed, theologically, in terms of an interdependence with Judaism. Among Jewish communities there is general recognition that a positive relationship with Christianity is possible, and for some a genuine partnership has now begun.

Conflicts and tensions remain, however, as witnessed, for example, by divergent attitudes towards the State of Israel (particularly, but not only, among the churches) and towards Christian mission.

When the World Council of Churches (WCC) was founded in 1948, it held its first meeting in Amsterdam and its *Report on the Christian Approach to the Jews* referred to the conference taking place 'within five years of the extermination of six million Jews'. The WCC acknowledged the Christian contribution to antisemitism, stating that 'the churches in the past have helped to foster an image of the Jews as the sole enemies of Christ, which has contributed to antisemitism in the secular world'. It called upon 'all churches we represent to denounce antisemitism'. Thus, the churches' awareness of the Christian contribution to antisemitism was placed firmly on the agenda of Christian–Jewish relations by an organisation that encompassed over 350 non-Catholic churches (today some 500 million Christians).

The magnitude of the WCC's step can be seen more clearly when compared with the failure of the Anglican Lambeth Conference in the same year even to mention antisemitism. Forty years later, the Lambeth Conference delivered a scathing denunciation of antisemitism and of the Christian teaching of contempt: *Jews, Christians and Muslims* (document 5). Other Protestant churches, such as the Leuenberg Church Fellowship (consisting of the Reformation Churches in Europe) in 2001, also issued statements which explicitly acknowledged the Christian contribution to Jewish suffering.

The same process cannot be seen among the Orthodox churches, although eleven formal meetings of Jewish and Christian academics and religious leaders have taken place since 1974, most recently in 2022, initially involving Greek theologians but since the 1990s including Orthodox Christians from eastern Europe and the Middle East. A small number of gatherings have taken place in Russia itself, such as in St Petersburg in 1997 on 'Theology after Auschwitz and the Gulag', but despite these meetings and occasional statements by Orthodox leaders (notably the Ecumenical Patriarch's speech at the US Holocaust Memorial Museum in 1997 and to a meeting of Jewish leaders in New York in 2009), there is no comparison with the western churches. To some extent, the uneasy relationship of the Orthodox churches with Judaism echoes the state of their involvement in the ecumenical movement.

The Roman Catholic Church's contribution to Christian–Jewish relations began to be recognised shortly before Easter 1961 when John XXIII changed the Good Friday liturgy during which Catholics had said, 'Let us pray also for the perfidious Jews'. A year later, the pope also received wide attention for publicly greeting Jewish visitors with the words, 'I am Joseph your brother.' Issued in 1965, *Nostra aetate* (document 2) marked the beginnings of a fresh approach to Judaism and, according to Edward Flannery, terminated at a stroke a millennial 'teaching of contempt' of Jews and Judaism. It condemned 'all hatreds, persecutions, displays of antisemitism leveled at any time or from any quarter against the Jews' (although it did not acknowledge Christian responsibility) (Flannery 1988: 128). As we shall see, the statement ushered in a new era and discourse never previously heard in the Catholic Church, and was deeply influential on subsequent Christian statements.

For the most part, Jews responded with distrust – a legacy of the consequences of the 'teaching of contempt'. There was, among Jewish communities, no widespread desire to engage in dialogue with Christians, although Nahum Goldmann and Gerhart Riegner, from the World Jewish Congress, established an international Jewish dialogue body, the International Jewish Committee for Interreligious Consultations (IJCIC), which still exists (and continues to issue statements, such as a formal response to the Vatican's 1998 document *We Remember: A Reflection on the Shoah* and on the fifty-fifth anniversary of *Nostra aetate* in 2020).

The lack of a Jewish response was due not only to suspicion of Christian intentions but also to the mark which the *adversus Judaeos* tradition had left on the Jewish psyche. Most Jews did not trust Christian motives, and while individual Jews, some synagogues and their communities did engage in Jewish–Christian dialogue, no significant institutional statements were published.

The lack of Christian institutional statements reflecting on the Holocaust, not just anti-semitism, added to Jewish distrust, the Synod of the Evangelical Church in the Rhineland's (Evangelische Kirche im Rheinland; EKiG) 1980 statement *Towards Renovation of the Relationship of Christians and Jews* being one of the first (document 4). In 1987 contro-versy arose following Pope John Paul II's reception of Austrian president Kurt Waldheim, who had been an active Nazi. In response, the pope asked the Pontifical Commission for Religious Relations with Jews to consider responses to the Holocaust, and *We Remember: Reflections on the Shoah* was published in 1998. This was not a formal apology, unlike that of the French Catholic bishops, who had publicly admitted 'the primary role played by the consistently repeated anti-Jewish stereotypes wrongly perpetuated by the Christians in the historical process that led to the Holocaust' (Catholic Bishops of France, *Declaration of Repentance*, 1997). *We Remember* spoke of those Christians who helped Jews and those who failed to do so, but implied a balanced picture. It differed significantly from contemporary Protestant documents on the Holocaust, as illustrated by the 1996 US United Methodist Church statement *Building Bridges of Hope*, which stated:

> Especially crucial for Christians in our quest for understanding has been the struggle to recognize the horror of the Holocaust as the catastrophic culmina-tion of a long history of anti-Jewish attitudes and actions in which Christians, and sometimes the Church itself, have been deeply implicated.

Yet an emphasis on the Holocaust carries a danger for Jewish–Christian relations since it is based on an edifice of guilt, transient, not easily passed to the next generation and unstable, inherently prone to sudden reversal. This is why the second theme, a reawakening among Christians to the Jewish origins of Christianity, is significant: it provided a positive foundation for Jewish–Christian relations.

Church statements from the *Ten Points of Seelisberg* onwards not only renounced triumphalist doctrines and antisemitism but also emphasised the Jewishness of Jesus and the early church. Indeed, they acknowledged an ongoing relationship, as illustrated by Protestant (e.g., the Evangelical Church of the Rhineland) and Roman Catholic statements (e.g., phrases such as 'the Jews remain very dear to God' in *Nostra aetate*). Pope John Paul II, for example, made clear that God's covenant with the Jewish people had never been broken and retained eternal validity (cf. Romans 11:29). If the Jews were not rejected, then Judaism was not a fossilised faith, as had been taught previously, but a living, authentic religion (see *The Jewish People and Their Sacred Scriptures in the Christian Bible*; document 8).

The ramifications were manifold. Christians were taught that Jesus, his family and his followers were Jewish, and the Jewish background to Christianity was highlighted, including the closeness of the relationship between Jesus and the Pharisees, to whom 'he was very near', and 'that from the Jewish people sprang the apostles' (1985 Vatican *Notes on the Correct Way to Present the Jews and Judaism in Preaching and Catechesis in the Roman Catholic Church*).

From the Jewish side, individuals such as Claude Montefiore (see Chapter 6, p. 333) had reminded Jews that Jesus was a fellow Jew (their 'great brother' as Martin Buber described him; see Chapter 8, p. 405). But this has rarely made an appearance in Jewish institutional statements, and even the publication of *Dabru Emet* (*Speak Truth*) in 2000 (document 7) failed to mention the Jewishness of Jesus, simply stating that 'Christians know and serve God through Jesus Christ and the Christian tradition'.

While the first theme illustrated a shift among the churches from what was, for the most part, an inherent need to condemn Judaism to a condemnation of Christian anti-Judaism, the second led to a closer relationship with Jews as 'the elder brother'. Although no significant Jewish statement was published before 2000, institutional engagement with the churches was becoming more common, notably through the various national Councils of Christians and Jews.

The third (shared) theme, common purpose, is partly the result of building a culture of trust between Jews and Christians, prompted in part by the Vatican's advice that 'Christians must strive to learn by what essential traits the Jews define themselves in the light of their own religious experience' (*Guidelines to Nostra aetate*, 1974). A similar view was expressed by Protestant churches such as the Leuenberg Church Fellowship, which stated that 'the relationship with Israel is therefore for Christians and for the churches an indispensable part of the foundation of their faith' (*Church and Israel*, 2001). The two Jewish statements *Dabru Emet* and *To Do the Will of Our Father in Heaven* (documents 7 and 13) also acknowledge the positive basis for relations with the churches, a 'common covenantal mission' in the words of the latter.

Christian institutional statements demonstrate that Christian theology has been profoundly revised at the official level: the churches are committed to the fight against anti-semitism and to teaching about the Jewishness of Christianity, the problem of mission to Jews has been reduced although not removed (see the Southern Baptist Convention's *Resolution on Jewish Evangelism*, 1996; document 6) and in the Roman Catholic Church has all but disappeared (see the Pontifical Commission for Religious Relations with the Jews' 2015 statement *The Gifts and the Calling of God Are Irrevocable*; document 14).

Yet there remains one significant area of tension: Zionism and the State of Israel. For Jews, the centrality of the land of the Bible, as well as the survival of over a third of world Jewry, is at stake. The churches, for their part, not only disagree as to the place of the land of Israel in Christian theology but feel particular concern for Christians who live in the nation state of Israel, as well as for Palestinians. There are also of course many Christians and Jews (and Muslims) who are deeply concerned about the 'other', making this a complicated picture.

Some churches are extremely critical of Israel, as represented by the statements *Relations with Believers of Other Religions* and the Kairos Document (documents 10 and 11) issued on behalf of churches from the Holy Land. For Christians in the Middle East, the relationship with Jews exists within the framework of a larger dialogue with Muslims. Christian Palestinians, in particular, are under pressure, concerned at the prospect of Hamas and other Islamist parties taking power and at the exodus of Christians from the region.

Other churches are vocal in their support for Israel, as witnessed by the General Synod of the Netherlands Reformed Church's 1970 statement *Israel: People, Land, and State* (document 3). Christian Zionists, most evident in the American Protestant fundamentalist and evangelical communities, are sympathetic to the more conservative elements in Israeli politics, as well as to the concept of a Greater Israel. They believe in the restoration of Israel in the days preceding the end of the world, and their support for the State of Israel is linked to the Second Coming of Jesus (see the International Christian Embassy in Jerusalem's 2013 statement *Swords into Ploughshares*; document 12). For such Christian Zionists, Israel becomes a pawn on the chessboard of history, used to fulfil a final predetermined game plan, but their support for the State of Israel has been appreciated by both secular and some religious Israeli Jews, including Orthodox settlers in the occupied West Bank. Indeed, since the late 1970s successive Israeli governments have been wooing Christian conservatives, increasingly influential in US Republican circles. Nevertheless, it would not be surprising if the increasing diversity of Jewish opinion about Israel, between liberals who are critical and conservatives who are more supportive, plays out in future Jewish institutional statements about Jewish–Christian relations and, in turn, influences Christian approaches to Israel. The most recent statement, *A Jewish–Christian Glossary* (document 15), explores the differences between Jewish and Christian approaches to Israel and is an example of the third theme, commonality of purpose, being jointly penned by the Office of the Chief Rabbi of the United Hebrew Congregations of the Commonwealth and the Church of Scotland. The document recognises divergent approaches to this area of contention and seeks to apply Jonathan Sacks' call to foster a 'dignity of difference'.

Finally, while there is an important agenda for top-level dialogue and the publication of official statements, there is also a growing trend towards regional and local levels. Consciousness of changes in Jewish–Christian relations has been largely confined to the elite (although in certain regions, such as the United States, it has been more widely disseminated). The object for many is to ensure that these changes are disseminated into the everyday understanding of the faithful around the world (see for example the WCC's *African Jewish Consultation*; document 9), in churches and synagogues, seminaries and yeshivahs, schools and universities, as well as in public education.

Giant strides have been made, but the Jewish–Christian relationship is a dynamic and evolving process. Jews and Christians will never be able to sit back and say that the work is done and the agenda completed, even though on many major issues today they find themselves on the same side of the fence, faced with the same challenges.

Bibliography

Brockway, Allan, van Buren, Paul, Rendtorff, Rolf, and Schoon, Simon (eds.), *The Theology of the Churches and the Jewish People: Statements by the World Council of Churches and Its Member Churches* (Geneva: WCC Publications, 1988).

Cunningham, Philip A., *Seeking Shalom: The Journey to Right Relationship between Catholics and Jews* (Grand Rapids: Eerdmans, 2015).

Cunningham, Philip A., Langer, Ruth, and Svartvik, Jesper (eds.), *Enabling Dialogue about the Land: A Resource Book for Jews and Christians* (Mahwah: Paulist Press, 2020).

D'Costa, Gavin, *Catholic Doctrines on the Jewish People after Vatican II* (Oxford: Oxford University Press, 2019).

Flannery, Edward H., *The Anguish of the Jews: Twenty-Three Centuries of Anti-Semitism* (New York: Macmillan, 1965).

Flannery, Edward H., 'Seminaries, Classrooms, Pulpits, Streets: Where We Have to Go', in Brooks, Roger (ed.), *Unanswered Questions: Theological Views of Jewish–Catholic Relations* (Notre Dame: University of Notre Dame Press, 1988).

Greive, Wolfgang, and Prove, Peter N. (eds.), *A Shift in Jewish–Lutheran Relations?* (Geneva: Lutheran World Federation, 2003).

Marshall, David, 'The World Council of Churches and the Theology of Jewish–Christian Relations', *Current Dialogue* 72, no. 5 (2020), 861–94.

Sherman, Franklin (ed.), *Bridges: Documents of the Christian–Jewish Dialogue*, 2 vols (New York: Paulist Press, 2011–14).

DOCUMENTS

I

International Council of Christians and Jews (ICCJ): The Ten Points of Seelisberg *(5 August 1947)*

Text

1. Remember that One God speaks to us all through the Old and the New Testaments.
2. Remember that Jesus was born of a Jewish mother of the seed of David and the people of Israel, and that His everlasting love and forgiveness embraces His own people and the whole world.
3. Remember that the first disciples, the apostles, and the first martyrs were Jews.

4. Remember that the fundamental commandment of Christianity, to love God and one's neighbour, proclaimed already in the Old Testament and confirmed by Jesus, is binding upon both Christians and Jews in all human relationships, without any exception.

5. Avoid distorting or misrepresenting biblical or post-biblical Judaism with the object of extolling Christianity.

6. Avoid using the word Jews in the exclusive sense of the enemies of Jesus, and the words 'the enemies of Jesus' to designate the whole Jewish people.

7. Avoid presenting the Passion in such a way as to bring the odium of the killing of Jesus upon all Jews or upon Jews alone. It was only a section of the Jews in Jerusalem who demanded the death of Jesus, and the Christian message has always been that it was the sins of mankind which were exemplified by those Jews and the sins in which all men share that brought Christ to the Cross.

8. Avoid referring to the scriptural curses, or the cry of a raging mob: 'His blood be upon us and our children', without remembering that this cry should not count against the infinitely more weighty words of our Lord: 'Father forgive them for they know not what they do.'

9. Avoid promoting the superstitious notion that the Jewish people are reprobate, accursed, reserved for a destiny of suffering.

10. Avoid speaking of the Jews as if the first members of the Church had not been Jews.

Source

An Address to the Churches (The Ten Points of Seelisberg), https://ccjr.us/dialogika-resources/
documents-and-statements/ecumenical-christian/seelisberg

Commentary

Soon after the end of World War II, sixty-five Jews and Christians took part in an Emergency Conference on Anti-Semitism, which met in the Swiss town of Seelisberg. The Christian participants issued a declaration originally titled *An Address to the Churches* but which soon became known as *The Ten Points of Seelisberg*, in which, in consultation with Jews, they tackled the problem of Christian antisemitism and proposed a new relationship between Christianity and Judaism. The declaration anticipated many later church statements in highlighting the Jewishness of Jesus and the early church and in its concern for care in preaching and catechesis.

Individual Christian theologians, such as James Parkes (see Chapter 7, p. 392) in his book *The Conflict of the Church and the Synagogue*, which was published in 1934, the year after the Emergency Conference was originally scheduled to meet, had argued for major revisions to Christian teaching about Jews and Judaism. Similarly, the French Jewish historian Jules Isaac (see Chapter 8, p. 402), whose wife and daughter had perished in the Holocaust but who devoted his life to reconciliation with Christianity, publishing *Jésus et Israël* in 1948, coined the term 'teaching of contempt' (*enseignement du mépris*, the title of his 1962 publication) to describe Christian anti-Judaism and called for a 'teaching of respect' towards the Jewish people. Both men encouraged church leaders to condemn antisemitism, eliminate anti-Judaism from church teachings and acknowledge the permanent value of Judaism, and Isaac was a key figure at the conference, where he presented his Eighteen Points for the 'rectification necessary in Christian teaching'.

The *Ten Points* focused on Christianity's roots in Judaism, called on Christians to avoid 'promoting the superstitious notion that the Jewish people are reprobate, accursed, reserved for a destiny of suffering', and challenged literalist or fundamentalist readings of biblical texts, pointing to the necessity of historical, cultural and theological context – assertions which may seem timid by today's standards but were still fairly revolutionary in 1947.

The impact of the document extended well beyond the number of participants, and in 1960 Jules Isaac met Pope John XXIII to ask him to place Christian anti-Judaism on the agenda of the upcoming Second Vatican Council. The pope agreed, and some of Isaac's recommendations were adopted in *Nostra aetate* (see document 2 below). The influence of the *Ten Points* can also be seen in documents published by Protestant churches, such as *On the Jewish Question* (Synod of the Evangelische Kirche in Deutschland, 1950) and *The Church and the Jewish People* (Lutheran World Federation, 1964).

The *Ten Points* became a cornerstone of modern Jewish–Christian dialogue and the study of Jewish–Christian relations, invigorating Christian efforts to renew the relationship with Jews and Judaism. In 2009 a revised and updated version of the *Ten Points* was issued by Jewish and Christian theologians under the auspices of the International Council of Christians and Jews (ICCJ), and in 2022 the ICCJ organised a series of events and publications to mark the Seelisberg Conference's seventy-fifth anniversary.

Bibliography

Isaac, Jules, *Jesus and Israel*, ed. Bishop, Claire Huchet, trans. Sally Gran (New York: Holt, Rinehart and Winston, 1971). (Originally published as *Jésus et Israël*, 1948.)

Rutishauser, Christian M., 'The 1947 Seelisberg Conference: The Foundation of the Jewish–Christian Dialogue', *Studies in Christian–Jewish Relations* 2, no. 2 (2008), https://doi.org/10.6017/scjr.v2i2.1421

Simpson, William W., and Weyl, Ruth, *The Story of the International Council of Christians and Jews* (Heppenheim: International Council of Christians and Jews, 1996).

2

Declaration on the Relation of the Church to Non-Christian Religions: Nostra aetate *(28 October 1965)*

Text

4. [... T]he Church cannot forget that she received the revelation of the Old Testament by way of that people with whom God in his inexpressible mercy established the ancient covenant. Nor can she forget that she draws nourishment from that good olive tree onto

which the wild olive branches of the Gentiles have been grafted (cf. Rom. 11:17–24). The Church believes that Christ who is our peace has through his cross reconciled Jews and Gentiles and made them one in himself (cf. Eph. 2:14–16).

Likewise, the Church keeps ever before her mind the words of the apostle Paul about his kinsmen: 'they are Israelites, and to them belong the sonship, the glory, the covenants, the giving of the law, the worship, and the promises; to them belong the patriarchs, and of their race according to the flesh, is the Christ' (Rom. 9:4–5), the son of the virgin Mary. She is mindful, moreover, that the apostles, the pillars on which the Church stands, are of Jewish descent, as are many of those early disciples who proclaimed the Gospel of Christ to the world.

As holy Scripture testifies, Jerusalem did not recognize God's moment when it came (cf. Lk 19:42). Jews for the most part did not accept the Gospel; on the contrary, many opposed the spreading of it (cf. Rom. 11:28). Even so, the apostle Paul maintains that the Jews remain very dear to God, for the sake of the patriarchs, since God does not take back the gifts he bestowed or the choice he made. Together with the prophets and that same apostle, the Church awaits the day, known to God alone, when all peoples will call on God with one voice and 'serve him shoulder to shoulder' (Soph. 3:9; cf. Is. 66:23; Ps. 65:4; Rom. 11:11–32).

Since Christians and Jews have such a common spiritual heritage, this sacred Council wishes to encourage and further mutual understanding and appreciation. This can be obtained, especially, by way of biblical and theological enquiry and through friendly discussions.

Even though the Jewish authorities and those who followed their lead pressed for the death of Christ (cf. John 19:6), neither all Jews indiscriminately at that time, nor Jews today, can be charged with the crimes committed during his passion. It is true that the Church is the new people of God, yet the Jews should not be spoken of as rejected or accursed as if this followed from holy Scripture. Consequently, all must take care, lest in catechizing or in preaching the Word of God, they teach anything which is not in accord with the truth of the Gospel message or the spirit of Christ.

Indeed, the Church reproves every form of persecution against whomsoever it may be directed. Remembering, then, her common heritage with the Jews and moved not by any political consideration, but solely by the religious motivation of Christian charity, she deplores all hatreds, persecutions, displays of antisemitism leveled at any time or from any source against the Jews.

The Church always held and continues to hold that Christ out of infinite love freely underwent suffering and death because of the sins of all men, so that all might attain salvation. It is the duty of the Church, therefore, in her preaching to proclaim the cross of Christ as the sign of God's universal love and the source of all grace.

Source

Flannery, Austin (ed.), *Vatican Council II: The Conciliar and Post Conciliar Documents*, Vatican collection, vol. 1, rev. ed. (Leominster: Gracewing; Dublin: Dominican Publications; Newtown, NSW: Dwyer, 1992), 740–2. (Translation by Father Killian, OCSO.)

Commentary

Nostra aetate (*In Our Time*) was proclaimed on 28 October 1965 by Pope John VI and consists of the fourth and most important section of Vatican II's *Declaration on Non-Christian Religions*. It is regarded as the most influential of the modern church documents on Jewish–Christian relations, achieving a radical reversal of the church's 'teaching of contempt' against Jews and Judaism and marking the beginnings of a fresh approach by the Roman Catholic Church.

The document was both formed in and generated controversy. Consideration of the church's relationship with the Jewish people was put on the Second Vatican Council's agenda by Pope John XXIII, who delegated the preparation to Augustin Bea. Abraham Joshua Heschel and Jules Isaac (see Chapter 8, pages 436 and 402) encouraged Bea to prepare a statement that condemned antisemitism, eliminated anti-Judaism from church teachings and acknowledged the permanent value of Judaism. While a statement on relations with Jews was one of the earliest on the Council's agenda and stimulated interest from the general public, it was among the last to be promulgated, meeting opposition from conservatives as well as from bishops representing minority Christian communities in the Muslim, especially Arab, world.

The document condemns antisemitism and rejects the charge of Jewish responsibility for the death of Jesus, undermining the view commonly expressed in the *adversus Judaeos* literature – see, e.g., John Chrysostom (Chapter 2, p. 91) and Martin Luther (Chapter 5, p. 241) – that Jews were divinely rejected. If Jews were not then and are not now collectively responsible for the death of Jesus, it is no longer possible to view the destruction of the Jerusalem temple in 70 CE and the dispersion of Jews as divine punishment. Later pontifical documents, such as the 1985 *Notes on the Correct Way to Present the Jews and Judaism in Preaching and Catechesis in the Roman Catholic Church*, developed this further.

Positively, *Nostra aetate* emphasises the Jewish origins of Christianity, importantly adopting the present tense (cf. Rom. 9) to show the ongoing relationship both between Judaism and Christianity and between Jews and God: the Church 'draws' spiritual sustenance from Jews; they 'remain' beloved; to them 'belongs' the covenant(s). Excerpts from Rom. 9–11 are regularly used in *Nostra aetate* and other church statements (e.g., Rom. 11:29, *The Gifts and the Calling of God Are Irrevocable*; see document 14). One consequence of *Nostra aetate* is that the ongoing relationship between God and the Jewish people has become central to both Roman Catholic and Protestant teaching (see, for example, *Towards Renovation of the Relationship of Christians and Jews* (document 4) and *Jews, Christians and Muslims: The Way of Dialogue* (document 8)). Pope John Paul II's oft-quoted description of the Jewish people as 'the people of God, of the Old Covenant never revoked by God' (see Chapter 9, p. 453) is illustrative.

However, *Nostra aetate* omitted a number of key topics, such as Zionism and Israel, and also exhibits a tension that runs through Jewish–Christian relations: both Jews and the church claim to be the true Israel (*verus Israel*). The theological implications of the latter, such as for mission, covenant and peoplehood, are explored in later documents (see, for example, documents 13 and 14 below) and continue to influence the Jewish–Christian relationship.

Bibliography

D'Costa, Gavin, *Vatican II: Catholic Doctrines on Jews and Muslims* (Oxford: Oxford University Press, 2014), 113–60.

Moyaert, Marian, and Pollefeyt, Didier (eds.), *Never Revoked: Nostra Aetate as Ongoing Challenge for Jewish–Christian Dialogue* (Leuven: Peeters; Grand Rapids: Eerdmans, 2010).

Schultenover, David G. (ed.), *50 Years On: Probing the Riches of Vatican II* (Collegeville: Liturgical Press, 2015), 207–70.

Sherman, Franklin, 'Protestant Parallels to *Nostra aetate*', *Studies in Christian–Jewish Relations* 10, no. 2 (2015), https://doi.org/10.6017/scjr.v10i2.9226.

3

General Synod of the Reformed Church of the Netherlands: Israel: People, Land, and State – Suggestions for a Theological Evaluation *(1970)*

Text

[…] If as Christians we feel ourselves connected with the biblical Israel, the implication is that there is also a special connection between us and the Jewish people of today. It is an essential part of the task of Christians to ponder upon this […] Today the State of Israel is one of the forms in which the Jewish people appear. We would be talking in a void and closing our eyes to reality, if today we were to think about the Jewish people without taking the State of Israel explicitly into consideration […]

[…]

[…] We have spoken about the unique destiny of the Jews to be God's covenant people and about the unique tie which binds them and the land of Palestine together. Even the rejection of Jesus Christ did not bring any change in this regard. Thereby the people have indeed affirmed their alienation which they had shown already, but they are still the chosen people, destined to fulfil a lasting and separate role. In our time many Jews have again gone to the land of Palestine. In this way the people, who were threatened with disappearance, partly through assimilation, partly through awful pogroms and acts of extermination, have again obtained a new, clearly visible form. Precisely in its concrete visibility, this return points to the special significance of this people in the midst of the nations, and to the saving faithfulness of God […] Therefore we rejoice in this reunion of people and land.

[…] However, we do not intend to imply that the return is the final stage of history, nor that the people can never again be expelled from the land. Indeed, in the return the grace of God's lasting election has become manifest, but this return carries with it a special threat. For it could be that the other peoples deny a place to the Jews who are in their midst. It could also be that Israel does not use the new chance which it has received to fulfill its destiny in the land. But both these perils cannot prevent us from understanding the return positively as a confirmation of God's lasting purpose with his people [...]

[...]

[...] The land is given to Israel as dwelling place; there it can have its state. But the boundaries of this state cannot be read from the Bible. The territory in which the Jewish people lived in OT times has had very different boundaries, and these never coincided with those of which the prophetic promises spoke. The only thing of which we are sure is that these boundaries must be such that they offer the Jewish people a dwelling place where they can be themselves. But it is a matter of a dwelling place, not a sphere of power and control. The necessity of protecting their dwelling place should not induce the Jews to make it into a nationalistic state in which the only thing that counts is military power. It is true that the so-called Christian states also have frequently succumbed to this temptation. But this is exactly the point, namely that in this way Israel is in danger of becoming a people like all other peoples, not worse and not better. Such a collective assimilation would be a denial of its true nature.

[...] The Jewish people are called to exercise justice in an exemplary way. This too is an essential aspect of their true identity. In this respect the problems caused by the founding of the State of Israel and its later military victories are a particular challenge for the people. Hundreds of thousands of Palestinian refugees live miserably, without rights, around the borders of Israel. It belongs to Israel's vocation that it should know itself to be responsible for them and that it should do all it can to put right the injustice done to them [...]

[...]

[...] In this time before the ultimate fulfillment, we as the church are called together with the people of Israel to be true to our vocation. The difference between us is that our starting point is the way of Jesus Christ, who is not yet recognized by Israel as the fulfillment of *its* destiny. But we ourselves also do not live truly and entirely on the basis of the salvation which we have received. Indeed, if we were to live in that way, the Jews would be made jealous. The fact that does not happen, shows how imperfectly the church fulfills her calling; the criticism which we make against the Jewish people comes back upon our own heads. The Christian church too has not yet reached her destiny, she too lives still in a transitional state. The Jewish people and the church are both travellers and both are preserved, each in its own way, in God's faithfulness.

Source

Croner, Helga (ed.), *Stepping Stones to Further Jewish–Christian Relations: An Unabridged Collection of Christian Documents* (New York and London: Stimulus Books, 1977), 92, 102–3, 105, 107.

Commentary

While antisemitism and the 'teaching of contempt' of Judaism were being explored by the churches, discussions on the land and State of Israel were proving more difficult. It was easier to condemn antisemitism as a misunderstanding of Christian teaching than to come to terms with the re-establishment of a Jewish state. *Israel: People, Land, and State* is one of the earliest Christian statements on Israel, issued by the oldest Dutch Reformed church in 1970.

There were a number of reasons for the delay. The churches had links with local Christian communities, including Palestinians who had experienced loss of land and were understandably concerned about a statement. The *adversus Judaeos* tradition might have been rejected, but did this mean accepting the State of Israel as fulfilling God's promise? Finally, the concept of peoplehood, especially of a people tied to a particular land, was difficult to understand, since most Christians viewed their faith as primarily connected to a personal relationship with God. As Geoffrey Wigoder put it, 'the relationship of covenant to Land as of the Jews to Israel is as much outside the Christian experience as the centrality of Jesus in the mystery of the triune God is outside the Jewish experience' (1988: 105).

The first steps were taken by Christian theologians, notably Reinhold Niebuhr and James Parkes (see Chapter 7, p. 392), but church statements were much slower to emerge. In 1948, the year in which the State of Israel was founded, the First Assembly of the WCC met in Amsterdam and its conference report acknowledged that 'the establishment of the state "Israel" [*sic*] adds a political dimension to the Christian approach to the Jews and threatens to complicate antisemitism with political fears and enmities. On the political aspects of the Palestinian problem and the complex conflicts of "rights" we do not undertake to express a judgement.' The second and third assemblies in the 1950s did not mention the subject, nor did the Roman Catholic document *Nostra aetate* in 1965 (see document 2 above).

The statement of the General Synod of the Reformed Church of the Netherlands challenged this prevailing attitude. It recognised the importance of Israel to Jews, noting that it is 'one of the forms in which the Jewish people appear'. Since a special connection exists between the Jewish people and the church, the State of Israel is 'a sign [...] that it is God's will to be on earth together with man'. Indeed, the church 'rejoice[s] in this reunion of people and land'.

Having traced the place of the land in Israel's covenant with God, the Synod concluded that if the election of the Jewish people remains valid, so does the tie between the people and the land. It called on the state to be 'exemplary' in its actions, a call criticised by the Lutheran scholar Alice Eckardt (see Chapter 8, p. 439).

Bibliography

Harries, Richard, 'The Response of the Churches to Israel', *European Judaism* 25, no. 1 (Spring 1992), 14–24.

Stuart, Geert H. Cohen, 'The Attitude of the Netherlands Reformed Church to *Israel: People, Land, and State*', *Immanuel* 22–3 (1989), 146–61.

Wigoder, Geoffrey, *Jewish–Christian Relations since the Second World War* (Manchester: Manchester University Press, 1988).

4

Synod of the Evangelical Church in the Rhineland (EKiG): Towards Renovation of the Relationship of Christians and Jews *(1980)*

Text

Thou bearest not the root, but the root thee (Rom. 11:18b).

1. According to its 'Message to the Congregations concerning the Dialogue between Christians and Jews' (12 January 1978) the Synod of the Evangelical Church in the Rhineland accepts the historical necessity of attaining a new relationship of the church to the Jewish people.

2. The church is brought to this by four factors:
   1) The recognition of Christian co-responsibility and guilt for the Holocaust – the defamation, persecution and murder of the Jews in the Third Reich.
   2) The new biblical insights concerning the continuing significance of the Jewish people within the history of God (e.g., Rom. 9–11), which have been attained in connection with the struggle of the Confessing Church.
   3) The insight that the continuing existence of the Jewish people, its return to the Land of Promise, and also the foundation of the state of Israel, are signs of the faithfulness of God towards his people (cf. the study 'Christians and Jews' III, 2+3).
   4) The readiness of Jews, in spite of the Holocaust, to (engage in) encounter, common study and cooperation.
   [...]

4. In consequence the Synod declares:
   1) We confess with dismay the co-responsibility and guilt of German Christendom for the Holocaust (cf. Thesis I).
   2) We confess thankfully the 'Scriptures' (Luke 24:32+45; I Cor. 15:3f.), our Old Testament, to be the common foundation for the faith and work of Jews and Christians (cf. Thesis II).
   3) We confess Jesus Christ the Jew, who as the Messiah of Israel is the Saviour of the world and binds the peoples of the world to the people of God (cf. Thesis III).
   4) We believe the permanent election of the Jewish people as the people of God and realize that through Jesus Christ the church is taken into the covenant of God with his people (cf. Thesis IV).
   5) We believe with the Jews that the unity of righteousness and love characterizes God's work of salvation in history. We believe with the Jews that righteousness and love are the commands of God for our whole life. As Christians we see both rooted and grounded in the work of God with Israel and in the work of God through Jesus Christ (cf. Thesis V).
   6) We believe that in their respective calling Jews and Christians are witnesses of God before the world and before each other. Therefore we are convinced that the

church may not express its witness towards the Jewish people as it does its mission to the peoples of the world (cf. Thesis VI).

7) Therefore we declare:

Throughout centuries the word 'new' has been used in biblical exegesis against the Jewish people: the new covenant was understood in contrast to the old covenant, the new people of God as replacement of the old people of God. This disrespect to the permanent election of the Jewish people and its condemnation to non-existence marked Christian theology, the preaching and work of the church again and again right to the present day. Thereby we have made ourselves guilty also of the physical elimination of the Jewish people.

Therefore, we want to perceive the unbreakable connection of the New Testament with the Old Testament in a new way, and learn to understand the relationship of the 'old' and 'new' from the standpoint of the promise: in the framework of the given promise, the fulfilled promise and the confirmed promise. 'New' means therefore no replacement of the 'old'. Hence we deny that the people Israel has been rejected by God or that it has been superseded by the church.

Source

Brockway, Allan, van Buren, Paul, Rendtorff, Rolf, and Schoon, Simon (eds.), *The Theology of the Churches and the Jewish People: Statements by the World Council of Churches and Its Member Churches* (Geneva: WCC Publications, 1988), 92–4.

Commentary

The EKiG, a member of the Evangelical Church in Germany, is a union of Reformed and Lutheran churches extending across the former Prussian Rhine province. It was created at the instigation of King Frederick William III (*r.* 1797–1840) shortly after the Congress of Vienna in 1815.

Towards Renovation is the first statement from a German Protestant church to recognise the theological importance of Jewish–Christian relations, and a number of striking conclusions followed. Although previous church statements had denounced antisemitism, the 1980 Rhineland Synod insisted that the churches must share responsibility for the Holocaust and are duty-bound to resist any manifestations of antisemitism. The statement echoes the Anglican minister James Parkes' comment that it was 'the Christian Church alone, which turned normal xenophobia and normal good and bad communal relations between two human societies into the unique evil of antisemitism' (1969: 123).

The document proposed a covenantal theology that functioned as a bridge between Christianity and Judaism, developing the *Nostra aetate* declaration (and other church statements) that the covenant of God with the Jewish people remained unabrogated. *Towards Renovation* argues that Jews and Christians represent one people of God, sharing sufficient common ground that the same covenant could be applied to both: 'We believe the permanent election of the Jewish people as the people of God and realize that through Jesus Christ the church is taken into the covenant of God with his people.'

Following the lead of *Israel: People, Land, and State* (document 3), the Rhineland Synod also addressed the establishment of the State of Israel, referring to the Jewish return to the land and the creation of the state as 'signs of the faithfulness of God towards his people'. Its view was later endorsed by a small number of Protestant denominations such as the United Methodist Church (USA) in 1994, but was rejected by the majority. The WCC, as well as the Roman Catholic Church, viewed the State of Israel as of political rather than theological importance.

Towards Renovation also tackled the subject of mission, a subject of vigorous debate among Protestants. In 1975 the German Evangelical Church produced a report, *Juden und Christen*, which outlined the divisions between advocates of active proselytism to Jews and those who emphasised dialogue. The 1980 document repudiated mission to the Jewish people, asserting that both Jews and Christians are 'witnesses of God before the world and before each other'. Thus, Jews represented a special case when it came to evangelism, and a more productive relationship was based on common witness, a theme developed further by the 1988 Lambeth Conference in *Jews, Christians and Muslims: The Way of Dialogue* (document 5).

Similar expressions of a new Jewish–Christian relationship are found in other church statements, although rarely as accessible or as relevant beyond their own denominational boundaries as the Rhineland Synod document. *Towards Renovation* had a profound impact, not only in its rejection of the evangelising of Jews and in discarding any sense of a triumphalist Christianity, but also in reflecting upon new positive views of Judaism and the theological implications for Christian self-understanding.

Bibliography

Hockenos, Matthew D., *A Church Divided: German Protestants Confront the Nazi Past* (Bloomington: Indiana University Press, 2004).

Holtschneider, Kirsten Hannah, *German Protestants Remember the Holocaust: Theology and the Construction of Collective Memory* (Munster: Lit, 2000).

Parkes, James, *Voyage of Discoveries* (London: Gollancz, 1969).

Sell, Alan P., *Reformed Theology and the Jewish People* (Geneva: World Alliance of Reformed Churches, 1986).

5

The Lambeth Conference: Jews, Christians and Muslims: The Way of Dialogue *(1988)*

Text

13 For Christians, *Judaism* can never be one religion among others. It has a special bond and affinity with Christianity. Jesus, our Lord and the Christ, was a Jew, and the Scriptures which informed and guided his life were the books of the Hebrew Bible. These still form part of the Christian Scriptures. The God in whom Jesus believed, to whom he totally gave himself, and

in whom we believe is 'the God of Abraham, Isaac and Jacob'. A right understanding of the relationship with Judaism is, therefore, fundamental to Christianity's own self-understanding.

14 *Christians and Jews* share one hope, which is for the realisation of God's Kingdom on earth. Together they wait for it, pray for it and prepare for it. This Kingdom is nothing less than human life and society transformed, transfigured and transparent to the glory of God. Christians believe that this glory has already shone in the face of Jesus Christ. In his life, death and resurrection the Kingdom of God, God's just rule, has already broken into the affairs of this world. Judaism is not able to accept this. However, Christian belief in Jesus is related to a frame of reference which Christians and Jews share. For it is as a result of incorporation into Jesus Christ that Christians came to share in the Jewish hope for the coming of God's Kingdom […]

16 Christians and Jews share a passionate belief in a God of loving kindness who has called us into relationship with himself. God is faithful and he does not abandon those he calls. We firmly reject any view of *Judaism* which sees it as a living fossil, simply superseded by Christianity. When Paul reflects on the mystery of the continued existence of the Jewish people (Rom. 9–11) a full half of his message is the unequivocal proclamation of God's abiding love for those whom he first called. Thus he wrote:

> God's choice stands and they are his friends for the sake of the patriarchs. For the gracious gifts of God and his calling are irrevocable. (Rom. 11.28–9, NEB)

God continues to fulfil his purposes among the Jewish people.

17 However, with some honourable exceptions their relationship has too often been marked by antagonism. Discrimination and persecution of the *Jews* led to the teaching of contempt; the systematic dissemination of anti-Jewish propaganda by Church leaders, teachers and preachers. Through catechism, teaching of school children, and Christian preaching, the Jewish people have been misrepresented and caricatured. Even the Gospels have, at times, been used to malign and denigrate the Jewish people.

Anti-Jewish prejudice promulgated by leaders of both Church and State has led to persecution, pogrom, and, finally, provided the soil in which the evil weed of Nazism was able to take root and spread its poison. The Nazis were driven by a pagan philosophy, which had as its ultimate aim the destruction of Christianity itself. But how did it take hold? The systematic extermination of six million Jews and the wiping out of a whole culture must bring about in Christianity a profound and painful re-examination of its relationship with Judaism. In order to combat centuries of anti-Jewish teaching and practice, Christians must develop programmes of teaching, preaching, and common social action which eradicate prejudice and promote dialogue.

[…]

The Way of Sharing

25 Dialogue does not require people to relinquish or alter their beliefs before entering into it; on the contrary, genuine dialogue demands that each partner brings to it the fullness of themselves and the tradition in which they stand. As they grow in mutual

understanding they will be able to share more and more of what they bring with the other. Inevitably, both partners to the dialogue will be affected and changed by this process, for it is a mutual sharing.

26 Within this sharing there are a variety of attitudes towards *Judaism* within Christianity today. At one pole, there are those Christians whose prayer is that Jews, without giving up their Jewishness, will find their fulfilment in Jesus the Messiah. Indeed some regard it as their particular vocation and responsibility to share their faith with Jews, whilst at the same time urging them to discover the spiritual riches which God has given them through the Jewish faith. Other Christians, however, believe that in fulfilling the Law and the prophets, Jesus validated the Jewish relationship with God, while opening this way up for Gentiles through his own person. For others again, the holocaust has changed their perception, so that until Christian lives bear a truer witness, they feel a divine obligation to affirm the Jews in their worship and sense of God who is, for Christians, the Father of Jesus. In all these approaches, Christians bear witness to God as revealed in Jesus and are being called into a fresh, more fruitful relationship with Judaism. We urge that further thought and prayer, in the light of Scripture and the facts of history, be given to the nature of this relationship.

27 All these approaches, however, share a common concern to be sensitive to *Judaism*, to reject all proselytising, that is, aggressive and manipulative attempts to convert, and, of course, any hint of antisemitism. Further, Jews, Muslims and Christians have a common mission. They share a mission to the world that God's name may be honoured: 'Hallowed be your name'. They share a common obligation to love God with their whole being and their neighbours as themselves. 'Your Kingdom come on earth as it is in heaven'. And in the dialogue there will be mutual witness. Through learning from one another they will enter more deeply into their own inheritance. Each will recall the other to God, to trust him more fully and obey him more profoundly. This will be mutual witness between equal partners.

Source

Anglican Consultative Council, *The Truth Shall Make You Free: The Lambeth Conference 1988: The Reports, Resolutions & Pastoral Letters from the Bishops* (London: Church House Publishing, 1988), 302–3, 305. *The Truth Shall Make You Free: The Lambeth Conference 1988* is copyright © The Secretary of the Anglican Consultative Council 1998. Reproduced by permission of the Anglican Consultative Council.

Commentary

This document originated during the decennial Anglican Communion conference in 1988. Originally called *Jewish–Christian Guidelines for the Anglican Communion*, it was significantly altered during the conference because a parallel document on Christian–Muslim relations had not been completed in time. By the end of the conference, representative of 80 million Anglicans, it had been renamed *Jews, Christians and Muslims: The*

Way of Dialogue. Clearly, the Anglican Communion did not feel it could comment on Christian–Jewish relations without reference to Christian–Muslim relations at a time when the Archbishop of Canterbury's envoy, Terry Waite, was still being held hostage in Lebanon and sensitivity levels were high.

As far as Jewish–Christian relations were concerned, the document delivered a scathing denunciation of antisemitism, the teaching of contempt and Christian triumphalism. No previous document had so explicitly argued that there should be a fundamental change in the Christian approach to Judaism. It illustrated the widespread shift from what was, for the most part, an inherent need to condemn Judaism to a condemnation of Christian anti-Judaism. Christian desire for a closer relationship with 'the elder brother' is illustrated in our excerpt by its discussion of mission.

Although the first time Christian–Jewish relations appeared on the Lambeth Conference agenda was in 1988, an Anglican report entitled *Witness of the Church to the Jews in London* was published in 1949, four years after the end of World War II. It stated that 'The first step in presenting the gospel to them [Jews] is the removal of those barriers which pre-dispose them against accepting it [...] Very little advance can be made in the matter of proclaiming the Christian gospel unless antisemitism is first attacked.' It then advised its readers to seek to convert Jews by inviting Jewish neighbours into Christian homes (*Mission to London Papers*, unpublished, Lambeth Palace, 1952: 28–30).

The 1988 conference took a totally different position. Christian mission was seen not in terms of the conversion of Jews, but rather of a common mission. Proselytism was to be rejected and the conference called for 'mutual witness between equal partners' so that 'God's name may be honoured'. This is not to imply that there are no Anglican missions to Jews today, but there has been a dramatic downscaling, and a distinction is drawn between 'mission' and 'witness'.

The Church of England continued to reflect on Christian mission and the Jewish people, producing documents in 2001 (*Sharing One Hope*) and in 2019 (*God's Unfailing Word*). These highlighted the key fault lines within the Anglican Communion, indeed among the Protestant churches as a whole, and three positions remain: first, those who seek the conversion of all Jews because there is no exemption from the need for salvation in Christ; second, those who witness to faith in Christ, without targeting Jews specifically, and believe in sharing the Christian faith with all people; and third, those who have no conversionary outlook towards Jews, where mission is understood as joint witness in an unredeemed world. This latter model has been termed 'critical solidarity' or 'mutual witness'.

Bibliography

Braybrooke, Marcus, *Time to Meet: Towards a Deeper Relationship between Jews and Christians* (London: SCM, 1990).

The Faith and Order Commission, *God's Unfailing Word: Theological and Practical Perspectives on Christian–Jewish Relations* (London: Church House Publishing, 2019).

Harries, Richard, *After the Evil: Christianity and Judaism in the Shadow of the Holocaust* (Oxford: Oxford University Press, 2003).

Mission to London Papers, unpublished MSS 1948–60, Lambeth Palace, 1952.

6

Southern Baptist Convention: Resolution No. 10 – On Jewish Evangelism *(1996)*

Text

WHEREAS, Jesus commanded that 'repentance and remission of sins should be preached in his name among all nations, beginning at Jerusalem' (Luke 24:47); and

WHEREAS, Our evangelistic efforts have largely neglected the Jewish people, both at home and abroad; and

WHEREAS, We are indebted to the Jewish people, through whom we have received the Scriptures and our Savior, the Messiah of Israel, and 'they are beloved for the sake of the fathers' (Romans 11:28); and

WHEREAS, There has been an organized effort on the part of some either to deny that Jewish people need to come to their Messiah, Jesus, to be saved; or to claim, for whatever reason, that Christians have neither right nor obligation to proclaim the gospel to the Jewish people; and

WHEREAS, There is evidence of a growing responsiveness among the Jewish people in some areas of our nation and our world.

Be it therefore RESOLVED, that we, the messengers of the Southern Baptist Convention, meeting in New Orleans, Louisiana, June 11–13, 1996, reaffirm that we are not ashamed of the gospel of Christ, for it is the power of God unto salvation to every one that believeth; to the Jew first, and also to the Greek (Romans 1:16); and

Be it further RESOLVED, that we recommit ourselves to prayer, especially for the salvation of the Jewish people as well as for the salvation of 'every kindred and tongue and people and nation' (Revelations [*sic*] 5:9); and

Be it finally RESOLVED, That we direct our energies and resources toward the proclamation of the gospel to the Jewish people.

Source

Atchison, David W. (ed.), *Annual of the Southern Baptist Convention: June 11–13, 1996* (Nashville: Southern Baptist Convention, 1996), 97.

Commentary

Christian mission to Jews is one of the most contentious areas in Jewish–Christian relations, partly because, for Jews, it indicates disrespect and conjures up images of forced conversions, and because, for Christians, the 'no' to Jesus from his Jewish coreligionists is troubling and raises awkward questions for Christian self-understanding. As we saw in document 5 above, the growth of modern Jewish–Christian dialogue as well as widespread acceptance by Christians of an ongoing covenantal relationship between the Jewish people and God have prompted the churches to reflect on the meaning of mission, with particular reference to the Jewish people.

The 1996 statement of the Southern Baptist Convention argues that Christians have a responsibility to evangelise Jews in order to convince them that Jesus is the messiah. One of the largest evangelical groupings in the United States, the Convention directs its members' 'energies and resources toward the proclamation of the gospel to the Jewish people', referring explicitly to Paul's conviction of the need to bring the gospel 'to the Jew first, and also to the Greek (Romans 1:16)'. Indeed, according to the Southern Baptist churches, Christians would be false to their faith if they failed to try to convert Jews. The Convention's charter states that 'we believe in the lost condition of every human being, whether Jew or Gentile, who does not accept salvation by faith in Jesus Christ, and therefore in the necessity of presenting the gospel to the Jews'. Alongside some others, such as the World Evangelical Fellowship in Willowbank, who met in Willowbank, Bermuda, in 1989 and produced a declaration calling for a mission to Jews, the Southern Baptist churches thus believe that the only positive future for the Jewish people lies in their conversion to Christianity, viewing active mission towards Jews as a priority for Christians.

Among the evangelical theologians who support this position is Richard de Ridder, for whom it is the divinely mandated mission of the church to preach the gospel to Jews (as well as to everyone else). While this remains the widely held evangelical view in the US – a 2017 survey of American evangelicals (released by LifeWay Research at the 2018 National Religious Broadcasters convention in Nashville) found 87 per cent agreed that 'sharing the gospel with Jewish people is important' because working for the conversion of all Jews to belief in Christ is a necessary requirement for their salvation – not all evangelical groups subscribe to it, some, such as the International Christian Embassy in Israel (see document 12) arguing that Christians should not focus on evangelising Jews but, in light of the history of Christian antisemitism, should 'Advocate for Israel around the world and combat antisemitism in all its forms' and that only after the Second Coming of Christ will all Israel be saved (www.icej.org/mission-statement/a-biblical-mandate/).

Bibliography

de Ridder, Richard R., *Discipling the Nations* (Grand Rapids: Baker Book House, 1975).
Kim, Kirsteen, Jørgensen, Knud, and Fitchett-Climenhaga, Alison (eds.), *The Oxford Handbook of Mission Studies* (Oxford: Oxford University Press, 2022).
Mittleman, Alan, Johnson, Byron R., and Isserman, Nancy (eds.), *Uneasy Allies? Evangelical and Jewish Relations* (New York: Lexington, 2007).

7

National Jewish Scholars Project/Institute for Christian and Jewish Studies:
Dabru Emet: A Jewish Statement on Christians and Christianity *(2000)*

Text

Jews and Christians worship the same God. Before the rise of Christianity, Jews were the only worshippers of the God of Israel. But Christians also worship the God of Abraham, Isaac, and Jacob; creator of heaven and earth. While Christian worship is not a viable religious choice for Jews, as Jewish theologians we rejoice that, through Christianity, hundreds of millions of people have entered into relationship with the God of Israel.

Jews and Christians seek authority from the same book – the Bible (what Jews call 'Tanakh' and Christians call the 'Old Testament'). Turning to it for religious orientation, spiritual enrichment, and communal education, we each take away similar lessons [...] Yet, Jews and Christians interpret the Bible differently on many points. Such differences must always be respected.

Christians can respect the claim of the Jewish people upon the land of Israel. The most important event for Jews since the Holocaust has been the reestablishment of a Jewish state in the Promised Land. As members of a biblically-based religion, Christians appreciate that Israel was promised – and given – to Jews as the physical center of the covenant between them and God. Many Christians support the State of Israel for reasons far more profound than mere politics. As Jews, we applaud this support. We also recognize that Jewish tradition mandates justice for all non-Jews who reside in a Jewish state.

Jews and Christians accept the moral principles of Torah. Central to the moral principles of Torah is the inalienable sanctity and dignity of every human being. All of us were created in the image of God. This shared moral emphasis can be the basis of an improved relationship between our two communities [...]

Nazism was not a Christian phenomenon. Without the long history of Christian anti-Judaism and Christian violence against Jews, Nazi ideology could not have taken hold nor could it have been carried out. Too many Christians participated in, or were sympathetic to, Nazi atrocities against Jews. Other Christians did not protest sufficiently against these atrocities. But Nazism itself was not an inevitable outcome of Christianity. If the Nazi extermination of the Jews had been fully successful, it would have turned its murderous rage more directly to Christians [...]

The humanly irreconcilable difference between Jews and Christians will not be settled until God redeems the entire world as promised in Scripture [...] Jews can respect Christians' faithfulness to their revelation just as we expect Christians to respect our faithfulness to our revelation. Neither Jew nor Christian should be pressed into affirming the teaching of the other community.

A new relationship between Jews and Christians will not weaken Jewish practice. An improved relationship will not accelerate the cultural and religious assimilation that Jews rightly fear [...]

Jews and Christians must work together for justice and peace. Jews and Christians, each in their own way, recognize the unredeemed state of the world as reflected in the persistence of persecution, poverty, and human degradation and misery. Although justice and peace are finally God's, our joint efforts, together with those of other faith communities, will help bring the kingdom of God for which we hope and long.

Source

Novak, David, Ochs, Peter, Signer, Michael, and Frymer-Kensky, Tikva, '*Dabru Emet: A Jewish Statement on Christians and Christianity*', *New York Times* (10 September 2000), 37.

Commentary

Dabru Emet (*Speak Truth*) is the first modern cross-denominational Jewish statement on Christians and Christianity, the significance of which is amplified by the previous lack of official Jewish statements about Christianity. It was issued in 2000 by four North American Jewish scholars and signed by 200 Jewish leaders, writers and rabbis, primarily from the United States but also from Europe and the Middle East. The document is addressed to the Jewish community and offers a positive evaluation of Christianity, calling for dialogue and deeper cooperation in the spirit of partnership in response to the modern transformation in Christian attitudes towards Jews. The Jewish people, the document explains, need to learn about the efforts of Christians to honour Judaism and to reflect on what Judaism may now say about Christianity.

Dabru Emet's positive affirmation of Christianity was generally well received by the churches and by Jewish communities, especially those involved in dialogue, although it was criticised by some evangelical Christians and strictly observant Jews – both groups oppose theological dialogue. For the latter, Christianity also remains an object of fear and anger which they continue to resist or ignore. However, the publication in 2015 of *To Do the Will of Our Father in Heaven* (document 13) indicates new Orthodox Jewish interest in dialogue with the church.

Some of the eight points in *Dabru Emet* caused widespread controversy for both Christians and Jews. For example, the assertion that Christians worship the God of Israel and legitimately draw on the Hebrew Bible was criticised by some Orthodox Jewish writers, such as David Berger, because, they argued, Christian doctrines (e.g., the Trinity and Incarnation) compromise the integrity of Jewish monotheism. For their part, some Christians were surprised to discover from this controversy that Christianity can still be criticised by Jews for a tendency towards idolatry.

The assertion that Nazism was not an inevitable outcome of Christianity prompted some Jewish leaders active in Jewish–Christian dialogue, such as Norman Solomon, not to sign the document. They criticised *Dabru Emet* for giving the impression that Christians might feel exonerated, while for some Christians it was troubling to learn that some Jews do view Nazism as the logical outcome of European Christian culture.

Some critics have also expressed disappointment about the omission of two major topics: the Palestinians and the Israeli–Palestinian conflict; and the significance of the fact that Jesus was a Jew. Both topics were regularly discussed in Jewish–Christian literature and dialogue but, in the view of the authors, remained too controversial for the Jewish audience for them to be included.

Dabru Emet continues to influence Jewish–Christian relations, notably Jewish views of Christianity. Its primary significance lies in the recognition that most mainstream

Jewish communities are willing to recognise and join Christian partners to explore commonalities and differences and work towards a mutually fruitful relationship.

Bibliography

Berger, David, *Persecution, Polemic, and Dialogue: Essays in Jewish–Christian Relations* (Boston: Academic Studies Press, 2010).

'Dabru Emet: 20 Years Later', *American Religion*, www.american-religion.org/dabruemet.

Frymer-Kensky, Tikva, Novak, David, Ochs, Peter, Fox Sandmel, David and Signer, Michael A. (eds.), *Christianity in Jewish Terms* (Boulder: Westview Press, 2000).

Sandmel, David Fox, Catalano, Rosann M. and Leighton, Christopher M., *Irreconcilable Differences? A Learning Resource for Jews and Christians* (Boulder: Westview Press, 2001).

8

Pontifical Biblical Commission: The Jewish People and Their Sacred Scriptures in the Christian Bible *(2001)*

Text

A Christian Understanding of the Relationships between the Old and New Testaments

[…] Affirmation of a Reciprocal Relationship

By 'Old Testament' the Christian Church has no wish to suggest that the Jewish Scriptures are outdated or surpassed. On the contrary, it has always affirmed that the Old Testament and the New Testament are inseparable […]

[…]

[…] The Unity of God's Plan and the Idea of Fulfillment

[…]

The notion of fulfillment is an extremely complex one, one that could easily be distorted if there is a unilateral insistence either on continuity or discontinuity. Christian faith recognizes the fulfillment, in Christ, of the scriptures and the hopes of Israel, but it does not understand this fulfillment as a literal one. Such a conception would be reductionist. In reality, in the mystery of Christ crucified and risen, fulfillment is brought about in a manner unforeseen. It includes transcendence. Jesus is not confined to playing an already fixed role – that of Messiah – but he confers, on the notions of Messiah and salvation, a fullness which could not have been imagined in advance; he fills them with a new reality; one can even speak in this connection of a 'new creation.' It would be wrong to consider the prophecies of the Old Testament as some kind of photographic anticipations of future events. All the texts, including those which later were read as messianic prophecies, already had an immediate import and meaning for their contemporaries before attaining a fuller meaning for future hearers. The messiahship of Jesus has a meaning that is new and original.

The original task of the prophet was to help his contemporaries understand the events and the times they lived in from God's viewpoint. Accordingly, excessive insistence, characteristic of a certain apologetic, on the probative value attributable to the fulfillment of prophecy must be discarded. This insistence has contributed to harsh judgments by Christians of Jews and their reading of the Old Testament: the more reference to Christ is found in Old Testament texts, the more the incredulity of the Jews is considered inexcusable and obstinate.

Insistence on discontinuity between both Testaments and going beyond former perspectives should not, however, lead to a one-sided spiritualization. What has already been accomplished in Christ must yet be accomplished in us and in the world. The definitive fulfillment will be at the end with the resurrection of the dead, a new heaven and a new earth. Jewish messianic expectation is not in vain. It can become for us Christians a powerful stimulant to keep alive the eschatological dimension of our faith. Like them, we too live in expectation. The difference is that for us the One who is to come will have the traits of the Jesus who has already come and is already present and active among us.

Source

Sherman, Franklin (ed.), *Bridges: Documents of the Christian–Jewish Dialogue*, Vol. 2: *Building a New Relationship (1986–2013)* (Mahwah: Paulist Press, 2014), 260–1, 263, 264–5.

Commentary

The Jewish People and Their Sacred Scriptures in the Christian Bible (*JPSSCB*) is the first statement on Jewish–Christian relations issued by the Pontifical Biblical Commission, demonstrating that Roman Catholic consideration of the Christian–Jewish encounter was of institutional concern for the wider church, not only for the Pontifical Commission for Religious Relations with the Jews.

The document begins with the reminder that the New Testament should not be viewed in opposition to the Old. Indeed, 'the Jewish Scriptures' (sometimes used as an alternative to 'Old Testament') form an integral part of the Christian Bible. Christianity and Judaism share a common heritage, the sacred scripture of Israel, which is no longer viewed as the exclusive preserve of the church.

JPSSCB explores difficulties raised by typological interpretations, which a previous Pontifical document, *Notes on the Correct Way to Present Jews and Judaism in Preaching and Catechesis in the Roman Catholic Church* (1985), warned should 'avoid any transition from the Old to the New Testament which might seem merely a rupture'. While *JPSSCB* acknowledged in a section not excerpted here that 'the New Testament cannot be fully understood except in the light of the Old Testament' (p. 265), links between the Old and the New were sometimes abused and scripture could easily be severed from its context. As a result, 'Interpretation [...] became arbitrary' (p. 263). The document points to the dangers of fundamentalist approaches, warning against considering 'the prophecies of the Old Testament as some kind of photographic anticipations of future events'. Christians can overcome an unhealthy dependence upon typology by increasing their knowledge of Jewish biblical interpretation. Indeed, a later section of the document states that Christians can and ought to admit that 'the Jewish reading of the Bible is a possible one, in continuity with the Jewish Sacred Scriptures from the Second Temple Period, a reading analogous to the Christian reading which developed in parallel fashion' (p. 266). This striking remark represents an application of Pope John Paul II's oft-repeated comment about the covenant remaining with the Jewish people, which implies that Jewish interpretation of scripture must, at the very least, remain 'possible'.

The document recognises that the church is dependent upon its participation in the election of the Jewish people even though only a few Jews accepted Jesus as Christ. It acknowledges a special status of elder brother for the Jewish people, thereby giving Jews a unique place among all other religions, although at the end time, the church expects Jews to realise the truth of Christianity. Nevertheless, 'Jewish messianic expectation is not in vain'. This is a particularly important assertion as it indicates that the Roman Catholic Church now teaches that Jews, alongside Christians, keep alive the messianic expectation. The difference is that for Christians 'the One who is to come will have the traits of the Jesus who has already come and is already present and active among us'. Both Jews and Christians share this anticipation.

JPSSCB concludes by tackling difficult New Testament texts which, it notes, were produced in a time of conflict. It explains that the situation has changed radically since and that the polemic has no relevance to contemporary Jewish–Christian relations.

Bibliography

Aitken, James K., and Kessler, Edward (eds.), *Challenges in Jewish–Christian Relations* (Mahwah: Paulist Press, 2006).

Bieringer, Reimund, Pollefeyt, Didier, and Vandecasteele-Vanneuville, Frédérique (eds.), *Anti-Judaism and the Fourth Gospel* (Louisville: Westminster John Knox Press, 2001).

Scripture Bulletin 1, no. 33 (2003), special issue dedicated to *The Jewish People and Their Sacred Scriptures in the Christian Bible*.

9

International Jewish Committee for Interreligious Consultations/World Council of Churches: African Christian–Jewish Consultation, Yaoundé *(2001)*

Text

(i) Christian–Jewish Consultation in Yaoundé, Cameroon, November 2001: Message of the Consultation

I.   The first Christian-Jewish consultation to be held in French-speaking Africa took place in Yaoundé, Cameroon, from 8 to 13 November 2001 under the auspices of the International Jewish Committee for Interreligious Consultations (IJCIC) and the World Council of Churches (WCC), with participants from Benin, Burundi, Congo/Brazzaville and Democratic Republic of the Congo, France, Israel, Ivory Coast, Kenya, Rwanda, South Africa, Switzerland, Togo, the United States, and Cameroon. [...]

II. We have particularly noticed convergences between certain concepts found in our lived traditions and our respective histories:

- Shalom and Ubuntu;
- the role of the word in Judaism and of palaver [discussion, consensus-formation] in African cultures;
- the idea of tikkun (repair) and the theology of reconstruction.

Unhindered by the bilateral disputes underlying the Jewish-Christian dialogue in Europe, our encounter here has been able to establish itself on a positive basis, free from suspicion and resentment, and emphasizing:

- the centrality of the biblical text in the Jewish and Christian traditions of all the participants;
- the convergence of Jewish and African memories.

III. Recommendations:

- Each participant will endeavor to give a media echo to this consultation.
- The participants pledge to transmit the message in their respective religious communities.
- We would like to see the minutes of this consultation published in order to bring it to the attention of a wider audience.
- We envision a study of biblical sources, particularly in Hebrew, that make reference to the African people.
- We propose creating a Jewish-African anthology.
- We would like to meet in the near future in Jerusalem.
- We encourage the idea of itinerant lecturers.
- We will undertake a study of biblical texts that can be used to support concrete struggles such as various social injustices, the condition of women, AIDS, conflicts, etc.
- We propose to set up an Internet forum for the sharing of knowledge, reflections, and information.

Condemning racist and antisemitic prejudices, we pledge to stay together, in our communities and wherever we find ourselves, as artisans of peace.

> '*Depart from evil and do good; seek peace and pursue it.*' (Psalm 34:14)

Source

'Christian-Jewish Consultation in Yaoundé, Cameroon, November 2001', jcrelations.net/fr/declarations/declaration/message-of-the-consultation-november-2001.html. Translated from the French by jcrelations.net. (The square-bracketed phrase is part of the original.)

(ii) Hans Ucko: [Travel Report] African Christian–Jewish Consultation in French-Speaking Africa: Yaoundé, 8–13 November 2001

Jewish-Christian dialogue is in Europe and North America a well-established experience. It continues to inspire many Christians, which is demonstrated in many church documents and theological writings. Lately it has also led to a reflection on the role and significance of Christianity for Jewish theology. I have referred to the document *Dabru Emet* in an earlier travel report. The Jewish-Christian dialogue builds upon the presence of Jewish communities and the problematic history of Jews and Christians in Europe. Anti-Judaism and antisemitism have left stains in history impossible to remove and impossible to forget.

There is of course another aspect of Jewish-Christian encounters or rather lack of encounters. The Israeli-Palestinian conflict is one major reason for the absence of dialogue between Jews and Middle East Christians [...]

Christians in other parts of the world, where there is no or insignificant Jewish presence or history, are not immediately part of the Jewish-Christian dialogue. They may for sure have other priorities. If there are any associations with Jews and Judaism, they are complex and contradictory. They may be related to what is said in the Bible about the Jews. They may refer to what was conveyed through missionary education. Attitudes encompass respect and esteem for the chosen people, the people of God but entail alas also classical theological positions between Jews and Christians expressed through polarisations such as old and new, Law and Gospel, merit and grace. There is the sympathy for Palestinians, living under occupation by the Jewish State. At the same time there is also in some places, where Islam is dominant and Christians live as minorities, a silent support for Israel in its struggle against Muslim neighbours, Israel vicariously doing what they would like to do themselves but cannot do.

[...]

A peak in the consultation was in the discussion about memories and experiences of violence. Here Shoah and Rwanda became the focal points.

The churches involved in violence live between being victims and being responsible, between memory and amnesia. In this situation, one cannot operate with a theology of liberation. A theology of reconstruction is needed. Everything was shattered after what happened in Rwanda. African cultures and values were shattered [...]

[...] How does one safeguard the memory and at the same time keep a way out for pardon and forgiveness?

African theology has dealt with both memory and violence. Memory is foundational and is celebrated in a liturgical manner in the theology of reconstruction. Countries, cultures, dignity have been destroyed repeatedly and yet one has to assume the responsibility to deal with memory in a constructive way.

[...]

The Jewish concept of *tikkun olam*, the reparation or betterment of the world, is also a kind of reconstruction. There is a risk with excessive memory, where the past conditions the present, where Arafat becomes the new Hitler. Such excessive memory will empty

Hitler of meaning and should make us reflect on the meaning of metaphors. One has to reckon with [the fact] that there is in the Jewish world sometimes an excessive paranoia, an excessive memory of the Shoah [...]

Is there a place for silence or amnesia in memory or how do we deal with excessive memory? One must be wary of simplistic metaphors, dividing the world into good or evil in too facile a way. One must realise that one sometimes has to consciously discontinue remembering. One must realise that there is a relationship between memory and idolatry. When you become a slave to your memory, there is a risk of becoming idolatrous. There is a challenge also in peace building: In the pursuit of peace, there is a danger in becoming overwhelmed by wrath and anger. Anger can become idolatry, when you lose the face of the other.

Source

Ucko, Hans, 'African Christian–Jewish Consultation in French-Speaking Africa', *Current Dialogue* 39 (June 2002), 52, 55–6.

Commentary

The third African Christian–Jewish consultation took place in Yaoundé in Cameroon in 2001, under the auspices of the IJCIC and the WCC and organised by its Programme Executive for Christian–Jewish Relations and Dialogue, Hans Ucko, whose 'travel report' on the consultation forms the second of our excerpts (document 9 (ii)). The first document (9 (i)) is from the summary of the consultation, which is an example of the WCC's desire to foster Jewish–Christian dialogue among member churches in the Global South. The WCC had previously organised consultations in Nairobi (1986), Hong Kong (1992), Cochin (1993) and Johannesburg (1995).

Since the WCC comprises approximately 350 mainline Protestant and Orthodox churches, some of its members would rarely have encountered Jews and Judaism. In addition, its large and disparate range of church bodies possess divergent attitudes on a great many topics, including Jewish–Christian relations and notably the impact of the Israel–Palestinian conflict. In 1971, the WCC established a Sub-unit for Dialogue with People of Living Faiths and Ideologies, which also provided a desk for Jewish–Christian dialogue, to help in this endeavour.

One of the challenges of Jewish–Christian relations in the Global South is a perception that the topic is of concern only to the Global North. Another is that discussion of the State of Israel can easily dominate, as acknowledged in document 9 (ii) by the expression of 'sympathy for Palestinians, living under occupation by the Jewish State' but also, where Christians live as minorities among Muslim majorities, 'silent support for Israel in its struggle against Muslim neighbours'.

As can be seen in document 9 (i), the Yaoundé consultation pointed to a number of 'convergences' in African theology and Judaism, which included the similarities between the concept of shalom and Ubuntu (humaneness or humanity), the role of the word and of palaver (discussion, consensus-formation) and the idea of *tikkun* ('repair') and the theology of reconstruction. African Christian emphasis on the Old Testament, especially biblical narratives on liberation (notably the Exodus and the journey of the Israelites from bondage to freedom) and life-cycle events (such as sacrifices at births, weddings and funerals and the rite of circumcision) also provided a link. The consultation noted the 'centrality of the biblical text in the Jewish and Christian traditions' and explored the topics of memory and violence, since Jews and Africans experienced a similar history of exclusion, exploitation and violence, as well as of survival. Thus, as Hans Ucko notes in document 9 (ii), the 'Shoah and Rwanda became the focal points' for the discussion.

The Yaoundé consultation demonstrates that Jewish–Christian encounters do not only take place in the Global North and in the Holy Land. While the number of Jews is few in comparison with Christians, the churches in the Global South are growing significantly and are becoming increasingly influential throughout the Christian world. As Christians decline as a percentage of the population in Europe and North America, the proportion of Christians from the Global South is increasing, as can be seen in recent Pew research, which shows that the number of Pentecostals and evangelical Protestants grew to 700 million by 2020, a more than tenfold increase since 1970, second in size only to that of Roman Catholics. It is likely that as the demographic shift unfolds further, this diverse and growing grouping of Christians will take more positions of leadership in the churches worldwide, not just in the Global South, which is bound to have an impact in the future on Jewish–Christian relations around the world.

Bibliography

Chireau, Yvonne, and Deutsch, Nathaniel (eds.), *Black Zion: African American Religious Encounters with Judaism* (New York and London: Oxford University Press, 2000).

Halpérin, Jean, and Ucko, Hans (eds.), *Worlds of Memory and Wisdom: Encounters of Jews and African Christians* (Geneva: WCC Publications, 2005).

Phan, Peter, *The Joy of Religious Pluralism: A Personal Journey* (Maryknoll: Orbis Books, 2017).

Ucko, Hans (ed.), *People of God, Peoples of God: A Jewish–Christian Conversation in Asia* (Geneva: WCC Publications, 1996).

10

Assembly of Catholic Ordinaries in the Holy Land: Relations with Believers of Other Religions *(2001)*

Text

The Foundations for This Relationship
Our relationship with Jews is founded on:

- *Shared history* in the region of the Middle East. In our countries, Muslims, Christians and Jews have lived together in fruitful social and cultural interaction, this being evident in the clear traces we find of this interaction in Arab civilization. There were certain dark moments in this history and responsibility for these must be assumed by all sides. This historic past is a foundational reference point for a new vision of these relations in the present and the future, without ignoring contemporary factors.

- In one way or another, we are in everyday contact with the *concrete Jewish presence* in this Holy Land, and this obliges us to reflect on how we might formulate the relationship, consonant with our faith, our Christian evangelical values and our reality. The Jewish other is a vibrant reality which we cannot forget or ignore.

[...]

Difficulties of the Relationship

Our relationship with members of the Jewish religion is confronted with real problems in our countries. These problems must be taken seriously if we desire to establish an honest and positive relationship in the future. The relationship must be between two groups which are real and true:

- *The political situation*: The first of these difficulties is the existing political situation in our countries, which has caused suffering to everyone, and which has overshadowed – and continues to do so – relations among the members of the three monotheistic religions, among them Christians and Jews. The reality of the ongoing struggle has a negative influence on mutual relations. Christians in this region are united in fate with their Muslim brothers and sisters, carrying on their bodies the scars of exile and forced dispersion, confiscation of land and civil discrimination, as well as violation of legitimate human rights.
- *Differing mutual regard*: The mutual regard between members of the three religions in our countries, Christians and Jews among them, is defined by different historical memories. Christians in our countries look on Jews through their painful experience in the modern period [...]

[...]

- *Personal relationship*: There is no doubt that personal relationship on the human level is a guarantee that psychological and social barriers which separate the two will be overcome. This requires of us practical steps toward the other at every occasion in our lives so as to transform the other from a labeled stereotype into a person of flesh and blood with his or her tendencies and particularities.
- *Action for truth, justice and peace*: The political struggle and the concomitant continuous tensions make sincere action for truth, justice and peace an essential element of any true relationship. This can be accomplished through collaboration with movements for justice and peace within Jewish society, and with all those of good will who seek justice and peace. This also requires a struggle against *discrimination*. Discrimination is an evil at odds with the truth of God, Creator of all humanity, who loves all. Religious differences and the political circumstances in which we live permit racist attitudes on both sides and these must be eradicated so that the true face of the other can be seen. This means that we must distinguish between what is political and what is religious,

between Judaism as a religion and Zionism as a political ideology, between the Israeli people and the policies of its government.

- *Means for establishing relationship*: Personal relationships must be supported by relations at the level of the official religious institutions of the three religions, and in our case Christian and Jewish institutions in our countries. Establishing such official bodies will help to construct bridges for mutual knowledge and understanding. We must, therefore, establish a church body in our dioceses, composed of the various church sectors, whose task would be to reflect on this subject and take appropriate initiatives at the local level […]

- *Relationship between Arab Christian and Christians of Jewish origin*: There is a group within the Jewish people who have come to know Christ as God and Saviour. They are part of our local church and they live in their own special conditions. They too have a right to develop their own relationship with Jews and Judaism from the vantage point of their reality and their situation, at the same time as remaining connected to the reality of the local Church and being open to it. We must preserve open bridges of communication between our Churches and this community in order to exchange experiences so that we can learn from one another and so that this community can develop according to its own particularity and as part of the community of faithful in our countries.

Source

Khader, Jamal, and Neuhaus, David, 'A Holy Land Context for *Nostra aetate*', *Studies in Christian–Jewish Relations* 1 (2005–6), 79–80, 82.

Commentary

The churches of the Holy Land, comprising the Roman Catholic Church and the major local Orthodox churches, began a synod in 1995 and published a General Pastoral Plan consisting of sixteen documents. These churches do not have the same starting point as their European counterparts, seeing themselves as free of antisemitic practice and also of responsibility for the Holocaust. Our excerpt comes from the thirteenth document, *Relations with Believers of Other Religions*, which deals with relations with Jews and Muslims and is the first Christian Arab document in modern times to reflect on relations with Israeli Jews. It begins by acknowledging the rich history of Abrahamic relations in the Holy Land and in the wider Middle East.

In this region, Christians are a minority, and in Israel, unlike anywhere else in the world, Christians live alongside a Jewish majority, representing only 2 per cent of the population. They are also a minority within an Arab minority, since 20 per cent of the Israeli population (excluding the West Bank) are Muslim. This unique situation means that Christians 'are in everyday contact with the *concrete Jewish presence*' and personally experience the sovereignty of the Jewish state, which includes occasional violent attacks by Jewish radicals as well as suspicion by Orthodox Jews. It is a challenging environment and has led Christians in the Holy Land to 'distinguish between what is political and what is religious, between Judaism as a religion and Zionism as a political ideology'.

Another factor is that *Relations with Believers* was issued during the Second Intifada (2000–5), when Christian Arab congregations demonstrated solidarity with the wider Palestinian cause, emphasising a shared Arab heritage ('united in fate with their Muslim brothers and sisters') and when Christian figures, such as Anglican theologian Naim Ateek, a leading voice in Palestinian liberation theology, were active in expressing their support for Palestinian rights (see Chapter 9, p. 491).

At the same time, Christians were concerned at the prospect of the gradual Islamisation of the nascent state of Palestine. The Christian population there mainly live in the Bethlehem area and are in decline, with many choosing to emigrate and join relatives abroad. In comparison, the numbers of Christians in Israel have remained steady, but this is primarily due to the immigration to Israel in recent decades of Christians with Jewish partners from the countries of the former Soviet Union, which has balanced those who left. The significant reduction in the numbers of Christians elsewhere in the Middle East adds to feelings of insecurity.

Although local Christians are primarily concerned with relations with the majority Muslim population rather than with Jews, some, such as the Jesuit David Neuhaus, engage in Jewish–Christian dialogue. Indeed, *Relations with Believers* highlights the value of personal relations to break down the barriers between Jews and Christians. However, in a context where Jews are an empowered majority and Christians an embattled minority, Jewish–Christian relations will continue to remain dominated by the Israeli–Palestinian conflict and the search for peace and justice.

Bibliography

Al-Liqa' Center, *Theology and the Local Church in the Holy Land*, 3rd ed. (Bethlehem: Al-Liqa' Center for Religious and Heritage Studies in the Holy Land, 2015).

Khader, Jamal, and Neuhaus, David, 'A Holy Land Context for *Nostra aetate*', *Studies in Christian–Jewish Relations* 1 (2005–2006), 67–88, https://ejournals.bc.edu/index.php/scjr/article/view/1360/1270.

Khoury, Rafiq, and Zimmer-Winkel, Rainer (eds.), *On Christian Theology in the Palestinian Context* (Berlin: AphorismA Verlag, 2019).

11

Kairos Palestine: A Moment of Truth: A Word of Faith, Hope and Love from the Heart of Palestinian Suffering *(2009)*

Text

1. The Reality on the Ground

1.1 *'They say: "Peace, peace" when there is no peace'* (Jer. 6:14). These days, everyone is speaking about peace in the Middle East and the peace process. So far, however, these are simply words; the reality is one of Israeli occupation of Palestinian territories, deprivation of our freedom and all that results from this situation [...]

[...]

1.1.5 Religious liberty is severely restricted; the freedom of access to the holy places is denied under the pretext of security. Jerusalem and its holy places are out of bounds for many Christians and Muslims from the West Bank and the Gaza strip. Even Jerusalemites face restrictions during the religious feasts. Some of our Arab clergy are regularly barred from entering Jerusalem.

[...]

2. *A Word of Faith*

[...]

2.3 We believe that our land has a universal mission. In this universality, the meaning of the promises, of the land, of the election, of the people of God open up to include all of humanity, starting from all the peoples of this land [...]

[...]

2.3.2 Our presence in this land, as Christian and Muslim Palestinians, is not accidental but rather deeply rooted in the history and geography of this land, resonant with the connectedness of any other people to the land it lives in. It was an injustice when we were driven out. The West sought to make amends for what Jews had endured in the countries of Europe, but it made amends on our account and in our land. They tried to correct an injustice and the result was a new injustice.

[...]

2.5 We also declare that the Israeli occupation of Palestinian land is a sin against God and humanity because it deprives the Palestinians of their basic human rights, bestowed by God. It distorts the image of God in the Israeli who has become an occupier just as it distorts this image in the Palestinian living under occupation. We declare that any theology, seemingly based on the Bible or on faith or on history, that legitimizes the occupation, is far from Christian teachings, because it calls for violence and holy war in the name of God Almighty, subordinating God to temporary human interests, and distorting the divine image in the human beings living under both political and theological injustice.

[...]

5. *Our Word to our Brothers and Sisters*

[...]

5.4 Our numbers are few but our message is great and important. Our land is in urgent need of love. Our love is a message to the Muslim and to the Jew, as well as to the world.

5.4.1 Our message to the Muslims is a message of love and of living together and a call to reject fanaticism and extremism. It is also a message to the world that Muslims are neither to be stereotyped as the enemy nor caricatured as terrorists but rather to be lived with in peace and engaged with in dialogue.

5.4.2 Our message to the Jews tells them: Even though we have fought one another in the recent past and still struggle today, we are able to love and live together. We can organize our political life, with all its complexity, according to the logic of this love and its power, after ending the occupation and establishing justice.

[...]

6. Our Word to the Churches of the World

6.1 Our word to the Churches of the world is firstly a word of gratitude for the solidarity you have shown toward us in word, deed and presence among us. It is a word of praise for the many Churches and Christians who support the right of the Palestinian people for self determination. It is a message of solidarity with those Christians and Churches who have suffered because of their advocacy for law and justice.

However, it is also a call to repentance; to revisit fundamentalist theological positions that support certain unjust political options with regard to the Palestinian people. It is a call to stand alongside the oppressed and preserve the word of God as good news for all rather than to turn it into a weapon with which to slay the oppressed. The word of God is a word of love for all His creation. God is not the ally of one against the other, nor the opponent of one in the face of the other. God is the Lord of all and loves all, demanding justice from all and issuing to all of us the same commandments. We ask our sister Churches not to offer a theological cover-up for the injustice we suffer, for the sin of the occupation imposed upon us [...]

[...]

6.3 We condemn all forms of racism, whether religious or ethnic, including anti-Semitism and Islamophobia, and we call on you to condemn it and oppose it in all its manifestations. At the same time we call on you to say a word of truth and to take a position of truth with regard to Israel's occupation of Palestinian land. As we have already said, we see boycott and disinvestment as tools of non-violence for justice, peace and security for all.

[...]

9. A Call to Our Palestinian People and to the Israelis

[...]

9.2 Education is important. Educational programs must help us to get to know the other as he or she is rather than through the prism of conflict, hostility or religious fanaticism. The educational programs in place today are infected with this hostility. The time has come to begin a new education that allows one to see the face of God in the other and declares that we are capable of loving each other and building our future together in peace and security.

9.3 Trying to make the state a religious state, Jewish or Islamic, suffocates the state, confines it within narrow limits, and transforms it into a state that practices discrimination and exclusion, preferring one citizen over another. We appeal to both religious Jews and Muslims: let the state be a state for all its citizens, with a vision constructed on respect for religion but also equality, justice, liberty and respect for pluralism and not on domination by a religion or a numerical majority.

Source

A Moment of Truth: A Word of Faith, Hope and Love from the Heart of Palestinian Suffering,
  www.kairospalestine.ps/index.php/about-kairos/kairos-palestine-document. © 2018
  Kairos Palestine. Reproduced by permission of Kairos Palestine.

Commentary

A Moment of Truth, commonly known as the Kairos Document or Kairos Palestine after the self-designation of the group of Palestinian Christians who issued it, was published on the sixty-first anniversary of UN Resolution 184 (which called for the repatriation of Palestinian refugees) and was signed by sixteen Christian leaders including Michel Sabbah (Roman Catholic), Atallah Hanna (Greek Orthodox) and Riah Abu El-Assal (Anglican), all of whom had recently retired from office. It was circulated around the Christian world by the WCC. *Kairos* (a Greek term meaning a propitious moment) refers to the necessity of speaking out and was used in the 1985 document issued by South African Christians calling for resistance to the apartheid regime.

The authors of the Kairos Document hold Israel responsible for the Israeli–Palestinian conflict and criticise 'the West' for trying to make amends for the suffering of Jews for which they were responsible: 'They tried to correct an injustice and the result was a new injustice.' The text, an example of Christian liberation theology (see also Leon Klenicki, Chapter 9, p. 460) is influenced by the writings of Naim Ateek (see Chapter 9, p. 491), one of the signatories. Our excerpt depicts the challenges facing Christians in the Holy Land and condemns both 'fundamentalist theological positions' (that is, Christian Zionism) and 'the Israeli occupation of Palestinian land', which it calls 'a sin against God and humanity'.

The excerpt begins by highlighting Christian solidarity with Palestinians, since most Christians in the Holy Land speak Arabic, identify as Palestinians and are integrated within Palestinian Arab society. Christians have often played a leading role in the Palestinian struggle for independence, which strengthened relations with Muslims, but the growth of the Islamist movement in recent times has unsettled Christian–Muslim relations. The Kairos Document expresses Christian support for the Palestinian cause.

But what of its relevance to Jewish–Christian relations? The document counters the view that the biblical election of Israel and the promise of the Land justify modern Zionism. In particular, it condemns the support of Christian Zionists and their interpretations of scripture. It also insists that Christians outside of the region should not ignore the Palestinians and their struggle for liberation.

Mainstream Jewish responses were, in general, critical, pointing out that the churches do not act similarly regarding human rights and state abuse in other countries, especially in the wider Middle East. The American Jewish Committee and the Anti-Defamation League both argued that the document and its Christian supporters damaged Christian–Jewish relations. Other mainstream Jewish groups were less strident but still criticised the document for being unbalanced; Liberal Judaism (UK), for example, highlighted its partiality but also acknowledged that narratives which express suffering are rarely objective. There was some Jewish support for the document, for example from the American academic Marc Ellis.

As for the churches, views were more divided. In general, the liberal churches were supportive, as illustrated by a group of American Christian churches, Kairos USA, who commended the document and called for reflections on its implications for interfaith relations. In the UK the Methodist Church adopted resolutions critical of Israel, explicitly basing its approach on the Kairos Document. The evangelical churches and theologians were more critical, as illustrated by Malcolm Lowe, a member of the Ecumenical Theological Research Fraternity in Israel, who called it a 'deception' and condemned its 'extreme language'.

In sum, the Kairos Document caused controversy and generated pressures on Jewish–Christian relations that had not been experienced for some decades. Since its publication, discussions about Israel–Palestine have not lost in intensity but illustrate increasing tensions within and between Jewish and Christian interlocutors, which have only just begun to be addressed together (see document 15).

Bibliography

Call to Action: U.S. Response to the Kairos Palestine Document (Carlton: Kairos USA, 2012), https://kairosusa.org/wp-content/uploads/2013/12/Kairos-USA-Call-to-Action.pdf.

Lowe, Malcolm, *The Palestinian 'Kairos' Document: A Behind-the-Scenes Analysis* (Heppenheim: International Council of Christians and Jews, 2010), www.jcrelations.net/articles/article/the-palestinian-kairos-document.html.

Nelson, Cary, and Gizzi, Michael C. (eds.), *Peace and Faith: Christian Churches and the Israeli–Palestinian Conflict* (Philadelphia and Boston: Presbyterians for Middle East Peace, 2021).

Stadler, Will, *Palestinian Christians and the Old Testament: History, Hermeneutics, and Ideology* (Minneapolis: Fortress Press, 2015).

Svartvik, Jesper, 'The Theology of the Land in Jewish–Christian Relations and Its Role in Misunderstandings between Jews and Christians', in Adams, Jonathan, and Hess, Cordelia (eds.), *The Medieval Roots of Antisemitism: Continuities and Discontinuities from the Middle Ages to the Present Day* (London: Routledge, 2018), 363–76.

12

International Christian Embassy in Jerusalem (ICEJ): Swords into Ploughshares: Christian Zionism and the Battle of Armageddon *(2013)*

Text

4) This time of restoration of Israel to her land and to her God in our day is vouched for by the holy prophets, affirmed in the faithful and true words of Jesus, and given prominent place in Peter's preaching of the Gospel and Paul's teachings as the Apostle to the Gentiles. Therefore, we can boldly state that no man's Gospel is complete without reference to and affirmation of the promised final restoration of Israel.

5) This promised time of restoration for Israel taking place in our day is also the divinely chosen and unmistakable warning sign openly seen before all nations, that He is coming to judge humanity's continuous rebellion against Him and will be justified in so doing.

6) The Battle of Armageddon foretold in the book of Revelation is to be understood as one final act of humanity's rebellion against God and will never be initiated by or result from some dark hidden agenda allegedly espoused by Christian Zionists.

7) Rather, we are Christians whose Zionism is founded upon and motivated by the promise of an epoch of righteousness and peace for the whole earth known in the Bible as the Millennial reign of Messiah, a vision of world peace that humanity has known about and aspired to for generations, while being largely ignorant of the manner in which God will birth it into being – the now raging controversy surrounding Israel's restoration.

8) We encourage all humanity that this Messianic age is open to anyone who would dare open their hearts to the Lord Who made them.

9) The Jewish people have not returned to Israel for another appointed time of God's wrath whereby two-thirds die in the Tribulation so that one-third will call on the name of the Lord, but for an incredibly life-giving repentance and revelation of the Messiah first promised to them.

10) Therefore, we encourage our long-suffering Jewish brothers and friends not to lose heart in the midst of the current struggle over the land of Israel, nor be fearful or reticent as to the comfort and support offered by sincere Christians, knowing that when your prolonged wait is over for *your* promised Messiah, He will be everything that God solemnly promised to you – a Redeemer, a Deliverer, a Comforter and a Righteous King to sit on the throne of David over an Israel and an earth finally at rest. Indeed, Messiah will reconcile all things within Himself.

Source

Parsons, David, *Swords into Ploughshares: Christian Zionism and the Battle of Armageddon* (Jerusalem: International Christian Embassy Jerusalem, 2021), 45–6.

Commentary

Swords into Ploughshares is a modern example of Protestant restorationist literature, which began in the late eighteenth century when Christian restorationists such as Lord Shaftesbury (see Chapter 6, p. 304) were actively supporting Jewish settlement in Palestine. Our excerpt is taken from the 'Conclusion' section of the document, which was published by the evangelical Christian Zionist organisation the International Christian Embassy in Jerusalem (ICEJ) and written by its Vice President, David Parsons.

Swords into Ploughshares presents an evangelical Christian Zionist view of the establishment of the State of Israel ('restoration of Israel to her land'), interpreting it as a sign of the beginning of the kingdom of God and a precursor to the day of judgement. The document combines apocalypticism and an end-of-times theology with God's covenantal promises to the Jewish people.

Evangelical Christian Zionism is influenced by dispensationalism and 'Judaeo-centric prophecy belief', a term first found among the Puritans in early seventeenth-century England. The former is commonly associated with John Nelson Darby (1800–82) of the Plymouth Brethren, who identified two peoples of God – Jewish and Christian – and argued that particular biblical prophecies only referred to the Jewish people. However, Aron Engberg and Faydra Shapiro suggest that Protestant Judaeo-centric prophecy belief is more influential, as illustrated by Parsons' comment in the 'Introduction' to *Swords into Ploughshares* that 'Our approach […] views both the Jewish people and Land of Israel as chosen by God long ago for purposes of world redemption. Thus we have the interest and fate of the entire world in heart and mind when we defend Israel's restoration to her land' (pp. 2–3).

A key moment for Christian Zionists was the Six-Day War (1967), which resulted in Israeli control of the Old City of Jerusalem and the West Bank. Military success generated euphoria among Jewish religious Zionist nationalists, such as *Gush Emunim* ('Block of the Faithful'), who began to build settlements in newly occupied territories, which they called Judah and Samaria after their biblical names. It also generated messianic fervour among Christian Zionists, who encouraged Jews to make *aliyah* ('go up') to Israel (in other words, immigrate). While other Christians were hesitant (e.g., the WCC) or critical (e.g., Ateek; see Chapter 9, p. 491), evangelicals were enthusiastic, viewing Israel's victory in terms of prophetic fulfilment, 'vouched for by the holy prophets', in the words of the document.

Swords into Ploughshares also demonstrates evangelical defence of the State of Israel in response to criticism from liberal Christians and others: 'we encourage our long-suffering Jewish brothers and friends not to lose heart in the midst of the current struggle over the land of Israel'. Even before the establishment of the ICEJ, the support of Christian Zionists was noticed by Israeli politicians and the general public. The Jerusalem Conference on Biblical Prophecy in 1971 attracted evangelicals from around the world, who were welcomed by former Israeli prime minister David Ben-Gurion. In 1977 Menachem Begin was elected prime minister, and the Likud leader fostered relations with US evangelical leaders such as Jerry Falwell. In 1980 the ICEJ was established, drawing support from fundamentalist Christians and evangelicals, especially in the USA. The ICEJ's Christian critics include both conservatives, who fault them for failing to evangelise Jews (see document 5), and Palestinian Christians and their supporters, who censure their unconditional support for the State of Israel (see document 11). However, some Israeli Jews (both religious and secular) expressed their appreciation to the ICEJ for defending the state and facilitating financial and political support abroad, as illustrated by *Swords into Ploughshares*.

Bibliography

Engberg, Aron, *Walking on the Pages of the Word of God: Self, Land, and Text among Evangelical Volunteers in Jerusalem* (Leiden: Brill, 2019).

Lux, Richard C., 'The Land of Israel (Eretz Yisra'el) in Jewish and Christian Understanding', *Studies in Christian–Jewish Relations* 3, no. 1 (2011), https://doi.org/10.6017/scjr.v3i1.1479.

McDermott, Gerald R., *Israel Matters: Why Christians Must Think Differently about the People and the Land* (Grand Rapids: Brazos Press, 2017).

Merkley, Paul, *Christian Attitudes towards the State of Israel* (Montreal: McGill-Queen's University Press, 2001).

Shapiro, Faydra L., *Christian Zionism: Navigating the Jewish–Christian Border* (Eugene: Cascade Books, 2015).

13

International Group of Orthodox Rabbis: To Do the Will of Our Father in Heaven: Toward a Partnership between Jews and Christians *(2015)*

Text

After nearly two millennia of mutual hostility and alienation, we Orthodox Rabbis who lead communities, institutions and seminaries in Israel, the United States and Europe recognize the historic opportunity now before us. We seek to do the will of our Father in Heaven by accepting the hand offered to us by our Christian brothers and sisters [...]

1. The Shoah ended 70 years ago [...]
2. We recognize that since the Second Vatican Council the official teachings of the Catholic Church about Judaism have changed fundamentally and irrevocably. The promulgation of *Nostra Aetate* fifty years ago started the process of reconciliation between our two communities [...] We appreciate the Church's affirmation of Israel's unique place in sacred history and the ultimate world redemption. Today Jews have experienced sincere love and respect from many Christians that have been expressed in many dialogue initiatives, meetings and conferences around the world.
3. As did Maimonides and Yehudah Halevi, we acknowledge that the emergence of Christianity in human history is neither an accident nor an error, but the willed divine outcome and gift to the nations. In separating Judaism and Christianity, G-d willed a separation between partners with significant theological differences, not a separation between enemies. Rabbi Jacob Emden wrote that 'Jesus brought a double goodness to the world. On the one hand he strengthened the Torah of Moses majestically ... and not one of our Sages spoke out more emphatically concerning the immutability of the Torah. On the other hand he removed idols from the nations and obligated them in the seven commandments of Noah so that they would not behave like animals of the field, and instilled them firmly with moral traits ... Christians are congregations that work for the sake of heaven who are destined to endure, whose intent is for the sake of heaven and whose reward will not [be] denied.' Rabbi Samson Raphael Hirsch taught us that Christians 'have accepted the Jewish Bible of the Old Testament as a book of Divine revelation. They profess their belief in the G-d of Heaven and Earth as proclaimed in the Bible and they acknowledge the sovereignty of Divine Providence.'

Now that the Catholic Church has acknowledged the eternal Covenant between G-d and Israel, we Jews can acknowledge the ongoing constructive validity of Christianity as our partner in world redemption, without any fear that this will be exploited for missionary purposes. As stated by the Chief Rabbinate of Israel's Bilateral Commission with the Holy See under the leadership of Rabbi Shear Yashuv Cohen, 'We are no longer enemies, but unequivocal partners in articulating the essential moral values for the survival and welfare of humanity'. Neither of us can achieve G-d's mission in this world alone.

4. Both Jews and Christians have a common covenantal mission to perfect the world under the sovereignty of the Almighty, so that all humanity will call on His name and abominations will be removed from the earth. We understand the hesitation of both sides to affirm this truth and we call on our communities to overcome these fears in order to establish a relationship of trust and respect [...]

5. We Jews and Christians have more in common than what divides us: the ethical mono-theism of Abraham; the relationship with the One Creator of Heaven and Earth, Who loves and cares for all of us; Jewish Sacred Scriptures; a belief in a binding tradition; and the values of life, family, compassionate righteousness, justice, inalienable free-dom, universal love and ultimate world peace. Rabbi Moses Rivkis (Be'er Hagoleh) confirms this and wrote that 'the Sages made reference only to the idolator of their day who did not believe in the creation of the world, the Exodus, G-d's miraculous deeds and the divinely given law. In contrast, the people among whom we are scattered believe in all these essentials of religion.'

6. Our partnership in no way minimizes the ongoing differences between the two com-munities and two religions. We believe that G-d employs many messengers to reveal His truth, while we affirm the fundamental ethical obligations that all people have before G-d that Judaism has always taught through the universal Noahide covenant.

7. In imitating G-d, Jews and Christians must offer models of service, unconditional love and holiness. We are all created in G-d's Holy Image, and Jews and Christians will remain dedicated to the Covenant by playing an active role together in redeem-ing the world.

Source

International Group of Orthodox Rabbis, *To Do the Will of Our Father in Heaven: Toward a Partnership between Jews and Christians*, https://cjcuc.com/2015/12/03/orthodox-rabbinic-statement-on-christianity/. (Footnotes omitted.)

Commentary

To Do the Will of Our Father in Heaven is the first modern Orthodox Jewish statement on Christianity, crafted by twenty-five prominent rabbis from Israel, US and Europe, each of whom was actively engaged in Jewish–Christian dialogue. It was published by the Center for Jewish–Christian Understanding and Cooperation and called for partnership with Christians, acknowledging the value of Christianity as part of God's plan for humanity.

Whereas *Dabru Emet* (document 7) was a cross-denominational Jewish statement, *To Do the Will* was exclusively the work of Orthodox rabbis who represent a movement within Judaism which tends to be less active in dialogue with Christianity. The document cited traditional opinions and rulings from past rabbinic authorities in support of its views, quoting, for example, the medieval philosopher Maimonides' (see Chapter 4, p. 199) description of Christianity as a 'willed divine outcome' and referring to the statement of the eighteenth-century German rabbi Jacob Emden (1697–1776), who praised the ethical teachings of Christianity, that Jesus 'strengthened the Torah' and that Christians 'work for the sake of heaven'.

More recent Orthodox figures were also quoted to strengthen the halakhic (legal) legitimacy of *To Do the Will* and to appeal to mainstream Orthodox Jews. These included Samson Raphael Hirsch (1808–88), regarded as the intellectual founder of the *Torah im Derech Eretz* ('the way of the land') school of contemporary Orthodox Judaism, which combined western culture with strict adherence to Jewish tradition, as well as Eliyahu Yosef Shear Yashuv Cohen (1927–2016), Chief Rabbi of Haifa, who was known for his interfaith activity with Christians (and Muslims).

The statement was welcomed by liberal Orthodox communities as well as by Christians, especially the Vatican as the document explicitly commended the endeavours of the Roman Catholic Church: 'Now that the Catholic Church has acknowledged the eternal Covenant between G-d and Israel, we Jews can acknowledge the ongoing constructive validity of Christianity as our partner in world redemption, without any fear that this will be exploited for missionary purposes.' Coincidentally, *To Do the Will* was published a few days before the Vatican's document *The Gifts and the Calling of God Are Irrevocable* (see document 14 below) which included a statement abandoning Catholic missionary activity to Jews.

Although *To Do the Will* stated that it did not minimise differences between Judaism and Christianity, it was criticised by more strictly observant communities for being a violation of Torah. The American Jewish author Yair Hoffman, for example, cited 'fundamental halachic errors', pointing to Maimonides' view of Christianity as *avodah zarah* ('idolatry') and describing the document's portrait of Christianity and Judaism as partners as 'tantamount to partnering with Avodah Zarah'.

Although it is too soon to gauge the long-term impact of *To Do the Will*, its significance will surely lie in the acceptance by mainstream Orthodox Jewish leaders of partnership with Christians and its promulgation of a positive theological status for Christianity.

Bibliography

Ahrens, Jehoschua, Greenberg, Irving, and Korn, Eugene (eds.), *From Confrontation to Covenantal Partnership: Jews and Christians Reflect on the Orthodox Rabbinic Statement of 'To Do the Will of Our Father in Heaven'* (Jerusalem: Urim Publications, 2021).

Ahrens, Jehoschua, Heil, Johannes, Blickle, Karl-Hermann, and Bollag, David (eds.), *Hin zu einer Partnerschaft zwischen Juden und Christen: Die Erklärung orthodoxer Rabbiner zum Christentum* (Berlin: Metropol Verlag, 2017).

14

Pontifical Commission for Religious Relations with the Jews: 'The Gifts and the Calling of God Are Irrevocable' (Rom 11:29): A Reflection on Theological Questions Pertaining to Catholic–Jewish Relations on the Occasion of the 50th Anniversary of 'Nostra ætate' (No. 4) *(10 December 2015)*

Text

5. The Universality of Salvation in Jesus Christ and God's Unrevoked Covenant with Israel

35. Since God has never revoked his covenant with his people Israel, there cannot be different paths or approaches to God's salvation. The theory that there may be two different paths to salvation, the Jewish path without Christ and the path with the Christ, whom Christians believe is Jesus of Nazareth, would in fact endanger the foundations of Christian faith. Confessing the universal and therefore also exclusive mediation of salvation through Jesus Christ belongs to the core of Christian faith. So too does the confession of the one God, the God of Israel, who through his revelation in Jesus Christ has become totally manifest as the God of all peoples, insofar as in him the promise has been fulfilled that all peoples will pray to the God of Israel as the one God (cf. *Is* 56:1–8). The document 'Notes on the correct way to present the Jews and Judaism in preaching and catechesis in the Roman Catholic Church' published by the Holy See's Commission for Religious Relations with the Jews in 1985 therefore maintained that the Church and Judaism cannot be represented as 'two parallel ways to salvation', but that the Church must 'witness to Christ as the Redeemer for all' (No. I, 7). The Christian faith confesses that God wants to lead all people to salvation, that Jesus Christ is the universal mediator of salvation, and that there is no 'other name under heaven given to the human race by which we are to be saved' (*Acts* 4:12).

36. From the Christian confession that there can be only one path to salvation, however, it does not in any way follow that the Jews are excluded from God's salvation because they do not believe in Jesus Christ as the Messiah of Israel and the Son of God. Such a claim would find no support in the soteriological understanding of Saint Paul, who in the Letter to the Romans not only gives expression to his conviction that there can be no breach in the history of salvation, but that salvation comes from the Jews (cf. also *Jn* 4:22). God entrusted Israel with a unique mission, and He does not bring his mysterious plan of salvation for all peoples (cf. *1 Tim* 2:4) to fulfilment without drawing into it his 'first-born son' (*Ex* 4:22). From this it is self-evident that Paul in the Letter to the Romans definitively negates the question he himself has posed, whether God has repudiated his own people. Just as decisively he asserts: 'For the gifts and the call of God are irrevocable'

(*Rom* 11:29). That the Jews are participants in God's salvation is theologically unquestionable, but how that can be possible without confessing Christ explicitly, is and remains an unfathomable divine mystery [...]

[...]

6. The Church's Mandate to Evangelise in Relation to Judaism

40. It is easy to understand that the so-called 'mission to the Jews' is a very delicate and sensitive matter for Jews because, in their eyes, it involves the very existence of the Jewish people. This question also proves to be awkward for Christians, because for them the universal salvific significance of Jesus Christ and consequently the universal mission of the Church are of fundamental importance. The Church is therefore obliged to view evangelisation to Jews, who believe in the one God, in a different manner from that to people of other religions and world views. In concrete terms this means that the Catholic Church neither conducts nor supports any specific institutional mission work directed towards Jews. While there is a principled rejection of an institutional Jewish mission, Christians are nonetheless called to bear witness to their faith in Jesus Christ also to Jews, although they should do so in a humble and sensitive manner, acknowledging that Jews are bearers of God's Word, and particularly in view of the great tragedy of the Shoah.

Source

Catholic Truth Society, *Reflections on Catholic–Jewish Relations: 'The Gifts and the Calling of God Are Irrevocable' (Rom 11:29): A Reflection on Theological Questions Pertaining to Catholic–Jewish Relations on the Occasion of the 50th Anniversary of 'Nostra Aetate' (No. 4)* (London: Catholic Truth Society, 2016), 37–9, 41–2.

Commentary

The Gifts and the Calling of God Are Irrevocable, the most recent document produced by the Pontifical Commission for Religious Relations with the Jews, was published in October 2015 to mark the fiftieth anniversary of *Nostra aetate* (document 2). It considers some of the key theological questions that lie at the heart of the Jewish–Christian relationship, in particular supersessionism (also known as 'replacement theology') and mission, both of which are discussed in the excerpt.

In sections not excerpted above, the document asserts that 'the New Covenant for Christians is therefore neither the annulment nor the replacement, but the fulfilment of the promises of the Old Covenant', a striking remark which rejects the *adversus Judaeos* claim that all God's promises to the Jewish people have been inherited by Christianity because of Israel's faithlessness. *The Gifts and the Calling of God Are Irrevocable* also repudiates any attempt to replace Judaism by the 'Church of the Gentiles', although it does not clarify how to avoid fulfilment sliding into replacement, which seems alive and well in both pulpit and pew.

Equally important, the document states that 'the Catholic Church neither conducts nor supports any specific institutional mission work directed towards Jews', which seems to mark the end of Roman Catholic institutional mission to the Jewish people, a seismic shift in the history of Christian–Jewish relations. Mission had been the subject of numerous Jewish–Christian dialogues, and well before *Nostra aetate* was promulgated the Anglican scholar James Parkes (see Chapter 7, p. 392) argued that there was a direct connection between Christian missionary activity and antisemitism and called for an elimination of Christian mission to Jews. More recently, the conservative Catholic scholar Gavin D'Costa suggested that 'Christians must seriously consider the appropriateness of mission to the Jews, in view of the Holocaust.' Although *The Gifts and the Calling of God Are Irrevocable* does not abandon individual conversionary activity, it rejects the wider mission.

How God will save Jews if they do not explicitly believe in Christ is declared 'an unfathomable divine mystery' but one which must be affirmed since Christians believe that God is faithful to his promises and therefore never revoked his covenant with the Jewish people. This is reminiscent of Paul's conclusion about the mystery of the ongoing covenant between God and the Jewish people: 'How inscrutable [are] his ways' (Rom. 11:33, NRSVue).

The document recognises elsewhere that the Jewish people have a genuine relationship with God and that 'The Torah is the instruction for a successful life in right relationship with God. Whoever observes the Torah has life in its fullness (cf. *Pirqe Avot* II, 7)' (p. 26). In this way, *The Gifts and the Calling of God Are Irrevocable*, which quotes extensively from rabbinic sources, reveals a deepening Christian recognition of the importance of Torah. It also emphasises the responsibility of educational institutions, particularly those for the training of priests, to integrate into their curricula both *Nostra aetate* and the subsequent documents of the Holy See, although this remains more of a (worthy) aspiration than current reality.

Bibliography

Cunningham, Philip A., 'Gifts and Calling: Coming to Terms with Jews as Covenantal Partners', *Studies in Christian–Jewish Relations* 12, no. 1 (2017), https://doi.org/10.6017/scjr.v12i1.9796.

Langer, Ruth, '"Gifts and Calling": The Fruits of Coming to Know Living Jews', *Studies in Christian–Jewish Relations* 12, no. 1 (2017), https://doi.org/10.6017/scjr.v12i1.9797.

Procario-Foley, Elena, 'Fulfillment and Complementarity: Reflections on Relationship in "Gifts and Calling"', *Studies in Christian–Jewish Relations* 12, no. 1 (2017), https://doi.org/10.6017/scjr.v12i1.9800.

Rutishauser, Christian M., 'Christian Mission to the Jews Revisited: Exploring the Logic of the Vatican Document "The Gifts and Calling of God Are Irrevocable"', *Studies in Christian–Jewish Relations* 14, no. 1 (2019), https://doi.org/10.6017/scjr.v14i1.11587.

Tapie, Matthew, 'Christ, Torah, and the Faithfulness of God: The Concept of Supersessionism in "The Gifts and the Calling"', *Studies in Christian–Jewish Relations* 12, no. 1 (2017), https://doi.org/10.6017/scjr.v12i1.9802.

15

Office of the Chief Rabbi and the Church of Scotland: A Jewish–Christian Glossary: Dialogue and Project Convened by Office of the Chief Rabbi and the Church of Scotland *(2023)*

Text

Importance of the Term [Israel] in Relation to Christian Identity

The issue that many Christians grapple with in relation to both the modern State of Israel and passages describing the military conquest of the land in the Old Testament, is that of any claim to exclusive possession of a land. There is a sense shared by many in the Church of Scotland that the land belongs to everyone and thus no one. Dismay is often expressed by some Christians when encountering an emphasis on the sovereignty of any one people or religious group given the diversity of people laying claim to the same land.

There is a reflection that while Christians claim to be untethered to a land, they have gained enormous power as a religion from the day the Roman Empire adopted Christianity as a state religion to its spread to the global North and West. With its subsequent dominance there and the global dominance of the North and West since the Industrial Revolution and colonialism, Christianity has never required sovereignty to survive whilst simultaneously benefitting enormously from its dominance in so many powerful countries.

Christians in the West have grappled with reflecting on the relative power of being a Christian in the Global North whilst listening and responding to theology developed by Palestinian Christians which urges all Christians to address Christian theological justification for Israeli policies and the occupation [...] How Christians in the West grapple with this theological response to an experience of occupation, requires a careful and empathetic ear. On the one hand, the lived experience of Palestinian Christians will inform a particular view of Zionism which is worthy of engagement. As part of this engagement, Christians also need to be aware that [... i]t is one thing to critique Christian reading of Christian Zionism into the scriptures, critiquing Jewish readings has more problematic ramifications. It helps when reading about another faith's engagement with their scripture, to be honest, open and aware that Christians will not be the experts.

[...]

Jewish Reflections on 'Israel'

Reading the entries above expresses more clearly how a classic Jewish theology of land differs from Christian theologies expressed here. Where the former is a boundaried connection to a piece of land, realised in sovereignty there, the latter considers a more 'untethered' relation to land. This may also explain a difference between a Christian universalism explained here in terms of the 'Kingdom of God' and a Jewish universalism which was described by the late Chief Rabbi Sacks as a 'dignity of difference'. This is a recurrent difference that is causing great misunderstanding between the two communities and great mistrust. If there is no place in Christian theology, and more specifically here Church of Scotland theology to understand a Jewish connection to the Land of Israel, this approach will quickly be connected with other approaches against Zionism that are understood to be sometimes antisemitic. In other words, a theology, or rather, as conveyed within this section, a political interpretation of the situation, that is untethered completely from borders, will find most result in Jews who relate to the State of Israel, whether from a religious or cultural identity, or from a historical perspective, being in a position of mistrust of the Church [...]

Christian Reflections on 'Zionism'

[...] Christian Zionism and Zionism are not the same thing. This differentiation proves that Zionism is almost a useless term without a prefix or qualifier even within the many shades and diverse roots of Christian Zionism. Most importantly for Christian readers it is important to reflect on Jewish Zionist developments through history and today, and the fact it developed independently of Christian perspectives. This carries with it the recognition that Judaism has developed independently for 2000 years, attempts to use Christian interpretations of scripture to argue against Zionist thinking is to misunderstand how Zionism has developed and why. In that vein, there needs to be reflection on what it means for a Jew to be a Zionist and to check the assumption that a Zionist will automatically defend everything that Israel does and even the idea that they should have to be asked. As Christians do not tend to ask patriotic immigrants from Pakistan what their beliefs on the blasphemy law are, when Christians meet Jews, we might ignore the temptation to immediately bring up events in Israel and the actions of the Israeli State.

Empathy is needed [...] The difficult next step in dialogue is the fact that the Church's Palestinian Christian partners deserve to be listened to when they express their discomfort with Zionism (both Christian and Jewish understandings of it). They do not carry the same privilege that White Scottish Christians have, and they live with the reality of a Jewish majority State and military occupation in a very different way.

Source

Office of the Chief Rabbi and the Church of Scotland, *A Jewish–Christian Glossary: Dialogue and Project Convened by Office of the Chief Rabbi and the Church of Scotland*, 2023, 32, 34, 82, https://churchofscotland.org.uk/__data/assets/pdf_file/0007/108745/ocr23-01_a-jewish-christian-glossary_a4_v4.pdf.

Commentary

We end this collection of institutional statements with a document jointly produced by the Office of the Chief Rabbi of the United Hebrew Congregations of the Commonwealth and the Church of Scotland. It is one of a small number jointly penned by Jewish and Christian organisations and deals with understanding and managing difference, specifically attitudes on Zionism and the land and State of Israel. Despite Jews and Christians finding themselves on the same side of the fence on most major issues, they still face challenges, the most contentious being related to the significance of Israel.

In 2013 the Church of Scotland published *Inheritance of Abraham? A Report on the 'Promised Land'*, which forcefully condemned Christian Zionism and in so doing also strongly criticised Jewish Zionism, stating for example that 'Christians should not be supporting any claims by Jewish or any other people to an exclusive or even privileged divine right to possess particular territory'. The report, and its call for a boycott and disinvestment from Israel, prompted an array of anguished and angry Jewish responses.

In its fraught aftermath, Chief Rabbi Mirvis, who had just succeeded Jonathan Sacks, attended the Church of Scotland Assembly and called for a dialogue between clerics from both communities. This *Glossary* is one outcome and exemplifies increased engagement by mainstream Orthodox (but not ultra-Orthodox) Jews in dialogue with Christians. It consists of a series of commentaries, followed by reflections on each other's remarks. While it is not uncommon for individual Jews and Christians to produce co-authored writings, joint official statements are rarer.

Our excerpts deal with different approaches to the concepts of Israel and Zionism. The Church of Scotland explains why Christians respond sympathetically to the views of Palestinian Christians and wish to remove the theological burden of Christian Zionism, rejecting any attempt to place Israel on a moral and spiritual pedestal as an outworking of God's plan. Its refutation of Christian Zionism reflects a contemporary discourse acknowledging Christianity's colonial past and repudiating the theological tools of that past. The *Glossary* acknowledges that many Christians are unaware of how Israel is understood by Jews and that the Church needs to understand the Jewish experience and reflect 'on what it means for a Jew to be a Zionist'.

For their part, Jewish contributors recognised that an emphasis on universalism and an '"untethered" relation to land', make it hard for Christians to understand the centrality of the land and State of Israel to Jewish self-understanding. In their explanation of the relationship between 'Jewish religion, Jewish law and a defined piece of land given to us for eternity by God' (p. 29), they reject the application of colonial discourse to Israel.

The importance of the document lies in its recognition of the need to understand divergent approaches, especially on a polarising topic. Its reference to Jonathan Sacks' book *The Dignity of Difference* is relevant here because he wrote of the need to 'feel not diminished, but enlarged' (p. 18) by difference and called for 'not only a theology of commonality, but also a theology of difference' (p. 21). The jointly written *Glossary* seeks to embody that call.

Bibliography

The Anglican Consultative Council, *Land of Promise? An Anglican Exploration of Christian Attitudes to the Holy Land, with Special Reference to Christian Zionism: A Report from the Anglican Communion Network for Inter Faith Concerns* (London: Network for Inter Faith, 2014).

Church of Scotland, *The Inheritance of Abraham? A Report on the 'Promised Land'* (Church and Society Council, 2013), www.scojec.org/news/2013/13v_cos/inheritance_of_abraham-original.pdf.

Cunningham, Langer and Svartvik, *Enabling Dialogue about the Land*.

Sacks, Jonathan, *The Dignity of Difference: How to Avoid the Clash of Civilisations* (London: Continuum, 2002).

Index of Documents and Sources

NON-SCRIPTURAL SOURCES

Index of Names and Subjects

Milton Keynes UK
Ingram Content Group UK Ltd.
UKHW050132081224
452061UK00010B/89